HITTITES

KIZZUWATNA
(QUE, CILICIA)

SAMAL

*Euphrates R.*

HANIGALBAT

• Karatepe

Carchemish •

HURRIANS

Harran •

• Arpad

• Alalakh

Antakya

*JEBEL EL-AQRA*

• Qarqar

Ugarit (Ras Shamra) •

*Orontes R.*

*JEBEL EL-ANSARIYE*

NUHASHSHE

• Halab (Aleppo)

• Ebla (Tell Mardikh)

Hamath •

CYPRUS
(ALASHIYA)

• Tartus

*Nahr el-Kebir*

Qadesh

• Homs

Palmyra •

MEDITERRANEAN SEA

• Tripolis

• Byblos

*Dog R. (N el-Kelb)*

• Beirut

• Sidon

*Leontes (N el-Litani) R.*

*LEBANON MTS.*

*EL-BIQA'*

Baalbek •

*ANTI- LEBANON MTS.*

SYRIA

AMORITES

SYRIAN-ARABIAN
DESERT

△ *MT. HERMON*

• Dan

• Damascus

• Tyre

*PHOENICIA*

Hazor •

*LAKE HULEH*

*SEA OF GALILEE*

CANAAN

*Jordan R.*

• Taanach

# MAP II
# SYRIA-LEBANON

# THE WORLD
# OF THE BIBLE

# THE WORLD
# OF THE BIBLE

**Bible Handbook, Volume I**

*General Editor*
**A. S. VAN DER WOUDE**

*Editors*
M. J. MULDER, B. J. OOSTERHOFF, J. REILING,
H. N. RIDDERBOS, W. C. VAN UNNIK

*Translated by*
SIERD WOUDSTRA

WILLIAM B. EERDMANS PUBLISHING COMPANY

*Reprinted, August 1986*

**Library of Congress Cataloging-in-Publication Data**

Wereld van de Bijbel.   English.
The World of the Bible.

(Bible handbook ; v. 1)
Translation of: De wereld van de Bijbel.
Includes index.
1. Bible — Introductions.   I. Woude, A. S. van der.   II. Series.
BS475.2.W4713   1986      220.9      86-2214

ISBN 0-8028-2405-6

# CONTENTS

# PREFACE

The results of modern biblical scholarship are little—all too little—known both inside and outside the churches. Prejudices of various sorts have caused much of the wealth of knowledge uncovered through the exploration of Scripture and of the world of the Old and New Testaments to remain unused. Nevertheless, in many quarters one can detect a need for responsible, contemporary, and scientifically grounded information about the land of the Bible and about the history, language, content, and interpretation of the Old and New Testaments.

We found many of the best-known comprehensive introductions of this sort to be antiquated or out of print, but in a happy contrast to the years before the Second World War, such a degree of consensus in the scientific investigation of the Bible exists today that the time seems right for a comprehensive work that leaves behind ecclesiastical division as it listens reverently to Scripture and history. We are happy to be able to present a work that offers a comprehensive survey of the present state of biblical research and is a sign of the happy cooperation of scholars of diverse spiritual backgrounds.

The *Bible Handbook* comprises four volumes—this one on the world of the Bible, one on the Old Testament, one on the intertestamental period, and one on the New Testament—which may be used independently. The present work is intended first of all to offer information to the general Bible reader. This information, however, will also be suitable as introductory material for students of Bible schools and institutes and for seminarians. Preachers and priests will find much in this book that they can use in their teaching, as will professors of religion.

Because of the nature of the work we have made no attempt to supply regular documentation. Consequently, we have kept footnotes to a minimum. The reader who wants to pursue the subjects further will find plenty of material for further study in the bibliographies accompanying the various essays.

A second mark of this work is its emphasis on spiritual history. The various writers proceed from the conviction that the Bible is not only the norm but also the product of tradition. For that reason, wherever possible they have set the historical and literary problems in the context of spiritual history without cutting down on the necessary information. That is also why they have devoted considerable attention to the history of the study of the Bible and to the history of methods of exegesis, in which religious and historical presuppositions are so important.

While the publication of this work was in preparation, W. C. van Unnik was taken from us by death. In him the editors lost a wise and widely esteemed scholar of international repute, as well as an unforgettable friend whose work we remember with gratitude and sadness. He was not able to write the essay he had promised to contribute, but because of his share in the preparation of this work we honor his memory by mentioning his name in the list of editors.

We present this work with sincere thanks to all who have given so much of themselves to make it a reality. A special word of thanks is due B. Jongeling, who assumed the thankless job of editing and supplying first corrections for the individual essays, and J. C. de Moor and C. H. J. de Geus, who provided help with the illustrations.

Please note that maps I and II are printed on the front endleaf and map III on the back endleaf. Where the source of individual illustrations is not mentioned, they have been made available by or are derived from: The Semitic Institute of the Theological Seminary of the Reformed Churches in the Netherlands, Koornmarkt 1, Kampen; the collection of the Institute for Semitics and Archeology of the Near East in Groningen; Dr. C. H. J. de Geus, Groningen; Prof. Dr. J. C. de Moor, 't Harde; Prof. Dr. K. R. Veenhof, Heemstede; Photo archive Kok, Kampen.

On behalf of the editors,
A. S. van der Woude

# I

# Geography of
# the Biblical Lands

*by J. H. Negenman and B. VanElderen*

# A. Geography of Palestine

*by J. H. Negenman*

## 1. PHYSICAL GEOGRAPHY

"The land of the Bible" is the part of "the Fertile Crescent" that today comprises the nations of Israel, Jordan, Lebanon, and Syria. In ancient times this coastal strip was the bridge between the cultural centers of Egypt and Mesopotamia. The southern part, which is uniquely "the land of the Bible," is known as Palestine, which may be divided into Cisjordan and Transjordan to designate the areas west and east of the Jordan River respectively. Because the northern part of this coastal strip, the territory of the state of Lebanon and of northwestern Syria, forms a kind of unity with Cisjordan and Transjordan, it should be included in a geography of "the land of the Bible."

Throughout history economic, political, and social factors have given Palestine its place in the Crescent. Long before human beings made their appearance there, however, the land already possessed certain features that affected their life. Situated between the Arabian peninsula and the Mediterranean Sea, this strip is approximately 600 kilometers (375 mi.) long and an average of no more than 120 kilometers (75 mi.) wide. It received its character during the millions of years of prehistory. With its diverse rocks, its mountains and valleys, and its coastal plains and wadis, Palestine, together with the present state of Lebanon and northwestern Syria, became the bridge between Egypt and Mesopotamia and the heartland of the Bible.

The entire coastal strip between Egypt and Mesopotamia originated through the interaction of the water and the mainland during the formation of the earth. This process may be pictured as an immense, slow cycle of low tide and high tide

that took millions of years each time. Every time the water receded after it had engulfed the land for millions of years, it left a thick layer of sediment behind. During the long dry period, which one might call low tide, this sediment became part of the mainland. This process repeated itself in the following cycle of low tide and high tide. That is how the various layers of limestone rock that cover this strip of land came into existence. In the process the solid mass, the mainland, did not remain passive. Because of their different composition, these layers exerted pressure on each other. Earthquakes and volcanic eruptions intensified that pressure. Fissures arose in the layers of limestone rock and many large areas were thrust upward. Eventually these areas became a definite part of the mainland and gave it its unique relief.

This relief is both regular and irregular. If at various places one draws straight lines from west to east, from the coast to the interior, one always encounters the same phenomenon. Viewed horizontally, the starting point of this line lies at sea level. This is followed by a quick and remarkable elevation, abruptly followed by a sharp drop. Then immediately there is a new elevation, after which the line ends with a low drop and continues to fluctuate on this higher level. Whether one draws this line from Sidon to Damascus, from Tel Aviv to es-Salt, or at the height of Beer-sheba, everywhere one observes the same up-and-down movement. Thus from north to south the eastern coastal strip of the Mediterranean Sea is divided into four bands or tracks. The first band is a narrow coastal plain beginning at ancient Ugarit and ending at the Suez Canal. The second band consists of mountainous land, beginning at Jebel el-Aqra and extending deep into the Sinai peninsula.

The third band is again lowland, a valley through which the Orontes, the Leontes, and the Jordan flow, and which in the south is made up of the Dead Sea, the Wadi el-Arabah, and the Gulf of Aqabah. The fourth band, the last, is again mountainous land, to which belong, among others, the Anti-Lebanon range, Mount Hermon, and the hills of Transjordan. Behind this fourth band begins the vast Syrian-Arabian desert.

Viewed from a north-south perspective, at first sight these four bands give to this area a simple relief. A closer look at each narrow band, however, reveals several irregularities.

## a. The Coastal Plain

### (1) NORTHWESTERN SYRIA

The coastal plain can be divided into six natural regions. The northernmost part is formed by the coastal plain of northwestern Syria. The mouth of the Orontes (or Nahr el-Asi) may be taken as the beginning. South of it the coastal strip is fairly narrow, and a mountaintop of the second track, the 1,729 meter (5,673 ft.) high Jebel el-Aqra, stands near the sea. Further to the south, near ancient Ugarit, the plain broadens to about 25 kilometers (15 mi.). From there it continues to the Nahr el-Kebir, the river that now forms the boundary between Lebanon and Syria. The total length of this first band is about 160 kilometers (100 mi.).

### (2) PHOENICIA

The second part of the first band includes Phoenicia, well known in antiquity. Extending from the Nahr el-Kebir to Ras en-Naqurah, it is about 190 kilometers (120 mi.) long. From west to east its width is for the most part no more than a few kilometers. Only at a few places is the coastal plain about 15 kilometers (10 mi.) wide—near Tripolis, near Beirut, and near Sur, the biblical Tyre. The shore itself consists of a winding line of rocks and numerous natural bays. This coastal plain is sometimes intersected by mountains from the second band. One of these points lies about 10 kilometers (6 mi.) north of Beirut. There the Nahr el-Kelb ("river of the dog"), flowing between steep cliffs, empties into the sea. From ancient times, therefore, this was a strategic point.

This small brook is not the only river that descends from the Lebanon toward the sea. More than ten brooks intersect the plain and have deposited much fertile soil. The longest and most important is the Nahr el-Litani, earlier called the Leontes. Its source is near Baalbek, from where it flows to the south and southwest. After about 150 kilometers (100 mi.) it takes a sharp turn to the west and breaks through the mountains of the second band; 8 kilometers (5 mi.) north of Tyre it flows into the sea. Even as the Nahr el-Kebir forms the northern boundary of Phoenicia, so the Nahr el-Litani could have been the southern boundary. But south of Tyre there is still another sharp break in the coastal plain called Ras en-Naqurah; it used to be called "the ladder of Tyre" because the rocks descend staircaselike toward the sea. These rocks closed off the plain to the south and therefore the area of Tyre always belonged to Phoenicia.

### (3) THE PLAIN OF ACCO

The third part of the first band runs from Ras en-Naqurah to Mount Carmel, a distance of about 30 kilometers (20 mi.) in a straight line. The city of Acco lies nearly in the middle of this coastal strip, hence the name "plain of Acco." Inland the part north of Acco has an average width of 7 kilometers (4 mi.). For the most part it is a fertile area, consisting of alluvial soils like those of the coastal plains of Phoenicia and northwestern Syria. But the coastal strip here is naturally swampy, because a line of sandy limestone, called *kurkar*, which came into existence along the coast during the next-to-the-last formative period of the earth, makes water drainage difficult.

The part south of Acco has an average width of 12 kilometers (8 mi.). Here the sea has formed a bay that is now called the Bay of Haifa. Inland for a few kilometers the soil is covered with a layer of sand deposited by the sea. The soil between this sand and the hills in the east is fairly swampy because the water from the hills has difficulty reaching the sea.

To the southeast the plain of Acco is connected with the Valley of Jezreel. At the place where the brook Kishon enters the plain of Acco the hills of Lower Galilee and the slopes of Mount Carmel do not touch each other.

### (4) MOUNT CARMEL

On the south side the plain of Acco is abruptly interrupted by Mount Carmel. This mountain ridge is one of the most conspicuous faults in the first track, rising rather sharply out of the sea.

Carmel as a whole has roughly the shape of a triangle. The northeastern and the southeastern sides are both a little over 20 kilometers (13 mi.) long, and the western side is over 30 kilometers (20 mi.) long. The northeastern flank is very steep. Along that side are also the highest peaks, which at times reach over 500 meters (1,650 ft.). To the southwest the mountain ridge slowly descends toward the plain of Sharon.

Geologically Carmel was formed during the Early Cretaceous Period; in this period the limestone layer of most of the hills of Judah and Samaria was also formed. Therefore Carmel is properly a spur of the second track that here as well as near Nahr el-Kelb and Ras en-Naqurah cuts through the first track. Nevertheless, the plain of Acco was connected with the plain of Sharon south of Carmel, because between Carmel and the central highland lie some tracks of soft limestone that made the formation of clefts and roads possible.

### (5) THE PLAIN OF SHARON

After Mount Carmel the first track continues with the plain of Sharon. Its average width is 15 kilometers (10 mi.), and in the south it extends to the Yarkon River (Nahr el-Awja) north of Tel Aviv, a total length of 75 kilometers (47 mi.). Today this coastal plain is a complete entity, but in the past it was not so. The northern part extending from the western point of Carmel to the Tanninim River (Nahr ez-Zerqa) constituted a separate part because the lower course of this brook was very marshy. This, too, was caused by the sand along the sea and a line of *kurkar*. Locked in between Carmel, the sea, and the Tanninim River, this area of about 25 by 5 kilometers (15 by 3 mi.) has never played an important role.

In the Bible the plain of Sharon is often used in parallelism with mountains like Lebanon and Carmel (Isa. 33:9; 35:2). Like those mountains, Sharon was known for its luxurious vegetation. The reason for this was the red clay, the so-called

*terra rossa,* which is found in many places along the Mediterranean Sea. In the rainy season this clay is very heavy, and in the summer it is as hard as stone. Moreover, here too a row of dunes and some *kurkar* along the coast held the water in the plain and away from the mountains for a long time. In earlier times that made agriculture too difficult in this area and gave nature a free hand.

### (6) PHILISTIA

After the plain of Sharon in the first track is the plain of Philistia, or simply Philistia. This area does not have a well-defined southern boundary; the river Besor (Nahr Ghazzeh), 8 kilometers (5 mi.) south of Gaza, runs along its borders. This gives the area a total length of about 80 kilometers (50 mi.); its width from north to south ranges from about 19 kilometers (11 mi.) near Tel Aviv to about 38 kilometers (24 mi.) near Gaza. The ground consists mainly of alluvial soil, mixed with loess deposited by the wind. Indeed, a strip of sand about 5 kilometers (3 mi.) wide runs along the coast, but there is no *kurkar;* moreover, the plain lies at an average elevation of 50 meters (165 ft.). Drainage is therefore no problem, and the area is naturally very suitable for the growing of grain.

### (7) THE COASTAL STRIP OF SINAI

The southernmost area of the first track is formed by the coastal strip of the Sinai peninsula. From the river Besor to the Suez Canal is approximately 200 kilometers (125 mi.). The coastline, which already at Mount Carmel bends southward, runs here mainly from east to west. Parallel with it the inland boundary of this coastal strip extends from Beer-sheba by way of Nizzana to the Bitter Lakes. This gives the plain an average width of 60 to 70 kilometers (40 to 45 mi.). Not only the length and breadth indicate that this area is different in nature from the coastal plain of Phoenicia or from the plain of Sharon. This coastal strip is nothing but desert, entirely covered with a thick layer of sand and gradually rising from sea level to about 400 meters (1,300 ft.). In the center, 50 kilometers (30 mi.) south of el-Arish, lies a mountain range (Jebel el-Maara) with peaks of over 700 meters (2,300 ft.).

## b. The Central Highlands

### (1) JEBEL EL-ANSARIYE

The second track consists of a number of mountain ranges running alongside the coastal plains. The first is Jebel el-Ansariye, bounded on the west by the coastal plain of northwestern Syria, on the north and east by the valley of the Orontes, and on the south by the Nahr el-Kebir. The earlier-mentioned Jebel el-Aqra is at the same time the northernmost and highest peak. Further to the south the mountains drop slowly. In the center, east of Latakia, are peaks with a height of about 1,500 meters (4,900 ft.). Further to the south, east of Tartus, the mountain range is generally no higher than 500 meters (1,650 ft.). From there it goes down to the valley of the Nahr el-Kebir.

### (2) THE LEBANON RANGE

The second part of the central highland comprises the well-known Lebanon range, bounded on the west by Phoenicia, on the north by the valley of the Nahr el-Kebir, and on the east by the valley between the Lebanon and the Anti-Lebanon ranges. This mountain range runs slightly more northeast to southwest and has a length of about 160 kilometers (100 mi.) and an average width of about 20 kilometers (13 mi.). Generally it is higher and wider in the north than in the south. Many peaks rise to over 2,000 meters (6,550 ft.). The highest point (3,088 m. or 10,132 ft.) is 30 kilometers (20 mi.) southeast of Tripolis. In winter this area is covered with a heavy layer of snow that in some places stays till far into the summer. The western as well as the eastern slopes of the Lebanon are crisscrossed by the many narrow, winding wadis that formerly made this whole mountain range a virtually insuperable barrier for human traffic.

The southern boundary of the Lebanon range is not sharply marked. Actually the Lebanon range continues in the mountains of Upper Galilee, though these are considerably lower. Because this difference in height begins especially at the place where the Nahr el-Kebir cuts through the mountains, this river may be regarded as the southern boundary.

### (3) THE HIGHLANDS OF GALILEE

The mountains and hills of Galilee border on the Litani River in the north, the Jordan Valley and the Sea of Galilee in the east, the Valley of Jezreel in the south, and the coastal plains around Tyre and Acco in the west. The area is about 75 kilometers (50 mi.) long, with an average width of about 30 kilometers (20 mi.). Certain differences between this region and Lebanon are immediately noticeable. For instance, peaks of over 1,000 meters (3,300 ft.) are an exception; also, the direction is once again more from north to south. This entire area is intersected by a great valley from west to east, a little to the north of the line from Acco to the Sea of Galilee. South of this rift lie hills, none of which is higher than 600 meters (1,950 ft.), while on the north the elevation is around 800 meters (2,600 ft.). This area is therefore rightly divided into Upper Galilee and Lower Galilee.

Using contemporary political terms, one might call Upper Galilee the Lebanese-Israelite plateau. It is a rough, windy, mountainous land that slowly widens and rises from north to south. Along the rift mentioned earlier lies the highest peak of Cisjordan, Mount Meron, which rises to 1,208 meters (3,963 ft.). At first sight Lower Galilee also looks like a land of mountains, especially because of the lower regions south and east of it, namely, the Valley of Jezreel and the Sea of Galilee. The average elevation of this area is, however, not more than 300 meters (1,000 ft.), and only about ten hills exceed 500 meters (1,650 ft.). The best known of these is Mount Tabor (588 m. or 1,929 ft.), 8 kilometers (5 mi.) east of Nazareth. Taken as a whole, Lower Galilee is a rolling country; the hills alternate with wide valleys, which occasionally widen to vast plains. In the southeast corner numerous basalt rocks lie within the red soil, a remnant of volcanic activity in the Diluvian Period. The rest of Lower Galilee also shows traces of earthquakes. There are numerous larger and smaller rifts in the earth's crust, running in a predominantly northeast-southwest direction in the north, east-west in the center, and southeast-northwest in the south. Despite its low elevation Upper Galilee is in many places not easily accessible from the surrounding territories.

### (4) THE VALLEY OF JEZREEL

The Valley of Jezreel is a unique section of the central highlands. It is a low, level territory situated between the hills of Galilee and Samaria. This large valley links the coastal strip in the west with the Jordan Valley in the east without one hill or mountain interrupting it. This is entirely unique in Palestine; here the normal relief disappears completely. The shape of the valley reminds one of an inverted triangle. At the low point lies the village of Jenin. The raised northwest line extends to the point where Mount Carmel and Upper Galilee come to within a few kilometers of each other. From there one can draw the top line from west to east to Mount Tabor. The line from Tabor to Jenin completes the triangle. The plain is not large; the sides of the triangle are about 31, 25, and 23 kilometers (19, 15, and 14 mi.) long respectively. From the surrounding hills one can easily look over the entire area. The city of Afula is near the center. East of it the rain and spring water drain toward the Jordan Valley and west of it toward the Mediterranean Sea. The drop is small, however, for Afula's elevation is only 50 meters (165 ft.). Because of this, in the past the Valley of Jezreel was often swampy, especially in the wet season.

### (5) THE MOUNTAINS OF SAMARIA

The highlands of Palestine that extend from Jenin past Hebron are geologically a complex territory. It can be divided into three major sections: the mountains of Samaria, the plateau of Benjamin, and the hill country of Judah.

The mountains of Samaria are bounded in the north by the Valley of Jezreel, in the east by the Jordan Valley, in the west by Mount Carmel and the plain of Sharon, and in the south by the plateau of Benjamin. These mountains do not constitute a unity, however. The primary reason is the variety of rocks, which were formed in successive geological periods. One finds three kinds of limestone rocks: stone-hard limestone rocks from the Early Cretaceous Period, soft layers from the Late Cretaceous Period, and again hard limestone from the Eocene Period, which followed the Cretaceous Period. The end result of their mutual interaction is the winding wadis, often with steep cliffs and pointed mountaintops,

and especially the wide valleys between the level, rounded hills. Their height also varies considerably. The mountains of Gilboa (Jebel Fuquah) reach 400 to 500 meters (1,300 to 1,650 ft.), between Tubas and Sebastiye are peaks of 600 to 700 meters (1,950 to 2,300 ft.), and the well-known Ebal and Gerizim are 940 meters (3,084 ft.) and 881 meters (2,890 ft.) respectively. Jebel Asur, 9 kilometers (6 mi.) northeast of Ramallah, is the highest peak of Samaria (1,016 m. or 3,333 ft.). This mountain, which is easy to ascend—today there is even a paved road leading to the top—is indicative of what many mountains of Samaria are like.

### (6) THE PLATEAU OF BENJAMIN

The plateau of Samaria gives way to the plateau of Benjamin. Its approximate shape is that of a square 15 by 15 kilometers (10 by 10 mi.); it lies directly north of Jerusalem. It is an undulating area without deep valleys and high peaks. The present road from Jerusalem to Ramallah continues over a distance of 14 kilometers (9 mi.) without sharp curves and on a level between 750 and 800 meters (2,452 and 2,600 ft.). To the south the Soreq River (Wadi es-Sarar), along which the railroad between Jerusalem and Tel Aviv runs today, is the boundary. In the east the plateau soon drops into the wilderness of Benjamin, and behind that is again the Jordan Valley. In the west, between the plateau and the coastal plain, lies an area dominated by soft rocks from the Late Cretaceous Period. Consequently the difference in height was bridged by eroded, sloping hills and the plateau of Benjamin was fairly open toward the coastal plain.

### (7) THE HILL COUNTRY OF JUDAH

South of the plateau of Benjamin lies the hill country of Judah. In the east the Dead Sea is the boundary, in the west Philistia, and in the south the Negeb. It is a complex area, consisting of three strips that run parallel from north to south. On the west side lies the Shephelah, in the middle the actual hill country of Judah, and in the east along the Dead Sea the well-known Judean desert.

The Shephelah, which extends from the present Beth-shemesh to about 18 kilometers (11 mi.) north of Beer-sheba, is a hilly strip 15 kilometers

(10 mi.) wide. The height varies from 250 to 450 meters (825 to 1,475 ft.). Because the name Shephelah means "low area," this name must have been given by people who lived in the more elevated hill country of Judah. The Shephelah consists primarily of hard rock from the Eocene Epoch; therefore, it has few level areas or straight valleys. Between the Shephelah and the hill country of Judah lies a strip of soft rock that shows considerably more erosion. Thus a natural division or barrier was formed that protected the hill country of Judah.

The hill country of Judah itself is about 50 kilometers (30 mi.) long and 25 kilometers (15 mi.) wide. This area consists primarily of hard rock from the Early Cretaceous Period. The mountain ridge itself is sloping; from Jerusalem past Bethlehem to the south of Hebron runs a track 5 to 8 kilometers (3 to 5 mi.) wide with slight differences in elevation. Near Bethlehem the elevation is on the average 800 meters (2,600 ft.), and near Hebron almost 1,000 meters (3,300 ft.). About 2 kilometers north of this city lies the highest peak (1,020 m. or 3,350 ft.), but that height is not conspicuous because it fits into the long line of the plateau. Behind the eastern edge of the mountain ridge the level soon drops 100 to 200 meters (330 to 660 ft.); the precipitation there is considerably less. On that line the Judean desert begins.

The Judean desert lies hidden behind the plateau of Benjamin and the mountain ridge of Judea. Its total length is about 55 kilometers (35 mi.) and its average width about 16 kilometers (10 mi.). It consists primarily of soft layers of rock from the Late Cretaceous Period, though in many places one also finds hard rock from the Early Cretaceous Period. Behind the mountain ridge the peaks are still 600 to 700 meters (1,950 to 2,300 ft.) high, but on the east side the highest points are 100 meters (330 ft.) below sea level. Along with the little but usually heavy rainfall, this geological formation has given the Judean desert its distinctive features, which resemble those of a moonscape. Most of the mountaintops are partly rounded and of a gray color, but the edges can be jagged and steep, with colors like red, brown, white, and black. As in most places in Cisjordan, the wadis run predominantly from northwest-west to southeast-east. In the vicinity

of the Jordan Valley and the Dead Sea these wadis usually end in a steep cliff because of the strip of hard rock that runs alongside it.

## (8) THE NEGEB

Modern maps call the entire triangle of Israel south of Beer-sheba the Negeb. Though in the Bible the Negeb refers to the area around Beersheba, we shall stay with the modern meaning. On the northwest the Negeb is bounded by the southern part of Philistia, on the east by the Wadi el-Arabah, and on the south by the Sinai peninsula. From north to south its length is about 185 kilometers (115 mi.) and from east to west its width is about 75 kilometers (50 mi.). Geologically it is a complex area. The northern part, the biblical Negeb, is not really hill country. Therefore there is no sharp divide from the coastal strip of Philistia. With rolling hills the Negeb slowly rises to about 500 meters (1,650 ft.), maintains this elevation for a great distance, and finally drops sharply to the northernmost part of the Wadi el-Arabah. The ground consists primarily of hard rock from the Early Cretaceous Period and the Eocene Period. Because the loess deposited by the wind on this fairly flat area stays, it is a fertile region as long as there is enough water. Southeast of this area lies a more hilly region. Rocks of many different kinds, numerous rifts in the earth's crust, a significant drop from west to east, and a great shortage of water have made this a wild, inhospitable land.

The most fascinating parts are the three enclosed valleys that cut through this mountainland: the Maktesh Qaton (Wadi Hadire) and the Maktesh Gadol (Wadi Hatire), 16 kilometers (10 mi.) southeast and 10 kilometers (6 mi.) south of Dimona respectively, and especially the Maktesh Ramon (Wadi Raman), 45 kilometers (28 mi.) south of Avdat. This last valley is about 35 kilometers (22 mi.) long and on the average 7 kilometers (4 mi.) wide. In this desert valley lying at an elevation of about 550 meters (1,800 ft.) and surrounded by mountain sides 200 to 300 meters (650 to 1,000 ft.) high, one of the oldest types of rock in Cisjordan comes to the surface, namely, limestone from the Triassic Period that is more than 200 million years old. The highest point of this whole area, Mount Ramon (Jebel Raman), is in the southwest corner of this valley; it is 1,035 meters (3,395 ft.) high. Still farther to the southeast the triad of hard-soft-hard limestone again appears regularly. Because of this one sees sloping mountains alternating with wide valleys, sharp peaks, and steep wadis. The oldest rock of Cisjordan, consisting of pre-Cambrian layers older than 600 million years, lies exposed near the present Timnah and northwest of Elath.

## (9) THE MOUNTAINLAND OF SINAI

Between the Negeb and the mountainland of Sinai there is today a political border, but the territories on either side of that border have for the most part the same character. Therefore the mountainland of Sinai may also be considered part of the second track. In the north these mountains are bounded by the coastal strip of Sinai, in the west by the Gulf of Suez, and in the east by the Gulf of Aqabah or Elath. Actually the entire Sinai rises staircaselike from north to south. First there is the coastal plain that over a stretch of about 60 to 70 kilometers (37 to 43 mi.) gradually rises to about 400 meters (1,300 ft.). Then follows a wide strip, on an elevation between 400 and 600 meters (1,300 and 1,950 ft.), that extends to the line from Elath to Suez; this area with its wide, flat plateaus is enclosed in the west by the passes of Mitla and Jidi and in the east by the central Negeb. South of the line from Suez to Elath, along which in the Middle Ages the pilgrims traveled the road (the Darb el-Hajj) toward Mecca, the Sinai rises to 800 meters (2,600 ft.), and has some peaks of about 1,000 meters (3,300 ft.). Nevertheless, these last two areas do not form an imposing mountain range. They are more like the area of the central Negeb. It is only in the southern corner of the peninsula that the mountains average 1,500 meters (4,900 ft.) high. In the vicinity of the traditional mountain of Sinai, that is, 90 kilometers (55 mi.) above the southernmost tip, the mountains reach their highest elevation. There one finds several peaks that are over 2,000 meters (6,550 ft.). The well-known mountains, known in Arabic as Jebel Musa and Jebel Qaterin, are 2,285 meters (7,497 ft.) and 2,641 meters (8,665 ft.) high respectively. In this area one finds, besides hard rock from the Early Cretaceous Period, Nubian sandstone and especially much coarse granite. There is no volcanic stone, despite the suggestion of certain biblical traditions. From this high mountain range, wadis run south, east, and west, but especially north. In this last direction they finally come together in the Wadi el-Arish. So the well-known "river of Egypt" is, as it were, the central drainage canal of the entire peninsula.

## c. The Valley between the Mountains

### (1) THE VALLEY OF THE ORONTES

The third geological track consists for the most part of the well-known crack in the earth's crust through which one can descend to the lowest point below sea level. From north to south the following parts can be distinguished: the valley of the Orontes, the valley between the Lebanon and the Anti-Lebanon ranges, the Jordan Valley, the Dead Sea, the Wadi el-Arabah, and the Gulf of Aqabah.

The Orontes is the most important river in the western part of Syria. Its source is 20 kilometers (12 mi.) north of Baalbek. From there it flows in a northeasterly direction between the Lebanon and the Anti-Lebanon, and after about 70 kilometers (43 mi.) it reaches the plateau near Homs and Hamath. In the vicinity of these cities one cannot really speak of "the valley of the Orontes," for here the river runs through a fairly flat area. In the west lie the lower hills of the Jebel el-Ansariye, but on the east one can look far into the undulating Syrian desert. Therefore the typical relief of the four tracks is absent here because the third and fourth track are lacking. Only about 30 kilometers (20 mi.) northwest of Hamath the Orontes begins to form its own valley. There it flows on a level of about 200 meters (660 ft.), with mountains rising up on both the west and the east: in the west the Jebel el-Ansariye and in the east the hills that lead to the plateau between Hamath and Halab. Because of the slow, winding current, the valley itself is about 10 kilometers (6 mi.) wide and rather swampy. Further to the north this valley narrows between hard, mountainous rocks. Finally the Orontes enters the valley of Antakya, bends there around the northern point of the second track, and after about 50 kilometers (30 mi.) empties into the sea. Thus this river does not go below sea level, and one cannot regard the valley of the Orontes as part of the well-known crack in the earth's crust.

## (2) THE VALLEY BETWEEN THE LEBANON AND THE ANTI-LEBANON RANGES

The flat area between the Lebanon and the Anti-Lebanon ranges is properly, without further designation, called el-Biqa, that is, "the valley." With its length of 120 kilometers (75 mi.) and its width of 8 to 12 kilometers (5 to 8 mi.), it is a unique phenomenon in these regions. Nevertheless, it is not lowland. It is on a level of about 900 meters (2,950 ft.). The highest point, 1,120 meters (3,675 ft.), is near Baalbek; from there it slowly drops toward the north-northeast and the south-southwest. This drop has prevented el-Biqa from becoming one extended swampy area. Because of its elevation this plain, like the valley of the Orontes, cannot be considered part of the crack in the earth's crust, which starts farther toward the south. Thus the Biqa continually narrows toward the south as the spurs of the Lebanon range and Mount Hermon gradually approach each other. Nevertheless, there remains an opening, for through a hilly terrain that quickly drops from about 780 meters (2,550 ft.) to about 100 meters (330 ft.), one reaches the Jordan Valley.

## (3) THE JORDAN VALLEY

The Jordan Valley starts near the modern city of Qiryat Shemona in the present nation of Israel. Because of its exceptional depth, this valley, together with the Dead Sea, has strongly determined the character of the land of Palestine. This natural state was at the same time a significant historical factor; because of it the Jordan functioned more as a dividing line than as a traffic artery such as the Nile and the Euphrates.

At the height of Qiryat Shemona one cannot yet speak of the Jordan, but only of rivulets that later form the Jordan. From the Biqa come the Nahr Baregit and the Nahr Hasbani, from the southern slopes of the Hermon the Nahr Leddan (the river Dan) and the Nahr Baniyas (the river Hermon). When they converge, the last three form the Jordan itself, and like the Nahr Baregit they formerly flowed into Lake Huleh. In biblical times this lake was about 6 kilometers (4 mi.) long and 4.5 kilo-

meters (3 mi.) wide. Today it is a lot smaller, the Jordan has been canalized, and the marshy region drained. All that, however, has not influenced the drop of the Jordan. At that place the drop is very small. It is difficult for the water to leave this area. In the west the steep hills of Upper Galilee rise to about 700 meters (2,300 ft.); in the east they climb slowly but eventually reach the same elevation as the Golan plateau. In the south the river finally meets a large area of basalt, through which it is difficult for the water to flow. Yet in this direction lies the only outlet; about 10 kilometers (6 mi.) north of the Sea of Galilee the Jordan reaches sea level.

The Sea of Galilee (Sea of Chinnereth, Lake Tiberias, Lake Gennesaret) is 21 kilometers (13 mi.) long at its farthest points, and its greatest width is almost 12 kilometers (8 mi.). Its level is about 212 meters (696 ft.) below that of the Mediterranean Sea and in places it reaches a depth of 50 meters (165 ft.). Looking from the water toward the surrounding mountains one gets the impression that on all sides they extend into the lake. Nevertheless, all around there are sloping shores and even some alluvial plains. The largest of these is on the northwest; it has an average length and width of 5 kilometers (3 mi.) and 2 kilometers (1 mi.) respectively. Flat areas are also found farther in the north near the mouth of the Jordan, in the southeast, and in the south where the river leaves the lake. In many places around the lake one can find larger and smaller basalt rocks. This rock and the sulfurous hot water springs near Tiberias indicate volcanic activity in this region from the Pleistocene Period (2 million—25,000 years), that is, before the rift of the Jordan Valley came into existence.

The Jordan Valley between the Sea of Galilee and the Dead Sea has a length of 105 kilometers (65 mi.) in a straight line and an average width of about 15 kilometers (10 mi.). From west to east and vice versa one can distinguish three bands: in the center the river; immediately beside it the wide shores, called ez-Zor; a little higher on both sides of it el-Ghor, the wide valley between the mountains. The drop of the river south of the lake is not as great as the drop north of the lake. The water drops from 212 meters (696 ft.) below sea level to 392 meters (1,286 ft.) below sea level, a total of 180 meters (590 ft.) over a distance of 105 kilometers (65 mi.). Moreover, the river is rarely straight. Because of its serpentine character, the water in effect travels a distance of about 320 kilometers (200 mi.), three times the distance it would go if it traveled in a straight line. Some of the curves are so sharp that in ten places the river flows due north. The many curves have produced a number of places where the river can be crossed. Most of these are difficult to reach, however, because of the dense foliage of the Zor.

From north to south this part of the Jordan Valley also shows remarkable differences. Three zones can be distinguished: the zone of Beth-shean, the narrow zone in the middle, and finally the region between ed-Damiye and the Dead Sea. The zone of Beth-shean stretches from the Sea of Galilee to about 17 kilometers (11 mi.) south of this city; its total length is about 40 kilometers (25 mi.). The following features are striking. About 9 kilometers (6 mi.) south of the lake, the Yarmuk River (Sheriat el-Menadire), coming from the east, runs into the Jordan. As such this is nothing strange; in addition to the Yarmuk more than thirteen rivulets enter the Jordan from the east, and about ten from the west. The Yarmuk, however, pours into it almost as much water as the main river. Near Beth-shean the Jordan Valley is at its widest, and in effect it is not closed off by mountains toward the west.

The narrow center strip, which begins about 17 kilometers (11 mi.) south of Beth-shean and continues about 25 kilometers (15 mi.), forms a sharp contrast with the zone of Beth-shean. On the west side the hard rocks from the Eocene Period in the highlands of Manasseh extend almost to the Jordan. Indeed, the easternmost peaks are on the average only 100 meters (330 ft.) below sea level high, but the difference in level with the Zor, which lies 300 meters (1,000 ft.) below sea level, is nevertheless impressive for a distance of barely 2 kilometers (1 mi.). On the east side the Ghor has its normal width of 3 to 5 kilometers (2 to 3 mi.).

The narrow center strip ends where the Jabbok (Nahr ez-Zerqa) from the east and the less well-known Wadi Fara from the west enter the Ghor. From this point to the Dead Sea the valley has its greatest width, sometimes more than 20 kilometers (12 mi.).

## (4) THE DEAD SEA

The valley between the mountains continues in the inland sea known since the fourth century A.D. as the Dead Sea. In the Bible it is also called the "Sea of the Plain" and the Salt Sea. This latter designation no doubt refers to the high salt content of the water, which is six times as high as that of the other seas of the world. Besides salt, the water contains a high percentage of bromium, magnesium chloride, and calcium chloride. This makes the water very heavy and oily; plant and animal life cannot exist in it.

The Dead Sea is 75 kilometers (50 mi.) long. Its greatest width is just south of Engedi where it is slightly over 17 kilometers (11 mi.). The narrowest part is near el-Lisan, the well-known "tongue," which protrudes into the sea from the east. At this point its width is only 4 kilometers (2 mi.). The Lisan divides the inland sea into two parts: the large northern part is 400 meters (1,300 ft.) deep in the middle, while the southern part is barely 10 meters (33 ft.) deep in places.

It is not just because of its high salt content that the Dead Sea is such a unique phenomenon. Salt lakes are also found elsewhere. The Dead Sea is unique for its unequalled low level; here one is at the lowest spot on the face of the earth, about 395 meters (1,300 ft.) below sea level. This low position is further accented by the surrounding mountains. In the west these are the hard cretaceous rocks of the Judean desert. At a distance of 2 to 3 kilometers (1 to 2 mi.) some of its peaks are already 100 to 300 meters (330 to 1,000 ft.) high, a difference in height of 500 to 700 meters (1,650 to 2,300 ft.)! In the east the mountains are composed mainly of Nubian sandstone. Generally these are even higher and leave little or no room for a flat beach. Therefore, low beaches are found only in the north near the mouth of the Jordan or in the east near the mouth of the Arnon and alongside the Lisan; of course, they are also found in the south where the Wadi el-Arabah begins, and finally in the west. The hot springs near Engedi (Hamman ez-Zara), of Kallirhoë (Hammam ez-Zara), and in the northeast corner of the Lisan point to the influence of volcanic activity in the formation of the Dead Sea.

Because of the enormous evaporation the atmosphere is sweltering and the horizon hazy. The rate of evaporation is so great that the level of the inland sea is fairly constant, notwithstanding the large quantities of water that pour into this basin from every side.

## (5) THE WADI EL-ARABAH AND THE GULF OF AQABAH

The last part of the third track is made up of the Wadi el-Arabah, which goes into the Gulf of Aqabah. From the southern point of the Dead Sea to the Strait of Tiran this part is almost 350 kilometers (217 mi.) long, almost twice as long as the entire Jordan Valley. With its average width of 25 kilometers (15 mi.), the Gulf of Aqabah is suitable for ocean vessels. Only in the north do ships with considerable draft face some danger; there the bottom of the gulf climbs slowly to the coastline near el-Aqabah.

Though the Wadi el-Arabah gives a monotonous impression, it is not everywhere the same. Directly south of the Dead Sea the plain is over 11 kilometers (7 mi.) wide and lies more than 375 meters (1,230 ft.) below sea level. This region is naturally marshy, for the water of the Wadi el-Hesa and of a few brooks and springs loses itself in the sand of the plain. Somewhat over 30 kilometers (20 mi.) south of the Dead Sea the plain already lies 200 meters (660 ft.) below sea level. At this point the mountains on the western side recede; the soft Late Cretaceous rock that is found here is very much eroded and has resulted in the formation of broad wadis. One has to go 15 kilometers (10 mi.) to the west, in the Negeb, to reach sea level. Toward the south the level of the Arabah continues to rise, and about 78 kilometers (48 mi.) south of the Dead Sea the valley reaches sea level. Already 35 kilometers (21 mi.) farther south it has climbed to 200 meters (660 ft.) above sea level. In that region there is even a peak of 288 meters (945 ft.). The soil is rocky here. Here too lies a damlike formation; all the water north of it runs into the Dead Sea, while the water south of it flows into the Gulf of Aqabah. This last part of the Arabah, which is about 45 kilometers (28 mi.) long, is considerably smaller; the width varies from 5 to 10 kilometers (3 to 6 mi.). The mountains on either side are much more impressive. Only a few wadis are

found along the entire east side of the Arabah; traveling along them one can, with difficulty, reach the plateau of Edom. The Nubian sandstone and the granite that dominate in the south rise steeply like a wall. South of the dam, on the western side, the same situation prevails; the Nubian sandstone and even the hardest granite also appear there.

The word *Arabah* probably means "dry land," an apt name for this valley. To be sure, north and south of the dam the ground consists of alluvial soil that as such is not infertile, but the climate is very bad for spontaneous growth.

## d. The Mountains Inland

### (1) EAST OF THE ORONTES

The fourth track comprises the mountains that run parallel with the central highlands. The hills and the peaks of the Syrian-Arabian desert are thus not included. The division of this band corresponds for the most part to the division found in the third track.

The land east of the Orontes is the northernmost part of the fourth track. It deviates considerably from the rest because it is not really mountainous land. The region between Halab and Hamath is better characterized as a hilly plateau intersected now and then by free-standing mountain ranges. This landscape continues to the Euphrates east of Halab and Hamath.

### (2) THE ANTI-LEBANON RANGE AND MOUNT HERMON

The large northern part of the mountain ridge that runs parallel with the Lebanon is called the Anti-Lebanon; the small southern part, Hermon. Like the Lebanon and the Biqa this mountain ridge runs in a northeast-southwest direction and has a total length of about 160 kilometers (100 mi.). In contrast to the Lebanon, the highest point here lies in the south, where the top of Mount Hermon (Jebel es-Sheh) rises to 2,814 meters (9,233 ft.). West of Damascus Mount Hermon becomes the Anti-Lebanon. At this point there is a dip in the mountains; the mountain pass between Damascus and the Biqa is no more than 1,200 meters (3,950 ft.) high. Soon after that, about 25 kilometers (15 mi.) north of Damascus, the Anti-Lebanon again reaches a height of over 2,000 meters (6,600 ft.). The highest peak (2,629 m. or 8,626 ft.) lies about 60 kilometers (37 mi.) north of Damascus. The rocks of this mountain ridge are varied. In the higher regions one can find formations from the Jurassic Period, which preceded the Cretaceous Period. Furthermore, one also finds here the familiar trio: rocks from the Early Cretaceous Period, from the Late Cretaceous Period, and from the Eocene Period. Consequently one finds here peaks as well as rounded tops. Toward both the west and the east the slopes decline gradually for the most part. It is, for instance, possible to reach the top of Mount Hermon on foot. To the east the Anti-Lebanon increases in size and takes on the shape of a triangle. From Damascus to Homs one can find detached hill ridges; these come closer together in the vicinity of Palmyra. But this triangle between Damascus, Homs, and Palmyra is no more a genuine mountain region than the land east of the Orontes. This territory is better described as an uneven plateau 800 meters (2,600 ft.) high, interrupted now and then by peaks and mountain ridges 200 to 300 meters (660 to 1,000 ft.) higher.

## (3) THE LAND OF BASHAN

Bounded by Mount Hermon in the north, the Jordan Valley in the west, the Yarmuk in the south, and the desert in the east is an area (about 90 km. or 55 mi. long and wide) called "the land of Bashan" (Hauran). In the center this region is very fertile, for the soil consists primarily of weathered remains of volcanic activity in the Quaternary Period. The name of the extinguished volcano is Jebel ed-Druz; it lies about 100 kilometers (62 mi.) east of the Sea of Galilee. This is the border territory of the land of the Bible, for the desert begins on the east side of these mountains. The so-called "oaks of Bashan" (Isa. 2:13; Ezek. 27:6) probably grew in the area south of Mount Hermon. Several mountain ridges of over 1,000 meters (3,300 ft.), currently known as the "Golan Heights" (Jolan), are found there. The land of Bashan drops gradually from the northeast to the southwest. This decline gives the Yarmuk, with its many tributaries, a lot of water.

## (4) THE LAND OF GILEAD

The Yarmuk just mentioned is one of the largest wadis to intersect Transjordan. About 150 kilometers (100 mi.) to the south the well-known Arnon does the same. The territory bounded by these two rivers and by the Jordan Valley plus the Dead Sea in the west and the vast desert in the east can be designated "the land of Gilead," even though historically this is not altogether correct. The proper territory of Gilead was probably found in the high mountainland that extended north and south of the Jabbok. Already at a distance of 15 kilometers (10 mi.) from the Jordan Valley, which lies here 300 meters (1,300 ft.) below sea level, its peaks have risen to around 1,100 meters (3,600 ft.). Because of this difference of 1,400 meters (4,600 ft.) in elevation, the heartland of Gilead was always difficult to reach from the west, for the ground of this region consists primarily of hard rocks from the Early Cretaceous Period; along the Jabbok even older rocks come to the surface.

North of this heartland, at an elevation of 600 meters (1,950 ft.), lies an uneven area whose rocks are younger, coming from the Late Cretaceous Period. The rock found here has suffered little erosion because the region is protected by strips of hard rock in the north, in the south, and especially in the west.

South of the heartland lies an uneven plateau whose average height is 750 meters (2,460 ft.). It stretches from the present Amman to the Arnon (Wadi el-Mojib), a distance of 55 kilometers (34 mi.) in a straight line. The old city of Medeba (Madaba) may be regarded as the center. This region consists primarily of soft rock from the Late Cretaceous Period, and is also protected on the west by hard rock from the earlier periods. Consequently the plateau has been able to maintain itself for a distance of 8 to 13 kilometers (5 to 8 mi.) from the Dead Sea. Only then do declining slopes follow abruptly. One of its peaks, 7 kilometers (4 mi.) northwest of Medeba, is regarded as the locale of Mount Nebo.

East of these three regions one soon reaches the end of inhabitable land. The region of Bashan is on the average 75 kilometers (50 mi.) wide because the Jebel ed-Druz affords some protection against the forces of the desert. The rest of Transjordan lacks this protection, however. Thus 50 kilometers (30 mi.) east of the Jordan and the Dead Sea the stony Arabian desert usually begins. Oases such as el-Azraq, 100 kilometers (62 mi.) east of Amman, are the only places where agriculture is possible.

## (5) THE MOUNTAIN COUNTRY OF MOAB

The area bounded by the Arnon in the north, the Zered (Wadi el-Hesa) in the south, the Dead Sea in the west, and the desert in the east may be regarded as the heartland of Moab. It is a relatively small area, no more than 50 kilometers (30 mi.) from north to south and from west to east. Its landscape resembles the region north of the Arnon; in the east it is flat and in the west it drops sharply toward the Dead Sea. Its plateau here, however, lies at an elevation of over 900 meters (2,950 ft.). The western side has several peaks of over 1,000 meters (3,300 ft.), and south of el-Kerak some exceed 1,200 meters (3,950 ft.).

The large wadis in this region are impressive. The Arnon is actually a winding crack in the plateau. Twenty kilometers (12 mi.) south of the Dead Sea it is 5 kilometers (3 mi.) wide, and the water flows 500 meters (1,650 ft.) lower in a shallow bedding. This makes the Arnon a natural barrier. Not until 30 kilometers (20 mi.) east of the Dead Sea does crossing get easier. In the center the Wadi el-Kerak runs toward the west. This river is less impressive because the walls of the valley drop terracelike and cliffs in the rock are rarely perpendicular. The Wadi el-Hesa in the south has more resemblance with the Arnon. This wadi is a deep, wide crack with steep walls rising to a height of 800 meters (2,600 ft.) and with a bedding on the level of 300 meters (1,000 ft.).

A little over 8 kilometers (5 mi.) south of the Arnon lies the Jebel Shihan (1,065 m. or 3,494 ft.). The eruptions of this extinguished volcano have given the soil of the plateau north and especially south of the Arnon its reddish-brown color. This indicates that the volcano was active before the Arnon had come into existence. For the rest the ground is mostly similar to that of the area north of the Arnon, soft rock from the Late Cretaceous Period.

Limestone rocks and Nubian sandstone from the Early Cretaceous Period are found in the valley of and alongside the Arnon. The same is true of the area along the Dead Sea. One also finds many older rocks here, some even Pre-Cambrian. The Lisan is of course an exception. It consists of sediment from the Tertiary Period and alluvial soil from the Quaternary Period.

## (6) THE MOUNTAINS OF EDOM

Even more than the land of Moab, the territory of Edom consists of a north-south mountain range that gradually disappears in the desert toward the east and has abrupt, steep cliffs in the west. This mountain range stretches 110 kilometers (68 mi.) from the village of et-Tafila to about 45 kilometers (28 mi.) south of Maan. As a whole this mountain range lies at an elevation of 1,200 meters (3,950 ft.), but many parts rise above 1,500 meters (4,900 ft.), and a few peaks are over 1,600 meters (5,250 ft.). The two highest mountains reach 1,736 meters (5,696 ft.) and 1,727 meters (5,666 ft.), the one a little over 8 kilometers (5 mi.) north and the other 13 kilometers (8 mi.) south of the well-known Petra. Behind this 20 kilometer (12 mi.) wide range there follows, to the east, a narrow strip (7 km. or 4 mi.), at an elevation of about 1,150 meters (3,775 ft.). This in turn is followed by a 10 kilometer (6 mi.) wide strip at an elevation of about 1,050 meters (3,445 ft.). Finally, Edom disappears in the Arabian desert. Thus the mountains of Edom are not cut apart by large wadis. The real breaks are found along the Wadi el-Arabah. They run predominantly from the north to the south and from the northwest to the southeast. This makes the mountain range of Edom difficult to approach from the west. From the south it is not easy either. About 65 kilometers (40 mi.) northeast of el-Aqabah the plateau suddenly stops. There the wide Wadi el-Hisma flows from the northwest to the southeast at an elevation of about 800 meters (2,600 ft.).

Geologically the mountains of Edom are a complex territory. From the east to the west one can observe the following. Along the entire east side lies a vast area of hard limestone rocks from the Eocene Period. This means that as late as the Tertiary Period the water of the sea covered everything for a long time. The plateau itself consists primarily of soft limestone from the Late Cretaceous Period. If it were not for the strips of hard rock that hem in this plateau on the west side, erosion would have worn it away. The elevation would then have risen slowly from the Wadi el-Arabah to Maan, whereas now steep, rocky walls mark off the Wadi el-Arabah on the east side.

The rocks on the west side of Edom are highly diverse. First there is a strip of hard limestone from the Early Cretaceous Period that covers the entire length. This is followed by several narrow bands toward the west. There is Nubian sandstone from the Early Cretaceous Period; this is wider in the north and narrower in the south. Then there is Nubian sandstone from the Cambrian Period, with roselike, greenish marl from the same period beside and above it. This last combination has given the rocks around Petra their fascinating colors and shapes. After this there are several areas where hard granite from the Pre-Cambrian Period lies exposed on the surface. In between one can find places with the roselike, greenish marl, again with Nubian sandstone and hard Cretaceous layers. The unique character of the different rocks makes this a diverse and fascinating area.

### (7) NORTHWESTERN ARABIA

The final part of the fourth band is a strip of rocky mountains that stretch from about 60 kilometers (37 mi.) north of el-Aqabah to the northwest point of Arabia. In the north lies a crumbling, 15 kilometer (10 mi.) wide mountain ridge with lonely peaks up to 1,400 meters (4,600 ft.). The ridge keeps the Wadi el-Hisma and the Wadi el-Arabah apart from each other. The ridge runs south to el-Aqabah, and about 15 kilometers (9 mi.) from the city its peaks reach almost 1,600 meters (5,250 ft.). This mountain ridge is nothing but a northern spur of the mountainland of northwestern Arabia; it is likely the locale of the biblical Midian. Like the Sinai mountains, this mountainland runs along the Gulf of Aqabah to the south and has many peaks of over 2,000 meters (6,600 ft.). Pre-Cambrian layers of rock are prevalent here, though one can also find Early

Cretaceous limestone rocks and volcanic ashes from the Quaternary Period. But the rosy granite, often mixed with the greenish diorite, predominates.

## 2. CLIMATE, FLORA, AND FAUNA

### a. Climate

The climate of Palestine can be called subtropical; the summer is dry and hot and the winter is humid and chilly.

The summer begins in May and lasts till October. In that season the weather is much the same from day to day, for it is determined by a large, stable low pressure system above the Persian Gulf and a high pressure system near the Azores. This pressure system creates a constant air current above the eastern basin of the Mediterranean Sea. The hot air that blows in from Turkey is, to be sure, somewhat cooled above the Mediterranean Sea, but it remains too dry to cause rain.

The winter, which includes the period from October to April, brings greater variety in the weather. A gulf of depressions that often goes across the Mediterranean Sea all the way to India causes a cool, mostly southwesterly wind. A high pressure system then covers central Asia. This system often extends as far as the eastern part of the Mediterranean. This stops the southwestern current as well as the rain clouds. As a result, sunny days alternate with cloudy days and days with heavy showers. Not every winter or summer day in this area is alike, however. Cisjordan, Transjordan, Phoenicia, and northwest Syria are only a narrow strip between the sea in the west and the desert in the east. These two forces are constantly competing with each other. This competition takes on the character of confusion on account of the rising and dropping terrain from west to east and vice versa. The boundaries between the fertile land, the steppe, and the desert are therefore highly erratic.

Because of the above-mentioned factors, the summer temperatures differ considerably from place to place. For August, the hottest month, it has been possible to compute the following temperatures from west to east:

|  | MEAN | | AVERAGE |
|---|---|---|---|
| COAST | | | |
| *night* | 23°C | (73.4°F) | 26°C (78.8°F) |
| *day* | 29°C | (84.2°F) | |
| CENTRAL HIGHLANDS | | | |
| *night* | 18°C | (64.4°F) | 24°C (75.2°F) |
| *day* | 30°C | (86°F) | |
| JORDAN VALLEY | | | |
| *night* | 23°C | (73.4°F) | 31°C (87.8°F) |
| *day* | 39°C | (102.2°F) | |
| TRANSJORDANIAN PLATEAU | | | |
| *night* | 18°C | (64.4°F) | 25°C (77°F) |
| *day* | 32°C | (89.6°F) | |

To gain a proper perspective on these variations in temperature, one should not forget the short distances: from the coast to the central highlands is about 50 kilometers (30 mi.), from the central highlands to the Jordan Valley is 30 kilometers (20 mi.), and from the Jordan Valley to the plateau is also about 30 kilometers (20 mi.). From north to south the distances are greater, but one can construct a similarly varying table in this direction. The hottest spots turn out to be the valley of the Dead Sea and the Wadi el-Arabah, because of the southeasterly location and the exceptionally low level.

The temperature and the wind determine the living conditions. For a normal summer day in Palestine one must reckon with the following factors. The air heats up faster above the land than above the sea. Thus as the temperature climbs during the day the air above the land rises faster than the air above the sea. At a certain time of the day this creates a current from west to east. The cooler, heavier air above the sea replaces the warmer, lighter air above the land. During the night, to a lesser degree, the reverse happens; the air above the rocky land cools faster than the air above the water. This creates a slight current from east to west.

Though clouds are not rare, the summer as such is without rain. Because of the proximity of the sea and the regularly arising westerly wind, the air contains sufficient moisture to cause dew. With the exception of the real desert areas the entire land profits from it in the summer. During the winter there is less dew because the higher amounts of moisture often condense into rain. Ob-

viously this dew greatly aids plant growth in the dry summer. Because the hot rays of the morning sun soon make the dew evaporate, one may also view it as a symbol of perishability.

No fixed dates can be given for the beginning and end of the summer. June, July, and August are the main summer months. May and September may also be included, though there is the possibility of some rain in early May or at the end of September. This rain marks the beginning (in September) or the end (in May) of the wet season. Because of the influence of the desert still another phenomenon sometimes marks the division between summer and winter; this is the so-called sirocco (Hebrew *sharab*; Arabic *hamsin*). This is a dry, hot desert wind that usually lasts three to seven days. When this *sharab* blows, the humidity is abnormally low and the temperature rises to above average. There is little cooling in the night and the air is full of fine dust, blurring the sun. The wearisome and even unbearable character of this east wind is caused especially by the dry atmosphere. The humidity in the air can drop to 30 percent or lower. The significance of this becomes clear if it is realized that the normal humidity lies between 40 and 75 percent. This helps us understand why the Bible views this "east wind" as a cause of infertility and death, an expression of the punishing activity of God.

The winter is entirely different from the summer. Rain is typical for this season. The precipitation is around 550 millimeters (22 in.) in the coastal region, 600 millimeters (24 in.) in the central highlands, 250 millimeters (10 in.) in the Jordan Valley, and 400 millimeters (16 in.) on the heights of Transjordan. When one compares this to the yearly precipitation in Paris (about 575 mm. or 23 in.) and in London (about 615 mm. or 25 in.), one can hardly call Palestine a land with little rain. The difference is that the precipitation is limited to a certain part of the year. An additional factor is that even in the winter the number of sunny days far exceeds the number of rainy days. Out of a total of 210 days an average of only 45 are rainy. Consequently, one can hardly put winter here on a level with the similar period in regions farther north such as Western Europe or Canada, or with the wet monsoon of tropical countries.

The first rains usually fall in October. After that there is often a break in the rainfall of more than a month. The real rainy months are December, January, and February. In March and April, toward the end of the winter, the so-called late rains fall and help to ripen the grain in the field.

Very often the rain comes down in heavy showers. These are most frequent in the month of December, though they are not unusual in November and January. This is because most of the time the high pressure system above Siberia has not reached its full intensity. This enables the cold, polar air to flow directly to the south. This air collides with the fairly warm air above the Mediterranean Sea, causing the autumnal storms there, while in northwestern Syria, Lebanon, and Palestine it causes heavy rains. This water runs from the higher to the lower areas from where it makes its way to the Mediterranean Sea or to the Jordan Valley and the Dead Sea. At times this rainwater becomes a raging mass that sweeps away the fertile soil, dilapidated homes, people, and animals.

Fortunately the rain does not always fall in this disastrous manner. It also comes in the form of an extended drizzle that gently rejuvenates everything. Hail or snow is also possible, though not frequent. Snow falling on the central mountain ridge or on the plateau of Transjordan never remains long, for during the day the temperature always rises above freezing. Snow of longer duration is found only on the higher mountains such as the Lebanon range, Mount Hermon, and Jebel ed-Druz.

Because southwesterly winds predominate in the winter, generally the north has more rain than the south. For the regions from west to east it has been possible to come up with the following figures:

NORTHWESTERN SYRIA

| | | | |
|---|---|---|---|
| coastal plain | about | 800 mm. | (32 in.) |
| Jebel el-Ansariye | about | 1,100 mm. | (44 in.) |
| Orontes Valley | about | 650 mm. | (26 in.) |
| around Aleppo and Hama | about | 450 mm. | (18 in.) |

LEBANON

| | | | |
|---|---|---|---|
| coastal plain | about | 850 mm. | (34 in.) |
| Lebanon range | about | 1,600 mm. | (64 in.) |
| the Biqa | about | 800 mm. | (32 in.) |
| Anti-Lebanon and Hermon | about | 1,000 mm. | (40 in.) |
| north of Damascus | about | 400 mm. | (16 in.) |

NORTHERN PALESTINE

| | | | |
|---|---|---|---|
| coastal plain | about | 600 mm. | (24 in.) |
| Galilee | about | 700 mm. | (28 in.) |
| Jordan Valley | about | 350 mm. | (14 in.) |
| Bashan | about | 550 mm. | (22 in.) |

CENTRAL PALESTINE

| | | | |
|---|---|---|---|
| coastal plain | about | 500 mm. | (20 in.) |
| central highlands | about | 650 mm. | (26 in.) |
| desert of Judah | about | 200 mm. | (8 in.) |
| Jordan Valley | about | 125 mm. | (5 in.) |
| heartland of Gilead | about | 600 mm. | (24 in.) |
| plateau of Medeba | about | 400 mm. | (16 in.) |

SOUTHERN PALESTINE

| | | | |
|---|---|---|---|
| coastal plain | about | 200 mm. | (8 in.) |
| around Beer-sheba | about | 200 mm. | (8 in.) |
| Wadi el-Arabah | about | 50 mm. | (2 in.) |
| around el-Kerak | about | 400 mm. | (16 in.) |
| around et-Tafile | about | 300 mm. | (12 in.) |

Using these figures one can make the following generalizations:

a. Precipitation decreases from north to south.
b. Precipitation decreases from west to east.
c. The higher the land, the greater the amount of precipitation.
d. The lower the land, the smaller the amount of precipitation.
e. Precipitation is greater on the west side of the mountains than on the east side.

These figures are not to be taken as infallible. The winters may be either dry or wet, and it is possible that in the same year one area receives more and another less than the average amount of rain.

In the winter the temperature is considerably lower than in the summer. Already with "the early rain" the temperature drops immediately, especially in the higher regions. January is the coldest month. There is of course a great difference between a sunny day and a day with clouds and rain. Taking the average for this month, however, from west to east one obtains approximately the following figures:

| | MEAN | AVERAGE |
|---|---|---|
| COASTAL PLAIN | | |
| night | 9°C (48.2°F) | 13°C (55.4°F) |
| day | 17°C (62.6°F) | |
| CENTRAL HIGHLANDS | | |
| night | 5°C (41°F) | 9°C (48.2°F) |
| day | 13°C (55.4°F) | |

JORDAN VALLEY

| | | |
|---|---|---|
| night | 10°C (50°F) | |
| day | 20°C (68°F) | 15°C (59°F) |

TRANSJORDAN

| | | |
|---|---|---|
| night | 4°C (39.2°F) | |
| day | 12°C (53.6°F) | 8°C (46.4°F) |

The coldest weather is thus found in the higher regions and in the eastern regions. However, these, too, are only general figures. They do not, for example, indicate that night frosts can occur in the mountain areas and that as a rule temperatures are a little higher in the southern areas than in the northern areas.

Despite the rainfall, which is more than sufficient because of the short distances and the sharp relief of the land, few large rivers have come into existence. The numerous wadis are much more characteristic. These clefts have originated through the interaction of the various rock layers and earth tremors. Here the rainwater collects and flows to the Mediterranenan Sea, to the central valley between the mountains, or to the desert in the east. The wadis were gouged out even deeper as the rainwater, often in enormous quantities and with terrific force, tried to find its way to those lower areas. For the greater part of the year these clefts in the rocks are dry, however. Occasionally, between the boulders one finds an insignificant brook that is fed from a spring located above it.

The real rivers are the Orontes in northwest Syria, the Litani in southern Lebanon, the Yarmuk in Transjordan, and of course the Jordan. In addition there are a number of larger or smaller brooks, such as the Jabbok and the Arnon. These brooks do not amount to much in the summer, but in the winter, especially after a heavy downpour, these rivers and brooks can turn into raging masses of water.

Because of the abundant rainfall and the thick layers of limestone rock there are numerous springs. The porous limestone rocks allow part of the rainwater to seep to the older and less porous layers beneath them. This is how the subterranean channels were formed that try to find their way out at the foot of a mountain or hill. The number of these springs is especially large in the transition areas between mountain regions and lowlands. For instance, there are over a hundred along the Jordan Valley, north of the Sea of Galilee. Because these springs are very much dependent on the rainfall, their number and force decrease from north to south and from west to east. They are found everywhere, however, even in the desert east of el-Aqabah and in the Sinai desert.

## b. Flora and Fauna

The rainfall has to a large degree determined the flora and the fauna. Three zones can be distinguished: the region with the Mediterranean climate, the narrow strip of the steppe, and finally the desert.

The coastal regions and the adjoining lowland as well as the mountain regions of northwestern Syria, Lebanon, and Cisjordan belong to the climate zone of the Mediterranean Sea. Even the highland of Transjordan, that is, the land of Bashan, the mountains of Gilead, the plateau of Medeba, and the central territory of Moab and Edom, may be included with it for the most part. All these territories have the flora and the fauna of most of the areas around the Mediterranean Sea. Oaks, cypresses, and pine trees are found in the mountainous regions. The cedars of Lebanon are also well known. Careless exploitation through the centuries has pushed the forests back considerably, so that now this land is covered with dense, low brushwood.

Every specific area of the Mediterranean Sea zone—the marshlands, the dunes, the sandy soil, the alluvial land, and the rocky mountains—used to have its own kind of vegetation, which cannot be enumerated here, for—to take one example—in the present state of Israel alone there are eleven kinds of tamarisks. How much this entire zone is dependent on rain is seen every spring. The winter rains bring forth new life out of the apparently infertile ground. Trees and shrubs get new leaves and become green again, new grass shoots up, and everywhere one sees flowers of the field, such as anemones, lilies, cyclamen, narcissi, and orchids. After a few weeks of hot sun in April and May, however, not much remains of it. Even the tough thistles and thorns wither, and the land turns arid, dry, and dusty.

This zone also has its own fauna. The Bible

distinguishes between domestic animals and "the beasts of the field," or wild animals. Of the latter one finds all kinds of species, which are also found in certain areas of Africa, Asia, and Europe. That Palestine lies at the pivotal point of these three continents has much to do with it. Even today the country has at least thirty-five kinds of snakes. Thus even a summary of all the kinds of animals is impossible in a few pages.

To the tame animals belong, first, the small livestock; the usually white, fat-tailed sheep, which were kept for their wool, milk, meat, and skin, and the black goats, which were useful for the same reason. The keeping of cattle was limited to definite areas. The ass or donkey, which was used as a beast of burden and for riding, and the ox, which was used as a draft animal, also played a large role. Of the wild animals the Palestinian lion was the most familiar. Smaller than its African kin, this animal made its habitat in areas covered with dense vegetation, but since the Crusades it has disappeared. Such is apparently not the case with the Syrian brown bear, which reportedly is still found in some impenetrable parts of the Lebanon mountains. The small crocodile is extinct. The fox still hunts on his own, and packs of jackals still appear regularly.

In view of the lay of the land, there have undoubtedly always been a large number of birds in Palestine. They can be divided roughly into four groups: (1) the migratory birds such as the storks, which in the spring go from south to north over the land and in the autumn from north to south; (2) the birds that enter the land from the south in the dry season and leave with the first rain; (3) the birds that enter Palestine from the north and spend the winter there; and (4) the animals that spend their entire life in this land.

The second climate zone is formed by the steppe. This is the region between the Mediterranean Sea and the desert, with an average rainfall of 200 to 400 millimeters (8 to 16 in.). In Palestine this steppe is very twisted; it is a narrow strip, 8 to 30 kilometers (5 to 20 mi.) wide, that snakes through the land. The steppe begins behind the dunes south of Gaza and from there, at a width of about 25 kilometers (15 mi.), it moves in the direction of Beer-sheba and Dimona. South of these two places it descends, pocketlike, almost into the heart of the Negeb. South of Dimona this zone runs in a narrow strip to the north, east of Hebron, Bethlehem, and Jerusalem, and just south of Bethshean. At this height the steppe continues its way on the other side of the Jordan along the Jordan Valley, the Dead Sea, and the Wadi el-Arabah till just past the famous ruins of Petra. There it skirts around the mountains of Edom and then goes past the east side of the mountainland of Moab to the north as far as the Jebel ed-Druz. From there the steppe continues along the east side of Damascus, fans out in a northeasterly direction up to Palmyra, and moves in a more easterly direction until it reaches the valley of the Euphrates. Thus the steppe, almost ribbonlike, borders the climate zone of the Mediterranean Sea. The possibilities for eking out a living in this area are limited. Little rain falls here, and when it does it is usually in the form of downpours, making farming a risky undertaking. Some agriculture is possible, but the area is more suitable for shepherds. There is enough food here for small livestock. If one knows where to find the springs and wells in the wadis, there is also sufficient water for a limited number of people and animals.

Annual plants, which need much water, are rare in these areas. Whatever grows soon withers. Even so, trees and shrubs such as the tamarisk and the acacia are found here. In the higher areas such a tree or shrub often stands by itself; woods are more often found near wadis and springs. Only a small number of animals feel fully at home in this steppe; the small gazelle is one of them.

The desert is the third climate zone. It extends south and east of the steppe. Therefore most of the Sinai peninsula, the heartland of the present Negeb, and the Syrian-Arabian desert are part of it. Precipitation is minimal, at most 200 millimeters (8 in.), and in most areas less than 100 millimeters (4 in.). Moreover, this rain falls mainly in the form of a few downpours, which do not leave the ground enough time to absorb the water. The temperatures, too, are more extreme than elsewhere; a difference of 20° C (36° F) between day and night is not rare. Therefore the desert offers few opportunities for living; the only exceptions are the often vast oases. The desert was mainly an area for passing through, not for inhabiting. This trekking through the desert did not become possible on a large scale until the domestication of the one-hump camel (dromedary); then this animal could be used as a burden and saddle animal.

A separate climate zone lies south of Beth-shean along the banks of the Jordan, along the Dead Sea, and in the Wadi el-Arabah. These regions are totally enclosed by the steppe and the desert, but in many places where there is an abundance of water they have a tropical character. The heat, the humidity, and their low position make for luxurious vegetation. This does not mean, however, that everywhere these areas are thickly grown over. In places where there is no water the steppe and the desert dominate.

## 3. HUMAN LIFE

Water is indispensable for every community. Because Palestine (like Greece) has hardly any rivers that hold water year-round, the springs are very important. Near these springs one was assured of water during the long, rainless summer. Attempts were undoubtedly made already very early to collect and store the rainwater in cisterns and to keep it for the summer. As long as the cisterns were hewn out of the limestone ground, however, they had little effect in most places. Limestone rocks are usually porous; the water slowly seeps through. The problem was solved about 1100 B.C. and, according to recent investigations in the mountains of Samaria, locally even several centuries before that, through the discovery of a plaster that was impervious to water. Spread over the bottom and along the sides of the cistern, this plaster made it possible to keep the water till the end of the summer and even longer. Because the quantity of "dead water" was totally dependent on the rains in the winter, and because the danger of spoiled water was ever present, however, the "living water" from springs remained preferable.

In addition to the availability of water, other factors determined whether a human community could exist in a certain place. For instance, a village had to have enough arable land as well as pastureland. Even in the zone of the Mediterranean Sea such land is not everywhere available. If a village was located in the valley of a river, such as Beth-shean, for example, or in the coastal plain,

such as Sidon, there was enough cropland. In the hill country or in the mountain regions the situation was much less favorable, however. In those areas a large community could develop only at localities with enough flat land, such as near Shechem. In other places the available arable land was increased by constructing small horizontal walls along the slopes, thus creating long, narrow terraces on the hills. Usually there was enough pastureland. Palestine does not have meadows like Western Europe, but in the winter sheep and goats usually found enough to eat in places that were unsuitable for agriculture, and in the summer they could graze on fallow land.

Another factor contributing to the rise and development of a community was the possibility of contact with other groups. As a community grew, work specialization created an overproduction of some goods and a shortage of others. At a certain stage in the development of the community, exports and imports thus became very important. In addition, the commerce between other cities and countries could bring much economic profit and political advantage to the community. Thus many cities were built along caravan routes, though the reverse—first cities, then caravan routes—also happened here and there. As a result, three types of roads can be distinguished i: Palestine and surrounding lands.

First, regional roads linked village to village and city to city; these were important for local trade and for the maintenance of family ties.

Second, highways, were constructed when the communities began to form larger political units. These roads facilitated the contacts between the major parts of the state. They were necessary for the economy and for the protection of the country. Examples of such roads are the highways that go over the mountain ridges and through the Negeb. The highway of the central highlands followed along the strip that has the highest peaks of Palestine. Nature itself dictates that in this area this is the best place for a road. If the road were to be shifted a little to the east or to the west, numerous wadis flowing eastward or westward from the mountain ridge would have to be crossed. In many places this was difficult, even impossible. Since this was such a natural route to follow, it is not surprising that alongside it lay several well-known cities such as Shechem, Bethel, Jerusalem, Bethlehem, and Hebron. According to Judges 21:19, at one time the route of this road was better known than the location of the sacred place of Shiloh. Another important highway connected Jerusalem with the Gulf of Aqabah. Recent investigations have shown that this road through the Negeb was protected by a large number of military posts.

Third, the international routes maintained contact with the surrounding countries. The most important of these was the one that connected Egypt with Mesopotamia. This road moved north of the Sinai desert, along the coast and the mountainland of Palestine, through the Valley of Jezreel, past Hazor, across the Jordan, past Damascus, and so northward to the Euphrates. The total length of this route was about 1,000 kilometers (620 mi.); it was about 200 kilometers (125 mi.) from Egypt to Palestine, about 250 kilometers (155 mi.) through Cisjordan, and about 550 kilometers (340 mi.) through Syria. Along this road were found such cities as Gaza, Ashkelon, Megiddo, Hazor, Damascus, Hamath, and Halab (Aleppo). Another important international road ran through Transjordan. Going through the territories of Ammon, Moab, and Edom, this road connected Mesopotamia and Syria with the Gulf of Aqabah; from there it had branches to the Arabian peninsula, eastern Africa, and Egypt. For a long time this Transjordanian route followed a line farther west, straight through Moab and Edom. A line farther east ran over the plateau of Transjordan along the desert zone. Because water was available at only a few places and there was little natural protection, this eastern route could be used extensively only when there was a strong central government, such as in the Roman era.

The unsafety of the eastern branch of the Transjordanian highway shows that safety was a fourth factor that was important for the develop-ment of human communities. The natural geographical divisions of Palestine and its surroundings made it difficult for the country to become a political unity. Because of their contrary interests, the various political powers constituted a permanent danger. Until the fall of Jerusalem in 587 B.C., the period of David and Solomon was the only significant exception. Consequently, from the beginning the communities were forced to settle at safe places. Wherever possible they located on hills or peninsular mountains. An added benefit was that this saved the fertile lands in the valleys for the growing of crops. A wall was constructed around the top of such a hill, which made the place look more like a fortress than a city. A great disadvantage of settling on the top was that one was rather far removed from the spring at the bottom of the hill. In times of siege this water even became unreachable. Thus ingenious methods such as shafts and tunnels were used to gain access to the water. The best-known example is the tunnel of Shiloah under the City of David in Jerusalem.

This situation changed after the Exile. Palestine was then a political unity, or rather, the country was a province made up of one large realm. During the Persian domination the cities remained at their old locations. This situation changed in the Hellenistic era. Cultural life required extensive public buildings, for which there was no room on a restricted hilltop. Consequently, the theaters, the gymnasiums, the stadia, and the like were put in the valley around the city, and the city itself became an acropolis. This meant, of course, that the cities were less secure and that the scarcity of fertile lands became a matter of permanent concern. Thus villages still arose in the old way; the cities, however, had to move along with the waves of the new culture. As a matter of fact, once the Roman empire was firmly entrenched, the defense of cities and villages was left to fortifications on the borders.

*I. The Jordan River flows through the plain of Gennesaret into the northern end of the Sea of Galilee. (L. T. Geraty)*

*II. Mount Gilboa (modern Jebel Fuquah) is between Megiddo and Beth-shean and southeast of Jezreel. (A. D. Baly)*

III. Snow-capped Mount Hermon as seen from Lebanon. (W. S. LaSor)

IV. An oak forest in Gilead (Transjordan). The trees stand far apart; if they were close together there would not be enough water for all of them, since moisture is in limited supply. These are remnants of old forests (cf. 2 Sam. 18:6–9). The "forest of Ephraim" was in this vicinity. Unlike our woods, these old oak forests could definitely have served as a battlefield. (C. H. J. de Geus)

*V. Landscape in the hill country of Judah. (C. H. J. de Geus)*

*VI. The creeping vines of Palestine. The grapes are led along the ground, so that the leaves can pick up as much moisture as possible. Especially in the summer, dew is a precious form of precipitation. (C. H. J. de Geus)*

VII. The shore of the Dead Sea in the vicinity of the present Sedom. (Rob Lucas, Enschede)

VIII. View of the Valley of Jezreel, the "breadbasket of Israel." In the foreground is the typical red earth. (Rob Lucas, Enschede)

# B. Geography of the Countries around Palestine

*by J. H. Negenman*

A brief description of the physical conditions, the climate, and the living conditions of the countries around Palestine might give the impression that Palestine functioned as the center. As far as history is concerned, such was obviously not the case. In addition, Palestine played a limited role in the formation process of the earth. We have presented the elaborate description of Palestine and its environs above and are offering this brief sketch of the neighboring lands only because of their role in biblical literature. This role presupposes a much greater knowledge of Palestine than of those other countries.

Palestine and its environs have had only a subordinate role in the formation process. Left to itself, the eastern strip along the Mediterranean Sea would never have become part of the mainland. The source of the forces that gave existence to the bridge between Asia and Africa, by pushing up the land, lay in the African and Asian massifs. Because of the converging movement of these blocks Palestine eventually emerged from the Mediterranean water.

This particular context does not allow space for a complete description of this formation process. For a good understanding of the history of Israel and of the early Church a broad outline of the surrounding countries is sufficient.

## 1. EGYPT

### a. Physical Geography

Because of the Nile, Egypt can be divided into four regions: the Delta in the north, the river valley from Cairo to Aswan, the western desert (es-Sahra el-Gharbiya), and the eastern desert (es-Sahra esh-Sharqiya). The land as a whole lies on the northern side of the African massif and owes its origin and shape to this massif and the sea. About 30 percent of the ground of present-day Egypt consists of Pre-Cambrian granite and Nubian sandstone. Everywhere in the south as well as in the east along the Red Sea these rocks lie exposed on the surface. Farther to the north all the way to the vicinity of Cairo, limestone rocks from the Eocene and Miocene Epochs (60-13 million years old) dominate, having been deposited there by the sea in the course of time. Between these rocks and north of them, in the valley of the Nile and in the Delta, lies a thick layer of alluvial ground. Near Aswan this layer is about 7 meters (23 ft.) thick and in the Delta more than 15 meters (49 ft.) thick. It is fertile soil, originating for the most part in Ethiopia and the Sudan. Since this ground was carried there mainly by the Nile and, moreover, since the river annually inundates the area, one may say with respect to this part of the land that Egypt is a gift from the Nile.

Since the last glacial period this river has made the valley habitable when changes in climate shaped the deserts of northern Africa into their present form. The river as such begins in Lake Victoria, which lies at an elevation of 1,135 meters (3,725 ft.). From that lake to the Mediterranean Sea it traverses a distance of about 6,650 kilometers (4,130 mi.). To Aswan, at an elevation of 100 meters (330 ft.), the course and the drop of the river are very irregular because of the hard subsoil; one time it flows slowly over a plateau, then again the water forces itself through all kinds of sharp turns, resulting in cataracts. From Khartum, where from the east the Nile is joined by the Blue Nile, to Aswan there are six such waterfalls. Ninety percent of the yearly inundation is caused by another tributary, the Atbara. Originating in the 2,000 meter (6,600 ft.) high Ethiopian plateau, in the rainy season this river pours its volumes of waters into the Nile about 270 kilometers (167 mi.) north of Khartum. Only at Aswan, after it has traveled 5,000 of the 6,000 kilometers (3,100 of the 3,700 mi.), does the Nile begin to flow more evenly. The granite and the Nubian sandstone end there, and the limestone, which is easier for the water to flow through, begins. There are no more cataracts, and the curves are less sharp. The drop, too, is more gradual: every 14 kilometers (9 mi.) the river drops only 1 meter (3 ft.). From there on the yearly flooding is the only change. This starts in early July and ends in November. Interestingly, this means that the Nile reaches its highest level when the Euphrates, the Tigris, and the Jordan are at their lowest.

Each of the four large regions—the Delta, the valley, the eastern desert, and the western desert—has its own features.

The Delta is a relatively level area that used to be known as Lower Egypt. From north to south it has a length of about 150 kilometers (100 mi.) and from west to east a width of about 300 kilometers (200 mi.). Today the Nile divides above Cairo, with one branch flowing to Rosetta (Rashid) to the west and the other branch flowing to Damietta (Dumyat) on the east. Formerly the river apparently split into seven branches. The thickness of the alluvial ground now fluctuates between 15 and 25 meters (49 and 82 ft.). Because the drop of the river is so gradual, hardly any salinization has occurred. From Cairo, which lies at a level of around 17 meters (56 ft.), the water drops at a ratio of 1 to 10,000, that is, 1 meter (3 ft.) for every 10 kilometers (6 mi.). Consequently, brackish soil is found only in the north along the sea.

The Nile valley itself, which used to be called Upper Egypt, extends from Cairo to Aswan, a length of about 1,000 kilometers (620 mi.). Despite its length, the surface area of this valley is only about half that of the Delta, because of its narrowness, which generally fluctuates between 8 and 15 kilometers (5 and 10 mi.). An exception is the area approximately 35 kilometers (22 mi.)

south of Cairo; there the valley widens to the west to 80 kilometers (50 mi.). In this depression lies Lake Qarun (Birket Qarun) at about 45 meters (150 ft.) below sea level. This lake is about 35 kilometers (22 mi.) long and 5 kilometers (3 mi.) wide, but with high water an area four to five times as large can be inundated. For this lake is fed by a branch of the Nile (Bahr Yusuf) that begins 15 kilometers (10 mi.) south of el-Amarna, as well as by the water from the surrounding areas above it. This depression, which is known as the Faiyum oasis (el-Fayyum), greatly enlarged the arable land. The eastern side of the valley is considerably smaller here, only 5 to 8 kilometers (3 to 5 mi.), but the many springs at the bottoms of the hills make this a very fertile area. Approximately 100 kilometers (62 mi.) south of Cairo the valley resumes its normal width, on the west about 9 kilometers (6 mi.) and on the east about 4 kilometers (2 mi.). This situation is maintained, notwithstanding the many curves, to about 20 kilometers (12 mi.) north of Aswan. There the actual valley ends and the first waterfall, caused by the hard granite ground, begins. For that reason the valley between Aswan and the Sudan border, which is now filled with the water of Lake Nasser, could not be reached by ship.

The western desert, also called the Libyan desert, occupies about three-fourths of modern Egypt. It is a plateau of sandstone and limestone rocks lying at an elevation of 200 to 300 meters (660 to 1,000 ft.). Occasionally, particularly in the southwest, peaks of nearly 1,000 meters (3,300 ft.) are found. In general it is a fairly level area. There are few real wadis. There are, however, a number of depressions that, because their level is below 200 meters (660 ft.), contain enough water to create oases. Two hundred fifty kilometers (155 mi.) west of the Nile, near Luxor (el-Uqsur), lies a depression (el-Wahat el-Hariya), a long strip from north to south. Approximately 100 kilometers (62 mi.) farther to the west lies a second but smaller depression (el-Wahat ed-Dahila). Fifty kilometers (30 mi.) northwest of it lies the next depression (el-Wahat el-Farafira). The smallest depression (el-Wahat el-Bahariyya) lies southwest of the Faiyum 150 kilometers (100 mi.) from the Nile. The largest depression is found at the latitude of Cairo, about 300 kilometers (200 mi.) to the west. It is the well-known Qattara depression, an area with a length of 250 kilometers (150 mi.) at the longest point and an average width of 100 kilometers (62 mi.). The entire depression lies below sea level, and its lowest point lies 134 meters (440 ft.) below. Caught between the limestone plateau in the south and the Libyan sand plateau in the northwest, this depression has few oases. Better known as a well-watered place is the Siwa oasis (el-Wahat Siwa) southwest of the Qattara depression and 500 kilometers (300 mi.) from the Nile.

The eastern desert, also known as the Arabian desert, covers approximately one-fifth of the land of Egypt. It differs considerably from the western desert. It is not a plateau but real mountain country. In the middle, close to the Red Sea, there is even a peak (Jebel Shaib) of 2,187 meters (7,176 ft.). The entire area is intersected by wadis that flow to the Nile valley, to the Gulf of Suez, or to the Red Sea. Particularly in the south, where sandstone is predominant, these wadis are reasonably passable. In the north, south of the Cairo-Suez line, these desert hills are rarely higher than 250 meters (820 ft.); north of this line the terrain quickly levels out and eventually merges into the Delta. The location of the present Suez Canal used to be the direct link between Egypt and Asia. Though this corridor has a length of 145 kilometers (90 mi.), this area had only two passages for leaving or entering Egypt, for the northern part between the present cities of Port Said and Ismailia is largely marshy and sandy. Only near Ismailia is the ground naturally quite passable; that is where the northern passage was. About 20 kilometers (12 mi.) south of Ismailia are the Bitter Lakes, with a total length of 40 kilometers (25 mi.). Between these lakes and Suez used to be the southern land connection between Egypt and the Sinai.

### b. Climate, Flora, and Fauna

The climate of Egypt is best characterized as a desert climate. This means that the summers are hot and dry and the winters cool and dry, and that there can be extreme differences in temperature between day and night. Locally there are, of course, variations. In the north, along the coast, the average precipitation comes to 300 millimeters (12 in.) per season. Because of the influence of the sea the variations in temperature are less extreme here. In Alexandria, for example, the variation is only about 8° C (14.4° F); the day and night temperatures during the summer are around 30° C (86° F) and 22° C (71.6° F) respectively, and during the winter around 18° C (64.4° F) and 10° C (50° F). The humidity is naturally higher here, too, than farther inland. Near Cairo, at the beginning of the valley, the situation has changed a lot already. Rain is rare here, approximately 25 millimeters (1 in.) per season. Temperature variations are greater too. The nighttime summer temperature averages 22° C (71.6° F), and the daytime temperature around 36° C (97° F). For the winter these figures are 7° C (44.6° F) and 18° C (64.4° F). Still greater contrasts are found near Aswan, at the end of the valley. There is little precipitation there, sometimes 3 millimeters (0.12 in.). In the summer the temperature may climb to 42° C (107.6° F) during the day and drop to 25° C (77° F) during the night, while in the winter the thermometer may go up to 23° C (73.4° F) during the day and go down to 9° C (48.2° F) during the night.

For the eastern and western deserts the contrasts are even greater. The western desert is part of the large Sahara and as such has for the most part the same climate as this immense area. Only the depressions with their oases form an exception. They are larger and, particularly in the south, richer in water than many oases in the Sahara. The proximity of the plateau of Sudan has something to do with it. Perhaps the Nile also helps by carrying water to these areas through the limestone soil.

The eastern desert has a somewhat different climate than the western desert. Because of its elevation the average temperature is a few degrees lower. The chance of precipitation is also somewhat greater. In all of Egypt the sun shines, unobstructed by clouds, nearly every day. The differences between summer and winter are mainly those of temperature. The heat in summer is fortunately tempered by the nearly constant north wind that is caused by the high pressure system above the Sahara and by the difference in temperature between the water of the sea and the air masses above central Africa. By contrast, conditions become virtually unlivable when the south wind arises. This can happen from April through June when there are depressions above the Sahara. The temperature can quickly rise 10 degrees (18° F), while the humidity in the air is often no more than 10 percent.

Vegetation and animal life in the desert areas differ, of course, from those along the Nile. Many aquatic plants grow in the valley and in the Delta. The papyrus plant, which was the symbol of Lower Egypt, is everywhere. Illustrations and texts show that this plant, which can reach a height of 2 to 5 meters (6 to 16 ft.), was found in abundance along the riverbanks and in marshy areas. The lotus flower must have been characteristic of Upper Egypt because this plant was the symbol of that region. In contrast, trees were rare. Date palms, some cypresses, and sycamores grew along the Nile and in the oases, while the tamarisk and the acacia grew in the wadis.

Wild animals such as the ibex, the gazelle, the hyena, and the leopard lived in the deserts and in the steppes. In and along the water lived, among others, the crocodile and the hippopotamus. In addition there were, of course, the birds. Even today the Nile Valley is a bird paradise; at least 150 kinds have their permanent habitat there, and approximately 200 kinds of migratory birds live there temporarily. It is doubtful whether the elephant and the lion were indigenous there in biblical times. Intensive human habitation of the Nile valley soon forced out or exterminated these and similar animals.

## c. Human Life

Changes in climate made life in the desert very difficult. The river valley, by contrast, offered all kinds of possibilities for sedentary communities. This valley guaranteed optimum safety and undisturbed development. The waterfalls in the south, the sea in the north, and the deserts in the east and in the west (called "the red land" by the Egyptians) constituted natural protection. The annual flooding that deposited fertile silt on the fields protected "the black earth" against depletion. The danger of salinization, as in Meso-

potamia, was virtually nonexistent, for the water receded by itself to the riverbed. The Egyptians therefore recognized only three seasons: the season of flooding (July-November), the season of sowing and harvesting (December-March), and the dry season (April-June). This flooding was highly regular, both in extent and in time. At its peak early in September the river was 15 meters (49 ft.) higher than normal near Aswan and still 7 meters (23 ft.) higher than normal near Cairo. Deviations rarely occurred; in summer there is always enough rain on the high plateau of Ethiopia with its peaks of up to around 4,000 meters (13,000 ft.). With a low Nile, as happened only occasionally, not enough fields could be flooded; too high a Nile jeopardized the scheme of sowing and harvesting. In both cases the result was the same: a shortage of grain and vegetables. The irrigation system was rather simple. Through canals with raised banks the rising water was directed to the sides of the valley and caught in basins, from which, wherever and whenever necessary, it was released over the fields, which were lined with dikes.

This irrigation made possible a prosperous existence in this rainless land. For in addition to the products of the field, the waterfowl and the livestock provided meat and the Nile yielded an abundance of fish. The moderate climate enabled the people to live in lightly constructed homes; because they were so light, however, few of them have survived. The ability to erect monumental structures was surely there, nevertheless. Especially the eastern desert yielded all sorts of stone for building. Good limestone was found in many places, for example, opposite Memphis. There were sandstone quarries on the east side between Luxor and Aswan, while granite was obtained from the vicinity of Aswan. Particularly between the rocks in the south there are many metamorphic rocks, that is, pieces of rock that have changed their structure through enormous pressure and high temperature; among them are alabaster, turquoise, and quartz. This material was transported by way of the Nile, which was an eminently suitable transport route. To the north one could go along with the stream, while the north wind made sailing upstream (i.e., south) possible. The papyrus forests had all sorts of uses.

The green parts of the papyrus provided food for the cattle, the root provided fuel, the bark the raw material for mats, baskets, cords, and sandals, the stems material for ships, and the pith was used for papyrus rolls.

Yet Egypt was no paradise. Certain goods were in short supply, making trade necessary. Good lumber, for example, was scarce. The interest of the Egyptians in the cedars of Lebanon is not surprising; the less so because the overland route and the coastal route were not too difficult. Other goods such as gold, ebony, ivory, and perfume were obtained from Nubia, the country south of the first waterfall; from Cush, the country south of the second waterfall; and from the Sudan. Near Aswan there was extensive barter trade. More than that was done, however. Already during the Sixth Dynasty (ca. 2300 B.C.) a canal was hewn around the first waterfall; with high water one could go farther south by boat toward Nubia, which came to be regarded as a conquered province. Successful attempts were made to navigate the wadis to get to the Red Sea, from whose harbors one could sail to eastern Africa or southern Arabia. There are indications that the Egyptians even dug a primitive canal for that purpose between the Nile and the Gulf of Suez.

The irrigation system and the expeditions abroad required some kind of organization. This led to the dynasties, which provided the necessary leadership. Upper and Lower Egypt soon united and Memphis (Egyptian *Men-Nofer*), a city on the boundary of the valley and the Delta, became the capital. During the Middle Kingdom, when Egypt was more isolationistic, Thebes (Egyptian *No-Amon*) for some centuries assumed that role. From there the Hyksos were driven out of their capital Avaris, somewhere in the eastern Delta. During the New Kingdom the insignificant city of Akhetaton (Tell el-Amarna) was briefly the center. Being more interested in Asia, Ramses II made Tanis (Egyptian *Pi-Ramses*) in the eastern Delta his new residence. Later, when Egypt was in a weakened condition, foreign rulers from Libya and Ethiopia took over. Egypt gained new stature under the Ptolemies. From Alexandria, the new capital located in the north, Egypt looked to the coasts of the Mediterranean Sea.

But the empire was no match for the powerful invading Romans. The country remained an important economic factor in the Roman empire, however, for Egypt became the granary of Rome. The contact with the Egyptian province was of vital importance for the residents of the imperial city. The shortest route between Rome and Alexandria was by way of the Mediterranean Sea. Because this route was not always safe, the land route through Palestine was also very important.

## 2. MESOPOTAMIA

### a. Physical Geography

Originally the name Mesopotamia referred only to the northern territory between the Euphrates (el-Furat) and Tigris (el-Dijla) rivers. Today it is customary to include the southern part of the Persian Gulf as well.

The name Mesopotamia ("between the rivers") points to the great importance of the Euphrates and the Tigris for this area. The two rivers wrap themselves around the land, which is surrounded by mountains in the east (the Zagros) and in the north (mountains of Kurdistan), is bounded by deserts in the west (Syrian desert) and in the southwest (Arabian desert), and touches the Persian Gulf in the southeast. The sources of the Euphrates are two mountain streams (Murat and Kara Su) in the high mountains of eastern Asia Minor, the area where the mountain ridges of eastern Turkey, which run in a southwesterly-northeasterly direction, meet the mountain ridges of the Caucasus and the Zagros mountains, which run in a northwesterly-southeasterly direction. It is an area with many high volcanic peaks, of which Mount Ararat (5,165 m. or 16,946 ft.) is the highest. It is no wonder that in antiquity people from the Near East regarded this mountainland as the top of the world. It was also the territory of Urartu and from the sixth century B.C. the heartland of Armenia, which as the borderland of the Roman empire experienced a turbulent period at the beginning of the Christian era. The source of the Tigris lies in the same mountainland, at a distance of about 60 kilometers (37 mi.) from the point where the Murat and Kara Su merge to form the Euphrates. A mountain ridge of over 2,000 meters (6,600 ft.) has kept the two rivers separate. The Euphrates was forced to go in a southwesterly direction, the Tigris in an easterly direction. After they leave the mountainland, both rivers lose their character of wild mountain streams and become quieter waterways at a level of around 400 meters (1,300 ft.).

At the border of Turkey and Syria, near Jarabulus, the Euphrates is still only a little over 150 kilometers (100 mi.) from the Mediterranean Sea. The plateau around Aleppo, and later the Syrian desert plus the mountain strips around Palmyra, however, force the river to continue in a southerly and southeasterly direction. In this northeastern part of present-day Syria the Euphrates is fed by two tributary rivers (Balikh and Habur), whose source is the southern slopes of the Armenian mountains. These tributaries often widen the Euphrates from 600 to 700 meters (1,950 to 2,300 ft.); numerous islets in the river, however, illustrate its erratic course. For the riverbanks rise rather fast here, so that in this northern area the Euphrates has only a relatively narrow valley. The river valley widens only after the confluence with the Nahr el-Habur, especially on the east side. From that point, however, the Euphrates is no longer being fed by the water of real rivers, with the result that it slowly enters the southern part of Mesopotamia.

The Tigris may be regarded as the drainage canal for the Armenian mountains in the north and the Zagros mountains in the east. Whereas the Euphrates makes a long detour along the Syrian steppe, the Tigris follows a more direct route to the lower area. Near Mosul in northern Iraq it already flows at a level of 250 meters (820 ft.). It takes the river about 650 kilometers (400 mi.) to reach this level, in contrast to the Euphrates, which needs about 1,400 kilometers (850 mi.) for that. The Tigris has therefore always been a faster and more turbulent river than the Euphrates. This character is strengthened by the large tributaries that feed the Tigris from the Zagros mountains, such as the Great Zab (Zab el-Kebir), the Little Zab (Zab es-Saghir), and especially the Diyala. Normally, therefore, the Tigris flows around 4,000 cubic meters (140,000 cu. ft.) per second near Baghdad, whereas at that level the Euphrates barely reaches 2,500 cubic meters (88,000

cu. ft.). South of Mosul the Tigris makes its way through a narrow valley in a south-southeasterly direction and so comes continually closer to the Euphrates. Near Baghdad the rivers are only about 30 kilometers (20 mi.) apart.

The land upstream around the Euphrates and Tigris looks like this: Flowing through what is now Syria, the Euphrates has to make its way through a limestone plateau. To the southwest stretches the stony, sloping Syrian desert. Northeast of the Tigris lies a relatively level area known today as "the island" (el-Jazirah). Its elevation fluctuates around 300 meters (1,000 ft.). Some mountain ridges break the monotony: in the center the Jebel Abd el-Aziz, whose highest peak reaches 920 meters (3,019 ft.), and farther to the east the Jebel Sinjar, which rises to 1,460 meters (4,790 ft.). The northernmost and most fertile part of this area used to be the interior of the country of the ancient Mitanni. The entire "island" consists of an alluvial plain of sand and loess, resting on a substratum of limestone and basalt that at times is exposed on the surface. The alluvial ground derives from the higher areas that, except in the southeast, surround the plain. The climate, the level, and the soil conditions have made for typical phenomena here. From the south side of the Jebel Sinjar runs a stream of wadis that lose themselves in the 350 kilometer (217 mi.) long Wadi Tartar, ending up in a marshy inland lake. There are more such inland lakes. For instance, about 70 kilometers (43 mi.) south of the Jebel Sinjar lies Lake Sunaisila. Approximately 80 kilometers (50 mi.) southeast of it, along the current border of Syria and Iraq, lies an entire area with such lakes. "Lakes" is perhaps not the right term; they are more like marshy, brackish valleys.

The area east of the northern Tigris is entirely different. This is already obvious from the Jebel Hamrin, which lies a short distance from the Tigris. This mountain ridge between the Little Zab and Diyala tributaries is a kind of outpost of the high Zagros. The farther one goes from here to the north and to the east, the more uneven the terrain becomes and the higher the plateau rises. In this area, between the Tigris, the Little Zab, and the mountains in the northeast, lies the so-called Assyrian triangle, the interior of Assyria with the ruins of Asshur, Nineveh, Dur Sharrukin, and other cities.

The southern part of Mesopotamia differs in many respects from the northern part. The delta, which runs from Baghdad to the Persian Gulf, is about 600 kilometers (375 mi.) long and 200 kilometers (125 mi.) wide, that is, it has the same length and width as the entire eastern coastal strip along the Mediterranean Sea with its four geological tracks. It is one immense alluvial plain of loam and loess. This alluvial soil often has a thickness of 10 meters (33 ft.) or more. Over millions of years the soil has been carried here from the mountains and the loess from the deserts. At one time it was thought that the sediment carried by the Euphrates and the Tigris might have shifted the coastline at the Persian Gulf farther to the south. But the thick layer of sediment that already starts directly south of Baghdad, the fact that most of the water of the Euphrates and the Tigris does not even reach the sea, and the difference of 2 meters (6 ft.) between high and low tide suggest that the coastline has not drastically changed. That the level of the delta has not risen very much, despite the enormous layers of sediment, must be explained as due to the gradual dropping of the hard underlayer of the delta. This also explains why today the oldest dwelling places of southern Mesopotamia are often below the level of the groundwater.

Through this yellow, clayish plain the Euphrates and the Tigris find their way, making numerous turns and frequently branching into side rivers. The winter rains and especially the melting snow often double the volume of water in the rivers. Because of the low level of the delta (37 m. or 121 ft. near Baghdad), this water can flood large areas, where it stays until it has seeped into the ground or been evaporated by the sun. In many places it does not even get that far. As a result, large, shallow lakes with marshy banks have formed. One extensive inland lake (100 by 30 km., or 62 by 20 mi.) lies on the south side of the end of the Euphrates, the Hawr el-Hammar. In this lake the Euphrates loses most of its water before it merges with the Tigris, and over a length of 110 kilometers (68 mi.) forms the Shatt el-

Arab. In addition, the Tigris becomes a lot calmer in this southern region. That the tributaries from the Zagros mountains can no longer reach the Tigris and already are swallowed up by the alluvial plains east of the Tigris has something to do with it. Deep in the south the Nahr Karun manages to do this, but by then the Tigris has already merged with the Euphrates. That has brought into being the narrow strip of land around the Nahr Karun connecting the territory of ancient Elam with southern Mesopotamia. By contrast, the nearly impenetrable barrier of the Arabian desert lay for centuries in a southwesterly direction. The level of this area lies higher than the valley of the Euphrates, but there are no constantly flowing rivers from this plateau to the valley. But a large number of wadis quickly carry away the scarce rainwater from the plateau. The most important of these, lying in the northwest, is the Wadi Hauran; it brings about a weak link between Transjordan and Mesopotamia.

## b. Climate, Flora, and Fauna

The weather in all of Mesopotamia is determined by the same climatological phenomena as in Palestine. In the summer there is a low pressure system above the Persian Gulf. As a result, a constant land wind, called the Shamal, blows from the northwest. This wind does not carry clouds and rain, but it can cause a sandstorm five or six times a season. In the winter there is a changing pressure zone above the Arabian peninsula. If there is low pressure, depressions from the Mediterranean Sea can move to the Persian Gulf. These cause a southeast wind, called the Sharqui, which can bring rain. If there is a high pressure above the peninsula, no depressions occur and a cold, dry northeast wind blows from the inland of Asia.

Because of the great distances, the difference in elevation, and the surrounding areas, this weather system has different consequences for the south than for the north. The city of Samarra, about 130 kilometers (80 mi.) northwest of Baghdad, may be taken as the north-south boundary. South of it the summer temperatures are very high. In the hottest months (July-August) the daytime temperature averages around 35° C (95° F), with highs of up to 50° C (122° F) in the shade. The water in the delta aggravates the situation even more, for it gives the hot air a high level of humidity. The winters, on the other hand, are mild. The average temperature stands around 10° C (50° F), and the freezing point is seldom reached. Northern Mesopotamia deviates from this pattern. In the summer the temperature does not reach such high figures, for in the hottest months the mercury averages around 30° C (86° F). Moreover, because of the higher elevation, the humidity is considerably lower. Therefore in the summer this region is less sultry. The winters, on the other hand, are more severe. It is not unusual for the mercury to dip below the freezing point for a brief period.

For both areas the winter (November-March) is the rainy season. The amount of precipitation is small, however. In the south and in large parts of the north there is never more than 200 millimeters (8 in.). The northeast gets more; the proximity of the mountains makes for an average of 200 to 400 millimeters (8 to 16 in.). Much more important, however, is the period from April through May, when the snow melts in the spring-area of the Euphrates and the Tigris. This snow water fills the entire river valley in the north and inundates vast areas in the south. Because the temperature has already risen considerably in this period, however, the water quickly evaporates and there is great danger of salinization. The salty marshes are one of the results. The position, the soil conditions, and the climate were not conducive to abundant vegetation. The expression "Fertile Crescent" is therefore applicable to this area only in comparison with the adjacent desert. In the north the region between the rivers has only steppe vegetation: some brushwood, clumps of grass, and creeping plants. Only the riverbanks and the marshy areas have more abundant vegetation; these areas have become the habitat of birds and small wildlife. At one time there were trees, particularly on the slopes in the north and the northeast. Unrestrained cutting and the erosion that followed left only a few small oak groves on the hills of the Zagros mountains; brushwood is now predominant. In the northern part there are some extensive oases of date palms

along the Euphrates, such as near Anah, about 300 kilometers (200 mi.) northwest of Baghdad.

The south is in a more favorable position because of the regular flooding, though the salinization for the most part eliminates this advantage. Here the woods of poplars and willow trees, the reeds and the high grass in the swampy areas, and especially the date palms along the riverbanks are most remarkable. Deep in the south the area along the Shatt el-Arab is one large date forest.

The wild animals have been greatly reduced. Old illustrations and texts show lions, ostriches, gazelles, wild boars, harts, and wild asses. This larger wildlife has virtually disappeared. The gazelle is still found in remote areas, as are animals such as the jackal and the wildcat. All sorts of lizards and snakes are still found in abundance. Of the fish in the rivers the most familiar is the so-called Tigris salmon, a carp-like fish that can reach a length of almost 2 meters (6 ft.).

### c. Human Life

Life was not equally easy for people living in the various parts of Mesopotamia. The first villages arose in the northeast, where there is fairly usable arable land. The situation in the south compelled the people to work more closely together. Only by managing the rivers, controlling the irrigation water, and constantly tending the crops in the fields could settled communities arise. If that was done, however, living in that area was certainly possible. This soon led to the rise of cities—not just villages—with all kinds of specializations. One had to work with poor building materials, however. Instead of blocks of rock, only clay and reeds were available. Only at a few places was there limestone near the surface. Fortunately there was bitumen along the Euphrates near Hit and Ramadi, west of Baghdad, that could be used as mortar for the bricks of baked clay. The lack of rock and especially of wood and metal forced the successive human communities to resort to raids and trade. Highways for that were already built along and on the Tigris and Euphrates. It is not surprising that the political powers in Akkad, Babylonia, and Assyria were driven by a desire for expansion in the northwest. Along the higher west side of the Euphrates it was easy to go in the direction of the Mediterranean Sea, or to pass from Assyria through the northern region of "the island" to Carchemish, where the most favorable crossing of the Euphrates lay. Going downstream, one could transport nearly everything on rafts that were kept floating by means of inflated goat-skins, as long as one reckoned with the flood in the spring. Therefore the cities were often positioned on a higher terrace along the rivers or canals. This position could also have unfavorable results, however. Sometimes the river changed its bedding, as is shown, for example, by the ruins of ancient Babylon. There the remains of a 123 meter (404 ft.) long bridge now lie completely on dry ground. Sometimes through negligence a canal became silted up. That made community life in such a place difficult; the city suffered economically and declined. It could happen, too, that the city did not protect itself against the rising waters or that the powers of nature were so strong that no dike was strong enough. That, too, brought an abrupt end to the community. Finally, the fields around the city could slowly become brackish, leading to a gradual decrease in productivity, eventually making it an unfavorable spot for human habitation.

The water was also an ally, however. Most cities in Mesopotamia lie fairly open and exposed in the plain; the natural protection of rock walls and mountain passes is lacking. Without encountering many natural obstacles, the inhabitants of the mountains in the east and in the north and of the steppe in the west could invade the valley. When that happened the water around the cities afforded a strong line of defense, the more so because the intruders were not familiar with this element.

Not all cities were located along the banks of a river or canal. Especially the oldest settlements in the south were often located at a considerable distance (about 200 m. to 20 km., or about 660 ft. to 12 mi.) from the water. Apparently in those days the people did not know how to cope with sudden flooding. Under such circumstances one often lay defenseless, exposed in the open plain.

This vulnerability may have been one of the factors in the military expansiveness of political powers such as Assyria and Babylonia. To the east the people of Mesopotamia were not able to overcome this weak position, except in the south (in Elam). Apparently the Zagros mountains were a difficult barrier for the dwellers of the plain. The final capture of Nineveh and Babylon by the Medes and the Persians came from the direction of these mountains. They could make the best use of their military apparatus by going westward, for between the high mountains of Armenia in the north and the Arabian desert in the south lay the steppe that carried them to the coastal strip of the Mediterranean Sea. Control of that coastal strip was easiest if there were no strong political power in that area, for the supply lines through the steppe were very long. The distance from Nineveh to Carchemish on the Euphrates is about 500 kilometers (300 mi.) in a straight line, and from Babylon to that point almost 750 kilometers (465 mi.). From the west to the east a similar situation prevailed. The pressure of the Parthians always made the eastern border of the Roman empire very vulnerable. Roman attempts to gain a solid foothold east of the Euphrates and to conquer all of Mesopotamia by means of "the island" never succeeded.

## 3. PERSIA

### a. Physical Geography

Persia consists of an enormous plateau surrounded on all sides by mountain ridges. To the west are the Zagros mountains, stretching from southeast to northwest over a length of about 1,000 kilometers (620 mi.); at 200 to 300 kilometers (125 to 200 mi.) wide, they constitute a natural boundary with Mesopotamia. To the north the Elburz mountains and the mountain ridge Koppet Dagh mark off the plateau. The Elburz mountains run south of the Caspian Sea over a length of about 1,100 kilometers (700 mi.) and a width of about 110 kilometers (70 mi.). The highest peak of this range, which is at the same time the highest peak in all of Persia, is 5,604 meters (18,387 ft.). The Koppet Dagh in the northeast is less imposing, though here there is also a peak of 3,496 meters (11,470 ft.). To the east several mountain ridges along the Indus Valley protect the plateau, and in the south several lower mountain ridges along the Gulf of Oman and near the southern slopes of the Zagros mountains along the Persian Gulf do the same.

The plateau itself moves for the most part at an elevation of about 1,000 meters (3,300 ft.). Two deserts are very important. They are the Dasht e-Kebir (the great desert) in the north, about 300 kilometers (200 mi.) long from west to east and about 150 kilometers (100 mi.) wide from north to south, and the Dasht e-Lut (desert of Lot) south of the plateau, similar in surface area but running more from north to south. The origin of these barren areas is not difficult to explain. The total amount of precipitation averages less than 100 millimeters (4 in.) because the surrounding mountains block the rains. These deserts are indeed at a somewhat lower elevation than the surrounding plateau; as a result the water from the higher regions can run off to it. The effect of this water is negative, however. The lower elevation makes drainage impossible; for the most part the water evaporates, so that through the centuries the soil has become mainly brackish and several salt marshes have come into existence.

A few regions of the vast country of Persia are of special importance to biblical literatures. These are Elam, Media, the heartland of Persia, and the heartland of the Parthians.

Elam lay partially outside the plateau, with mountains surrounding it. It was positioned between the Shatt el-Arab in Mesopotamia and the southwestern hills of the Zagros mountain ridge. The life-giving river of this area was the Nahr Karun; coming from the Zagros mountains it made the low plain fit for human habitation.

Media was situated in the northwest between the Zagros ridge and the Elburz mountains. The region consists of wide valleys at an elevation of about 1,500 meters (4,900 ft.), intersected by mountain ridges of up to 3,000 meters (9,850 ft.). The Zagros range offered solid protection. Very often these mountains rise above 3,000 meters (9,800 ft.), with some peaks higher than 4,000 meters (13,100 ft.). At the same time this mountain ridge, which consists partially of granite but mainly of hard and soft limestone rocks, offered good possibilities for human habitation in its lower areas. On the east there were even greater possibilities for human habitation because of the central mountain ridge of Persia, which runs parallel to the Zagros mountains. This mountain ridge, volcanic in origin, has many faults and depressions that allow for easy access to the groundwater.

The heartland of Persia lay southeast of Elam in the southern part of the Zagros ridge. The region has many valleys at an elevation of about 800 meters (2,600 ft.), vast plateaus at an elevation of around 1,500 meters (4,900 ft.), and a large number of mountain ridges between 2,000 and 3,000 meters (6,600 to 9,800 ft.) with peaks up to around 4,000 meters (13,100 ft.). The composition of the ground is similar to that in the northern part of the Zagros: hard and soft limestone intermixed with granite.

The center of the living area of the Parthians was southeast of the Caspian Sea, north of "the great desert," and south of the mountain ridge Koppet Dagh and the Elburz mountains. The land is flatter than that of Media and Persia, and consists primarily of vast limestone plateaus at an elevation of 1,000 to 2,000 meters (3,300 to 6,600 ft.). Small rivers flow through this area of the Koppet Dagh to the south, to "the great desert," where they come to an end.

## b. Climate, Flora, and Fauna

The climate is determined by the same pressure systems as in Mesopotamia. During the winter a high pressure system is found above Siberia and one of changing pressure above the Persian Gulf, while in the summer the low pressure system above the Persian Gulf is determinative. However, the numerous, high mountain ridges as well as the great distance often cause this metereological system to have different effects than in Mesopotamia. For example, throughout Persia there are much greater variations in temperature and in precipitation. The summers are generally hot and dry, but high in the mountains and along the Caspian Sea the temperature is considerably lower. In the winter little rain falls in the south (about 50 mm. or 2 in.), in the north along the Caspian Sea there is an abundance (about 1,000 mm. or 40 in.), and in the mountains the precipitation often takes the form of snow and hail. Therefore in the northwest the temperature can drop to around $-20°$ C $(-4°$ F). For the areas mentioned, the following precipitation figures can be cited: in Elam 50 to 400 millimeters (2 to 16 in.), in Media around 400 millimeters (16 in.), in Persia 200 to 500 millimeters (8 to 20 in.), and in Parthia 100 to 500 millimeters (4 to 20 in.).

These variations in temperature, in precipitation, and in terrain have given the flora and fauna of Persia great diversity. All these regions—the steppe and the deserts, the southern lowland, the northern lowland, and the mountains in the west, north, east, and south—have their own distinct vegetation and the animals that go with it. For example, the oak, and even the willow and the poplar, grow in the valleys of the Zagros mountains, and wild animals such as the lion and the bear live there. It is worthy of note that the two-hump camel lived almost everywhere in Persia, while the one-hump African camel was known in Palestine. Old drawings from Mesopotamia show both kinds.

## c. Human Life

Already around 2000 B.C. there was a highly developed society in Elam. Because of its position outside the mountain chain of Persia, this region always had close contacts with Sumer and Akkad, and later with Asshur and Babylon. Nevertheless, this community never became fully one with the powers of Mesopotamia. The marshes along the southern Tigris formed a natural barrier, and in times of trouble one could escape from the dwellers in the lowlands of Mesopotamia by seeking refuge in the Zagros mountains. Thus these people had a fairly peaceful life in the plain along the Nahr Karun, which was navigable over a long distance. This area also gets more rain than Mesopotamia because of the Zagros mountains in the north, even though it is in the form of heavy downpours. At any rate, the water of the Nahr Karun could be used to inundate large areas. The governing center of this region was Susa, a city in the northern part of the plain of Elam. Elam reached the zenith of its power about 1200 B.C. It conquered Babylon and carried the famous stele of Hammurabi to Susa.

The second important area of human habitation lay in Media around the city of Ecbatana, the present Hamadan. Possibly the Medes came here around 1000 B.C., carried on a wave of Indo-Europeans. The city was located on the southern edge of a vast plain at an elevation of 1,826 meters (5,991 ft.). Because of the mild summers and the abundance of rain and snow on the mountains during the winter, the valleys in this area are suitable for agriculture. Even during the summer enough water was available in the numerous subterranean streams to sustain life. Moreover, it was possible to go from here, by means of the many valleys, to the north, the east, the south, and even the west, because for mountain people the Zagros is not an insuperable obstacle. About 700 B.C. the Medes acquired considerable political power and soon gained control over many surrounding territories (e.g., the heartlands of the Persians and the Parthians). In history the Medes have become known especially for the capture and destruction of Nineveh in 612 B.C. To do that they had to march straight through the Zagros mountains in a northwesterly direction over a distance of about 520 kilometers (320 mi.), as the crow flies.

The heartland of the Persians, who took over power from the Medes, lay in the southeastern part of the Zagros. They probably came from the north with the same wave of Indo-Europeans that carried the Medes to Persia about 1000 B.C. The territory of the Persians is not as fertile as that of Media. There are winters in which no more than 200 millimeters (8 in.) of rain falls on the plateaus and valleys; this makes the regular growing of grain difficult. The royal city of Pasargadae and the holy city of Parsa (Persepolis), built about 500 B.C., were the centers of community life. Persepolis was situated on a vast plateau with an elevation of around 1,570 meters (5,150 ft.). Not only was the natural wealth of this area less than that of Media, but it was also less accessible. Having established their empire, therefore, the Persians shifted the residence of their rulers. During the winter they preferred to rule from the Elamite Susa, 500 kilometers (300 mi.) to the northwest in a straight line. This cut the distance to Babylon by half. The summer residence was usually in Ecbatana, which lies about 680 kilometers (420 mi.) from Persepolis in a straight line. These figures indicate that the Persians were not afraid of great distances. The famous royal highway went right through a large part of the empire, beginning at Susa and extending to Sardis in the western part of Asia Minor, a distance of about 2,500 kilometers (1,550 mi.).

Originally the territory of the Parthians lay about 300 kilometers (200 mi.) east of the present Tehran. Their center was Hecatompylos, a city whose location so far has not yet been identified with certainty. Conditions allowed for simple communities. The mountains in the north and especially the salt desert in the south, however, prevented any expansion. As they increased in numbers and power, the Parthians therefore moved farther and farther to the west. Their war with the Seleucids for the possession of Mesopotamia is well known. After they had gained full victory in the second century B.C., the Parthian princes established their summer residence in Ecbatana and their winter residence in Ctesiphon on the Tigris, 30 kilometers (20 mi.) southeast of Baghdad. Their conflicts with the Romans along the Euphrates in northern Syria and in the Armenian mountains date from that time.

## 4. ASIA MINOR

### a. Physical Geography

Asia Minor forms a kind of bridge between Asia and Europe. Here, too, the horizontal activity of the seas and the upward force of the earth's mass played their roles during the formation of the earth. Eventually, during the Tertiary Period, the sediments of the sea together with old earth layers were thrust up in a line that runs from India across Persia and Asia Minor and to the Balkans and the Alps. Even today this movement continues in many places, as is evident from the many earth tremors along this line. This explains why the relief of Asia Minor is similar to that of Persia. Here, too, one finds a central plateau in the middle, surrounded on all sides by high mountain ridges.

In the north are the Pontus mountains. They extend along the Black Sea from Bithynia in the west through Paphlagonia and Pontus to the Armenian plateau. The differences in elevation are considerable: in the west, hills of 600 meters (1,950 ft.); in the middle, mountains of around 2,000 meters (6,600 ft.); and in the east, peaks of over 3,000 meters (9,800 ft.). The highest peak, the Kisir Daghi (3,937 m. or 12,917 ft.), lies near the southeast point of the Black Sea. The entire chain consists mostly of elongated limestone mountains running from east to west, 100 kilometers (62 mi.) wide in places, and separated by long depressions. Connections from east to west are therefore much easier than from north to south. The mountains have left little room for coastal plains; very often the rocks protrude into the sea. Along the south coast, as the counterpart of the Pontus mountains, are the Taurus mountains. This mountain range, likewise consisting primarily of Cretaceous rocks, runs from the Caria region in the southwest, through Lycia, Pamphylia, southern Lycaonia, northern Cilicia, and Cappadocia, to the Armenian highlands in the east. So the Pontus mountains and the Taurus mountains clasp the central part of Asia Minor like a tong. In a sense the Taurus mountains do this even more than the Pontus mountains. Already in Lycia, in the southwest, the Taurus has peaks that are higher than 2,500 meters (8,200 ft.). In Pamphylia and western Cilicia the elevation dips somewhat; there the highest peaks reach about 2,000 meters (6,600 ft.). In central Cilicia the mountains become much more pronounced again. There one finds a double row of mountains running from southwest to northeast, with a number of peaks of the northern line lying at an elevation of above 3,000 meters (9,800 ft.). In eastern Cilicia and in Cappadocia, the Taurus, now called Anti-Taurus, fans out and together with the Pontus mountains reaches the Armenian highlands. Around the Gulf of Iskenderun, there is even a spur of the Taurus, Mount Amanus (Gavur Dagh), that nowhere rises above 1,800 meters (5,900 ft.). In addition, the Taurus does not leave much room for coastal plains along the sea. There is a long strip (about 100 km. or 62 mi.) in Pamphylia, but its average width is no more than 10 kilometers (6 mi.). Of greater significance is the plain of Cilicia, which is at least 150 kilometers

(100 mi.) long and in places over 50 kilometers (30 mi.) wide.

The high plateau of Anatolia lies clamped between these two imposing mountain ranges. Its core is made up of the regions of Galatia, northwestern Cappadocia, and eastern Phrygia. Though the plateau nowhere drops below 800 meters (2,625 ft.), the area is not everywhere equally flat. It is rather an uneven plateau, ranging between 800 and 1,500 meters (2,625 and 4,900 ft.). In between lie scattered mountain ridges whose peaks reach 3,000 meters (9,800 ft.). The highest peak lies south of Kayseri (3,916 m. or 12,848 ft.). Between these mountains and plateaus lie several depressions, low, level areas covered with an alluvial layer derived from the hills and the mountains. In places these depressions are so low that they lack an outlet to the sea; as a result there is always water standing there. The best known of these is the large salt lake Tuz Golu, over 100 kilometers (62 mi.) south-southeast of Ankara; it is longer, wider, and even more salty than the Dead Sea. Southwest of it lies "the lake district" of Asia Minor. These lakes, about fifteen in number, also lack a link with the sea. Their salt content is lower, however, because they are located on a higher level between mountains, resulting in less evaporation. This is an indication that it is difficult for the river water that comes down from the plateau of Anatolia to reach the sea. The surrounding mountains in the north and the south force the streams to make long detours. For example, the sources of the well-known Halys (Kizil Irmak) are in the mountains north of the present Siwas, 160 kilometers (100 mi.) from the Black Sea in a straight line. The river has to make a long detour to the southwest, however, before it can discharge its water through the Pontus mountains into the Black Sea. This gives the Halys a length of 1,150 kilometers (715 mi.).

Besides the Pontus mountains, the Taurus mountains, and the plateau of Anatolia, the west has still a fourth area with distinct features. The heart of this area is composed of the regions of Mysia and Lydia. Parts of Bithynia and Caria may also be included here. In this area, too, the mountain ridges run mainly from east to west. Thus here the mountains do not close off the way to the sea. They often continue all the way into the sea, forming islands, peninsulas, and sharp bays. Between these mountains, however, wide valleys reach far inland; this means that toward the west the center of Asia Minor has the easiest connection with the sea. Conversely, from the west it was easy to penetrate the plateau of Anatolia. Centuries-long deforestation and erosion have left these western mountain ridges, which rise to about 2,000 meters (6,600 ft.), virtually bare. The eroded soil was, and still is, carried to the valleys and from there by rivers such as the well-known Meander (Buyukmenderes) to the coast. So the formation of deltas has caused many natural harbors to fill up.

North of this region lies the territory around the Sea of Marmara, the Dardanelles, and the Bosporus. These expanses of water may be regarded as the westernmost depressions of the Pontus mountains. Because they are all connected and are 50 meters (165 ft.) below sea level, they form a link between the fresh water of the Black Sea and the salt water of the Mediterranean Sea. Along their north side few natural harbors are found because the coastline is fairly straight. The opposite is true of the south side; there the coastline is full of bays. The rapidly rising hinterland, however, makes the coast inhospitable, so that few harbors could come into existence. As a consequence, the most favorable passages are on the extremes, through the Dardanelles and through the Bosporus. Halfway through the almost 60 kilometer (37 mi.) long Dardanelles the coasts of Asia and Europe come within 1,270 meters (4,170 ft.) of each other, and two small bays serve as mooring places. The connection with Europe is even easier along the 26 kilometer (16 mi.) long Bosporus. The average width of this strait is no more than 1,500 meters (4,900 ft.), and the coastline has numerous small bays.

## b. Climate, Flora, and Fauna

Because of the long, high mountain ridges and the proximity of seas in the north, the west, and the south, Asia Minor has a widely varying climate. In general four types can be distinguished: a moderate climate along the coast of the Black Sea, a Mediterranean Sea climate along the west and the south coast, a continental climate in central Anatolia, and a mountain climate in the Armenian highlands.

There can be abundant rainfall along the northern coast throughout the entire year. In the east the average rainfall is above 1,000 millimeters (40 in.) per year, while in the west, the territory bordering the Mediterranean Sea, there is still around 700 millimeters (28 in.). There are no extreme temperatures in the winter or the summer. January, the coldest month, has an average temperature of 7° C (45° F); August, the warmest month, an average of around 22° C (72° F). Because of the abundant rains and the moderate temperatures, the Pontus region is heavily forested. As high as 1,300 meters (4,250 ft.) there are all kinds of foliage trees, while beyond that elevation the mountains are covered with pine trees.

The area around the Sea of Marmara is a transition territory. During the summer some rain falls inland, east of this sea, but there is no rain along the coast; the summers are warm and dry.

The western and the southern coasts have the familiar Mediterranean Sea climate, that is, humid, mild winters and dry, hot summers. Along the valleys in the west this climate penetrates far inland, while in the south, due to the braking influence of the Taurus, it covers only the true coastal areas. In the mild winter, when the temperature seldom dips below freezing, this rain (about 650 mm. or 26 in.) causes luxuriant vegetation of greenery and flowers. In late spring when the sun gains in intensity and the rain stays away, however, everything quickly withers, leaving the land brown and bare during the hot summers. This is, of course, also true in mountainous regions such as the Taurus, where the pine trees have managed to remain up to the tree line.

The eastern part of Asia Minor, that is, the area where the Pontus mountains and the Taurus come together and where the Armenian highland lies, has a rough climate. The summer is rather chilly, for in the hottest month the temperature as a rule does not rise above 17° C (62.6° F). The winter is definitely cold. Therefore precipitation often takes the form of snow; it stays on the high-er places until the month of May. In the summer the fertile volcanic soil benefits from this snow. The valleys and slopes turn green and up to the tree line vast forests of oaks and birches hold their own among the pine trees.

Central Anatolia, the heart of Asia Minor, has entirely different weather conditions. Because this area is surrounded by the climates of the regions just mentioned and because of the considerable differences in elevation, weather conditions are not everywhere the same in central Anatolia. One can, however, give a general characterization for this area. It can be called a steppe climate because precipitation is limited to the winter and because it amounts to no more than 400 millimeters (16 in.). One might also call it a continental climate because the winters are cold and the summers dry. The coldest month has an average temperature of 2° C (35.6° F), and the hottest month averages 22° C (72° F). Therefore precipitation is often in the form of snow. This precipitation makes it possible for the uneven plateau of Anatolia to be covered with green in the spring, but the summer turns it into a steppe area. Only the higher areas have a few trees. It is a good area for keeping livestock, and it is possible to grow crops in many places, though only to a limited extent.

The animal world of Asia Minor reflects the same variety as the terrain and the climate. This enormous area, extending from west to east over a length of about 1,700 kilometers (1,050 mi.), had plenty of room. Animals such as lions, bears, and wolves made the wooded areas their habitat, while the steppelike areas offered a good habitat to deer, gazelles, and jackals. The great local differences make a more detailed description impossible within the confines of a brief chapter.

### c. Human Life

The above description indicates that Asia Minor had some accessible and some less accessible areas. In Anatolia it was not difficult for people to go from one place to another, though the Halys, like other rivers in Asia Minor, was virtually unnavigable. Toward the east (the Armenian highland), the terrain becomes more and more difficult to traverse because the mountains increase in height, number, and size. Northward and southward the situation is somewhat more favorable. The Pontus mountains are the smallest obstacle. As long as one is prepared to make long detours around the mountains, it is relatively easy to reach the coast of the Black Sea, especially in the west and in the center. In the south the Taurus is a greater obstacle. It is obvious that people were especially interested in a link with the two large coastal plains in the south, those of Pamphylia and Cilicia. Traces of caravan inns and of Roman Hellenistic theaters show that they reached Pamphylia from the north. Leaving the lake district one had to climb slightly, but one could avoid the higher peaks of the Taurus. Moreover, the plain of Pamphylia rises terracelike, making the descent toward the sea easier. The plain of Cilicia was likewise reached from the north. The journey through the Taurus was somewhat shorter here, but at the same time more difficult. The road climbed to about 1,500 meters (4,900 ft.). The descent after that seemed easy; however, at an elevation of about 1,200 meters (3,950 ft.), one was unexpectedly confronted by a second mountain massif, intersected by many clefts. The small river Cakit uses one of the clefts to drain its water in the sea. At the narrowest spot in this cleft lies the so-called Cilician gate. After one leaves this small split behind, the descent toward Tarsus is no longer long and difficult. In the winter and in the spring, when the Cakit can overflow its banks, this route must have been terribly dangerous.

Anatolia lay most open to the west. Therefore the contacts with the west have always been intensive. Even the name Anatolia derives from the west, for it is simply a derivation of the Greek *anatole*, meaning sunrise or east.

Anatolia's connections with the outside world were mainly by way of the coastal strips. Wherever nature offered ships a safe place with enough hinterland, contacts could be made with and from overseas. These contacts were made through the passes of the Taurus, through the valleys of the Pontus, and especially through the valleys from the west coast. In the east, contact was more difficult. The wide Anti-Taurus made connections with Mesopotamia and Syria difficult. Four roads could be followed. From Cilicia there was a route through the south of the Amanus mountains; this was the Syrian gate, which lies at an elevation of

only 664 meters (2,179 ft.). The Amanus could also be crossed along the north at a height of 1,150 meters (3,773 ft.). In either case, however, connection was made only between the plateau of Syria and the plain of Cilicia. The third road went through the Anti-Taurus proper. Viewed from the south, one went first through the valley of the Aksu River and then reached some brooks of the Euphrates near the present Malatya, the continuation of the Roman Melitene and the Hittite Milid. From there, following mountain passes of about 1,180 meters (3,872 ft.) and 1,800 meters (5,900 ft.), one could cross the Anti-Taurus and reach the plateau of Anatolia. The fourth route was nothing but a segment of the Persian royal road between Susa and Sardis. From Malatya one went in a more southeasterly direction, crossed the Euphrates, and soon reached the upper course of the Tigris. The road followed a winding course through ravines, enabling the traveler to avoid mountain passes that were too high.

Human life existed at a very early time in all of Asia Minor. The numerous caves in the limestone mountains and the fertile valleys offered a good basis for it. It is not surprising that sedentary life developed early. On the basis of archeological discoveries such as those near Hacilar in the lake district, about 25 kilometers (15 mi.) southeast of Burdur, and in the ruins of Çatal Hüyük near Konya, it may be said that Asia Minor was one of the first locations where the growing of crops and animal husbandry were done systematically. The next phase, urban culture, was not long in coming, particularly because copper and iron were easily accessible in a number of places. In contrast to Egypt and Mesopotamia, however, in that phase the art of writing did not evolve immediately. Consequently Asia Minor entered history at a later point in time.

Relative to the Bible, central Anatolia played a significant role at an early time. More than the closed coastal plains, this area lent itself to the formation of a large state. Moreover, the trade routes crossed the center of this region, going from the west coast to Assyria and from Cilicia and Pamphylia to the Black Sea. Thus, from the eighteenth to the fifteenth century, the Old Hittite empire arose around the big curve of the Halys. For political and economic reasons the Hittites tried to expand their power beyond the Anti-Taurus. A few times they conquered Aleppo, and apparently around 1600 B.C. they even destroyed Babylon. In addition, bear in mind that the distance between their capital Hattushash (Boghazköy) and Babylon amounted to about 1,700 kilometers (1,050 mi.).

The Neo-Hittite empire existed from the fifteenth to the twelfth century. In that period the Hittites expanded their power to the west coast and obtained a solid foothold in the northern part of Syria. In this expansion they encountered the power of Egypt at the beginning of the thirteenth century. This confrontation eventually resulted in "the everlasting peace," which made it possible to establish commercial relations between Egypt and Anatolia through the land of Palestine.

The mass migrations around 1200 B.C. resulted in the demise of the Hittite empire. For centuries afterward Asia Minor remained an area of regional city-states, enabling the Greeks to extend their influence, especially along the coasts. The Lydian empire began to form around 600 B.C., beginning from Sardis (about 70 km. or 43 mi. east of Izmir), and it extended its power as far as the Halys in central Anatolia. At the time the northeast belonged to Media, and the south, Pamphylia and Cilicia, to the Neo-Babylonian empire. Soon afterward the Persians gained control; Lydia in the west became the ninth satrapy and Cappadocia with everything else the eighth.

After Alexander the Great, Asia Minor did not become an independent political entity either. It was largely controlled by the Seleucids, who ruled this territory from Antioch in Syria. Asia Minor remained politically weak when the Romans, from 200 B.C., increasingly pressed toward the east. Not even the city-state of Pergamum (about 80 km. or 50 mi. north of Izmir), which flourished from the middle of the third century, could change this. Consequently the political division of the Romans approximated the regional boundaries. The province of Asia comprised the western coastal regions of Lydia, Mysia, Caria, and a part of Phrygia. Northwest lay the province of Bithynia, to which were added Paphlagonia and part of Pontus.

In 25 B.C. the Romans changed central Anatolia into the province of Galatia. To it belonged the old heartland of Anatolia, where since the third century Celtic tribes had penetrated, as well as the eastern part of Phrygia, the territories of Pisidia and Lycaonia north of the Taurus, and the southern part of Pontus. The region of Cappadocia, which bordered on rebellious Armenia, was made into a province by Tiberius in A.D. 17. Soon the coastal region of Cilicia also obtained provincial status, first as part of the province of Syria and later, in A.D. 17, as an independent entity.

Initially the island of Cyprus, which consists of two mountain ridges that run east-west, with a flat depression between them, was reckoned to Cilicia. But as early as 22 B.C. Augustus followed the geographical partition: the copper-rich island became a separate senate province. The same happened with Lycia and with the coastal region of Pamphylia, which became an independent province in 36 B.C.

This history makes it very clear that the geographical diversity of Asia Minor constantly prevented the area from uniting politically. It was not until the Persian empire that the area became politically unified. But as in Palestine, neither under the Persians nor under the Seleucids and the Romans did this mean independence. The territory was a division of a foreign world empire and nothing more.

## 5. GREECE

### a. Physical Geography

The geographical conditions of Greece are strongly determined by two factors, the sea and the mountains.

With the exception of the north, the land is surrounded on all sides by the sea. Everywhere this presence of the sea makes itself felt. No part inland is more than 100 kilometers (62 mi.) from the sea. To the west lies the Ionian Sea, to the south the Mediterranean Sea, and in the east the Aegean Sea. The sea reaches far inland through inlets and bays, the best-known inlet being the Gulf of Corinth, which divides the land nearly in half.

The other geographical factor is the mountains. In its entirety Greece with its islands belongs to the line of mountain ridges that was shaped in the

Tertiary Period and that extends from India over Persia and Asia Minor to the Alps. Limestone is predominant in these mountains, though sandstone and even granite are also present. The Aegean Sea is a break in that line, though not a complete one. Everywhere rocky islands rise up out of the water. The familiar island of Crete together with Rhodes and three other islands to the south are the end of this system. So about a fifth of the total surface area of present-day Greece consists of islands.

About 80 percent of Greece is covered with mountains. Extensive alluvial plains are found only in the northeast, in Thrace, Macedonia, and Thessaly. No peak, however, reaches higher than 3,000 meters (9,800 ft.). Even peaks between 2,000 and 3,000 meters (6,600 and 9,800 ft.) are the exception rather than the rule. The proximity of the sea and the frequently steep slopes often make the mountains look higher than they are.

The chief mountain range is the Pindus, which extends from the northern border with Albania to the Gulf of Corinth to the south and thus divides the land into a western and an eastern part. This partition is quite drastic, for the central ridge of the Pindus mountains fluctuates at an elevation of 2,000 meters (6,600 ft.), with some twenty peaks over 2,000 meters (6,600 ft.). Spurs to the west and the east in turn divide the regions along the Ionian and the Aegean Sea. Thus in the northwest lies the region of Epirus, a small strip along the Ionian Sea that, terracelike, extends inland. In the sea overlooking it lies the island of Corfu. South of Epirus the territory of Aetolia stretches along the Ionian Sea and the Gulf of Corinth. East of the Pindus mountains lie more familiar areas. First Macedonia, which to the south is bounded by a spur of the Pindus (the center of this spur is Mount Olympus, at 2,917 m. or 9,571 ft. the highest peak in all of Greece), to the west by the northernmost peaks of the Pindus, and to the north by the Balkan mountains. Between these mountains and the Aegean Sea in the southeast, the wide alluvial plain of Macedonia has come into being along some brooks from the Balkans. East of it, as far as the Sea of Marmara, lies Thrace; currently it is partitioned off among Greece, Turkey, and Bulgaria. The northern part is a mountainous area, fluctuating at an elevation of 1,000 to 2,000

meters (3,300 to 6,600 ft.). The southern part, along the Aegean Sea and the Sea of Marmara, is predominantly level and intersected by some small rivers.

South of Macedonia lies the greatest plain of what is properly Greece. This is the district of Thessaly; to the south it is closed off by another spur of the Pindus mountains.

Still farther to the south lie two other spurs of the Pindus. One of these reaches the water of the sea on the south side of the Gulf of Lamia; this is the location of the famous mountain pass of Thermopylae that connects the northern part of Greece with the middle. Southeast of it begins the plain of Boeotia; overlooking it in the west is Mount Parnassus (2,457 m. or 8,061 ft.), and to the south it is closed off by the last and lowest spur of the Pindus. This spur penetrates the Attica peninsula, which has several flatter areas along the sea.

South of the Pindus mountain range and its adjoining areas lies the Peloponnesus; its greatest width is about 170 kilometers (105 mi.), and its greatest length about 230 kilometers (140 mi.). Technically this peninsula is now an island because the canal of Corinth now cuts through the approximately 8 kilometer (5 mi.) long isthmus. The core of this area is formed by the mountainland of Arcadia, which consists of very porous limestone. In the north a few peaks exceed 2,000 meters (6,600 ft.), in the middle the mountainland drops to around 1,000 meters (3,300 ft.), and in the south it climbs again to 2,000 meters (6,600 ft.). Near the well-known Sparta is even a peak that reaches 2,407 meters (7,897 ft.). Very little space remains for flat, low areas. The most important plains lie near Sparta in the region of Laconia and near Argos in the region of Argolis.

With its length of about 255 kilometers (160 mi.) and its width of about 50 kilometers (30 mi.), Crete is by far the most important island. It consists of an east-west mountain chain made up of limestone. Its highest points are the White mountains in the west (2,452 m. or 8,045 ft.), the massif of Mount Ida in the middle (2,456 m. or 8,058 ft.), and Mount Dikta (2,148 m. or 7,048 ft.) in the east. Low, flat areas are found along large sections of the north side of the island and in the middle of the south side.

## b. Climate, Flora, and Fauna

Seas and mountains are not only determinative factors for geographical conditions; they are also important for climate. The almost ubiquitous sea with its relatively high winter temperatures gives Greece a mild climate. Thus in Athens the average temperature in January is around 10° C (50° F). Rain falls mainly in the winter, caused by a low pressure system from the Atlantic Ocean. The mountains meanwhile cause local variations. In the west, along the Ionian Sea, they bring about an abundant rainfall, sometimes over 1,000 millimeters (40 in.). Further inland there is less precipitation, but because of the high elevation, such precipitation can take the form of snow in Thrace, in the Pindus mountains, in Arcadia, and even on Crete. Therefore below-freezing temperatures are not exceptional in these high regions. The least amount of rain falls on the eastern coast, behind the Pindus. Athens, for example, receives no more than 400 millimeters (16 in.). The influence of the mountains on the amount of precipitation is also evident on Crete. The northern coast gets on the average 500 millimeters (20 in.), while along the southern coast on the other side of the mountains there is hardly 200 millimeters (8 in.)

In the spring flowers bloom everywhere. In the summer, however, the weather is dry and rather warm; temperatures of around 30° C (86° F) are normal at that time of the year. The proximity of the sea causes an almost constant movement of air; in the morning a wind blows inland and toward the evening a wind blows away from the land. This makes the climate much more pleasant.

Despite the considerable amount of rain, Greece is virtually devoid of important rivers. During the summer they are often dry or shrink to rivulets, while in the winter, due to the terrain, the water drops toward the sea or seeps into the porous rock. The ideal place to live, therefore, is near the springs.

Vegetation in the higher regions remains abundant up to the tree line. Pine trees and even foliage trees such as beeches and oaks are not a rarity there. On the lower slopes, however, grows mostly the typical brushwood of the countries around the Mediterranean Sea. As a result of de-forestation, erosion, and pasturing by sheep and goats, the trees have virtually disappeared there. Large wild beasts of prey, such as lions, are no longer to be found in any part of Greece, but wildcats, wolves, jackals, and wild goats are still seen there.

## c. Human Life

Seas and mountains also had a great influence on the course of human existence. The presence of alluvial soil and sufficient precipitation made the lower regions very fertile. Marshes were found only in Macedonia. In the rest of the land the porous limestone, the differences in elevation, and the proximity of the sea provided sufficient drainage. For the same reason there were virtually no rivers suitable for irrigation and navigation. The rivers were too shallow, too narrow, and too fast for that.

On the other hand, the sheltered valleys offered safe living conditions. The mountains and the inlets of the sea constituted a natural barrier and thus provided protection. The ancient warlike city of Sparta in Laconia, for example, did not even need protective walls. The same was true of the Minoan center of Crete. These natural dividing lines had their negative aspects, too, however. Much more than the central ridge in Palestine, they hindered the development toward political unity; for a long time the land connections were too difficult for such a unity. Having such a restricted territory was an even greater disadvantage for the spread of the community itself. There was no possibility of gaining additional land, and as a result overpopulation was a constant threat. This threat could be removed only through emigration and importing food. The land available for growing vegetables and fruit and for agriculture and pasture was too limited. The sea provided the solution. The numerous islands were an easy beacon by day and the usually clear starry heaven served the same purpose by night. Furthermore, the constant wind provided enough energy for the primitive sailing boats. A disadvantage was that many harbors were vulnerable from the sea.

About 3000 B.C., when Egypt and Mesopotamia had already developed an urban culture,

Greece had only villages. Cities did not develop until 2600 B.C., possibly under the influence of Asia Minor and Egypt. From 2000 B.C. on, the Minoan culture was augmented and eventually even displaced by that of the Acheans; they were Indo-Europeans who likely entered Greece at the time the Hittites settled in Asia Minor. Around 1600 this first Greek culture prevailed from the Peloponnesus to Crete. Power was divided over a number of small states, the most important of which was Mycenae in Argolis. In this cultural period stone fortresses were built, tablets were used for writing (Linear B), beautiful gold ornaments were crafted, and the pottery that has been found in many places around the eastern basin of the Mediterranean Sea was made.

Around 1100 a new wave of Indo-Europeans, called Dorians, entered the south from the north; they put an end to the Mycenaean civilization. The restoration started only slowly. After the Phoenician alphabet had been adopted around 900 and after the coinage from Lydia had been accepted in the seventh century, however—which greatly simplified the export of wine and oil and the import of grain—culture reached new heights.

During the classical period, in the fifth and fourth centuries, Greece reached its cultural, economic, and political zenith. A unique combination of forces made it possible even to withstand the powerful Persian empire. The conquests and policies of Alexander the Great enabled Greek culture to spread through the entire Near East during the Hellenistic period.

From around 200 B.C. the Roman power forced itself into Greece; this gave rise to the political constellation that ruled there during the first years of the Christian Church. Initially the Romans divided Greece into four districts, called tetrarchies, but in 148 B.C. they combined them all into one province with Thessalonica as the capital. After the destruction of Corinth in 146 B.C., the rest of Greece was also added to that province. On account of its location, Greece was strategically very important to the Romans, as is apparent from the fact that in the first century B.C. it became the place where the Romans fought their decisive battles for power. Near Pharsalus in Thessaly,

Caesar defeated Pompey in 48 B.C.; at Philippi, Octavian and Antony defeated the murderers of Caesar in 42 B.C., and at Actium, on the west coast, Antony had to yield to Octavian in 31 B.C. At the time, traffic in that area was made easier by the Via Egnatia, a Roman highway that ran from Byzantium through Philippi, Thessalonica, and Pella to Apollonia on the west coast.

The Romans so appreciated Greek culture that in 27 B.C. they gave the south the status of a separate province, called Achaia. Corinth, which had been rebuilt by Caesar in 44 B.C., became the capital. Under Tiberius, Achaia was again made part of Macedonia, but Claudius returned the status of provincehood to Achaia in A.D. 44.

Politically nothing was in store for fractured Greece in the later centuries. It was not until the modern era that it became an independent political unity in its own right.

# 6. ITALY

## a. Physical Geography

The sea and the mountains are also determinative factors for the geography of Italy. In the north the Alps skirt around the land in a wide arch, while the Apennines form the spine of the entire peninsula. The sea is just as nearby as in Greece. The distance to the sea is never more than 100 kilometers (62 mi.) in a straight line; the only exception is the area near the Alps in the north. The similarity between Italy and Greece is even greater than that, for only a slightly larger area of Italy (23 percent) may be regarded as part of the low, level areas, and of that the greatest part is taken up by the (formerly uneconomic) Po Basin immediately south of the Alps. The remainder (77 percent) consists of hilly (42 percent) and mountainous terrain over 700 meters (2,300 ft.) high.

The arch of the Alps is about 1,200 kilometers (750 mi.) long and has a width that varies from 120 to 200 kilometers (75 to 125 mi.). On the average this mountainland has an elevation of 1,300 meters (4,250 ft.), with eleven peaks going over 4,000 meters (13,100 ft.). The highest is the well-known Mont Blanc in the northwest

(4,807 m. or 15,772 ft.). The Alps were likely formed at the beginning of the Tertiary Period as part of the folding that extends from the Balkans to India. The mountains are composed mainly of hard limestone, some of which dates from the Cambrian Period, interspersed with numerous metamorphic rocks. Like the Peloponnesus, the eastern part of the Alps is known for its karst phenomena. This is a process by which parts of the limestone ground are dissolved through the influence of water. This leads to the formation of clefts and caves in which small rivers disappear. For that reason there are few river valleys in the Alps, while to the south of it numerous springs irrigate the Po Basin.

The Apennine mountains start at the southwestern tip of the Alps and run down the entire peninsula to the western tip of Sicily. In length (about 1400 km. or 875 mi.) they surpass the Alps, while their width varies from 40 to nearly 200 kilometers (25 to 125 mi.). Their main difference from the Alps is their lower elevation. Less than ten peaks rise above 2,000 meters (6,600 ft.) and the highest point is only 2,914 meters (9,561 ft.) (Monte Corno, 95 km. or 59 mi. northeast of Rome). As a mountain range the Apennines are younger than the Alps, and they continue to fold, as is evident from active volcanoes such as Mount Vesuvius, Mount Stromboli, and Mount Etna.

Few low, level areas lie on the edge of the Apennines. In most places, especially on the east side, the rocky foothills encroach on the surrounding seas. In the east this is the Adriatic Sea, in the south the Ionian Sea, and in the west, extending to Corsica, Sardinia, and Sicily, the Tyrrhenian Sea. The shoreline is less jagged than in Greece. To be sure, the line is not as straight as in Palestine south of Haifa, but compared to the long coastline the number of beautiful natural harbors is small.

No important rivers were formed because of the relief of the peninsula. The drop in the terrain was too great and the distance to the sea too short for that. After the Po, the longest river is the Tiber; it originates between Florence and the Adriatic Sea on the foot of the Monte Fumaiolo (1,408 m. or 4,620 ft.). Winding its way to the sea over a distance of about 400 kilometers

(250 mi.), the river carries a large quantity of soil. This gives the water a murky color, causes delta formation near the mouth of the river, and makes for poor navigability. The same holds true to a greater or lesser degree for all other rivers.

## b. Climate, Flora, and Fauna

The mountains and the seas have a great influence on the climate. In the north the Alps bring about a divide between the oceanic and continental climate of western and central Europe and the Mediterranean Sea climate. The climate of the entire peninsula is Mediterranean, with mild, humid winters and dry, hot summers, though the crossline of the Apennines and the length of the "boot" cause variations from west to east and especially from north to south.

The amount of precipitation in the north is considerably greater than in the south; even the rainy periods are not the same. The Po Basin and the central part of the peninsula have two periods of maximum precipitation, namely, the autumn and the spring. In contrast, the south and the Alps have only one maximum period, namely, the winter. The temperatures vary greatly, too, especially in the winter. In Milan, for example, the average January temperature is only 1° C (33.8° F), while in Palermo on Sicily this figure is 10° C (50° F). In one year Rome gets about 900 millimeters (36 in.) of precipitation, the most in October (140 mm. or 5.6 in.) and the least in July (22 mm. or 1 in.). The average January temperature there fluctuates around 7° C (45° F), and in July the temperature fluctuates around 24° C (75° F). Thus the conditions for agriculture and the keeping of livestock are favorable here, though the torrential rainfall and the sharp relief have an adverse effect on it. Centuries of deforestation and subsequent erosion have left little of the original forests. The oak trees and the pine tree forests have given way to the Mediterranean brushwood, and only the cypress has managed to hold its own. The populated hilly land shows a greenish color in the winter, blossoms luxuriously in the spring, and exhibits a parched appearance in the summer.

Not much is left of the original animals either. In

the higher mountain regions, the wolf, the brown bear, the ibex, and the chamois are still found, but in the lower regions they have virtually disappeared.

## c. Human Life

The hilly land of Italy possesses a more gradual relief than that of Greece and is therefore more suitable for agriculture. This is true of the peninsula proper as well as of the southern half of Sicily. Malta is similar to it. To be sure, on the northeast side this island has a few natural harbors, but the small surface area of only 30 by 15 kilometers (20 by 10 mi.) prevented economic development, and therefore it had only strategic importance. The limited number of natural harbors along the coast of the "boot" likewise stimulated agriculture. Therefore, unlike the Greeks, the old inhabitants of Italy were not a seafaring people but rather farmers and keepers of livestock. These favorable agricultural conditions also induced the Greeks, who from the eighth century B.C. spread out over the Mediterranean Sea, to establish not only trading posts here but also complete colonies for the growing of food for the home country. All of Sicily and the southern coast as far as Cumae in the vicinity of the present Naples were taken over by the Greeks; in the home country this area was even called "Greater Greece."

Another group of immigrants, the Etruscans, settled north of Rome in Tuscany, about 1000 B.C. In the course of the centuries they extended their power farther north, to the Po, and further south, to Rome. Between these two power blocks, Italian tribes such as the Latini, the Sabini, and the Umbri inhabited the middle part of the "boot."

The Romans introduced further change in the fifth century B.C. The city of Rome had been founded as far back as the eighth century, at the point where the north-south trade route crossed the Tiber, which was also as far as ships coming from the sea could sail up the river. The Romans did away with the pressure of the Etruscans, assumed the leadership of the Italian tribes, and gradually enlarged their territory in a northerly and especially a southerly direction. As early as 312 B.C. they began construction of the first high-way, the Via Appia, which eventually would run from Rome through the Apennines to the southeast tip of the peninsula. Their wars with the Greeks and Carthage in the third century made the Romans familiar with seafaring and made them aware that the Alps were not an insuperable barrier for their armies. With that the conditions for aggressive expansion and for the establishment of a world empire were present. From that moment on every threat from the outside was met as soon as possible, and as a result in a few centuries Rome ruled large parts of Europe and all the coastal areas of the Mediterranean Sea. This development also carried its dark side for the city. It disturbed the old economy of the Italian tribes, which was based mainly on simple agriculture and the keeping of livestock. Rome became a cosmopolitan city whose needs increased enormously because of the large population and the high standard of living, while the country became depopulated and not enough people were left to till the land. It became necessary to import food. Fortunately, the extensive road system and the intensive shipping on the safe Mediterranean Sea, which was proudly called *Mare Nostrum* ("Our Sea"), made it possible to bring in enough grain, wine, and oil from the provinces.

## LITERATURE

F. M. Abel, *Géographie de la Palestine* I-II (Paris, 1938).

Y. Aharoni, *The Land of the Bible* (London, 1968[2]; Philadelphia, 1979[3]).

Y. Aharoni and M. Avi-Yonah, *The Macmillan Bible Atlas* (New York, 1976[8]).

A. Alon, *The Natural History of the Land of the Bible* (London, 1969).

S. Applebaum, *Jews and Greeks in Ancient Cyrene* (Leiden, 1979).

*Atlas of Israel* (Jerusalem, 1970).

M. Avi-Yonah, et al., *Encyclopedia of Archaeological Excavations in the Holy Land* I-IV (Jerusalem/Englewood Cliffs, N.J., 1975-78).

D. Baly, *Geographical Companion to the Bible* (London/New York, 1963).

_____, *The Geography of the Bible* (London, 1967[7]/New York, 1974[2]).

D. Baly and A. D. Tushingham, *Atlas of the Biblical World* (New York, 1971).

P. Beaumont, G. H. Blake, and J. M. Wagstaff, *The Middle East: A Geographical Study* (London/New York, 1976).

M. A. Beek, *Atlas van het Tweestromenland* (Amsterdam, 1960).

W. Berg, *Historische Karte des alten Aegypten* (St. Augustine, 1973).

G. Cansdale, *Animals of Bible Lands* (Exeter, 1970).

M. du Buit, *Géographie de la terre sainte* I-II (Paris, 1958).

N. Feinbrun-Dothan and R. Koppel, *Wild Plants in the Land of Israel* (Tel Aviv, 1968²).

W. B. Fisher, *The Middle East* (London, 1978⁷).

*Geological Map of Israel* (Jerusalem, 1975).

L. H. Grollenberg, *Atlas of the Bible* (Camden, N.J., 1956).

_____ , *Israel* (Paris, 1961).

W. Helck, *Wirtschaftsgeschichte des Alten Ägypten im 3. und 2. Jahrtausend vor Chr.* (Leiden, 1975).

A. A. M. van der Heyden, *Atlas van de antieke wereld* (Amsterdam, 1962).

Y. Karmon, *Israel. A Regional Geography* (London, 1971).

H. Kees, *Ancient Egypt: A Cultural Topography* (London, 1961).

*Map of Israel, 1:100,000* (Jerusalem, 1975).

H. G. May, *Oxford Bible Atlas* (London/New York, 1974³).

*Moyen-Orient: Libya, Syria, Jordan, Iraq, Iran* (Paris, 1956).

J. H. Negenman, *Een Geografie van Palestina* (Kampen, 1982).

_____ , *Geografische Gids bij de Bijbel* (Boxtel, 1981).

_____ , *New Atlas of the Bible* (Garden City, N.Y., 1969).

J. Neumann, "On the Incidence of Dry and Wet Years," *Israel Exploration Journal* 6 (1956) 58–63.

F. E. Noel-Baker, *The Land and the People of Greece* (London, 1960²).

E. Orni and E. Efrat, *Geography of Israel* (Jerusalem, 1971).

A. Parmelee, *All the Birds of the Bible* (London, 1960).

N. Peelman and B. F. Kocian, *The Beasts, Birds, and Fish of the Bible* (New York, 1975).

_____ , *The Plants of the Bible* (New York, 1975).

A. Phillipsow and E. Kirsten, *Die griechischen Landschaften: eine Landeskunde* I-IV (Frankfort, 1951–59).

N. Shalem, "La stabilité du climat en Palestine," *Revue biblique* 58 (1951) 54–74.

D. Sharon, "Variability of Rainfall in Israel: A Map of the Relative Standard Deviation of the Annual Amounts," *Israel Exploration Journal* 15 (1965) 169–76.

J. Strange, *Caphtor/Keftiu: A New Investigation* (Leiden, 1980).

D. S. Walker, *A Geography of Italy* (London, 1967²).

W. Walker, *All the Plants of the Bible* (New York, 1979).

M. Zohari, "Ecological Studies in the Vegetation of the Near Eastern Deserts," *Israel Exploration Journal* 2 (1952) 201–15.

_____ , *Plants of the Bible* (Tel Aviv, 1982).

## GEOLOGICAL TABLE

The chronology in the scheme below is given only with reservations. Because of the time span, the periods can be indicated only in millions of years and then only approximately. Moreover, the formation of the earth happened in such a way that nowhere are all geological layers present.

PRE-CAMBRIAN
—the archaic era that includes about 80 percent of geologic time

Before 600 million years

PALEOZOIC
—era of the oldest life, divided into periods:

| | |
|---|---|
| Cambrian | 600-500 million years |
| Ordovician | 500-440 million years |
| Silurian | 440-400 million years |
| Devonian | 400-350 million years |
| Carboniferous | 350-270 million years |
| Permian | 270-225 million years |

MESOZOIC
—era of life in the middle, divided into periods:

| | |
|---|---|
| Triassic Period | 225-180 million years |
| Jurassic Period | 180-135 million years |
| Cretaceous Period | 135-70 million years |
| Albian | |
| Early Cretaceous Period | |
| Late Cretaceous Period | |
| Danian | |

CENOZOIC

—era of the new life, divided into the Tertiary and Quaternary Periods, each subdivided:

Tertiary Period, subdivided into epochs:

| | |
|---|---|
| Paleocene | 70-60 million years |
| Eocene | 60-40 million years |
| Oligocene | 40-25 million years |
| Miocene | 25-12 million years |
| Pliocene | 12-2 million years |

Quaternary Period, subdivided into epochs:

| | |
|---|---|
| Pleistocene or Glacial | 2 million-25,000 years |
| Holocene or Alluvial | 25,000 years-present |

# C. New Testament Geography

*by B. VanElderen*

The Gospels report only a few occasions when Jesus went outside of Palestine proper. The three areas visited are the Decapolis region (Matt. 8:28–34 = Mark 5:1–20 = Luke 8:26–39; Mark 7:31), the region of Tyre and Sidon (Matt. 15:21–28 = Mark 7:24–30), and Perea ("beyond the Jordan") (Matt. 19:1; Mark 10:1).

## 1. DECAPOLIS

The term Decapolis describes a loose confederacy that at first consisted of ten cities, all but one located east of the Jordan River and the Sea of Galilee. These were Hellenistic cities founded or settled by Greek immigrants who came to the Middle East after the conquests of Alexander the Great. These settlements were Hellenistic in culture, religion, architecture, government, and politics. They modeled the freedom and independence of the Greek city-state and generally enjoyed such status within the larger political entity. They were conquered by Alexander Janneus in the 80s B.C., but liberated and given considerable autonomy by Pompey in 64 B.C. Such was their status in the first century A.D.

Initially, according to Pliny (*Natural History* 5.16), ten cities comprised the Decapolis: Scythopolis, Pella, Dion, Gerasa, Philadelphia, Gadara, Raphana, Canatha, Hippos, and Damascus. Ptolemy lists eighteen names, dropping Raphana and adding nine new names: Heliopolis, Abila, Saana, Ina, Samulis, Abida, Capitolias, Adra, Gadora (*Geography* 5.14, 22).

These cities were located on the major trade routes from the east to Palestine and the Mediterranean Sea. The one city west of the Jordan, Scythopolis (Old Testament Beth-shean), was strategically located at the eastern end of the plain of Esdraelon and at the junction of three major roads entering Transjordan. Most of the other cities are on these three roads or on connecting arteries. Each of these cities had political control of a certain amount of territory around it, but the extent has not been adequately defined. Little is known about the interrelationships of these cities, and it is doubtful that they were united in a central or federal government. Hence the term "league" or "confederation" is hardly adequate (cf. S. T. Parker, "The Decapolis Reviewed," *Journal of Biblical Literature* 94 [1975] 437–41).

The healing of the demoniac(s) reported in Matthew 8:28–34 = Mark 5:1–20 = Luke 8:26–39 cannot be precisely located since the area is designated *he chora* ("the district," "the region"); in addition, the textual evidence is very mixed— Gerasa, Gadara, and Gergesa are all attested in the manuscripts.

The religion of these cities is amply evident in their Greco-Roman temples dedicated to Artemis, Zeus, Herakles, Dionysus, Pallas, Tyche, and the like. In some places Astarte worship was practiced. The cultural interests of these cities can be seen in the extensive ruins of theaters and other public monuments. Some cities, such as Gadora, had impressive educational institutions. In many of the cities the Roman influence can be seen in the colonnaded *cardo maximus,* forum, and theater(s).

The Decapolis functioned very significantly in the ministry of Jesus, especially in Mark. This was Gentile territory—also to be penetrated with the gospel. Here the injunction to silence is not necessary (Mark 5:19 = Luke 8:39). Later, when Jesus went northward to Tyre and Sidon, Mark adds that he returned by way of the Decapolis (Mark 7:31), where he healed a deaf-mute and fed the four thousand (7:32–8:10). Similarly, Matthew's inclusion of the Decapolis in his summary of the followers of Jesus (4:25) is not without great significance.

The spread of Christianity east of the Jordan is not reported in the New Testament, but believers were located in Damascus when Saul went there (Acts 9:3). Christians fled to Pella in the Decapolis during the sieges of Jerusalem in A.D. 70 and 135. Evidence of Christianity in Transjordan and in the Decapolis region is very extensive from the early Byzantine period.

## 2. TYRE, SIDON, CAESAREA PHILIPPI

On two occasions the Gospels report that Jesus traveled north of Palestine. One of these was his journey through the district of Tyre and Sidon along the Mediterranean coast (Matt. 15:21–28 = Mark 7:24–30), when he had the encounter with a Gentile woman (identified in Mark 7:26 as a "Greek, Syrophoenician by birth," and in Matt. 15:22 as a Canaanite). The history of these cities of Phoenicia dates far back into pre-Christian times. In New Testament times this territory was part of the province of Syria. Tyre and Sidon were important coastal cities linked to Galilee by a major road and by a direct trade route to Damascus. Hence the itinerary in Mark 7:24 and 31, at times criticized by commentators, is a plausible and efficient one since it follows the major highways in the area.

Jesus' other northern excursion was to Caesarea Philippi, located directly south of Mount Hermon (Matt. 16:13 = Mark 8:27; Luke does not locate this event). The modern name Banias reflects the ancient name Panias, alluding to the worship of Pan in this area. At the time of Christ, Philip, son of Herod the Great, was tetrarch of this territory. He rebuilt and enlarged ancient Panias and renamed it in honor of the emperor (Philippi was added to the name to distinguish it from Caesarea Maritima on the Mediterranean coast). Earlier Herod the Great had built a temple in honor of Augustus. In this setting of the worship of nature (Pan) and political power (emperor worship), Jesus received the confession of Peter

and introduced his disciples to his impending death (cf. Smith, pp. 306–308).

## 3. PEREA

As Jesus made his final journey to Jerusalem, he passed through "the region of Judea beyond the Jordan" (Matt. 19:1 = Mark 10:1), that is, Perea, a portion of the tetrarchy of Herod Antipas. It is the southern part of the east bank of the Jordan and part of the plateau along this part of the Jordan Valley as far south as Machaerus. By passing through Perea, one could avoid traveling through Samaria while going from Galilee to Jerusalem.

## 4. ANTIOCH IN SYRIA

Early in the history of the Church, Antioch in Syria became the center of Christianity and the sending church of Paul and his associates. Today the city is Antakya—since World War I part of Turkey. The city is on the Orontes River about 30 kilometers (20 mi.) from the Mediterranean coast. Its harbor was Seleucia. Near Antioch were the gardens of Daphne, noted for their excesses in pagan worship and immoral practices.

In the first century A.D. Antioch was a leading city of the Roman empire and the capital of the Roman province of Syria. The city was very cosmopolitan, with a mixed population enjoying equal citizenship rights. The political, commercial, and cultural status of this city in the eastern Mediterranean world readily qualified it as a center for first-century Christianity.

## 5. CILICIA

The birthplace of Paul was Tarsus (e.g., Acts 9:11), a major city not far from the junction of the two main trade routes from the east that went through the Amanus Pass and the Syrian Gates. Westward and northward from Tarsus this major road passed through the Cilician Gates, the principal pass from east to west. At the time of Paul, Tarsus was the capital of the Roman province of Cilicia and a commercial and cultural center with a famous university.

## 6. CYPRUS

On his first missionary journey Paul with Barnabas first visited the island of Cyprus (Acts 13:4). The island was made a separate province of the Roman empire and was ruled by a proconsul. In Acts 13:7 Sergius Paulus is named as a proconsul, but so far attempts to identify him in other documents have not been convincing. (Cf. B. Van-Elderen, "Some Archaeological Observations on Paul's First Missionary Journey," in W. Gasque and R. Martin, eds., *Apostolic History and the Gospel* [Festschrift F. F. Bruce; Grand Rapids, 1970], pp. 151–56.)

## 7. ASIA MINOR

The greater part of Paul's first and third missionary journeys was spent in Asia Minor. Although this part of the Roman empire had a fine network of overland routes, Paul actually traveled as much by sea as by land in his mission activity. Even Tarsus, located about 15 kilometers (10 mi.) from the Mediterranean, could be reached by navigation on the river Cnydus in the first century. Generally Paul concentrated his work in the coastal areas, and it is not without significance that the three centers of early Christianity (Antioch, Ephesus, Corinth) were seaport cities where important land and sea routes joined. These major commercial centers also provided ready communication with other parts of the Roman empire.

The topographical features of Asia Minor resulted in the major concentrations of population being in the coastal areas. The interior high plateau was not very hospitable, being separated from the northern and southern coasts by high mountain ranges. Paul traveled through this area at the beginning of his second missionary journey (Acts 15:41; 16:1, 6), but was directed by the Spirit to the western coast (Acts 16:6, 7). Similarly, at the beginning of the third missionary journey he went overland from Antioch to Ephesus (Acts 18:23). Only during the first missionary journey did Paul cross the Taurus mountains from the southern coast and evangelize certain cities on the southern plateau—Pisidian Antioch, Iconium, Lystra, and Derbe. These cities were located in the Roman province of Alatia, and generally are considered the recipients of the epistle to the Galatians. The mixed population of these inland cities contained a sizable Jewish element, with synagogues in which Paul preached and with significant authority to influence public opinion against the Christian missionaries. Local dialects such as Phrygian and Lycaonian were spoken. It is out of this mixed cultural background that Timothy came (Acts 16:1)—occasioning his reticence in the more cultural and cosmopolitan cities, such as Ephesus (cf. 1 Tim. 4:12).

Coastal cities visited and evangelized by Paul were Perga, Attalia, Ephesus, Miletus, and Troas. These cities were located in Roman provinces; hence Paul was guaranteed the rights and privileges of Roman citizenship. Paul's longest residence at any place on these missionary journeys was at Ephesus, where he stayed almost two and a half years (Acts 19:8, 10). During this time he made some hasty visits to Corinth and may also have evangelized other towns in western Asia Minor. Ephesus's strategic location at the junction of land and sea routes for trade and travel, its cultural history spanning many centuries, and its religious importance as the center of Artemis worship resulted in a large, heterogeneous, and mixed population representing all facets of life and culture in the Roman empire. Ephesus's prominence in the early Church was a natural consequence of these features and Paul's sustained mission activity.

## 8. GREECE

Acts records Paul's first visit to Greece as occurring during the second missionary journey. In answer to the Macedonian call (Acts 16:9–10), Paul sailed from Troas to Neapolis (modern Kavalla) and then went on the Via Egnatia to Philippi. Founded by Philip the father of Alexander the Great, Philippi became a Roman colony with special privileges because of involvements in Rome's internecine struggles during the first century B.C. From Philippi Paul went southwest on the Via Egnatia to Thessalonica, a major Macedonian seaport with a Jewish community that was initially receptive to the gospel, but eventually forced the missionaries to leave.

After a brief visit to Berea, Paul went by sea to

Athens, the epitome of all the culture, religion, architecture, and art of ancient Greece. No doubt Paul thrilled to see all of this, just as the modern visitor to Athens does, but he was also shocked by its moral and religious bankruptcy when compared to Christianity. Here was perhaps the first major confrontation of Christianity and the best of pagan culture and thought (Acts 17:16–34).

From Athens Paul went to Corinth, the thriving commercial center of Greece. Situated on the narrow isthmus connecting central Greece and the Peloponnesus, Corinth received trade from east and west. Although destroyed in 146 B.C. by the Romans, it was rebuilt in 46 B.C. by Julius Caesar and by the time of Paul had become one of the great commercial centers of the Roman empire. It was the capital of Achaia and the residence of the proconsul (Acts 18:12). The numerous problems that existed in this church (cf. 1 Corinthians) reflect the mixed population and attendant tensions that arise in a commercial city.

Acts does not report further mission activity in Greece, but in a summary of his ministry Paul wrote that he went as far as Illyricum (Rom. 15:19), a district located northwest of Macedonia along the Adriatic Sea (also known as Dalmatia). Reference is made in Titus 3:12 to Nicopolis, located on the Ionian Sea in northwest Achaia.

Acts concludes with Paul's visit to Rome after a disastrous sea voyage from Caesarea (Acts 27:1–28:14). The route followed was the usual one, but involved certain difficulties because of the season and unfavorable conditions. Paul had desired frequently to go to Rome, and the New Testament story of the spread of the Church concludes with his limited, two-year ministry in Rome. As the capital of the Roman empire, this city displayed all the achievements of the Romans in government, architecture, culture, religion, and amusement. In the subsequent history of the Church, this city was to play a major role in ecclesiastical organization, theological development, liturgical expression, and political involvement.

## 9. OTHER NEW TESTAMENT SITES

Peter addressed his first letter to the believers in Pontus, Galatia, Cappadocia, Asia, and Bithynia. These are Roman provinces in the northern half of Asia Minor representing not only the Black Sea coastal areas but also the central plateau. It is not reported who evangelized this large area—possibly Peter and others after his departure from Jerusalem, but hardly the apostle Paul. The recipients of 1 Peter appear to have been predominantly Gentiles. That Christians became a significant part of the population of Bithynia is evident from the correspondence between Pliny and Emperor Trajan in A.D. 110.

In Revelation 2 and 3, John addresses letters to seven churches in western Asia Minor. The seven are located in a large semicircle in western Asia Minor and are listed in sequence beginning with Ephesus in the west. It appears from the New Testament that Paul had contact with only two of these—Ephesus, where he resided for more than two years, and Laodicea, to whom he wrote an epistle (Col. 4:16).

Early Church tradition reports that the apostle John went to Ephesus with Mary the mother of Jesus shortly before the fall of Jerusalem in A.D. 70. Whether this John was the author of Revelation is disputed. Dionysius challenged the apostolic authorship and reported a traveler's account that there were two tombs of John in Ephesus. The reliability of this report is questioned and the two Johns are unidentified. In any case, the author must have been sufficiently well known to the recipients that he did not have to identify himself further.

The second city mentioned by John was Smyrna (modern Izmir), lying north of Ephesus with a protected harbor. It was an attractive city in the first century and had a number of temples, including one in honor of Tiberius and his mother. With its harbor and trade connections the city played an important role in the economic life of Asia Minor. The ruins of an earlier city may have been the alleged birthplace of Homer. In A.D. 155 Polycarp the bishop of Smyrna suffered martyrdom at the hands of the Jews, whose earlier opposition to the Christians is referred to in Revelation 2:9.

Pergamum (modern Bergama) lies directly north of Smyrna on the Caicus River. In the first century A.D. it was the capital of the Roman province of Asia and the residence of the proconsul. On the acropolis overlooking the modern city stood a beautiful temple of Athena with a huge altar of Zeus nearby (identified by some with the "throne of Satan" in Rev. 2:13). Other buildings included a library, large theater, temples of Dionysus and Demeter, colonnades, and agora. At a lower level a complex of buildings in Roman times honored the god Asklepios, whose healing powers gave great prominence to Pergamum.

East of Pergamum lies Thyatira (modern Akhisar), the home of Lydia, the seller of purple goods who assisted Paul at Philippi (Acts 16:14). Epigraphical evidence indicates that the city was a manufacturing center with numerous trade guilds. A special purple dye, used for textiles in Thyatira, was derived from certain roots found in the area. The city had its own patron hero, Tyrimnos, who was worshiped along with Artemis. No doubt problems confronting the Thyatiran church related to the commercial and industrial character of the city.

South of Thyatira lies the famous city of Sardis, one-time capital of the Lydian empire whose opulently rich king Croesus was conquered by Cyrus the Great in 546 B.C. The Sardis of John's time had been rebuilt after extensive destruction by an earthquake in A.D. 17. The temple of Artemis near the Pactolus stream was not only large but also impressively decorated—later partially reused as a church. The Roman city was very large and included a Jewish synagogue.

The sixth city mentioned by John was Philadelphia (modern Alashehir), lying east of Sardis on a tributary of the Hermus River. Its position at the entrance into the main plateau of central Asia Minor may explain the statement: "I have set before you an open door" (Rev. 3:8). The earlier city was extensively destroyed by the earthquake of A.D. 17. Virtually no archeological work has been done at the site, and traces of the ancient walls are visible in the modern town built over the site.

The last of the seven churches is Laodicea, whose ruins lie some 9 kilometers (6 mi.) from modern Denizli. Laodicea lies between Hierapolis (Col. 4:13) and Colossae, forming in the Lycus valley a triad of cities with first-century churches. The ruins of Hierapolis are very extensive and the lukewarm mineral springs nearby have deposited startling white surfaces on the nearby cliffs (the modern name Pammakale ["cotton-castle"] reflects this phenomenon). The piping of some of this lukewarm water to Laodicea may explain the words: "So, because you are lukewarm, and neither cold nor hot . . ." (Rev. 3:16). Some remains (theater, hippodrome, colonnaded streets) of ancient Laodicea are visible, but very little archeological work has been done on the site.

John was exiled on the island of Patmos when he wrote Revelation (1:9). The island is located off the southwest coast of Asia Minor, almost directly west of Miletus. It is about 16 by 10 kilometers (10 by 6 mi.) in size and contains volcanic hills and rugged shorelines. The first-century town must have been sheltered between two bays on the west side. In this vicinity John was incarcerated and in the midst of these experiences wrote about the promising and perilous future.

## 10. CONCLUSION

A geographical survey of the main sites mentioned in the New Testament shows that the entire Mediterranean world was deeply affected in the first century by the work of the early Christian missionaries. In varying ways many New Testament accounts reflect the geographical setting of the events and recipients. A look at the Mediterranean world and its topography makes Paul's catalog of experiences in 2 Corinthians 11:23–27 all the more astounding. The dangers there recounted are very real when one considers the terrains traversed and distances covered by the Apostle. Thus the challenge of his example takes on greater dimensions.

### LITERATURE

M. Avi-Yonah, *Gazeteer of Roman Palestine* (Jerusalem, 1976).

D. Baly, *Geographical Companion to the Bible* (New York, 1963).

———, *The Geography of the Bible* (New York, 1974²).

A. A. M. van der Heyden, *Atlas van de antieke wereld* (Amsterdam, 1962).

G. A. Smith, *The Historical Geography of the Holy Land* (repr. London, 1966).

# II

# Archeology of Palestine and Other Biblical Lands

*by H. J. Franken and C. H. J. de Geus*

# A. Archeology of Palestine: Problems and Task

*by H. J. Franken*

## 1. ARCHEOLOGICAL METHODOLOGY

The archeology of one part of the world is different from that of other parts. This diversity can be explained in terms of the history of the origin and development of archeological activities in those regions. This also holds true for the archeology of the Near East: it has a long history, it has developed its own methods, and thus it has acquired its own distinctive features. The archeology of Palestine bears all the marks of the archeology of the Near East.

Today there is a tendency to bring about a closer alignment of the goals and techniques of archeology as it is practiced worldwide. At present, however, it is not yet possible to formulate precisely the nature and purpose of archeology; there are too many mutually contradictory formulations, reflecting the different developments through which archeologies have gone. Moreover, individual archeologists have their own ideas or follow definite schools, resulting in diversity even within a specific area.

Not every archeologist is a digger, though for the practice of the discipline there are advantages in taking part in excavations. Digging itself falls under the rubric "techniques," and modern archeology places more and more activities under this category. Most of these activities have a scientific background and lead to the scientific study of the material. In a modern excavation it is customary to examine the ground using modern laboratory equipment. As a rule, this work is not done by the archeologist himself. The archeologist becomes more and more the scientist; his challenge is to arrive at a meaningful collation of data that

have been acquired by all kinds of investigative methods, which he himself does not have to know or master. By combining the results of various investigations, he can gain insight into the nature and the history of ancient civilizations. The great increase in the available data, acquired by the application of the knowledge of the exact sciences, has not made the task of the archeologist easier. We are familiar with the image of the archeologist who studies the great achievements of ancient civilizations, who writes history and publishes texts. On the basis of such activities one could give a definition of archeology. Now that other data are added and the emphasis may be put on other aspects, giving a definition of what archeology is or should be becomes more difficult. Theories are made in which the nature of the contribution to our knowledge of the past is less dependent on the traditional placement of the so-called historical facts, but comes more from the area of social and cultural history.

Much of the current archeological effort lies in the area of prehistory and concerns peoples and places whose history has not been preserved in any form of literary remains; all that we have are material remains. Newer forms of investigation have made archeologists increasingly critical in their interpretation of archeological finds. On good grounds they have doubted the current explanation of changes that are apparently observable in certain cultures and that were related to invading tribes, migrations, earthquakes, and the like. They have also cast suspicion on the identification of specific sites with events that are known from historical sources. They have not doubted the reliability of the historical sources, but only the procedure followed in using the finds for identification. Generally, the intensification of the effort to master the basic procedures by expanding the investigative methods with techniques derived from the exact sciences has resulted in the search for new principles of explanation.

These new developments have also begun to make their impact on biblical archeology. In general the research has followed the paths mapped out in the years between the two World Wars. Philologists, historians, and theologians have put their stamp on this archeology. This has resulted not only in recognized advantages but also in disadvantages. An important disadvantage now manifesting itself is that the system of explaining finds has acquired a kind of one-sidedness; as a result, little new information is obtained in comparison with the mass of newly uncovered material. As a rule the excavation reports discuss extensively the pottery that has been dug up and use it for stratigraphic dating. A person who is accustomed to this method of researching pottery will wonder whether anything can be added to the discussion of pottery. For a vessel is described as carefully as possible, accurately drawn and pictured, and typologically classified and dated. What could be wrong with this methodology? If this method is uncritically accepted as valid and effective, it implies that progress in this field is at a standstill. In what follows this example will be elaborated. It is a more concrete or tangible example than the one that concerns the procedure used to identify antiquities by means of historical data with which we are familiar; here it is more difficult to detect stagnation in the reflection on methodology. In the past too much was required of the latter archeological approach, both by some archeologists and by the public, which had a great interest in antiquities. The burden that was laid upon it was to support biblical truths by providing historical data that, if they could not prove the correctness of those biblical data, at least would make them plausible. The need for this kind of use of archeological data is contradictory in itself because it conflicts with the nature of biblical revelation that it tries to make plausible. Here, however, we ought to concern ourselves with arguments that can be directly derived from the archeological method.

## 2. THE NATURE AND PROCESSING OF ARCHEOLOGICAL DATA

Archeology works mainly with data acquired by excavation. The purpose of an excavation is to produce new study material in an area in which the archeologist has a special interest. This material consists of raw ingredients that need processing in order to turn them into useful data. Three kinds of processing are often necessary before new information can be derived from them.

The first kind involves the *study of the setting* of a specific object in the ground. The concept "object" must be taken in a very broad sense; it may refer to a particular type of soil as well as to a man-made artifact. Thus, this first requirement concerns the study of the context or relationship of an object to its setting. In an earlier stage of the history of archeology, this context, the ground in which an object was discovered, was regarded as "wrapping paper" and simply thrown away. In a later stage the researcher began to note the relation between the object and the man-made environment in which it was placed, such as the floor and the walls within which the object was discovered. The object was also studied in relation to other objects that were found in that same space. An even more recent development is the study of the influence the environment has had on the object during the time the two were together. The degree of preservation of the object is directly related to the nature of the milieu in which it was located: dry or humid, acid ground or soil rich in lime, etc. Thus the study of the context must be done before "the object" has been discovered. Stated in different and better terms: the nature and layers of the ground in which objects might be found are themselves objects of research.

The next step is *preservation and restoration*. A good illustration is the discovery of a text. Texts are found on all kinds of materials: stone, clay, metal, papyrus, wood, leather, wall plaster, faience (earthenware decorated with opaque colored glazes), frit (partly treated glass), pottery, and glass. Letters or words can be written by cutting or chipping stone out of stone, by engraving in stone, metal, potsherd, or a mold for making pottery by the use of metal oxides such as paint on pots, by the use of ink (carbon) on potsherds, papyrus, and so on. Extensive texts on stone cannot be preserved without great expense, and the need is not always evident. But all texts on other materials, including stony materials such as faience, frit, or glass, must sooner or later be preserved. Texts written in ink must be preserved as soon as possible after their discovery, after they have been subjected to a thorough laboratory examination of the object's condition. Similar treatment should also be given to texts found on metal (bronze, copper). Because the need for preservation is still not universally recognized, many texts become irreparably lost in a time span that is very brief compared with the many centuries in which they were preserved in the ground (and would have remained preserved if they had not been suddenly exposed to light and air).

The third treatment of the text is its *interpretation*. This requires the aid of an arsenal of ancillary disciples that have been built up and expanded by generations of experts. The content of the text is a datum by itself. One of the questions that comes up in connection with the interpretation concerns the date. As a rule, texts that derive from Palestine cannot be dated with the use of information in the texts themselves, because they contain no reference to a chronology with which we are familiar. In attempting to reconstruct the time of origin, one must consider the circumstances of the find as well. This makes texts once more part of the general problem of the dating of artifacts, of groups of artifacts, and of the archeological context in which such groups have been found. So the problems of dating texts become part of a larger context from which all too often they are wrongly detached. For example, archeologists sometimes attempt to date inscriptions by an analysis of the development of the script. The underlying assumption is that reliable data are available for particular stages of the development of the script and that there has been a synchronistic development of all the letters and signs wherever the script was used. Thus the problem remains that there are no other possibilities for verification than the presuppositions that are being used. We mention this problem here because it bears on many other aspects of the study of artifacts, in particular the study of pottery.

Readers who are aware of the dating problems posed by the texts sometimes look for help to the results of the archeological study of the context. In so doing they encounter an extensive but far from transparent arsenal of arguments in favor of certain datings that are defended by the authors against other opinions. A fine, though complicated, example is the discussion on the dating of the so-called *la-melek* seals (ill. 1). A conclusive argument for a particular dating is lacking for two reasons: first, the selective use of all the aspects adduced in the discussion, and second, many authors come with arguments derived from stratigraphy and site of discovery that cannot be harmonized with each other and sometimes directly contradict each other.

The so-called reliable data and synchronistic development of artifacts spread through a large part of the land are, as it were, cornerstones for the construction of the picture of cultural developments in Palestine in the Iron Age. If archeology is to have a clear dividing line in obtaining a date that is indisputable and that it can use to work backward or forward in time, the obvious fixed point of reference is the culture at the eve of the Babylonian captivity. This historically fixed date is an ideal starting point because the capture of Judah by the Babylonians must have left clearly detectable traces in the ground. There can be no doubt that the Judean cities were captured and thoroughly destroyed. The discussions among archeologists, however, have not furnished decisive criteria that would enable us to attribute an earlier destruction to the first Babylonian invasion or to the Assyrian conquest, which took place over a century earlier. So far, neither pottery nor inscriptions—if they exist—nor other artifacts (in the broadest sense of the term) can give a definite answer. We know, for example, what seventh-century pottery is, but we do not know to what extent or whether it differs from pottery in the last decades of the eighth century B.C. Again we should note that the arguments that are used to fix a certain date within this time span of at least 125 years for the particular age of an object rest on a conglomerate of data that individually are insufficient to prove the point. Conversely, it should be possible, on the basis of probabilities, to use part of the data for an earlier and part for a later dating.

IX. This aerial photo provides a good view of the narrow strip of land that the Nile irrigates and the abrupt change from vegetation to desert. (C. H. J. de Geus)

X. The upper Euphrates River at Kale, between Malatya and Elazis in Anatolia. (A. D. Baly)

XI. Aghri Dagh in eastern Turkey, the highest peak of the Ararat range and the traditional landing place of Noah's ark. (W. S. LaSor)

1. One of the royal seals: a winged/flying scarab with the inscription lmlk, "royal" (above) and ḥbrn, "Hebron" (below). See pp. 51–52.

2. Excavations along the southwest corner of the retaining wall surrounding the temple mount in Jerusalem. An inscription found in this area confirmed that a tower stood here, from which a priest sounded the beginning of the sabbath. (Consulate General of Israel in New York)

3. Middle Bronze and Late Middle Bronze Age (ca. 2000–1500 B.C.) pottery from Megiddo, a period of prosperity but little peace, indicated by numerous strata and phases of strata. (Oriental Institute, University of Chicago)

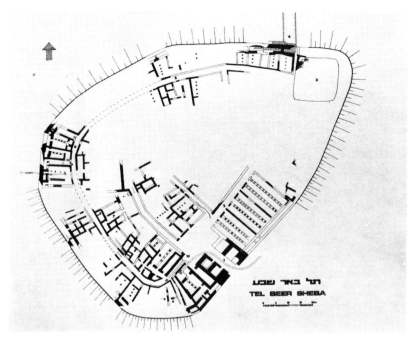

4. *A map of Beer-sheba in the time of the monarchy. Beer-sheba was a fine example of a small Israelite city. (1) City gate. (2) Store rooms (see ill. 92). (3) Large shaft for water system. (4) Small trench cut by excavators. (5) and (6) Road around the city, parallel to the city wall. On both sides of this road were found the better homes (see ill. 96). (7, 8, 9) Public buildings. (10) Square behind the gate (cf. Gen. 19:2). In the period of the monarchy Beer-sheba was not much larger than 2 hectares (5 acres). See p. 57.*

5. *A group of female clay figurines from the earliest period of Israel. Their function is uncertain; they may have been goddesses. The depicted group is of the "pillar type." These and similar figurines remained very popular for a long time, both within and outside Israel.*

XII. The famous theater at Ephesus where the Ephesians nearly rioted in response to Paul's preaching (cf. Acts 19:29, 31). (W. S. LaSor)

XIII. The Via Egnatia from Kavalla (Neapolis) to Philippi. (W. S. LaSor)

XIV. The altar of Zeus on the acropolis at Pergamum. Some identify this altar as the ''throne of Satan'' mentioned in Rev. 2:13. (W. S. LaSor)

XV. Gerasa, Jordan, was one of the cities of the Decapolis in New Testament times. View of the large colonnade, the main street, of this once-elegant Greco-Roman city. (C. H. J. de Geus)

XVI. A detail from a capital at Gerasa. (C. H. J. de Geus)

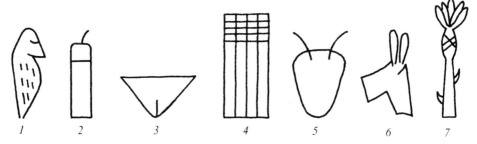

6. Pictographic signs from Mesopotamia, ca. 3000 B.C. (1) Hairy torso: "man," "a human," Sumerian lú. (2) Male pubic part: "male," "manly," Sumerian gìš. (3) Female pubic part: "woman," "female." Sumerian mì or munus. (4) Rectangle divided into small squares: "house," Sumerian é. (5) Head of a bull: "bull," Sumerian gud. (6) Head of an ass: "ass," Sumerian anše. (7) Stylized palm: "date palm," Sumerian gišimmar. See pp. 78–79.

7. Elaborating on the same basic form: (1) Stylized head: "head," Sumerian sag. (2) Head with arched mouth: "mouth" or "word," Sumerian ka. (3) Head with piece of bread: "eating," Sumerian kú. See pp. 78–79.

8. Predynastic Sumerian tablets from Jemdet Nasr (ca. 3000 B.C.) inscribed with linear characters immediately derived from pictographs. They contain accounts of fields, crops, and commodities. (Trustees of the British Museum)

|  | I | II | III | IV | V |
|---|---|---|---|---|---|
| 1 | | | | | |
| 2 | | | | | |
| 3 | | | | | |
| 4 | | | | | |
| 5 | | | | | |
| 6 | | | | | |
| 7 | | | | | |

9. *Development of cuneiform writing (cf. p. 79). I. Pictographic signs; see ill. 6 for the explanation. The signs are tipped 90°, because the clay tablets began to be held differently in the hand. II. Development of cuneiform, ca. 2500 B.C. III. Forms of the same signs in the Old Babylonian period, 20th-16th centuries B.C. The signs become more cursive. IV. Sign forms in the Neo-Assyrian period, 9th-7th centuries B.C. V. Sign forms in the Late Babylonian period, after 625 B.C.*
  *Besides the shapes given here, each period also had all sorts of variants of its own. Moreover, besides designating a word, many signs also acquired syllabic values. For example, sign no. 3 can represent the following syllables: sal, shal, rag/k/q, mim, mam, min.*

10. *Classroom at Mari. For the location of this city, see map III (see also A. Parrot, Mari capitale fabuleuse [Paris, 1974], p. 129, fig. 77). See p. 79.*

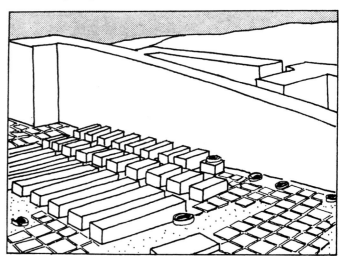

XVIII. The library of Celsus at Ephesus. Celsus was a pagan philosopher who wrote the oldest literary attack on Christianity that has survived, albeit as part of Origen's response in defense of Christianity, Contra Celsum. (W. S. LaSor)

XVII. The island of Patmos where the exiled John wrote Revelation. (A. D. Baly)

XIX. Looking south from the temple of Artemis at Gerasa: the forum, the temple of Zeus, and the south theater, which could hold 5,000 people. (L. T. Geraty)

Why are these circular arguments not eliminated? The answer is that they often "lurk" in the use of external data not derived from the material, such as the identification of places and of historical events. If one assumes that Tell ed-Duweir is Lachish and that a certain layer is the "Assyrian" stratum, one employs two a priori arguments by which other data are, as it were, forced to fit into the scheme. If it is thought that the numerous recent excavations have provided the answer to these questions, it would be good to verify the proof that has been adduced with the starting points described here. When a certain thesis, which can neither be substantiated nor denied, is used often, it eventually comes to be regarded as an established fact and as such is used by some and contested by others.

This problem cannot be solved, however, even with the best of stratigraphic data. We referred already to the use of external data in the argumentation (identification with respect to time and place). The correctness of the classification of pottery, however, is also subject to doubt, at least in regard to its refinement for use in dating within the margin of a few decades.

## 3. INVESTIGATION AND DATING OF POTTERY

Time as such is not an obvious given of pottery, though this is often thought to be the case. That a vessel can contain an element of age is a discovery of modern physics. The equipment needed to measure that age does not possess nearly the kind of refinement that would make it possible to determine, in terms of biblical time, within a few hundred years the time when a vessel was made. As a matter of fact, a pot is not a calendar; it was not made to show time. In the archeological literature of the Near East, however, pottery is almost always used to determine the time and the culture, though today a greater number of archeologists share the view that there is more to pottery than that. The thesis that the material itself must be thoroughly studied before it can be used or applied—a fixed rule in the applied sciences—should also become a rule in archeology. In other words, the material itself should be carefully studied and analyzed before conclusions are drawn from it.

The modern methods of analyzing pottery can be divided into two main groups. The one most used is that of analyzing the substance and investigating the various characteristics of the elements of which it is composed. A pot is made of the substance of clay minerals that through the application of heat has been changed into stone and now presents itself as a conglomerate of many elements. The characteristics of this stone are altogether different from the original substance, the clay. It is not possible to return this stone to that original condition. In a laboratory, various aspects of pottery can be examined: hardness, porosity, the heat applied to it in the oven, and its mineral composition. This research is entirely based on methods of examination that have been developed for the ceramic industry and for advanced developments in physics. Such analysis not only makes it possible to explain certain features that are observed on the pottery, but also to determine whether among a group of pots there are some that have not been made in the same place as most of the others. A trained archeologist will soon sense that a few pots do not belong in that group, even in cases where the untrained eye does not see any difference. The microscopic examination of coarser grains of minerals or grit in such a group, whether intentionally added or not, may indeed show that these pots have a different origin.

The other form of analysis, which is the most recent development in this field, concerns the craft of making pottery in antiquity. For the most part this investigation has no other given to work with than the product of that craft, namely, the pottery. It is nothing short of amazing, however, how many givens about that craft (and thus about the methods used) have been preserved in the form of a variety of features on the surface of an old pot. This is not work that is done in a laboratory; it is the domain of the expert in the potter's craft and its history. The difference between the two approaches is that the first uses chemical-physical means to explain processes that must have happened to the substance, while the latter uses the study of the craft of the potter to explain the origin of the shape and the unity in a particular group of shapes. The technological difference between two apparently identical shapes may be so great that it is not likely that these two shapes come from the same workshop. Of necessity these two investigations must eventually converge.

An objection raised against newer methods of examining pottery is that archeology is a discipline that typically belongs to the humanities and that it may not lose its character by trying to become an exact science. Both approaches, however, have long been advocated by researchers who believed that the traditional description of pottery (the typological method), in which a pot is used as a "label" for a particular period and a particular culture, was a poor means to trace the maker of the vessel and the people who used it. Historically, therefore, archeologists with training in cultural anthropology were the first to call in the aid of the exact sciences in the investigation of pottery.

The following example will show the need for this broadening of the examination of pottery. In archeology the pottery that was made in Israel's preexilic period is regarded as well-thrown pottery, comparable to pottery that is made on a modern kick wheel. This wheel enables one to make pots in rapid succession. The clay that is used for the process must be of a particular quality, however. If vessels are made without the use of such an easily turning wheel, the clay needs other qualities. Its characteristics must then be similar to those of our chamotte clay, and a light manual disk is sufficient to form pots. Thus we can infer that the transition from manual disk to kick wheel is rather drastic. Production can be increased tenfold. If the demand for the product remains the same, it makes no sense to change over to a fast wheel, for it would create overproduction and many small potters' shops would become superfluous. We are familiar with this problem in our own day. The question whether ancient Israelite pottery—using that term for the sake of convenience—was made by the one method or the other is thus related to specific societal situations. Technological examination performed in the division of Palestinian antiquities at the University of Leiden has shown that this ancient Israelite pottery cannot have been made on a fast-turning wheel. Certain characteristics of the types of clay that were used make it impossible to fashion a vessel from it on a fast wheel. The modeling and finishing of a bowl must have taken at least a whole day of intensive work, for someone had to polish it with a small piece of stone or bone from sunrise to sunset.

We can go a step further and establish that if such bowls were fired in a kiln, roughly 10 to 20 percent would be lost. Thus for every thousand bowls one hundred to two hundred workdays would be lost. Knowing these things, one looks differently at a pot than the traditional typologist does.

Also, the idea that handmade pottery would be more "primitive" than that made on a wheel is definitely shown to be wrong, unless one considers what is done slowly to be "primitive." Technological investigation of so-called primitive pottery has in many cases shown that its makers fashioned an outstanding product with the clay available to them.

Another presupposition in traditional pottery typology is that similarity in form is proof of simultaneity. This is regarded as an axiom. If all the pottery in a certain area would come from one or two production centers, this axiom would become plausible. Such an occurrence is very rare, however, or it cannot be demonstrated cogently. For pottery obtained through excavation may originate from a number of potters' shops scattered throughout the country. That makes it very difficult, if not impossible, to explain that their products would all simultaneously have gone through the same evolution in form.

That an examination of the potter's craft leads to different conclusions than the typological method can be illustrated by a study of pottery from Jericho. This pottery comes from a trench at Tell es-Sultan (not the Jericho of the Old Testament), and it is assumed that it dates from the seventh century B.C. The buildings that were found with it may have belonged to the settlement that is mentioned at the end of the list of exiles who returned to Judah (Ezra 2:34—345 people). The identity cannot be proved. The typological approach caused no real problems, for the shapes were familiar from other digs. There were, however, some "old-fashioned" types among them that one would like to date a few centuries earlier. Technological examination, however, showed the following. Most pots proved to have been fashioned from substances (clay and added minerals) that were found at the site. Consequently they were most likely local vessels. They were made on a slowly turning wheel. The method of fabrication was the same as the one already found toward the end of the second millennium B.C. Larger pots were constructed by putting clay rings on top of each other. The desired form was obtained by scraping clay from the thicker parts when the pot was being made, lest it would collapse while still wet. Among the pottery there was, however, also a smaller group that was made on a fast-turning wheel and that had a very small amount of tempering material, namely, quartz, which is not found at Tell es-Sultan. This is a newer development that may be related to the introduction of more advanced techniques by the Assyrian conquerors. The other small group of pot fragments, which typologically might belong to earlier centuries, was found to contain a different tempering material and can be related to the making of pottery in Transjordan. It is entirely possible that occasionally people carried pottery across the Jordan to Tell es-Sultan and left the pottery behind there. The best explanation, however, is that here is a case of nonsynchronistic evolution in form. There were potters whose product was "behind" that of, for example, Tell es-Sultan in terms of shape.

This example enables us to point out two shortcomings of the traditional typological method. First, there is no way to distinguish two totally different techniques, and second, the thesis "identity in shape means simultaneity" is not always true. The customary method of dating is thus not without its problems. Questions can be asked which that method cannot answer.

If the evolvement of the shape of pottery proceeds synchronistically in all sorts of places, nearly all the pottery that is found in a particular layer at a particular place should be compared with all the pottery that is found in certain layers at other places. In practice this is not done, however. Shapes that are considered characteristic for a certain period are selected to serve as comparative material. Next, this select group is further subdivided, because some shapes from place A are found at B and C, but others not at B are found at C and D; and others are found at B and D, but not at C.

A possible explanation for this situation may be that the method has been wrongly applied. The demand that an excavator publish all the shapes that are found in a certain layer and mention how many of these shapes have been found is not always met. If a publication does not provide certainty on this point, or if it is certain that this demand has not been met, the procedure lacks a reliable basis.

Moreover, the sampling—the collection of pottery—may be unreliable. In the experience of this writer, a trench, say, 10 meters (30 ft.) wide, dug into a tell, is not enough to furnish a reliable sample from a layer. Such a layer ought to be dug up at least over an area of 30 meters (100 ft.). An average of at least one recognizable shape should be found in a surface of a square meter. If approximately three hundred identifiable shapes have been reconstructed from the pieces (10 x 30, which is a steep requirement), one begins to obtain a reliable insight into the numerical relations the various shapes have to each other. This assumes, of course, that the situation found in that layer is not a unique one, but is representative of, for example, a normal living quarter. Statistically the margin of uncertainty would then be roughly 9 percent. By contrast, if a large part of the excavated area is occupied by, for example, a "public" building, one cannot be certain of the pottery data for dating purposes. If the material comes from a long, narrow trench, it may furnish one-sided data because it is not possible to give a closer identification of the place where it is found. Utilizing these insights in the study of excavation reports, one soon discovers that in many cases the basis for making comparisons is too small. From the excavation one cannot determine whether the sample of pottery is statistically reliable.

The above discussion deals with a number of defects that could inhere in the application of the method. The method itself also has defects. What conclusion might one come to if it were determined that the total group of pottery found at place A was 50 percent directly comparable with that found at place B, 30 percent with that of place C, and 20 percent with that of place D? Only 20 percent of what is found at A can be directly compared with pottery from all three of the other places. For the evaluation of this situation it is necessary to have a criterion that would make it possible to say whether the comparison of pottery from place A with that from place B may still lead to results. To obtain that criterion an explanation is needed for the low comparison between D and A. Is the distance between places A and D the cause? Or is there too much of a difference in time so that somewhere in place D there must be a layer that furnishes a better comparative result? Or is trade between the two places the explanation for the 20 percent that can be compared? Also, the 50 percent comparative value of place B with A calls for an explanation. While many shapes from both places can be compared with each other, it is precisely the segment that cannot be compared that points to a problem; there is the additional possibility that not all A-shapes that can be compared with C and D belong to the category that can be compared with B.

The problem inherent in this method of comparison becomes particularly evident if technical questions are brought to bear: How was a particular vessel made and from what material? Where were these materials obtained? How were they used? The investigation of these matters furnishes all sorts of new data. For example, there turns out to be a relationship between the composition of the clay and the shape of the vessel, kiln temperature, length of baking, etc. The making of pottery at Tell es-Sultan took place in various civilizations and covered a time span of several thousand years. Almost without exception it is a relatively soft type of pottery. The clay substance could not be baked into a hard product because its lime content is much too high for that and because the lime contains many coarse impurities that have been added as tempering material. Particularly in the case of the latter, a low oven temperature and a quick firing method are necessary; both provide economic advantages. No matter how it is fired, this pottery does not become really red. To obtain a harder product or a beautiful red color, it would have been possible to mix the local clay with some kinds of clay that are found east of the Jordan or in the mountains. If among the collection of potsherds from that place some really hard potsherds are found, these generally contain a tempering mineral that according to the geological map is not found at Tell es-Sultan. Pots that have been tempered with quartz or basalt can stand higher temperatures than those tempered with lime.

These examples are sufficient to show that the usual typological method is defectively applied and that it is based on presuppositions that are valid within the method but not outside it. If pottery is studied from different perspectives, the defects of the typological method become evident.

From the perspective of the craft it is possible to determine a type, a particular shape of a pot, if one knows the operations that go into its making in the proper sequence. If these operations are followed, the normal result is a fairly simple typological system that is based on the possibility of determining whether two quite similar shapes have been made in the same way. Moreover, this investigation provides a reliable basis for the statistical use of ceramic data. That statistical use appears to be more and more necessary for the study of the use of pottery and for use in dating.

In this section much attention has been given to the description of problems related to the study and dating of pottery. This is in line with the space given to the study of pottery in the literature and excavation reports. Students of archeology are expected to know the pottery they study and to be able to deal with it. In all the discussions on the dating of strata, the description of shapes of pottery has a dominant role. See ill. 3.

## 4. PROCESSING A DISCOVERY

Recent literature has a much broader conception of the context of a discovery—using the word in a comprehensive sense—than used to be the case. To classify a discovery, earlier archeology used to be satisfied to describe the object, to determine its date, and to compare it with similar objects that had been found and published elsewhere. A group of pots that were found together on a floor or in a grave constituted a "collective object." This find could be combined with other objects (made, e.g., of metal, glass, or stone) found at the same site and so constitute a "collective discovery or find." Next, the location of the collective find, such as the floor and four walls, could be added to it, forming a closed collective discovery. In a dig, a series of such collective finds can be combined so that they constitute one collective find. This combining into larger units is done by comparing objects (pottery) that exhibit such a great degree of correspondence that it is assumed that they are also from the same time. The result is a complex of data that have been defined with respect to space and time, and this group can be used to classify other larger or smaller finds in other places.

In this connection the significant stratigraphic datum is that the mound containing ruins has older and younger strata. Of necessity the younger layers are excavated first because they cover the older ones. In publications the oldest layer is usually described first. This method, briefly touched on here, is sometimes called the "locus-to-stratum method"; it still has its proponents.

But a study of the context of a find, as this is understood today, includes more and other data. For instance, the relationship among the elements that compose the mound is no longer determined mainly by a study of the objects associated with those elements, such as pottery, but by an examination of the deposits of which the mound consists, including the traces of human activity such as walls and floors. These deposits consist for the most part of layers of debris originating from the demolition—whether by human beings or through natural forces such as rain, wind, or fire—of a great variety of buildings ranging from stables and barns to city walls and palaces. So far the archeology of the Near East has paid too little attention to the complexities of tell stratigraphy. The traces of human activity are often stressed, and the tell is described without paying attention to the numerous evidences of erosion that also determine how everything fits together. The danger with this procedure is that connections are made among loose elements in the stratigraphy that are not or need not be correct. For instance, layers are linked to each other because they lie at the same height or have the same type of pottery. A simple rule of thumb says that elements such as houses, yards, and pits that were in use simultaneously must have been connected with each other by the existing surface over which one goes from point a to point b. That surface indicated what belonged together. Though it sounds simple, it may be very difficult to determine what was part of the surface. Techniques have, however, been developed to do that, and they are a much more reliable method of combination than the one just mentioned. See ill. 2–4.

There is much more to this matter of context than can be mentioned in detail in this section. Just a few brief suggestions must suffice. In the various strata one may find identifiable carbonized traces of plants as well as remains of animal skeletons. Moreover, the composition of the ground may contain clues concerning both the history of the mound and human activity. These aspects will increasingly call for the attention of the archeologist. One aspect of the associations between ground and object remains to be mentioned. Methods of investigation are developed to determine the age of the traces of human life in the past. The best known of these is the so-called carbon-14 dating method.

## 5. ARCHEOLOGY AND THE OLD TESTAMENT

Reading books and reports about excavations in biblical lands, many might be inclined to think that there is a close relation between archeological finds and biblical data in the sense that traces of events or persons mentioned in the Old Testament can be found in the ground. This is only partially true. Most of the archeological data now available from the biblical period have no connection with people, places, events, or objects with which we are familiar from the Bible. Here we touch on the problem of the identification of data we know from the Bible with antiquities we have learned about through excavation or some other way. Some archeologists treat this problem lightly. For example, Deuteronomy 34:6 states "no man knows the place of his [Moses'] burial to this day," but elsewhere in this chapter Moses' death is described as well as the place where he was buried: ". . . in the valley in the land of Moab opposite Beth-peor. . . ." In rabbinic and patristic literature this text has been the subject of much discussion; without further elucidation, however, what can be derived from this text is that the place where the grave is to be sought is limited and circumscribed, but that the location of the grave was not marked by a stone or other monument. We may also infer that the biblical passage did not intend that the site of this grave should become known. In addition, for thousands of years every valley in this area has been used as a nomad cemetery; thus we have two reasons for not searching for the grave of Moses—a religious one and the practical reason that there are no signs of recognition. There is nothing by which the grave of Moses might be recognized. Nevertheless, in recent times expeditions have tried to find this grave!

Both perspectives can be used in many instances. For example, the Jericho of Joshua cannot be identified with Tell es-Sultan. On the one hand, all the collapsed city walls look alike, making it impossible to declare a divine word as the literal cause of the fall. On the other hand, there is little certainty on two points: the date of the fall of Jericho (a biblical datum), and the date of the ruins of Tell es-Sultan (an archeological datum), which would have to be identified with Jericho. This brings us back to the archeological dictum that the archeologist should classify his finds without bringing in nonarcheological data, and only afterward compare them with data derived from historical sources. The Bible student who reads and interprets the text in the light of the excavations at Tell es-Sultan (which many identify with the Old Testament Jericho) commits a serious methodological error. The archeologist can make a similar error. If the archeologist is guided by a name for a ruin that sounds biblical (e.g., Heshbon and Tell *Hesban*) and excavates the ruin with the history of the biblical city in mind, he may be faced with strange surprises. This does not alter the fact that a number of identifications are correct. It happens, too, however, that proof is forced. This has happened with Tell ed-Duweir and Lachish, el-Jib and Gibeon, Tell el-Ful and Gibeah, Tell Deir Alla and Succoth. Occasionally archeology has degenerated into a search for relics (e.g., the well where Jesus talked with the Samaritan woman and the piece of a jar from Herod's temple).

## 6. WHAT IS ARCHEOLOGICAL INTERPRETATION?

A large part of the task of interpretation consists of making comparisons. New findings are compared with similar objects found at the site or elsewhere. To use a simple, neutral example: in a certain locality archeologists find remnants of buildings all of which have an oblong shape and are approximately the same dimensions. In the center they find remnants from one building that form a cross. If it may be assumed, for whatever reason, that the inhabitants of this settlement were all Christians, it may be concluded that the ruins represent homes with a church in the center. This conclusion is based on the assumption that in this cultural period a similar situation obtained in various places, namely, a central building surrounded by dwellings of a known type. Here is another example. If a similar pattern is found regularly—for instance, an open courtyard next to an area closed in by four walls and containing a particular type of vessel and two rubbing-stones—it may be assumed that what is found represents a normal domestic situation. However, if it should happen that the rubbing-stones are identical in pairs every time they are found, but that this familiar situation is once interrupted by a stone artifact of a totally different shape, the problem of interpretation surfaces. The more objects appear to be related to each other, that is, occur in a particular constellation, the more numerous are the possibilities of coming up with an interpretation of the whole and the parts.

The same problem surfaces with the clay tablets of Deir Alla. Three tablets with writing have been found; these are the only pieces known so far. Therefore one can only theorize about the language and significance. If, however, there would be a hundred such texts, it would be strange if it were not possible to decipher them.

One of the problems encountered in the archeology of the Near East is that the unknown is explained by fitting it in with what is known, often at the cost of certain concrete data. In the Jordan Valley, for example, some so-called Philistine pottery has been discovered. Some archeologists see here an indication that the Philistines, known from, among other places, the Old Testament, began to extend their power beyond the Jordan. But is that the only possible explanation of the occurrence of certain shapes of pottery in a certain area? It would be difficult to maintain that the presence of Chinese pottery in the Near East in the early Middle Ages would be related to Chinese invasions in that area.

It is therefore not surprising that in reaction to such premature conclusions archeologists search for and try to test entirely different means of explanation. One approach is to determine whether and in what way a new group in an area might be recognized with archeological means as such. For a long time already, some archeologists have been aware that the arrival of Israelite tribes in Canaan can in no way be determined by archeology, let alone be demonstrated. Biblical scholars have different views about the time of the events connected with Joshua. In these disputes the decision cannot be left to archeologists as long as they themselves do not offer unambiguous arguments for their datings and logical definitions of "old" and "new" inhabitants.

Here are some examples of the criticism of present archeological statements. Both critical remarks concern logic. If on the basis of biblical data Israel's entry into Canaan is dated in the second half of the thirteenth century B.C., the changes that, archeologically speaking, occurred about 1200 B.C. must be attributed to the Israelites. In that case the cities, pottery, dwellings, organizations, and the like are Israelite. Whenever this new situation is discovered in excavations, a date of about 1200 B.C. will be assigned to it. Everything from an earlier time is considered Canaanite. If the invasion is dated in the course of the fourteenth century B.C., however, one may on the same ground identify as Israelite the newly built cities, pottery, and so on, simply because it is not known whether there was a difference in what the Israelites could make and build before and after their settlement in Canaan. The "correctness" of the archeological dating does not come from the archeological data but from the answer discovered in biblical study. The reasoning here is circular. The statement that the pottery changes after 1200 B.C. and that the reason for

that change is the presence of the Israelites in the land is no proof either. This argument is based on the assumption that the Israelites possessed the skill of making pottery and that this skill replaced that of the Canaanites. This does not in the least solve the problem of the change in pottery in the twelfth century B.C. Today we are familiar with several factors that can effect a change in pottery, such as the need for change in the style or quality of the product or new ideas from the outside. Of these two possibilities we may choose the second and suppose that these new ideas are from the Israelites. Here, too, the argument is circular: because the Israelites are in the land there is new pottery, and because there is new pottery it must be Israelite; wherever there is new pottery, there the Israelite tribes must have been. The question is not whether there were tribes in Canaan or where they were there at a certain time. That is a matter of understanding the biblical text. The question is whether the argumentation that is used in archeology proves anything.

To make comparisons is one of the most important archeological activities, and the more comprehensive the units that are being compared, the clearer it will become whether one is dealing with the same things or with something new. A comparison of larger units will increase the likelihood of being able to discover new elements and formulating explanations for such new elements. In other words, it is very important to keep in mind the nature of archeological proof if it is thought that antiquities confirm a historical datum. This question must be narrowed and applied to the question that was raised earlier, namely, whether biblical data can be confirmed, altered, or denied on the basis of archeological statements. From the perspective of the hermeneutics of the literary-historical and theological study of the Bible this question must be answered negatively. This same answer must be given from the perspective of archeology.

## 7. INQUIRY INTO THE CULTURE

Not the findings of the archeologist but the interpretation of the findings determines whether the archeologist makes a genuine contribution toward a better understanding of the land, the culture, and to a certain extent the people of ancient Israel. It has long been known that ancient Israel did not produce significant art treasures. This conclusion from an earlier investigation has never been freshly tested and then thoroughly evaluated. Instead, every small piece of "popular art," whether it be a small sculpture in stone or a clumsy terra-cotta, is recorded as a special find and reproduced in many publications (ill. 5). On this basis one might argue with some cogency that ancient Israel must have been a fairly barbaric sort of people—one has only to compare the Phoenician ivory carvings from that time. This is, however, not legitimate archeological reasoning. To begin with, it would be possible to formulate an archeological question that would make clear to the reader the possibilities and use of archeology. The questions to be asked would be: What were the natural conditions of the people's life in a particular area at a particular time? What possibilities were offered by nature and how did they make use of these possibilities? The Old Testament describes the promised land as a land flowing with milk and honey. This kind of statement, of course, contains no indication as to the natural condition of the land and does not belong in archeological studies. Nor is a statement such as "your eyes are doves" (Cant. 1:15) pertinent in archeology. Archeologically important issues are climatic influence on the types of homes that were constructed, the composition of the settlement, agriculture, and the like. If one studies these things using modern means of investigation, one may expect that the prophetic books and the Psalms in particular provide better comparative material than the history itself.

A rather simple statistical use of the pottery finds from Deir Alla showed that the inhabitants did not use lamps in the evening. Apparently their use was reserved for special occasions. Compared to other pottery, a small lamp was a cheap product. Whether the fuel that was used for the light was also cheap we do not know. The inhabitants of Deir Alla did not work after sundown. Deir Alla was not a city. Would lamps have been lighted in a town when darkness fell? Eventually it may be possible, using this kind of archeological data, to write an economic and social history of

parts of the population of Canaan and to compare this with earlier and later times. At the present time archeology is too much oriented toward the identification of historical events and the ethnic interpretation of finds.

A very comprehensive comparative investigation might give some insight into the spread of all kinds of artifacts over an area that comprises both the tribal territories of Judah and Israel and surrounding areas. Moreover, those artifacts and their spread would have to be compared with the geological map of the area. The relationship between home construction and building materials that are dependent on the geological formation—for instance, kinds of wood on sandy soil, limestone rock, clay, and swamps—would have to be researched. Could it be that the people in marshy areas and alongside rivers lived in reed huts plastered with loam, while elsewhere they built flat-roofed homes from clay bricks, and that in mountainous limestone areas they preferred roughly hewn stone? Might the same not be true in antiquity of the people who lived in Lebanon, Syria, and Jordan?

Next, a comparison should be made between the material culture of the cities and of the country. Such an investigation belongs within the realm of archeology. As a consequence, certain questions that arise from the study of the Bible may coincide with the problems archeology faces: How does the picture change as the result of the introduction of royal courts and the accompanying concentration of power? Is a growing contrast noticeable between city and country regarding standards of living? Did religion put a stamp on the material culture of the land so that it could be distinguished from that of the surrounding cultures? So far such questions have not been asked systematically and few answers have been given. As long as there is no better insight into these problems with respect to the material culture, we cannot say what was typically Israelite.

Concerning the rich, we need only call to mind the commercial activities of Solomon to become aware that archeology does not offer criteria to determine what was specifically Israelite. The fairly soft marlstone, structurally somewhat similar to alabaster, was used in the Iron Age to make all kinds of vases and bowls. In archeological literature they are called luxury articles because it is assumed that they were used in connection with cosmetics and because they were rare. When these stony objects fell into disuse they were thrown away. It is one of the few kinds of "luxury articles" that have been preserved. Ornaments of gold and silver were preserved only if they were lost accidentally and were buried under the debris. Graves from that time are rare and hardly ever contain objects of art. All this illustrates the problems involved in archeologically determining what may be called Israelite culture.

Basalt bowls, rubbing stones, and stampers have been found everywhere in and around ancient Israel. This kind of stone is found in volcanic areas. Its products may have been manufactured in the places where the stone is found and have been traded by donkey caravans. Such trade is not restricted by political boundaries. It is my impression—that is the most we can say considering the present level of our knowledge—that what is today regarded as typical Israelite culture in, for example, the eighth century B.C., is much less determined by so-called ethnic elements than by the above-named factors. At this point I also touch on the relationship between archeology and the Old Testament; differently, however, than is commonly done. In the days of the writing prophets the "cosmopolitan" character that urban culture had acquired was being attacked. It may have been less the city itself than the concentration of wealth in certain groups that caused misery for segments of the people and that also changed the character of the cities. These are familiar sounds in our time.

## 8. THE TASK OF ARCHEOLOGY

The question concerning the task of archeology can hardly be answered satisfactorily considering the many definitions of archeology that are given today. From what has been said above it can be inferred that (1) archeology tries to make comparisons between the largest possible units, and (2) the units may be highly complex "objects" such as a stratum (e.g., the remnants of a destroyed city as they are preserved at a particular time in the ruins). If this is regarded as the most significant activity in archeology, an important task would be to describe the conclusions that can be drawn from comparative studies with respect to the society to which the ruins bear witness. This type of work constructs a kind of identity and picture that can be used to identify the inhabitants of a certain locality at a particular moment in their history. That identity is usually designated by the modern name of the place where the basic traces were first discovered.

The examination of individual finds is certainly part of the task of archeology. The more exceptional such a find is the fewer the points of contact that can be used in making comparisons. The examination is therefore limited mainly to a very careful description of the object. What the object was intended for and how it was used often remain a mystery. Purpose and use may remain mysterious, even when many objects have been dug up (e.g., pottery).

On the periphery of these studies are possibilities related to external data, that is, data that cannot be derived from the material itself but that stem from reliable historical sources. To this belongs, among others, the chronology, at least for the biblical period. In this case the chronology is built out of Egyptian historical data. Shortly before the time of the New Testament, coins took over the role of the Egyptian cartouches in stone. Once a number of fixed points have been established, it may be possible, too, to do something in the area of dating pottery; the ground plan, however, is based on genuine historical information.

For the connection with historical events two external data are needed: time and place. Not only is a reliable dating in both areas (historical and archeological) required, but there must also be a reliable identification of the locality; that requirement was not always equally carefully adhered to in the past. For that reason this chapter has paid a lot of attention to the archeological work done in establishing the identity of the excavated antiquities. Whether and to what extent this identification of antiquities is a useful element in exegetical studies of the Old and New Testaments is something that cannot be left solely to the archeologist. The final yield of the harvest can only be tabulated in a close cooperation between exegete and archeologist.

## LITERATURE

M. Avi-Yonah, ed., *Encyclopedia of Archae-ological Excavations in the Holy Land* (Jerusalem/Englewood Cliffs, N.J., 1975-78).

D. L. Clarke, *Analytical Archaeology* (London, 1968).

H. J. Franken, "Palestine in the Time of the Nineteenth Dynasty," in *Cambridge Ancient History* II/2 (Cambridge, 1975).

_____, "The Problem of Identification in Biblical Archaeology," *Palestine Exploration Quarterly* (1976) 3–11.

K. Galling, et al., *Biblisches Reallexikon* (Hand-buch zum Alten Testament, Erste Reihe 1) (Tübingen, 1977²).

K. M. Kenyon, *Digging up Jerusalem* (London, 1974).

_____, *Archaeology in the Holy Land* (London/New York, 1979⁴).

*Palestine Exploration Quarterly* (published by the Palestine Exploration Fund, London, 1869- ).

D. W. Thomas, ed., *Archaeology and Old Testament Study* (Oxford, 1967).

*World Archaeology* (London, 1969- ).

# B. The Development of Palestinian Archeology and Its Significance for Biblical Studies

*by C. H. J. de Geus*

## 1. THE BEGINNING

A certain nostalgia for the past is a common human trait that betrays a vague awareness of the importance of history. As far as we can tell, the desire to reestablish contact with that past by means of its material remains has always been there. Many Mesopotamian kings declare in their building inscriptions that they have restored walls, temples, and the like to their original condition. We know that this was often preceded by careful research. Moreover, antiquities have always been collector's items, though no doubt their "value" has something to do with it. The prewar excavations at Megiddo unearthed a collection of ivories that had clearly been hidden away; some of the objects were at least two centuries old when they were put away. Rome boasted an active market of antiquities, for the Roman aristocracy liked to flaunt genuine Attic vases that were centuries old. The oldest museum we know is the collection of local antiquities brought together at Ur in the sixth century B.C. by the Neo-Babylonian princess Bel-Shalti-Nannar for the benefit of visitors to that ancient city.

Though it is very likely that earlier attempts were made to search the Palestinian soil for traces of the past, as far as we know St. Helen was the first to engage in Palestinian archeology. In 326 she carried out intensive investigations concerning the site and possible remains of the holy sepulchre and the cross of Jesus. In subsequent centuries, interest in the Holy Land and in remnants of the sacred history that transpired there was especially of an individual-religious nature. For centuries pilgrims visited Palestine to see the places where "it happened" so that in this way they might get as close as possible to this sacred history. Travelers from later times, whose background was more humanistic, also visited the country for individual, personal reasons.

The student of Palestine is in the fortunate position of having two bibliographies containing virtually all the publications that have been preserved. These are P. Rohricht, *Bibliotheca Geographica Palestinae* (Berlin, 1890), which lists all the publications from the years 333 through 1878, and P. Thomsen, *Die Palästina-Literatur. Eine internationale Bibliographie in systematischer Ordnung mit Autoren und Sachregister* I-VI (1895–1939). Currently L. Rost is working on a volume (the first part has appeared) to fill the gap between 1878 and 1895. For the literature after World War II the best place to go is the regularly appearing bibliographical information and indexes in the most important periodicals such as *Palestine Exploration Quarterly, Zeitschrift des deutschen Palästina-Vereins, Biblical Archaeologist, Bulletin of the American Schools of Oriental Research,* and *Israel Exploration Journal.*

## 2. PHASES IN THE STUDY OF PALESTINE

The specifically scientific character of the study of Palestine arose in the nineteenth century. It originated from the need for illustrations to elucidate the Bible. Everyone who has to teach a Bible story and who asks, What is the location of Bethlehem or Mamre? What kind of clothes did Abraham wear? What did a house look like in Jesus' days? Who were the Levites? asks questions that the student of Palestine also asks. Something preceded this, however, namely, the awakening consciousness that a time factor is involved here. One who inquires about Abraham's clothes is aware that Abraham lived in a different time; one accepts this fact and is prepared to make a study of it. This was not always the case. Art to illustrate Bible stories goes back a long time. The early Church had an extensive iconographic tradition. Even Judaism had its art. From the talmudic period are mosaic floors in synagogues with pictures of the sacrifice of Isaac (Beth Alfa in Galilee), Daniel in the lions' den (Naaran near Jericho), the ark of Noah (Gerasa in Jordan), not to mention the murals of prophets (Isaiah, Jeremiah) and prophetic visions (e.g., of Ezekiel 37) on the walls of the synagogue of Dura Europos in northern Mesopotamia.

Like all early Christian and medieval art, this art portrays episodes and persons as the artists imagined them from their own time. The artists' intent was to get the viewer intimately involved in the message contained in the biblical narratives.

Romanticism, with its discovery of the past, created the need for a method of illustration that reproduced the past as authentically as possible. This resulted in auxiliary means such as biblical archeologies or Israelite antiquities. From its origin in the nineteenth century to the present, three phases can be distinguished in the study of Palestine: the literary phase, the historical phase, and the prehistorical phase.

In this context *literary phase* means the pursuit of archeology (i.e., the collecting of authentic data) was intended to illustrate a particular literary work. Therefore there arose not only biblical, but also talmudic, Homeric, and Thucydidean archeologies.

The old biblical archeologies include all three components of which the study of Palestine is still made up today:

*Geographia Sacra:* the historical topography and geography, including the physical geography (soil conditions, climate, etc.), of Palestine.

*Realia:* the concrete, tangible objects ranging from fortresses and city walls to domestic objects, clothing, and coins. The remains of flora and fauna, including human remains, also belong to it.

*Institutiones:* institutions such as the state, the system of justice, the organization of religious life, the economy, and the military. Many of these institutions are partially or totally identical with what the modern historian understands by the "structures" of a particular culture.

These archeologies also had three methods. During the literary phase, the literary method was by far the most important. The past was reconstructed not only on the basis of biblical passages but also through the use of data from ancient authors and from ancient travel accounts. An Israelite home could be reconstructed by collecting, comparing, and combining all the texts that say something about a house. This method must still be used in all cases in which authentic objects are lacking, for example, in the case of the tabernacle.

The analogy with the Arabian world was used alongside the literary method from the start. In the previous century Arabian culture was regarded as a primitive civilization, a culture that had either come to a standstill or that had slowed down greatly. As late as 1935 the famous Dutch scholar J. Simons called the Arabian population of Palestine simply "natives."

Every picture of Abraham as a bedouin sheikh or of Jesus as an Arab (but with blond hair and blue eyes), overly familiar from Sunday School material, goes back to this. Though here, too, the historical and anthropological presuppositions of this method have become completely antiquated, it is definitely not true that the material that has been collected is now worthless for the biblical archeologist. Certain segments of the culture, especially of the Arab farmer in Palestine, have hardly changed through the centuries, simply because they proved to be the most efficient under the circumstances. We are referring here to special irrigation techniques, agriculture on terraces constructed on mountain slopes, certain techniques of making pottery, and forms of social organization (e.g., communal ownership of the land). Particularly in our time we are again becoming aware of this aspect.

Only in the third place do we mention direct research. This was done first in the field of geography. Without exaggeration Edward Robinson, an American, may be called the father of the modern study of Palestine. In 1838 he spent seven months in Palestine, in which time he crisscrossed the land on horseback, searching everywhere for ruins and visible antiquities. With his friend Eli Smith, who spoke and wrote Arabic fluently, he also fixed Arabian place-names and traditions. On May 4 and 5 he traveled north of Jerusalem and on the basis of Arabic place-names established nine identifications with biblical places: Anathoth, Geba, Rimmon, Michmash, Bethel, Ophrah, Beeroth, Gibeon, and Mizpah. Of these only the identification with Beeroth has proved to be uncertain. His notes appeared in 1841 in his classical work *Biblical Researches in Palestine.* Along the same lines is the great work *Survey of Western Palestine,* done by competent officers of the British army under the auspices of the Palestine Exploration Fund (established in 1865 for the purpose of engaging in scientific research in Palestine, ". . . for purposes of Biblical Illustration"). The work of these pioneers clearly brought out the strong side of the nineteenth-century scholars, namely, their fully developed gift— almost incredible to us—of observing and recording.

The Palestine Exploration Fund also mandated the first excavations in Palestine. Those were the days when the excavations of Layard and others in Mesopotamia yielded the shiploads of art objects that were filling the large museums in Europe. The first "diggers" in Palestine were De Saulcy, who emptied the so-called royal graves, and another British officer, Charles Warren. Warren dug in Jerusalem, for example, near the Western Wall, and at a few other places in the land, including Jericho. He used methods derived from mining, namely, tunnels and shafts. After all, his search was for treasures in the ground. He hardly knew what to do with his finds because it was impossible to date them.

The great handbooks from this literary phase are J. Benzinger, *Hebräische Archäologie,* and W. Nowack, *Lehrbuch der hebräischen Archaeologie,* both from 1894 and reprinted many times. In these titles the word "archeology" must also be understood in its old comprehensive sense of "study of antiquity."

The subdivisions of geography, *realia* and *institutiones,* were described in a strictly literary fashion. "Excavations" were hardly within the purview of the writers, for these were thought to belong to "travel accounts." On p. 267 of volume I of his book Nowack pictured a potsherd found by Warren, a handle of a jar from his shaft near the Western Wall. He regarded it as modern Palestinian; today the imprints of two concentric circles and a flying beetle show without a doubt that it came from the Iron Age. Nowack did, however, recognize that a potsherd with a letter from the Phoenician alphabet found together with this handle belonged to the time of the Siloam tunnel (end of the 8th century B.C.). Nowack always rejected as absurd the idea that pottery itself might be a means of dating. On pp. 261–66 of his book Benzinger already revealed a much more modern conception (the one of Flinders Petrie; see below), though he, too, was clearly skeptical.

Another of the most important travelers in Palestine was C. Clermont-Ganneau. He, too, made use of every available hour to describe the land. He had a surprisingly keen eye for inscriptions, of which he collected a great many. He has the distinction of managing to salvage the famous Moab stele with the Mesha inscription from the hands of the bedouin; in addition, he demonstrated the spuriousness of the so-called "Moabite Antiquities" (counterfeit antiquities—mainly ceramic—that had been purchased by the Germans on a large scale) and of a scroll of Deuteronomy that had purportedly been written by Moses himself and that had been offered to England for a million pounds.

The start of scientific excavations in Palestine is commonly regarded as 1890. This coincided with the beginning of a new phase in the study of Palestine: the historical phase.

One of the great merits of the study of the Bible in the previous century has been that it was able to demonstrate that the Bible contains older and younger parts and that the dating of these makes it possible to reconstruct Israel's history and spiritual development. For proponents as well as opponents of what was then the modern study of the Bible this provided an enormous stimulus toward historical investigation. Initially archeology as the science of excavation played no role in the fierce debates, particularly that concerning such scholars as Wellhausen in Germany and Kuenen in the Netherlands. The great problem of archeology was that it could date its finds only if they contained texts, or at least letters—in other words, only in a literary way.

This changed in 1890 when Sir W. M. Flinders Petrie excavated for six weeks at Tell el-Hesi in southwestern Judah. Previously Flinders Petrie had dug in Egypt for many years and had noted how the shapes of pottery had changed through the centuries. Because in Egypt he excavated primarily in the graves of the pharaohs, the dating of the finds was a secondary problem; normally it was known to which pharaoh the grave being excavated belonged. In 1890 Flinders Petrie started digging in Palestine to test his budding theory of a pottery chronology. Actually he made two discoveries at Tell el-Hesi:

(a) He discovered that a tell was not a natural hill with remains of buildings on top of it as had always been assumed, but an artificial hill that had been built up because new buildings were constantly erected on the remains of earlier occupations of the site. After a destruction a new city was built atop the ruins of the old. Thus a tell consists of the remains of various cities. Thereby Flinders Petrie laid the basis for a most important possibility for dating—stratigraphy, that is, dating on the basis of the stratum or layer in which the object to be dated was found. Petrie's own report appeared as early as 1891 in *Tel el Hesy*. However, the book of his American assistant F. J. Bliss, carrying the expressive title *A Mound of Many Cities* (London, 1894), became much better known.

(b) Petrie's theory with respect to pottery was confirmed; indeed, every layer contained a distinctive type of pottery. With that he laid the foundation for what is still the most important dating method in the archeology of the Near East, the typology of pottery. From that time on archeologists have attempted to determine the layer from which each find comes and to date this layer on the basis of the pottery.

This particular type of dating results in most cases in a relative dating, that is, the determination whether an object is earlier or later than another object. The typological and stratigraphic methods are not able to establish an absolute chronology, that is, a specific year. That can only be done, directly or indirectly, by means of texts or scientific methods such as the carbon-14 method.

The excavations at Tell el-Hesi were followed by an increasing number of excavations. A survey of the most important excavations since 1890, along with the excavation reports, is found in Kathleen M. Kenyon, *Archaeology in the Holy Land* (London, 1970[3]; New York, 1979[4]). More extensive is Eleanor K. Vogel, "Bibliography of Holy Land Sites," *Hebrew Union College Annual* 42 (1971) 1–96. For the most recent excavations and finds one can turn to the surveys in the *Israel Exploration Journal, Qadmoniot* (Hebrew), and the "Chronique archéologique" of the *Revue biblique*.

Though there is an immense difference between the oldest excavations and the large campaigns of the 1930s (e.g., Megiddo, Lachish, Samaria) or the 1950s (Jericho, Hazor), all these excavations may be reckoned to the historical phase because the purpose of the excavators was predominantly historical: the desire to gain insight into the history of the tell and into the development of the culture or cultures found there. The possibility of dating the finds led to ambitious attempts to reconstruct the past of a particular place. It was discovered that there was a history in the ground. In the interpretation of archeological findings this discovery had three results:

First, consciously or unconsciously, archeologists searched for objects that would make it possible to illuminate a portion of political history. This led to a pronounced preference for texts, coins, and buildings such as fortresses, gates, and city walls. Moreover, there was always a diligent search for layers created by the destruction of sites. The decision concerning which tell to excavate was also strongly influenced by this orientation. Until very recently hardly any excavation has been done in Palestine of sites that do not play a specific role in the Bible.

Second, the object of the search was always to discover what had changed. This led to a heavy accent on observed *discontinuity*. The historical interpretation of an observed discontinuity—a destruction, a new type of ceramics, a sudden enlargement of the city, and the like—was obtained by means of the principle of *ethnic designation*.

This principle rests on an extensive equation of the concepts "people" and "culture." The search was first of all for traces of the political history. Because peoples are the subjects of this history, it was very important to make these peoples "visible." Every slightly important change in the pottery is therefore always ascribed to a particular, at times entirely hypothetical, people. The most important thing that can be said of a piece of pottery is that it is "Canaanite," "Israelite," "Philistine," "Phoenician," and so on.

Third, it is obvious that the identification of the material remains with people and events known from the texts was done with Bible in hand. Because the Bible is the most important literary source for the archeologist of Palestine, and because it is a religious book, there was a decided preference for objects that could be designated as remnants of the religious life. In the excavation reports, cultic installations and objects are always extensively treated. Especially the older literature describes many "cultic" objects that after further investigation were shown to have had an entirely different function.

Until 1930 the dating techniques (stratigraphy and typology) introduced into Palestinian archeology since 1890 remained more theory than practice. Though since about 1890 the digs were done mainly by means of the trench method—the digging of a number of trenches through a tell, parallel with or at right angles to each other—one can hardly speak of a genuine archeological dating. R. A. S. Macalister, who from 1902 to 1909 excavated in Gezer and made undeniably significant finds, still published them systematically (after the manner of the archeologies from the literary phase) and not chronologically. In 1908 Americans introduced a significant technical innovation. A large team from Harvard University, directed by G. A. Reisner and C. S. Fisher, dug from 1908 to 1910 at Samaria and tried to uncover the city layer by layer. Here for the first time in Palestine an attempt was made to devise a technique that tied in with the theory. With added improvements—mainly as a result of the better functioning of the pottery typology—this method was the basis of all large excavations between the two World Wars. (At Jericho [1908–09] the Germans E. Sellin and C. Watzinger, and at Shechem [1913–14 and 1926–28] Sellin and Welter stayed with the trench system, mainly for financial reasons.) The most familiar example is the large excavation of Megiddo, where again it was Americans who tried to excavate this enormous city layer by layer (excavation of the Oriental Institute of Chicago under the direction of C. S. Fisher [1925–27], P. L. O. Guy [1927–35], and G. Loud [1935–39]). In retrospect these large excavations—and even more the smaller ones—are being deplored; to dig up is to destroy: what has been dug up once cannot be dug up again. Neither the technique of that time nor the training of the excavators was adequate for such undertakings. Indeed, much was found and sometimes a reasonably good job was done in publishing it, but in the final analysis dating and interpretation were in most cases of a literary nature. In essence, scholars used the Bible to interpret finds rather than using archeology as an independent science to "illustrate" the Bible. In addition, this interpretation with the use of the Bible was in many cases entirely dependent on the subjective judgment of the digger.

From the time of World War I, W. F. Albright incessantly pressed for improved techniques, for better methodological reflection, and, if possible, for the formation of a core of professional diggers. He too started with the horizontal method of Reisner and Fisher, but because his strategy was to dig on a much smaller scale and to open up small fields, he succeeded in gaining a better insight into the stratification of a tell and as a consequence in obtaining a more reliable pottery typology. In fact, the excavations of, for example, Megiddo and Lachish became increasingly dependent on the pottery chronology that Albright had established with his excavation of Tell Beit Mirsim (1926–32) southwest of Hebron. It can be said without exaggeration that after Flinders Petrie, Albright took the second important methodological step on the road toward turning Palestinian archeology into a science.

After World War II, especially when the British archeologists of Palestine had come in contact with the techniques that had been developed in England, Kathleen M. Kenyon took a third important step forward. Building upon techniques developed by Sir Mortimer Wheeler, she again began to dig in Jericho using the trench technique (1952–58). Her method was based on the principle of *three-dimensional* determination (horizontal as well as vertical) and is characterized by great carefulness. Initially this led some to call this method of investigation "teaspoon digging." Besides the excavations of Dame Kenyon at Jericho and Jerusalem (1961–67), particularly those of H. J. Franken at Tell Deir Alla in Jordan are a good example of this technique. Characteristic of this method is the step-trench; the steps constitute the most important layers of the tell. After the excavations in Jericho, where an entire generation of postwar archeologists was trained, the methods introduced by Dame Kenyon were also gradually adopted by the Americans and the Israelis (ill. 2).

After many ups and downs the Palestinian archeology of the 1960s (almost a century after its beginning) reached the point at which it was able independently, using its own questions and methods, to arrive at an archeological interpretation of the material.

We have observed that so long as pottery typology was not a reliable instrument for dating layers and so long as the digging techniques were not sufficiently refined to uncover the complicated structure of a tell, the interpretation remained necessarily very subjective. Till late in the 1950s it was a common occurrence for a digger to date a group of graves as being from the Late Bronze Age and later for someone else to regard them as from the Late Iron Age. Whenever a somewhat deviating type of pottery surfaced, the whole chronological system threatened to collapse. Also, gross mistakes were made in the area of stratigraphy. Because of the primarily horizontal mode of operation, later disturbances remained unnoticed; for instance, a glazed medieval bowl from an Arabian grave at Beth-shean could be ascribed to the time of Pharaoh Amenophis III (15th century B.C.). Moreover, many interpretations, even datings, were derived from the Old Testament, such as those of the "royal stables" at Megiddo. Here a faulty interpretation—in reality they are warehouses—became the basis for dating the entire layer as Solomonic, over a century

too early. Surveying this chaos, one is not surprised that all this impressed critical outsiders as being absolutely arbitrary.

This led many European scholars, especially Germans, to introduce a sharp methodological distinction between conclusions derived from literary-historical investigation and those derived from archeological research. Martin Noth made a principal distinction between the oftentimes disputed results of archeology and those of his own literary investigation; for that reason he may be regarded as an exponent of this methodological approach. Noth would not agree to a combination of the two kinds of data until both the archeological material and the texts gave occasion for such a combination. For example, the Assyrian king Sennacherib had the capture of Lachish depicted on wall reliefs in his palace at Nineveh, and these reliefs showed the Assyrian helmets. In the excavations of Lachish, remains of the same Assyrian helmets were discovered in the destruction layers of about 700 B.C. On that basis this destruction is connected with the reliefs and with Sennacherib's annals (also by Noth). In by far the majority of cases, however, the archeological material itself provides no occasion to link it with literary data. Only at a later stage would Palestinian archeology learn to ask adequate questions about the material. Noth practiced a similar reservation with the use of texts and cultural-historical data from the *Umwelt* as he did with the archeological material: before it can be used one must do painstaking research. An eventual combination is again the ultimate stage; in many cases, however, this stage cannot be reached because many questions in the study of the Old Testament and in that of the *Umwelt* necessarily remain open. Yet Noth was one of the first to point out the great significance of the Mari Texts for the Old Testament. With respect to the relevance of much Ugaritic material he remained very restrained, however.

Though Noth could build on a head start of at least a century that the literary disciplines had on archeological research, frequently he had a sharper eye for the shortcomings of archeology than for those of the literary disciplines. These, too, remain highly subjective. Also, the work of Noth himself teems with words such as "to be sure" and "probably." Noth's great counterpart was the earlier-mentioned W. F. Albright. His knowledge was at least as encyclopedic as that of Noth or Alt. He had a more pragmatic bent than Noth, however, and he put more stock in his often well-founded intuition. Albright was at least as interested in methodological questions, but in sharp contrast to the European use of these questions he was inclined to test them against the results. "Result" in this context means a better understanding of the Old Testament. That "better" hides a lot of theological and historical presuppositions did not bother him; he openly admitted it. When shortly after World War I Albright began to work in Palestine, the school of Wellhausen still had a great influence in the United States. With respect to the history of Israel, Wellhausen also followed a strictly literary method, augmented with analogies derived from Arabian culture. He always persisted in his denial of the decipherment of the cuneiform script! And he put aside as irrelevant the first published Assyrian royal annals, the Amarna Letters, and the Code of Hammurabi. Albright fought with all his might against this pride and shortsightedness clothed in methodological arguments. His own standpoint was always that Israel was part of the whole of the ancient Near Eastern cultures and that Israel could be understood only from that perspective; only so does Israel's uniqueness become clear. Albright saw keenly the subjectivity of many literary and historical conclusions. To bring about a greater objectivity he introduced the concept of "external evidence." The reasoning behind this concept is that growing knowledge of the ancient oriental cultures and history renders one literary conclusion more probable than another. Though it was never Albright's intention to prove "the truth of the Bible," he was inclined to regard a conclusion closer to the traditional understanding of the Bible as more "probable" than one further removed from that tradition. This enormously broad starting point led him to stimulate the archeology of the Near East with an unquenchable enthusiasm and with an incredible personal drive. Every new discovery was hailed enthusiastically, even if it made questionable an earlier conclusion or position.

The discussion between Noth and Albright focused on the problem of the historicity of the conquest traditions in the book of Joshua, sparked by the publication of Noth's commentary on Joshua in 1935. In this book he contested the historicity of most of the conquest traditions in Joshua 1–10. He did this mostly on literary grounds, but in part also on archeological grounds, as in the case of Ai where excavations had demonstrated that it was not in existence at the time of Joshua. Noth's literary argumentation is based mainly on the *form-critical* standpoint that these traditions are essentially *etiologies*, making the historical element secondary. Etiologies are stories that explain "why something is the way it is." They deal mostly with peculiarities in the landscape, and in some form they contain the information that something is "until the present day." It would be wrong to say of Noth that the results of the excavation of Ai caused him to ask: if the story is historically impossible, why then was it told? and to move from there to an etiological explanation (*ai* = ruin). On the contrary, in the 1930s the discovery of etiologies and the investigation of folk stories was very much in vogue in the study of literature. Noth considered the results at Ai a strong affirmation of his method.

Albright fiercely attacked Noth, mainly with archeological arguments that supposedly contained the "external evidence." To maintain this argumentation it was imperative that the conquest be archeologically discernible in the places mentioned in Joshua 1–10. A destruction layer is not enough; strata are difficult to date and, moreover, many cities around that time (ca. 1200 B.C.) turned out to have been destroyed more than once. A type of pottery that Albright had first found at Bethel and that he believed was "Israelite" became the *Leidfossiel* (guide fossil) to establish Israelite presence. Wherever this pottery was found, Albright saw the coming of the Israelites. Noth objected, and rightly so, that there was nothing in this pottery, nor in the context in which it was found, that pointed compellingly to the Israelites. Albright and his disciples could get no further than "probability." This "probability" was further weakened when this pottery was also discovered in areas and cities that never, or only much later, passed into Israelite hands.

Currently, forty years after this heated discussion, it is generally acknowledged that this pottery by itself allows no ethnic designation and that the historical problem is in fact irrelevant here. Everywhere in the world, archeology has gone through a historical phase in one form or another, though of course it felt the strongest impetus to develop its own questions and techniques with respect to those cultures in which no literary data were available. This resulted in the paradoxical situation that archeology and prehistory could obtain a methodological and technical advantage with the scriptless cultures. The abundance of literary sources for the history and culture of the ancient Near East, particularly for Palestine, was one of the reasons that the historical phase of Palestinian archeology lasted so long and was so important. A second reason was that in Europe and the United States the study of Palestine happened to be closely tied to theology. Until recently, theological thinking was strongly historically determined. "Biblical revelation is mediated in historical events. Hence the biblical scholar, or indeed the serious Christian or Jew, is necessarily a historian of the ancient past. And the best way to increase historical knowledge of the biblical era is to dig up the Near East," as F. M. Cross, Jr., said in his sermon at the funeral of G. E. Wright (Sept. 8, 1974). This meant, of course, that most people who felt attracted to Palestinian archeology did so from historical and theological motives and not primarily out of a purely archeological interest. Archeologists such as Kathleen Kenyon from England and H. J. Franken from the Netherlands were clear exceptions. The rapid change now occurring is primarily due to the rise of a secular archeology in modern Israel. This archeology maintains few contacts with biblical studies and increasingly dissociates itself from the often exclusively historical orientation of the older generation, which was almost entirely formed by Albright. This detachment from the historical phase is thus concomitant with a strong *professionalization* of this science.

After World War II a movement arose among archeologists in Anglo-Saxon countries that wanted to strike out in entirely different directions and that was particularly allied to the natural sciences. This "New Archeology" has a preference for abstract models and has fiercely opposed the historical interpretation of archeological finds. Parallel to this is the ahistorical tendency that for years has characterized anthropology. Recall in this connection that in many countries, especially in the United States, "history" and "archeology" are divisions of the social sciences. In many American universities archeology is the same as paleoanthropology. In Dutch universities, too, prehistory is viewed as a subdivision of anthropology and/or human ecology. In America as well as in the Netherlands the danger is that the classical and Near Eastern archeologies will become isolated from their literary faculties. In practice this means that a connection between an archeological find and a literary or historical datum that is entirely obvious to a theologian or historian is not at all obvious to the professional archeologist and in many cases is regarded as irrelevant. In view of increasing professionalization this tension will become more and more important, also in Palestinian archeology; therefore it is worthwhile to point out that a combination of literary and archeological data is as such not unscientific, and is even mandatory. Properly combined, the two kinds of data supplement each other, making it possible to acquire a much more richly variegated picture of a culture, cultural development, or period. In the future archeologists in the Near East should still be able to read their texts, and the exegete will need a knowledge of archeology. Attempts to play the two disciplines against each other by assailing or proving the results of the one with those of the other have failed. Archeology can only confirm what was already historically sure: the campaigns of Sennacherib or Nebuchadrezzar, the building activities of Herod, Phoenician influence on Israel under the Omrides, the tragic events at Masada, etc. In reality it is always a matter of *complementation*. Archeology elucidates figures such as an Ahab or Herod much more than the Old Testament or Assyrian texts. The same holds even more for a king like Solomon, of whose activities traces have been found at Megiddo, Hazor, Beersheba, Arad, and Jerusalem. On the other hand, these finds would necessarily be able to say much less if no texts from the same culture were available. A purely literary study of a culture can commit terrible blunders; a purely archeological one, no less.

Fortunately, time has worn down the sharp edges of this old conflict between archeology and literary method. The modern study of history sets much less store by actual events and persons or groups that are not archeologically visible. In contrast, quantitative data, social and economic structure, and the like have become much more important; particularly here archeology can contribute many data. Anthropologically oriented archeologists have also become increasingly conscious that what they call "culture" is an arbitrary snapshot of a development, even regarding the so-called primitive and ancient cultures.

Now, we should still briefly consider the *prehistorical* phase. What was said above will have made clear that "prehistorical" in this sense is not the same as "scriptless," such as when we speak of "scriptless cultures or peoples." Nor can it mean a- or even anti-historical. Currently archeology is understood as the systematic study of antiquities. In most cases these antiquities are material remains or elements of a culture. For a long time already the archeologist has not been dealing exclusively with dead cultures. If the remains or elements are not material, they concern ecological givens or institutions. If they are material, their systematic study involves the acquisition of such remains, mostly by way of digging; then the study and description of these remains, including the context in which they were found; and finally the care for their preservation and proper storage. Archeology is consequently always an *analytical* discipline. In contrast, the science of prehistory occupies itself with *synthesis*. The prehistorian combines the results of the archeological analysis with those of other disciplines such as anthropology, paleobotany and paleozoology, (ancient) history, linguistics, and the study of religion. Archeology is thus more a technique than a science.

The science of the past that gives full weight to the results of archeology is called prehistory. In general the modern prehistorian would like the archeologist to furnish data that can give insights into the following aspects of the particular culture: (1) human ecology in the broadest sense of the term, including questions of a geographical (course of old rivers, coastlines, etc.), topographical (earlier cities, problems of identification), and physical-geographical nature (climate); (2) economy and production techniques; (3) social structure; (4) technology, including art; (5) economic, cultural, and military contacts with other cultures. In good excavations it is almost always possible to say something about all these points.

## 3. RESULTS

What implications and bearing does all this have on the study of the Bible? The first observation to be made is that the answer to the question, What is the importance of the science of prehistory for the study of the Bible? depends in part on the extent to which one wishes to read the Bible historically, that is, circumscribed by its own time. The more historical the exegetical methods are, the greater becomes the relevance of prehistory. Below is an indication of the value of prehistory for the scientific study of the Bible, following the traditional threefold division:

The *geography* of Palestine and the Near East remains of great importance:

a. A constantly growing knowledge of the historical geography of these areas is of the greatest importance for the interpretation of historical texts, both biblical and extrabiblical. This concerns both the identification of places mentioned in those texts, including rivers, mountains, areas, etc., and a better understanding of strategic positions, distances, and the economic importance of cities, areas, and the like.

Here the exegete should be warned to make sure that the data he wishes to use are not *exclusively* the result of *surveys*. This surface investigation, however necessary and useful, can never produce more than provisional conclusions derived from surface remains, such as parts of walls, pieces of pottery, or coins. Examples of places where later diggings resulted in much more nuanced conclusions than the earlier surface examination are numerous.

b. From the perspective of longer periods, a better insight into the historical geography results in conclusions with respect to changes in the settlement pattern. Such changes may be due to economic, social, political, or physical causes. Knowledge of this kind of data is indispensable for insight into the historical processes that have taken place in and around Palestine. To give one example: why were the Canaanite city-states situated in the plains and the oldest Israelite settlements in the hill country, and what was the importance of that? Why did the Romans have a preference for the plains and why did cities arise in the Negeb? The history of production techniques and of the landscape are also closely intertwined with these questions.

c. Knowledge of the historical topography of Palestine and surroundings makes it possible to date certain texts. A document transmitted in the Old Testament mentioning a number of cities will most of the time have been written in a period when all these cities were in existence. Familiar examples are Joshua 12 and 15 and 1 Kings 4:7–20.

The greatest advance in Palestinian archeology has been made in the area of *realia*, so much so that it has been possible to illustrate much of the Bible. Today we have a fairly good picture of the homes and living conditions of the Israelites or Jews. We know what their homes looked like and know many of the usual items in them. We possess reasonably good insight into the techniques and technical possibilities of that time, though it still remains very difficult, for example, to identify specific building terms mentioned in the Old Testament. Many questions must remain open. Where there are questions about items of a highly perishable nature, such as food and clothing, we remain dependent on purely literary methods. For the Roman period we now possess important remnants of clothing from caves in the wilderness of Judah, and we have contemporary pictures. With respect to daily food, we can only guess whether the adoption of the Roman cooking pot in the beginning of the Roman period indicates the adoption of Roman eating habits. Or was this new model very suitable as well for preparing the traditional food? Questions like these still await an answer, first because so little is known of the daily food, and second because the *experiment* has hardly been introduced into Palestinian archeology. By experiment we mean the reconstruction and use of homes, pottery, irrigation works, tools, etc., in order to discover their possibilities and shortcomings. It hardly needs saying that however useful these experiments may be, they can never prove anything.

The study of *realia* also makes historical developments visible. *Realia* have clearly shown the great influence of Egypt on the culture of Canaan and later also on that of Israel. For a while we can recognize the Philistines as an independent group. Much clearer than is evident in the Old Testament we can see already in Iron Age I a distinct difference between north and south, the later states of Israel and Judah. Likewise, the influence of Phoenicia, Assyria, or Hellenism becomes much clearer from the material culture than from the Old Testament itself.

In the area of *institutiones*, the relevance of archeology grows every year, certainly now that more and more anthropologically trained archeologists are available. Here the developments mentioned above have their greatest impact. Owing to the many excavations, we now know more about the military situation and the economy of the ancient Near East than we could ever have known solely from the texts themselves. In recent years digs at Hazor, Arad, and Beer-sheba have yielded many data about the social, political, and administrative structure of Judah and Israel; the data from the last two places have come especially from a few dozen ostraca discovered there. Here again it is true that the combination of texts and material remains produces the greatest number of possibilities for obtaining new insights. A sensation in the 1960s was the discovery of the first authentic Israelite temple, from the citadel of Arad. Moreover, this was the first genuine Iron Age temple discovered. This structure was remarkable for its similarity to the regulations found in the Old Testament (e.g., concerning the altar). In contrast, the large altar of burnt offerings from Beer-sheba, which is from the same period, conflicts with these regulations; this large altar with "horns" is made entirely of hewn blocks of stone.

Today if an archeological analysis leads to conclusions that are difficult to reconcile with the texts, it no longer means having to choose between the two or to correct one of them. That someone acts differently from the way he should according to his own expressed beliefs is such a well-established anthropological phenomenon that it would be strange if it were not found. Nor should one lose sight of the difference between the spiritual and material aspects of a culture: the fanatic Jewish zealots of Bar Kochba wore Roman togas and ate from imitation terra-sigillata plates! Older handbooks often say that for the ancient Israelites life after death was not very real, a conclusion derived from the study of the Old Testament. But the funeral ritual with gifts of food and drink and the care of graves seems to conflict with it. To get out of the difficulty it used to be maintained that all the Iron Age graves that have been found happened to be Canaanite graves. Today we speak of complementation on this point, too; on this matter we are in the fortunate position that we can learn something about both the theory and the practice. In every culture, theory and practice belong together, no matter how much they may appear to clash with each other—at least for the uninformed observer. Theory and practice can each have their own significance. In all these developments the analogies with Arabian culture, particularly that of the bedouin, become less and less important. First, the volume of authentic data from the world of the Old and New Testaments overshadows the Arabian data, since the Arabs were always a fringe element. Until the second half of the nineteenth century the Arabian culture was the only Semitic culture outside Israel that could be used for making comparisons. This situation is now altogether different. Especially the excavations and finds at ancient Mari along the central Euphrates have been a tremendous incentive to a new study of the rural population of the Syrian interior and of northern Mesopotamia. Second, the Arabian culture, certainly that of the bedouin, is fairly recent. Modern researchers agree that it arose in the late Roman period, thus after the time of the Bible. This does not alter the fact that knowledge of the life and culture of the Arabian population, especially the sedentary aspect, is still relevant, because a large measure of continuity has been preserved in agricultural methods and irrigation techniques as well as in social structure.

## LITERATURE

W. F. Albright, *The Archaeology of Palestine* (Harmondsworth, 1949; rev. ed. Magnolia, Mass., n.d.).

_____, *Archeology and the Religion of Israel* (Garden City, 1968).

J. Bright, *Early Israel in Recent History Writing* (London, 1956).

F. M. Cross, "Albright's View of Biblical Archaeology and Its Methodology," *Biblical Archaeologist* 36 (1973) 1–5.

W. G. Dever, *Archaeology and Biblical Studies* (Evanston, Ill., 1974).

_____, "Archaeological Method in Israel: A Continuing Revolution," *Biblical Archaeologist* 43 (1980) 97–103.

_____, "The Impact of the 'New Archaeology' on Syro-Palestinian Archaeology," *Bulletin of the American Schools of Oriental Research* 242 (1981) 15–31.

_____, "Retrospects and Prospects in Biblical and Syro-Palestinian Archaeology," *Biblical Archaeologist* 45 (1982) 103–108.

M. I. Finley, "Archaeology and History," *Daedalus* (1971) 168–86.

H. J. Franken, *A Primer of Old Testament Archaeology* (Leiden, 1963).

K. M. Kenyon, *Archaeology in the Holy Land* (London, 1970[3]; New York, 1979[4]).

H. D. Lance, "American Biblical Archaeology in Perspective," *Biblical Archaeologist* 45 (1982) 97–103.

P. W. Lapp, *Biblical Archaeology and History* (Cleveland, 1969).

J. M. Miller, "Approaches to the Bible through History and Archaeology: Biblical History as a Discipline," *Biblical Archaeologist* 45 (1982) 211–16.

R. Moorey, *Excavation in Palestine* (Grand Rapids, 1983).

M. Noth, *The History of Israel* (New York/Evanston, 1960[2]).

_____, *The Old Testament World* (London, 1966).

A. F. Rainey, "Historical Geography: The Link between Historical and Archaeological Interpretation," *Biblical Archaeologist* 45 (1982) 217–24.

I. Rouse, *Introduction to Prehistory. A Systematic Approach* (New York, 1972).

J. A. Sauer, "Syro-Palestinian Archaeology, History and Biblical Studies," *Biblical Archaeologist* 45 (1982) 201–10.

D. W. Thomas, ed., *Achaeology and Old Testament Study* (Oxford/New York, 1967).

D. Ussishkin, "Where is Israeli Archaeology Going?" *Biblical Archaeologist* 45 (1982) 93–97.

R. de Vaux, "On Right and Wrong Uses of Archaeology," in J. A. Sanders, ed., *Near Eastern Archaeology in the Twentieth Century* (Festschrift N. Glueck; New York, 1970), pp. 64–82.

M. Weippert, *The Settlement of the Israelite Tribes in Palestine* (London, 1970).

G. E. Wright, "Archaeological Method in Palestine: an American Interpretation," *Eretz-Israel* 9 (1969) 120–33.

———, "Biblical Archaeology Today," in D. N. Freedman and J. C. Greenfield, eds., *New Directions in Biblical Archaeology* (New York, 1971), pp. 167–86.

———, "What Archaeology Can and Cannot Do," *Biblical Archaeologist* 34 (1971) 70–76.

———, *Biblical Archaeology* (Philadelphia, 1962).

---

### CHRONOLOGICAL TABLE OF THE CULTURAL PERIODS IN PALESTINE

| | |
|---|---|
| 12,000-8500 B.C. | Mesolithic |
| 8500-4000 B.C. | Neolithic |
| 4000-3150 B.C. | Chalcolithic |
| 3150-2850 B.C. | Early Bronze I (also Early Canaanite; usual abbreviation: EBA) |
| 2850-2650 B.C. | Early Bronze II |
| 2650-2350 B.C. | Early Bronze III |
| 2350-2200 B.C. | Early Bronze IV (earlier regarded as a transition period, called EB-MB or IB) |
| 2200-2000 B.C. | Middle Bronze I |
| 2000-1750 B.C. | Middle Bronze IIA |
| 1750-1550 B.C. | Middle Bronze IIB (also called Middle Canaanite; abbreviation MBA) |
| 1550-1400 B.C. | Late Bronze I |
| 1400-1300 B.C. | Late Bronze II (also Late Canaanite; abbreviation LBA) |
| 1300-1200 B.C. | Late Bronze IIB |
| 1200-1000 B.C. | Iron Age I (also Israelite Age; abbreviation IA) |
| 1000-900 B.C. | Iron Age IIA |
| 900-800 B.C. | Iron Age IIB |
| 800-587 B.C. | Iron Age IIC (some call it Iron Age III; the Persian period is also sometimes called Iron Age III) |
| 587-332 B.C. | Persian Period |
| 332-152 B.C. | Hellenistic I |
| 152-37 B.C. | Hellenistic II (also: Hasmonean) |
| 37 B.C.–A.D. 70 | Herodian Period |
| A.D. 70-324 | Roman Period |
| A.D. 324-640 | Byzantine Period |
| A.D. 640-1099 | Early Arabian Period |
| A.D. 1099-1291 | Crusader Period |
| A.D. 1291-1516 | Mamluk Period |
| A.D. 1516-1920 | Turkish Period |

N.B. Today the following abbreviations are often used after the years: B.C.E.: Before the Common Era, and C.E.: Common Era.

# III

---

# Systems of Writing and Languages in the World of the Bible

---

*by J. C. de Moor, J. Hoftijzer, and G. Mussies*

---

## Introduction

It is impossible to give a complete survey of all the script forms, languages, and dialects of the Near East in this chapter. We shall therefore limit ourselves to the languages of the Bible (Hebrew, Aramaic, and Greek) and to those languages that have proved to be especially important for the study of the Bible. That in this latter category we will still touch on more than thirty languages shows that ancient Near Eastern studies have become an inseparable part of the study of the Bible.

In the discussion we will always set forth script, language, and literature in capsule form. Only the actual languages of the Bible will receive more elaborate treatment. Moreover, we will always make reference to the literature in the area to make further study possible. For a more comprehensive knowledge of the subject the reader should, however, follow the special courses in this field that are offered by most universities and theological schools.

### GENERAL BIBLIOGRAPHICAL INFORMATION

J. H. Hospers, ed., *A Basic Bibliography for the Study of the Semitic Languages* I-II (Leiden, 1973–74) (also several non-Semitic languages!).

Of general interest for the history of the literature:

*Handbuch der Orientalistik* (Leiden/Köln), many volumes published since 1953.

W. Röllig, ed., *Neues Handbuch der Literaturwissenschaft, I: Altorientalische Literaturen* (Wiesbaden, 1978).

Several collections of translations for the important Old Testament texts:

W. Beyerlin, ed., *Near Eastern Religious Texts Relating to the Old Testament* (Philadelphia, 1975).

R. Borger, et al., *Texte aus der Umwelt des Alten Testaments* I- (Gütersloh, 1982– ).

K. Galling, ed., *Textbuch zur Geschichte Israels* (Tübingen, 1968[2]).

H. Gressmann, ed., *Altorientalische Texte zum Alten Testament* (Berlin/Leipzig, 1926) (somewhat outdated).

R. Labat, et al., *Les religions du Proche-Orient asiatique* (Paris, 1970).

J. B. Pritchard, ed., *Ancient Near Eastern Texts* (Princeton, 1968[3]).

Many volumes in a new series: *Littératures anciennes du Proche-Orient* (Paris).

Several collections of translations of important texts of the intertestamental and New Testament periods:

J. Carmignac, et al., *Les Textes de Qumran* I–II (Paris, 1961–63).

R. H. Charles, ed., *The Apocrypha and Pseudepigrapha of the Old Testament* I–II (Oxford, 1913; New York, n.d.) (various reprints).

J. H. Charlesworth, ed., *The Old Testament Pseudepigrapha* I–II (Garden City, 1983–85).

E. Hennecke and W. Schneemelcher, eds., *New Testament Apocrypha* I–II (Philadelphia, 1963–65)

E. Kautzsch, ed., *Die Apokryphen und Pseudepigraphen des Alten Testaments* I–II (Tübingen, 1900).

W. G. Kummel, ed., *Jüdische Schriften aus hellenistisch-römischer Zeit* (Gütersloh, 1973– ).

E. Lohse, *Die Texte aus Qumran* (Darmstadt, 1964).

J. Maier, *Die Texte vom Toten Meer* I–II (Munich/Basel, 1960).

M. E. Stone, ed., *Jewish Writings of the Second Temple Period* (Assen, 1984).

H. L. Strack and P. Billerbeck, *Kommentar zum Neuen Testament aus Talmud und Midrasch* I–IV (Munich, 1922–28). Rabbinical index, ed. J. Jeremias and K. Adolph (Munich, 1956).

Additional volumes in series:

*Nag Hammadi Studies* (Leiden, 1971– ).
*Studies in Veteris Testamenti Pseudepigrapha* (Leiden, 1970– ).
*Studies on the Texts of the Desert of Judah* (Leiden, 1957– ).

# A. Systems of Writing and Nonbiblical Languages

*by J. C. de Moor*

## 1. THE ORIGIN OF WRITING

No invention has had a greater impact on the history of mankind than that of writing. Unfortunately we will probably never know to whom we owe this ingenious invention. Though already in the hoary prehistorical past simple communication via pictures and symbols occurred rather frequently, this was not yet the same as writing. By "writing" we mean a system of symbols that by common consent can be used for recording information given in natural language. Such systems were developed almost simultaneously in Mesopotamia and Egypt toward the end of the fourth millennium B.C. It cannot be seriously maintained that one of these two types of writing is derived

from the other, though there is a measure of correspondence between the principles that lie behind the two systems. It may be that people in Mesopotamia and in Egypt independently drew similar conclusions from earlier, less successful attempts to construct a system of writing. This type of coincidence happens often in epoch-making discoveries.

For purely practical reasons we have maintained geographical divisions in this chapter, discussing first of all the script dominating that particular area in antiquity. Because, as will be seen, more than one type of script was used almost everywhere, this kind of division does have its flaws. Yet a classification according to the type of script is not satisfactory either, because every

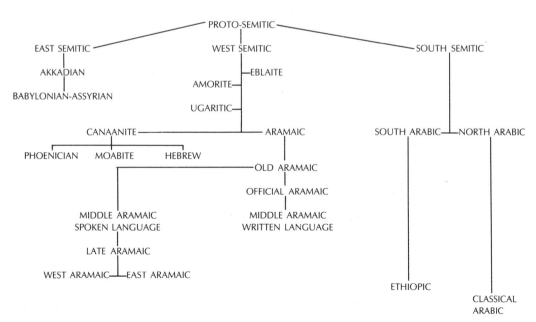

type has been used for several languages. A linguistic arrangement of the material likewise has its problems. Not only is there the problem of the many noncognate languages, but scholars are far from unanimous about the classification of Near Eastern languages even if they do apparently belong to the same linguistic family. Much research remains to be done in this field. Nevertheless, it may be useful, at least for the Semitic languages that will figure prominently in what follows, to provide a family tree that the writer of this section considers defensible.

---

### SOME LITERATURE
### Writing:

D. Diringer, *The Alphabet* I–II (London, 1968³).

G. R. Driver, *Semitic Writing* (London, 1973³).

J. Friedrich, *Entzifferung verschollenner Schriften und Sprachen* (Berlin, 1966).

_____, *Geschichte der Schrift* (Heidelberg, 1966).

I. J. Gelb, *A Study of Writing* (Chicago/London, 1963²).

H. Jensen, *Die Schrift in Vergangenheit und Gegenwart* (Berlin, 1958²).

M. Heerma van Voss, et al., *Van beitel tot penseel* (Leiden, 1973).

P. K. McCarter, *The Antiquity of the Greek Alphabet and the Early Phoenician Scripts* (Missoula, Montana, 1975).

J. Naveh, *Early History of the Alphabet* (Leiden, 1982).

### General Semitic Languages:

See the bibliography by J. H. Hospers cited above, especially Vol. I, pp. 365–86. In addition:

P. Fronzaroli, ed., *Studies on Semitic Lexicography* (Firenze, 1973).

S. Moscati, et al., *An Introduction to the Comparative Grammar of the Semitic Languages* (Wiesbaden, 1969).

---

## 2. MESOPOTAMIA: CUNEIFORM SCRIPT

The idea of using clay tablets as the bearers of written information likely arose in Mesopotamia

out of the so-called *bullae* used in administration before the invention of writing as such. These *bullae* were balls of clay containing a number of small beads, disks, cones, and similar objects inaccessible to outsiders. Those small objects were identical in number with, for example, the animals involved in a transaction. In order to know what was inside the ball of clay, the contents were pictured on the outside. The pictures of these objects became, as it were, written signs. They have continued to function like that.

Obviously, filling the ball of clay with small objects became unnecessary as soon as one could be certain that the signs scratched into the clay would not be obliterated. This could be achieved by baking the clay in an oven. Thus it was no longer necessary to retain the shape of a ball; more information could be put on a flattened piece of clay, hence the clay tablet.

Soon people began to realize that it was not necessary to limit themselves to the pictures of the objects just mentioned. With a stylus one could picture any other thing in the wet clay. This is called *pictography*, a system of writing in which a word is expressed by a simple drawing called a word sign, logogram, or ideogram (ill. 6). From the start the number of signs was intentionally kept small, for example, by adding certain elements to the existing signs (ill. 6,7).

The tablets were usually not big, often less than 10 centimeters (3.9 in.) long. After the one side had been filled, they were turned around the horizontal axis so that the other side could be filled. Later the Mesopotamians made other bearers of information from clay, for example, thick "nails" driven into the wall, four- to ten-faceted prisms, and bulky "cylinders." These conspicuous forms were used mostly for texts having a monumental or ceremonial function. Extensive literary works for library use were simply written on more tablets, later often numbered. In that case there was a "series." Because the writers always tried to get the same lines on a tablet with the same number, this numbering may be compared with our pagination. In modern references the old numbering of the tablets is often indicated by Roman numerals.

Soon after the evolvement of the pictographic script, people found out that it was very difficult to draw curved lines in the clay. Therefore they began to use a heavier stylus with a triangular point, making the signs more angular and giving a wedgelike shape to the impressions made by the slanted stylus. This shape is the origin of the English adjective "cuneiform." The cuneiform script was even used when, in exceptional cases, the writing was not on clay but had to be done on natural stone or metal. Though the wedges have remained the components of the Mesopotamian writing system, the form of the signs changed considerably through the centuries. The signs were also written differently in different places (ill. 8,9).

A pictographic script in which virtually every word has its own sign is usable only for the simplest forms of information. Even then writer and reader must have agreed on the meaning of a very large number of signs. At an early stage this led to the elaboration of the system by using the signs for syllables, too. Possible combinations were vowel (V), consonant-vowel (cV), vowel-consonant (vC), consonant-vowel-consonant (cVc), and, rarely, consonant-vowel-consonant-vowel (cVcV). In principle this made it possible to record graphically, at least approximately, all the words of the spoken language (cf. the principle of the rebus). This resulted in a reduction of the number of required signs from about 1,500 (ca. 3100 B.C.) to a few hundred (after 2000 B.C.).

Nevertheless, in Mesopotamia there was never a complete break with the principles on which the original script was constructed. In every period we encounter *logograms,* that is, signs or combinations of signs designating an entire word without phonetically representing every syllable of that word. Because most of them designate frequently used concepts, these logograms were probably maintained because they made a briefer form of writing possible (cf. the use of symbols for frequently used concepts in modern texts).

Besides these word and syllable signs, Mesopotamian cuneiform developed so-called *determinatives,* signs that were not read but gave an indication of the semantic or grammatical nature of the word to which they were added. For instance, the determinative indicates whether the word is to be taken as the name of a country or a city, as an occupation, as an object of wood or stone, as a plural, and so on. To facilitate the correct reading of a sign or a group of signs, *phonetic*

*complements,* that is, syllables of the word to be read, were sometimes added.

Thus in cuneiform the same sign can have more than one meaning; it can stand for whole words, various syllables, and determinatives. In addition, the form of the sign could differ from place to place and from period to period. Obviously it was not easy to learn to read and write. This art remained the privilege of a small group of learned professional writers. The seats in a Babylonian classroom are silent witnesses of the large number of dropouts; of the special seats, which were most likely meant for the "advanced," far fewer were necessary (ill. 10). The masses, including people in the highest positions, remained illiterate.

Notwithstanding this high level of difficulty, cuneiform continued in use for over three thousand years. As late as A.D. 50 it was used to copy astronomical texts. Many peoples in the ancient world used it and a variety of languages were written in it: Sumerian, Akkadian (Babylonian and Assyrian), Eblaite, Hittite, Elamite, Hurrian, Ugaritic, Urartian, Aramaic, and Persian. This widespread use of cuneiform was in part due to the tremendous cultural and political impact of the civilizations of Mesopotamia on the entire western Asiatic world. An additional factor was no doubt that cuneiform had definite advantages over other ancient Near Eastern systems of writing. For example, the baked clay tablets were extremely durable; moreover, they were difficult to falsify and syllabic writing had the capability of expressing the vowels. As far as we know, only in Ugaritic cuneiform (see section 5.a below) was a conscious attempt made to combine these advantages with the simplicity of an alphabet.

Babylonian cuneiform was deciphered only in the previous century. Important contributions to that effect were made by G. F. Grotefend, H. Rawlinson, E. Hincks, and J. Oppert. Since then it has been customary to publish cuneiform texts in the form of drawn copies. Initially the signs were highly stylized; today the attempt is made to reproduce the original as faithfully as possible. Because the tablets are often broken and many pieces are scattered, an important task of specialists in this field is to find and join the pieces that belong together. Checking the correct reading of a sign with the use of the original tablet is called "collation." Of the hundreds of thousands of clay tablets dug up in the last 150 years, only a small part has been published.

In addition to a copy and a photograph, a transcription can be made, that is, a reproduction of the text in a form that in some ways has been adapted to our alphabet. Illustrations 11 and 16 give examples of such transcriptions. In the transcription the person working with the text reproduces what he or she thinks is the correct reading of the cuneiform text. In that transcription one must abide by international agreements that in principle should always make it possible to determine which sign was used in the original cuneiform text. Unfortunately, these agreements have been subject to frequent change, and they have not always been applied equally consistently. For that reason alone it is advisable, if possible, to verify the transcription with copies of the cuneiform text.

The transcription is in reality already an interpretation of the text. Often the editor makes the interpretation explicit through an added translation and/or a linguistic commentary. Sometimes this interpretation will be questionable or even antiquated. That circumstance makes it particularly advantageous to be able to consult the cuneiform text itself. But if a transcription or a translation has to suffice, it is advisable to find a recent edition from an acknowledged expert.

## LITERATURE

R. Borger, *Akkadische Zeichenliste* (Neukirchen, 1971).

———, *Assyrische-babylonische Zeichenliste* (Neukirchen, 1978).

R. Caplice, *Introduction to Akkadian* (Rome, 1980).

R. Labat, *Manuel d'épigraphie akkadienne* (Paris, 1976[5]).

B. Meissner and K. Oberhuber, *Die Keilschrift* (Berlin, 1967[3]).

K. R. Veenhof, "Klei, kleitablet en spijkerschrift," *Phoenix* 24 (1978) 15–30.

W. von Soden and W. Röllig, *Das akkadische Syllabar* (Rome, 1967[2]).

### For an introduction to the cultural history of Mesopotamia:

M. A. Beek, *Atlas van het Tweestromenland* (Amsterdam/Brussels, 1960).

B. Landsberger, *Die Eigenbegrifflichkeit der babylonischen Welt* (Darmstadt, 1965).

B. Meissner, *Babylonien und Assyrien* I–II (Heidelberg, 1920–25).

A. L. Oppenheim, *Ancient Mesopotamia* (Chicago, 1964).

H. W. F. Saggs, *The Greatness that was Babylon* (London, 1962).

W. von Soden, *Leistung und Grenze sumerischer und babylonischer Wissenschaft* (Darmstadt, 1965).

### Two important reference works:

R. Borger, *Handbuch der Keilschriftliteratur* I–II (Berlin, 1967–75) (with the help of this book one can find editions, transliterations, and translations of cuneiform texts).

*Reallexikon der Assyriologie* I– (Berlin, 1932– ).

See also the annual "Cuneiform Bibliography" in the periodical *Orientalia*.

---

## a. Sumerian

The oldest legible cuneiform texts are written in a language called Sumerian. It is one of the so-called agglutinative languages, that is, grammatical significance is indicated by appending elements to the root of the word (prefixes, infixes, and suffixes); each of these has its own meaning. No use is made of inflection or conjugation.

Here are some examples: *é* "house," *gal* "large," *é-gal* "large house (temple, palace)"; *é-a-ni* "his house," *é-gal-a-ni* "his palace"; *é-a-ni-a* "in his house." *dù* "build," *gim* "as, such as, like," *é-dù-gim* "like someone who builds a house"; *i(n)-dù*, "he has built." *lú* ("man") *é* ("house") *dnin-gír-su-ka(k)* (the determinative d shows that it is the name of a god) *in-dù-a* ("who has built"): "he who has built the house of Ningirsu."

So far it has proved impossible to include Sumerian in any known language family.

Sumerian was the language of a people who must have arrived in Mesopotamia already in prehistoric times (ca. 3500 B.C.). The name "Sumerians" given to these people is a general term found regularly in the cuneiform texts themselves since the end of the third millennium. In reality this designation must have included more groups of people. At least one Sumerian dialect, the so-called *eme-sal*, is rather well known.

During the first half of the third millennium B.C. Sumerian remained the predominant written language of Mesopotamia. Scribes who belonged to the old indigenous population or to the Semitic immigrants, as indicated by their names, and who in many cases spoke another language, nevertheless wrote good Sumerian. It may be assumed that the group that was the most prominent, socially speaking, not only wrote but also spoke Sumerian. Next to nothing is known about the origin of these "real" Sumerians.

The growing influence of Semitic immigrants led, however, to the founding of the kingdom of Akkad about 2370 B.C. A period followed when Sumerian was used much less in writing, presumably because the increasing self-awareness of the Semites promoted the development of written languages of their own (see section 2.b below).

Around 2150 B.C. a Sumerian renaissance started, culminating in tremendous literary activity at the time of the kings of the so-called Third Dynasty of Ur (ca. 2120-2006 B.C.; often abbreviated "Ur III"). It seems likely that then, too, Sumerian was the official spoken language of the ruling class. But there are many indications, such as a large number of Semitic proper names and Semitic loanwords, that the Semitic-speaking Mesopotamians maintained their influence, and that therefore a great number of people must have been bilingual at that time.

The admiration with which these people of the Ur III period greeted Sumerian literature has had far-reaching consequences. Though around 1850 B.C. Sumerian ceased to be a commonly spoken language, the knowledge of this "dead" language continued to be cultivated for centuries. In Old Babylonian writing schools, Sumerian texts were copied as a form of exercise; moreover, because texts whose original may be assumed to have been Babylonian were translated into Sumerian, it is fairly certain that at least some of the Babylo-

nian scribes also mastered Sumerian. Priests used Sumerian as the mysterious language of worship. Until the first century B.C., numerous generations of Babylonian scribes faithfully copied the Sumerian literary works, even when they themselves were no longer able fully to understand these texts. In more than one respect this situation parallels the role of Latin in the Middle Ages.

Because Mesopotamia dominated the political and cultural development of the ancient Near East more often than Egypt, this continuously transmitted legacy of the Sumerians is also important for the understanding of various ideas and institutions in the world of the Old Testament. Moreover, the oldest known examples of a variety of literary genres and forms are to be found in Sumerian literature. Scholars made giant strides forward in the understanding of Sumerian only after World War II; thus much exploration remains to be done in this area.

The oldest Sumerian texts are mainly of an administrative and juridical nature. Apart from the word lists, duplicated for the benefit of the writers themselves, the number of literary fragments from the earliest period is very small. It is, however, not unthinkable that this may be accidental. Among the many tablets dug up at Fara and Abu Salabikh, dating from about 2600 B.C., are pieces of a highly literary caliber, including hymns and wisdom proverbs ("The Instructions of Shuruppak," ill. 11). Most literary tablets, however, are of a more recent date. At best, they come from the Ur III period or the beginning of the Old Babylonian era. Examples of a more recent date are often less carefully copied.

Today a large number of Sumerian literary compositions are known. Among these are myths—for example, myths on the creation and ordering of the universe. The god Enki plays an important role in it. Many hymns and songs are about Inanna, the goddess of love and war. They sing about her love for Dumuzi, the god of vegetation, his unhappy death, and his journey to the netherworld. Motifs from these stories were later incorporated into the mythology of other ancient Near Eastern peoples. For example, the Babylonians spread the cult of Dumuzi, under the name of Tammuz, through the entire ancient Near East (cf. Ezek. 8:14). Favorite texts were those belonging to the ceremony of the sacred marriage, where the king played the role of Dumuzi and a priestess acted as his beloved Inanna. See ill. 12.

Important epic texts deal with legendary rulers such as Enmerkar, Lugalbanda, and Bilgamesh (later Gilgamesh). Hymns, prayers, and songs of lamentation provide material that shows great similarity in form with the poetry of the Old Testament. Parallel in content are parts of the extensive wisdom literature and the "law books" of Ur-Nammu and Lipit-Ishtar (ill. 13). The greatest impact of Sumerian culture on Israel, however, came indirectly through other people, particularly through those who spoke a Semitic language. For that reason we do not deal extensively with the content of the Sumerian literary texts in this chapter.

---

## LITERATURE

A. Falkenstein, *Grammatik der Sprache Gudeas von Lagaš* I–II (Rome, 1949–50).

_____, *Das Sumerische* (Leiden, 1959).

S. N. Kramer, *The Sumerians* (Chicago, 1963).

### History of literature:

O. Edzard and C. Wilcke, in *Kindlers Literatur Lexikon* VI (Zürich, 1971) 2109–55.

W. H. Ph. Römer, "Fünf und zwanzig Jahre der Erforschung sumerischer literarischer Texte," *Bibliotheca Orientalis* 31 (1974) 207–22.

---

## b. Old Akkadian, Eblaite, and Amorite

Sumerian loanwords and personal names are also found in the Sumerian tablets of Fara and Abu Salabikh (ca. 2600 B.C.; cf. map III). We may therefore assume that already in prehistoric times people speaking a Semitic language found a place to live in Mesopotamia. It was only in the twenty-fourth century B.C. that the founding of Semitic kingdoms made the development of written Semitic languages apparently desirable.

In the south, Sargon I acquired the hegemony and brought his kingdom Akkad to great prosperity. He is probably the person who strongly promoted the attempts to use the Sumerian cuneiform script for the writing of Semitic texts. We call this Semitic language written in Akkad Old Akkadian, though the designation "Akkadian" does not occur until much later, among the Babylonians, in documents from the Old Babylonian period.

Only recently have scholars learned that this does not complete the picture. Recent excavations at Tell Mardikh in northern Syria (map II) have brought to light that this tell hides the capital of a large West Semitic empire extending over all of northern Mesopotamia and Syria during the Old Akkadian period. The city was called Ebla. Here, too, cuneiform was used to record documents in the language spoken at the time. The royal archives comprise more than 15,000 tablets, about 80 percent written in Sumerian and about 20 percent in the indigenous Eblaite (ill. 14). An initial inventory has shown that this Eblaite was even used for literary texts and multilingual vocabularies. Because Eblaite seems closely related to the Canaanite languages, to which Hebrew also belongs, it may be expected that the publication of these texts will in many respects be important for the study of the Old Testament. According to some scholars (e.g., G. Pettinato and M. Dahood), various biblical names appear in these texts, including cities such as Salem (cf. Gen. 14:18), Sodom, and Gomorrah, and personal names such as Israel, Ishmael, Michael, Micaiah, and Hananiah. These last names are particularly astonishing because they seem to suggest that the God of Israel (Yahweh) was worshiped in northern Syria long before the time of the patriarchs (cf. Gen. 4:26). Other scholars (e.g., A. Archi and H. P. Müller) read these names differently, however, and deny any connection with the Bible. Resolution of the problem must await publication of more texts and further study.

As far as we know now, after the Old Akkadian period Eblaite as a written language was entirely pushed aside by Sumerian and Akkadian. Especially in northern Mesopotamia, however, several dialects resembling Canaanite were spoken. As a rule they are subsumed under the term *Amorite;* "Eastern Canaanite" is also used. Because hardly any written documents in this language have been discovered thus far, we know

Amorite almost exclusively from personal names and loanwords. The speakers of these dialects, often inaccurately called "Amorites," played an important role in the society of Mesopotamia in the Old Babylonian period. They are known primarily from the Old Babylonian texts from Mari.

## LITERATURE
## On Old Akkadian:

I. J. Gelb, *Glossary of Old Akkadian* (Chicago, 1957).

_____, *Old Akkadian Writing and Grammar* (Chicago, 1961²).

H. H. Hirsch, "Die Inschriften der Könige von Agade," *Archiv für Orientforschung* 20 (1963) 1–82 (transcription and translation).

E. Sollberger and J. R. Kupper, *Inscriptions royales sumériennes et akkadiennes* (Paris, 1971) (translation).

### On Eblaite:

Ch. Bermont and M. Weitzman, *Ebla: A Revelation in Archaeology* (New York, 1979).

E. Cagni, ed., *La lingua di Ebla* (Naples, 1981).

P. Matthiae, *Ebla: An Empire Rediscovered* (Garden City, 1981).

G. Pettinato, *The Archives of Ebla* (Garden City, 1981).

Articles by G. Pettinato in *Orientalia* 44 (1975) 361–74; *Biblical Archaeologist* 39 (1976) 44–52; *Archiv für Orientforschung* 25 (1974/77) 1–36; *Oriens antiquus* 15 (1976) 11–15; *Reallexikon der Assyriologie* V (Berlin/New York, 1976) 9–13; P. Matthiae, *Biblical Archaeologist* 39 (1976) 94–173; I. J. Gelb, *Thoughts about Ibla* (Malibu, 1977); K. R. Veenhof, *Nederlands Theologisch Tijdschrift* 32 (1978) 1–11; *Phoenix* 23 (1977) 7–25; D. N. Freedman, *Biblical Archaeologist* 41 (1978) 143–64; etc.

### On Amorite:

Th. Bauer, *Die Ostkanaanäer* (Leipzig, 1926).

G. Buccellati, *The Amorites of the Ur III Period* (Naples, 1966).

I. J. Gelb, *Computer-aided Analysis of Amorite* (Chicago, 1981).

H. B. Huffmon, *Amorite Personal Names in the Mari Texts* (Baltimore, 1965).

## c. Akkadian (Babylonian and Assyrian)

Akkadian is a further development of Old Akkadian. For over two thousand years it was used in many places as the written language. The two factors of time and space provided the impetus for the rise of numerous dialects that we today are only partially able to classify. They have so many features in common, however, that in present parlance all these dialects are subsumed under the names *Akkadian* or *Babylonian-Assyrian*. The latter name designates the two most important dialects that are recognizable since about 2000 B.C., Babylonian in the southern part of Mesopotamia and Assyrian in the north.

In comparison with other Semitic languages, Akkadian exhibits a number of special features, for example, with regard to the morphology, particularly that of the verb, and syntax. Its vocabulary likewise exhibits remarkable deviations; for instance, the word for "son" is not based on the consonants *bn* (as in Hebrew and most other Semitic languages) but instead is *māru*. It is more difficult to determine whether there were also great phonological differences. For, as we have seen, the Akkadians did not develop a script of their own but used Sumerian cuneiform. However, this offered insufficient possibilities for expressing a variety of typical Semitic sounds, for example, the laryngeals and the emphatic consonants. Furthermore, in many cases it is not possible to express a sharp distinction between voiced and voiceless consonants. Some vowels, for example, *o*, cannot be expressed.

The following division is customary in Assyriology:

*Old Akkadian* (2500–2000 B.C.)

Relatively few documents, primarily royal inscriptions and administrative texts.

*Old Babylonian* (2000–1530 B.C.)

Many documents, covering all areas of public, religious, and private life. Conscious cultivation of language and literature.

*Old Assyrian* (2000–1750 B.C.)

Known mainly from letters and contracts of the Assyrian trade colony Kanish (Kültepe) in Asia Minor (see map III).

*Middle Babylonian* (1530–1000 B.C.)

Especially administrative texts from Nippur,

Ur, Dur-Kurigalzu, and—interesting in many ways for the Old Testament—Nuzi (map III). Furthermore, important diplomatic correspondence and administrative texts from Palestine, Syria, and Asia Minor, including the famous *Amarna Letters,* correspondence between the Egyptian royal court and the small kingdoms of Canaan, discovered in excavations at Tell el-Amarna in Egypt. Meanwhile, similar archives have also been discovered in many places in Syria-Palestine itself, for example, in the mounds of the ancient cities of Ugarit, Alalakh, Taanach, and Emar (map III). That in all these places Babylonian was used shows that it had become the first lingua franca of the world.

*Middle Assyrian* (1500–1000 B.C.)

Influenced by Middle Babylonian. The best-known genre of texts is the laws (cf. ill. 16).

*Neo-Babylonian* (1000–625 B.C.)

It still reflects the living language, which was being neglected more and more owing to the rise of Aramaic. The literary texts were, however, written in a somewhat archaic dialect called *Young* (or *Standard*) *Babylonian.* Many tablets were found in the library of King Ashurbanipal (669–627 B.C.) in Nineveh (map III). This ruler was interested in literature and had tablets from every part of his empire copied for his personal collection.

*Neo-Assyrian* (1000–600 B.C.)

Like Neo-Babylonian, it betrays the influence of the spoken language and therefore is found mainly in everyday documents such as letters and contracts. Though for official pieces and literary works Standard Babylonian was normally used, in Assyria a chauvinistic tendency in favor of the language spoken by the Assyrians themselves is noticeable.

*Late Babylonian* (625 B.C.–A.D. 50)

In this period Aramaic had virtually pushed Akkadian aside as the spoken language. For a long time, however, Babylonian continued to be cultivated as the written language for royal inscriptions, science, and literature.

In addition to linguistic differences, each period is characterized by the altered form of the signs (cf. above, ill. 9). To give an idea of the resultant changes, illustration 16 offers fragments from an Old Babylonian text as well as from a Middle As-

syrian text, both supplied with a transcription and a translation.

For the study of the Old Testament, Akkadian has assumed a position of eminence, not only on account of the many historical contacts with Assyrian and Babylonian armies, but also on account of the silent influence exerted by the highly developed civilization of Mesopotamia on the relatively "provincial" Canaan. This cultural influence was accomplished through various classes of people: emigrants, merchants, diplomats, artists, and soldiers. According to the book of Genesis, this traffic was intensive already at the time of the patriarchs. Unfortunately, many Jews later came to know Assyria and Babylonia all too well as exiles. Obviously, these numerous contacts have left traces in the Old Testament.

In 1872 George Smith became the first to discover a Babylonian clay tablet containing a story of a deluge strongly resembling that of the biblical tradition; this find created an enormous sensation and was the beginning of the so-called "Babel and Bible" conflict, with scholars taking extreme positions in both directions. Some scholars boundlessly exaggerated the similarities between the Akkadian texts and the Bible, while others all too desperately defended the uniqueness of Israel's legacy.

Today there is a greater awareness that it is inappropriate to weigh the differences and the similarities against each other. The similarities show only that the Israelites were fully people of their own time. As for the differences, they are as characteristic of the one as of the other culture. If we have a greater appreciation for what is unique in the Old Testament, we should be aware that this rests on personal conviction.

Within the compass of this section it is impossible to give even an approximately complete survey of the Akkadian texts that are of importance to Old Testament scholars. We have to restrict ourselves to a few categories.

## (1) MYTHS AND EPICS

Even in their oldest form, myths and epics are elaborate stories often incorporating motifs already found in Sumerian literature. It is often assumed that the Sumerian version is the oldest, but in many cases it is quite possible that in an

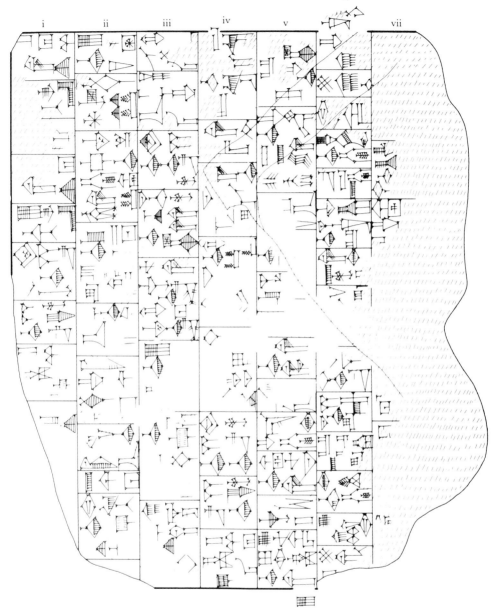

11. *Copy of the front of a Sumerian clay tablet from Abu Salabikh (ca. 2600 B.C.) containing part of the Instructions of Shuruppak. The transcription and translation of the bottom three panels of column iv are reproduced below. The form used is similar to that of the book of Proverbs (cf. Prov. 1:1, 8; 2:1; 3:1; etc.). See p. 81.*

      iv.6   shuruppak dumu na na-mu-ri
             *Shuruppak gave instruction to his son:*
      iv.7   dumu-mu na ga-ri
             *My son, let me give you instruction,*
      iv.8   GISH.PI. TUG he-ma-ak
             *incline your ear to it.*

        *(from R. D. Biggs,* Inscriptions from Tell Abu Salabikh *[Chicago, 1974], plate 111)*

13. *A fragment of the Lipit-Ishtar law code from Nippur (ca. 1900 B.C.) that deals with boat rental, orchards, and slaves. (University Museum, University of Pennsylvania)*

12. *The clay conical nail of Entemena, recording in Sumerian cuneiform script the building of the temple of Dumuzi (Tammuz) and Inanna (Ishtar) at Badtibra (ca. 3000 B.C.). (Royal Ontario Museum)*

15. *A fragment of the third tablet of* Enuma Elish, *the Assyrian creation epic recounting the struggle between cosmic order and chaos. This copy from Ashurbanipal's library at Nineveh is similar to older Babylonian versions, which in part may be traced to Sumerian originals of the 3rd millennium B.C. (Trustees of the British Museum)*

14. *Tablets of the palace library as discovered at Tell Mardikh (Ebla), the most recent major archeological find in the Near East. These administrative texts document an extensive commercial empire in the 3rd millennium B.C.* (Biblical Archaeologist)

21. *Phonetic complements and determinatives in the Egyptian script (cf. pp. 93–94). The hieroglyphic "swallow" has the phonetic value of* wr *and is thus a so-called two-letter sign. The word* wr *means "great" and is pronounced* wer. *To prevent mistakes, the Egyptian writers usually added the one-letter sign "mouth" (= r) to it. This is thus a phonetic complement, separately mentioning, as it were, the* r *of* wr. *To write the word* wrs, *"headrest" (example above), it was only necessary to add to* wr + r *the one-letter sign "folded cloth" (= s) (transcription:* wrs; *pronunciation:* weres). *To make absolutely sure the writers finally added a picture of a headrest as a determinative.*

*Something similar was done with the verb* wrh, *"to be anointed" (example below). To* wr + r *was added the one-letter sign "string of flax" (= h). In this case the determinative was the jar of oil.*

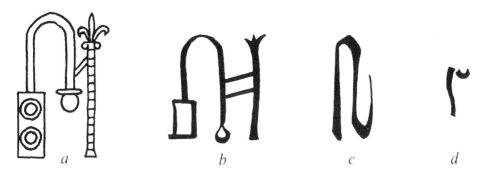

22. *Types of Egyptian writing. The ideogram for "to write" is shown successively as (a) a hieroglyph on a monument (ca. 1300 B.C.), (b) a hieroglyph from the Book of the Dead (ca. 1500 B.C.), (c) a hieratic sign (ca. 1300 B.C.), and (d) a demotic sign (ca. 400 B.C.). See p. 94.*

23. *Egyptian writers at work, ca. 2410 B.C. Each has a piece of papyrus, a palette with two colors (black and red), and reeds for writing, which they have put behind their ears. Between the writers are cases with rolls of papyri. See p. 94.*

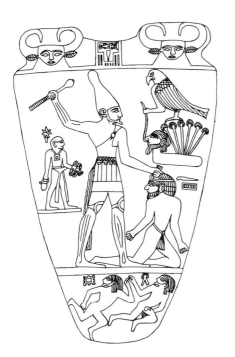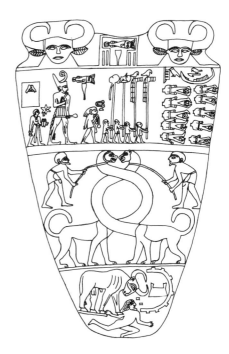

19. *Between pictogram and script. A palette of slate stone belonging to King Narmer, ca.*
*3000 B.C. We see here very graphic pictures of the king as victor. But several representations*
*also have a symbolic meaning. Thus in the bottom register of the front (above left) destitute*
*enemies flee from their city and from their farming village. The place they are from is "written"*
*with a small symbol. In the bottom register of the other side (above right) the king is depicted*
*as a bull, who tramples the enemy and with his horns breaches the wall of a schematically*
*indicated fortress.*

*The falcon (= the king in the shape of the god Horus) who drags away prisoners (= head*
*on a rope) out of the Nile Delta (= papyrus on piece of land) is clearly an advanced form of*
*pictogram. Beside it are signs that can be regarded as pure hieroglyphics. Thus on the back it*
*is, for example, hieroglyphically indicated that the king who is pictured in or by the procession*
*is King Narmer. The picture does not indicate this; it is something one must be able to read.*
*The Horus-name of the king also occurs in the center above, between the heads of Hathor,*
*the cow-goddess who symbolizes fertility. See p. 93.*

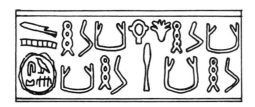

20. *A cylinder seal of a high official, ca. 3000 B.C. The name of the man, Hemaka, occurs*
*four times, but the order of the three signs that stand for the name is changed in the bottom line,*
*probably because it was thought to look better. In later times such transpositions were also made*
*for aesthetic reasons. The name is phonetically written; the string of flax represents* he, *the*
*sickle* ma, *the raised hands* ka. *The string of flax is a so-called one-letter sign (ḥ), the other*
*two are two-letter signs (m3, k3). The pronunciation of the name as "Hemaka" is modern;*
*in general the Egyptian script does not indicate vowels. See p. 93.*

17. *A fragment of Tablet XI of the* Gilgamesh Epic, *which contains a Babylonian flood account, written in Assyrian cuneiform. This tablet details the building of the ship, the storm, and the landing on Mount Nisir. (Trustees of the British Museum)*

18. *A tablet of the so-called Sumerian Job ("Man and His God") from Nippur (18th century* B.C.*). This poem, originating in the late 3rd millennium, tells of an innocent man who, like Job, meets misfortune, prays for deliverance, is finally saved from his afflictions, and then praises his god. (University Museum, University of Pennsylvania)*

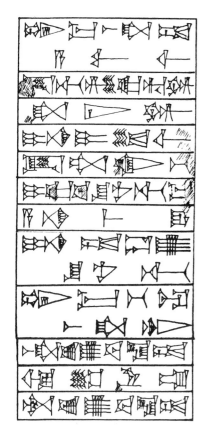

## CODE OF HAMMURABI, ARTICLE 129

Transcription

§ 129.42) šum-ma aš-ša-att a-wi-lim 43) [it-ti]-zi-ka-ri-im 44) ša-ni-im 45) i-na i-tu-lim 46) it-ta-aṣ-bat 47) i-ka-sú-šu-nu-ti-ma 48) a-na me-e 49) i-na-ad-du-ú-šu-nu-ti 50) šum-ma be-el aš-ša-tim 51) aš-ša-sú ú-ba-la-aṭ 52) ù šar-ru-um 53) waras (ÌR)-sú ú-ba-la-aṭ

Translation

"If someone's wife, while she had relations with another, was caught, they shall be bound and thrown into the water. If, however, the husband of that woman lets his wife live, then also the king shall let his servant live."

16. Copy (left), transcription, and translation (above) of an article from the Old Babylonian Code of Hammurabi. Below is a similar article from the Middle Assyrian laws. The differences between the two scripts are evident. But all kinds of grammatical differences can also be noted. Thus the Old Babylonian word awīlum corresponds with the Assyrian aīlu; the dropping of the w and of the final m (the so-called mimation) are characteristic developments.

Note that in cuneiform the words are constructed of syllables, separated in the transcription by a hyphen. Logograms are indicated by capital letters. In the above transcriptions they are placed in parentheses, while they are preceded by the Akkadian word that was pronounced in the reading of the text.

It is remarkable that the Middle Assyrian laws elaborate more on the incident. The main rule is, however, that in a case of adultery the woman and her friend are punished by death, unless the deceived husband shows mercy. The Old Testament does not specifically mention this type of mercy (cf. Lev. 20:10; Deut. 22:22). See p. 80.

## MIDDLE ASSYRIAN LAWS, ARTICLE 15

Transcription

§ 15, Col. II.41) šum-ma aīlu (LÚ) iš-tu aššitī (DAM-ti)-su aīla (LÚ) 42) iṣ-ṣa-bat 42) ub-ta-e-ru-ú-uš 43) uk-ta-i-nu-ú-uš 44) ki-la-al-le-šu-nu-ma 45) i-du-uk-ku-šu-nu 46) a-ra-an-šu la-áš-šu 47) šum-ma iṣ-ṣa-ab-ta lu-ú a-na muḫḫi (UGU) šarre (LUGAL) 48) lu-ú a-na muḫḫi (UGU) dayyānē (DI.KUD.MEŠ) it-tab-la 49) ú-ub-ta-e-ru-ú-uš 50) ú-uk-ta-i-nu-ú-uš 51) šum-ma mu-ut sinnište (MÍ) aššas (DAM)-su i-du-ak 52) ù a-i-la i-du-ak-ma 53) šum-ma ap-pa ša aššitī (DAM)-šu i-na-ki-is⁵ 54) aīla (LÚ) a-na ša re-še-en ú-tar 55) ù pa-ni-šu gab-ba i-na-qu-ru 56) ù šum-ma aššas (DAM)-[su] [ú-uš-šar] 57) [aīla (LÚ) ú]-[uš-šar]

Translation

If someone has caught another with his wife and accused him and given proof against him, both shall be put to death — that is not punishable. However, if after having caught him, one has brought him before the judges, accused him and given the proof against him, then things will be as follows:

If the husband kills his wife, he shall also kill that man.

If he cuts off her nose, he shall also make a eunuch of that man and his whole face shall be mutilated.

But if he spares his wife, he shall also spare that man.

24. *The Rosetta Stone, a fragment of a stele commemorating the coronation of Ptolemy V Epiphanes as king of all Egypt (186 B.C.). The Greek inscription (bottom) was a major key to the decipherment of the Hieroglyphic (top) and Demotic (middle) Egyptian scripts. (Trustees of the British Museum)*

25. *The victory stele of Merneptah with a hymn (or series of hymns) commemorating the pharaoh's defeat of the Libyans and Asiatic peoples. The boast that "Israel is laid waste and has no seed" (line 27) is the only mention of the name Israel in ancient Egyptian writing. (Oriental Institute, University of Chicago)*

26. *Part of the Theban Book of the Dead in cursive Hieroglyphs with some Hieratic signs (ca. 1200–1000 B.C.). (University Museum, University of Pennsylvania)*

28. A fragment from the Coptic Gospel according to Thomas. The text of logion 20 contains a variant version of the parable in which the kingdom of heaven is likened to a mustard seed (Matt. 13:31–32; Mark 4:30–32; Luke 13:18–19). See p. 99.

29. A copy of a stamp seal with the portrait and name of a Hittite prince (Tarkondemos) in Hittite cuneiform and hieroglyphs. (Ashmolean Museum, Oxford; picture W. S. LaSor)

27. A papyrus containing column 12 of the Instruction of Amenemope (in Hieratic script, ca. 1000 B.C.), which talks about the destructive speech of an angry man. (Trustees of the British Museum)

earlier phase the Sumerians took over the motif from the Akkadians.

Not only epics but also myths make use of a special epic style. Linguistic archaisms, repetitions, cliches, parallelism, and a rhythmic division of the verse lines characterize this special style. Today some scholars are of the opinion that the epic form of poetry derives from the living oral tradition of which the tablets known to us would be only a more or less "canonical" written fixation. This would explain why there is often more than one version of the same story, all of which manifest considerable differences depending on the time and place of writing.

Here follows a brief summary of some of the frequently cited myths and epics:

### (a) THE EPIC OF ATRA-HASIS

The story begins in mythological times when there were only gods. The universe is divided among three gods: Anu (heaven), Enlil (earth), and Ea (subterranean freshwater ocean; also called Enki). On earth the younger gods are forced to do labor for Enlil and they rebel. Ea proposes the creation of humankind to take over the work. In other Mesopotamian creation traditions, too, the motive for humankind's creation is that the gods had to be served.

Ea and the mother-goddess Mami (also called Nintu or Ninharsag) form seven men and seven women from loam and the blood of a butchered god. Thus, according to this epic, human beings are a combination of something earthly and something heavenly (cf., e.g., Gen. 2:7; Job 4:19; 10:9; 33:6; Psalm 8).

Humankind multiplies so rapidly, however, that the god Enlil can no longer sleep on account of the noise on earth. By various means he tries drastically to reduce the number of people: epidemics, severe drought, famine. Every time, however, his evil intent fails because Enki intervenes at the request of Atra-hasis (a human king). At last Enlil decides to destroy humankind with a flood. Bound by an oath, Enki is unable to help this time. He can only advise Atra-hasis to construct a watertight ship, in which only the man and his family survive the catastrophe.

Immediately the gods deplore the flood because the human beings no longer provide them with food. Therefore, like flies they are attracted to the smell of the first sacrifice brought by Atra-hasis after the flood. Only fragments of the end of the epic are known.

As a rule the *Epic of Atra-hasis* was written on three (later two) large tablets.

### RECOMMENDED LITERATURE

W. G. Lambert and A. R. Millard, *Atra-hasis. The Babylonian Story of the Flood* (Oxford, 1969) (with transcription and translation).

### (b) THE CREATION EPIC, OR ENUMA ELISH

The latter name is the original Babylonian title. As was the custom later among the Jews, the Babylonians often titled their literary works with the opening words, in this case *enuma elish*, "When above. . . ." Some scholars prefer to call this work of art, consisting of seven tablets averaging one hundred fifty lines each, a myth because it deals entirely with the primordial history of the gods. Moreover, the text had a definite function in the cult. Each year at the celebration of the New Year, the Babylonians recited *Enuma elish* before the image of Marduk, the hero of the story and the chief god of Babylon since the Old Babylonian period.

In the beginning, so the story goes, there were only the male freshwater ocean (*Apsu*) and the female saltwater ocean (*Tiamat,* which is related etymologically to Hebrew *tehom*; cf. Gen. 1:2). The union of these two produces the first life, namely, the gods. Eventually there are so many gods, however, that Apsu and Tiamat can no longer sleep because of the noise. They decide to destroy their own progeny. The crafty god Ea prevents this by causing Apsu to fall into a deep sleep and then locking him up in the depths (groundwater). Initially Tiamat does not react.

Ea begets Marduk, who receives the four winds as a gift. But when he starts playing with them, he disrupts the quiet of the gods. A number of them incite Tiamat to avenge herself. She creates fearful monsters and prepares herself for a terrible war against the younger gods under the leadership of Ea and Marduk. Finally, Marduk defeats Tiamat in a duel.

> When he had rested, Marduk, observing her corpse, wondered how he would divide the body to create pieces of art. He split her in two like a stockfish. One half of her he put down and covered the heaven with a roof of it.

Marduk shapes heaven like a temple-tower with different levels. Next he creates the stars, assigns them their circuits, and so fixes the division of the year. He creates moon and sun, day and night. From Tiamat's saliva he makes clouds and winds, rain and cold. From the head and the other half of her body he fashions the earth. He declares his intention to establish a sanctuary for himself and his helpers on earth with the name "Babylon." The gods want to do things themselves, but Marduk knows something better:

> "Blood I want to collect and cause bones to be, I want to bring into existence a human being, 'man' shall be his name. Truly, a human being I want to create! He shall be charged with serving the gods, so that they can be free."

He then creates man from the blood of one of the enemy gods who stood on the side of Tiamat, in order to do forced labor for the gods. With miraculous speed the sanctuary of Marduk is built in Babylon. The epic concludes with an enumeration of the fifty names of Marduk, which extol his greatness. See ill. 15.

---

### RECOMMENDED PUBLICATIONS

W. G. Lambert and S. B. Parker, *Enuma elis. The Babylonian Epic of Creation* (Oxford, 1966) (only cuneiform text).

An edition of the entire epic has been announced by Lambert.

For the present the following works should prove helpful:

A. Heidel, *The Babylonian Genesis* (Chicago, 1951[2]) (translation).

R. Labat, *Le poème babylonian de la création* (Paris, 1935) (transcription and translation).

E. A. Speiser and A. K. Grayson in Pritchard, ed., *Ancient Near Eastern Texts*[3], pp. 60–72, 501–503 (translation).

---

### (c) THE GILGAMESH EPIC

Gilgamesh, or Bilgamesh as he is called in older texts, was a historical king of the city-state of Uruk (see map III). He probably lived around 2700 B.C. Like other kings, he was deified after his death. His fame was so great, however, that soon his name was included in the official lists of great gods. All kinds of legends sprang up around him, preserved in part in Sumerian. As far as we know, these stories were not put in a series.

The Akkadian epic is the work of a brilliant (unfortunately unknown) poet, probably living in the Old Babylonian period. Borrowing freely from motifs in the old legends, he reworked them into a coherent whole. The development of the theme and the narrator's art are so magnificent that the *Gilgamesh Epic* has rightly been called a precursor of Greek tragedy. The epic was famous already in antiquity. Fragments of the original text have been found, for example, at Megiddo and Ugarit. There were even translations in circulation (e.g., in Hittite and Hurrian).

We still do not have the complete text of all the versions of the epic. The most complete is the version from Nineveh, probably comprising about 3,600 lines divided over twelve tablets (ill. 17). The last tablet of this version is a later addition, however, possibly a substitute for an older epilogue.

The epic begins with a description of the walls of the city of Uruk looming in the distance (cf. Ps. 48:13–14). The storyteller as it were takes the reader along to the city where King Gilgamesh rules. The population suffers from his despotic actions, especially the young women. The people appeal to the gods for help against their king. Their prayer is heard and the gods create the wild, primitive man Enkidu, who is to be the godlike equal of Gilgamesh. Enkidu lives among the wild animals until he is discovered by a hunter.

Next the poet gives a moving description of the clash between the primitive Enkidu and the bearers of culture, pictured as being somewhat decadent. Seduced by a harlot, Enkidu finally goes to the city of Uruk to fight Gilgamesh, whose arrogance becomes more and more intolerable. The fight is inconclusive, however, and the two heroes become friends. Gilgamesh takes Enkidu along from feast to feast. Eventually Enkidu tires of it, and Gilgamesh proposes that they have an adventure. He wants to defeat the giant Humbaba, who lives far to the west in a huge cedar forest.

In the discussions about this venture the thread running through the whole epic becomes visible for the first time: the problem of human mortality. At this point Gilgamesh still says: man must die, so why should we be afraid of danger and death? If we are killed in battle, we will be praised, and is not that the only way in which man can continue to live after his death?

After a difficult trek, the two friends reach the cedar forest. In a heroic combat they defeat Humbaba. Returning to Uruk in triumph, Ishtar, the goddess of love and of war, falls in love with the hero Gilgamesh. She proposes, but Gilgamesh refuses crudely. This is the tragic moment in the epic. On the one hand, the deprivations and the struggle have apparently purified and steeled Gilgamesh so that he no longer succumbs to every erotic temptation, not even if his seductress is the goddess of love. On the other hand, his answer to the goddess bespeaks a pride unfit for any mortal in the presence of the gods.

The vengeful Ishtar manages to set the bull of heaven, a devouring monster, on Gilgamesh and his men. There follows a vivid description of the struggle with this animal in which Gilgamesh and Enkidu manage to kill the monster. Ishtar is furious and curses Gilgamesh. This time it is Enkidu who goes too far. He taunts Ishtar and throws a shank of the animal at her. In so doing he signs his own death sentence.

After a severe illness in which he is tormented by feverish dreams about death and the realm of the dead, Enkidu dies. Gilgamesh is inconsolable and mourns bitterly for his friend. Having experienced death at such close range, he can no longer accept human mortality. Alone he leaves Uruk to visit Utnapishtim, the only human who ever obtained immortality. After an arduous journey with many dangers, breathtakingly described by the poet, Gilgamesh at last reaches the distant place where Utnapishtim lives.

At first Utnapishtim does not want to reveal the secret of his immortality. Eventually he is persuaded to tell his story, which consists of the story of the flood. In this version of the story, Utnapishtim is the hero of the flood. In some respects this version is closer to the biblical story of the flood than the corresponding episode from the Atra-hasis epic. Utnapishtim tells Gilgamesh that after the flood he was given eternal life as a gesture of repentance by the god who had caused the catastrophe. That possibility is, of course, not available to Gilgamesh. He may have a chance, however, if he will go without sleep for seven days.

The bone-tired Gilgamesh is barely seated, however, when he falls into a deep sleep from which he awakens only on the seventh day. The attempt has failed.

Utnapishtim feels sorry for him and permits him to bathe once in the fountain of life so that, renewed, he can assume the homeward journey. Eventually Utnapishtim even tells him the secret of the strength of the fountain of life: at the bottom grows the herb of life. If Gilgamesh could cut off part of that plant he himself would be able to make life-giving water in Uruk.

Gilgamesh seizes this final opportunity. With heavy stones attached to his feet, he dives into the spring and indeed is able to secure the herb of life. Alas, on the way back to Uruk, a serpent steals the plant from him—and to prove her rejuvenation immediately strips off her old skin. Everything has been in vain; disillusioned, Gilgamesh drags himself home. The poet underlines the senselessness of the whole undertaking by concluding the epic with lines that are virtually identical with the opening lines: the description of the walls of Uruk looming up.

---

## RECOMMENDED PUBLICATIONS

A new edition of the epic is in preparation (W. G. Lambert). Meanwhile one can manage with R. C. Thompson, *The Epic of Gilgamesh* (Oxford, 1930) (text, transcription, and translation), in addition to the literature in R. Borger,

*Handbuch der Keilschriftliteratur* I (pp. 555ff.) and II (pp. 292ff.).

On the transmission of the Gilgamesh Epic:

J. H. Tigay, *The Evolution of the Gilgamesh Epic* (Philadelphia, 1982).

Good translations are:

F. M. Th. de Liagre Böhl, *Het Gilgamesj Epos* (Amsterdam, 1958³).

A. Heidel, *The Gilgamesh Epic and Old Testament Parallels* (Chicago, 1949²).

A. Schott and W. von Soden, *Das Gilgamesch-Epos* (Stuttgart, 1958).

E. A. Speiser and A. K. Grayson, in Pritchard, ed., *Ancient Near Eastern Texts,* pp. 72ff., 503ff.

---

## (d) THE ERRA EPIC

Some scholars prefer to call this epic, too, a "myth," because the chief characters are exclusively gods. The text is relatively recent (ca. 1050 B.C.; others prefer an even later date) and covers five tablets. A striking difference from other epic texts is the distinct preference for long dialogue.

Incited by the fearful "Seven (gods)," the plague-god Erra (Irra) prepares to destroy the earth. In this case, too, one of the causes is the noise of the people, making it impossible for the gods to get their sleep. The real reason, however, seems to be that the image of the god Marduk is neglected in Babylon.

Erra's vizier Ishum tries vainly to restrain the furious god from his evil plan. With beautiful promises Erra succeeds in persuading Marduk to leave his earthly abode in Babylon for a while. But this absence of Marduk destroys the balance of the entire cosmos. Erra makes use of this imbalance to bring about unimaginable destruction and chaos. Only after long talks does Ishum manage to calm him down, after which Babylon can start its rebuilding.

---

### LITERATURE

L. Cagni, *L'Epopea di Erra* (Rome, 1969) (transcription and translation).

_____, *Das Erra Epos—Keilschrifttext* (Rome, 1970) (cuneiform only).

_____, *The Poem of Erra* (Malibu, 1977) (translation and commentary).

R. Labat, et al., *Les religions du Proche-Orient asiatique* (Paris, 1970), pp. 114–37.

For a Dutch summary see R. Frankena, "Het Epos van de Pestgod Irra," *Jaarbericht Ex Oriente Lux* 15 (1957–58) 160nd76.

---

## (2) HYMNS AND PRAYERS

Though reference has already been made to the similarities between the biblical and the Babylonian psalms, no comprehensive systematic research has been done in this area. It can be shown that the Babylonian poets used Sumerian examples as models. Many tablets with hymns and prayers were made in two languages for that matter; it is not certain, however, that in all cases the Sumerian version is the oldest.

From many insertions it is evident that the Babylonian psalms were used in the ritual in which prayer was thought to possess magical power. This may explain why the language and style seem rather formal and stereotyped. Nevertheless, these songs also express an intimate personal piety, as indicated by the following fragments from a Babylonian penitential psalm:

> Who is there who has never sinned against his god?[1]
> Who has always kept the command?
> All people are sinners. . . .
> I, your servant, have sinned in every respect.
> I would serve you, but I acted faithlessly.
> I spoke lies, smoothed over my transgression.
> I spoke unseemly things, you know them all.[2]
> . . . . . . . . . . . . . . . . . . . . . . . . . . . . . . . . . . . .
> Enough, my god! Let your heart be at rest!
> May the angry goddess be totally quieted!
> Let go of the anger that filled your heart![3]
> May your inner soul by which I swore be reconciled to me.
> Though my transgressions are many, deliver me from my guilt![4]
> Though my offenses are many, let your heart be at rest!

Though my sins are many, show me your grace!
My god, I am exhausted—seize thou my hand![5]

1. Cf. Ps. 143:2; Job 4:17; 15:14; Prov. 20:9.
2. Cf. Pss. 69:6; 139:1–4.
3. Cf. Pss. 6:2; 38:2.
4. Cf. Ps. 25:11.
5. Cf. Ps. 73:23.

## LITERATURE

A. Falkenstein and W. von Soden, *Sumerische und akkadische Hymnen und Gebete* (Zurich/Stuttgart, 1953).

M.-J. Seux, *Hymnes et prières aux dieux de Babylonie et d'Assyrie* (Paris, 1976).

Both books constantly refer to the original publications.

W. Mayer, *Untersuchungen zur Formensprache der babylonischen "Gebetsbeschwörungen"* (Rome, 1976).

G. Widengren, *The Accadian and Hebrew Psalms of Lamentation as Religious Documents* (Stockholm, 1937).

F. J. Stephens and S. N. Kramer, in Pritchard, ed., *Ancient Near Eastern Texts*, pp. 383–92, 455–63, 573–86, 611–19.

## (3) WISDOM LITERATURE

Besides collections of proverbs and fables that in the Near East as elsewhere intend to pass on practical instructions for everyday life, this genre also contains more comprehensive works. The didactic poem *Ludlul bel nemeqi* ("I will praise the Lord of Wisdom"—again the opening words of the poem are used as the title) probably contained 400 to 500 lines, divided over three tablets. We listen here to the laments of a pious nobleman who has fallen into disgrace and has become seriously ill besides. Only after a long time and much inner struggle is this suffering righteous man rehabilitated. The poem has been likened to the book of Job.

A greater affinity with the theme of Job, however, is found in the so-called *Babylonian Theodicy*. In it a skeptic and a pious man alternately

articulate their views on life. The misfortune of the pious contrasts glaringly with the success of the godless. See ill. 18.

## RECOMMENDED PUBLICATIONS

W. G. Lambert, *Babylonian Wisdom Literature* (Oxford, 1960) (text, transcription, translation).

For the opening hymn of *Ludlul*, see D. J. Wiseman, *Anatolian Studies* 30 (1980) 102ff.; W. L. Moran, *Journal of the American Oriental Society* 103 (1983) 255ff.

## (4) JURIDICAL TEXTS

A large number of the clay tablets that have been found are of a juridical nature. Occasionally they are edicts of kings or protocols of judicial affairs, but for the most part they are contracts in which business transactions are settled in the presence of witnesses. Such agreements included, among others, marriages, adoptions, and testaments. The juridical basis for these texts is common law, for ordinary, universally accepted lawbooks did not exist. Various attempts were made to codify this law. The most famous example of such an attempt is the *Code of Hammurapi* (formerly read Hammurabi). This code is written on a diorite pillar over 2 meters (6.5 ft.) high and was made by order of the Old Babylonian king Hammurapi. There are reasons to believe that this ruler at first tried to unify the administration of justice in his kingdom via the oral and written promulgation of this text. He also tried to push through certain renewals in this way. Though little came of it in practice, as a literary creation the codex demanded such respect that until the Late Babylonian period copies of it were made in clay.

Other significant codifications are the somewhat older *Laws of Eshnunna* and the *Middle Assyrian Laws*. All these "laws" are of the casuistic type, that is, laws that are restricted to regulating individual cases without trying to formulate a universally valid juridical principle. Both in respect to this point and in terms of content it is interesting to make comparisons with the juridical parts of the Old Testament. To get an idea of this literary genre see the fragments cited in illustration 16.

Precisely because it is doubtful that the "laws" ever acquired general validity, it is regrettable that comparative research has often limited itself to this type of text. Much important material concerning the actual administration of justice can be found in the protocols and contracts mentioned above, but so far this material has not been fully exploited by Old Testament scholars.

## LITERATURE
### Code of Hammurapi:

E. Bergmann, *Codex Hammurabi textus primigenius* (Rome, 1953³) (cuneiform text).

R. Borger, *Babylonisch-assyrische Lesestücke* II (Rome, 1963) 2–46 (transcription).

G. R. Driver and J. C. Miles, *The Babylonian Laws* I–II (Oxford, 1952–55) (transcription, translation, and commentary).

A. Finet, *Le Code de Hammurapi* (Paris, 1973) (translation).

T. J. Meek, in Pritchard, ed., *Ancient Near Eastern Texts*, pp. 163–80 (translation).

### Laws of Eshnunna:

A. Goetze, *The Laws of Eshnunna* (New Haven, 1946) (text, transcription, translation, and commentary).

―――――, in Pritchard, ed., *Ancient Near Eastern Texts*, pp. 161–63 (translation).

R. Yaron, *The Laws of Eshnunna* (Jerusalem, 1969) (transcription, translation, and commentary).

### Middle Assyrian Laws:

G. Cardascia, *Les lois assyriennes* (Paris, 1969) (translation and commentary).

G. R. Driver and J. C. Miles, *The Assyrian Laws* (Oxford, 1935; repr. with supplementary additions and corrections, Aalen, 1975) (transcription, translation, and commentary).

T. J. Meek, in Pritchard, ed., *Ancient Near Eastern Texts*, pp. 180–88 (translation).

### Contracts:

See the bibliography in R. Borger (Vol. III, pp. 45ff., 161) as well as:

G. Cardascia and J. Klima, *Droits cunéiformes* (Brussels, 1966).

V. Korošec, *Keilschriftrecht* (Leiden, 1964).

## (5) HISTORICAL TEXTS

The annals and chronicles of the kings of Babylonia and Assyria frequently mention kings of Israel and Judah, speak of military campaigns against the states near the Mediterranean Sea, and record the tributes Israel paid. No history of Israel can be written without taking into account the historical cuneiform texts.

Nevertheless, generally accepted terms such as "annals," "chronicles," and "historical texts" might give the impression that the ancients wrote history in the modern sense of the word. Today the historian tries to reproduce the facts as objectively as possible, however much he is convinced that he will never fully reach this ideal. In the ancient Near East, however, history was usually written as it was *experienced*. The writers did not want to record the dry facts, but the glory of god and king that could be so clearly perceived in those facts. Barring a few exceptions, such as the so-called *Babylonian Chronicles*, these texts are not characterized by a deliberate attempt to write objective history. The writers apparently had no qualms about concealing facts, or retouching or regrouping them for the greater glory of conquerors or deliverers. That there is good ground for defending the proposition that Israel's historiography is "more honest" than that of the Babylonians and Assyrians will be admitted by anyone who has become better acquainted with the boastful inscriptions of the Mesopotamian kings. That does not alter the fact that in Israel, too, interpreted history was written.

It is understandable that under those circumstances considerable differences could arise between historiographies written from opposing points of view. For example, compare the fragment below from the Assyrian king Sennacherib with the same history recorded in 2 Kings 18 and 19. Though the Assyrian text confirms the biblical narrative on the most important point, Sennacherib's siege of Hezekiah and his failure to capture Jerusalem, on several details Sennacherib's account falls short of inspiring confidence:

As concerns Hezekiah of Judah, who had not submitted to my yoke: with stamped-down earthen ramps, with battering rams, with attacks of the foot soldiers, with breeches, tunnels, and scaling-ladders, that is how I laid siege to 46 of his walled, fortified cities, besides innumerable neighboring villages, and I captured them. 200,150 people, young and old, men and women, horses, mules, donkeys, camels, large and small cattle without number I carried off from their midst and considered them booty.

He, Hezekiah, who was overwhelmed by fear for my lustrous lordship, and who handed over the Urbi [irregular troops?] and even his elite troops, which served to strengthen his residence Jerusalem (as hostages) and so obtained a truce (?), sent me later in my residence at Nineveh: 30 talents of gold, 800 talents of silver, top quality mascara, large blocks . . . stone, couches inlaid with ivory, chairs with ivory, an elephant-hide, an elephant-tooth, ebony-wood, walnut-wood, all kinds of valuable treasures, also his daughters, his concubines, male and female singers. To deliver the tribute and to do obeisance he sent his ambassadors.

Himself I shut up like a caged bird in Jerusalem, his residence. I made entrenchments before him and made it unthinkable for him to dare to go outside the gate of his city. His towns which I had plundered I cut off from his country and gave them to Mitinti king of Ashdod, Padi king of Ekron, and Sillibel king of Gaza. Thus I reduced his country. In addition to the earlier tribute, annually to be paid by them, I imposed upon them an extra tribute as proof of their faithfulness to my sovereignty.

## LITERATURE

Almost every historical text important for the Old Testament has been translated in the an-

thologies of Pritchard and Galling, already mentioned above. One could also consult, for example:

R. Borger and W. Schramm, *Einleitung in die assyrischen Königsinschriften* I– (Leiden/Köln, 1961– ).

A. K. Grayson, *Assyrian and Babylonian Chronicles* (Locust Valley, 1975).

_____, *Assyrian Royal Inscriptions* I– (Wiesbaden, 1972– ).

### (6) OTHER TEXTS

Other genres can also be of incidental importance. Occasionally letters yield material useful for explaining certain expressions or customs. Deserving of special mention are the letter archives of Tell el-Amarna, Mari, and Ugarit, because like the Israelites the writers belonged to the Northwest Semitic cultural environment.

Certain genres of literature found in abundance in Mesopotamia are altogether lacking in the Old Testament. An example is the so-called omen-literature, fortune-telling with the use of all kinds of usual and unusual events. The same is true of grammatical, lexicographical, medical, mathematical, and astronomical compilations—the pre-scientific legacy of Mesopotamia. Nevertheless, occasionally these texts yield material that sheds light on the everyday life of the biblical world.

## RECOMMENDED LITERATURE FOR THE STUDY OF AKKADIAN

R. Borger, *Babylonisch-assyrische Lesestücke* I–III (Rome, 1979²).

R. Caplice, *Introduction to Akkadian* (Rome, 1980).

K. K. Riemschneider, *An Akkadian Grammar* (Milwaukee, 1976²).

A. Ungnad and L. Matouš, *Grammatik des Akkadischen* (Munich, 1969).

W. von Soden, *Grundriss der Akkadischen Grammatik* (Rome, 1969²) (with Supplement).

### Lexicons:

A. L. Oppenheim, et al., *The Assyrian Dictionary of the Oriental Institute of the University of Chicago* (Chicago/Glückstadt, 1956– ).

W. von Soden, *Akkadisches Handwörterbuch* I-III (Wiesbaden, 1965–81).
See further the bibliography cited under section 2.b above.

life after this life are difficult to explain if the Old Iranian religion is not taken into account. Also, the rise of apocalyptic in the later parts of the Old Testament and in the Intertestamental Period, as well as the rise of gnosticism, can be fruitfully studied in the light of Iranian religious literature.

## d. Elamite and Persian

Only rarely are these languages chosen as secondary subjects in the biblical disciplines. This is not hard to explain. The people of Israel had no more than incidental contacts with the Elamites, who already toward the end of the third millennium B.C. began to write on clay (the so-called Proto-Elamite) and later began to use cuneiform. Israel maintained extensive contacts with the Medes and the Persians, as is evident from the postexilic parts of the Old Testament. In the Persian empire, however, a lot of use was made of Babylonian and Aramaic in international communications.

Nevertheless, the little interest in the Persian language is not justified. It goes without saying that the inscriptions of the Achaemenidian kings, such as the famous Behistun inscription of Darius I, are indispensable for good insight into a period of history that became crucially important for the Jewish people. The language of these inscriptions, which were recorded in a simplified cuneiform, is called *Old Persian* (ca. 500–330 B.C.).

From the standpoint of religion, the holy books of the religion of Zarathustra (Zoroaster) are especially important. A distinction is made between *Old Iranian*, to which the language of the Avesta belongs, and *Middle Iranian*, to which the so-called Pahlavi literature is assigned. Both were written in a script derived from the Semitic alphabet. A peculiarity of Pahlavi is its ideogram-like use of Aramaic words for certain Persian terms. The Pahlavi literature comprises theological writings of the Zoroastrian priests who were active between A.D. 200 and 600.

The importance of the teaching of Zarathustra for the study of the Bible should not be underestimated. Scholars are generally agreed that the difference between Old Testament and New Testament with respect to ideas concerning the

### LITERATURE
#### General Bibliographical Orientation:

R. N. Frye, ed., *Neue Methodologie in der Iranistik* (Wiesbaden, 1974).

*Handbuch der Orientalistik*, Sect. 1, Vol. IV.

L. de Meyer, in J. H. Hospers, ed., *A Basic Bibliography for the Study of the Semitic Languages* I (Leiden, 1973) 118–26.

Y. M. Nawabi, *A Bibliography of Iran* I (Tehran, 1969).

J. D. Pearson, ed., *A Bibliography of Pre-Islamic Persia* (London, 1975).

J. Rypka, et al., *History of Iranian Literature* (Dordrecht, 1968).

#### Elamite:

F. W. König, *Die elamischen Königsinschriften* (Graz, 1965).

E. Reiner, in *Handbuch der Orientalistik*, Sect. 1, Vol. II, 1/2 (Leiden, 1969), pp. 54–118.

#### Old Persian:

W. Brandenstein and M. Mayrhofer, *Handbuch des Altpersischen* (Wiesbaden, 1964).

W. Hinz, *Altpersischer Wortschatz* (Leipzig, 1942; repr. 1966).

———, *Neue Wege im Altpersischen* (Wiesbaden, 1973).

R. G. Kent, *Old Persian* (New Haven, 1953[2]; repr. 1961).

G. Walser, ed., *Beiträge zur Achämenidengeschichte* (Wiesbaden, 1972).

F. H. Weissbach, *Die Keilinschriften der Achämeniden* (Leipzig, 1911; repr. 1968).

F. H. Weissbach and W. Bang, *Die Altpersischen Keilinschriften*, 2 Lief. (Leipzig, 1893–1908).

#### Old Iranian:

C. Bartholomae, *Altiranisches Wörterbuch* (Berlin, 1961[2]).

_____, *Handbuch der altiranischen Dialekte* (Leipzig, 1883; repr. 1968).

J. Darmesteter, *La Zend-Avesta* I-III (Paris, 1892–93; repr. 1960).

W. Geiger, *Handbuch der Awestasprache* (Erlangen, 1879; repr. 1972).

F. Geldner, *Avesta* I–III (Stuttgart, 1885–95).

S. Insler, *The Gathas of Zarathustra* (Liege, 1975).

A. V. W. Jackson, *An Avesta Grammar* (Stuttgart, 1892; repr. 1968).

_____, *Avesta Reader* (Stuttgart, 1893; repr. 1975).

B. Schlerath, *Awesta-Wörterbuch* I– (Wiesbaden, 1968– ).

F. Wolff, *Avesta* (Strassburg, 1910; repr. 1960).

**Middle Iranian and Pahlavi:**

E. G. Browne, *A Literary History of Persia* I (Cambridge, 1902; repr. 1969).

O. Hansen, *Mittelpersisches Lesebuch* (Berlin, 1963).

D. N. MacKenzie, *A Concise Pahlavi Dictionary* (London, 1971).

H. S. Nyberg, *A Manual of Pahlavi* I–II (Wiesbaden, 1964–74).

J. C. Tavadia, *Die mittelpersische Sprache und Literatur der Zarathustrier* (Leipzig, 1956).

E. W. West, *Pahlavi Texts* I–V (London, 1880–97; repr. 1965).

**Three Introductions to the Teaching of Zarathustra:**

M. Boyce, *A History of Zoroastrianism* I– (Leiden, 1975– ).

J. Duchesne-Guillemin, *La religion de l'Iran ancien* (Paris, 1962).

G. Widengren, *Die Religionen Irans* (Stuttgart, 1965).

---

## 3. EGYPT: HIEROGLYPHICS

### a. Egyptian

As in Mesopotamia, so in Egypt the first script was pictorial. The oldest fragments discovered in this script are from about 3000 B.C. For a number of reasons, however, it must be assumed that the principles of this system of writing were developed several centuries earlier. It seems likely that this script originated in the Nile Delta.

The invention of the art of writing played a large role in the unification of the whole of Egypt under King Narmer (ill. 19). He is regarded as the founder of the First Dynasty of Egypt, though he does not appear in that capacity in the later lists of kings. The pharaohs of the First Dynasty were able to rule over a much more extensive area than their predecessors because they could avail themselves of an administrative system that for the first time possessed a reliable method of communication. Many inscriptions of the First Dynasty have been found at Abydos, a site of royal burials, and the predynastic capital of Nekhen, later known as Hierakonpolis.

The strong bond that initially existed between the plastic arts and writing was never abandoned in Egypt. Nowhere in the ancient Near East has such a perfect harmony been achieved between calligraphy, painting, and sculpting. Furthermore, nowhere in the Old World has the word been illustrated with such eagerness and verisimilitude. Because it is often difficult to obtain an idea of what was meant on the basis of written texts alone, archeologists, orientalists, and Old Testament scholars frequently turn to Egyptian art for clarification.

Like the Mesopotamians, the people of Egypt soon hit upon the idea of using word-signs for words or syllables that had a sound similar to the pictured word. Because only the *consonants* were taken into account, however, Egyptian script, unlike cuneiform script, did not evolve into a syllabic script. It became a purely consonantal script in which characters were used that could represent one, two, or three consonants. It is customary to speak of one-, two-, or three-letter signs (see ill. 20). The one-letter signs, 24 in number, are especially intriguing because they would have allowed the Egyptians to write alphabetically. Nevertheless, the Egyptians never took the decisive step of using these signs exclusively. The word-signs or *ideograms* remained in use, though a small vertical line was added to make them more easily recognizable. Also, the two- or three-letter signs were not abandoned. Furthermore, as in Mesopotamia, *determinatives* indicating the class or group to which the word belonged were added to facilitate reading, as were the *phonetic complements* with which a word was "spelled," partially or totally (see ill. 21).

Because the Egyptian script leaves out the vowels, the pronunciation of the language is in most cases unknown. Only the so-called *group-spelling*, which especially in the New Kingdom was used for the writing of strange names and words, might be regarded as a partially successful attempt to record the proper pronunciation. This is of course especially important for biblical names. For the rest we have to be satisfied with the consonants. In books and articles on Egypt, the signs transcribed into our Latin script (complemented with a number of special signs) are always vowelless forms. To make academic communication possible, a short *e* is inserted between the consonants when the Egyptian language is pronounced. Furthermore, certain transcription signs are read as vowels in modern pronunciation; for example, *w* at the end of a word is pronounced as *oo* (or *u* as in *put*). It has proved impossible, however to construct an academically satisfactory transcription system for Egyptian. For that reason many Egyptologists prefer to use standardized types of the original signs. Some printers and plotters, too, possess these types.

The name "hieroglyphics" (Greek for "sacred inscriptions") is due to the early Christian writer Clement of Alexandria. The designation is correct in that hieroglyphics were often used for religious purposes. They were also used, however, for recording all kinds of profane texts, provided of course that these were important enough. Because hieroglyphs (ill. 22a) are actually miniature drawings or reliefs, it was naturally very time-consuming to draw the innumerable fine details. The scribes rigorously maintained the correct execution of the signs, with the result that in thousands of years the form of the hieroglyphs barely changed. Yet this calligraphic writing was not very practical. This was the reason for the early invention of cursive scripts with less intricate signs, the so-called *Hieratic* script (ill. 22c), and since the seventh century B.C. the still more simplified *Demotic* script (ill. 22d).

If the signs were not carved into stone or wood,

they were usually written on papyrus or potsherds (ostraca). The invention of the procedure for making papyrus must have nearly coincided with the origin of the script itself (ca. 3000 B.C.). Papyrus was kept in the form of scrolls. By attaching sheets of papyrus to each other the Egyptians made scrolls that in some cases were over 40 meters (130 ft.) long. The ideogram for the concept "write" consists of a picture of the classical scribal equipment: a belt with a writing reed (in a case), a paint or water napkin, and a palette (ill. 22). Words that were considered important for some reason were written in red. Hence the palette contained red as well as black ink.

Though the Egyptian script has hundreds of signs and the use of these signs is very complicated, with some practice it is not very difficult to distinguish the various hieroglyphs by memorizing their characteristic shapes. It is therefore entirely possible that more people were able to "read" to some extent in Egypt than, for example, in Mesopotamia. Some kings and courtiers are said to have mastered the art of writing. Even so, the genuine mastering of the script, including that of the more difficult Hieratic and Demotic scripts, was reserved for professional scribes (ill. 23). They constituted the backbone of the Egyptian state. They were the people who knew the old literature, which they had to memorize and copy at school. They handled all correspondence, took care of administration, collected taxes for temple and palace, and made calculations. They are also the people who have made it possible for us to gain access to the glorious civilization of ancient Egypt after so many centuries, despite the fact that the meaning of their hieroglyphs had passed into oblivion for more than 1,400 years (the last hieroglyphic inscription known is from A.D. 394).

As is generally known, the decipherment of Egyptian is based largely on the so-called Rosetta Stone. For centuries attempts to decipher the mysterious signs of the Egyptians had been in vain. This changed in 1799 when Napoleon's soldiers discovered a text near the small city of Rashid (Rosetta) that apparently was in three languages and that seemed to offer the key to the solution. The upper text, unfortunately severely damaged, was written in hieroglyphics. The middle text was written in a script that we now know as

Demotic; this part thus offered the same text as the one above it, only in a different phase of the script. The bottom part was easy to read, for it was written in Greek. Apparently the stone contained decisions of an Egyptian synod of priests from 196 B.C. Yet it was not until 1822 that the young French scholar Jean-François Champollion was able to unravel the principles of the Egyptian writing system. The famous Rosetta Stone can be seen in the British Museum in London. (When the French capitulated in Egypt in 1802, the stone passed into British hands.) See ill. 24.

The Egyptian language is often called Hamito-Semitic, meaning that it has an affinity with the Hamitic languages (among others the Berber languages) as well as with the Semitic languages. Because this "mixture" must have occurred in prehistoric times, the results of comparative research remain uncertain.

The following periods are distinguished in the history of the Egyptian language:

*Old Egyptian* (3000–2200 B.C.)

Language of the Old Kingdom; the Pyramid Texts, among others, are written in it.

*Middle Egyptian* (2200 B.C.–A.D. 200)

Originally the language of the Ninth through the Twelfth Dynasties, around 2240–1990 B.C. Later regarded as the classical written language, it continued to be cultivated for writing down literature until the time of the Roman emperors.

*Late Egyptian* (1370–660 B.C.)

Designation of the spoken language; since the so-called Amarna period it was also used for writing, along with classical Middle Egyptian. It may be assumed that Late Egyptian was spoken earlier than this, toward the end of the Middle Kingdom. Because the scribes were also trained in classical Egyptian, there is often a mixture of old and new language in their writings.

*Demotic* (660 B.C.–A.D. 470)

Designation of later Egyptian in Demotic script (the term "demotic" thus stands for both a type of script and a phase in the development of the language). Demotic was used especially for contracts, deeds, and administration. Gradually Demotic petrified into a purely written language, while the spoken language continued to live on in Coptic (see below section 3.b).

Egyptian literature is important in many re-spects for the study of the Old Testament. According to the Old Testament itself, the early history of Israel as the people of God happened in Egypt. The traditions about the Exodus belong to the oldest strata of the Old Testament. For a large part of the second millennium, Egypt ruled over the land of Canaan. Egyptian annals, lists of Canaanite cities, and especially travel accounts from that period, such as the *Tale of Sinuhe* (ca. 1962 B.C.) and the *Journey of Wen-Amon* (ca. 1076 B.C.), provide valuable information. Mention should also be made of the *"Israel Stele" of Merneptah* (ca. 1219 B.C.) in which the people of Israel are mentioned specifically beside city-states such as Ashkelon and Gezer and the land of the Hurrians (ill. 25). It seems likely that the Egyptian loanwords in the Canaanite languages, including Hebrew, are mainly from this period.

The period from about 1100 to 650 B.C. is sometimes called the Third Intermediate Period. This was a dark episode in the history of the country. Libyans and Nubians occupied the throne and the country was torn by internal dissensions. Canaan was viewed more as a shield against Assyria than as a territory belonging to the Egyptian sphere of influence. The *Journey of Wen-Amon* gives a vivid account of the rough treatment an Egyptian emissary received in Canaan as early as about 1100 B.C. Diplomatic marriages between Egyptian princesses and princes from this formerly despised province (1 Kings 3:1; 11:19) plainly indicate that the power structures had changed considerably. Therefore it is not surprising that not a single Egyptian historical document from this period refers to Israel, which just then, under the judges and kings, experienced a large degree of independence.

The cultural and religious influence of Egypt on Israel is markedly smaller than that of Mesopotamia. This was not only because of the just-mentioned political circumstances. Nor were the geographical and linguistic factors decisive, though they were decidedly in favor of Mesopotamia. More important was that Egypt had always prided itself on its independence from the then known world. This has given Egyptian literature its great but lonely height. The style and genre of Egyptian literature often differ markedly from that found elsewhere. Also, Egyptian religion might be called a chapter by itself. Unfortunately, this means that in the scope of this handbook we have to pass over the nucleus of Egyptian religious literature: the *Pyramid Texts*, the *Sarcophagus Texts*, the *Book of the Dead*, and the *Myth of Osiris*. For those who wish to become familiar with these texts we shall mention recent translations in the bibliography. See ill. 26.

In cases where a direct relationship between Egyptian and Hebrew literature must be rejected on good grounds, it may be possible to point to interesting analogies. One example is the creation through the word, occurring among other places in the so-called *Memphite Theology* (cf. Genesis 1; Isa. 41:4; 44:26–27; 48:13; 50:2; 55:10–11; Ps. 33:6, 9; 148:5; Job 37:5–6). In the so-called *Prophecy of Neferti* one can hear motifs reminiscent of the Old Testament prophets, though obviously the analogies are purely formal.

The similarities between Egyptian and Israelite wisdom literature are striking. The *Instruction of Ptah-hotep*, the *Instruction of Merikare*, the *Instruction of Ani*, the *Instruction of Amenemope* (ill. 27), and similar texts contain proverbs whose purport and even the words themselves agree markedly with the practical wisdom written in Israel. In many cases one can speak of a highly developed ethical and religious awareness. For instance, Merikare is instructed that "The mind of the righteous is more pleasing than the ox of the wicked" (cf. Prov. 15:8; 21:3). Other wisdom texts such as the *Counsels of Ipu-wer* and the *Conversations of One Tired of Life with his Soul* deal with problems taken up in the book of Job. An exhortation to enjoy life while it is still possible is found in the *Song of the Harpist*, whose view of life may be compared with that of the writer of Ecclesiastes (Eccl. 3:12–13; 5:17ff.; 9:7ff.; 11:8ff.). The Egyptian *love songs* are as roguish as those in the Song of Songs (Canticles).

Accustomed as we are to the Psalms, the religious songs of the Egyptians impress us as being rather stiff and formal. This must have something to do with their close connection with magic ritual. Nevertheless, songs such as the *Hymn to the Sun* of Akhenaten, the monotheistic heretical king, in many ways come close to the conceptual world of Old Testament songs of praise such as Psalm 104. Particularly in the period after the Amarna Age, the Egyptians composed songs of deep personal piety. Especially the hymns to Amon-Re, the father and creator of god and man, impress even the modern reader. As an example we give here a number of fragments from the so-called *Stele of the draughtsman Nebre*, who lived in the thirteenth century B.C. (as in *Documents from Old Testament Times*, D. W. Thomas, ed.):

Giving praises to Amun:
I compose hymns to him in his name,[1]
I render him praises to the height of heaven
And to the breadth of earth;[2]
I recount his might to him who sails
   downstream
And to him who sails upstream.

Beware of him![3]
Proclaim him to son and daughter,
To great and small;
Tell of him to generations of generations
Which have not yet come into being.[4]

Tell of him to the fish in the deep,
To the birds in the sky;[5]
Proclaim him to the one who knows him not
And to the one who knows him.[6]

Beware of him!
Thou art Amun, the Lord of the silent man,
One who comes at the cry of a poor man.[7]
Were I to call upon thee when I am ill,
Thou comest, that thou mightest rescue me,[8]
That thou mightest give breath (to) him who
   is weak
And rescue the one who is shut in.[9]
Thou art Amon-Re, Lord of Thebes,
Rescuer of him who is in the underworld.[10]

. . . . . . . . . . . . . . . . . . . . . . . . . . . . . . . . . . . .

The servant was bent on doing wrong,
Yet the Lord is bent on being merciful.[11]
The Lord of Thebes does not spend a whole
   day angry;
As for his anger, in the completion of a
moment nothing is left.[12]

1. See, e.g., Ps. 66:2.
2. Cf., e.g., Pss. 48:11; 57:10–12; 96:1, 11; 148:7, 13.
3. This is reminiscent of the biblical exhortations to fear the Lord, Ps. 34:10; Prov. 3:7; 24:21; etc.
4. Cf. Pss. 22:31–32; 45:18; 48:14; 71:18; 79:13; 89:2; 135:13; and especially 78:1–8.
5. Cf. Ps. 148:7–10.
6. Cf. Jer. 31:34; Pss. 46:11; 100:3.

7. Cf. Ps. 34:7.
8. Cf. Ps. 34:5, 7, 18.
9. Cf. Pss. 18:5-6; 116:3; 119:61.
10. Cf. Pss. 30:4; 49:16; 56:14; 86:13; 89:49, etc.
11. Cf., e.g., Ps. 103:8–11.
12. Cf. Pss. 30:6; 103:9.

The reader of this beautiful Egyptian psalm will no doubt be struck by its strong similarities with the biblical Psalms. This is true not only of the contents but also of the form. The parallelism familiar to us from Israel's poetry is clearly recognizable in this song.

Thus it is especially poetic literature (wisdom sayings, profane and cultic songs) that shows parallels with the Old Testament. As was mentioned earlier, the poetry of Mesopotamia also exhibits these kinds of similarities, and as we shall see, the Canaanites, too, were familiar with this mode of composing poetry. Even today it remains difficult to explain this remarkable phenomenon. Perhaps it goes back to the fact that the poetry of the ancient world, at least in regard to form, was based on the improvisations of poet-singers who like bards moved from place to place. They made use of stereotyped patterns, fixed sentence constructions that were easy to remember and follow. These they made to fit the music, which, as is still true today, is much less bound by national borders than language. Even when poetry was composed in a purely literary manner, the composers patterned themselves after the stereotyped forms of these "bards." This makes it understandable why much poetry in the ancient world was of "professional" quality. Because similar methods were used, similar formulations could readily arise, without the necessity of any direct literary dependency or even similarity in content.

## LITERATURE
### On Egyptian Writing:

H. Brunner, *Hieroglyphische Chrestomathie* (Wiesbaden, 1965).

J. Capart, *Je lis les hieroglyphes* (Brussels, 1968[4]).

J. Černý, *Paper and Books in Ancient Egypt* (London, 1952).

H. Grapow, *Sprachliche und schriftliche For-* *mung ägyptischer Texte* (Glückstadt/New York, 1936).

J. M. A. Janssen, *Hiërogliefen. Over lezen en schrijven in Oud-Egypte* (Leiden, 1952).

H. Kees, et al., *Ägyptische Schrift und Sprache* (Leiden, 1973[2]).

G. Möller, *Hieratische Paläographie* I-III (Osnabrück, 1965[2]).

S. Schott, *Hieroglyphen, Untersuchungen zum Ursprung der Schrift* (Wiesbaden, 1951).

H. Sottas and E. Drioton, *Introduction à l'étude des hiéroglyphes* (Paris, 1922).

### Recommended Literature for the Study of Egyptian:

A. Erman, *Ägyptische Grammatik* (Berlin, 1929; repr. 1972).

A. Erman and H. Grapow, *Ägyptisches Handwörterbuch* (Berlin, 1921; repr. 1961).

_____, *Wörterbuch der ägyptischen Sprache* I–XII (Berlin/Leipzig, 1926–63; repr. 1971).

### Old Egyptian:

E. Edel, *Altägyptische Grammatik* I-II (Rome, 1955–64) (list of citations published by R. Gundlach and R. Schwarzkopf [Rome, 1967]).

### Middle Egyptian:

H. Brunner, *Abriss der mittelägyptischen Grammatik* (Graz, 1967[2]).

A. de Buck, *Grammaire élémentaire du Moyen Égyptien* (Leiden, 1952).

_____, *Egyptian Readingbook* (Leiden, 1970[3]).

J. B. Callender, *Middle Egyptian* (Malibu, 1975).

R. O. Faulkner, *A Concise Dictionary of Middle Egyptian* (Oxford, 1962; repr. 1976).

A. H. Gardiner, *Egyptian Grammar* (London, 1973[3]).

### The Amarna Age:

F. Behnk, *Grammatik der Texte aus el Amarna* (Paris, 1930).

### Late Egyptian:

A. Erman, *Neuägyptische Grammatik* (Leipzig, 1933[2]; repr. 1968).

J. Černý and S. I. Groll, *A Late Egyptian Grammar* (Rome, 1975).

## Demotic:

W. Erichsen, *Demotische Lesestücke* (Leipzig, 1937).

———, *Demotisches Glossar* (Copenhagen, 1954; repr. 1972).

F. Lexa, *Grammaire démotique* (Praha, 1949).

W. Spiegelberg, *Demotische Grammatik* (Heidelberg, 1925).

Recent translations of important categories of texts (see also the literature at the end of the introduction to Chapter III):

## General:

A. Erman, *The Literature of the Ancient Egyptians* (London, 1927).

R. O. Faulkner, et al., *The Literature of Ancient Egypt* (New Haven, 1972).

G. Roeder, *Die ägyptische Religion in Texten und Bildern* I–IV (Zurich, 1959–61).

W. K. Simpson, ed., *The Literature of Ancient Egypt* (New Haven, 1973).

## Literature on the Dead:

P. Barguet, *Le Livre des Morts* (Paris, 1967).

R. O. Faulkner, *The Ancient Egyptian Pyramid Texts* I–II (Oxford, 1969).

———, *The Ancient Egyptian Coffin Texts* I (Warminster, 1973).

J. C. Goyon, *Rituels funéraires de l'ancienne Égypte* (Paris, 1972).

E. Hornung, *Ägyptische Unterweltsbücher* (Zurich, 1972).

## Stories:

J. F. Borghouts, *Egyptische sagen en verhalen* (Bussum, 1974).

E. Brunner-Traut, *Altägyptische Tiergeschichten und Fabel* (Freiburg, 1970³).

## Wisdom:

F. W. von Bissing, *Altägyptische Lebensweisheit* (Zurich, 1955).

I. Grumach, *Untersuchungen zur Lebenslehre des Amenemope* (Munich, 1972).

## Songs:

J. Assmann, *Ägyptische Hymnen und Gebete* (Zurich, 1975).

A. Herrmann, *Altägyptische Liebesdichtung* (Wiesbaden, 1959).

S. Schott, *Altägyptische Liebeslieder* (Zurich, 1950²).

## For an Introduction to the Cultural History of Egypt:

H. Altenmüller, et al., *Ägyptologie: Literatur* (Handbuch der Orientalistik I, Abt. 1/2) (Leiden, 1970²).

J. von Beckerath, *Abriss der Geschichte des alten Ägypten* (Darmstadt, 1971).

H. Brunner, *Grundzüge einer Geschichte der altägyptischen Literatur* (Darmstadt, 1966).

E. Brunner-Traut and V. Hell, *Ägypten. Studien-Reiseführer mit Landeskunde* (Stuttgart, 1966²).

F. Daumas, *La civilisation de l'Égypte pharaonique* (Paris, 1967²).

E. Drioton and J. Vandier, *L'Égypte* (Paris, 1962⁴).

W. Helck, *Die Beziehungen Ägyptens zu Vorderasien im 3. und 2. Jahrtausend v. Chr.* (Wiesbaden, 1971²).

E. Hornung, *Einführung in die Ägyptologie* (Darmstadt, 1967).

E. Otto, *Ägypten. Der Weg des Pharaonenreiches* (Stuttgart, 1966⁴).

W. Wolf, *Kulturgeschichte des alten Ägypten* (Stuttgart, 1962).

## Important Reference Works:

*Annual Egyptological Bibliography*, since 1948 (Leiden).

H. Bonnet, *Reallexikon der ägyptischen Religionsgeschichte* (Berlin, 1971²).

W. Helck and E. Otto, *Kleines Wörterbuch der Ägyptologie* (Wiesbaden, 1970²).

*Lexikon der Ägyptologie* I– (Wiesbaden, 1972– ).

G. Posener, et al., *Dictionnaire de la civilisation égyptienne* (Paris, 1970²).

## Art:

C. Vandersleyen, *Das alte Ägypten* (Propyläen Kunstgeschichte, 15) (Berlin, 1975).

W. Westendorf, *Het Oude Egypte* (Kunst in Beeld) (Amsterdam/Brussels, 1968).

---

# b. Coptic

As we mentioned above, the Egyptians did not take the step from their one-letter signs to an alphabetic system of writing. From the third century B.C. Egyptian had often been transcribed with Greek letter signs, yet these were no more than incidental attempts. At the time of the Ptolemies, in the kingdom of Meroe (now northern Sudan), an alphabet of twenty-three signs was developed from the Demotic script, but that, too, must be regarded as incidental.

The *Coptic* language became much more important. By the third century A.D., the classical art of writing had virtually died out in Egypt. Moreover, the spoken language only barely resembled Demotic Egyptian. Therefore it was decided to write the Egyptian language in Greek characters. From that point on, the language is no longer called Egyptian but Coptic, though this designation is actually no more than a corruption of the Greek *Aigyptios*. Because Greek lacks certain necessary phonemes, seven characters derived from the Demotic script were added.

Soon Coptic became the language of the Christian church in Egypt, which after the Council of Chalcedon (A.D. 451) separated from the Byzantine church.

There are several Coptic dialects, the most important of which are:

(1) *Sahidic.* Used from the third to the tenth century in southern Egypt, it is the classical Coptic language in which most documents are written.

(b) *Subachmimic.* Once spoken in the vicinity of the city of Achmim, linguistically it is the most archaic dialect.

(c) *Bohairic.* Since the eleventh century A.D. the ecclesiastical language of the Copts; by then it was dead as a spoken language, having been replaced long before by Arabic.

The Coptic versions of the Bible are of some significance for textual criticism. There is, however, a much greater interest in the numerous apocryphal books and Gnostic tracts written in Coptic. The research of this kind of writings has in recent years received new impetus through the discovery of no less than thirteen codices from the fourth century A.D. at Nag Hammadi, about 100 kilometers (60 mi.) downstream from Luxor on the Nile. This discovery included a variety of New Testament apocrypha, among which were the *Gospel according to Thomas* (ill. 28) and the *Gospel according to Philip.* Others included the *Gospel of the Truth,* the *Gospel of the Egyptians,* the apocryphal *Acts of the Apostles,* the letters of *James,* and a number of apocryphal *Revelations.*

Though these documents are saturated with the spirit of Gnosticism, they are interesting to biblical scholars because they may contain authentic traditions from the earliest Christian church; according to some scholars they may even contain genuine words of Jesus. At any rate, they do give information about early Christian traditions that were rejected as heretical by the church. For that reason they were rarely passed on and consequently did not become well known. This is true, among others, of the Gnostic school of Valentinus (born ca. A.D. 100).

## LITERATURE

M. Cramer, *Koptische Paläographie* (Wiesbaden, 1964).

W. E. Crum, *A Coptic Dictionary* (Oxford, 1939).

A. Fuchs and F. Weissengruber, *Konkordanz zum Thomasevangelium* (Linz, 1978).

R. Kasser, *Compléments au dictionnaire copte de Crum* (Le Caire, 1964).

————, *Dictionnaire auxiliaire, étymologique et complet de la langue copte,* fasc. 1– (Geneva, 1967– ).

W. Kossack, *Lehrbuch des Koptischen* I–II (Graz, 1974).

J. M. Robinson, ed., *The Nag Hammadi Library in English* (Leiden, 1977).

F. Siegert, *Nag-Hammadi Register* (Tübingen, 1982) (index of important concepts).

R. Smith, *A Concise Coptic-English Lexicon* (Grand Rapids, 1983).

W. C. Till, *Achmimisch-koptische Grammatik* (Leipzig, 1928).

————, *Koptische Dialektgrammatik* (Munich, 1961[2]).

————, *Koptische Grammatik, Saïdischer Dialekt* (Leipzig, 1970[4]).

W. Westendorf, *Koptisches Handwörterbuch,* Number 1 (Heidelberg, 1965– ).

For the ever increasing literature on the new Coptic texts one should refer to D. M. Scholer, *Nag Hammadi Bibliography (1948–1969)* (Leiden, 1971), continued yearly in the periodical *Novum Testamentum* from Vol. 13 (1971). In addition, one can turn to the yearly Coptic bibliography in the periodical *Orientalia*. An overview of Coptic literature also appears from time to time in the periodical *Enchoria*.

---

## 4. ASIA MINOR: HIEROGLYPHICS, CUNEIFORM, AND ALPHABET

### a. Anatolian Languages

Around 2000 B.C. waves of Indo-European tribes invaded Asia Minor. Of the former inhabitants of that area we know little more than that a *Hattic*-speaking people lived in the central highland. Though a developed people, as far as we know the speakers of this agglutinative language were not able to write. Because in later times the Hittites were interested in Hattic religious texts and recorded them, however, some of the Hattic language has been preserved.

The invading Indo-Europeans spoke various dialects, of which the most important are *Palaic, Luwian,* and *Hittite*. In the eighteenth century B.C. the Indo-Europeans developed their own hieroglyphic script. This script, whose details have not been completely deciphered, remained in use to the seventh century B.C. for certain Luwian texts, and thus is called Hieroglyphic Luwian.

Since the middle of the seventeenth century B.C., however, the great majority of texts were written in cuneiform derived from Mesopotamia. Only much later was the alphabet introduced into Anatolia: Old Phrygian texts from the eighth century B.C. and Lydian and Lycian inscriptions from the sixth century B.C.

Most Anatolian cuneiform texts were written in Hittite, between 1650 and 1200 B.C. The archives of Boghazköy (formerly Hattushash; see map III) have yielded an especially large number of tablets. It is remarkable that in addition to Hittite texts a large number of Babylonian tablets were discovered, including copies of literary works. This shows that Hittite culture was strongly influenced by Mesopotamia. Cf. ill. 29.

Though the Hittites do not belong to the Semitic-speaking peoples, and though historically their role was virtually over by about 1200 B.C., Hittite literature is by no means unimportant for the

Old Testament scholar. The religious texts, particularly the rituals and prayers, sometimes provide comparative material that is both literary and religio-historical. A complicating factor is that many Hittite myths and epics are translations or adaptations of literary texts from other peoples. Translations of the Gilgamesh Epic, of Canaanite myths (e.g., about the goddess Asherah), and especially of Hurrian myths (e.g., about the god Kumarbi and the dragon Hedammu) have been found. It is not surprising that this lively interest in other religions resulted in syncretistic tendencies in the Hittite religion.

According to some scholars, the construction of a number of Hittite international contracts exhibits a certain formal similarity with the texts that regulate the covenant between YHWH and his people. This is not surprising, for the Hittite "lawbooks" are entirely in line with the ancient Near Eastern traditions. Here, too, casuistic law is codified. The absence of the *ius talionis* ("an eye for an eye"), which frequently occurs in the Old Testament and in Mesopotamia, is remarkable.

---

### LITERATURE
#### On the Anatolian Languages:

J. Friedrich, et al., *Altkleinasiatische Sprachen* (Handbuch der Orientalistik, I, Abt. 2/2) (Leiden, 1969).

P. H. J. Houwink ten Cate, in J. H. Hospers, ed., *A Basic Bibliography for the Study of the Semitic Languages* I (Leiden, 1973) 84–109.

#### Hittite:

J. Friedrich, *Hethitisches Elementarbuch, I: Kurzgefasste Grammatik* (Heidelberg, 1960²); *II: Lesestücke in Transkription* (Heidelberg, 1967²).

——, *Hethitisches Keilschrift-Lesebuch* I–II (Heidelberg, 1960).

——, *Hethitisches Wörterbuch* (Heidelberg, 1952); 3 Ergänzungshefte (Heidelberg, 1957–66).

—— and A. Kammenhuber, *Hethitisches Wörterbuch*, Lief. 1– (Heidelberg, 1975²– ).

H. A. Hoffner, et al., *The Hittite Dictionary of the Oriental Institute of the University of Chicago* (Chicago, 1980– ).

**Hittite Laws:**

J. Friedrich, *Die hethitischen Gesetze* (Leiden, 1959; repr. 1971).

One important new series of editions (transcription, translation, and commentary) is *Studien zu den Boğazköy-Texten* (Wiesbaden, 1965ff.).

**Some Books on Anatolian Culture:**

A. Goetze, *Kleinasien* (Munich, 1957²).

O. R. Gurney, *The Hittites* (Harmondsworth, 1966, rev. ed.).

A. Kammenhuber, *Die Arier im Vorderen Orient* (Heidelberg, 1968).

Several chapters in *The Cambridge Ancient History* II/1 (Cambridge, 1973) and II/2 (Cambridge, 1975).

---

## b. Hurrian and Urartian

Actually, it is defensible to deal with these languages here only if it is assumed that the designation "Asia Minor" describes a territory that nearly coincides with present-day Turkey. The territory of the Hurrians and Urartians lies for the most part in eastern Turkey (Kurdistan). As early as the Old Akkadian period, fortified Hurrian cities were located here. This was also the area of the Hurrian kingdom of the Mitanni, which grew into one of the most powerful states of the ancient Near East between 1500 and 1350 B.C.

More important, however, than the Hurrian political influence has been their cultural influence. Because of their geographical position they controlled the roads from Mesopotamia to Asia Minor and northern Syria. It appears that they not only made full use of this favorable position in the negative sense, but that they also saw themselves as intermediaries. Hurrians settled in many places in northern Mesopotamia and Syria as merchants, interpreters, scribes, horse breeders, and even as priests.

It appears that they easily adapted themselves to the local situations. Therefore it is not always easy to determine what may properly be called Hurrian. Their influence is clear, however, from the large number of Hurrian loanwords and names in Akkadian (Nuzi), Hittite, and Ugaritic texts.

As far as we know, the Hurrians did not invent a script of their own. The relatively small number of *Hurrian* texts that have been published thus far are written mainly in Babylonian cuneiform or in the Ugaritic alphabet. Almost all these texts are from archives outside the actual territory of Mitanni: Hattushash, Nuzi, Ugarit, Amarna (see map III). It is therefore possible that a native script may have been used in the home country.

Owing to the limited number of available texts, our knowledge of the Hurrian language is still deficient. This much is certain: Hurrian did not resemble any other ancient Near Eastern language except *Urartian*, which was written during the first half of the first millennium B.C. in the same area. Even so, Urartian cannot be directly derived from Hurrian.

Urartu is important for the Old Testament because it was such a troublesome neighbor for the Assyrian kings (see Chapter V). That gave the West a relatively quiet time. The Hurrians are often connected with the Horites who, according to the Bible, played a role already at the time of the patriarchs (see, e.g., Gen. 14:6). Currently the correctness of this identification is in doubt. It is true, however, that in Hurrian milieus such as Nuzi, a number of interesting parallels have been found with customs that the biblical writers place in the period before Israel became a nation.

---

### LITERATURE

F. W. Bush, *A Grammar of the Hurrian Language,* microfilm/xeroxcopy (Ann Arbor/High Wycombe, 1964).

I. M. Diakonoff, *Hurrisch und Urartäisch* (Munich, 1971).

I. J. Gelb, *Hurrians and Subarians* (Chicago, 1944).

V. Haas, et al., *Das hurritologische Archiv* (Berlin, 1975).

P. H. J. Houwink ten Cate, in J. H. Hospers, ed., *A Basic Bibliography for the Study of the Semitic Languages* I (Leiden, 1973) 110–13.

F. Imparati, *I Hurriti* (Firenze, 1964).

B. B. Piotrovsky, *Urartu* (Geneva, 1969).

E. A. Speiser, *Introduction to Hurrian* (New Haven, 1941).

For lexicographical resources see also above under Hittites.

---

## 5. CANAAN: THE ALPHABET

Of the older scripts, particularly cuneiform was used in places that had no written language. Canaan was one of those places. As far as we know, only this script was used in Canaan until the middle of the second millennium B.C. A difficulty, however, was that cuneiform could reproduce the phonemes of the Canaanite languages only poorly. In addition, cuneiform greatly taxed the ability of the scribes, who preferably received their training in Mesopotamia. Therefore it was easier for these writers to translate a text dictated in Canaanite into Babylonian, and in reading it aloud to translate it back into Canaanite, than laboriously to find Babylonian equivalents for Canaanite phonemes.

This was, of course, an unsatisfactory situation, the more so if due to circumstances no experienced scribes were available. This may have been the case with a number of Canaanites who were captured and consigned to forced labor in the turquoise mines in the Sinai by the Egyptians about 1535 B.C. It is not inconceivable that the brilliant inventor of the alphabet may have been among these outcasts. In that case the alphabet was literally born out of need. Some scholars believe that the alphabet was invented simultaneously in other places; so far, however, the Sinai alphabetic texts are the oldest ones that have been discovered. Moreover, it was especially in the Egyptian labor camps that conditions were favorable for the origin of the alphabet. Finally, certain characteristics of later alphabets are hard to explain unless it may be assumed that all go back to the same archetype.

The oldest inscriptions, written in so-called *Proto-Sinaitic*, are from the sixteenth century B.C. It seems likely that the inventor was inspired by the script of his Egyptian masters, especially, of course, the principle of one-letter signs. He also consulted the available hieroglyphics for the shape of certain symbols. It seems that initially he did not completely dissociate himself from the logographic principle (one symbol representing a word of several letters, as is often the case in Egyptian; cf. ill. 30). His great discovery, however, was that the spoken language is composed of a relatively small number of different sounds that recur constantly. This implied a drastic reduction in the number of signs needed to reproduce the language. He became aware that only twenty-seven signs were needed. To facilitate the memorization of these signs, he chose simple pictures in which the first letter of the pictured word represented the phoneme he had in mind (the acrophonic principle). For example, Canaanite *alpu* for ' (Greek *alpha*), *betu* for *b* (Greek *beta*), etc. Presumably we owe our word "alphabet" to the order chosen by this man.

This new, easy-to-learn script was quickly accepted by the small, isolated group of Canaanites in the Sinai. That they were not hindered by a centuries-old writing tradition of their own now turned out to be an advantage. The new invention soon reached the "homeland" Canaan, as is shown by finds at Gezer and Lachish. This somewhat later form of the alphabet is named *Proto-Canaanite.*

That the alphabet was in part based on the consonantal graphemes of the Egyptians may explain why the oldest alphabets do not have vowels. The need for vowels was not immediately felt, for initially the new script was not intended for the recording of important literary works. Its purpose was to provide administrative help, to write addresses and brief dedication inscriptions. Moreover, in the West Semitic languages, to which Canaanite belongs, the meaning of a word is determined more by the consonants, especially those of the so-called "root," than by the vowels. In most cases it is possible to guess the correct pronunciation of a written word.

Even so, the ambiguities inherent in a vowelless alphabet could be overcome only if the written text were read by someone who had at least a general knowledge of the content. Even in the cases of letters, however, this was not an overriding objection because in those days a (brief) letter was always carried by a messenger who was familiar with the content. Usually he gave his message orally before handing over the letter.

The disadvantage of a vowelless script continued in later forms of the West Semitic alphabet. Whatever helps were devised, for instance, the introduction of the so-called *matres lectionis* (consonants used as vowels), only the oral tradition of the text could guarantee completely correct interpretation of the text. Especially when the great literary works began to be recorded, this became a problem. A correct reading is most important in religious literature. But centuries had to pass before the next logical step was taken. This was done when the Greeks added the most frequently occurring vowels to the alphabet. Thereby they gave certain Semitic consonants a new function; for instance, the sign for *ayin*, ', a sound not found in Greek, was used for *o*. It was not until the Middle Ages that systems were devised for adding vowels to Semitic languages such as Hebrew, Arabic, and Syriac. Because the consonantal text had to remain unchanged, these systems never amounted to much more than a makeshift solution. Moreover, in many cases it is a question whether the correct vowels were added. For further information regarding these attempts at vocalization, see the section below on the Hebrew language by J. Hoftijzer.

The development of the West Semitic alphabet was greatly influenced by its basic simplicity. Many could learn to write it in a relatively short time, and initially little time was spent on good handwriting. Under the pressure of wanting to write faster, the shape of the signs became more simple (ill. 31). A second factor that had a great impact on the evolution of the alphabetic signs was the material used for writing. The intensive trade between the Levant and Egypt made it easy to introduce papyrus from the Nile Delta. For this commerce the Phoenician city of Byblos often served as a transit harbor; hence this city gave its name to familiar words such as "Bible" and "bibliography." Papyrus was chosen because it was so much lighter than the clay tablets known from Mesopotamia. Later, leather was also used. Reed pens, fine brushes, and ink required an altogether different way of writing than the stylus of the Babylonians.

Unfortunately, documents of organic material are much less durable than baked clay tablets. They can be erased, burned, and are subject to decay. That the climate of Syria and Palestine is in most places so unfavorable that papyrus and leather soon decay in the ground was not considered a serious drawback in antiquity. As a consequence, however, almost no written texts have been found in excavations. Only inscriptions on monuments and brief notations on potsherds or metal have been able to withstand the ravages of time. So far not a single manuscript of the West Semitic literature, including the books of the Old Testament, has been found that is older than about the second century B.C.

The vulnerability of the writing material must have been one of the reasons why, toward the end of the second millennium B.C. (i.e., shortly after the invention of the alphabet), several attempts were made to write on clay. The most successful attempt was made in Ugarit (see section 5.a below), but in *Deir Alla* (Jordan), too, a Dutch archeological expedition led by Dr. H. J. Franken discovered three clay tablets with an alphabetic script that thus far has not yet been satisfactorily deciphered. Other more durable materials were also tried. At Izbet Sartah, 15 kilometers (10 mi.) east of Tel Aviv, potsherds were found in which a pupil had scratched the alphabet. The excavators date these pieces about 1200 B.C. and assume that there is reason to believe that the pupil was an Israelite. Also, the text of the Gezer calendar was scratched into durable material (limestone). Nevertheless, all these attempts led nowhere because papyrus and small brushes were so much easier to handle.

About 1100 B.C. a kind of standardization was introduced into the alphabet. The number of characters was set at twenty-two, and the linear shape and slant of the signs were slowly being fixed (ill. 35). Of course, further development could not be stopped; locally all sorts of variants arose through the centuries. Though experts distinguish between two or three large categories—namely, *Phoenician, Aramaic,* and, according to some, *Old Hebrew* letter types—and in these groupings a great number of stages of evolution are said to be found, one has to be careful with such classifications, all the more so if a very precise dating is proposed exclusively on the basis of the form of the characters. Wherever necessary, we will pay attention to the later development of the alphabet in our discussion of the separate languages.

## LITERATURE

For some literature on the development of the alphabet see first of all section A.1 above. In addition, one should be aware of the following:

W. F. Albright, *The Proto-Sinaitic Inscriptions and Their Decipherment* (Cambridge, Mass., 1966).

F. M. Cross, "The Origin and Early Evolution of the Alphabet," *Eretz-Israel* 8 (1967) 8ff.

P. Kyle McCarter, "The Early Diffusion of the Alphabet," *Biblical Archaeologist* 37 (1974) 54ff.

A. F. Rainey, "Notes on Some Proto-Sinaitic Inscriptions," *Israel Exploration Journal* 25 (1975) 106ff.

W. Röllig, "Die Alphabetschrift," in U. Hausmann, ed., *Allgemeine Grundlagen der Archäologie* (Munich, 1969), pp. 289ff.

K. R. Veenhof, "Nogmaals 'Van Beitel tot Penseel,'" *Phoenix* 19 (1973) 284ff.

Several works of a general nature in the area of West Semitic inscriptions:

G. A. Cooke, *A Text-book of North-Semitic Inscriptions* (Oxford, 1903).

*Corpus Inscriptionum Semiticarum* (Paris, 1881– ).

R. Degen, W. W. Müller, and W. Röllig, *Neue Ephemeris für semitische Epigraphik* I- (Wiesbaden, 1972- ).

H. Donner and W. Röllig, *Kanaanäische und aramäische Inschriften* I–III (Wiesbaden, 1966–69²).

J. C. L. Gibson, *Textbook of Syrian Semitic Inscriptions* I–III (Oxford, 1971–82).

C.-F. Jean and J. Hoftijzer, *Dictionnaire des inscriptions sémitiques de l'ouest* (Leiden, 1963).

## a. Ugaritic

Since 1929 hundreds of clay tablets inscribed with an alphabetic script have been found in excavations at Ras Shamra (Ugarit), a tell about 12 kilometers (7 mi.) north of Latakia on the Syrian coast (map II). H. Bauer, E. Dhorme, and Ch. Virolleaud soon succeeded in deciphering this script. The tablets turned out to have been written between 1400 and 1200 B.C. in the ancient city of Ugarit.

The Ugaritic alphabet was not an independent invention. The inventor of the script must have been familiar with an older alphabet, presumably a form of the Proto-Canaanite alphabet that was derived from the Proto-Sinaitic script. This presupposition is based on the number of letters (27, to which the Ugaritic inventor added 3), the apparently already fixed order of the letters, as well as the shape of certain characters (ill. 32). The international trade city of Ugarit used Babylonian cuneiform mainly for everyday purposes, such as lists of goods delivered and personnel. That script always required the services of a trained scribe. Toward the beginning of the fourteenth century B.C. one of these scribes must have perceived the advantages of the recently invented alphabet. The use of this novelty would make it possible for people with little schooling to read such things as lists. It would also make it possible to record religious texts in their native tongue, something that had been possible only defectively in cuneiform.

The scribe, trained as he was in Babylonian, also perceived keenly the advantages of cuneiform over the alphabet. The durability of the clay tablets was a great advantage, even more because this writing material was widely used and would continue to be used, for it would not be in the interest of international trade to give up the use of Babylonian, the lingua franca of that time. Therefore our hypothetical scribe decided to adapt the shape of the characters of the alphabet for writing on clay. He constructed the characters out of the same wedges used in Babylonian cuneiform. In the process he worked fairly systematically, though in many cases he tried to approximate the shapes of the Proto-Canaanite alphabetical characters.

He introduced still another innovation in this Proto-Canaanite alphabet, probably suggested to him by cuneiform. To overcome, at least in part, the lack of vowels he introduced three syllabic signs. The sign for *aleph* he used for *aleph + a* (*'a*) or *a + aleph* (*a'*). He also devised signs for *'i/i'* and *'u/u'*. Later the scribes of Ugarit sometimes used these signs as genuine vowels, that is, without reckoning with the *aleph*.

The third Ugaritic addition to the alphabet is likely connected with the presence of a large group of Hurrians in Ugarit. The extra sign *ś*, apparently a phoneme closely resembling that of *s*, is found especially in Hurrian loanwords. Interestingly, however, the sign is absent in the alphabetically written Hurrian texts from Ugarit.

As far as we know today, the Ugaritic alphabet did not spread much beyond the kingdom of Ugarit. Isolated discoveries of Ugaritic inscriptions have been made at various localities in Canaan (on Mount Tabor, at Beth-shemesh, Taanach, Kadesh, Sarepta, Aphek), but not too much may be deduced from that. Furthermore, all these texts are written in a shorter alphabet than the Ugaritic. For example, the signs for *'i* and *'u* are lacking. In Ugarit itself, too, some texts have been discovered written in this shorter alphabet. Though there are various explanations for this variant, it was most likely a *later* development. Certain letters dropped out because the phonemes for which they stood disappeared from the spoken language. We see the same thing happening in the contemporary linear alphabet, which apparently no longer needed some of the signs that were still present in the Proto-Sinaitic alphabet. Precisely the fact that at that time the linear alphabet started its irresistible advance may also explain why in the abbreviated Ugaritic alphabet the syllabic *aleph* signs were again abandoned. For this innovation did not fit the usual spelling, which was adapted to a purely consonantal alphabet.

It has proved difficult to classify the Ugaritic *language*. Though it is certain that Ugaritic belongs to the same group of (North) West Semitic languages to which Phoenician and Hebrew belong, there are remarkable differences. In part the explanation may well be that we possess insuffi-cient comparative material of the same age as the Ugaritic documents. Nevertheless, there appear to be enough reasons to classify Ugaritic as a Canaanite language. The affinity between Ugaritic and Hebrew is very important for the deepening of our insight into the history of the Hebrew language. More than once Ugaritic has also proved useful in clarifying linguistic problems in the text of the Old Testament. Research in this area is still going on; as happens more often with a new discovery, enthusiasm sometimes takes the upper hand so that it is all too readily concluded that a certain grammatical peculiarity also occurs in Ugaritic. It is important to be careful with the linguistic comparisons with Ugaritic, which are even found in commentaries on the Old Testament that are intended for the general public.

The literary texts of Ugarit show that Hebrew poetry was quite similar to Canaanite traditions, which in turn go back to the principles by which all ancient Near Eastern poetry was guided. Precisely because of the close linguistic affinity, the formal similarities between Ugaritic and Hebrew poetry are undeniably significant. Frequently the same words are found in parallel construction, identical figures of speech are employed, and the rhythmic structures of the verses hardly differ.

By far the most important contribution, however, is the religious information provided by the Ugaritic documents. Apart from sparse information in classical authors and some data that could be deduced from later Canaanite inscriptions, until 1930 scholars were mainly dependent on the Old Testament for their knowledge of the religion of the Canaanites. But precisely because the Old Testament was so fiercely opposed to the worship of the Baals, it was difficult to obtain a good picture of Canaanite religion. This is where the Ugaritic discoveries have been very helpful. What has also been learned is that the relationship between Israel and its neighbors was more complex than is suggested by the Old Testament. Israelite religion did not develop in the strict isolation that was the ideal of the Deuteronomist and his followers. The Israelites were fairly well acquainted with the religious literature of the Canaanites (cf. ill. 34). It is even certain that some elements in Israel's religion were taken over from the Canaanite religion. It should be added immediately, however, that the content of such derived terms and images was in most cases radically altered in Israel. See ill. 33.

Unfortunately, in getting to know the Ugaritic material, one is hampered by various circumstances. The difficulty begins already in referring to the texts. So far there is no unanimity about the best way of numbering the tablets, with the result that many systems are being used simultaneously. Regrettably, even the latest system, that of Dietrich, Loretz, and Sanmartin, is open to serious criticism. A second problem is the lack of satisfactory editions of the texts, even though the most recent edition, prepared by the above-mentioned scholars, does something to meet the need. A third problem concerns the linguistic interpretations of the texts. Comparing various translations of the same Ugaritic text, one soon notices considerable differences. These differences are due in part to the fact that Ugaritology is still a young discipline; in part they are also caused by fundamental differences in approach, however. For these reasons it is strongly recommended that the first steps in this field be made under the guidance of experts.

The most important literary texts from Ugarit are the following: (1) The *Myth of the Seasons* or the *Baal cycle*. To this belong at least three tablets (numbered 4, 5, 6 in Herdner's edition), but according to many three additional tablets (1, 2, 3 in Herdner's edition) as well. Read in the 3-1-2-4-5-6 sequence, these tablets would describe chronologically the mythological prototypes of the climatological, agrarian, and cultic events that normally took place in Ugarit in the course of a year. While formally giving an account of what happened in prehistoric times, the poet intended to explain why it is that the seasons follow each other with a fixed regularity. Just as in our ecclesiastical year the life of Jesus is always being actualized in a short span of time, so in the cult of Ugarit the prehistoric times, recorded in the *Myth of the Seasons*, were actualized. It should be added, however, that not all specialists subscribe to the seasonal interpretation of the tablets.

The chief character of the myth is Baal, the youthful god of rain and fertility. He is assisted by his consort Anat, who is not only goddess of love but also of war and hunting. His counterparts are Yam, the god of the sea, and Mot, the god of death. Both are sons of the old god El, the head of the Ugaritic pantheon. Baal's triumphs and defeats mirror the course of the seasons. From the perspective of the history of religion, his death (the beginning of the dry summer) and resuscitation (the beginning of the wet autumn) are particularly important; these episodes are dealt with elaborately in the myth. They were also known among other Canaanites outside Ugarit.

(2) The *Legend of King Keret*. The text deals with the tragic history of King Keret (others vocalize Kirtu or Kuritu), who was probably regarded as one of the ancestors of the Ugaritic dynasty. After many unhappy marriages, Keret, directed in a dream by the god El, acquires a new wife for himself. She gives him many sons and daughters. But at this peak of his happiness Keret falls seriously ill because he failed to honor a promise to the goddess Asherah. When against all expectations he recovers, his oldest son rises up against him. This forces Keret to curse his own child. Unfortunately, the story breaks off at this point. But there is reason to believe that in one way or another Keret also loses all his other children except the youngest girl, who in this way unexpectedly becomes the firstborn.

(3) The *Legend of Aqhat*. King Daniel does not have a son and is terribly sad about it. At the intercession of Baal, El gives him an heir whom he names Aqhat. On a certain day Daniel gets a miraculous bow. He gives this weapon to Aqhat, who successfully uses it in hunting. This arouses the jealousy of Anat, the hunting goddess. She promises Aqhat everything, including eternal life, if only he will give her the bow. Initially he turns a deaf ear to the proposal, even answering the goddess rudely. In so doing he signs his own death sentence. Anat has him assassinated by a helper. Only much later does Daniel learn of the murder of his only son. Naturally he is inconsolable. It is possible that Daniel's sister avenged him. In a few fragmentary tablets we see Daniel active in calling up the spirits of the dead in order that in this manner he may see his son again.

In every one of the three texts mentioned, the poet wrestles with such problems as human sin and mortality on the one hand, and the arbitrariness and impotence of gods who mutually oppose each other on the other. In every one we encounter a somber, fatalistic view on life. Besides these, other texts of a lighter genre have been found in Ugarit, in which eroticism and excessive drinking are dominant themes. These reflect the Baal religion against which Israel's prophets warned. It is, however, entirely obvious that such frivolity was not the only theme. Apparently, at the time of Israel's entrance into the promised land, there were also doubters among the Canaanites who dared to ask questions that were no longer answered by their religion.

## LITERATURE
### For Bibliographic Information See:

M. Dietrich, et al., *Ugarit-Bibliographie 1928–1966* I–IV (Neukirchen, 1973).

J. P. Lettinga in J. H. Hospers, ed., *A Basic Bibliography for the Study of the Semitic Languages* I (Leiden, 1973) 127–45.

A brief overview of the finds from Ras Shamra and their significance is given by A. S. Kapelrud, "Ugarit," in *Interpreter's Dictionary of the Bible* IV (Nashville, 1962) 724–32; J. C. de Moor, "Ugarit," in *Interpreter's Dictionary of the Bible, Supplementary Volume* (Nashville, 1976), pp. 928–31; and P. C. Craigie, *Ugarit and the Old Testament* (Grand Rapids, 1983). See also L. R. Fisher, ed., *Ras Shamra Parallels* I–III (Rome, 1972–81).

A volume with most of the alphabetical texts is: M. Dietrich, O. Loretz, and J. Sanmartin, *Die keilalphabetischen Texte aus Ugarit*, I– (Neukirchen, 1976– ).

This work should be compared with older studies, which are given with their diverse enumerations of the texts in:
M. Dietrich and O. Loretz, *Konkordanz der ugaritischen Textzahlungen* (Neukirchen, 1972).

A very good textbook is:
C. H. Gordon, *Ugaritic Textbook* I–III (Rome, 1965).

No complete lexicon is presently available. For an overview of lexicographical studies, see J. C. de Moor, "Ugaritic Lexicography," in P. Fronza-

roli, ed., *Studies on Semitic Lexicography* (Firenze, 1973), pp. 61–102; see also the work of Dietrich, Loretz, and Sanmartin cited above.

### Concordance:

R. E. Whitaker, *A Concordance of the Ugaritic Literature* (Cambridge, Mass., 1972).

A recent and overall good translation of the literary texts is:
A. Caquot, M. Sznycer, and A. Herdner, *Textes ougaritiques, I: Mythes et Legendes* (Paris, 1974). See also M. D. Coogan, *Stories from Ancient Canaan* (Philadelphia, 1978); J. C. L. Gibson, *Canaanite Myths and Legends* (Edinburgh, 1978[2]).

A specialized annual journal is *Ugarit-Forschungen* (since 1969).

## b. Phoenician and Punic

As we know from the Old Testament itself, in the first millennium B.C. the territory north of Israel was ruled over by Tyre and Sidon. As a rule, the inhabitants of that region called themselves after those cities. Sometimes they used the more general term "Canaanite." Following the practice of the Greeks and the Romans, however, we are accustomed to speak of "Phoenicians." This name is derived from the Greek word for "purple," the manufacture of which was one of the most important industries in this area. Later the Romans corrupted the name "Phoenician" to "Punic"; that term referred especially to the Phoenician residents of Carthage and other trade settlements in the western part of the Mediterranean Sea region.

In philology it has become customary to make the same distinction between Phoenician as the language of the home country and Punic as the language of the trade colonies. In reality the languages overlap somewhat grammatically. Moreover, some inscriptions exhibit peculiarities that are thought to indicate a "dialect." For these reasons scholars have not yet been able to agree on a further subdivision of Phoenician and Punic.

Phoenician texts may be of varying ages; they may be old, such as texts from Byblos from the eleventh century B.C., or young, such as texts from the Roman era. Texts that may be designated

"Punic" go no further back than the fifth or sixth century B.C.

The Phoenician alphabet of twenty-two consonants (cf. ill. 35) bears a great resemblance to the Old Hebrew alphabet. To the extent that we are able to judge on the basis of the unvocalized script, the language also shows great affinity with Hebrew. Both languages are reckoned to the same language family. Some important differences should, however, be mentioned. For example, segholization is mostly absent (*malk* > Hebrew *melek*). The feminine ending -*at* does not change to -*ah* in the absolute state, as in Hebrew. The pronouns have deviating forms, for instance, *mnm*, "something," and the -*y* suffix for the third person masculine singular. The active causative stem of the verb is not *Hiphil* but *Yiphil*.

The Phoenicians undoubtedly continued the literary traditions of the older Canaanite nations. Classical authors often mention Phoenician books, some of which have even been translated. Philo of Byblos (1st century A.D.) translated an important work on Phoenician religion into Greek. The Phoenician author was a certain Sanchuniathon, who supposedly lived in the ninth century B.C.

Other reasons, too, such as literary sentence constructions and allusions to mythological imagery, suggest that the Phoenicians must have had a rich literature. Unfortunately, since most of it was written on papyrus, hardly anything of it has been preserved. Our knowledge of the language is virtually limited to inscriptions in stone: epitaphs, commemorative stones, dedication texts, and a few cultic regulations. In addition, a few inscriptions on metal and in ivory should be mentioned, besides some ostraca. The majority of these texts are from northern Africa. Thus far only about a hundred of these epigraphical documents have been discovered in the Phoenician home country. It is obvious that the content of these texts, since they are mainly of a dedicatory and official nature, is fairly monotonous and does not provide a good picture of the literary ability of the Phoenicians. Only the inscriptions from kings occasionally contain more historical information. This means that the importance of Phoenician and Punic for the Old Testament is limited. One can, however, point to similar names, expressions, and figures of speech; these inscriptions also offer some interesting information on the history of the Canaanite religion (cf. ill. 36, 37).

---

## LITERATURE
### Bibliography:

K. R. Veenhof, in J. H. Hospers, ed., *A Basic Bibliography for the Study of the Semitic Languages* I (Leiden, 1973) 146–71. See also pp. 308–33 of the grammar by Segert cited below.

### Script:

J. B. Peckham, *The Development of the Late Phoenician Scripts* (Cambridge, Mass., 1968).

Textbooks, commentaries, etc.: see the literature above under section 5: works of a general nature in the area of West Semitic inscriptions.

### Grammar:

A. van den Branden, *Grammaire phénicienne* (Beyouth, 1969).

J. Friedrich, *Phönizisch-punische Grammatik* (Rome, 1970²).

Z. Harris, *A Grammar of the Phoenician Language* (New Haven, 1936).

S. Segert, *A Grammar of Phoenician and Punic* (Munich, 1976).

### Lexicons:

M. J. Fuentes Estanol, *Vocabulaire Fenico* (Barcelona, 1980).

R. S. Tomback, *A Comparative Semitic Lexicon of the Phoenician and Punic Languages* (Missoula, Montana, 1978).

---

### c. Hebrew

This paragraph will be limited to the discussion of the evolution of the Hebrew script and the epigraphy. The history of the language of the Old Testament will be taken up by Dr. Hoftijzer in a separate section below.

At an early stage the Israelites must have taken over the alphabet. It is not inconceivable that already during their wanderings in the desert they became acquainted with the Proto-Sinaitic script.

According to the Old Testament, leaders such as Moses (Exod. 17:14; 24:4; Num. 5:23) and Joshua (Josh. 24:26; cf. 8:32) were able to write. Judges 8:14 contains the incidental information that a young man of Succoth who had been captured was able to write the names of seventy-seven men. This presupposes a widespread acquaintance with the art of writing, something that was possible only with the use of the alphabet.

Thus far excavations have not yielded alphabetical texts that are undoubtedly Hebrew and are older than the tenth century B.C. The oldest find is the so-called Gezer calendar (ill. 38), presumably written by a pupil at the time of King Solomon when Gezer was an Israelite city (1 Kings 9:16). The young man seems to be answering questions about the importance for agriculture of certain astronomical or meteorological phenomena.

Its two months are ingathering;
[middle of Sept.—middle of Nov.]
Its two months are sowing;
[middle of Nov.—middle of Jan.]
Its two months are late sowing;
[middle of Jan.—middle of March]
Its month is cutting of flax;
[middle of March—middle of April]
Its month is harvest of barley;
[middle of April—middle of May]
Its month is harvest (of wheat) and measuring;
[middle of May—middle of June]
Its two months are watching (the fruit);
[middle of June—middle of Aug.]
Its month is summer fruit (harvest).
[middle of Aug.—middle of Sept.]

It is obvious that this text is highly significant for our knowledge of the agrarian year in ancient Israel. But script and language, too, deserve our attention. The writer makes use of a variant of the linear Phoenician alphabet, yet it is clear that this alphabet was not made for the writing of Hebrew. It lacks a number of phonemes that apparently were absent from Phoenician but not from Old Hebrew. The word for "barley" is spelled with *sh* (*shin*). The verb *zmr*, "watch," is spelled with a *z*, just like the archaic Hebrew word *zimrah*, "protection," whereas later *shmr*

was used. This may be an indication that the oldest Hebrew still had the phoneme *dh*, for which, however, there was no character in the Phoenician alphabet.

According to many, from the ninth century a separate typical *Old Hebrew* script began to be developed. Others maintain that it is very difficult to say how this script, in this early period, may have differed from, for example, the contemporary Phoenician or Moabite script. In part this difference in viewpoint can be attributed to the small number of available documents, for in Israel, too, the main writing material was papyrus. Except for an occasional fragment, all the texts written on this material have perished.

It is certain that as time progressed the Old Hebrew script assumed more and more cursive forms. This happened because the writing was mostly done with a reed pen and ink. The quick, cursive script of trained writers can especially be seen on *ostraca*, pieces of pottery inscribed with brief notations. Famous collections of ostraca have been found in Samaria, Arad, and Lachish (ill. 39). The cursive script continued to be used when the writing was done on stone. This can be seen, for instance, in the *Siloam inscription*, discovered accidentally in 1880 in the tunnel that carried the water from Spring Gihon to the pool of Siloam in Jerusalem (ill. 40). The inscription records the moment when the break in the rock wall was made. Work crews had been cutting through the rock simultaneously from both directions, a remarkable engineering feat for those days:

(. . .) cutting through. And this is the story of how they cut through: While the hewers, working toward each other, were still swinging their pickaxes, and while there were still three cubits to be cut through, there was heard the voice of a man calling to his fellow. For from both the right and the left side progress was made in the rock. And on the day of the cutting through, the hewers cut toward each other, axe against axe; and the water flowed from the spring toward the reservoir for 1,200 cubits. And the height of the rock above the heads of the hewers was 100 cubits.

The elegant shape of the letters points to a trained writer, and it must be assumed that the inscription was made by order of the authorities. Most likely it was Hezekiah who had the tunnel hewn out (cf. 2 Kings 20:20; 2 Chron. 32:30; Sir. 48:19). His name is not mentioned, however. And though the text betrays some justified pride about the achievement, there is none of the bragging with which other rulers in the ancient Near East claimed for themselves the honor for similar tasks ordered by them.

The remaining epigraphical material in the Old Hebrew script consists mainly of brief inscriptions on seals and vessels. This material is important for our knowledge of old Israelite names.

Until the fifth century B.C. the Old Hebrew script was generally used. After that, when the Aramaic language began to take over (see section 5.e below), the Aramaic script gradually began to prevail. Nevertheless, certain conservative groups kept using the Old Hebrew script for particular purposes. Coins from the period of the Maccabees, even as late as from the years after the revolt of Bar Kochba (A.D. 132–135), still bear the old characters. The Zadokite priests at Qumran had some manuscripts of the Pentateuch made in Old Hebrew letters. In other manuscripts they had the name of God (YHWH) written in the Old Hebrew script. These should not be interpreted as conscious attempts to reintroduce the old script. Rather it is similar to the custom, occasionally still practiced today, of writing Bible verses or name plaques in "old-fashioned" German letters.

One group remained faithful to the Old Hebrew script. These were the Samaritans, who in the third or second century B.C. separated from the Jews. This sect still makes use of a more developed form of the Old Hebrew script, be it only for religious texts, especially of course for the preparation of manuscripts of the Samaritan Pentateuch.

From the above it follows that the books of the Old Testament, or at least their forerunners, were passed on for many centuries in a script that differed considerably from the current square Hebrew script. It so happens that in the Old Hebrew script certain letters are easily confused that in the square script do not look at all alike, for example, *bet, resh,* and *dalet; yod* and *he; kaph, mem,* and *nun.* Unfortunately, Old Testament

textual criticism still does not take this sufficiently into account.

Though used as early as the fifth century for Jewish documents in the Aramaic language, it was the third century B.C. before the official Aramaic script, which was definitely simpler than the Old Hebrew script, came to be so commonly used that Hebrew texts and even biblical scrolls were written in it. Then at an early stage a special Jewish variant of the Aramaic script developed. From Matthew 5:18 we learn that already in Jesus' day it was customary for the Bible to be written in this script, for in the Old Hebrew script the *yod* is certainly not the smallest letter of the alphabet. The oldest fragments of the Old Testament discovered thus far, parts of the books of Exodus and Samuel, were already written in the Jewish Aramaic script. They were found among the manuscripts of Qumran (the Dead Sea Scrolls) and are probably from the second half of the third century B.C. Particularly owing to the wealth of younger manuscripts in the caves near that same Qumran, in the Wadi Murabba'at, and in the fortress of Masada, we know that there has been a slow evolution from the somewhat compressed form of the Jewish Aramaic script to the more or less square form of the familiar Hebrew square script. Old Testament textual criticism has to be very much aware of this gradual development, too. A look at illustration 41, for instance, shows that in the Jewish Aramaic script of the second century B.C., *aleph* and *het, waw* and *yod, kaph* and *pe* could easily be interchanged, something that would not happen so easily in the later square script.

Not until the ninth century A.D. did the Jewish calligraphers reach the letter form that has been in general use ever since, despite the fact that the various Jewish communities in the Dispersion later added their own refinements. With a not altogether correct but yet descriptive name, this script is called the *Hebrew square script* (ill. 58).

The Qumran finds, already mentioned above, are of great importance for our knowledge of the Intertestamental Period. The Essene sect, which had withdrawn to this place in the desert of Judah on the northwestern shore of the Dead Sea about A.D. 68, hid its extensive library in the caves around the settlement. It is likely that already in the Middle Ages a small part of these documents was discovered. They passed into the hands of another Jewish sect, the Karaites, who copied some of the manuscripts for their own purposes. Most of the Qumran scrolls and fragments, however, came to light between 1947 and 1967, having been relatively well preserved through the ages by the dry desert climate. For the most beautiful scrolls the nation of Israel built a special museum, the *hekal ha-sepher* (Shrine of the Book) in Jerusalem.

In addition to the earlier-mentioned biblical manuscripts, parts of numerous apocryphal and pseudepigraphal books have been discovered, including Jubilees, Tobit, Enoch, Testaments of the Twelve Patriarchs, and Jesus ben Sirach. Most of these books were well known, but not, or only in part, in the original Hebrew (or Aramaic) version. This indicates, too, that at least for the Essene sect, the canon of the Old Testament contained more than thirty-nine books. In contrast, thus far not a trace of the book of Esther has been found at Qumran.

Besides these sacred scriptures, the community of Qumran composed an extensive body of literature. *Commentaries* on a variety of biblical books show how the community applied the Scriptures and so legitimized itself. *The Manual of Discipline* prescribed to the members how they were to conduct themselves. A scroll of *Hymns* is composed for the most part of Bible passages. Some texts elaborately describe the messianic and apocalyptic expectations of the sect, for example, *The War Scroll,* which describes the final battle between the children of light and the children of darkness (cf. Luke 16:8; John 12:36; Eph. 5:8; 1 Thess. 5:5). Part of this sectarian literature is probably the work of the Teacher of Righteousness, the probable organizer of the sect.

Although the language of most of the scrolls is Hebrew, some are in Aramaic (see section 5.e below). As far as the Hebrew is concerned, Qumran Hebrew differs somewhat from the language of the Old Testament. These differences agree in part with those of the language of the Mishna, a collection of rabbinic statements compiled about A.D. 225, which belongs to the recognized religious traditions of official Judaism and which for that reason alone would be important for biblical studies. From about the same time are the *Tosefta*

(additions to the Mishna) and the *Tannaitic Midrashim* (commentaries on Exodus–Deuteronomy). All this later Hebrew is often subsumed under the name *Middle Hebrew*. In Qumran as well as among the rabbis, Middle Hebrew was used mainly for religious purposes. The regular spoken language was likely a Hebraically colored Aramaic.

---

## LITERATURE
### History of the Hebrew Script:

S. A. Birnbaum, *The Hebrew Scripts* I–II (London, 1954–71).

**Hebrew Inscriptions:**
See the Bibliography under Section 5 Above. In Addition:

D. Diringer, *Le iscrizioni antico-ebraiche palestinesi* (Firenze, 1934).

*Inscriptions Reveal,* Israel Museum (Jerusalem, 1973).

H. Michaud, *Sur la pierre et l'argile* (Neuchâtel/Paris, 1958).

S. Moscati, *L'epigrafia ebraica antica 1935–1950* (Rome, 1951).

D. Pardee, et al., *Handbook of Ancient Hebrew Letters* (Chico, 1982).

**Apocrypha, Pseudepigrapha, and Qumran Writings:**

M. A. Beek, *Inleiding in de Joodse apocalyptiek van het Oud-en Nieuw-Testamentisch tijdvak* (Haarlem, 1950).

C. Burchard, *Bibliographie zu den Handschriften vom Toten Meer* I–II (Berlin, 1959[2], 1965).

J. A. Fitzmyer, *The Dead Sea Scrolls. Major Publications and Tools for Study* (Missoula, 1975).

B. Jongeling, *A Classified Bibliography of the Finds in the Desert of Judah, 1958–1969* (Leiden, 1971).

W. S. LaSor, *Bibliography of the Dead Sea Scrolls 1948–1957* (Pasadena, 1958).

*Qumran-Handschriften* (Heidelberg, 1971).

L. Rost, *Einleitung in die alttestamentlichen Apokryphen und Pseudepigraphen, einschliesslich der Grossen Qumran-Handschriften* (Heidelberg, 1971).

See also the bibliography published in consecutive issues of the specialized periodical *Revue de Qumran* (since 1958).

## Mishna:

C. Albeck, *Einführung in die Mischna* (Berlin/New York, 1971).

G. Beer, K. H. Rengstorf, et al., *Die Mischna* I– (Giessen/Berlin, 1912– ) (text, translation, commentary).

P. Blackmann, *Mishnayoth* I–VII (New York, 1965³) (text, translation, commentary).

H. Danby, *The Mishnah* (Oxford, 1954⁶) (translation, commentary).

J. Neusner, *The Modern Study of the Mishnah* (Leiden, 1973).

## Tosefta:

G. Kittel, K. H. Rengstorf, et al., *Die Tosefta* (Stuttgart, 1933– ) (translation, commentary).

M. S. Zuckermandel, *Tosephta* (Jerusalem, 1963³).

### Tannaitic Midrashim:

L. Finkelstein, *Siphre zu Deuteronomium* (Breslau, 1935–39) (text, commentary).

G. Kittel, K. H. Rengstorf, et al., *Tannaitische Midraschim* (Stuttgart, 1933– ) (translation, commentary).

J. Z. Lauterbach, *Mekilta de Rabbi Ishmael* I–III (Philadelphia, 1949) (on Exodus; text, translation, commentary).

J. Winter, *Sifra-Halachischer Midrasch zu Leviticus* (Breslau, 1938) (translation, commentary).

### Middle Hebrew:

G. H. Dalman, *Aramäisch-neuhebräisches Handwörterbuch zu Targum, Talmud und Midrasch* (Göttingen, 1938³; repr. Hildesheim, 1967).

M. Jastrow, *A Dictionary of the Targumim, the Talmud Babli and Yerushalmi, and the Midrashic Literature* I–II (New York, 1886–1903; repr. 1950).

K. G. Kuhn, ed., *Konkordanz zu den Qumrantexten* (Göttingen, 1960) (Supplement: *Revue de Qumran* 4 [1963–64] 163–234).

————, ed., *Rückläufiges Hebräisches Wörterbuch* (Göttingen, 1958).

J. Levy, *Wörterbuch über die Talmudim und Midraschim* I–IV (Berlin/Vienna, 1924²; repr. Darmstadt, 1963).

M. H. Segal, *Grammar of Mishnaic Hebrew* (Oxford, 1927).

# d. Moabite, Ammonite

The script of the oldest inscriptions from Transjordan bears a strong resemblance to the Old Phoenician and Hebrew alphabets. From the seventh century B.C., however, the influence of Aramaic becomes increasingly evident. Moabite and Ammonite belong to the group of West Semitic or, more precisely, Canaanite languages. The number of preserved inscriptions is small. The best known is the *Moabite (or Mesha) Stone* (ill. 42). In recent years, Ammonite inscriptions have come to light, but for the Old Testament scholar the Moabite Stone remains the most interesting text because it speaks extensively of the relations between Moab and Israel. In the inscription on this stone, King Mesha prides himself on his victories over Israel. The Bible records only his defeat by Joram (2 Kings 3).

---

## LITERATURE
### Moabite:

F. I. Andersen, "Moabite Syntax," *Orientalia* 35 (1966) 81–120.

H. Donner and W. Röllig, *Kanaanäische und aramäische Inschriften*, no. 181.

E. Lipinski, "Etymological and Exegetical Notes on the Mesa Inscription," *Orientalia* 40 (1971) 325–40.

S. Segert, "Die Sprache der moabitischen Königsinschrift," *Archiv Orientalni* 29 (1961) 197–267.

A. H. van Zijl, *The Moabites* (Leiden, 1960).

### Ammonite:

There is good information in K. R. Veenhof, *Phoenix* 18 (1972) 170–79; 19 (1973) 299–301. In addition see, for example:

E. Puech, *Revue biblique* 80 (1973) 531ff.; 83 (1976) 59ff.; G. Garbini, *Journal of Semitic Studies* 19 (1974) 159ff.; P. E. Dion, *Revue biblique* 82 (1975) 24ff.; A. van Selms, *Bibliotheca Orientalis* 32 (1975) 5ff.; W. H. Shea, *Palestine Exploration Quarterly* 111 (1979) 17ff.; 113 (1981) 105ff.; V. Sasson, *Palestine Exploration Quarterly* 111 (1979) 117ff.; D. Sivan, *Ugarit Forschungen* 14 (1982) 219ff.

## e. Aramaic

In the turbulent transition period in the Near East between 1200 and 1000 B.C., several Aramaic-speaking, seminomadic tribes settled at various places in the civilized world. Though not the first Aramaic wave of immigration, they were undoubtedly the most important. In the territory of modern northern Syria and Jordan, they even became the ruling power, so that from the tenth century B.C. small Aramaic kingdoms were found there. In addition to taking over other cultural and religious achievements of the Canaanites, they soon adopted the simple Phoenician alphabet.

The Aramaic immigrants infiltrated many places in Mesopotamia, too, as is evident, for instance, from lists of names and a growing number of Aramaic loanwords in Assyrian and Babylonian. Consequently, Aramaic-speaking people gained a measure of prominence in the West as well as in the East. It is not surprising that this made the Aramaic language a convenient international mode of communication (cf. 2 Kings 18:26). This was true not only of oral contacts but also of correspondence. Thus far cuneiform had served this purpose; however, in comparison with the alphabet this was an archaic kind of script. When a language arose that could be internationally understood, had a simple grammatical structure, and was written in the efficient alphabet at an early stage, it was only natural to start using it as the language of correspondence. That this did not remain limited to international contacts is evident from the *Assur ostracon* (ca. 650 B.C.), a letter from a ranking Assyrian officer to a colleague, written in the Aramaic language and script.

Favored by these circumstances, Aramaic became a lingua franca in the Persian period (see the section on Official Aramaic below). Many peoples adopted this language not only as the written language but also as the spoken language; naturally, in the course of the centuries all sorts of dialects developed from it. Most Aramaic languages and dialects have fallen into disuse; but there are some areas in the Anti-Lebanon and in the vicinity of Mosul and Tur-Abdin where Aramaic is still spoken.

The division of the Aramaic languages and dialects has caused much discussion and so far there is no unanimity. A simple family tree will show which division lies behind the brief survey that now follows.

### (1) OLD ARAMAIC

To this language are reckoned the Aramaic inscriptions from the tenth century B.C. Specialists disagree about the end of this period, but for the time being it seems wise to label all Aramaic texts from the period extending to about 700 B.C. as Old Aramaic. It should be kept in mind that this name includes local dialects that differed from each other, such as *Damascene* and *Yaudian* Aramaic. Particularly in the early inscriptions, the Old Aramaic script varies little from Phoenician. Only from the seventh century, especially in the cursive texts written in ink, does a more or less characteristic Aramaic script begin to appear.

The Old Aramaic inscriptions are interesting in many ways for the study of the Old Testament. Historiographically it is of interest that Israel's contemporaries and neighbors are heard here. Some of them are also mentioned in the Old Testament, for example, Barhadad (= Benhadad, 1 Kings 15:16–17; 20:1–2) and Hazael (2 Kings

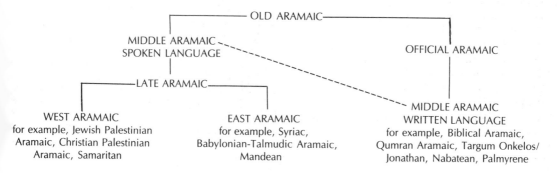

| OLD ARAMAIC | | |
|---|---|---|
| MIDDLE ARAMAIC SPOKEN LANGUAGE | | OFFICIAL ARAMAIC |
| LATE ARAMAIC | | |
| WEST ARAMAIC for example, Jewish Palestinian Aramaic, Christian Palestinian Aramaic, Samaritan | EAST ARAMAIC for example, Syriac, Babylonian-Talmudic Aramaic, Mandean | MIDDLE ARAMAIC WRITTEN LANGUAGE for example, Biblical Aramaic, Qumran Aramaic, Targum Onkelos/ Jonathan, Nabatean, Palmyrene |

8:7–8). Linguistically, similar expressions and syntactic constructions can be noted. For the history of religion it is important that the religion of the writers of these inscriptions does not differ much from that of other inhabitants of Canaan, even though, in distinction from, for example, the Phoenicians, they spoke Aramaic. By way of example, a translation is given here of the beginning of the Old Aramaic *Zakkur stele* from the beginning of the eighth century B.C.

Stele set up by Zakkur, king of Hamat and Luath, for Iluwer in Hazrek. I was Zakkur, the king of Hamat and Luath. I was a pious man. And Baal-of-Heaven delivered me and stood by me, and Baal-of-Heaven made me king in Hazrek. Barhadad, the son of Hazael, the king of Aram, united a coalition against me, seventeen kings . . . [an enumeration of these enemies follows]. All these kings laid siege to Hazrek. They made a wall higher than the wall of Hazrek and dug a moat deeper than the moat of the city. Then I lifted up my hands to Baal-of-Heaven and Baal-of-Heaven answered me. Baal-of-Heaven spoke to me through seers and through messengers, and Baal-of-Heaven said to me: "Fear not! For I have made you king and I shall stand by you. I shall deliver you from all these kings who set up a siege against you!"

Particularly interesting is the presence of seers and messengers who apparently speak on behalf of the deity. In form and content their message resembles that of many other ancient Near Eastern and Old Testament promises of deliverance (see, e.g., 2 Chronicles 20). In the large Aramaic inscription that was dug up by a Dutch expedition under the guidance of Dr. H. J. Franken in Deir Alla (Jordan) and published by Dr. J. Hoftijzer, a seer also speaks, namely, the prophet Balaam (Numbers 22–24). The text of this inscription contains much material that is suitable for comparison with the Old Testament.

## (2) OFFICIAL ARAMAIC

Naturally, the international usefulness of Aramaic was determined to a large degree by uniformity in spelling, grammar, and vocabulary. Therefore, a trend toward standardization began as early as the eighth century B.C. As a result, the dialect of Damascus probably became the standard. The movement toward uniformity really began, however, when in the sixth century B.C. Persian officials elevated Aramaic to the position of lingua franca of the vast Persian empire. This language is called *Official Aramaic.* Though everywhere the writers did their best to write this "ideal" Aramaic, certain grammatical deviations frequently betray something of their background.

A significant collection of papyri was found near Elephantine, a small settlement on an island in the Nile opposite the present Aswan. Already before the Persians conquered Egypt, an army of Jewish mercenaries was stationed here. Probably they were forced into this service as prisoners of war. The Aramaic papyri, mainly letters and contracts, yield valuable historical and legal material (ill. 43). The religion of the Jews in Elephantine was a strange mix of Yahwism and paganism. They had their own temple (cf. Isa. 19:19), in which besides Yahu (= YHWH) two Canaanite goddesses were worshiped. In contrast, the famous *Passover papyrus* from Elephantine, containing detailed prescriptions about the celebration of the Jewish Passover, is entirely in keeping with the Torah. Because this letter can be very precisely dated (419 B.C.), it is of special importance for the dating of the so-called Priestly document.

Though no fragments of biblical books were found in Elephantine, among the finds were an Aramaic wisdom text (*Ahiqar*) and fragments of an Aramaic version of the Behistun inscription of Darius. Important Aramaic literary texts in Demotic script were discovered in the Papyrus Amherst 63. Among them is a hymn resembling the biblical Psalm 20.

## (3) MIDDLE ARAMAIC (WRITTEN LANGUAGE)

The biography of Ahiqar is preceded by a biography written in an eastern variant of Official Aramaic. In subsequent centuries this dialect developed into a literary written language that, with slight mutations, remained long in use, among the Jews up to the Middle Ages. Though local variants can be noted in the development of the Middle Aramaic written language, the grammatical similarities are predominant. The differences may be due to the influence of the spoken

Middle Aramaic dialects that were contemporaneous with Official Aramaic and written Middle Aramaic. Unfortunately, we know almost nothing of this spoken language.

The Aramaic sections of the Old Testament (Dan. 2:4–7:28; Ezra 4:8–6:18; 7:12–26; Jer. 10:11; two words in Gen. 31:47) are written in the Middle Aramaic language. Thus it is also called *Biblical Aramaic*. A number of texts from Qumran are also in a more modernized form of the Middle Aramaic written language, among others a Genesis apocryphon, translations of the apocryphal books Tobit and Enoch, and a description of the new Jerusalem. To the surprise of excavators, an Aramaic translation (targum) of the book of Job was found. The publication of this Job targum was handled by the Dutch scholars Dr. J. P. M. van der Ploeg and Dr. A. S. van der Woude. The language of this targum shows much similarity with that of the targums that were later officially accepted by the Jews, *Targum Onkelos* on the Pentateuch and *Targum Jonathan* on the Prophets (that is, Joshua-Malachi). Both these translations give a fairly literal translation of the original text. A more detailed discussion of the background of these targums is given elsewhere in this handbook.

Other documents in the literary Middle Aramaic are the *Megillat Taanit* from the first century A.D., letters and contracts from the second century A.D., the still more recent *Scroll of Antiochus*, and the poems that were meant to serve as the setting of the readings from the targums.

*Nabatean* and *Palmyrene* may also be included with the Middle Aramaic written language, even though both languages developed a script of their own. The Nabateans lived in the territory south of the Dead Sea, with Petra as their capital, while the center of Palmyrene power was in and around Palmyra, in the northern part of the Syrian desert (map III). Nabatean and Palmyrene are to be regarded purely as written languages. It is likely that those who used it spoke Arabic most of the time. The datable inscriptions fall between the first century B.C. and the third century A.D. The content is one-sided: epitaphs, votive inscriptions, and the like. Relative to the Old Testament, these inscriptions provide some comparative material with respect to tribal structure. The religion of Palmyra may be regarded as a late offshoot of the Canaanite religion.

## (4) LATE ARAMAIC

Late Aramaic developed from spoken Middle Aramaic. It breaks up into two language families, *East Aramaic* and *West Aramaic*. To East Aramaic are reckoned *Syriac, Babylonian-Talmudic Aramaic, Mandean,* and some other dialects. To West Aramaic are reckoned *Jewish Palestinian Aramaic,* also called Galilean Aramaic, *Christian Palestinian Aramaic,* also called Syro-Palestinian, and *Samaritan.* Of these languages only Syriac and Jewish Palestinian Aramaic are of such importance for the study of the Bible that a separate discussion is warranted.

*Syriac* deserves mention especially because of the translation of the Bible in this language. For the Old Testament these versions are the Peshitta and the Syro-Hexapla, for the New Testament the Diatessaron (the first harmony of the Gospels) and the Vetus Syra (also known as the Peshitta). For more information on these translations of the Bible, see the chapter below on textual criticism. In addition, some apocryphal books of which we do not possess the original Hebrew text, such as the Odes of Solomon and the Baruch Apocalypse, have come down to us in Syriac.

Because already in the apostolic era Christianity spread to the western part of Syria (Antioch, Damascus) and about A.D. 150 it also gained entrance in the eastern part (Edessa, Arbela), Syrian theologians such as Tatian (died at the end of the 2nd century), Bardesanes (154–222), and Afraates (ca. 275–345) have had a great influence on the church in the eastern part.

The split of the Syrian church in 484 into a Nestorian and a Jacobite group also had consequences for the script and the language. From the original, highly cursive *Estrangela* alphabet each church developed its own variant: the *Nestorian* and the *Jacobite* scripts; the latter is also called *Serto* (ill. 44). In modern editions especially Estrangela and Serto are used. The linguistic differences are mainly differences in pronunciation. For the history of the Aramaic language, it is of special importance that Syriac was supplied with vowels at an early stage, initially through *matres lectionis* and dots above or below the letters, later also by means of more complete vowel signs.

*Jewish Palestinian Aramaic* is probably closest to the spoken language used by Jesus and his disciples. It therefore figures prominently in the discussions of the Semitic background of the New Testament. In that connection, a controversial question of long standing is whether one should speak of the Hebrew or the Aramaic background of the New Testament. It is questionable, however, whether this is a proper dilemma. To begin with, in their teaching the rabbis used mostly Hebrew, even when their everyday language was Aramaic. It is highly possible that this was also true of the teaching of Jesus and the apostles. But even if they spoke the Aramaic vernacular, it must be borne in mind that the Jewish Palestinian Aramaic we know is laced with Hebraisms. What else could one expect when a people that originally spoke Hebrew gradually went over to Aramaic?

At least as important as the language question is the very free way in which the rabbis in Palestine were accustomed to interpret the Scripture in the vernacular. The systematic analysis of their exegetical methods is far from complete. The available sources for that are:

(a) *Palestinian Targums.* These originated in the Aramaic translation (*targum*) recited by special interpreters in the synagogues of Palestine after the reading of the Hebrew text of the Bible, which had become unintelligible for most of the believers. This shows that what we have here is a genuine spoken language that can have had little resemblance to the Middle Aramaic written language in which, for example, Targum Onkelos and Jonathan were written. The interpreters did make some attempts to introduce an element of uniformity into their translations. Little came of it, however, because initially it was strictly forbidden to put a targum in writing; as a result, everything was dependent on oral tradition. Consequently, several versions continued to exist, even when in the third or fourth century A.D. it was occasionally decided to record the targums.

The most complete targum is the one on the Pentateuch that was discovered not so long ago in the Vatican manuscript *Neofiti I.* Some scholars are of the opinion that this targum also contains the most archaic Palestinian Aramaic we know. In addition to the Neofiti targum there were at least two other Palestinian translations of the Pentateuch: *Targum Yerushalmi I* (also called Targum Eretz Israel or Targum Pseudo-Jonathan) and *Yerushalmi II* (also called Fragmentary Targum). The latter is incomplete and contains only translations of separate verses, sentences, and words.

These free Palestinian translations were not always transmitted with equal care. Because later there was a greater familiarity with Babylonian-Talmudic Aramaic and with Targum Onkelos, the text and language of these Palestinian targums were often brought in line with Onkelos.

To be sure, there have also been Palestinian targums on the prophets; little remains of these, however, and we do not know whether such targums were ever fully put in writing. Though the targums on the Hagiographa (*Ketubim*) were in general edited late, the present assumption is that much old Palestinian material has been incorporated into them.

(b) *Palestinian Talmud.* The technical term "Talmud" is a designation of the discussions and guidelines composed by the rabbis in the third to the fifth centuries A.D. as an addition to the Mishna, which by that time had been closed. This material came to be incorporated into two huge compilations, the *Jerusalem* or *Palestinian Talmud* and the *Babylonian Talmud*, named after the areas of origin. These additions to the Mishna are for the most part written in Aramaic. Babylonian-Talmudic is an East Aramaic dialect, while the language of the Palestinian Talmud is Palestinian Aramaic.

The Babylonian Talmud, which went through its final editing about A.D. 500, later came to have greater authority among the Jews than the Palestinian Talmud, which, probably, because of persecution by Christians in the fourth century A.D. had been hastily edited. Large parts are missing and the received text is corrupt in many places.

(c) *Palestinian Midrashim.* The situation here is analogous to that of the Palestinian targums. We possess only fragments of the original form in which these Bible commentaries (*midrashim*) were transmitted. In part they are included in the

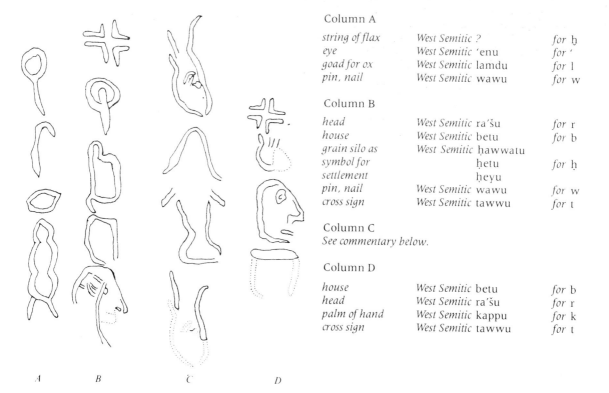

Column A

| | | |
|---|---|---|
| string of flax | West Semitic ? | for ḫ |
| eye | West Semitic ʿenu | for ʿ |
| goad for ox | West Semitic lamdu | for l |
| pin, nail | West Semitic wawu | for w |

Column B

| | | |
|---|---|---|
| head | West Semitic raʾšu | for r |
| house | West Semitic betu | for b |
| grain silo as symbol for settlement | West Semitic ḥawwatu ḥetu ḥeyu | for ḥ |
| pin, nail | West Semitic wawu | for w |
| cross sign | West Semitic tawwu | for t |

Column C

See commentary below.

Column D

| | | |
|---|---|---|
| house | West Semitic betu | for b |
| head | West Semitic raʾšu | for r |
| palm of hand | West Semitic kappu | for k |
| cross sign | West Semitic tawwu | for t |

A        B          C          D

30. A Proto-Sinaitic inscription (16th century B.C.). The text is badly worn and the correct interpretation is still far from certain. The "lines" are vertical and probably are to be read from bottom to top, beginning at bottom left.

In all these cases the writer has applied the so-called acrophonic principle, that is, he uses the symbols as one-letter signs, whereby the pictured word represents the first consonant. In column C this leads to problems, however. Therefore it seems better to read this column logographically (according to the rebus principle):

| | | |
|---|---|---|
| head of ox | West Semitic ʾalpu | for West Semitic ʾlp, "thousand" |
| kind of fish | West Semitic samaku | for West Semitic smk, "support" |
| head of ox | West Semitic ʾalpu | for West Semitic ʾlp, "thousand" |

This means that the signs would still have the same function as the Egyptian three-letter signs. Also, the very first sign, the string of flax, is evidently derived from Egyptian (cf. ill. 20, 21). This argues for the supposition that the inventor of the alphabet was inspired by the Egyptian script.

The complete text of the inscription would then read: ḫʿlw rb ḥwt ʾlp smk ʾlp brkt, "Hialwu, the ruler of the settlement, (may receive) a thousand supports, a thousand blessings." The name Hialwu means "the Most High is my brother," and in form may be compared with biblical names such as Hiel and Hiram, while the divine name "Most High" is found later among the Canaanites as well as in Israel (cf. Gen. 14:18–20; Num. 24:16; Deut. 32:8; etc.). See p. 102.

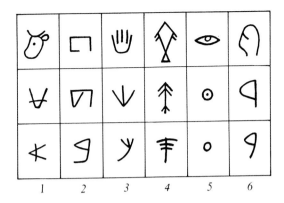

31. The early development of the alphabet. Column I shows the Proto-Sinaitic signs, already in a somewhat simplified form relative to the signs in the very old inscription of ill. 30. Column II offers Proto-Canaanite transitional forms from the 12th century B.C. To be sure, the sign II.4 has not yet been found, but may be supposed on the ground of the Ugaritic ṡ as well as of the form of the letter in the later linear alphabet. Column III finally offers Old Canaanite sign forms, which were used in the 10th century B.C. by Phoenicians and Israelites. Column 1 = 'aleph; column 2 = beth; column 3 = kaph; column 4 = samekh; column 5 = 'ayin; column 6 = resh. Several signs exhibit already the form that is still used today. See p. 103.

32. A bronze axe head from Ugarit inscribed with the name and title of its owner in the Ugaritic alphabetic cuneiform: ḫrṣn rb khnm, "ḪRṢN, chief priest." (Louvre)

33. The Ugaritic alphabet. As an exercise the student-writers had to write the alphabet on clay tablets. This undamaged specimen shows that the student did not make the best use of the available space. The first line became too long and was written partly on the side of the tablet.

The transcription of the alphabet is as follows: 'a, b, g, ḫ, d, h, w, z, ḥ, ṭ, y, k, š, l, m, ḏ, n, ẓ, s, ', p, ṣ, q, r, ṯ, ġ, t, 'i, 'u, ṡ. The phonetic system is thus richer than that of the later West Semitic languages, such as Hebrew, but corresponds almost totally with that of the somewhat older Proto-Sinaitic inscriptions. The Ugaritic alphabet was adapted to the needs of writing on clay, with the result that the shape of many of the signs varies from that of the Proto-Sinaitic and Proto-Canaanite alphabet. Nevertheless, several of the signs give evidence that the designer must have been acquainted with this older form of the alphabet (e.g., b, g, ḫ, z, k, ', ṡ). See pp. 104–105.

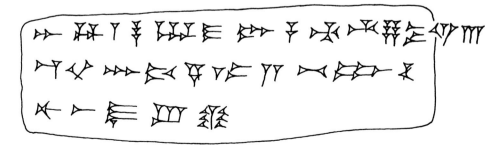

34. A copy of a mythological text from Ugarit, ca. 1360 B.C. On the top left are the following lines: "When you [Baal] slew Lotan [Leviathan], the slippery [or fleeing] serpent, when you destroyed the twisting serpent . . ." (Ugaritic ktmḫṣ ltn bṯn brḫ, tkly bṯn ʿqltn). It is obvious that the author of Isa. 27:1 ("Leviathan the fleeing serpent, Leviathan the twisting serpent," Hebrew lwytn nḥš brḥ lwytn nḥš ʿqltwn) must have been acquainted with these lines. However, he applies them to the Lord, who in the end time will defeat this sea monster, the personification of all godless powers. See pp. 105–106.

35. The Phoenician linear alphabet in the 10th century B.C. The top line (A) shows the sign forms of the Ahiram inscription (ca. 975 B.C.), the bottom shows the signs of the Yehimilk inscription (ca. 950 B.C.). See p. 103.

36. *A copy of a Phoenician inscription on the sarcophagus of King Tabnit (end of the 6th century B.C.). For the Old Testament scholar the text contains some interesting details. The kings of Sidon, for example, were at the same time priests of the goddess Astarte (cf. Gen. 14:18). The opening of the sarcophagus is described as "an abomination before Astarte," an expression that bears strong similarity to the biblical "an abomination to the Lord" (Deut. 7:25; 12:31; 17:1; etc.). For the spirits of the dead the word* rp'm *is used, which also occurs in the Old Testament with this meaning. See p. 108.*

37. *The sarcophagus of Eshmunazar king of Sidon (5th century B.C.) reflects Egyptian style. The Phoenician inscription lists the accomplishments of the king, who was "snatched away before [his] time," and warns against tampering with his resting place. (Religious News Service)*

38. *The Gezer calendar (10th century B.C.), so far the oldest Hebrew inscription. The letters, etched into soft limestone, are irregularly formed. Evidently it is the work of an unskilled student. See p. 109.*

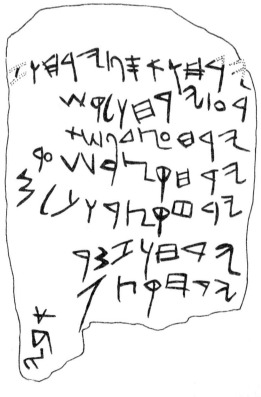

39. The front and back of Lachish ostracon no. 4, ca. 586 B.C. That the alphabet enabled many people to learn to write is indicated by the neat handwriting of this ostracon, which is from a lower army officer. The writer ends with the note that he can still see the signals from Lachish, but no longer those from Azekah. Jer. 34:7 shows that these were the last two cities which still held out for some time, before Jerusalem itself would fall (2 Kings 25). See p. 109.

42. The Mesha inscription (Moabite Stone), ca. 850 B.C., is the longest Moabite inscription found thus far. The script differs little from the Old Hebrew script. In the previous century the text was heavily damaged but fortunately could be restored with the use of a squeeze made earlier. The original is now in the Louvre, Paris, but copies of the stele can be seen in many archeological museums. See p. 112.

40. The Siloam inscription, ca. 700 B.C. King Hezekiah probably commissioned a skilled writer to make this inscription. See pp. 109–110.

41. A fragment of the large Isaiah scroll from Qumran (1QIsᵃ). The shape of the letters differs markedly from that of the later square script. Depicted is Isa. 53:9–12, where the text differs on several points from that of the Massoretic text. So in 53:10 it reads "and he pierced him" instead of "he has made him sick." And in 53:11 "he shall see light" instead of "he shall see it." The meaning of this reading may be that the Servant of the Lord will be delivered from the realm of the dead (cf. Job 33:28–30). These variants are important for the history of the messianic interpretation of this part of Scripture. See pp. 110–111.

43. *An unopened papyrus from Elephantine. A string was put around the folded papyrus, which was then sealed. On the outside (front and back) it reads: "Deed concerning the house which Anani, the son of Azariah, has put in the name of his daughter Yehoyishma." Anani was custodian of the sanctuary of Yahu in Elephantine. See p. 114.*

44. *Examples of Syriac script. Above: Estrangela; center: Serto; below: Nestorian (various texts). See pp. 115–116.*

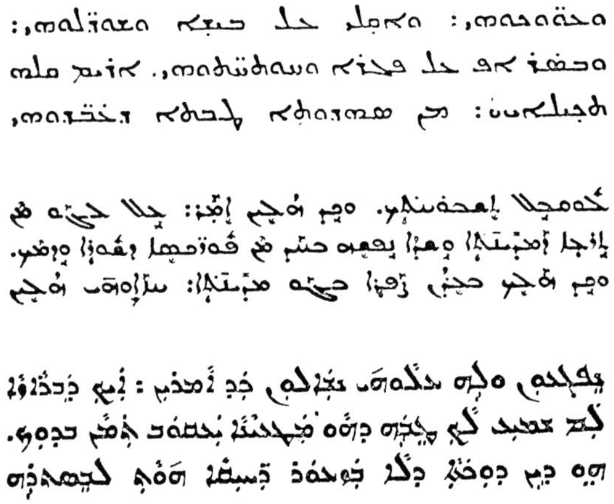

ܘܚܘܕܘ ܗܡܐܘܚܡܗܐ؛؛ ܘܐܡܕܝ ܕܐ ܚܒܕ ܐܪ̈ܝܐܡ؛
ܘܚܦܙ ܐܕ ܚܕ ܚܚܕܐܘ ܐܪ̈ܝܐ ܡܐܕ̈ܘܐܘܐܘ؛ ܐܪ̈ܝܐ ܪܡܝܚܐ
ܗܐܓܠܐܘ؛ ܡ ܘܡܡܐܘ ܐܪ̈ܝܕܐ ܠܐܪ̈ܕܐ ܘܚܬܐܘ،ܗܐܚܙܐܘ،

ܐܘܢܐܡܓܠܐ ܐܚܕܝܡܕܢܐܡܝ. ܘܘܡ ܗܘܓܡ ܐܡܓ؛ ܚܠܐ ܚܚܝܗ ܗܢ
ܝܐܪ̈ܓܠ ܐܡܕ̈ܝܡܬܐܟܐ ܘܚܡܐ ܝܚܡܝܗ ܚܡܡ ܗܢ ܩܘܐܕܚܡܐ ܘܩܘܐܕܝ ܘܝܩܚܘ.
ܘܘܡ ܗܘܓܡ ܚܚܝܢ ܚܚܝ̈ܢ ܙܗܐܝ ܚܚܝܗ ܗܡܬܐܟܐ؛ ܣܐܪ̈ܐܘܗܘܬ ܗܘܓܡ

ܘܟܚܠܕܘܡ ܘܟܕܡ ܚܚܓ̈ܕܗܗܟ ܚܚܓ̈ܠܗ ܚܕ ܐܡܚܚܝ؛ ܐܝܚܝ ܕܝܚܕܚܘܕܘܙ
ܠܚܕ ܚܚܚܝܕ ܠܚܝ ܚܚܚܝܙܚ ܘܕܗܗܘ ܚܚܓ̈ܚܚܚܙܟ ܚܚܚܚܗܕ ܐܚܚܙ ܚܝܚܘܘܝ.
ܘܗ ܕܝܚ ܕܘܩܚܐܝ ܘܠܐ ܚܘܩܚܗܕ ܚܚܝܚܚܚ ܕܝܣܚܚܐ ܚܗܦܚ ܠܟܝܚܚܕܙܚ

45. *An Old South Arabic inscription from Marib dedicating a building named Yafud by three brothers in the reign of Karibil Watar Yuhamin, King of Saba (1st century B.C.). (W. S. LaSor)*

47. One of the most significant finds in recent years, this large bulla is inscribed: "Belonging to Berechiah, the son of Neriah, the scribe." This is almost certainly Baruch, the son of Neriah, the scribe so familiar to us from the book of Jeremiah.

46. A recently discovered private seal from the time of the monarchy. It is important for two reasons. (1) It is the most detailed picture of the biblical lyre. (2) Though several seals from princes have been found, this is the first seal of a princess from the house of David that has been discovered. The text reads: "Belonging to Ma'adana, daughter of the king." Unfortunately the text does not mention who her father was.

49. An Amarna Tablet (no. 252) from Labaya, prince of Shechem. He protests to the pharaoh that his hostile activity was only to repel aggression against his home town. This tablet is remarkable for its language, which is almost pure Canaanite (written in Akkadian cuneiform). For a translation see Pritchard, ed., Ancient Near Eastern Texts, p. 486. (Trustees of the British Museum)

48. Fragments of clay tablets with cuneiform (from Aphek); these demonstrate that this script and the languages of Mesopotamia were known and studied in Palestine in the Late Bronze Age.

50. *A page from a tenth-century manuscript in the Hebrew square script (British Museum, London, Ms. Or. 4445, true size 42 by 33 cm. or 16½ by 13 in.), showing Gen. 50:23 – Exod. 1:13.*

*Midrash Rabba*, which was completed much later. Unfortunately, here, too, later hands have freely tampered with the original text of the Midrash.

---

## LITERATURE
### General Literature with Respect to Aramaic:

H. Donner, "Aramäische Lexikographie," in P. Fronzaroli, ed., *Studies on Semitic Lexicography* (Firenze, 1973), pp. 127–43.

H. J. W. Drijvers, in J. H. Hospers, ed., *A Basic Bibliography for the Study of the Semitic Languages* I (Leiden, 1973) 283–335.

A. Dupont-Sommer, *Les Araméens* (Paris, 1949).

J. J. Koopmans, *Aramäische Chrestomathie* I–II (Leiden, 1962).

E. Y. Kutscher, "Aramaic," *Current Trends in Linguistics* VI (1970) 347–412.

———, "Aramaic," *Encyclopedia Judaica* III (Jerusalem, 1971) 259–87.

E. Lipinski, *Studies in Aramaic Inscriptions and Onomastics* I– (Leuven, 1975– ).

J. Naveh, *The Development of the Aramaic Script* (Jerusalem, 1970).

F. Rosenthal, *Die aramäistische Forschung seit Th. Nöldeke's Veröffentlichungen* (Leiden, 1975).

F. Rosenthal, ed., *An Aramaic Handbook* I–IV (Wiesbaden, 1967) (a selection of exercises from diverse dialects).

S. Segert, *Altaramäische Grammatik* (Leipzig, 1975) (including not only Old Aramaic but also Official Aramaic and Biblical Aramaic).

For Aramaic inscriptions see the bibliography and the conclusion of the general introduction to section 5 (above, pp. 102–104).

### Old Aramaic:

R. Degen, *Altaramäische Grammatik* (Wiesbaden, 1969).

P.-E. Dion, *La langue de Ya'udi* (Canada, 1974).

J. Hoftijzer and G. van der Kooij, *Aramaic Texts from Deir Alla* (Leiden, 1976).

### Official Aramaic:

F. Altheim and R. Stiehl, *Die aramäische Sprache unter den Achaimeniden* I– (Frankfurt, 1963– ).

P. Grelot, *Documents araméens d'Égypte* (Paris, 1972) (translation and commentary on all the important texts, including Elephantine; bibliography).

P. Leander, *Laut- und Formenlehre des Ägyptisch-Aramäischen* (Göteborg, 1928).

J. M. Lindenberger, *The Aramaic Proverbs of Ahiqar* (Baltimore, 1983).

B. Porten, *Archives from Elephantine* (Berkeley/Los Angeles, 1968) (a good summary; bibliography).

J. B. Segal, *Aramaic Texts from North Saqqara* (London, 1983).

S. P. Vleeming and J. W. Wesselius, "An Aramaic Hymn from the fourth century B.C.," *Bibliotheca Orientalis* 39 (1982) 501–509 (on Papyrus Amherst 63).

### Biblical Aramaic:

H. Bauer and P. Leander, *Grammatik des Biblisch-Aramäischen* (Halle, 1927).

J. J. Koopmans, *Arameese grammatica (O. T. Aramees)* (Leiden, 1957[2]).

F. Rosenthal, *A Grammar of Biblical Aramaic* (Wiesbaden, 1961).

The large Hebrew lexicons have sections in the back and special sections for Biblical Aramaic.

### The Aramaic of Qumran and Murabba'at:

See the bibliographies cited under section 5.c, to which may be added, for example:

T. Muraoka, *Revue de Qumran* 8 (1972) 7–51; S. A. Kaufman, *Journal of the American Oriental Society* 93 (1973) 317–27, as well as the following important books:

A. Beyer, *Die aramäischen Texte vom Toten Meer* (Göttingen, 1984).

J. T. Milik, *The Books of Enoch, Aramaic Fragments of Qumran, Cave 4* (Oxford, 1976).

M. Sokoloff, *The Targum to Job from Qumran Cave XI* (Jerusalem, 1974).

### Nabatean and Palmyrene:

J. Cantineau, *Grammaire du palmyrénien épigraphique* (Le Caire, 1935).

———, *Le Nabatéen* I–II (Paris, 1930–32).

F. Rosenthal, *Die Sprache der palmyrenischen Inschriften* (Leipzig, 1936).

### Samaritan:

R. Macuch, *Grammatik des samaritanischen Aramäisch* (New York, 1982).

### Jewish Palestinian Aramaic:

G. Dalman, *Aramäische Dialektproben* (Leipzig, 1927²; repr. Darmstadt, 1960).

_____, *Grammatik des jüdisch-palästinischen Aramäisch* (Leipzig, 1905²; repr. Darmstadt, 1960).

H. Odeberg, *The Aramaic Portions of Bereshit Rabba, II: Short Grammar of Galilaean Aramaic* (Lund/Leipzig, 1939).

W. B. Stevenson, *Grammar of Palestinian Jewish Aramaic* (Oxford, 1962²).

### The Aramaic Background of the New Testament:

M. Black, *An Aramaic Approach to the Gospels and Acts* (Oxford, 1967³).

J. A. Fitzmyer, *Essays on the Semitic Background of the New Testament* (London, 1971).

M. McNamara, *Targum and Testament* (Grand Rapids, 1972).

P. Nickels, *Targum and New Testament* (Rome, 1967).

H. Ott, "Um die Muttersprache Jesu," *Novum Testamentum* 9 (1967) 1–25.

### Targums:

See the bibliography of Chapter IV below.

### Talmud and Midrash:

H. L. Strack, *Einleitung in Talmud und Midrasch* (Leipzig, 1921⁵) (several reprints).

J. L. Palache, *Inleiding in de Talmoed* (Amsterdam, 1955²).

### Syriac:

A. Baumstark, *Geschichte der syrischen Literatur* (Bonn, 1922; repr. Berlin, 1968).

C. Brockelmann, *Lexicon Syriacum* (Halle, 1928²; repr. Hildesheim, 1965).

_____, *Syrische Grammatik* (Leipzig, 1968¹¹).

L. Costaz, *Grammaire syriaque* (Beirut, 1955²).

W. Jennings, *Lexicon to the Syriac New Testament* (Oxford, 1926).

O. Klein, *Syrisch-griechisches Wörterbuch zu den vier kanonischen Evangelien* (Giessen, 1916).

R. Kobert, *Vocabularium Syriacum* (Rome, 1956).

P. Margoliouth, *Supplement to the Thesaurus Syriacus of R. Payne Smith* (Oxford, 1927).

Th. Nöldeke, *Kurzgefasste syrische Grammatik* (Leipzig, 1898²; repr. Darmstadt, 1966 [with appendix by A. Schall]).

I. Ortiz de Urbina, *Patrologia Syriaca* (Rome, 1965²).

R. Payne Smith, *Thesaurus syriacus* I–II (Oxford, 1879–1901).

R. Payne Smith and P. Margoliouth, *A Compendious Syriac Dictionary* (Oxford, 1903; repr. 1957).

A. Ungnad, *Syrische Grammatik* (Munich, 1932²).

T. H. Robinson, *Paradigms and Exercises in Syriac Grammar* (Oxford, 1962⁴, rev. by L. H. Brockington).

---

# 6. ARABIA AND ETHIOPIA: THE ALPHABET

The alphabet must have made its way into southern Arabia at an early stage, even though the inscriptions discovered so far are no older than the sixth century B.C. At that time, flourishing kingdoms in southern Arabia constructed extensive irrigation works and engaged in trade with Canaan. Among these was the kingdom of Saba, called Sheba in the Bible (cf. 1 Kings 10). It is customary to call the dialects spoken in southern Arabia *Old South Arabic* or *Epigraphic South Arabic*. The letters on monumental inscriptions in southern Arabia were written in elegant characters (ill. 45). The content of these texts, the most recent of which dates back to the sixth century A.D., is not exactly fascinating, yet occasionally the Old Testament scholar can find useful comparative material here. Unfortunately, a detailed comparative examination remains to be done. Such an examination would also have to include the somewhat more recent *North Arabic* inscriptions, consisting for the most part of graffiti from wandering tribes. In these Old North Arabic inscriptions, too, different dialects can be recognized (*Thamudic, Lihyanite, Safaitic*).

With respect to sound, all Arabic dialects are close to Proto-Semitic, a language that, in the opinion of experts today, can be reconstructed on the basis of the presently known Semitic languages. To explain certain changes in sound in this group of languages it is necessary to assume the existence of an original set of sounds that was virtually identical with that of Arabic. For that reason the Arabic dialects are particularly useful in determining the etymology of words in other Semitic languages, including Hebrew.

This explains, too, why *Classical Arabic* is so important for the Old Testament scholar, despite the fact that this language did not become prominent until after the rise of Islam in the seventh century A.D. The Classical Arabic script is derived from the Aramaic script and has twenty-eight consonants. For certain phonemes, not present in Aramaic, recourse was taken to adding a diacritical mark to an existing sign. Here, too, vowel signs were added only later.

Arabic lexicographers have composed extensive lexicons that are used by Hebraists not only for trying to find the etymological equivalents of familiar Hebrew words, but also those of words whose meaning may have been forgotten by later generations. This is not an illegitimate assumption, for the text of the Hebrew Bible has for centuries been transmitted by people who themselves no longer used Hebrew as their regular language. It can even be established that in some cases the meaning of a word or expression was no longer understood. In some cases present-day scholars have been able to recover the original meaning by way of Classical Arabic.

Yet a warning against frivolous "browsing" in the treasures of Arabic lexicography is in order. It should be borne in mind that these lexicons contain material of diverse age and origin, even many loanwords from other languages. Moreover, except in an occasional instance, they do not measure up to the scientific requirements modern dictionaries have to meet. Finally, often the etymology of a word says nothing about its meaning. For example, anyone who tried to determine the meaning of the English *slight* on the basis of its external resemblance to the Dutch *slecht*, now meaning "evil, bad," would evidently go astray. At an earlier stage, however, the Dutch word meant "simple, unimportant," which comes much closer to the meaning of the English cognate. The same must have happened in the case of the old Semitic languages. This is an important reason to be careful with new interpretations of the original Hebrew text that are based exclusively on a supposed etymological affinity

with a word in Arabic (or, for that matter, any other Semitic language).

Of the remaining South Semitic languages, classical Ethiopic, also called *Ge-ez*, using the indigenous term, briefly deserves mention. The art of writing was imported into Ethiopia from southern Arabia, presumably in the second century A.D. Ethiopic is of some importance for the study of the Bible because a number of pseudepigraphal books (e.g., Enoch and Jubilees), whose original Hebrew or Aramaic text is for the most part lost, have been transmitted in this language.

---

## LITERATURE
### Old South Arabic:

A. F. L. Beeston, *A Descriptive Grammar of Epigraphic South Arabian* (London, 1962).

J. C. Biella, *Dictionary of Old South Arabian* (Chico, 1982).

K. Conti Rossini, *Chrestomathia Arabica Meridionalis Epigraphica* (Rome, 1931).

M. Höfner, *Altsüdarabische Grammatik* (Leipzig, 1943).

J. Ryckmans, *Les inscriptions anciennes de l'Arabie du Sud: points de vue et problémes actuels* (Leiden, 1973).

### General:

J. H. Hospers, ed., *A Basic Bibliography for the Study of the Semitic Languages* I (Leiden, 1973) 336–58 (A. J. Drewes, "Old South Arabic Inscriptions); pp. 359–62 (J. H. Hospers, "The Ethiopic Language"); Vol. II (Leiden, 1974) (Classical Arabic).

### Classical Arabic:

A. F. Beeston, *Written Arabic* (Cambridge, 1968).

R. Blachère and M. Gaudefroy-Demombynes, *Grammaire de l'arabe classique* (Paris, 1952[3]; repr. 1970).

W. Fischer, *Grammatik des klassischen Arabisch* (Wiesbaden, 1972).

J. A. Haywood, *Arabic Lexicography* (Leiden, 1960) (cf. A. Spitaler, *Orientalische Literaturzeitung* 63 [1968] 50–58).

W. Wright and M. J. de Goeje, *A Grammar of the Arabic Language* I–II (Cambridge, 1896–1898[3]; repr. 1951).

Continuous bibliographical information is offered, among others, by *Abstracta Islamica,* supplemented by *Revue des Etudes Islamiques* (since 1927), and J. D. Pearson, *Index Islamicus 1906–1955* (Cambridge, 1958) with supplements in 1962, 1967, and 1973, and a bibliography till 1970; yearly supplements after that.

#### Ethiopic (Ge-ez):

E. Cerulli, *La letteratura etiopica* (Firenze, 1968³).

A. Dillmann, *Chrestomathia aethiopica* (Berlin, 1950²; repr. Darmstadt, 1967).

_____, *Ethiopic Grammar* (London, 1907²).

_____, *Lexicon linguae aethiopicae* (Leipzig, 1865; various reprints).

T. Lambdin, *Introduction to Classical Ethiopic (Ge-ez)* (Missoula, Montana, 1978).

W. Leslau, *An Annotated Bibliography of the Semitic Languages of Ethiopia* (The Hague, 1965).

# B. Hebrew and Aramaic as Biblical Languages

*by J. Hoftijzer*

## 1. HEBREW

The bulk of the original text of the Old Testament is written in Hebrew, and only a small part (see p. 135) in Aramaic. This Hebrew is best described as *Classical Hebrew*, first of all, to distinguish it from later forms of this language, such as Rabbinic Hebrew (also called Mishnaic Hebrew or Tannaitic Hebrew), Medieval Hebrew, and Modern Hebrew (Ivrit). This distinction makes sense because, despite the similarity, there are real differences between Classical Hebrew and these other forms, and it would be scientifically wrong to ignore these differences. Second, the term Classical Hebrew is preferable to another much-used term, *Biblical Hebrew*. This latter designation might create the impression that this form of Hebrew was (virtually) alone used for recording writings of a religious nature that (later) became canonical. Some epigraphical material, though unfortunately scarce (e.g., the Siloam inscription, the ostraca of Lachish, Yavne Yam, and Tell Arad), proves the contrary. See ill. 46, 47.

Classical Hebrew is the oldest known form of Hebrew in which texts have been preserved. Linguistic comparison shows, however, that when the oldest texts known to us originated (probably the 12th or 11th century B.C.), the language had already gone through a long history of development. The youngest Classical Hebrew texts are from the second century B.C. (We leave out of the picture here the Dead Sea Scrolls; it is not certain whether they are Classical Hebrew.)

At first sight it seems obvious that Classical Hebrew was the language of ancient Israel as we meet this people on the pages of the Old Testament. However plausible this may seem, the real-ity was much more complex. The available materials that bear on it are limited but very significant. According to Judges 12:6, the Gileadites from Transjordan pronounced the word for "ear of grain" as *shibboleth*. But members from the tribe of Ephraim who came from the territory west of the Jordan were unable to pronounce the word like that, not even when their life was at stake; they said *sibboleth*. The narrative presupposes that both groups could understand each other. Yet at the same time there were characteristic differences. The Ephraimites were not able to produce the *sh* sound as this was pronounced in the east (and likely also in the south), or they pronounced it altogether differently.

Both the Gezer calendar (probably 10th century B.C.) and the Samaria ostraca (8th century B.C.?) have their grammatical peculiarities; these cannot possibly be fitted into the pattern of Classical Hebrew. This is all the more remarkable considering the small chance for such differences between the available Classical Hebrew texts and the epigraphical texts mentioned here to become visible. The spelling does not help (see pp. 124ff.), nor does the nature of texts such as the Gezer calendar and the Samaria ostraca. The scarcity of the materials, however, makes it impossible to determine the extent of these differences. Both kinds of epigraphical material are from the territory called the Northern Kingdom; Classical Hebrew was the language spoken in (a part of) the south. At least in the eighth century B.C. a prophet from the south, Amos (from Judean Tekoa, Amos 1:1), had apparently little difficulty in making himself understood in the north, where he prophesied (see especially his meeting with the high priest of Bethel, Amaziah, 7:12ff.). It is not possible to say whether this mutual "comprehensibility" between north and south was also true in preceding centuries and in all areas of north and south. At any rate, ancient Israel definitely had dialectical differences, with Classical Hebrew being one of the dialects. Whether there were other more far-reaching linguistic differences remains uncertain (though the possibility cannot be absolutely excluded).

As indicated, Classical Hebrew was the language of (a part of) the south. In this connection the designation *Judean* is appropriate for this language. This designation occurs in 2 Kings 18:26, 28 (= Isa. 36:11, 13; cf. 2 Chron. 32:18). There it is recorded that at a siege of Jerusalem (ca. 700 B.C.) the Assyrian negotiators spoke Judean in the hearing of the people on the walls. The designation was used at least into the fifth century B.C., according to Nehemiah 13:24.

The name *Hebrew* for the language may not be used as an argument that Classical Hebrew must have been the language of ancient Israel in its entirety, since the name is rather late. The first reference we know of is in the introduction to the apocryphal book Sirach (line 22). This introduction was written by the grandson of the author, who also translated the work of his grandfather from Hebrew into Greek; in all likelihood it is from the second half of the second century B.C. (other old texts containing this designation are the book of Revelation [9:11], the work of the Jewish author Flavius Josephus in the first century A.D., and the Mishna).

Besides being called Hebrew, in later Jewish literature the language is also called the *Holy Language* or the *Language of the Sanctuary*. In a free translation of Genesis 31:47, Targum Pseudo-Jonathan has the patriarch Jacob speak the language of the sanctuary in an encounter with his opponent Laban. The use of such terms arose from the need to mark off Hebrew from other languages, particularly the Aramaic used for centuries by the Jews. One should be careful not to draw the same wrong conclusions from such a designation, as one could draw from a name such as Biblical Hebrew.

Still another name leads us to the origin of Hebrew, the name *language of Canaan* mentioned in Isaiah 19:18. This name indicates that the language was regarded first of all as belonging to *the land*. This argues for the assumption that the ancestors of the people made the language their own when they settled in the land and that before that time they spoke another language. This has happened with many groups of (semi)nomads who in the course of history, coming from the outside, settled in the cultivated areas of Syria and Palestine. The close affinity between Hebrew and a language such as Phoenician, which had been indigenous in the Levant much longer, also argues in favor of it.

It remains a question to what extent the ancestors' original language (or languages) influenced the language they took over. Many assume that there was such influence (which is very well possible). A noted scholar, Hans Bauer, has characterized Hebrew as a *mixed language* on the premise of such a theory. In view of our scant knowledge on this point, it seems better, however, to be cautious.

We do not know the language of Israel's ancestors who entered Canaan. The Old Testament calls them Arameans. In the confession mentioned in Deuteronomy 26:5, the Israelite of a later generation says that his father was a "wandering Aramean." The tradition that the members of the family of the patriarchs were Arameans points in the same direction. In Genesis 31:47 the name Laban gives to Gilead is clearly Aramean. He himself is also called an Aramean (Gen. 25:20; 28:5). The land in which this family lives is called *Aram-Naharaim* (Gen. 24:10) or *Paddan-Aram* (Gen. 28:2, 5, 7, etc.). The most obvious conclusion would seem to be that the ancestors of the people spoke a form of Old Aramaic. But even if this should be the case (it is by no means excluded), this does not help us very much. The oldest Aramaic text known to us is the Tell Fekheriyeh inscription; it is probably from the ninth century B.C., thus a long time after the settlement of the Israelites in Palestine. Besides, many features of the language that we regard as typically Aramaic arose only in the first half of the first millennium B.C. This should make us aware that a responsible reconstruction of the original language of Israel's ancestors, even if it was a kind of Aramaic, is presently impossible for us. For this reason, it would be preferable to be reserved where the establishing of ancient Aramaic influence is concerned.

Of course, it is possible to say something about the evolution of the Hebrew language in the period preceding the one from which we have our oldest Classical Hebrew texts, by applying the principles of linguistic comparison and by arguing back from certain data in Classical Hebrew. For instance, it can be determined that the article and the particle indicating the object (found both in Classical Hebrew prose and somewhat less in poetry) must have been (at least in this function) comparative latecomers in the language. In a number of cases it is even possible to indicate the evolutionary sequence; for instance, the article functioned as such before the particle indicating the object. The precise dating of such phenomena is much more difficult, however, let alone the reconstruction of the language. The lack of texts is painfully felt here. Therefore our knowledge is insufficient to determine with certainty whether the language of the invading ancestors influenced the language of the country, and if so, to what extent. Though the small number of traces of a native language that appear in Akkadian letters from Palestine, from a period prior to those of the oldest Classical Hebrew texts, may be very interesting, they are unable to help us to find an adequate solution to the problem discussed here. (In this connection we should not forget either that Classical Hebrew was the language of *a part* of ancient Israel.) See ill. 48, 49.

The number of preserved Classical Hebrew texts (the bulk of the Old Testament, the now known fragments of the original version of Sirach from the first half of the second century B.C., and a limited amount of epigraphical material) may appear insuperably large to the beginner, but for an extensive linguistic study it is only a limited amount. There are other reasons, too, why this kind of study is difficult to pursue.

Consulting a current edition of an original copy of the Hebrew Old Testament, one finds a text made up of consonantal characters with points and other small signs below, above, and within them (ill. 50). These points and signs indicate the vowels, the stress, the pronunciation of certain consonants, and whether a consonant is single or double. It would be wrong to assume that the entire text in this form is from the authors of the Bible. The system of signs around the consonantal text is centuries later than the consonantal text itself. The latest Hebrew in the Old Testament (the Hebrew part of the book of Daniel) is from about the middle of the second century B.C. The so-called vocalization and punctuation system found in current editions of the Old Testament text originated and evolved roughly between A.D. 600 and 900. It is called the *Tiberian system*. This name distinguishes it from other systems used in the past, for instance, the Palestinian and the Babylonian. These systems differ not only in the form of the signs or in their placement (for instance, only within or above the consonants), but in other respects as well. Behind each system lies a specific linguistic tradition. The long time span between the latest Hebrew document in the Old Testament and these systems (though some originated somewhat earlier than the Tiberian) inevitably brings up the question to what extent such a system can contribute to the knowledge of Classical Hebrew as such. There is no doubt that such systems do not provide *direct* access to Classical Hebrew. On the other hand, it would be wrong to undervalue their importance for the linguistic study of Hebrew. Let us take an example.

The well-known scholar Paul Kahle, who did fine work in this area, was of the opinion that the shape of the language as presented by the Tiberian system bears unmistakable traces of later artificial construction of the language. This would supposedly demonstrate that what is presented in the relevant instances as Hebrew had nothing to do with the language as it was spoken in the past. Transcriptions of Hebrew words in Greek writing (e.g., in Origen, a scholar who lived ca. A.D. 185–254) and in a Latin reproduction (in the works of Jerome, ca. A.D. 400), thus from a period prior to the origin of the Tiberian system, seemed to confirm this opinion. Further investigation has shown that Kahle's argument—and thus his conclusions—are much weaker than was thought previously. Those who developed systems such as the Tiberian were undoubtedly scholars (they are called Massoretes). It also seems plausible that, for example, in a system such as the Tiberian the language was systematized. But this need not imply that in the area of phonetics and morphology the Massoretes construed all sorts of phenomena that have no basis in history. One should be all the more careful with such conclusions now that it is also clear that the transcription system mentioned above has many more problems than earlier investigators thought. Here one could also adduce the existence of the *different* vocalization and punctuation systems with their different language traditions, as well as the fact that in the above-mentioned transcriptions, forms occur that in no way can be linked to corresponding forms in the Tiberian language system. It is better, however, to ascribe this phenomenon to different Hebraic traditions from which the scholars of the various schools drew, traditions that possibly go back to different types of Classical Hebrew (on this see also p. 125). Thus one must reckon with the possibility that the study of the vocalization and punctuation systems may make a welcome contribution, though *indirectly,* to the knowledge of Classical Hebrew. Such a contribution is welcome because on the points in question there are large gaps in our knowledge of Classical Hebrew (see also pp. 125ff.).

What we have said so far implies that our direct knowledge of Classical Hebrew is based on the consonantal text. (Non-Old Testament Classical Hebrew texts have no vocalization or punctuation system at all.) In what follows we shall consider problems that this consonantal text poses for linguistic investigation. (Text-critical problems will not be discussed, though they are certainly important philologically; they will be taken up elsewhere in this book.)

The Hebrew alphabet on which the consonantal text is based has twenty-two characters. The sequence of the characters, which we still know today, goes back to traditions at least as old as the mid-second millennium B.C. Witnesses to the existence of this alphabetical sequence in ancient Israel are still found in a few psalms and some other pieces of poetry in which each new line starts with the next letter of the alphabet (for instance, Psalms 9–10, 25, 34, etc.).

The alphabet itself was not designed for any form of Hebrew. It must have served first for another language and later have been taken over by Hebrew-speaking people, as suggested by the fact that Classical Hebrew had at least one more consonant than there were consonantal characters. (There was only one character for *sin* and *shin*; only later, when punctuation was introduced, were the two distinguished.) The shape of the characters has not always been the same. Present editions use the square script. According to tradition, this type of script was introduced at the time of Ezra (5th century B.C.). But the first evidence of its use is from the second century B.C. Before the rise of the square script (and also sometime after that) a script was used that looks much like the scripts found in the ancient West Semitic world, for instance, among the Phoenicians and Moabites. It must thus be assumed that a large part of the Old Testament was originally written in this older script and that later these texts were replaced by texts written in the square script. (It may be noted here that there are all kinds of variants of both the square script and the older script type, depending, e.g., on the time and the place of the writing of the text.)

The consonantal script operates on the principle that for every consonant there is one consonantal character. We noted already that in the Classical Hebrew texts there is at least one case in which this is not so. In a pure consonantal script, vowels are not indicated. Good examples of the use of such a script are found, for example, in the older Phoenician texts. The extant texts in Classical Hebrew contain no example of a pure consonantal script (not even if the vocalization and punctuation signs are removed; it cannot be stated with certainty whether such a script has ever been used for Classical Hebrew). In the material available to us, the characters, besides indicating consonants, also serve to indicate long vowels. If a consonantal character serves to indicate a vowel—only a few serve that function—it is said to serve as a *mater lectionis* (mother of reading). This term is entirely proper considering that the use of these signs greatly simplifies the reading of pure consonantal texts. Investigation of epigraphical texts has shown that the use of *matres lectionis* for long vowels *within* a word must have been introduced about the seventh century B.C. At that time (barring a few exceptional cases), *matres lectionis* were in common use *at the end* of a word. Traces of this are found in all the later Classical Hebrew texts. The long vowels at the end of a word are *always* indicated with a *mater lectionis* (except in certain cases just mentioned); the use of *matres lectionis* did remain optional for indicating long vowels *within* a word.

From the fact that *matres lectionis within* a word were introduced about the seventh century B.C. it may be concluded that they were later inserted in older Old Testament texts in which they now occur. This conclusion is not devoid of significance because many a word would be open to more than one interpretation without them, even if the context in which they stand is known. The insertion of *matres lectionis within* a word in older texts in which they were not used can, in many cases, imply a decision as to the proper explanation of such a text, a decision that is by no means always obvious. Similarly, the addition of a vocalization system such as the Tiberian was at the same time a decision as to the meaning of the text. The scholars engaged in this work did not just fix the pronunciation they regarded as the correct one, but they also made decisions (also on the basis of tradition) on the meaning of the text.

Another reason why we have discussed at length the situation of the script and the problems connected with it is that it has far-reaching consequences for our knowledge of Classical Hebrew. As we have said, vocalization and punctuation systems do not contribute directly to our knowledge on this point. It is obvious that a system such as the consonantal script (with *matres lectionis*) used for Classical Hebrew does not give sufficient information about all facets of the language, certainly not in the areas of phonetics and morphology. For short vowels are not indicated and long vowels not in all instances (an additional consideration is that a *mater lectionis* is normally used for more than one long vowel, e.g., $h = a, e$). A grammar of Classical Hebrew itself (not of Classical Hebrew as this is presented in much later vocalization and punctuation systems) would have to be prepared on the basis of philological comparison and the evidence of Greek (and Latin) transcriptions referred to above. Recently Klaus Beyer has tried to provide such a reconstruction. However interesting (and useful) such attempts at reconstruction may be, it is better not to ascribe absolute value to them. Too many things are uncertain. For instance, a number of

specific forms are found in the Greek transcriptions that cannot be linked with the forms that are found in (certain parts) of the Classical Hebrew texts, not even in the relationship of a younger form to an older form from which it may have come. In the case of other morphological phenomena, too, this should warn us against drawing conclusions too easily from these transcriptions for Classical Hebrew. These kinds of data (and certain data from the Dead Sea Scrolls) argue rather for different traditions of Classical Hebrew and for the existence (in certain periods) of diverse kinds of Classical Hebrew (see also p. 124).

Above we spoke a few times of philological comparison as an aid in the study of Classical Hebrew. For that matter the study of other Semitic languages (in particular those belonging to the same category) can greatly assist in the investigation of Classical Hebrew. This is particularly the case in the study of the historical evolution of the language. At this point, too, however, a warning is not out of place: this comparative philological study should never be pursued in such a way that the unique character of the language that is being studied is—perhaps unconsciously—denied. That this danger is not imaginary is seen in the tendency to postulate that all sorts of phenomena occurring in related languages are almost self-evidently to be found in Hebrew. Occasionally almost forced attempts are made to detect these phenomena in Classical Hebrew. For example, various related languages (e.g., the often-used Ugaritic) contain a so-called nominal ending *-m*. Unmistakable traces of it are also found in Classical Hebrew, and philological comparison helps us to understand it better. There are cases, however, in which an author becomes so overzealous in trying to find such traces that one cannot escape the impression that he has checked all the words beginning with *m-* in a concordance in order to see whether this consonant cannot in some way be made part of the preceding word.

As we said above, the texts in Classical Hebrew cover a period from the twelfth (or 11th) century to the second century B.C. It is unthinkable that the language would have remained unchanged over such a long period. Though the orthography by no means shows all the changes, a number of them can be noticed. Unfortunately, here too there are many problems. Many Old Testament documents are hard to date or cannot be dated with certainty, while some can be. Telling illustrations are the book of Lamentations and Psalm 137; both must be from the period shortly after 587 B.C. (fall of Jerusalem). In contrast, many parts of the so-called five books of Moses cannot even be dated to a particular century. Obviously, this does not make the study of the developments within Classical Hebrew easier. An additional factor is that spelling in the ancient West Semitic world was very traditional. It could happen that a form was still used in writing that was no longer extant in the spoken language of that time but, owing to the evolution of the language, had been replaced by another form. The new form entered the written language only slowly, often first as an error in writing, and eventually pushed out the old form. Therefore one can never be certain that the spelling in a certain document correctly reflects the language situation at that time or for which forms it holds. We already noted above that there are reasons to assume the existence of different kinds of Classical Hebrew (see p. 124). There are other reasons, too, however. The idiom of prose texts is so different from that of poetic texts that it would be advisable to keep the two strictly separate in a grammatical description, and certainly in the areas of morphology and syntax. (The vocabulary of poetry, in part due to the special requirements of this type of literature, is also clearly distinct from that of the "ordinary" texts. The frequent use of synonyms, required by the use of parallelism, has resulted in the preservation of many words and word roots in poetry that became lost or were rarely used in "ordinary" language.)

It is regrettable that many grammatical studies in the area of Classical Hebrew do not observe this distinction or do so insufficiently. In some cases this has been clearly detrimental to the interpretation of the text. Prophetic literature is difficult in this respect. Part of it can be regarded as prose, for instance, the bulk of the book of Ezekiel (it has only some songs, such as the lamentation over Israel's princes in ch. 19). Another part, however, is clearly poetic in character, for example, Isaiah 40–66. But there are also many prophetic passages that are neither typical prose nor typical poetry, and yet do not represent a separate idiom besides prose and poetry. This, too, does not simplify grammatical investigation. We already stated above (see p. 123) that the available texts in Classical Hebrew are fairly limited for purposes of grammatical study. That it is necessary to differentiate within the available Classical Hebrew texts can only aggravate the problem. In certain respects the material will be altogether insufficient to answer all the questions asked by the grammarian. It is not easy to find an adequate solution to this kind of problem. But to ignore the problems, as sometimes happens, can never be the right attitude.

The developments in Classical Hebrew must in part be viewed as strictly internal evolutions. In addition, there must have been an influence from the outside. Thus the vocabulary was enriched by borrowing first from Akkadian and later from Persian. The strongest influence, however, has come from Aramaic, which—considering the circumstances—is understandable. (I refrain from coming back to the possibility of the existence of an Aramaic legacy, derived from the language once [presumably] spoken by the ancestors; see pp. 122–23.)

As early as 700 B.C. a particular form of Aramaic must have served as diplomatic and commercial language in the Near East. An indication of this is found in the above-mentioned (p. 122) story of the discussions of the besieged Judeans with the representatives of the Assyrian king. The Judeans ask the Assyrians not to speak in Judean but in Aramaic, which the latter for obvious political reasons refuse (2 Kings 18:26 Isa. 36:11). In the context of this history it is the higher official classes who are able to speak Aramaic; apparently the common people could neither speak nor understand it. Though in this way Aramaic already had a kind of universal importance in the Assyrian period, it was particularly predominant in the Persian era (538-330 B.C.). During that period, Aramaic served, among other things, as the vehicle for official correspondence (on this Aramaic see also pp. 135–36).

There is no doubt that this internationally dominant position of Aramaic contributed significantly to the influence of Aramaic on the Hebrew language. This is particularly noticeable in postexilic writings, and for centuries it remained noticeable in Hebrew. Among others, especially Emil Kautzsch and more recently Max Wagner have done much to describe those cases where there has been Aramaic influence. In addition to their emphasis on morphology, their studies are heavily based on the derivation of words and word roots from Aramaic. It is a pity that the influence of Aramaic on Hebrew syntax does not get the attention this subject deserves. For it is here that Aramaic influence has been very great, if not the greatest. It should be added that this deficiency is understandable, because Hebrew syntax is a comparatively less developed part of Hebrew grammar.

As to the question when one may speak of derivations from the Aramaic vocabulary, greater care should be exercised than some are now doing. In a fair number of cases derivation is unmistakable. But there are also many words and word roots in later Classical Hebrew that are generally presented as *Aramaisms* without sufficient grounds. In such cases it would be better to present them as doubtful cases for which there is no solution as yet. (The same holds true for the socalled grammatical Aramaisms.) In the study of languages where, due to the limited and fragmented nature of the available material, no comprehensive knowledge is possible (this is true of Classical Hebrew as well as of older forms of Aramaic), it is better not to conceal the existing uncertainties. Ultimately a discipline suffers if it operates with apparent certainties.

As we noted, the study of Hebrew encounters many "problem areas." The greatest of these problem areas lies, however, in the realm of syntax and concerns the function of the verbal system. The problems here are so great that such a well-known scholar as Godfrey Rolles Driver regarded the Classical Hebrew verbal system in its entirety only as the product of historical development—meaning that in Old Testament times it was not really a functioning system. In contrast, those who do not regard the entire system as a nonfunctioning product of a highly complicated and confused historical development agree that its function clearly differs from such a verbal system as that of the English language. The usual assumption is that the forms used in Hebrew do not indi-

cate the *time* (present, past, future) of an action, but (opinions differ greatly on this point) whether the described action was complete or incomplete, or whether in its context it was important. In my judgment the most plausible assumption is that in its classical stage the Hebrew verbal system was functionally extremely complicated and that a lot more research is needed to do justice to all the nuances. In this research it is important to recognize the specific character of Classical Hebrew and not to force the language too much into the framework of certain cognate languages. At this point, too (cf. p. 125), it is dangerous to use the same denominator in the description of the cognate languages.

Though there are investigators, for instance, Francis I. Andersen, who apply modern linguistic methods in their research of Classical Hebrew, much is left to be desired on this point. While it is wrong to absolutize modern linguistic methods over against older methods of approach, one should not be blind to the fact that at least certain modern linguistic methods (such as structuralism) can contribute significantly to a better understanding of Classical Hebrew idiom and—equally important—show us where there are gaps in our knowledge.

Of course, that the Classical Hebrew texts we possess are limited in number also has its consequences for the study of words and word meanings. Several words and word roots occur only a few times, in some cases only once, in the texts we have. Despite the sometimes centuries-old traditions we have at our disposal, this limitation has caused difficulties in interpretation. Material from cognate languages can be of use in this connection. Here are some examples of cases in which the discovery and decipherment of texts in a West Semitic language have helped. Verbal forms of the root *sh-t-'* are found in Isaiah 41:10 and 23. These are the only passages in which this root occurs in Classical Hebrew, at least in the material available to us. That is the reason why these verbal forms were not recognized by scholars as forms of this root, a fact that also entailed interpretative problems. Ugaritic and Phoenician texts discovered and published in the course of this century have shown a number of unmistakable examples of this root and have also provided the meaning ("to be afraid"). The combination '*l-mwt* (I reproduce only the consonantal text here) is found in Proverbs 12:28; the Tiberian vocalizers rendered it as if it read '*al-mawet* (= absence of death, immortality). Some scholars doubted the correctness of this vocalization (which is at the same time an interpretation), contending that this type of combination could not be Hebrew. This was the only instance and there were no examples in cognate languages. Recently, however, a similar combination has been found in a text in a dialect from Transjordan: '*l-ngh* (= not-light, darkness). This has its implications for the interpretation of Proverbs 12:28. Consequently, it is certain that parallel material from the West Semitic world, and indeed from all of the Semitic world, can give and has provided fine services in determining the meaning and interpretation of words. Here too, however, one should beware of quick and methodologically facile conclusions; finding as many hidden and unrecognized roots in Classical Hebrew as possible should not become a game. James Barr, who has done much to trace and expose errors in Hebrew philology, has sounded a warning here too—and rightly so.

As we noted above, the latest Classical Hebrew texts known to us are from the second century B.C., at least if the Dead Sea Scrolls are not included in the picture. It is hard to say to what extent these latter texts are Classical Hebrew. Could it be a bad kind of Classical Hebrew, written by people who spoke another kind of Hebrew (Rabbinic)? The problems are formidable here and concern the difficult question of the precise demarcation of Classical and non-Classical Hebrew.

A related difficult question is how long Classical Hebrew was a spoken language. Today, as in the past, some scholars contend that Hebrew ceased to be a spoken language at an early date. Klaus Beyer, for instance, contends that Hebrew was spoken at the very latest in the sixth century B.C. This seems unlikely, however; a text such as Nehemiah 13:23–24 presupposes that Judean was spoken in the fifth century B.C. (Judean here means Classical Hebrew; see p. 122), even though its use was diminishing at the time, partly because of mixed marriages. It is impossible to say to what extent the countermeasures taken by Nehemiah were effective. At any rate, the Hebrew found in the books of Chronicles, that is, in those parts not derived from older documents, gives clear indications that it was a living language when those books were written (probably 4th century B.C.). Moreover, it seems entirely unlikely that the earlier theory that Rabbinic Hebrew was only an artificial written language, never spoken, can be right. In fact, there are strong indications that it was a living language. This already makes plausible a permanent tradition of Hebrew as a living language. Presently the most acceptable theory is that the end of Classical Hebrew as a spoken language was not the end of Hebrew as a spoken language. It is better to view the end of Classical Hebrew as a spoken language as a gradual transition process out of which an altogether different type of Hebrew (Rabbinic Hebrew) eventually emerged. There is no way of determining how many people or which groups may have spoken Classical Hebrew in the last centuries it existed. In any case, as we noted, the language did have its competitors.

We conclude this discussion with some remarks about the translation of Classical Hebrew texts, in particular of the Old Testament. Translation work is never easy; to translate from a language that contains the kinds of difficulties just shown is even more difficult (I leave aside here for the time being the problems encountered in respect to the content). Since the seventeenth century (when the Authorised or King James Version was made) much progress has undoubtedly been made in the study of Hebrew, and today we have many data that the translators of the King James Version did not have. It would be a mistake, however, to think that the number of uncertainties the present generation faces with respect to the Old Testament text is less than those that were faced three and a half centuries ago. The widely held notion that the increase of knowledge concerns exclusively the solution of earlier problems is wrong. It implies equally, or at least it ought to, that new problems come into focus that were not noticed at an earlier stage because of more limited knowledge. In the translation of the Classical

Hebrew texts, it is proper that we show not only the same reverence but also the same hesitancy that characterized our ancestors.

Another problem concerns the question *how* one should translate. Must one try to render the same thoughts found in the Classical Hebrew text in the best possible English, or does reverence for the text demand that one stick as closely as possible to a literal reproduction of the text? (Here I do not consider paraphrases, which try not only to render the text from one language into another but also attempt to substitute twentieth-century images for those of the world of the 1st millennium B.C.). It is obvious that a translator should stay as close as possible to the text he wishes to reproduce, and that he should follow the text literally as long as this can be done. The same holds for the translation of identical words; it is definitely preferable to translate them consistently by the same word in English as long as this is possible. The question is how far one should go with this principle. The most reasonable answer seems to be so long as the text of the translation can still be called English; so long as the translation does not cause misconceptions and confusion to the reader who does not know the original; and so long as the methodology followed in the translation is not in conflict with philological data. Let us give an example.

In translating it is methodologically wrong to ignore the altogether different structure of (Classical) Hebrew. Classical Hebrew contains a special form of the imperfect that the grammars often designate with the (inappropriate) term *cohortative*. This verbal form indicates that the subject would like something, regardless of whether the decision to do what is desired is dependent on him or another. This form is used in Genesis 11:7, where God announces his decision to come down and to bring about the confusion of tongues at Babel. It also occurs in Deuteronomy 2:27, where the Israelites kindly ask King Sihon of Heshbon for permission to pass through his land. The form is also found in Exodus 5:8, 17, where the Israelites humbly ask Pharaoh to give them the opportunity to sacrifice to their God. In these cases, the Hebrew does not state, in words or forms of words (as would have to be done in English, for

example), whether the subject is dependent on a second party. (It remains possible that this was expressed by intonation, but that is something of which we know next to nothing.) That in these Hebrew texts we do not find separate forms or circumscriptions indicating which of the possibilities is meant does not mean, of course, that an Israelite was unacquainted with the distinction between an independent decision and being dependent on the willingness of another. It would also be wrong to think that something that is not explicitly expressed is necessarily insignificant. Furthermore, English does not have one single way of expressing the connotations of the Hebrew cohortative, at least not in such a way that it never conveys wrong ideas to the reader who is unfamiliar with Hebrew. Only one way remains open: depending on its particular meaning in its context, translate the cohortative into good English. (I have not even mentioned here those cases in which a cohortative, occupying a particular place in a particular clause type and preceded by a special kind of clause, has a function altogether different from the one referred to above: in that case the cohortative indicates the consequence of an act mentioned in the antecedent. This makes it totally impossible to have just one translation for all cohortatives.)

We encounter similar problems with individual words and their meanings. In many cases, the semantic field of a Hebrew word does not coincide with that of its English equivalent (which is not surprising to anyone familiar with philology). To translate the same Hebrew word always with the same English word would lead to confusion. For instance, the verb *'anah* is usually employed in cases where we would use "answer." There are, however, clear instances where such a translation would be altogether wrong. In Job 3:2 this verb is used in a sentence in which Job does not answer someone (it would be best to translate it with something like "to begin"); in Exodus 23:2 the verb is used to indicate bearing witness, etc. To use one translation for all these cases seems inadvisable because there is not one translation that—at least if one wishes to write meaningful English—would satisfy all contexts. Most of the time the Hebrew word *mishpat* can properly be translated "justice" or "righteousness." But in some cases this rendering makes no sense at all. Thus King Ahaziah of Northern Israel, hearing that his messengers met an unknown prophet, asks, "What is his *mishpat*?" (2 Kings 1:7). The answer (verse 8) is that it was a man with a garment of haircloth and a girdle of leather. Here *mishpat* must mean something like "kind, type": the king asks for a description of the person. Any translation with "justice," "righteousness," or a similar word would be foolish here. Here, too, it is impossible to find one English word that covers all cases, unless one is content to write a kind of English that does not deserve the name and that can only mislead those who do not know Hebrew.

At this point it is useful to say something about the so-called basic meaning of a word or a stem of a word. It is widely held that in Classical Hebrew, among other Semitic languages, a word or stem of a word, from which various words are derived, has one basic meaning. This implies that a common basic meaning would be applicable in all cases where this word or word stem is used, regardless of the date of the text, and regardless of the literary genre, context, and situation with which the text deals. A method of translation, as described above, that always uses the same translation for a specific word seems to operate (probably unaware) from such a presupposition. To be sure, in the case of many words it is possible to find a common denotation for all (at least very many) instances where the word occurs. This, however, should not lead us to the mistaken notion that there *must* be such a common denotation for all cases. In research, the question should seriously be asked whether there *can* be such a denotation. To assume its existence is bound in some cases to result in a translation that is linguistically forced. Here are some examples.

In many cases the stem *sh-m-'* means "to hear." Here the central meaning is to perceive via the hearing. In a large number of instances, derivations from this stem indicate the granting of a prayer, etc., as for example in Genesis 17:20, where God says to Abram that he has heard him with respect to Ishmael. In other cases, derivations from this stem indicate *obedience,* as in Exodus 24:7, where the people say that they will do

and "hear" everything the Lord has said. It is obvious that it would be wrong to assume that there is one common denotation that holds for all cases. In Genesis 17:20, the perception by hearing is not (exclusively) central but the favorable divine reaction to it. Likewise in Exodus 24:7, the perception by hearing is not exclusively central but the obedient response. In these special cases the word *hear* will do as a translation. But this is more the exception than the rule. It rarely happens that one word or stem with more than one denotation, depending on the context or the time in which it is used, has one English equivalent that holds in all cases. Take, for example, the stem *q-l-l.* In some cases, the idea of "swiftness" is particularly central (so in 2 Sam. 1:23), in others, the idea of being "small in number, in quantity" (so in Gen. 8:11, which speaks of the quantity of water that is subsiding), and in still other passages the idea of being "unimportant, despised" (so in Gen. 16:4, where Sarah is of little importance in the eyes of her maidservant because of her childlessness). Obviously, there was once a time when there was one denotation of the stem from which these diverse meanings arose; that, however, is no reason to deny this diversity and the lack of one common denotation for the time from which our texts come.

An argument made frequently by those who insist on one consistent translation of a Hebrew word is that in this way the translator does justice to plays on words (which can be very important in the story) and so-called keywords. Otherwise certain essential features would be lost in translation. To transpose plays on words from one language to another is, however, extremely difficult to do—if it is possible at all. Another question is whether such a "translation" would still be acceptable English. If not, more is lost in such a rendering than in a free translation. It is undeniable that Old Testament literature may contain certain keywords that are significant for the content and the meaning. It would be ideal to translate such a keyword consistently by one word in English; in that way something essential in the original narrative would be retained. But here, too, if the result would not be meaningful English or would be misleading, the loss would be greater than in a nonuniform rendering. Moreover, one cannot escape the impression that for some the tracking down of keywords becomes a kind of sport in which a measure of arbitrariness is undeniably present. In this case, too, it is best to be strictly methodological and always to ask why a particular word would be a keyword, what the criteria are for establishing this, and the like.

## LITERATURE

One can find a general overview of the modern study of the whole subject of Hebrew in *Encyclopaedia Judaica* XVI (Jerusalem, 1971) 1560–1662 (Hebrew language). See especially the contributions of J. Blau ("Classical Hebrew," pp. 1560–83) and E. Y. Kutscher ("The Dead Sea Scrolls," pp. 1583–90).

See also E. Y. Kutscher, *A History of the Hebrew Language* (Jerusalem/Leiden, 1982).

The following publications offer good insight into the development of the modern study of Classical Hebrew:

J. Hempel, "Zur alttestamentlichen Grammatik," *Zeitschrift für die alttestamentliche Wissenschaft* 45 (1927) 234–39.

D. W. Thomas, "The Language of the Old Testament," in H. W. Robinson, ed., *Record and Revelation* (Oxford, 1938), pp. 374–402.

B. Gemser, "Die merkwaardigste verskynsel in die Hebreeuse Taal en sy verklaring," *Tydskrif vir Wetenskap en Kuns* 2 (1941) 197–217.

W. Baumgartner, "Was wir heute von der hebräischen Sprache und ihrer Geschichte wissen," *Anthropos* 35/36 (1940/41; published 1944) 593–616 (repr. in W. Baumgartner, *Zum Alten Testament und seiner Umwelt* [Leiden, 1959], pp. 208–39).

R. Meyer, "Probleme der hebräischen Grammatik," *Zeitschrift für die alttestamentliche Wissenschaft* 53 (1951) 221–35.

H. Cazelles, "Hébreu," in G. Levi Dela Vida, ed., *Linguistica semitica: presente e futuro* (Rome, 1961), pp. 91–113.

W. J. Moran, "The Hebrew Language in Its Northwest Semitic Background," in G. E. Wright, ed., *The Bible and the Ancient Near East* (Festschrift W. F. Albright; London, 1961), pp. 54–72.

J. P. Lettinga, *De 'Tale Kanaans'. Enkele beschouwingen over het Bijbels Hebreeuws* (Groningen, 1971).

### Grammars of Classical Hebrew:

F. E. König, *Historisch-kritisches Lehrgebäude der hebräischen Sprache* I–III (Leipzig, 1881–97). Especially the third volume, which discusses syntax, is still very useful, in spite of the author's method, which is in many respects antiquated. König's work is a real mine of information that is difficult to obtain elsewhere. (Grammars older than this one are not mentioned here, although some are still quite useful.)

W. Gesenius, E. Kautzsch, and A. Cowley, *Gesenius' Hebrew Grammar* (Oxford, 1910[2]; repr. London, 1970[2]). Still a very good and applicable grammar.

G. Bergstrasser, *Hebräische Grammatik* I–II (Leipzig, 1918–29; repr. Hildesheim, 1962). A thorough execution of Gesenius's grammar. An excellent work that regrettably remained unfinished (e.g., syntax is not discussed).

H. Bauer and P. Leander, *Historische Grammatik der hebräischen Sprache* (Halle, 1922; repr. Hildesheim, 1965). In spite of recent developments still a very useful and solid work. Syntax is not treated. The Introduction has an interesting synopsis of the earlier grammatical study of Classical Hebrew.

P. Joüon, *Grammaire de l'hébreu biblique* (Rome, 1947[2]). Among the newer grammars one of the best. It is, to a high degree, based on independent research.

A. Sperber, *A Historical Grammar of Biblical Hebrew* (Leiden, 1966). Actually a collection of originally independent publications. In spite of the valuable material that can be found in this work, as a whole the material is not well organized.

A. Bendavid, *Biblical Hebrew and Mishnaic Hebrew* I–II (Tel Aviv, 1967–71) (Hebrew). A very useful book.

K. Beyer, *Althebräische Grammatik. Laut- und Formenlehre* (Göttingen, 1969). An effort to reconstruct the actual Classical Hebrew.

R. Meyer, *Hebräische Grammatik* I–IV (Berlin/New York, 1966–74). A grammar not without merit, with references to more recent literature.

J. Blau, *A Grammar of Biblical Hebrew* (Wiesbaden, 1976). A somewhat more general grammar with references to newer literature; as a whole, not without merit.

W. S. LaSor, *Handbook of Biblical Hebrew* I–II (Grand Rapids, 1979).

Of the numerous teaching grammars we mention:

T. O. Lambdin, *Introduction to Biblical Hebrew* (New York, 1971). Very useful.

J. P. Lettinga, *Grammatica van het Bijbels Hebreeuws* (Leiden, 1976[8]). An excellent and careful grammar.

J. F. A. Sawyer, *A Modern Introduction to Biblical Hebrew* (Stocksfield, 1976).

W. Schneider, *Grammatik des biblischen Hebräisch* (Munich, 1978[2]). Methodically very interesting (cf. also the remarks of E. Talstra, "Text Grammar and Hebrew Bible, I: Elements of a Theory," *Bibliotheca Orientalis* 35 [1978] 169–74; idem, "Text Grammar and Hebrew Bible, II: Syntax and Semantics," *Bibliotheca Orientalis* 39 [1982] 26–38).

H. Irsigler, *Einführung in das biblische Hebräisch* I–II (St. Ottilien, 1979–81). A solid piece of work.

For the Hebrew of the Dead Sea Scrolls see E. Y. Kutscher, *The Language and Linguistic Background of the Isaiah Scroll (1Q Isaᵃ)* (Leiden, 1974).

E. Qimron, *A Grammar of the Hebrew Language of the Dead Sea Scrolls* (Jerusalem, 1976) (Hebrew).

For problems in teaching Classical Hebrew see:

D. Vetter and J. Walther, "Sprachtheorie und Sprachvermittlung, Erwägungen zur Situation des hebräisches Sprachstudiums," *Zeitschrift für die alttestamentliche Wissenschaft* 83 (1971) 72–96.

J. H. Hospers, "Some Observations about the Teaching of Old Testament Hebrew," in M. A. Beek, et al., eds., *Symbolae biblicae et mesopotamicae F. M. Th. de Liagre Bohl dedicatae* (Leiden, 1973), pp. 188–98.

————, "The Teaching of Old Testament Hebrew and Applied Linguistics," in M. S. H. G. Heerna van Voss, et al., eds., *Travels in the World of the Old Testament* (Festschrift M. A. Beek; Assen, 1974), pp. 94–101.

See also the volume of papers on this subject: J. H. Hospers, ed., *General Linguistics and the Teaching of Dead Hamito-Semitic Languages* (Leiden, 1978).

Separate publications on the syntax of Classical Hebrew:

A. Kropat, *Die Syntax des Autors der Chronik verglichen mit der seiner Quellen* (Giessen, 1909).

A. B. Davidson, *Hebrew Syntax* (repr. Edinburgh, 1924[3]). An excellent and valuable work.

C. Brockelmann, *Hebräische Syntax* (Neukirchen, 1956). Although the book is not unattractive methodologically, it is disappointing when used on a regular basis.

R. J. Williams, *Hebrew Syntax: An Outline* (Toronto/Buffalo, 1967). As the title indicates, this is a general synopsis, and useful as such.

M. Z. Kaddari, *Studies in Biblical Hebrew Syntax* (Ramat Gan, 1976) (Hebrew).

D. Michel, *Grundlegung einer hebräischen Syntax* I (Neukirchen-Vluyn, 1977).

M. Rothenberg, *Hidden Rules of Syntax in Biblical Hebrew* (Tel Aviv, 1979) (Hebrew).

For the problems of the verbal system compare:

R. Meyer, "Das hebräische Verbalsystem im Lichte der gegenwärtigen Forschung," *Supplements to Vetus Testamentum* 7 (1960) 309–17.

P. Kustár, *Aspekt im Hebräischen* (Basel, 1972).

T. N. D. Mettinger, "The Hebrew Verb System. A Survey of Recent Research," *Annual of the Swedish Theological Institute* 9 (1973) 64–84.

J. Hoftijzer, *Verbale vragen* (Leiden, 1974).

See also more recent studies:

W. Gross, *Verbform und Funktion, wayyiqtol für die Gegenwart?* (St. Ottilien, 1976).

O. Rössler, "Zum althebräischen Tempussystem. Eine morpho-syntaktische Untersuchung," in O. Rössler, ed., *Hebraica* (Berlin, 1977), pp. 33–57.

B. Johnson, *Hebräisches Perfekt und Imperfekt mit vorangehendem we* (Lund, 1979).

R. Bartelmus, *HYH. Bedeutung und Funktion eines hebräischen "Allerweltswortes"* (St. Ottilien, 1982).

L. McFall, *The Enigma of the Hebrew Verbal System* (Sheffield, 1982).

H. P. Müller, "Zur Geschichte des hebräischen Verbs. Diachronie der Konjugationsthemen," *Biblische Zeitschrift* 27 (1983) 34–57.

J. Hoftijzer, *The Function and Use of the Imperfect Forms with nun paragogicum in Classical Hebrew* (Assen/Maastricht, 1985).

For the verbal system, cf. also E. Jenni, *Das hebräische Pi'el* (Zurich, 1968); and W. T. Claassen, "On a Recent Proposal as to a Distinction between Piel and Hiphil," *Journal of Northwest Semitic Languages* 1 (1971) 3–10; idem, "The Declarative-estimative Hiphil," *Journal of Northwest Semitic Languages* 2 (1972) 5–16.

For the use of modern linguistics in research of Classical Hebrew see:

E. A. Nida, "Implications of Contemporary Linguistics for Biblical Scholarship," *Journal of Biblical Literature* 91 (1972) 73–89.

R. Kieffer, "Die Bedeutung der modernen linguistik für die Auslegung biblischer Texte," *Theologische Zeitschrift* (Basel) 30 (1974) 223–33.

Examples of studies of syntax that apply modern linguistic methods are:

F. I. Andersen, *The Hebrew Verbless Clause in the Pentateuch* (Nashville/New York, 1970) (cf. J. Hoftijzer, "The Nominal Clause Reconsidered," *Vetus Testamentum* 23 [1973] 446–510).

————, *The Sentence in Biblical Hebrew* (The Hague, 1974).

T. Givon, "The Drift from VSO to SVO in Biblical Hebrew. The Pragmatics of Tense-Aspect," in C. N. Li, ed., *Mechanisms of Syntactic Change* (Austin/London, 1977), pp. 181–254.

W. Richter, *Grundlagen einer althebräischen Grammatik* I–II (St. Ottilien, 1978–80).

J. Hoftijzer, *A Search for Method* (Leiden, 1981).

H. Schweizer, *Metaphorische Grammatik. Wege zur Integration von Grammatik und Textinterpretation in der Exegese* (St. Ottilien, 1981).

See also publications in a journal like *Afroasiatic Linguistics* (an annual publication).

For the use of modern statistical methods and the computer in analyzing Classical Hebrew see:

Y. T. Radday, *The Unity of Isaiah in the Light of Statistical Linguistics* (Hildesheim, 1973).

*The Computer Bible* (begun in 1972 by the Biblical Research Associates).

O. Schwarzwald, ed., *Hebrew Computational Linguistics: A Bulletin for Formal, Computational, Applied Linguistics, and Modern Hebrew* (Ramat Gan, 1975) (partly English, partly Hebrew).

R. E. Bee, "The Use of Statistical Methods in Old Testament Studies," *Vetus Testamentum* 23 (1973) 257–72.

————, "Statistics and Source Criticism," *Vetus Testamentum* 33 (1983) 483–88.

M. P. Weitzman, "Verb Frequency and Source Criticism," *Vetus Testamentum* 31 (1981) 451–71.

For studies on internal differences within Classical Hebrew, see:

R. Polzin, *Late Biblical Hebrew: Toward an His-*torical Typology of Biblical Hebrew Prose (Missoula, 1976).

J. Hoftijzer, *A Search for Method* (Leiden, 1981).

A. Hurvitz, *A Linguistic Study of the Relationship between the Priestly Source and the Book of Ezekiel* (Paris, 1982).

Comprehensive literature concerning the vocalization and punctuation systems and related problems is available; recommended for introductory study are:

P. E. Kahle, *Die hebräische Bibeltext seit Franz Delitzsch* (Stuttgart, 1961).

————, *The Cairo Geniza* (London, 1959²).

————, "Pre-Masoretic Hebrew," *Textus* 2 (1962) 1–7. For a sharp critique of Kahle's standpoint, see E. Y. Kutscher, "Contemporary Studies in North-western Semitic," *Journal of Semitic Studies* 10 (1965) 21–51.

S. Morag, *The Vocalization Systems of Arabic, Hebrew and Aramaic, Their Phonetic and Phonemic Principles* (Gravenhage, 1962).

————, "On the Historical Validity of the Vocalization of the Hebrew Bible," *Journal of the American Oriental Society* 94 (1974) 307–15.

H. M. Orlinsky, ed., *1972 and 1973 Proceedings of the International Organization of Masoretic Studies* (New York, 1974).

E. J. Revell, *Biblical Texts with Palestinian Pointing and Their Accents* (Missoula, 1977).

B. Chiesa, *The Emergence of Hebrew Biblical Pointing: The Indirect Sources* (Bern/Frankfurt am Main, 1979).

I. Yeivin, *Introduction to the Tiberian Masorah* (Missoula, 1980).

J. C. L. Gibson, "The Massoretes as Linguists," in *Studies in Hebrew Language and Biblical Exegesis* (= *Oudtestamentische Studiën* 19; Leiden, 1974), pp. 86–96.

For Greek and Latin transcriptions of Hebrew see:

G. Lisowsky, "Die Transkription der hebräischen Eigennamen des Pentateuch in der Septuaginta" (Diss., Basel, 1940).

E. Brønno, *Die Aussprache der hebräischen Laryngale nach Zeugnissen des Hieronymus* (Aarhus, 1970).

————, *Studien über hebräische Morphologie und Vokalismus* (Leiden, 1943; repr. Nendeln, 1966).

G. Janssens, *Studies in Hebrew Historical Linguistics Based on Origen's Secunda* (Leuven, 1982).

See also the grammar by Sperber (listed above, p. 131) for an extensive treatment of this particular subject.

For script and the alphabet see:

A. R. Millard, "The Practice of Writing in Ancient Israel," *Biblical Archaeologist* 35 (1972) 90–111.

M. Heerma van Voss, et al., eds., *Van Beitel tot Penseel* (Leiden, 1973) (a popular introduction to the problems).

G. R. Driver, *Semitic Writing: From Pictograph to Alphabet* (London, 1973³).

P. K. McCarter, *The Antiquity of the Greek Alphabet and Early Phoenician Scripts* (Cambridge, Mass., 1975).

_____, "The Early Diffusion of the Alphabet," *Biblical Archaeologist* 37 (1974) 54–68.

J. Naveh, *Origins of the Alphabeth* (Jerusalem, 1975). An attractive, popular work with beautiful pictures.

_____, *Early History of the Alphabet: An Introduction to West Semitic Epigraphy and Palaeography* (Jerusalem/Leiden, 1982).

S. Warner, "The Alphabet: An Innovation and Its Diffusion," *Vetus Testamentum* 30 (1980) 81–90.

For spelling problems see:

F. M. Cross and D. N. Freedman, *Early Hebrew Orthography: A Study of the Epigraphic Evidence* (New Haven, 1952).

Z. Zevit, *Matres Lectionis in Ancient Hebrew Epigraphs* (Cambridge, Mass., 1980).

For the use of other Northwest Semitic languages in the interpretation and description of Classical Hebrew materials see:

M. Dahood, "Hebrew-Ugaritic Lexicography," appearing in *Biblica* 44 (1963) through 55 (1974).

_____, *Ugaritic-Hebrew Philology* (Rome, 1965).

L. R. Fisher, ed., *Ras Shamra Parallels* I–III (Rome, 1972–81).

For criticism of the above-mentioned works see:

J. C. de Moor, "Ugaritic Lexicography," in P. Fronzaroli, ed., *Studies on Semitic Lexicography* (Firenze, 1973), pp. 61–102.

J. C. de Moor and P. van der Lugt, "The Spectre of Pan-Ugaritism," *Bibliotheca Orientalis* 31 (1974) 3–26.

P. C. Craigie, "Ugarit and the Bible: Progress and Regress in 50 Years of Literary Study," in G. D. Young, ed., *Ugarit in Retrospect: Fifty Years of Ugarit and Ugaritic* (Winona Lake, 1981), pp. 99–111.

S. B. Parker, "Some Methodological Principles in Ugaritic Philology," *Maarav* 2 (1979/80) 7–41.

For the methodology in semantics research see:

J. Barr, *The Semantics of Biblical Language* (Oxford, 1961).

_____, *Comparative Philology and the Text of the Old Testament* (Oxford, 1968).

_____, "Etymology and the Old Testament," in *Language and Meaning. Studies in Hebrew Language and Biblical Exegesis* (= Oudtestamentische Studiën 19; Leiden, 1974), pp. 1–28.

R. Meyer, *Gegensinn und Mehrdeutigkeit in der althebräischen Wort- und Begriffsbildung* (Berlin, 1979) (cf. his article with the same title in *Ugarit-Forschungen* 11 [1979] 601–12).

J. Margain, *Essais de sémantique sur l'hébreu ancien. Monèmes fonctionnels et autonomes. Modalités* (Paris, 1976).

For lexicons of Classical Hebrew see:

W. Gesenius and F. Buhl, *Hebräisches und Aramäisches Handwörterbuch über das Alte Testament* (Leipzig, 1915¹⁷; repr. Berlin, 1962). Still very useful.

F. Brown, S. R. Driver, and C. A. Briggs, *A Hebrew and English Lexicon of the Old Testament* (Oxford, 1929; repr. 1968). Still very valuable.

F. Zorell and L. Semkowski, *Lexicon Hebraicum et Aramaicum Veteris Testamenti* (Rome, 1940–54; repr. 1968).

L. Koehler and W. Baumgartner, *Lexicon in Veteris Testamenti Libros* (Leiden, 1958²). The Aramaic part of this lexicon is of much better quality than the Hebrew part. The authors also issued *Supplementum ad Lexicon in Veteris Testamenti Libros* (Leiden, 1958). A third edition of this lexicon takes into account the results of more recent work: W. Baumgartner, with B. Hartmann and E. Y. Kutscher, *Hebräisches und aramäisches Lexicon zum Alten Testament von Ludwig Koehler und Walter Baumgartner* I– (Leiden, 1967– ).

For words from non-Old Testament texts see:

C. F. Jean and J. Hoftijzer, *Dictionnaire des Inscriptions sémitiques de l'Ouest* (Leiden, 1965).

J. C. L. Gibson, *Textbook of Syrian Semitic Inscriptions, I: Hebrew and Moabite Inscriptions* (Oxford, 1971).

Y. Aharoni, *Arad Inscriptions* (Jerusalem, 1981).

For lexicons geared to students see:

G. Fohrer, *Hebrew and Aramaic Dictionary of the Old Testament* (Berlin, 1973).

W. L. Holladay, *A Concise Hebrew and Aramaic Lexicon of the Old Testament* (Leiden, 1971).

For lexicography see:

J. Barr, "Hebrew Lexicography," in P. Fronzaroli, ed., *Studies on Semitic Lexicography* (Firenze, 1973), pp. 103–26.

For text editions of Classical Hebrew texts see:

K. Elliger and W. Rudolph, eds., *Biblia Hebraica Stuttgartensia* (Stuttgart, 1976).

R. Kittel, ed., *Biblia Hebraica* (Stuttgart, 1937³).

N. H. Snaith, *Torah Nebiim u Ketubim* (United Bible Society, 1958).

For the fragments of the Hebrew text of Sirach see:

F. Vattioni, *Ecclesiastico: Testo ebraico con apparato critico e versioni greca, latina e siriaca* (Naples, 1968).

For epigraphical material:

J. C. L. Gibson, *Textbook of Syrian Semitic Inscriptions, I: Hebrew and Moabite Inscriptions* (Oxford, 1971).

Y. Aharoni, *Arad Inscriptions* (Jerusalem, 1981).

A. Lemaire, *Inscriptions hébraïques* (Paris, 1977).

D. Pardee, et al., *Handbook of Ancient Hebrew Letters* (Chico, 1982).

Concordances for the above-mentioned material:

S. Mandelkern, *Veteris Testamenti Concordantiae Hebraicae atque Chaldaicae* (Leipzig, 1937). This work has been reprinted many times; a concise edition has also been issued, but it is much less useful than the complete edition.

G. Lisowsky, *Konkordanz zum hebräischen Alten Testament* (Stuttgart, 1958).

D. Barthélemy and O. Rickenbacher, *Konkordanz zum hebräischen Sirach mit syrisch-hebräischem Index* (Göttingen, 1973).

For the influence of other languages on Classical Hebrew see:

M. Ellenbogen, *Foreign Words in the Old Testament: Their Origin and Etymology* (London, 1962).

M. Wagner, *Die lexikalischen und grammatikalischen Aramaismen im alttestamentlichen Hebräisch* (Berlin, 1966).

————, "Beiträge zur Aramaismenfrage im alttestamentlichen Hebräisch," in *Hebräische Wortforschung* (= *Supplements to Vetus Testamentum* 16; Festschrift W. Baumgartner; Leiden, 1967), pp. 355–71.

For some translation problems connected to the Old Testament see:

A. R. Hulst, *Old Testament Translation Problems* (Amsterdam, 1960).

M. J. Mulder, "*ḥayil* in het boek Ruth. Een vertaalprobleem," in M. Boertien, et al., eds., *Verkenningen in een stroomgebied* (Festschrift M. A. Beek; Amsterdam, 1974), pp. 120–31. This article refers to literature of different signatures.

K. A. Deurloo, "Enkele notities bij de Verdeutschung der Schrift van Buber-Rosenzweig," *Vox Theologica* 38 (1968) 39–45.

D. Crystal, "Some Current Trends in Translation Theory," *The Bible Translator* 27 (1976) 322–29.

A. R. Müller, *Martin Bubers Verdeutschung der Schrift* (St. Ottilien, 1982).

---

## 2. ARAMAIC

A very small part of the Old Testament is written in Aramaic. It includes the following verses: Genesis 31:47 (two words that together are the Aramaic designation for the heap of stones brought together by Jacob, *gal-ʿed*); Jeremiah 10:11; Ezra 4:8–6:18 and 7:12–26; and Daniel 2:4–7:28. Most of these passages (with the exception of Gen. 31:47 and Jer. 10:11) are postexilic, that is, from after the sixth century B.C. It is no accident that the bulk of the Aramaic passages is from such a late period. It agrees with the fact—noted above, p. 126—that particularly in the Persian period Aramaic began to have a dominant influence in the Near East.

The Aramaic that was already a diplomatic and commercial language throughout the Near East about 700 B.C. (see p. 126) and reached a zenith in the Persian period was and is usually regarded as one language, designated as *Official Aramaic*. (It bears this name to distinguish it from various other Aramaic languages and dialects from an earlier or later period. As such Aramaic is not the designation of one language but of a whole group of languages.) According to the noted Aramaic scholar Franz Rosenthal, the Aramaic of the Old

Testament is virtually identical with Official Aramaic as used in official (Persian) documents. This approach makes the name given to the Aramaic in the Old Testament (*Biblical Aramaic*) misleading, properly speaking, for the term suggests a separate idiom with an internal unity, something that did not exist.

Objections can, however, be raised against the above-mentioned conception of Official Aramaic. Recently Jonas C. Greenfield argued that the so-called Official Aramaic texts exhibit a far smaller linguistic unity than is often thought. According to him an official Aramaic did indeed exist, and it had great influence particularly in the Persian period. Many writers, however, were more or less influenced by the special Aramaic dialect they themselves spoke. That means that in many texts there is no "pure" Official Aramaic. Greenfield's view is probably correct. The Hermopolis papyri found in Egypt provide a fine example. Though they are from the Persian period (second half of the 5th century B.C.), the Aramaic of these texts has so many special features that influence from the Aramaic of the writers themselves is undeniable. Then, too, the well-known Elephantine Papyri (5th century B.C.), also originating in Egypt and much more in agreement with the pattern of Official Aramaic, betray an occasional trait pointing to an influence other than that of Official Aramaic. It would therefore seem to be out of the question still to be able to speak of one official Aramaic language, with universal validity in a particular period, and which, at least in writing, had crowded out all other Aramaic languages.

The influence of Official Aramaic—which was very great—diminished slowly. This waning probably started during the fourth century B.C. at the end of the Persian period and the beginning of the Greek influence. But centuries later, traces of Official Aramaic can be found in Aramaic texts, for instance, in various Palmyrene inscriptions. The evaluation of Official Aramaic as described above should also have its consequences for the evaluation of the Aramaic of the Old Testament. If the material that is strongly influenced by an Official Aramaic, that is, the material customarily designated as Official Aramaic, already is linguistically much less uniform than was thought previously, we must raise anew that question concerning the relationship of the Old Testament language to the official language. One can no longer unquestioningly assume that it was virtually identical with that official language.

The first thing to be noted is that there are internal variations in the Old Testament material. Jeremiah 10:11 contains an example of older orthography that is not found elsewhere in the Aramaic of the Old Testament, even though there was reason enough to use it; in the Jeremiah verse we also find the newer spelling at this point (the same spelling used in Ezra and Daniel). In addition, this verse contains an older form of what, for the sake of convenience, we shall call the personal pronoun; this older form is also found in Ezra but not Daniel. Furthermore, we find there a form of the imperfect plural that is virtually lost in the rest of the material (exceptions are in Dan. 5:10), though there were certainly reasons to use it.

Besides the above-mentioned difference, there are other linguistic variations between the Aramaic parts of Ezra and Daniel. In Daniel, for example, a form of the demonstrative pronoun occurs that is lacking in Ezra. In turn all of the Old Testament material exhibits linguistic and spelling differences from the Aramaic used in the Persian empire in official government documents, of which some have survived. A typical example of this type of Aramaic is the Arsames correspondence, letters sent by the satrap of Egypt, who at that moment happened to be in one of the capitals (Susa?), to his district (end of 5th century B.C.). Thus all of the Old Testament material varies to some extent from the "pure" Official Aramaic. Jeremiah 10:11 is closest to it, though it, too, contains deviations. Daniel is furthest from it. As such, this is, of course, no proof that the Old Testament material as a whole must be from a later period than, for instance, the Arsames correspondence, because at the time that Official Aramaic was written in the administrative centers, less "pure" Aramaic could and was used elsewhere. (I leave aside Gen. 31:47, because the two Aramaic words found there do not help us here.) In a number of cases it is very likely that the variations in the Old Testament material are caused by the Aramaic dialect of the writer himself.

It is striking that the Aramaic parts of the book of Ezra contain the texts of a number of official documents: (a) a letter written by Transjordanian dignitaries to the Persian king (Ezra 4:11[end]-16); (b) a letter written by the king to these dignitaries (Ezra 4:17[end]–22); (c) a letter written by Transjordanian dignitaries to the Persian king (Ezra 5:7[second half]–17); (d) a decree issued by an earlier Persian king (Ezra 6:2[end]–5); (e) part of a letter to the dignitaries from Transjordan, written by the Persian king (6:6–12); (f) a decree issued by the Persian king (7:12–26). The language and spelling of these documents, one presumably from the sixth century B.C. and the others from the fifth century B.C., occasionally vary considerably from documents in Official Aramaic such as the Arsames correspondence. These variations are also much greater than those (except for an occasional exception) found in the Elephantine Papyri from the fifth century B.C., despite the fact that the majority of those papyri are not government documents or letters to public authorities, but contracts and letters to private individuals. This fact—there are other reasons as well—argues for the assumption (assuming that we have a reproduction of genuine documents here) that the person who composed the book of Ezra made changes in these documents; he left out certain parts that were considered less important or offensive, and adapted the language and spelling to that of his own time and situation. Therefore it seems plausible that the texts as we have them now are from a somewhat later time (4th century B.C.) and from a milieu that was less bound to Official Aramaic.

Another solution to these problems in the book of Ezra might be that in the copying of the Old Testament writings through the centuries small changes crept in by which, for instance, the original Aramaic of a text was slowly adapted to that of later generations and eventually was even lost altogether. One should indeed reckon with this, for such changes do happen to some extent. But to use it as an explanation for the sometimes great differences in language and spelling between the documents in Ezra and those in Official Aramaic goes too far. Precisely the fact that there are obvious differences between Jeremiah 10:11, Ezra, and Daniel argues against it. The small, sometimes unintentional changes were never so great that the internal differences were erased. (In the

Hebrew texts, too, one cannot escape the impression that the repeated copying did not, for example, obliterate the differences between older and younger texts.) The general impression is that those who in antiquity transmitted the text that is still being used in our editions of the Hebrew and Aramaic Old Testament were very precise and disciplined in their work. (I leave aside here the question concerning the relationship of this text to the sometimes divergent texts in the Dead Sea Scrolls.) On the basis of content, the most likely dating for the Aramaic texts in Daniel would appear to be the second century B.C., probably not long before the middle of the century. At that time one is already nearly two centuries beyond the end of the Persian period, when the influence of Official Aramaic began to wane. This is not at all in conflict with what we noted above, namely, that the Aramaic in the book of Daniel is further removed from the Official Aramaic than are all other Aramaic sections in the Old Testament.

From the above it also follows that, even if one shares the view of Greenfield, strictly speaking it is less correct to speak of *Biblical Aramaic*. To be sure, we were able to note obvious variations from Official Aramaic, and it appears to be a misconception to treat the so-called Official Aramaic material as a virtually closed unity. But we were also aware that the internal differences in the Old Testament Aramaic material are fairly large and that they do not allow us to follow an approach that ignores these variations. The use of the term Biblical Aramaic, to the extent that it might suggest a linguistically uniform body of material, can in that case be very confusing.

It appears that the authors of the Aramaic parts of Ezra and Daniel were Aramaic-speaking people. That is also how one can explain the deviations from the official language. Of course, this need not imply that they did not speak Hebrew. They may very well have been bilingual or at least proficient in more than one language. This agrees with what we said above about the expanding influence of Aramaic in the second half of the first millennium B.C. This influence continued to grow, even when Official Aramaic was past its peak. This meant that part of the Jews spoke a Hebrew that increasingly showed traces of Aramaic influence while another part either began to speak Aramaic exclusively or at least acquired Aramaic as a second language. One of the consequences of this development was that a considerable number of the later rabbinic writings are composed in some form of Aramaic (see also below, p. 139).

In the linguistic study of the Aramaic material in the Old Testament, one encounters the same problems as in the study of Classical Hebrew. In the case of Aramaic, too, the vocalization and punctuation systems were developed and added centuries later. Such a system, for instance, the Tiberian (see p. 123) used in the present editions, therefore provides no *immediate* access to the Aramaic language (or, perhaps better, languages) represented in the Old Testament text. In some cases it is very clear that the Aramaic of the vocalizer deviates sharply from that presupposed in the text and, in fact, cannot even be regarded as a younger form of it. For a more direct linguistic study of Biblical Aramaic one is dependent here, too, on the consonantal text (cf. p. 124). Since the oldest Aramaic texts in the Old Testament are in any case younger than the oldest Classical Hebrew texts (Jer. 10:11 is possibly from the 6th century B.C.), Aramaic does not have the problem that some of the texts were written before the introduction of *matres lectionis* for long vowels within a word (cf. p. 125). Moreover, their use in Aramaic was probably introduced somewhat earlier than in Classical Hebrew (in the course of the 8th century B.C.).

At the beginning of the first millennium B.C., Aramaic had at least five consonants more than the number of consonantal characters in the script (22, as in Hebrew). It appears that about the middle of this millennium, due to the decline in the number of independent consonants (a normal phenomenon in the Semitic languages), there was an equal number of consonants and consonantal characters in the language, though because of the conservative spelling, particularly in Official Aramaic, traces of the old situation remained. In the Aramaic of the Old Testament these traces are not found, except in Jeremiah 10:11. That Aramaic originally had so many consonants for which the script did not have a separate character shows that this type of script with its twenty-two characters was no more designed for Aramaic than for

Hebrew; the use of this script for Aramaic was a secondary development.

In the present editions the square script (see p. 124) is used for the Aramaic parts of the Old Testament just as for the Hebrew parts. A kind of cursive script was originally used for Aramaic. A number of variants of this script are possible, depending on time and locality. Though it is not exactly certain when the square script arose (see p. 124), it would seem certain that at least the older Aramaic parts of the Old Testament were not originally written in this script.

Foreign languages have put their stamp on Aramaic, too; clear traces of such influence are recognizable in the Old Testament. The greatest influence is in the area of the borrowing of words, especially from Akkadian and Persian. This is not surprising for a number of reasons. Aramaic arose as a language of diplomacy and commerce during the Assyrian hegemony over the Near East; Aramaic also enjoyed this dominant position during the Babylonian empire; and Official Aramaic played a central role during the Persian rule (see also p. 135). In addition to borrowing from Akkadian and Persian, Aramaic also borrowed from Greek. That language contributed three of the names of the musical instruments in Daniel 3 (not surprisingly, for Daniel was written in the 2nd century B.C., more than a century and a half after the time of Alexander the Great). This may be viewed as a harbinger of the great influence Greek was to have on Hebrew and especially on Aramaic, which borrowed many Greek words.

Though the syntax of Aramaic is not without its problems and difficulties, and the function of the verbal system is more complicated than is sometimes thought, difficulties such as in the area of verbs in Classical Hebrew do not occur in Aramaic. What is a problem is the very small number of available texts, which are much more limited than those of Classical Hebrew, even if one considers all the older Aramaic texts, including those in the Old Testament. Thus a grammatical study regularly encounters problem areas about which little (or nothing) is known. The highly heterogeneous character of the older Aramaic material (the Old Testament material is definitely not an exception) does not improve the situation. An additional complication is that one may have two languages in one text—for instance, Official Aramaic with traces of the language of the writer himself (often recognizable only with difficulty). Relative to the translation problems and questions associated with it, the situation is similar to the one in Classical Hebrew (as described above, pp. 128ff.).

A remaining question is why people started writing in Aramaic in addition to Hebrew. One reason is of course the position of Aramaic as international medium. This led to a weakening of the position of Hebrew, though it did not—as has been thought at times—lead to the demise of Hebrew. The way in which a switch from Hebrew to Aramaic is made in a document remains puzzling. The beginning of Daniel 2 is written in Hebrew; verse 4 says that the Chaldeans spoke to the king in Aramaic; the direct speech that follows is indeed in Aramaic, but when this speech is finished (in v. 7) the history continues in Aramaic. A similarly remarkable transition occurs in Ezra. Ezra 4:7 says (in Hebrew) that a number of officials wrote a letter to King Artaxerxes; this verse ends with the word *Aramaic*. The next verse (v. 8), which contains information about a letter of other important officials to King Artaxerxes, is then written in Aramaic. (Only Ezra 7:12–26 deals with an Aramaic document cited in an entirely Hebrew context.) These remarkable kinds of transitions from one language to another are understandable only if the authors of the texts were equally proficient in Aramaic and in Hebrew. Similar abrupt transitions are found in later Jewish literature, particularly in the Midrashim.

The New Testament is not written in a Semitic language, but in a certain kind of Greek called *koine*. But at the time of Jesus and his disciples, and of the origin of the New Testament, Aramaic played a large role in Palestine and surrounding countries (the Jews spoke a lot of Aramaic), and this was not without consequences. For instance, occasionally a statement from Jesus is quoted directly in Aramaic: *Ephphatha* at the healing of the deaf-mute (Mark 7:34), *Talitha cumi* at the healing of the daughter of Jairus (Mark 5:41), the abusive word *Raca* ("empty-headed," Matt. 5:22), and *Abba* as an epithet for God (Mark 14:36; this way of invoking God is also found in

Rom. 8:15 and Gal. 4:6). Therefore it is clear that Jesus did speak Aramaic. Occasionally also a Hebrew word spoken by Jesus is quoted directly: *Corban* (Mark 7:11; the verb might also be Aramaic, but in this case one expects it to be Hebrew; in Matt. 27:6 a Greek transcription of the Aramaic equivalent is given). The words from the cross, "*Eli, Eli, lama sabachthani*" (Matt. 27:46; cf. Mark 15:34) are a quotation from Psalm 22:2, though the last word is clearly in Aramaicized form. Though the example from Mark 7:11 opens the possibility that Jesus also spoke Hebrew, in most quotations the emphasis is on the Aramaic. Elsewhere in the Gospels traces of Aramaic are also found, for instance, in the title *Rabboni* that a blind man gives to Jesus (Mark 10:51; according to John 20:16 Mary Magdalene addressed the resurrected Lord with this title), in the designation of Peter as Simon Bar Jonah (Matt. 16:17, where *bar* is the Aramaic word for son), and in personal names, for example, Barabbas and Martha. The title of address *Rabbi* (Matt. 23:7, 8; 26:25, etc.) is probably Hebrew, and the greeting of which the word *Hosanna* is part (Matt. 21:9; Mark 11:9–10; John 12:13; *Hosanna* also occurs in Matt. 21:15) is a free quotation from Psalm 118:25–26. (In the New Testament passages, however, Hosanna is Aramaicized.) Outside the Gospels the words *Marana tha* (our Lord come) are found in 1 Corinthians 16:22. Though there is a slight trace of Hebrew influence, that of Aramaic is thus much greater. Words like *Amen* (Matt. 5:18, 26; 6:2, etc.) and *Hallelujah* (Rev. 19:1, 3, 4, 6) say little about the influence of contemporary Hebrew because these exclamations are taken over from the Old Testament. It is remarkable that beyond that Hebrew is quoted only in the book of Revelation: *Abaddon* (the netherworld; Rev. 9:11) and *Armageddon* (Rev. 16:16).

Besides this derivation from Aramaic (and Hebrew) words in a Greek text, a much greater influence of Aramaic should be mentioned, namely, the direct influence of Aramaic on the Greek of the writers of the New Testament. Particularly in regard to syntax, this influence can hardly be overestimated.

Fortunately, the idea is now widely accepted that insight into the Jewish-Rabbinic thought-world is indispensable for understanding the

New Testament. It is just as necessary that those who desire to interpret the New Testament to the best of their ability possess a thorough knowledge of the Aramaic *language* (in this case the various kinds of western Jewish Aramaic) in order to be able to detect Aramaic influence. Neglect of this does not help the exegesis of the text.

As we said, western Jewish Aramaic was not a linguistic unity. The texts reflect this variety. It is understandable that people have asked which of these dialects Jesus spoke. It would have been better, however, if the energy of the investigators had not been so one-sidedly expended on this question. If a part of this energy had been devoted to the linguistic study of western Jewish Aramaic texts (many texts are written in more than one kind of Aramaic)—possibly not as spectacular a subject for study—it would certainly have helped our understanding and, eventually, have been a better contribution toward answering the question what kind of Aramaic Jesus spoke.

## LITERATURE

A general overview of the modern study of all of Aramaic may be found in:

E. Y. Kutscher, "Aramaic," in T. A. Sebeok, ed., *Current Trends in Linguistics* VI (The Hague/Paris, 1970) 347–412 (repr. in E. Y. Kutscher, *Hebrew and Aramaic Studies* [Jerusalem/Leiden, 1977], pp. 90–155).

————, "Aramaic," *Encyclopaedia Judaica* III (Jerusalem, 1971) 259–87.

J. A. Fitzmyer, "The Phases of the Aramaic Language," in *A Wandering Aramean: Collected Aramaic Essays* (Missoula, 1979), pp. 57–84.

————, "The Languages of Palestine in the First Century A.D.," *Catholic Biblical Quarterly* 32 (1970) 501–31 (repr. in *A Wandering Aramean*, pp. 29–56).

A still very valuable work is:

F. Rosenthal, *Die aramaistische Forschung* (Leiden, 1939) (see also by the same author, "Aramaic Studies during the Past Thirty Years," *Journal of Near Eastern Studies* 37 [1978] 81–91).

For the problem of Official Aramaic see:

J. C. Greenfield, "Standard Literary Aramaic," in A. Caquot and D. Cohen, eds., *Actes du pre-*

*mier congrès international de linguistique sémitique et chamito-sémitique, Paris 16–19 juillet 1969* (The Hague/Paris, 1974), pp. 280–89.

See also:

J. Whitehead, "Some Distinct Features of the Language of the Aramaic Arsames Correspondence," *Journal of Near Eastern Studies* 37 (1978) 119–40.

F. Rundgren, "Aramaica IV. The Rise of Imperial Aramaic," *Orientalia Suecana* 30 (1981) 173–84.

And compare:

J. C. Greenfield, "The Dialects of Early Aramaic," *Journal of Near Eastern Studies* 37 (1978) 93–99.

T. Muraoka, "The Tell-Fekheriye Bilingual Inscription and Early Aramaic," *Abr Nahrain* 22 (1983–84) 79–117.

Grammars of Biblical Aramaic:

H. Bauer and P. Leander, *Grammatik des Biblisch-Aramäischen* (Halle, 1927; repr. Hildesheim, 1962). An excellent grammar which is still very useful.

F. Rosenthal, *A Grammar of Biblical Aramaic* (Wiesbaden, 1963²). A concise but good grammar for classroom use.

S. Segert, *Altaramäische Grammatik mit Bibliographie, Chrestomathie und Glossar* (Leipzig, 1975). A classroom grammar that treats Biblical Aramaic in connection with the older textual material; useful, although it has some weak points (cf. the reaction of R. Degen, *Göttingische Gelehrte Anzeigen* 23 [1979] 8–51).

Important general grammatical studies of Biblical Aramaic include:

W. Baumgartner, "Das Aramäische im Buche Daniel," *Zeitschrift für die alttestamentliche Wissenschaft* 45 (1927) 81–133 (repr. in W. Baumgartner, *Zum Alten Testament und seiner Welt* [Leiden, 1959], pp. 68–123).

H. H. Rowley, *The Aramaic of the Old Testament. A Grammatical and Lexical Study of its Relations with Other Early Aramaic Dialects* (Oxford, 1929).

H. B. Rosen, "On the Use of the Tenses in the Aramaic of Daniel," *Journal of Semitic Studies* 6 (1961) 183–203.

K. A. Kitchen, "The Aramaic of Daniel," in D. J. Wiseman, et al., *Notes on Some Problems in the Book of Daniel* (London, 1965), pp. 31–79.

T. Muraoka, "Notes on the Syntax of Biblical

Aramaic," *Journal of Semitic Studies* 11 (1966) 151–67.

D. R. Cohen, "Subject and Object in Biblical Aramaic: A Functional Approach Based on Form-Content Analysis," *Afroasiatic Linguistics* 2 (1975) 2–24.

P. W. Coxon, "The Syntax of the Aramaic of Daniel. A Dialectical Study," *Hebrew Union College Annual* 48 (1977) 107–22.

A. Vivian, *Studi di sintassi contrastiva; dialetti aramaici* (Firenze, 1981).

For vocalization and punctuation systems see above, pp. 133–34, especially the work of Morag.

For scripts and the alphabet, in addition to the works on p. 134, see:

J. Naveh, *The Development of the Aramaic Script* (Jerusalem, 1970).

For lexicons, in addition to those listed on pp. 134–35 which combine Hebrew and Biblical Aramaic, see:

E. Vogt, *Lexicon linguae aramaicae Veteris Testamenti documentis antiquis illustratum* (Rome, 1971).

A great deal of the Official Aramaic vocabulary may be found in the lexicon of Jean and Hoftijzer (listed above, p. 134).

For Aramaic lexicography see:

H. Donner, "Aramäische Lexicographie," in P. Fronzaroli, ed., *Studies on Semitic Lexicography* (Firenze, 1973), pp. 127–43.

J. C. Greenfield, "Some Reflexions on the Vocabulary of Aramaic in Relationship to the Other Semitic Languages," in P Fronzaroli, ed., *Atti del secondo congresso internazionale di Linguistica Camito-Semitica Firense 16–19 Aprile 1974* (Firenze, 1978), pp. 152–56.

For text editions see the three works listed on p. 135; for concordances see those of Mandelkern and Lisowsky.

For the influence of Akkadian on Aramaic see:

S. A. Kaufman, *The Akkadian Influences on Aramaic* (Chicago/London, 1974).

For the Aramaic background to New Testament Greek see:

M. Black, *An Aramaic Approach to the Gospels and Acts* (Oxford, 1966³).

K. Beyer, *Semitische Syntax im Neuen Testament* I/1 (Göttingen, 1962).

R. A. Martin, *Syntactical Evidence of Semitic Sources in Greek Documents* (Cambridge, Mass., 1974).

F. Zimmerman, *The Aramaic Origin of the Four Gospels* (New York, 1979).

J. A. Fitzmyer, "The Study of the Aramaic Background of the New Testament," in *A Wandering Aramean: Collected Aramaic Essays* (Missoula, 1979), pp. 1–27.

_____, "The Contribution of Qumran Aramaic to the Study of the New Testament," *New Testament Studies* 20 (1973–74) 382–407 (repr. in *A Wandering Aramean*, pp. 85–113).

For studies on the language that Jesus spoke, see:

G. Dalman, *The Words of Jesus* (Edinburgh, 1902).

J. A. Emerton, "Did Jesus Speak Hebrew?" *Journal of Theological Studies* 12 (1961) 189–202.

J. Barr, "Which Language Did Jesus Speak?" *Bulletin of the John Rylands Library* 53 (1970) 9–29.

H. Birkeland, *The Language of Jesus* (Oslo, 1954).

A. Díez Macho, "La lengua hablada por Jesu Cristo," *Oriens Antiquus* 2 (1963) 95–132.

H. Ott, "Um die Muttersprache Jesu. Forschungen seit Gustav Dalman," *Novum Testamentum* 9 (1967) 1–25.

M. Black, "Aramaic Studies and the Language of Jesus," in *In memoriam Paul Kahle* (Berlin, 1968), pp. 17–28.

M. Delcor, "Le Targum de Job et l'Araméen du temps de Jésus," *Exégese biblique et judaisme* (Leiden, 1973), pp. 78–107.

P. Lapide, "Insights from Qumran into the Language of Jesus," *Revue de Qumran* 8 (1972–76) 483–501.

The literature presented here is not intended to be complete; but by consulting the above works the reader can find most of the literature from the last century. For those who want to make an in-depth study of these matters, the following bibliographic aids are recommended:

J. H. Hospers, ed., *A Basic Bibliography for the Study of the Semitic Languages* I (Leiden, 1973). Although this bibliography does not pretend to be complete, under the headings "Hebrew" and "Aramaic" one may find a reasonably wide choice of publications.

The systematically arranged listings of new books and articles added to the installments of *Biblica*; for more than 20 years now these bibliographical synopses have appeared in separate volumes as *Elenchus Bibliographicus Biblicus* (ed. P. Nober), a very helpful aid for tracing literature dealing with a specific area in biblical studies and in related fields.

The *Zeitschriften* and *Bücherschau* sections of *Zeitschrift für die alttestamentliche Wissen-* *schaft* also give information on recently published literature. Because the above-mentioned *Elenchus* tends to appear one or more years overdue, the synopses offered by this *Zeitschrift* are quite helpful in finding the most recent literature.

# C. Greek as the Language of the New Testament

*by G. Mussies*

In the Gospel of John (7:34–35) we read that, with respect to his words "Where I am you cannot come," the adversaries of Jesus ask themselves, "Does he intend to go to the Dispersion among the *Greeks* [i.e., Greek-speaking Jews]?" In the same Gospel we read (19:19–20) that the Roman governor had the superscription "Jesus the Nazorean, the King of the Jews" affixed to the cross not only in the language of the Roman rulers of Palestine and in that of the subjected people but also—at a distance of 1,300 kilometers (800 mi.) from Athens—in *Greek*. The addition "the Nazorean" found here (i.e., "the Nazarene"), or "the Messiah" (John 1:41), and the name "Nazoreans" for his disciples and followers (Acts 24:5), all three of which are (half-)Aramaic, have not become the customary designations, but "Christ," the *Greek* translation of "Messiah" (John 4:25), and "Christians," derived from it (Acts 11:26). Add to this the familiar fact that the whole New Testament, including the many quotations from the Old Testament, is written in Greek, and any reader who is rather unacquainted with the ancient world will wonder why this language, not indigenous to Palestine, played such a large role in this land and in connection with Jesus and the emerging Christendom, a role about which the New Testament is almost silent.

The above-mentioned texts raise a number of questions with respect to the use of Greek. On a closer look they can, however, be reduced to two main questions: How did the Greek language come to Palestine? Why was the New Testament written in Greek?

The answer to these two questions demands more than a look at the New Testament, more even than a look at the New Testament era. The answer necessarily leads us back to a time centuries before the events mentioned in the Gospels happened and were recorded. At the same time, owing to the scarcity of data from the first century, the answers must take subsequent centuries into account to some extent.

## 1. HOW DID THE GREEK LANGUAGE COME TO PALESTINE?

From the half-mythical records about the oldest period of Greek history one can infer that already at that time the Greeks and their language had spread outside the homeland along the coasts of the Mediterranean Sea and the Black Sea. Homer's poetry about the Trojan War not only carries us to the city of Troy in northwest Asia Minor, but also speaks in passing (*Iliad* vi.215ff.) of old relations between central Greece (Aetolia) and southwestern Asia Minor (Lycia). The *Odyssey* carries us to the western part of the Mediterranean Sea, if not farther, and it also tells us about Cyprus, Phoenicia, Egypt, and Libya (iv.83ff.). The famous journey of the Argonauts had as its destination Colchis, at the extreme eastern part of the Black Sea. Consequently, trade posts and permanent settlements began to be established at an early age: Ephesus and Miletus in Asia Minor in the eleventh century B.C., Salamis in Cyprus probably even earlier. Later the settlements were farther and farther away from the homeland: in Mainake in southern Spain in the seventh century, in Massilia (Marseille) around 600, in Cyme in Campania and in east Sicily in the eighth century; Cyrene was founded in 630, Naucratis on the western branch of the Nile about 650, both Pantikapeum on the eastern point of the Crimea and Olbia near the mouth of the Dnieper in the seventh century.

By enlisting as mercenaries in the armies of oriental rulers, the Greeks and their language traveled far from their land. Familiar to readers are the Ionians who were a regular part of the army of the pharaohs of the Twenty-sixth Dynasty of Egypt, such as Apries (called Hophra in Jer. 44:30), and especially Xenophon and his soldiers, who were mercenaries in the army of Cyrus the Younger of Persia when he rebelled against his brother Artaxerxes II in 401 B.C., and the retreat of this mercenary army to the west as described in the *Anabasis*. It so happens that the first Greeks whom we know by name to have been in Palestine belonged to the military category: "Iamani," that is, "the Ionian," the man who in 712 B.C. usurped the throne of Ashdod, and Antimenidas, who in 604, while in the army of Nebuchadrezzar, participated in the siege of Ashkelon and who was a brother of the lyric poet Alceus. Possibly the "Kittiyim," who occur a number of times in the Arad ostraca about military supplies, were Greek mercenaries from Cyprus in the army of King Josiah (see Y. Aharoni, *Arad Inscriptions* [Jerusalem, 1981], nos. 1, 2, 7, 8, 10, 11, 14, and pp. 12b–13a; I owe this reference to Dr. Helga Weippert of Heidelberg). See ill. 51.

The spread of Greek throughout the Near East, initially through trade or temporary military service, occurred especially when Alexander III, "the Great," of Macedonia conquered the immense Persian empire (334–324 B.C.) and stationed officials and army detachments at strategic points, for instance in the city of Samaria. Eventually this new empire extended from the Ionian Sea in the west to the Indus in the east, and from Maracanda (now Samarkand) north of Afghanistan to Syene (now Aswan) in southern Egypt. The army by which this was accomplished had been organized after the model of the Theban army by Philip II of Macedonia, who had spent three years as a hostage in Thebes; more than half of it consisted of Thessalians and other Greeks, while the rest was made up of Macedonians. The language used by all these Greeks was Attic, the dialect of Athens, the city that for a long time played a dominant role in Greek politics and still maintained extensive trade connections with the rest of the Greek world. The Greeks and the Macedonians, who themselves were not Greek but had superficially been hellenized, used Attic as their vehicle of communication. Attic was also used by the Macedonian royal house as the language of the court in its Pella residence.

The official language of the empire of Alexander could therefore hardly be other than Attic, though slightly colored by the Ionian dialect. For instance, the Attic *-tt-* was consistently replaced by the Ionian *-ss-*, as in *thalatta* "sea," which became *thalassa*. After the death of Alexander, when his empire virtually disintegrated, Attic remained the official language of the new kingdoms that were formed. This was also the case in Palestine, which soon became part of the Egyptian kingdom of Ptolemy I and his successors and remained so until 198 B.C. Because of its function this language was called the *koine dialektos*, the "common language," hence "Koine Greek" is the Attic that was used outside Attica after 330 B.C. The brief period when Palestine was ruled by the Seleucids, the Macedonian dynasty that controlled Syria (198–168 B.C.), brought no change in this matter.

Even the Maccabean revolt in 167 B.C. against the hellenizing politics of the Seleucids, which resulted in an independent Jewish state, did not cause a large shift, except that Hebrew again received official status beside Greek. The purely Jewish territory in this state, however, covered only Jerusalem and its environs. By contrast the entire coastal strip was hellenized. There were many centers of Hellenism inland as well: Marisa in Idumea, the city of Samaria, Scythopolis (Bethshean), Gadara across the Sea of Gennesaret (Sea of Galilee), and the other cities of the Decapolis. The expansion of the Maccabean state entailed, of course, the annexation of hellenized cities and countrysides, but it is obvious that the Greek language remained predominant in the governmental structure of those cities and regions. This dominance of Greek is reflected in the names of the Maccabean royal family; as early as the second generation, names occur both in Hebrew and in Greek. Maccabean coins tell the same story. Initially they bore only Hebrew inscriptions;

after some time, under Alexander Janneus (103–76 B.C.), bilingual Hebrew-Greek coins were also made, while as far as we know his grandson Antigonus Mattathias (40–37 B.C.) had only bilingual and Greek coins made. That Jonathan, the brother of Judas Maccabeus, could carry on a correspondence with rulers of Sparta (1 Macc. 12:2, 5ff.) is therefore no more surprising than the earlier correspondence between King Arius I of Sparta and the high priest Onias (1 Macc. 12:7, 20ff.).

After the arrival of the Romans and the Herodian dynasty they supported, Greek remained the language of government, though Latin, of course, now appeared alongside it; Julius Caesar had the decree whereby Hyrcanus II was appointed high priest and "ethnarch" inscribed on bronze plates in Greek and in Latin, and these plates were placed in Rome, Tyre, Sidon, and Ashkelon. According to Josephus (*Jewish War* 6.125), the inscription affixed to the temple in Jerusalem that denied access to non-Jews was also in Greek and in Latin, though only the Greek (ill. 52) has been found (in two copies): "No stranger (may) enter within the fence and the wall around the sanctuary. The person who is caught there is himself responsible because it is punishable by death" (Frey, no. 1400). According to John (19:20) and Luke (23:38, but not in all manuscripts), the superscription above Jesus' cross also contained a Latin version, something that cannot have surprised those passing by. Possibly the fact that it was also written in Hebrew is the most important, because with this language the Roman governor also spoke on behalf of the Sanhedrin.

As an administrative and juridical language Greek developed strong roots, as is evident from the following illustration. The eastern part of the Seleucid realm (Mesopotamia-Persia) gained its total independence under the Parthians in 139 B.C. Yet two sale contracts, made by native Iranians in 88 B.C. and 22/21 B.C., were still written in Greek (known as the Avroman parchments, named after the place in Persian Kurdistan where they were discovered). So far no comparable examples from first-century Palestine have been found. From the second century there are, however, several dated legal documents, such as the remarriage contract of Eleaios, son of Simon, and Salome, daughter of John, from Galoda in northern Judea (A.D. 124; see P. Benoit, J. T. Milik, and R. de Vaux, *Discoveries in the Judaean Desert II. Les grottes de Murabba'ât* [Oxford, 1961], no. 115). There is also the collection of documents from the years A.D. 110–132 that together constitute the so-called archive of Babatha, a woman who owned possessions near the Dead Sea and who lived in Maoza, southeast of it (*Israel Exploration Journal* 12 [1962] 258ff.). Looking again to a familiar administrative event, the census of Luke 2, we may safely assume that the orders were written in Greek.

So far we have discussed Greek in Palestine as the language of government. To what extent was it also the language of the population? Above we noted that when the Maccabean revolt broke out, the area where the Jews lived was not much larger than Jerusalem and the surrounding countryside. In the south this area stopped just short of Hebron, and in the north it did not go beyond the line that can be drawn eastward from Joppa. It was only in this part of Palestine that the hellenizing policies of the Ptolemies and the Seleucids evoked revulsion and revolt, particularly when the hellenizing attempts touched on the cult. During the Egyptian and the Syrian rule, the hellenizing party had its supporters especially among the priests and the aristocracy, such as the family of the Tobiads. When Antiochus IV attempted to introduce the Zeus cult in Jerusalem, the Maccabees, supported by the Hasideans, were sparked into armed revolt. Everywhere else, however, Hellenism could flourish most of the time undisturbed; colonists settled in Palestine, especially in the Decapolis ("Ten Cities") district. Alexander the Great himself probably established there the small city of Dion, which received its name from the identically named holy city of the Macedonians at the northern foot of Mount Olympus. Other cities were reestablished, that is, they received a city government after the Greek model and were renamed: Pahel was given a name resembling it, Pella, after the royal residence in Macedonia; Beth-shean was now called Scythopolis; Rabbah "of the children of Ammon" was now named Philadelphia after Ptolemy II Philadelphus; Susitha (i.e., "mare") was simply translated into Hippos (or Hippe).

As we mentioned, the expansion of the Maccabean kingdom always meant that more or less hellenized territory was added to Judea: battles were waged repeatedly in and about the Pentapolis (Philistia) west of Judea (1 Macc. 5:68; 10:76ff.; 11:59ff.; 13:43). South of it lay Idumea, inhabited by the Edomites, who had been forced out of their earlier tribal territory south of the Dead Sea and in the course of the fifth century B.C. had settled in the region west of it. Their chief city, Marisa, was a center of Hellenism; many tombs with murals and inscriptions in Greek have been found there. After the conquest by the Maccabeans, when circumcision was made obligatory about 126 B.C., it also became a part of Judaism religiously (Josephus, *Antiquities* 13.257). The same happened to the population of a part of Iturea in the extreme north, around 105 B.C. (Josephus, *Antiquities* 13.319), after the intervening districts of Galilee (only in part inhabited by Jews) and the territory of the Samaritans had been conquered. In Samaria a Macedonian settlement had been established already in 331 B.C. In 167 B.C. a colony of Sidonians attempted to hellenize the non-Jewish but related cult on Mount Gerizim (Josephus, *Antiquities* 12.258ff.). In 129/128 the Maccabeans took action and destroyed the temple (Josephus, *Antiquities* 13.255-56), then took Shechem and later the city of Samaria (Josephus, *Antiquities* 13.275ff.).

Already in the pre-Christian era many of these Hellenistic cities in Palestine had produced significant authors and scholars. The philosopher Antiochus, one of the teachers of Cicero, came from Ashkelon (ca. 68 B.C.). Gadara, across the Sea of Gennesaret, was the birthplace of no less than four familiar men: Menippus (3rd century B.C.), author of satirical works; his younger contemporary Meleager, author of some fifty epigrams, preserved in the *Anthologia Palatina,* the greatest collection of that kind of poems; furthermore, the Epicurean philosopher Philodemus (ca. 50 B.C.); and Oinomaus, a Cynic philosopher who sharply opposed soothsaying (though with him we are already in the 2nd century A.D.).

Of these men, the one of whom we have the most vivid picture is the poet Meleager. Almost all his epigrams are love songs, often addressed directly to the beloved. Some are addressed to his maid Dorcas—her name, like Tabitha in Acts 9:36, means "gazelle"; addressing her in poetic language he asks her to give a message to the beloved from her master. In one of these he laments that his girlfriend Demo has found another, apparently a Jewish lover; "but," says he, "if a sabbath love has caught you, no wonder: even on cold sabbaths love is warm" (*Anthologia Palatina* 5.160). Remarkably, he also wrote no less than three epitaphs for his own tomb, in which he also says something about his own life. In a free translation one of them reads:

> The island of Tyre was my nurse, but as for my home city, I was begotten from the Attic city of Gadara, located in Assyria.
> From Eucrates sprang I, Meleager, who first with the help of the Muses, contended with the Graces of Menippus.
> If I am a Syrian, what does it matter? Stranger, we dwell in one country: the world; the one Chaos brought forth all mortals.
> In my old age I wrote these lines on my tablet, before my death: for old age is the next-door neighbor of the grave.
> But greet me, the loquacious old man, and may you reach a garrulous old age yourself.
> (*Anthologia Palatina* 7.417)

Thus the poet addresses, as it were, those passing by his future tombstone. He calls Gadara "Attic" and locates it in Assyria (in antiquity Assyria and Syria were often used interchangeably). Apparently he did not spend his youth in his native city, but in Tyre, and in a second epitaph he tells us that he spent his old age in the island of Cos (cf. Acts 21:1). If he could call Gadara a "Syrian Athens," the city must have been very Greek. The herd of swine in the story of the two demon-possessed men in the land of the Gadarenes (Matt. 8:28ff.) is also significant in this respect, though according to Josephus, Gadara also had some Jews in A.D. 66. Meleager's third epitaph is interesting for its ending, where he keeps in mind that those passing by his grave may be of various origins and speak different languages. He greets them in various languages and asks for their greeting:

> But if you are a Syrian (I say): "*salam*"; if you are a Phoenician: "*naidios*"; if a Greek:

*"chaire"*; and say you then the same yourself.
(*Anthologia Palatina* 7.419)

Not only in these typically Hellenistic parts was Greek known and spoken. Besides at the court, it must also have been used in Jerusalem within priestly circles. According to the pseudepigraphic Letter of Aristeas to Philocrates, written perhaps in the first century B.C., Ptolemy II summoned seventy-two scribes from Jerusalem to translate the Jewish law for his library (at that time he did not have a copy). It is highly possible that an Egyptian king was interested in such a translation; it was, however, more a juridical than a bibliophilic interest: it made sense to possess a copy of the law code that enjoyed such great authority in a territory belonging to his realm and with a sizable minority of the population of the capital city Alexandria (observation of J. W. Doeve, Utrecht). Possibly at first only the "Law" (i.e., the Pentateuch) was translated. The rest of the Old Testament was done much later, as can be inferred from the postscript to the book of Esther in the Septuagint: "In the fourth year of the reign of Ptolemy [V?] and Cleopatra, Dositheus, who said that he was a priest and a Levite, and Ptolemy his son brought to Egypt the preceding letter concerning Purim. They said that it had been sent [reading *heinai* for *einai*] and translated by Lysimachus the son of Ptolemy, one of the residents of Jerusalem" (Esth. 10:3 LXX).

All this points to a tradition of instruction in Greek in Jerusalem, not so much with an eye to the wisdom of the Greeks (1 Cor. 1:22), but more for contact with the Jews living in the Dispersion and the spreading of Jewish writings abroad. Whether the information is historically true or not, apparently the notion that there were so many scribes in Jerusalem who knew Greek was not at all strange. For that reason it has been assumed that even before the beginning of our era the books Judith, Susanna, 1 Maccabees, the Testament of Job, the Testaments of the Twelve Patriarchs, and parts of the Enoch literature were written in Palestine. A similar center of Greek studies, possibly maintained by priests, may also contain the explanation for the excellent Greek later written by James in his letter to the "twelve tribes in the Dispersion" (James 1:1), though

many have considered it impossible that a Palestinian Jew could have such a mastery of Greek. Likewise Paul, who most likely came to Jerusalem at a very early age, must have been able to perfect his Greek style there. His answer, "I am a Jew, from Tarsus in Cilicia, a citizen of no mean city," refers not only to "Do you know Greek?" but just as much, if not more, to "Are you not the Egyptian, then?" (Acts 21:37ff.). Finally, Josephus, who was from a priestly family, undoubtedly learned his Greek in Jerusalem, but as he tells us, he never managed to learn the correct pronunciation (Josephus, *Antiquities* 20.263). This instruction alone could be the reason that there are a relatively large number of Greek loanwords in the Hebrew and Aramaic of later rabbinic literature such as the Talmud. Because these loanwords are not from one particular segment of life but from various areas of life, it is obvious that their source was a more widespread use of the Greek language. The first words we know still made it into the Old Testament; these are the terms for musical instruments in the Aramaic of Daniel 3:5 and 7 (e.g., *sumponyah*, RSV "bagpipe," from Greek *symphonia*). At a later time Greek legal and commercial terms, architectural terms, names of minerals, and the like are also found.

Apart from the purely pagan (e.g., the list of priests of the temple of Zeus Olympius in Samaria from the 2nd century B.C.) and the Christian inscriptions (e.g., the captions in the mosaic map of Palestine in the church of Medeba, A.D. 560–565), over 450 Greek inscriptions of Jewish origin have been found west of the Jordan alone. Most of these are brief epitaphs, often consisting only of names or short stereotyped sentences: "Josepus [sic!] son of Jairus," "Ammia from Scythopolis," "Here lies Isakis, oldest of the (congregation of) the Cappadocians, linen merchant from Tarsus" (Frey, nos. 1368, 1372, 931). They are for the most part from the cemeteries of Bethshearim (1st-4th centuries), Joppa (2nd-3rd centuries), Caesarea Maritima (Roman period), and Jerusalem (2nd century B.C.-2nd century A.D.); especially the last are significant for the New Testament era on account of their date. They are mainly on ossuaries, stone caskets containing the bones of the departed. So there were numerous Jews who even at the end of their life made use of Greek rather than the old Hebrew. It is natural to assume that these were Greek-speaking Jews who had repatriated from the lands of the Dispersion, such as the above-named Isakis in Joppa, or their descendants. But when one considers the relatively large number of these Greek inscriptions on ossuaries, 64 over against 97 in Hebrew or Aramaic, the question arises whether these were exclusively Jews of the dispersion. In a city such as Joppa that was hellenized much longer, the ratio between Greek and Hebrew inscriptions was even more lopsidedly in favor of Greek; of the inscriptions found at the cemetery there, only seven are in Hebrew over against fifty-seven in Greek (among the latter we have included those that contain only the Hebrew word *shalom* or the letter *shin* as its abbreviation, but for the rest are entirely in Greek). In all probability there was also a continually increasing number of hellenized Palestinian Jews. Together these two groups comprised the category of "Hellenists" that are mentioned in Acts 6:1 and 9:29. In their synagogue(s) the Law was probably still read in Hebrew but then translated into Greek and interpreted in this language. To these "Hellenists" belonged no doubt the Libertines, Cyrenians, Alexandrians, and others mentioned in Acts 6:9. These "Libertines" were released people (RSV "Freedmen") who had returned from Italy to Palestine. In view of the typically Latin name of his father, Theodotus, a ruler of the synagogue, may have belonged to this group. He had the following inscription (ill. 53), found at the ridge of Ophel, made:

> Theodotus, son of Vettenus, priest and synagogue-president, son of a synagogue-president and grandson of a synagogue-president, has built the synagogue for the reading of the Law and the teaching of the commandments and (he has built) the hostelry and the chambers and the cisterns of water in order to provide lodgings for those from abroad who need them—(the synagogue) which his fathers and the elders and Simonides have founded. (W. F. Albright, *Recent Discoveries in Bible Lands* [New York, 1955], p. 112)

The Qumran library also contained fragments of the Septuagint, suggesting that in the first century almost every group of Jews had some who spoke Greek in its midst. One of the Qumran scrolls, containing the Minor Prophets in a different Greek translation, is an indication that there was a need for a Greek Old Testament. Even the fortress of Masada near the Dead Sea, the Jewish stronghold that held out the longest against the Romans (until A.D. 73), where a Hebrew copy of Sirach was found, has also yielded a Greek letter about the delivery of vegetables and beverages, addressed to a certain Judas (*Israel Exploration Journal* 15 [1965] 110). Still later, three languages were used side by side in the army of Simon Bar Kochba that fought for freedom from the Romans (A.D. 132–135). One of these letters mentions the language problem: "Sumaios to Jonathan (son of) Baianos and to Masabalas: greetings. Because I have sent Agrippa to you, make haste to send me sticks and citrons. You must deliver these before the Citron Feast [Feast of Booths] of the Jews and not do otherwise. This is written in Greek because [Her]mas could not be found to write in Hebrew. Send him [Agrippa] quickly in view of the feast and do not otherwise. Sumaios. Farewell." Though the addition "[Her]" may not be altogether certain, two things are clear: the addressee Jonathan should have been approached in Hebrew, but he also understood Greek, while Sumaios for one reason or another had to fall back on Greek, possibly because he did not know any Hebrew; the addition "of the Jews" is unnecessary when dealing with a Jew and leads one to think that Sumaios himself was not a Jew (see B. Lifshitz, "Papyrus grecs du désert de Juda," *Aegyptus* 42 [1962] 240ff.; the addition "Her" to make the name Hermas is taken over from G. Howard and J. C. Shelton, "The Bar-Kokhba Letters and Palestinian Greek," *Israel Exploration Journal* 23 [1973] 101–102).

During the reign of Herod I and his successors, Palestine offered, if possible, even more opportunity for the learning of Greek and the study of Greek culture in all its facets. Not only did Herod found new Hellenistic cities, among others Caesarea and Sebaste, the old Samaria (now Sebastiye), while his son founded Tiberias (now Tabariye), but he tried especially to make Jerusalem equal to other cultural centers by constructing parks, building palaces, a circus, and a theater, and introducing festivals and games. At his court were Greek scholars, best known of whom is the historian-philosopher Nicolaus of Damascus who, among other things, was a teacher of the children of Anthony and Cleopatra. All this in the heart of Judea! Conversely, in the Hellenistic cities outside Judea lived Jews who in some cases constituted sizable minorities. On the eve of the great rebellion of A.D. 66, large numbers of them were killed. Josephus mentions 20,000 dead in Caesarea, 13,000 in Scythopolis, and 2,500 in Ashkelon, while there were also victims in Gadara and Hippos. There were also Jews in Gerasa, but these were allowed to leave without harm (*Jewish War* 2.457, 468, 477–80). He adds that all cities were divided into two camps and that the continuation of the one party depended on the destruction of the other (2.462). This shows how much the two population groups were mixed, something that advanced Greek as a second language even more.

In this kind of language situation a great need for interpreters is hardly to be expected. For that reason the New Testament never mentions them when Romans and Jews had to communicate—in Greek, of course—with each other: Jesus and the centurion (Matt. 8:5), Jesus and Pilate (Mark 15:1–11 par.), Peter and the centurion Cornelius (Acts 10), and later Titus and the inhabitants of Jerusalem (Josephus, *Jewish War* 5.361). The same is true of the conversations between Philip and the "Greeks," whether or not these were Dispersion Jews or proselytes (John 12:20–21). Perhaps the conversation between Jesus and the Gadarenes and other inhabitants of the Decapolis (e.g., Matt. 8:28, 34; Mark 5:17) and between Jesus and the Syrophoenician "Greek" woman (Mark 7:27)—"Greek-speaking" or "pagan"?— may also be mentioned here. In both cases it is just as possible, even more likely, that Aramaic was used. Meleager of Gadara (see above) was multilingual, and we read in Matthew 4:25 that among the multitudes following Jesus were many people from the Decapolis; could it be that Greek was spoken just for their sake or was what was said always translated into Greek? From Acts 21:27, 40 and 22:2 it might be inferred that many common people in Jerusalem could understand Greek. For Jews from Asia (western Asia Minor) stirred up a crowd against Paul and when he, contrary to expectation, did not begin to address these people in Greek but in "Hebrew," "there was a great hush" because the majority of them understood that language better; of course, the initial hush (21:40) may also have been due to the tense expectation of what was going to happen. The tribune expressed his amazement that Paul knew Greek because he thought he was dealing with an Egyptian bandit whom he did not expect to have that knowledge. This widespread knowledge of Greek shows that the question whether Jesus himself knew Greek must be answered affirmatively.

In our judgment, though, the number of people who spoke only Greek should not be overestimated, not in regard to the Hellenistic cities either, while on the other hand there must have been many people who spoke only Aramaic. Even from a much later period there are indications that some people in the cities did not know Greek, for example in the Christian church at Scythopolis. Of Procopius, who died a martyr's death under the emperor Diocletian (A.D. 303), it is known that he read the Scriptures in Greek but interpreted them in "Syriac" (Aramaic). About the beginning of the fifth century, a woman named Aetheria, perhaps from southern France, made a pilgrimage to the Holy Land and wrote about the worship service in Jerusalem:

> A portion of the population in this province knows both Greek and Syriac; another segment knows only Greek; and still another, only Syriac. Even though the bishop may know Syriac, he always speaks Greek and never Syriac; and, therefore, there is always present a priest who, while the bishop speaks in Greek, translates into Syriac so that all understand what is being explained. Since whatever scriptural texts are read must be read in Greek, there is always someone present who can translate the readings into Syriac for the people, so that they will always learn. (*Peregrinatio Aetheriae* 47.3–4; *Ancient Christian Writers*, no. 38)

It is thus correct to say that first-century Palestine was trilingual, provided one makes clear what precisely is meant by it. There were not three territories, each with its own language, as in modern Switzerland. It is even doubtful that there was still a separate area where Hebrew was spoken in addition to Aramaic. In regard to

Greek, it is best to speak of both a geographical and a social factor. First of all, for many people, if not the majority, Greek was a "second" language, as was the case with the Romans. Among Jews and Jewish Christians, Greek unilingualism was likely found mainly among the repatriates living in the cities. A knowledge of Greek in addition to the native tongue (Aramaic or Hebrew) was found more in the cities than in the villages, and generally speaking more among men than among women, more among merchants, priests, and lower officials than among the agricultural population. We are in the dark as to the extent to which one or the other was the case. There may have been priests who did not know Greek and farmers who did understand it, as can be illustrated by an example from a later period. Huna, a rabbi from the fourth century who had returned from Babylonia to Palestine, was given a legal problem. There was a court case about a document in Greek in which only the syllable -konta (= Eng. "-ty") was legible of the word for the amount of money, while someone had intentionally written "eigh-" over "fif-." He was asked to send someone to find out which Greek numeral ending in "ty" had the lowest value. Huna interpreted the contract on the basis of that numeral (30 in Greek; it would have been 20 in English) and noted, after the litigating parties had left: "This party wanted to make 30, but lost 20" (Baba Bathra 10.1.17c). Perhaps the two second cousins of Jesus who were brought to Rome and led before Domitian, suspected of being Christians on account of their descent from the royal house of David, were two Greek-speaking farmers. Hegesippus, who is cited by Eusebius, writes: "He [the emperor] asked them if they were of the house of David and they admitted it." Next he inquired about their property, and discovering that they possessed only a small parcel of land from which they made a living, he permitted them to return to their country unharmed (Eusebius, Ecclesiastical History 3.20.1–6). One gets the impression that the emperor talked directly to them, though it is possible that the use of an interpreter in such interrogations was such a common occurrence that, unless there would be a special reason for it, it was never mentioned. Similarly, the first conversation of Joseph with his brothers is told in Genesis 42:7–22 in a way that makes it appear as if Joseph talked directly with his brothers; only in verse 23 does it become clear that an interpreter was present because Joseph also understands what Reuben says to his brothers and is touched by it, even though what he said had not been translated.

## 2. WHY WAS THE NEW TESTAMENT WRITTEN IN GREEK?

This question cannot be answered by referring to the official status of Greek in Palestine as the language of government nor by pointing to its significance there as the second language. For the answer we must turn to the Diaspora. Jews who moved abroad, particularly to the coastal regions of Cyrene, Egypt, Syria, and Asia Minor, could communicate with the resident population only in the common language, which since Alexander the Great had been Koine Greek. As early as the prophecy of Joel (400 B.C.?) we read of Israelites who were carried away to the harbor cities of Philistia and Phoenicia and sold as slaves to the Ionians (3:4–5). No doubt some of them were eventually set free and remained in their new country. At Delphi, inscriptions have been found of Greeks who, in order to release their Jewish slaves, sold them to the god Apollo: "During the archonship of Emmenidas, (son) of Kallias, (162 B.C.) in the month Apellaios, Cleon, (son) of Cleudamos, with the approval of Xenophania, the mother of Cleudamos, sold to Apollo Pythius a male slave, called Joudaios (Judah), of Jewish descent, at the price of four silver minas, on condition that he shall be free and untouchable by anyone for his whole life, while Judaios may do what he wants to in accordance with the fact that he has entrusted the sale to the god" (followed by the names of two guarantors and ten witnesses). A second inscription from Delphi mentions a similar release of a Jewish mother, Antigona, and her daughters Theodora and Dorothea, while in a third Delphic inscription a Jewish owner, Judaios, son of Pindaros, releases a slave in this manner (Frey, nos. 710, 709, 711). Of course, Jews did not go abroad only as slaves. During his stay in Asia Minor (ca. 345 B.C.) the philosopher Aristotle met a traveling Jew who spoke good Greek.

Traveling inland to Syria, Arabia, Mesopotamia, or Persia, the first language Jews would use for communication would be some form of Aramaic; this was the language that had been the vehicle of communication in the Persian empire until Alexander and that remained important for a long time afterward. But in this territory, too, where so many Greek cities had been founded and which in the first century belonged for the most part to the realm of the Parthians, Greek was an important language. Two illustrations will demonstrate this. Under the Seleucids, Susa (Esth. 1:2) had been made into a Greek city as far as government was concerned, and remained so under the Parthians, as is shown from numerous inscriptions. As late as A.D. 21 the Parthian king Artabanos III confirmed the reappointment of a certain Hestiaios as manager of city finances in a decree to the city council of Susa that was written in Greek. The other officials that are mentioned, except one, also have Greek and Macedonian names (see C. B. Welles, *Royal Correspondence in the Hellenistic Period. A Study in Greek Epigraphy* [*Studia Historica* XXVIII] [New Haven, 1934; repr. Rome, 1966], no. 75).

Parallel to this is the case of the new capital of the Seleucid realm, called Seleucia, which was founded about 312 B.C. in the vicinity of old Babylon and which was entirely Greek in character. In the second half of the first century, Pliny the Elder wrote in his *Historia Naturalis*, a general encyclopedia completed in A.D. 77: "Seleucia . . . is now a free city [that is, in the realm of the Parthians] and has its own laws; its morals and customs are Macedonian; the city reportedly has a population of 600,000 souls" (6.122). There were Jews living both in Susa and in Seleucia—in Seleucia even a large colony. Thus many Greek-speaking Jews could come from the East and attend the Feast of Pentecost in Jerusalem (Acts 2). The sermon of Peter could easily be made understandable to all the people mentioned in the New Testament table of nations, that is, the Jews who lived among these people: it is virtually certain that the apostles, if not each individually at least together, knew both world languages. The Aramaic-speaking Peter converses later with the centurion Cornelius without the help of another, thus in Greek (Acts 10:25–28). If Acts 2 and Genesis

10–11 are exegeted as counterparts, the mere fact that Palestine was situated in the region where both world languages were overlapping already put an end to the confusion of tongues of Genesis 11. The lists of nations in the two accounts cover pretty much the same territory, with the exception of the Romans, who are not found in Genesis 10.

The Jewish emigrants who had been in their new country for some generations had only a scanty knowledge of Hebrew and Aramaic at best. They had also abandoned their native tongue in their conversations at home; though still able to read and understand it, they no longer used it as their everyday language. Many probably knew no Hebrew or Aramaic at all. So it is doubtful that Philo of Alexandria (died ca. A.D. 45), the leading Greek spirit of Hellenistic Jewry, whose extensive literary work deals mainly with the Old Testament, could still read it in the original languages, because he uses exclusively the Septuagint and sometimes gives strange explanations of Hebrew names. Aramaic or Hebrew was thus hardly the natural vehicle for communications between these hellenized Jews and the homeland. This alone enables us to understand why the letters addressed to the Jewish Christians of the Dispersion were written in Greek—not only the letters addressed to those who lived somewhere in Greece, in Corinth or Thessalonica, in Macedonia, or in Philippi, but everywhere: in Rome, in western Asia Minor (letters to the Ephesians, Colossians, Laodiceans, and the "Seven Churches in Asia" in Rev. 1:4, 11), the province of Galatia, the whole of Asia Minor (1 Peter), and finally all the Jews of the Dispersion (James). Concerning the letters to individuals: Timothy was a half-Greek from Lystra in Lycaonia (Acts 16:1), Titus a Greek (Gal. 2:3); nothing certain is known of Philemon and Gaius (3 John 1), and the addressees of the remaining epistles (2 Peter, 1 and 2 John, Jude) are not further indicated.

The "letter" to the Hebrews is left (ill. 54); it is actually the text of a sermon, which the leader, a friend of Timothy, for some reason was unable to preach at the particular place and which was therefore sent to the "hearers" (Heb. 13:22–23). He sends greetings to all the leaders and "all the saints," and he himself sends the greetings of "those (brothers) who come from Italy." Actually not "specially" from them, but not emphatically from "all" the brothers there either. So at the time the writer was visiting some congregations in Italy, not a church or churches elsewhere where there were also some believers from Italy; if the latter were the case, in his greetings he would no doubt have mentioned the larger community to which they belonged. Because we know nothing more of the author and his nationality, we are ignorant of the reason why he wrote in Greek. The addressees do not help us much either. Since he wrote from Italy, it is strange—assuming that the address "to the Hebrews" is authentic and complete—that no place was added, for every Jewish community in the Dispersion could call themselves "Hebrews." A "synagogue of the Hebrews," for instance, is mentioned in inscriptions (Frey, nos. 510, 718, 754) from Rome, Corinth (cf. also 2 Cor. 11:22), and the region of Philadelphia (Rev. 1:11), but letters sent from elsewhere to these churches were addressed to the "Romans," to the "Corinthians," and to the church "in Philadelphia" (Rev. 3:7). Because, moreover, the "letter" mentions an impending visit (Heb. 13:23), it is impossible that the Jewish Christian churches as a whole would be meant, as in the epistle of James. "Hebrews" must therefore be the designation of a relatively small group of churches outside Italy for which a more precise designation was unnecessary. That group can only have been Hebrews who had remained in the homeland Palestine, the churches in Judea (cf. Gal. 1:22). There happened to be a special group of Jewish Christians in Jerusalem who, owing to their language, called themselves "Hebrews" in distinction from the "Hellenists" (cf. Acts 6:1). In the city the address "to the Hebrews" would have been natural, but in the case of a letter from Italy, the further designation "in Jerusalem" would have been necessary. From the fact that the author occasionally adduces very familiar material, such as the daily sacrifice of the high priest (7:27), some have tried to infer that the addressees can hardly have been Jewish Christians but were more likely converted Gentiles who still needed this information. Presenting familiar facts as new is a characteristic trait of sermons in general, however, and it says nothing of the knowledge of the hearers. Perhaps an Aramaic sermon would have been more to the point for the "Hebrews," though a Greek one cannot have posed an insuperable difficulty.

With the Gospels the situation is entirely different. Greek was the only suitable language in which to write them. Such summaries, which had become necessary after the death of the eyewitnesses, would have remained restricted to those reading Aramaic if they had been composed in that language. The use of the Greek language made it possible to reach the entire Greco-Roman world and even countries east of it. It is of course altogether possible that there were also Gospels for non-Greek-reading people; but even in that case a wider circulation made translation into Greek unavoidable. This is exactly what Papias, bishop of Hierapolis about A.D. 130, reports about the Gospel of Matthew: "Matthew composed (or collected) the sayings of Jesus in the Hebrew language, but everyone translated these according to ability."

Moreover, the Gospel of Luke and the book of Acts are dedicated to Theophilus, who is accorded the title "most excellent" in Luke 1:3 and therefore must have been a person of rank, for instance in the senate or among the nobility. Through this preface Luke deliberately addressed a wider circle of readers, which included non-Jewish higher circles, for instance the proconsul Sergius Paulus (Acts 13:7). In this case, Greek was the only language to be used, if one did not know Latin.

## 3. THE GREEK OF THE NEW TESTAMENT

In conclusion, we will make some remarks about the kind of Greek in which the New Testament is written. A casual glance at an edition of the Greek text of the New Testament that prints the citations from the Old Testament in bold letters, or in some other way distinguishes them from the rest of the text, shows how full of Old Testament quotations the New Testament is. Those quotations are written in Greek, and virtually all of them are from the Septuagint translation. Only the ones from the book of Daniel are from another Greek translation. As noted above, according to the Letter of Aristeas the Septuagint was completed in one year, during the reign of Ptolemy II (ca. 250 B.C.). The addition to the book of Esther, discussed above, proves, however, that in reality the translation of the canonical Old Testament was a process of much longer duration. Because the New Testament originated between A.D. 48 and 100, the Old Testament quotations may reflect a vocabulary and a use of the language that occasionally is three centuries older than those of the New Testament writers themselves. Moreover, because the Septuagint is a translation that has rendered many specifically Hebrew idioms into fairly literal Greek, there are a considerable number of "translation Hebraisms" in the Old Testament quotations. Here is an example. To express in Biblical Hebrew that something was definitely the case, a second, special verbal form could be added to the conjugated verb, the infinitive of the same stem, which created a repetitive sound effect. One way in which the translators of the Septuagint tried to preserve this was through a combination of a verb and a present participle of the same stem, for instance: "*seeing* I *saw* the misery of my people . . ." (Exod. 3:7). The New Testament writers themselves never use such an un-Greek construction, except when quoting from the Old Testament, as in the speech of Stephen where Exodus 3:7 is quoted literally from the Septuagint. In English translations this peculiarity is as a rule expressed in other ways: "I have *surely* seen the ill-treatment of my people in Egypt . . ." (Acts 7:34).

In addition, the New Testament contains many Hebraisms and Aramaisms that do not derive from Septuagint Greek, particularly in the Gospels and the Revelation of John. In the story of the first miraculous feeding we read in Mark 6:39–40: "Then he commanded them all to sit down by companies upon the green grass. So they sat down in groups, by hundreds and by fifties." However, the Greek reads literally: "And he commanded them to sit down, all, (drinking) parties-(drinking) parties on the green grass. And they sat down (garden) plots-(garden) plots, by hundreds and by fifties." In Greek a noun could not be repeated in this manner. Aramaic, however, contains this kind of construction, giving it a distributive meaning, as is shown in the translation of the Revised Standard Version: "in groups." "Drinking party" and "garden plot,"

"plot of leeks," are the original meanings of the Greek words here. By extension they also came to mean any other "party" and any other "plot" in the sense of "group." We do not know whether this influence on New Testament Greek is due to translation (Matthew?) or to a mixing of the languages; possibly both influences have been at work. Because of these peculiarities the language of the Septuagint and that of the New Testament differ considerably in style from the Greek that was written by pagan contemporaries. On the other hand, both collections also contain writings that are similar linguistically to the profane use of the language, such as 3 Maccabees and the epistle of James.

---

## LITERATURE

The subject of the entire chapter has been treated comprehensively by:

J. N. Sevenster, *Do You Know Greek? How Much Greek Could the First Christians Have Known?* (Supplements to *Novum Testamentum* XIX; Leiden, 1968).

Later surveys:

G. Mussies, "Greek in Palestine and the Diaspora," in *Compendia Rerum Iudaicarum ad Novum Testamentum* II (Assen, 1976) 1040–64.

E. M. Meyers and J. F. Strange, *Archaeology, the Rabbis, and Early Christianity* (Nashville, 1981), pp. 62–91.

For the pre-Christian era see:

M. Hengel, *Judaism and Hellenism* (Philadelphia, repr. 1981), especially pp. 58ff.

For the period following the first century see:

G. Bardy, *La question des langues dans l'Eglise ancienne* (Paris, 1948).

G. Mussies, "Greek as the Vehicle of Early Christianity," *New Testament Studies* 29 (1983) 356–69.

S. Lieberman, *Greek in Jewish Palestine. Studies in the Life and Manners of Jewish Palestine in the II–IV Centuries C.E.* (New York, 1965²).

A book that is still very useful as a general introduction to Koine Greek:

A. Thumb, *Die griechische Sprache im Zeitalter des Hellenismus* (Strassburg, 1901).

Of the various grammars of New Testament Greek we would mention:

F. Blass, A. Debrunner, and R. Funk, *A Greek*

*Grammar of the New Testament* (Chicago, 1961).

J. H. Moulton, W. F. Howard, and N. Turner, *A Grammar of New Testament Greek* I–IV (Edinburgh, 1908–76[3]).

A grammar including the Greek of the Septuagint:

F. M. Abel, *Grammaire du grec biblique suivie d'un choix de papyrus* (Paris, 1927).

For the Aramaic-Hebrew influence on New Testament Greek:

M. Black, *An Aramaic Approach to the Gospels and Acts* (Oxford, 1967[3]).

M. Wilcox, *The Semitisms of Acts* (Oxford, 1965).

G. Mussies, *The Morphology of Koine Greek as Used in the Apocalypse of St. John. A Study in Bilingualism* (Supplements to *Novum Testamentum* XXVII; Leiden, 1971).

The Jewish inscriptions have been collected by:

J. B. Frey and B. Lifshitz, *Corpus Inscriptionum Iudaicarum* (New York, 1975[2]). New inscriptions and better versions of already published inscriptions can be found in the various volumes of *Supplementum Epigraphicum Graecum*.

The Jewish papyri, chiefly those coming out of Egypt, have been published by:

V. A. Tcherikover, A. Fuks, M. Stern, and D. M. Lewis, *Corpus Papyrorum Judaicarum* (Cambridge, Mass., 1957–64).

For a geographical picture of the real Jewish domain in Palestine consult:

D. H. K. Amiran, et al., *Atlas of Israel* (Jerusalem/Amsterdam, 1970), section IX, maps 5–8.

# IV

# Textual Witnesses and Textual History of the Old and New Testaments

*by E. Tov and J. Smit Sibinga*

# A. The Text of the Old Testament

*by E. Tov*

## 1. INTRODUCTION

### a. The Nature and Goals of Old Testament Textual Criticism

The goal of Old Testament textual criticism is to analyze the text of the Hebrew Bible and to trace in broad outline the history of this text. For that purpose it collects the relevant data from the Hebrew sources and reconstructs them from the ancient translations (versions). At the same time it examines these data critically by comparing them with parallel material in the Massoretic text (see section 5 below).

The nature of Old Testament textual criticism is best exhibited by comparing it with that of other works of literature. Such a comparison shows that the textual criticism of the Old Testament has its own character in the following respects:

(1) In contrast to the textual criticism applied to many works of literature, that pertaining to the Old Testament (the same holds for Homer's *Iliad* and *Odyssey*) does not seek to reconstruct the *original* form of the complete text of the biblical books, let alone try to determine the *ipsissima verba* of the authors of these books. The most that this could achieve would be to determine the text of the Old Testament current in a particular period (usually one thinks of the 4th or 3rd century B.C.) and to reconstruct individual "original" readings. Adherents of the "oral tradition" theory, however, are compelled to have a broader definition of the goals of Old Testament textual criticism, because in their view the books of the Old Testa-

ment never existed in one original text but only in various oral formulations (see Nyberg and van der Ploeg).

(2) It is often thought that textual criticism aims to produce *eclectic editions* of the text, that is, editions that attempt to reconstruct the original text of the Bible through a selection of readings from various sources. For theoretical as well as practical reasons this cannot be its task, for not all scholars agree that at one time there was an original text of a biblical book. Even if there had been such a text, practical problems make its reconstruction difficult (see further section 2.d.[1] below).

Because of these problems most of the existing critical editions of the Old Testament are not eclectic but diplomatic editions, that is, they reproduce a particular form of the *textus receptus* of the Old Testament as the original text, while recording divergent readings (variants) from Hebrew and non-Hebrew sources in an added critical apparatus. In contrast, modern translations of the Old Testament are usually eclectic in character.

A generally accepted principle in biblical studies is that the task of textual criticism begins at the point where literary criticism stops. Literary criticism deals with the history, authorship, and origin of the biblical books, stopping at the point where they have received their final literary shape, while textual criticism deals with the transmission of the completed works. Though this rule is applicable to all books of the Bible, in practice it is hard to follow, since the complex history of the formation of most books implies that some texts represent intermediate stages in the growth of the writings in question.

## LITERATURE

One can find the most recent précis in the articles "Text, Hebrew, History of" (D. Barthélemy) and "Textual Criticism, OT" (J. A. Thompson) in the *Interpreter's Dictionary of the Bible, Supplementary Volume* (Nashville, 1976), pp. 878–84, 886–91; in the article "Bible" in the *Encyclopaedia Judaica* IV (Jerusalem, 1971) 816–64; and in the relevant articles in the *Encyclopaedia Biblica* VIII (1982) (Hebrew). Other works deserving mention are:

D. Barthélemy, "Problématique et tâches de la critique textuelle de l'Ancien Testament hébraïque," in *Études d'histoire du texte de l'Ancien Testament* (Orbis biblicus et orientalis 21; Freiburg/Göttingen, 1978), pp. 365–81.

F. Buhl, *Kanon und Text des Alten Testaments* (Leipzig, 1891).

F. E. Deist, *Towards the Text of the Old Testament* (Pretoria, 1978).

O. Eissfeldt, *The Old Testament: An Introduction* (New York, 1965), pp. 669–721.

R. W. Klein, *Textual Criticism of the Old Testament* (Philadelphia, 1974).

E. König, *Einleitung in das Alte Testament* (Bonn, 1893).

M. Noth, *The Old Testament World* (Philadelphia, 1965), pp. 301–63.

B. J. Roberts, *The Old Testament Text and Versions* (Cardiff, 1951).

C. Steuernagel, *Lehrbuch der Einleitung in das Alte Testament* (Tübingen, 1912), pp. 19–85.

A. van der Kooij, *Die alten Textzeugen des Jesajabuches* (Orbis biblicus et orientalis 35; Freiburg/Göttingen, 1981).

J. Weingreen, *Introduction to the Critical Study of the Text of the Hebrew Bible* (Oxford/New York, 1982).

E. Würthwein, *The Text of the Old Testament* (Grand Rapids, 1979²).

## b. The Importance of Old Testament Textual Criticism

The realization that the Old Testament must be examined text-critically is relatively new. It has come about slowly through the discovery of new sources and through an increase in critical awareness. Meanwhile the necessity of a text-critical analysis of the Old Testament can be justified not only on the basis of historical considerations but also in view of the nature of the sources for the Old Testament text.

Except in the case of photographic reproductions of the same text, no two editions of the Hebrew Bible are identical. The differences among them generally have to do with minimal, even minute, details of the text (consonants, vowel signs, accents, text arrangement, numbering of verses, division into chapters and paragraphs, Massoretic notes). In a few cases, however, they concern entire words (e.g., some editions of Prov. 8:16 read *ṣedeq*, "righteousness," but others *ares*, "earth"). Older printed editions contain many misprints. This is even true of some modern editions. Thus some printings of the familar edition of Letteris (1852) read *moshet* (nonexistent word) instead of *mosheh* (Moses) in Numbers 11:30, and *shalakta* (wrong spelling of "you sent") instead of *shalahta* ("you sent") in Jeremiah 29:25.

These differences in the printed editions go back to differences in the manuscripts on which they are based. With the exception of the chapter and verse divisions, which are not found in them, these manuscripts differ from each other in the same manner as the printed editions referred to above. The differences between the Massoretic manuscripts are small. In contrast, older sources such as the Qumran scrolls display more than minor variations among themselves (see further section 4.d below).

In parallel versions of one biblical passage, such as 2 Samuel 22 and Psalm 18, Psalm 14 and Psalm 53, and in parts of the books of Samuel–Kings and Chronicles (for the sources see Vannutelli and Bendavid), it is possible to trace the textual variants in an early stage of the history of the text. Apart from redactional, linguistic, and stylistic variations among these passages, the remaining differences give a good idea of the mutual relationship between the texts in an early stage of the transmission (for examples see section 4 below). It is exactly these parallel biblical passages that have prompted the development of Old Testament textual criticism (see esp. Owen), because they made necessary the comparison of texts.

Not only the comparison of parallel texts in the Old Testament but also the differences among the Massoretic manuscripts and the independent analytical examination of the Massoretic text led very early to the conclusion that the biblical text is corrupt in a number of places. This conclusion has provoked many theological and philological discussions about the authority of the Massoretic text as well as that of the Septuagint and the Samaritan Pentateuch.

## c. The History of Investigation

The first rather complete analyses of the Old Testament text are those of J. Morinus, *Exercitationes biblicae de hebraei graecique textus sinceritate* (Paris, 1633, 1660[2]) and of L. Cappellus, *Critica sacra* (Paris, 1650, 1675–78[2]). After the middle of the seventeenth century there are a great number of treatises on the Old Testament text, though it should be noted that in this and the following century the borderline between textual criticism and theology is often unclear. Of the scholars who at that time made a critical study of the Old Testament text we mention in particular Buxtorf, Hottinger, Morinus, Cappellus, Spinoza, Richard Simon, Houbigant, Kennicott, and de Rossi (see p. 160).

The works of these scholars have been described in detail by Rosenmüller, Keil, and Barthélemy. Of the many names that could be mentioned from the nineteenth century, we single out those of Lagarde, Perles, Cornill, and Wellhausen because of their remarkable insight into textual criticism. However strange it may sound, in many areas of Old Testament textual criticism it is best to start with older works. In textual criticism (called an art by some and a science by others) an intuitively correct description of textual witnesses is just as important as recent data. Particularly Wellhausen in his commentary on Samuel (Göttingen, 1871) and König and Steuernagel in their Introductions exhibited that kind of intuition (see literature above).

## LITERATURE

D. Barthélemy, *Critique textuelle de l'Ancien Testament* (Orbis biblicus et orientalis 50; Freiburg/Göttingen, 1982), pp. 1*–63*.

A. Bendavid, *Parallels in the Bible* (Jerusalem, 1972).

S. L. Greenslade, ed., *The Cambridge History of the Bible, III: The West from the Reformation to the Present Day* (Cambridge, 1963[3]).

C. F. Keil, *Lehrbuch der historisch-kritischen Einleitung in die kanonischen Schriften des Alten Testaments* (Frankfurt am Main, 1853).

M. L. Margolis, "The Scope and Methodology of Biblical Philology," *Jewish Quarterly Review* 1 (1910–11) 5–41.

H. S. Nyberg, *Studien zum Hoseabuche, zugleich ein Beitrag zur Klärung des Problems der alttestamentlichen Textkritik* (Uppsala, 1935).

H. Owen, *Critica Sacra; or a Short Introduction to Hebrew Criticism* (London, 1774).

E. F. C. Rosenmüller, *Handbuch für die Literatur der biblischen Kritik und Exegese* I (Göttingen, 1797).

J. van der Ploeg, "Le rôle de la tradition orale dans la transmission du texte de l'Ancien Testament," *Revue biblique* 54 (1947) 5–41.

P. Vannutelli, *Libri synoptici Veteris Testamenti* I–II (Rome, 1931–34).

## 2. TEXTUAL WITNESSES

### a. The Hebrew Textus Receptus

The elements of the Hebrew text of the Old Testament to which the textual critic directs himself concern on the one hand the consonantal text and on the other hand the vocalization and accents. The modern reader is familiar with these through the printed editions of the *Biblia Hebraica*, which give the *textus receptus* of both elements. The *textus receptus* of the consonantal text preceded the one that includes the vocalization and accents. Here we deal only with the development of the text of the Hebrew Bible in the period after the fixation of the consonantal text. The developments prior to that will be dealt with in section 3 below.

## (1) THE TEXTUS RECEPTUS OF THE CONSONANTAL TEXT:

The Development of the Hebrew Text
from the Second Century A.D.
to (and including) the Printed Editions

In the first and second centuries A.D. the textual tradition of the Massoretic text resulted in the *textus receptus* of Rabbinic Judaism, a text that displaced other traditions (see section 3 below). Consequently all sources since that time exhibit a textual form that differs from the Massoretic text only in minor details. Except for the Septuagint, most of the old translations (which will be discussed in sections b-d below) indeed reflect a text that is closely akin to the Massoretic text; in fact, it is occasionally almost identical with it. This is also true of the Hebrew sources from this period (e.g., some of the scrolls from the Judean desert; see p. 166). Moreover, the biblical quotations in talmudic literature and in the *piyyut* (hymns) as a rule reproduce the Massoretic text, though sometimes they deviate from it in details. These variants are already described in the literature that appeared from the time that the Rabbinic Bibles were produced. It was not until the investigations of Aptowitzer, however, that they were taken seriously. Meanwhile, especially due to the influence of Kahle (see p. 182), the significance and the number of the variants in the rabbinic sources have in general been exaggerated in scholarly literature.

Readings deviating from the Massoretic text during the period mentioned here were also found in sources that are now lost. But talmudic and later rabbinic literature have preserved some of them. The best known of these sources is a copy of the Pentateuch connected with Rabbi Meir that according to tradition was brought by the Romans to the "synagogue of Severus" in Rome after the fall of Jerusalem (A.D. 70). Here we should also mention Codex Hilleli, Codex Zambuki, and Codex Yerushalmi (see further Ginsburg, pp. 410–37). Still other textual variants are found in the Massoretic *madinhae-* and *maarbae*-readings (see p. 163) and in the Massoretic handbook *Minhat Shay*. As with the Bible quotations in the talmudic literature, these sources differ only in minor details from the *textus receptus*; for the most part the variants have to do with spelling.

All the Massoretic manuscripts constitute an integrated group. That does not alter the fact that none of the extant scrolls or manuscripts is entirely identical with any other. The work of copying, certainly in earlier times, resulted in variations between the copy and the basic text. Though the consonantal text was consolidated in the first and second centuries A.D., all the manuscripts from that period, too, differ from each other in numerous details, details that often carried over to the medieval period.

In the description of the development of the consonantal Massoretic text two periods are to be distinguished, though, due to insufficient information, they cannot be totally separated from each other. The first period begins in the first two centuries A.D. (the scrolls from the Judean desert are the best witnesses), the second probably in the eighth century (the "Massoretic" manuscripts, first found in the geniza of Cairo; see p. 163).

In the first and formative stage of the development of the Massoretic text a conscious attempt was made to consolidate the text. This aim, however, could not overlook the presence of textual variants; it could not do so even in those circles where a serious attempt was made to transmit the text as accurately as possible. The variants current in this period are mainly from earlier textual traditions and often can still be found in the Septuagint and in the Qumran scrolls. In contrast, in the second period—that of the pointed "Massoretic" manuscripts—few variants came from earlier periods. Almost all variants from this period are the result of the frequent copying of manuscripts.

Due to lack of data it is not easy to determine the beginning of the second period. The first *dated* Massoretic manuscripts are from the ninth century. Therefore the second period may roughly be regarded as "medieval." A good description of the typical characteristics of medieval manuscripts is given by Goshen-Gottstein. For the text-critical analysis of these manuscripts it is important to remember that they should not be regarded as one source. Every individual manuscript must be compared separately with non-Massoretic sources. Goshen-Gottstein mentioned some manuscripts (Kennicott 30, 93, 96, 150; see below) that contain more substantive variants than others. Further, it can be demonstrated that the medieval manuscripts are to be subdivided into different geographical groups (Italy, Germany, France, Spain), some of which, according to Cohen, contain more substantive variants than others. Nevertheless, the consonantal text of no one manuscript is of greater importance than that of any other manuscript.

The variants in the medieval manuscripts from the twelfth century on are brought together in the large collections of B. Kennicott, *Vetus Testamentum hebraicum cum variis lectionibus* I–II (Oxford, 1776–80), and J. B. de Rossi, *Variae lectiones Veteris Testamenti* I–IV (Parma, 1784–88; repr. Amsterdam, 1969). A summary edition that includes the variants of these two editions was published by J. C. Döderlein and J. H. Meisner (Halle-Berlin, 1818). The more recent editions of C. D. Ginsburg, *The Twenty-four Sacred Books* . . . (London, 1896), *Biblia Hebraica Stuttgartensia,* and *The Hebrew University Bible* (see p. 188) also refer to older medieval manuscripts.

## (2) THE MASSORA

The Massora (literally, "transmission," "tradition") is an apparatus of references and remarks about details (esp. orthographic) in the biblical text, composed to facilitate its accurate transmission ("Massoretic text" refers to the consonantal text transmitted by the Massoretes; in some cases they provided it with vocalization, accents, and "Massora," and in other cases not). The best-known and most influential Massora at present is the Tiberian, which we will discuss in some detail here. Fragments of a so-called Palestinian and Babylonian Massora have also been preserved.

The Massora was composed in the period between A.D. 500 and 1000 by generations of scribes who busied themselves with the transmission of the biblical text. Little is known of the background of these Massoretes (*baale ha-massorah,* "masters of the Massora").

In the composition of the Massora, the Massoretes built on the work of earlier generations of scribes, traditionally called *soferim.* The word literally means "scribes," and it is further reinterpreted as men who occupied themselves with counting (*sfr*) the letters and words of the Old Testament (cf. Babylonian Talmud *Qiddushin* 30a: "The older men were called *soferim* because they counted all the letters in the Torah"). The work of the *soferim* began long ago; according to tradition the copying of the Pentateuch started with Ezra, who is called a *sofer mahir* (fast writer) in the Bible and is considered the writer par excellence in rabbinic tradition.

The Massoretes not only transmitted the consonantal text, but they also devised vocalization and accent systems for it (see sections [3-5] below). Hence their labors have both creative and secondary aspects. The secondary aspect of their work concerns the copying and counting of letters, words, and verses. The creative aspects pertain to the recording of the vocalization and accents. While doing this the Massoretes also created mechanisms to assure that great care would be exercised in the transmission. Far beyond the original design, these mechanisms expanded into volumes of detailed observations about the biblical text, especially with respect to orthography.

The three above-mentioned aspects of the secondary work of the Massoretes—the transmission of the text, the counting of letters, words, and verses, and the description of the orthography—have determined the form and content of the Massoretic corpus. This corpus is recorded in the text (a), in an apparatus of remarks around the text (b), and further in separate handbooks (c).

### (a) IN THE TEXT

The Massoretes were painstaking in recording accurately all the peculiarities in their manuscripts for future generations. For a detailed description of these points see Ginsburg. The most important are:

### (i) Paragraphs

With painstaking care the Massoretes transmitted the earlier division into paragraphs (*parashah,* plural *parashiyyot*), which are also found in the Qumran scrolls (see p. 166). They distinguished between small textual units that were separated from each other by open spaces between verses (*parashah setumah*) and larger textual units that were separated from each other by spaces that leave the whole line blank (*parashah petuhah*) after the final word in a paragraph (see esp. Oesch).

*(ii) Inverted nuns* (e.g., before and after Num. 10:35–36)

The original purpose of these signs was to indicate that the particular passage does not belong in the present context (cf. *Sifre* 84 on Num. 10:35). In the Massoretic tradition the form of the sign became an inverted *nun,* but originally it may have had the form of an *antisigma* ( ɔ ), which the Alexandrian textual critics also used to indicate elements that did not belong to the text (cf. Liebermann, pp. 38–43). Similar signs have been found in some of the Qumran scrolls.

*(iii) Puncta extraordinaria*

Supralinear (occasionally in combination with infralinear) points are found in fifteen places in the Old Testament (e.g., Gen. 33:4; Ps. 27:13). These points probably indicate that the elements thus designated are uncertain or should be deleted (cf. Butin and Talmon and the explanation in *Abot de Rabbi Nathan,* version A, 34). Similar conventional signs are found in the Qumran scrolls and in Hellenistic texts (cf. Liebermann, pp. 43–46).

*(iv) Tiqqune soferim* (Corrections of the *soferim*)

This term refers to words (18 or 11 depending on the sources; the most important source is the *Mekilta* on Exod. 15:7) that tradition says were changed by the *soferim,* for instance "my wickedness" (Num. 11:15 Massoretic text) instead of an original reading "your wickedness." All supposed corrections concern minor changes in words that the *soferim* deemed inappropriate for God or (in one instance) Moses (Num. 12:12). In some sources such corrections are called *kinnuye soferim* (euphemisms of the *soferim*), implying that the *soferim* had a different understanding of these words, without, however, changing the text itself.

Many details in the list of *tiqqunim* are dubious. Nevertheless, it is considered likely that alterations have been made in the text (see p. 187), even though the transmitted *tiqqune soferim* do not give the best examples of this process (cf. McCarthy).

*(v) Suspended Letters (litterae suspensae)*

In the manuscripts some letters are intentionally placed higher than those around them; they are as it were suspended between the other letters. A good example is the suspended *nun* in Judges 18:30, where the text with the *nun* can be read as *mnshh* (*menashsheh,* Manasseh) or without this letter as *mshh* (*mosheh,* Moses). The suspended letters probably indicate later additions or omissions.

*(vi) Litterae minusculae* (e.g., Gen. 2:4) and *majusculae* (e.g., Lev. 13:33)

The special form of these letters directs the reader's attention to details that were important for the Massoretes, such as the middle letter or the middle word in a book. The background of some special letters is not entirely clear.

*(b) THE APPARATUS AROUND THE TEXT*

*(i) Massora parva (massora qetanah)*

The *Massora parva,* written in the spaces between the columns, contains observations about the number of times a word (or phrase) occurs in a biblical book or in the Old Testament, about grammatical peculiarities, about the Qere (see p. 162), and especially about orthography. The *Massora parva* deals only with the orthography of words whose spelling deviates from the rules devised by the Massoretes themselves. For a summary of these rules see Elias Levita, *Massoret ha-Massoret* (Venice, 1538), especially in the edition of C. D. Ginsburg (London, 1867; repr. New York, 1968). Levita noted, for example, that words of the type *shalom* and *qarob* are as a rule written *plene* (i.e., with a *waw*; see p. 187); hence the *Massora parva* records only the exceptions to this rule, that is, the defective spellings of words of this type. Similarly, *meod* and *koah* are as a rule written defectively, so that the *Massora parva* refers only to these words if written *plene.*

In the use of the *Massora parva* it is well to bear in mind that the notes are often neither consistent noraccurate. One reason for this is that the *Massora parva* was initially transmitted with its companion manuscript but later also separately or even copied in other manuscripts. Thus not one but several Massora texts were in circulation. The invention of the art of printing increased the confusion because the Second Rabbinic Bible (see p. 165), which would later become the *textus receptus,* contained an eclectic *Massora parva,* composed by Ben Hayyim from various sources.

In our time Weil has facilitated the study of the Massora (see p. 163).

*(ii) Massora magna (massora ge̱dolah)*

The space between the columns was not sufficient for all the Massoretic notes. Hence the *Massora parva* contains only the most necessary data (e.g., the frequency with which the particular word occurs in the Old Testament), whereas the *Massora magna* describes these data in greater detail (i.e., it mentions the exact verses the *Massora parva* refers to). The *Massora magna* is written in the spaces under and above the columns and sometimes in the margin itself.

*(iii) Massora finalis*

The *Massora finalis* contains various lists for which there was no space in the *Massora parva* and *Massora magna*. The first time the *Massora finalis* occurs is not in the manuscripts but in the Second Rabbinic Bible (see p. 165).

*(iv) Ketib (K) and Qere (Q)*

In many places (ranging from 848 to 1566 in the various manuscripts) the *Massora parva* mentions words that should be read instead of the ones found in the text (indicated by a small circle in the text), for instance, *napsho (K)* for *napshah (Q)* in Jeremiah 2:24. The *Ketib* indicates the word "that is written," and the *Qere* the word "that is read." Early manuscripts indicate the presence of a *Qere* by a sign in the margin, resembling final *nun* (a vertical line); in later manuscripts the *Qere* is indicated by the letter *qof* (for *Qere*). In most manuscripts and printed editions the consonantal text of the *Ketib* is pointed with the vowels of the *Qere*. In that case the *Qere* itself is left unvocalized.

In some cases whole words were "written but not read" (*ketib wela qere*) and others "read but not written" (*qere wela ketib*).

The *Qere* words can be subdivided into various categories. Lists of such categories are found in the Massoretic handbooks *Okhlah we-Okhlah* and Elias Levita's *Massoret ha-Massoret* (see p. 161). The classification and analysis of Gordis is the best modern introduction to the problem of the *Ketib* and *Qere*.

Opinions vary about the background of the *Qere*. The Massoretes regarded the *Qere* as a correction of the *Ketib* and therefore they ignored the *Ketib*. In line with this tradition some modern scholars maintain that all *Qere* words were indeed intended as a correction of the *Ketib*. That is doubtful, however, for the following reasons.

1. Some words that constitute the *Qere* word in one case are the *Ketib* word in other verses.

2. Every category of *Qere* words contains words that are not "corrected" elsewhere.

3. In some passages the *Qere* words are impossible for grammatical or contextual reasons.

The summary—and subjective—statistics of Gordis show that as a rule the *Qere* and *Ketib* are equal in value and that the *Ketib* sometimes offers a better reading than the *Qere*. Moreover, for purely theoretical considerations, it is improbable that the *Qere* would offer a correction of the *Ketib*, because the aim of the *soferim* and Massoretes was to preserve the text intact, not to correct it. For that reason some scholars believe that the *Qere* words were originally textual variants that later were regarded as corrections. That idea, too, is doubtful.

Gordis offers a middle course between these two ideas. He has detected two stages in the development of the *Qere*. Initially the *Qere* was intended as a correction, particularly to discourage blasphemy, such as the *Qere perpetuum* (the constant *Qere*) of the tetragrammaton (*YHWH*) as *adonay*. Later, the already existing system of marginal notes was used to preserve deviating readings for posterity. Still later these notes were regarded as corrections. Recently, Barr suggested that the *Qere* words (always one word) originated in the "reading tradition." This reading tradition was always consulted with reference to another, more authoritative text, which contained the *Ketib* words.

*(v) Sebirin*

The *Massora parva* notes by various words in the Massoretic text: *sebirin* . . . , followed by an almost identical word (e.g., in Jgs. 11:34). The category of *sebirin* resembles that of the *Qere;* various words are indeed indicated as *Qere* in some manuscripts but as *sebirin* in others. *Sebirin* does not mean, as is often assumed, that "it is likely" (*sbr*) that *x* must be read instead of *y;* the term is an abbreviation of *sebirin wematin*, that is, one might think (*sbr*) that *x* must be read instead of *y*, but that is a wrong assumption (*matin*).

## (vi) Maarbae and Madinhae

The *Massora parva* mentions various textual variants between Palestinian (*maarbae* = western) and Babylonian (*madinhae* = eastern) readings.

### (c) MASSORETIC HANDBOOKS

The Massoretes collected the data of the *Massora parva* in several handbooks. Conversely, such handbooks offered guidelines for the *Massora parva*. The most extensive of these is *Okhlah we-Okhlah*, named after the first list that contains all pairs of *hapax legomena* (i.e., words occurring only once in the Bible) that are written once with a *waw* and once without a *waw*. Published by S. Frensdorff (Hannover, 1864; repr. Tel Aviv, 1968), this book contains 374 separate lists.

### Editions of the Massora

For a long time the Massora of the Second Rabbinic Bible (see p. 165) was regarded as the codification of the Massora. However, this Massora was composed from later and less accurate manuscripts. An improvement came with the publication of C. D. Ginsburg, *The Massorah Compiled from Manuscripts* I–IV (London-Vienna, 1880–1905). Based on various accurate manuscripts, this work, formerly the standard edition of the Massora, also has proven to be inaccurate. Presently the best resource is that of G. Weil, *Massorah Gedolah selon le manuscrit B 19a de Léningrad* I (Rome, 1971); it contains a diplomatic edition of the Massora based on one source.

The technical terms of the Massora are explained in *Okhlah we-Okhlah*, in *Biblia Hebraica (Stuttgartensia)* (see p. 188), and in Yeivin (*Introduction*; see literature).

### (3) VOCALIZATION AND ACCENTS

The modern editions of the Old Testament reproduce the *textus receptus* both of the consonants and of the vocalization. This is also true of most manuscripts, even though recent findings and studies have demonstrated that this *textus receptus* is only one of many systems. Other systems are represented in manuscripts that have been discovered in the last two centuries, especially those that have come from the geniza (a storeroom for sacred writings) in a synagogue in Cairo.

The history of vocalization is roughly as follows. Initially the vocalization of the biblical text indicated only a few vowels. Under the influence of Syrian and Arabic literature, later systems indicated the vocalization in full. It is not known when manuscripts were completely supplied with vowels for the first time; the first *dated* manuscript is the Cairo Manuscript of the Prophets from A.D. 895.

The following vocalization systems are known: (1) the Tiberian; (2) the Palestinian (supralinear); (3) the Babylonian (supralinear), divided into "simple" and "complex" (according to the terminology of Kahle); (4) that of Codex Reuchlinianus (A.D. 1105). This codex is considered a separate entity because it does not fit into one of the earlier-mentioned groups. Some label this manuscript "proto-Massoretic," others "non-Massoretic," and still others as an unaccepted form of the Tiberian traditions.

The vocalization systems differ from each other in the shape of the signs, the conception of the vocalization (e.g., in the use of the *shewa*), and pronunciation (e.g., the *patah* [a] and *segol* [e] of the Tiberian system are represented by only one sign in the Babylonian system). The vocalization systems are discussed by Kahle, Ben-Hayyim, Yeivin, and Dothan, among others.

In addition to vowel signs, the Massoretic manuscripts also indicate accents (*teamim*), whose shape and musical value vary from tradition to tradition. Moreover, in the Tiberian tradition the signs that are used in the books of Job, Proverbs, and Psalms differ from those of the rest of the Old Testament writings. The accents indicate not only the pitch of the words in the recitation of the biblical text in the synagogue, but also the syntactic relationship among words and parts of a sentence. Hence the accents are called dividing (*distinctivi* or *domini*) and connecting accents (*conjunctivi* or *servi*).

### (4) THE TIBERIAN VOCALIZATION (THE TEXTUS RECEPTUS OF THE VOCALIZED TEXT)

Of the various vocalization systems, the Tiberian has become the most widely accepted. More and more details of the other systems are becoming known through the discovery of Palestinian and Babylonian manuscripts.

The vocalization of the manuscripts dating from A.D. 850 to 1100 is of greater importance for the reconstruction of the vocalization systems than those of the later manuscripts. For the early sources (the Aleppo Codex, Codex Leningrad B 19a, the Cairo Manuscript of the Prophets, British Museum *Or.* 4445, Sassoon 507, 1053, and various manuscripts from the collection of Firkowitch in Leningrad) indicate the original systems of the Massoretes, whereas later sources have been corrupted.

In the school that occupied itself with the vocalization of the biblical text from the seventh to the tenth century A.D. in Tiberias, the most prominent families were those of Ben Asher and Ben Naftali.

Of the Tiberian tradition, the system of Ben Asher was later accepted universally, while that of Ben Naftali was rejected. It is not known whether one of the transmitted manuscripts offers a pure Ben Naftali tradition. Hence not all details about the vocalization of Ben Naftali are known, even though one learns much from the "variants"—*hillufim*—between Ben Asher and Ben Naftali listed by Mishael ben Uzziel, *Kitab al-Khilaf,* published by L. Lipschutz, *Publications of the HUB Project* (Monograph Series 2; Jerusalem, 1965).

In the family of Ben Asher, the most developed system is that devised by the last grammarian of that family, Aharon ben Moshe Ben Asher (ca. 925). The assumption used to be that the Second Rabbinic Bible (see p. 165) contained the text of Ben Asher. It is now generally assumed that this edition contained an eclectic text from various manuscripts and that in the preparation of this text the editor was often guided by his own grammatical rules (e.g., with respect to the *metheg,* the sign for secondary emphasis). Some scholars presently hold that Codex Leningrad B 19a (A.D. 1009) is the best representative of the Ben Asher text; hence *Biblia Hebraica* and *Biblia Hebraica Stuttgartensia* (see p. 188) are based on this codex. Many, however, have come to see that the Aleppo Codex is the best representative of the tradition of Ben Asher, because this codex was vocalized and supplied with Massora by Aharon

ben Moshe himself. The fame of this manuscript must largely be attributed to Maimonides, who declared it to be the authoritative text of the Bible. Kept for centuries by the Jewish congregation of Aleppo (Syria), this manuscript was thought to have been lost in a fire in 1948, but only the Pentateuch was lost; the other books were saved. A facsimile edition of the Aleppo Codex was published by M. H. Goshen-Gottstein (Jerusalem, 1976); its vocalization is described in detail by Yeivin (*Aleppo Codex*). This codex is the basis for the edition of the Hebrew University Bible Project (see p. 188). See ill. 58.

## (5) THE CHARACTER
## OF THE MASSORETIC VOCALIZATION

Transcriptions of biblical texts in the second column of the Hexapla (see section d.[2] below) and in Jerome's Bible commentaries (see section d.[5] below) often present traditions that differ from the Massoretic vocalization. Because of these data, several scholars (esp. Kahle, pp. 149–88) have contended that the Massoretic vocalization is an artificial system, devised by the Massoretes themselves, that rejected earlier systems. Kahle based his view especially on the double pronunciation of the letters *b, g, d, k, p, t,* and the form of the suffix of the second person masculine singular personal pronoun; in the Massoretic tradition this is *-eka,* but in the above-mentioned sources *-ak.* However, the Qumran scrolls have strengthened the status of the Massoretic pronunciation, in this respect as well as in other details (see esp. Ben Hayyim).

## (6) PRINTED EDITIONS
## OF THE HEBREW BIBLE

In our judgment the most ideal edition would be based on only one manuscript. Such editions have appeared only recently, however. Editors used to compose their own text from a variety of manuscripts that they deemed suitable. The editors did not mention their sources; moreover, they allowed their own grammatical ideas to influence the text. Even though the differences between the printed editions are minor, these small variations are important for the grammatical analysis of the Old Testament.

The first printed edition of the complete Old

Testament appeared in 1488 in Soncino, a small city in the vicinity of Milan.

Particularly important for the advance in biblical research have been the so-called polyglots, multilingual editions that give the text of the Bible in parallel columns in Hebrew (Massoretic text and Samaritan Pentateuch), Greek, Aramaic, Syriac, Latin, and Arabic, accompanied by Latin translations and introduced by grammars and lexicons. The first is the Complutensian Polyglot (1514–17; ill. 60), prepared by Cardinal Ximenez in Alcala (Latin *Complutum*). The second was published in Antwerp (1569–72), the third in Paris (1629–45), and the fourth, the most extensive, in London (1654–57), edited by B. Walton and E. Castell.

The so-called Rabbinic Bibles have proved to be of great importance for determining the *textus receptus* of the Old Testament. These editions contain in parallel columns the Massoretic text and the Aramaic targums, along with various rabbinic commentaries. The earliest editions of the Rabbinic Bible were printed in Venice by Daniel Bomberg, the first (1516–17) edited by Felix Pratensis, the second (1524–25) by Jacob Ben Hayyim. The latter edition differs from the former in the addition of the *Massora parva* and *Massora magna*. Perhaps because of this Massoretic apparatus, subsequent generations regarded this edition as the *textus receptus* of the Hebrew Bible. For that reason by far the majority of the editions of the Bible (with the exception of some modern editions) contain the text of Ben Hayyim. They differ only where they remove errors, introduce new ones, or add details from manuscripts that the editor deemed important.

In the course of the centuries, hundreds of editions of the Hebrew Bible have appeared, of which the most important are those of J. Buxtorf (1611), Athias (1661), Leusden (1667[2]), Jablonski (1699), Van der Hooght (1705), Michaelis (1720), Hahn (1831), Rosenmuller (1834), and Letteris (1852). See also the editions of Kennicott and de Rossi (p. 160).

From the end of the previous century, scholars have been aware of the need for more accurate editions that are based on critical principles. F. Baer and F. Delitzsch tried to reconstruct the text of Ben Asher on the basis of (among others)

Ben Asher's grammatical treatise *Diqduqqe hateamim*, which was published jointly by Baer and H. L. Strack (Leipzig, 1879). C. D. Ginsburg hoped to reconstruct the tradition of Ben Asher on the basis of his thorough knowledge of the Massora (see p. 163). His analysis of the Massora induced him to make the Second Rabbinic Bible the basis of his edition (London, 1894), to which he added a critical apparatus containing variants from manuscripts and printed editions. For the modern critical editions of the Old Testament, see p. 188.

In recent years the full text of the Hebrew Bible (editions as well as manuscripts) has been made available in machine-readable (computer) form.

## LITERATURE

V. Aptowitzer, *Das Schriftwort in der rabbinischen Literatur*, I–IV (Vienna, 1906–15; repr. New York, 1970).

J. Barr, "A New Look at Kethib-Qere," *Oudtestamentische Studiën* 21 (1981) 19–37.

Z. Ben-Hayyim, *Studies in the Traditions of the Hebrew Language* (Madrid/Barcelona, 1954).

R. Butin, *The Ten Nequdoth of the Torah* (Baltimore, 1906; repr. New York, 1960, with a prolegomenon by S. Talmon).

M. Cohen, "Orthographic Systems in Ancient Massorah Codices" (Ph.D. diss., Hebrew University, Jerusalem, 1973; Hebrew).

A. Díez Macho, *Manuscritos hebreos y arameos de la Biblia* (Rome, 1971).

L. Díez Merino, *La biblia babilónica* (Madrid, 1975).

A. Dothan, "Massorah," *Encyclopaedia Judaica* XVI (Jerusalem, 1971) 1401–82.

C. D. Ginsburg, *Introduction to the Massoretico-Critical Edition of the Hebrew Bible* (London, 1897; repr. New York, 1966).

R. Gordis, *The Biblical Text in the Making: A Study of the Kethib-Qere* (New York, 1971[2]).

M. H. Goshen-Gottstein, "Hebrew Biblical Manuscripts: Their History and Their Place in the HUBP Edition," *Biblica* 48 (1967) 243–90 (repr. in F. M. Cross and S. Talmon, eds., *Qumran and the History of the Biblical Text* [Cambridge, Mass., 1975], pp. 42–89).

P. E. Kahle, *The Cairo Geniza* (Oxford, 1959[2]).

———, *Masoreten des Ostens* (Leipzig, 1913).

———, *Masoreten des Westens* I–II (Beiträge zur Wissenschaft vom Alten Testament VIII, XIV, 1927, 1930).

S. Z. Leiman, ed., *The Canon and Masorah of the Hebrew Bible: An Introductory Reader* (New York, 1974).

S. Lieberman, *Hellenism in Jewish Palestine* (New York, 1962²).

C. McCarthy, *The Tiqqune Sopherim* (Orbis biblicus et orientalis 36; Freiburg/Göttingen, 1981).

M. Medan, "Teamim," *Encyclopaedia Miqra'it* III (Jerusalem, 1958) 394–406.

J. M. Oesch, *Petucha und Setuma* (Orbis biblicus et orientalis 27; Freiburg/Göttingen, 1979).

A. Sperber, *A Historical Grammar of Biblical Hebrew* (Leiden, 1966).

G. E. Weil, "La Massorah," *Revue des Etudes Juives* 131 (1972) 5–103.

I. Yeivin, *The Aleppo Codex of the Bible: A Study of Its Vocalization and Accentuation* (Jerusalem, 1968) (Hebrew).

_____, "Massorah," *Encyclopaedia Miqra'it* V (Jerusalem, 1968) 130–59.

_____, *Introduction to the Tiberian Masorah* (Masoretic Studies 5; Missoula, Montana, 1980).

---

## b. Scrolls from the Judean Desert

### (1) INTRODUCTION

In 1947 a young bedouin of the Ta'amireh tribe discovered some jars with scrolls at Qumran (12 km. or 7 mi. south of Jericho). These have become known as the Dead Sea Scrolls. Presently the preferred designation is "Scrolls from the Desert of Judea," because these writings have been found at various places in the desert of Judea, some not far from the Dead Sea but others farther inland. The first scrolls were discovered accidentally, but later ones were found after systematic digging in the entire area. The story of the first finds ("the shepherd with his goat") is described in great detail by van der Ploeg and Cross (*Ancient Library*; see literature).

The scrolls and fragments that were found are now for the most part in the Israel Museum and the Rockefeller Museum in Jerusalem. An international group of scholars has taken on the task of publishing the fragments, often making use of infrared photos to heighten the legibility of the script.

The majority of the scrolls so far remain un-

published. But all of them have been described and the most important have been published either entirely or partially. This makes it possible already to obtain a good idea of the importance of the new sources, though publication of further scrolls may of course augment the present knowledge.

In the relatively short period since the discovery of the first manuscripts, thousands of studies have been written on the Dead Sea Scrolls, both about the biblical manuscripts and about the sectarian documents of the Qumran community that have come to light. The following subjects are discussed at length in the literature: the identity of the Qumran community (Essenes?), the background of their writings, the ideas of the Qumran community, and the importance of the scrolls for the background of the late biblical period and early Christendom (on all these subjects see the bibliographies of Burchard, Jongeling, and Fitzmyer). Here we will deal only with the biblical scrolls.

The scope of the documents differs from scroll to scroll. The Isaiah Scroll from Cave 1 (1QIsa) contains all 66 chapters of the book, but often only fragments of other scrolls have been preserved.

With the exception of Esther, fragments or complete scrolls have been found of all the books of the Old Testament. In addition, fragments of some apocryphal and pseudepigraphal books (in Hebrew or Aramaic), which thus far were known only in Greek or other translations, have been found. Therefore it is generally assumed that the Qumran community had no fixed ideas about the scope of the biblical canon. The Psalms Scroll 11QPsa may serve as an illustration; besides Psalms from the Bible it also contains a few poems also found in the so-called Apocrypha as well as psalms that were previously unknown.

The inventory of the number of biblical scrolls from Cave 4 (see Skehan, "Biblical Scrolls," p. 88) illustrates the number of writings that have been found at Qumran: Genesis 11; Exodus 11; Leviticus 4; Numbers 2; Deuteronomy 18; Joshua 2; Judges 2; 1 Samuel 3; 1 Kings 1; Isaiah 15; Jeremiah 3; Minor Prophets 7; Psalm 17; Job 3; Proverbs 2; Ruth 2; Song of Songs 3; Ecclesiastes 2; Lamentations 1; Daniel 5; Ezra 1; Chronicles 1.

In most cases, only fragments of scrolls have remained, but it is nevertheless possible to distinguish them from each other by the form of their script. See ill. 59.

The scrolls from the Judean desert are designated as follows. The number of the cave where the scroll was found is given first, followed by an abbreviation of the place of origin, next the name of the biblical book, and finally a letter indicating which manuscript in the series it is (e.g., 4QJer[b] is the second manuscript of Jeremiah from Cave 4 at Qumran). If the scroll is written in the Old Hebrew script (cf. p. 186), this is specially indicated (e.g., 4QpaleoEx[m]); several of the Pentateuch scrolls and one scroll of Job are so written.

The majority of the published scrolls have appeared in the series *Discoveries in the Judaean Desert (of Jordan)*, I– (Oxford, 1955–). A detailed list of the contents of this series as well as bibliographic details about other scrolls is found in J. Fitzmyer (see literature).

The importance of the scrolls for biblical research can hardly be exaggerated. Aside from the Nash Papyrus (1st or 2nd century A.D.; ill. 55), which contains the combined text of Exodus 20 and Deuteronomy 5 (published in 1903), only these scrolls reveal what a biblical scroll looked like at the time of the Second Temple. Many details about the transmission and history of the text of the Old Testament have now become clear (cf. sections a.[3–5] above). Another gain for biblical studies has been that many new readings have become known that are important for exegesis.

Based on archeological and historical considerations, the chronological period of the Qumran community is from roughly 150 B.C. to A.D. 68. The oldest Qumran scrolls were written before that time, however, because the first residents of the Qumran community brought some scrolls with them (based on paleographic data the oldest scrolls are dated toward the end of the 3rd century B.C.).

The scrolls discovered at Nahal Heber, Nahal Se'elim, and in the Wadi Murabba'at date from about A.D. 130, those of Masada from about A.D. 70. These scrolls offer a text that is virtually identical with the Massoretic text (see p. 185).

## (2) THE CHARACTER OF THE QUMRAN SCROLLS

The Qumran scrolls are from eleven caves. Presently it cannot be determined whether the scrolls differ textually from cave to cave. Clearly most of the scrolls that are important for the reconstruction of the history of the text are from Caves 4 and 11.

The biblical text of the Qumran scrolls is best described in relation to the *textus receptus* (Massoretic text):

1. Most scrolls from Caves 1, 2, 3, 5, 6, and 8 are virtually identical with the Massoretic text, barring occasional (esp. orthographic) variants (e.g., 1QIs[b]). In view of the early date of these scrolls their text tradition is often called "proto-Massoretic."

2. Some scrolls, while reflecting the tradition of the Massoretic text, contain a larger number of variants than the ones just mentioned (e.g., 11QPs[a]).

3. Other scrolls, though based on the tradition of the Massoretic text, represent a different approach to the text. These scrolls are written in a much fuller orthography (cf. p. 187) and contain a relatively large number of secondary readings, that is, readings that eliminate grammatical and contextual difficulties (e.g., 1QIs[a]).

4. Some scrolls exhibit great similarity with two non-Massoretic textual witnesses: the Septuagint and the Samaritan Pentateuch. The two scrolls that are akin to the Samaritan Pentateuch are described on p. 171. 4QJer[b] is closely akin to the Septuagint, which in Jeremiah reflects a Hebrew text that is shorter by one-seventh than the Massoretic text and arranges verses, pericopes, and chapters differently than the Massoretic text. 4QJer[b] resembles the Septuagint in both respects. In the literature, however, the existence of Qumran scrolls of a so-called Septuagint type is overemphasized. In the past a scroll was prematurely labeled a "Septuagint type" without considering the problem of the relationship between the Septuagint and these scrolls (cf., e.g., section 3.d below). Moreover, the Septuagint does not contain a text-type but it reflects a text (cf. pp. 181–82).

5. All other scrolls are "independent" in relation to the Massoretic text, Septuagint, and (in the Pentateuch) Samaritan Pentateuch. A large scroll such as 11QpaleoLev agrees with the Massoretic text over against other textual witnesses, though occasionally with the Septuagint and at other times with the Samaritan Pentateuch. But it also contains many independent readings, that is, readings not found in other sources (see esp. p. 185). This is also true of the Samuel scrolls from Cave 4, which in the research are linked with the Septuagint. This supposed relationship with the Septuagint is misleading, however, because the Samuel scrolls often coincide with the Septuagint in instances where they contain a (probably) original reading, while the Massoretic text is corrupt. To determine the relationship it is especially important that faulty readings they have in common are taken into consideration, not common original readings.

## LITERATURE

C. Burchard, *Bibliographie zu den Handschriften vom Toten Meer* (Beiheft zur Zeitschrift für die alttestamentliche Wissenschaft 76 and 89; Berlin, 1957, 1959², 1965).

J. A. Fitzmyer, *The Dead Sea Scrolls. Major Publications and Tools for Study* (Missoula, 1975).

B. Jongeling, *A Classified Bibliography of the Finds in the Desert of Judah 1958–1969* (Leiden, 1971).

See further:

F. M. Cross, *The Ancient Library of Qumran and Modern Biblical Studies* (New York, 1961²; repr. Grand Rapids, 1980).

———, "A New Qumran Fragment Related to the Original Hebrew Underlying the Septuagint," *Bulletin of the American Schools of Oriental Research* 132 (1953) 15–26.

F. M. Cross and S. Talmon, eds., *Qumran and the History of the Biblical Text* (Cambridge, Mass., 1975).

E. Y. Kutscher, *The Language and Linguistic Background of the Isaiah Scroll (1QIsaᵃ)* (Leiden, 1974).

P. W. Skehan, "The Biblical Scrolls from Qumran and the Text of the Old Testament," *Biblical Archaeologist* 28 (1965) 87–100 (repr. in Cross and Talmon, eds., *Qumran and the History of the Biblical Text*, pp. 264–77).

———, "The Qumran Manuscripts and Textual Criticism," *Supplements to Vetus Testamentum* 4 (1957) 148–60 (repr. in Cross and Talmon, eds., *Qumran and the History of the Biblical Text*, pp. 212–25).

———, "The Scrolls and the Old Testament Text," in D. N. Freedman and J. C. Greenfield, eds., *New Directions in Biblical Archaeology* (New York, 1971), pp. 99–112.

———, "Qumran, textes bibliques," *Dictionnaire de la Bible, Supplement* IX (Paris, 1979) 805–22.

E. Tov, ed., *The Hebrew and Greek Texts of Samuel* (Jerusalem, 1980).

G. Vermes, *The Dead Sea Scrolls: Qumran in Perspective* (London, 1977).

See also the bibliography on p. 188.

## c. The Samaritan Pentateuch

### (1) ORIGIN AND BACKGROUND

The Samaritan Pentateuch contains the sacred writings of the Samaritans, presently a community of a few hundred members, living mainly in two places, on Mount Gerizim (near Shechem, modern Nablus) and in Cholon (near Tel Aviv). Since the origin of the community is shrouded in mystery, opinions vary about how it arose. Some think that the first Samaritans were pagans who had converted to Judaism. According to others they belonged to the lost ten tribes of Israel. The Samaritans themselves believe that the origin of their community goes back to the time of Eli (11th century B.C.). This community had withdrawn from Shechem to establish a new cult in Shiloh, which was later brought to Jerusalem. According to this conception, the Jews split off from the Samaritans, not the other way around.

The great majority of scholars, however, are inclined to think that the Samaritans are a sect that separated from Judaism at the time of the Second Temple. According to some this schism took place in the Persian period (cf. Ezra 4:1–5), according to others at the time of Alexander the Great (cf. Josephus, *Antiquities* 11.302–25). Recently, cogent arguments have been advanced for a later date. According to Purvis (pp. 98–118), the schism cannot have happened before the destruction of Samaria by John Hyrcanus in 128 B.C.

That the Samaritan script does not resemble the Old Hebrew type but a later development of it from the Hasmonean period also favors a later date. A further argument for the late date of the Samaritan Pentateuch is the full orthography of this text (see p. 187; ill. 57). On the other hand, that the Samaritans accepted only the Pentateuch might be an argument for an earlier date.

## (2) EDITIONS AND TRANSLATIONS

Several manuscripts of the Samaritan Pentateuch are known. The first of these is the manuscript that was brought to the West in 1616 by Pietro della Valle and later printed in the Polyglot of Paris (1629–45). Since then many other manuscripts of the Samaritan Pentateuch have become known.

Presently, no satisfactory critical edition of the Samaritan Pentateuch is available. The best critical edition is by A. von Gall, *Der hebräische Pentateuch der Samaritaner* I-V (Giessen, 1914–18; repr. Berlin, 1966). The eclectic principles on which this edition is based are not always convincing, however. For example, von Gall prefers defective readings and grammatically "more correct" readings. Another problem in the use of this edition is that von Gall knew only a limited number of manuscripts. The important Abisha Scroll, for example, became known only later; cf. the edition of F. Perez Castro (Madrid, 1959). The colophon of this scroll states that it was written in the thirteenth year after the entrance into Canaan. Though this dating cannot be right (the scroll was probably written in the 15th century A.D.), the manuscript contains many original readings. On the basis of the Abisha Scroll and other old manuscripts, A. and R. Sadaqa issued a modern edition of the Samaritan Pentateuch, *Jewish and Samaritan Version of the Pentateuch* (Jerusalem, 1965). In this edition the Samaritan Pentateuch and Massoretic text are printed in parallel columns that indicate typographically the differences between the two texts. The most recent edition of the Samaritan Pentateuch is L. F. Giron Blanc, *Pentateuco hebreo-samaritano, Genesis* (Madrid, 1976), which contains the text of Codex Add. 1846 Univ. Lib. Cambr. (A.D. 1100) and offers variants from fifteen unpublished manuscripts.

The Samaritan Pentateuch was translated into Aramaic, Arabic, and perhaps also Greek. While not of direct significance for the textual criticism of the Hebrew Bible, these translations do give the Samaritan tradition of the vocalization, which constitutes a supplement to the unvocalized text of the Samaritan Pentateuch.

The manuscripts of the Samaritan targum contain different but related translations. The most used editions are the ones of H. Brüll, *Das samaritanische Targum zum Pentateuch* (Frankfort am Main, 1873–76; repr. Hildesheim, 1971), and A. Tal, *The Samaritan Targum of the Pentateuch* I–III (Tel Aviv, 1980–83).

An Arabic translation from the eleventh century was published by P. Kahle, *Die arabischen Bibelübersetzungen* (Leipzig, 1904). For a partial, critical edition and an extensive discussion of this Arabic translation, see H. Shedadeh, "The Arabic Translation of the Samaritan Pentateuch, Prolegomena to a Critical Edition" (Ph.D. diss., Hebrew University, Jerusalem, 1977; Hebrew).

The status of the Greek translation is fairly complicated. A fragment of a Greek translation of Deuteronomy was published by Glaue and Rahlfs and attributed to the Greek translation of the Samaritan Pentateuch. Yet it is not certain whether there has ever been a complete Greek translation of the Samaritan Pentateuch. The assumption that such a translation existed is based on some marginal notes in hexaplaric manuscripts (see p. 176) that quote from a *samareitikon*.

## (3) THE HISTORY OF INVESTIGATION

When the Samaritan Pentateuch became known in Europe in the seventeenth century, many greeted it as a more original version of the Pentateuch than the Massoretic text. This idea was influenced by the use of the Old Hebrew script (see, however, above) as well as by the similarities that were soon discovered between the Septuagint and the Samaritan Pentateuch. The Polyglot of London contains a list of non-Massoretic similarities between the Samaritan Pentateuch and the Septuagint in 1900 instances, that is, one-third of the total number of readings in which the Samaritan Pentateuch deviates from the Massoretic text. These data have given rise to many theories, which are discussed by Gesenius. For example, it has been propounded that the Septuagint was translated from a Samaritan text; also that the Septuagint was revised on the basis of the Samaritan Pentateuch (or vice versa, the Samaritan Pentateuch was revised on the basis of the Septuagint). Gesenius's own view was that both the Samaritan Pentateuch and Septuagint derived from a "recension" that differed from the Palestinian recension of the Old Testament (i.e., the Massoretic text). Such opinions, which find defenders even today, are based neither on accurate data nor on critical editions (for this antiquated view on the history of the text see further pp. 181–82). The relationship between both texts needs to be reexamined. The likely result will be that the Samaritan Pentateuch and the Septuagint are not as closely related as was thought in the past.

More important than the relationship between the Samaritan Pentateuch and the Septuagint is that between the Samaritan Pentateuch and the Massoretic text. Before Gesenius, the Samaritan Pentateuch was usually described as a more original text than the Massoretic text. Gesenius proposed a new view on the relationship of both. In a now classical study he carefully described ten categories of differences between the Massoretic text and Samaritan Pentateuch that illustrate the secondary character of the Samaritan Pentateuch evident especially in harmonizing changes. Even though Gesenius's analysis is now in several respects antiquated and shown to be inaccurate, his classification still remains valuable. For the grammatical analysis see now especially Ben Hayyim and Macuch.

## (4) THE CHARACTER OF THE SAMARITAN PENTATEUCH

Most readings of the Samaritan Pentateuch constitute secondary developments of parallel details in the Massoretic text, subdivided into the following four categories:

### (a) SECTARIAN CHANGES

The ideas of the Samaritans differed from those of the Jews in a number of important details. Nevertheless, from the standpoint of text-critical analysis, the Samaritan Pentateuch does not contain a sectarian text since it has few sectarian readings.

The most important doctrinal difference between the groups concerns the location of the central sanctuary: Jerusalem for the Jews and Mount Gerizim for the Samaritans. To reinforce this belief the Samaritans added a commandment to the Decalogue (after Exod. 20:14 and Deut. 5:18) that secured the centrality of Mount Gerizim in the cult. This commandment is composed of a series of biblical pericopes that mention a central cult in Shechem (Deut. 11:29; 27:2–7; 11:30 [in this sequence]).

Closely connected with this addition are various alterations in Deuteronomy where the characteristic expression "the place which the Lord your God *will* choose" is changed to "the place which the Lord your God *has* chosen" (e.g., Deut. 12:10, 11). From the Samaritan perspective, Shechem was already the chosen place in the time of Abraham, whereas from the historical perspective of Deuteronomy, Jerusalem, the (anonymous) location envisioned in Deuteronomy, still had to be chosen.

### (b) HARMONIZING ALTERATIONS

The Samaritan Pentateuch contains various kinds of harmonizing alterations that by definition are secondary. The presence of these alterations does not display a consistent pattern, and in the present state of scholarly investigation the harmonizing technique used in those days is not sufficiently known.

The most frequent type of harmonizing alterations happens when one of two variant parallel verses in the Samaritan Pentateuch is adapted to the other. Thus in the Massoretic text the fourth commandment in Exodus 20:8 begins with *zakor* (remember) and in Deuteronomy 5:12 with *shamor* (observe), but the Samaritan Pentateuch reads *shamor* in both verses. As a rule, however, the Samaritan Pentateuch puts both parallel verses (or parallel details) after each other in one of the two texts. Thus the parallel verses from Deuteronomy 1:9–18 are added to Exodus 18:24.

Another kind of harmonizing change concerns the addition of details in the Samaritan Pentateuch with which the reader should actually be familiar but which are not explicitly mentioned in the Bible. In Exodus 14:12 the Israelites murmur against Moses after he has led them through the Red Sea: "Is not this what we said to you in Egypt, 'Let us alone and let us serve the Egyptians'?" This complaint is not mentioned earlier in the Massoretic text, however, and therefore the Samaritan Pentateuch mentions the "source" of this quotation in an addition to an earlier verse (Exod. 6:9). Another illustration is in Genesis 31:11–13, where Jacob tells a dream to his wives that is not known to the readers of the earlier verses. In the Samaritan Pentateuch the content of this dream is added after 30:36.

It is characteristic of the style of the biblical narrative to relate commands in great detail but their execution only briefly, with the words ". . . and he [etc.] did as. . . ." In the Samaritan Pentateuch also, the execution of such commands is often elaborately narrated by repeating the details of the command. For example, in the first chapters of Exodus God gives Moses and Aaron commmands whose execution is briefly mentioned in the Massoretic text; the Samaritan Pentateuch, however, mentions their execution in detail after Exodus 7:18, 29; 8:19; 9:5, 19.

## (c) ORTHOGRAPHIC AND PHONOLOGICAL DIFFERENCES

The use of *matres lectionis* (see p. 187) in the Samaritan Pentateuch differs in several respects from their use in the Massoretic text. Macuch and Cohen have shown that it is an oversimplification to say that the orthography of the Samaritan Pentateuch is fuller than that of the Massoretic text: in some word categories the Massoretic text is fuller than the Samaritan Pentateuch, while in other categories the Samaritan Pentateuch is fuller than the Massoretic text.

The phonological background of the Samaritan Pentateuch often differs from the Massoretic text. This is true especially of the gutturals because the Samaritan Pentateuch represents a different dialect than that of the Hebrew of the Massoretic text (see esp. the studies of Ben-Hayyim and Macuch). Thus in Genesis 49:7 the Samaritan Pentateuch reads *we-ḥebratam* instead of the Massoretic text's *we-'ebratam*; in Genesis 36:13, 17 the Samaritan Pentateuch reads *shammaḥ* instead of the Massoretic text's *shammah*.

## (d) MORPHOLOGICAL DIFFERENCES

The Massoretic text and Samaritan Pentateuch exhibit a large number of morphological differences. For example, in the Samaritan Pentateuch many "unusual" forms of the Massoretic text are changed into more "usual" forms. Thus *nahnu* (we) in Genesis 42:11 is changed in the Samaritan Pentateuch to the more usual form *anahnu*. A remnant of an old case suffix *-o* in *wehayeto eres* in Genesis 1:24 is removed in the Samaritan Pentateuch (*wehayyat haares*).

In addition to these four categories of secondary readings, the Samaritan Pentateuch contains many nonsecondary readings that cannot be put under one rubric. These are old readings that are often more original than the parallel readings in the Massoretic text (cf. p. 183).

## (5) THE SAMARITAN PENTATEUCH IN MODERN RESEARCH

In modern research the Samaritan Pentateuch is basically regarded as an originally nonsectarian text exhibiting typological similarities with the following texts:

(a) The greatest similarity with the Samaritan Pentateuch is found in 4QpaleoEx[m]. The harmonizing readings this scroll has in common with the Samaritan Pentateuch have been described by Skehan. The similarity between the Samaritan Pentateuch and 4QNum[b] has been described by F. M. Cross, *Ancient Library*, p. 186.

(b) 1QIs[a] (see p. 167) shares a number of characteristics with the Samaritan Pentateuch, both in orthography and in changes on the basis of the context.

(c) The Samuel scrolls from Cave 4 of Qumran contain many readings derived from the parallel texts in Chronicles.

(d) The typological similarity between the Samaritan Pentateuch and Massoretic text of Chronicles has been described by Gerleman. According to him, both texts contain "vulgar" text traditions in contrast to the carefully edited Massoretic text.

Like the Samaritan Pentateuch, all these texts show evidence of editorial manipulation and of an orthography representing an approach to the biblical text that differs from the character of the Massoretic text (cf. pp. 183–85). The secondary character of these texts does not exclude that occasionally they contain more original readings than the Massoretic text. However, in the analysis of these texts one must continually be aware of their special characteristics.

## LITERATURE

L. A. Mayer, *Bibliography of the Samaritans* (Supplement to Abr Nahrain; Leiden, 1964).

R. Weiss, *Leqet bibliografi al ha-shomronim* (Jerusalem, 1974[3]) (Hebrew).

See further:

Z. Ben-Hayyim, *The Literary and Oral Traditions of Hebrew and Aramaic among the Samaritans* I–V (Jerusalem, 1956–79) (Hebrew).

M. Cohen, "The Orthography of the Samaritan Pentateuch," *Beth Miqra* 64 (1976) 54–70; 66 (1976) 361–91 (Hebrew).

G. Gerleman, *Synoptic Studies in the Old Testament* (Lund, 1948).

W. Gesenius, *De Pentateuchi samaritani origine, indole et auctoritate commentatio philologico-critica* (Halle, 1815).

P. Glaue and A. Rahlfs, "Fragmente einer griechischen Übersetzung des samaritanischen Pentateuchs," *Mitteilungen des Septuaginta-Unternehmens* I/2 (Berlin, 1909–15) 31–64.

R. Macuch, *Grammatik des samaritanischen Hebräisch* (Berlin, 1969).

J. D. Purvis, *The Samaritan Pentateuch and the Origin of the Samaritan Sect* (Harvard Semitic Monographs 2; Cambridge, Mass., 1968).

P. W. Skehan, "Exodus in the Samaritan Recension from Qumran," *Journal of Biblical Literature* 74 (1955) 182–87.

B. K. Waltke, "The Samaritan Pentateuch and the Text of the Old Testament," in J. B. Payne, ed., *New Perspectives on the Old Testament* (Waco, 1970), pp. 212–39.

## d. The Ancient Versions

### (1) THE TEXT-CRITICAL VALUE OF THE VERSIONS

The textual criticism of the Old Testament aims at tracing Hebrew readings that differ from the *textus receptus* (Massoretic text). It is not enough to search for such readings in Hebrew sources because non-Hebrew sources, particularly the ancient translations (versions), also contain many data that are important for reaching the goal just mentioned. These data are used in the text-critical analysis of the Old Testament, but by definition they cannot be used in the language of the translations, for the aim is to discover deviating *Hebrew* text traditions. Therefore the textual critic must first determine whether a particular deviation from the Massoretic text in an ancient translation reflects a Hebrew variant. The first step in the text-critical analysis of the versions is thus that the translation be retranslated (retroverted) into the assumed Hebrew-Aramaic original text, in order that the elements that have been retranslated, together with original Hebrew readings, can be compared with the Massoretic text.

Until recently, Old Testament textual criticism has paid much attention to the versions. This interest was justified because the oldest Hebrew manuscripts were from the Middle Ages, whereas some of the manuscripts of the Septuagint, Peshitta, and Vulgate are from the fourth and fifth centuries. This situation has now changed because the Hebrew scrolls from the Judean desert (see section 2.b above) are not only considerably older than the oldest manuscripts of the versions but also substantively more important. It is therefore likely that in the coming decades the text-critical interest will be focused more on Hebrew sources than on the versions, even though text-critically the latter remain of great importance, especially the Septuagint.

Text-critical analysis reconstructs the Hebrew text—the *Vorlage*—on which the translation was based. Scholars are divided about the possibilities and methodology of this reconstruction. There are no firm systematic criteria for such reconstruction of the text, but important aspects of the procedure followed have been described by Margolis, Ziegler, Goshen-Gottstein, Barr, and Tov (see literature), mainly in reference to the Septuagint. These methodological treatises can also be applied to other versions.

When a detail in a translation differs from the Massoretic text, one need not immediately assume that its *Vorlage* differed from the Massoretic text. Such differences are also caused, even in larger measure, by other factors such as exegesis, translation technique, and the transmission of the text of the versions.

If analysis leads to the conclusion that a particular deviation in the Massoretic text is not caused by one of the above-mentioned factors, one may assume that the translation is based on a Hebrew consonantal text that differed from the Massoretic text. We have various means at our disposal, especially concordances of translations, by which this text can be reconstructed. The following is a good illustration: the Septuagint of Deuteronomy 31:1 reads, "and Moses finished speaking" (*kai synetelesen Mouses lalon*) instead of the Massoretic text's "and Moses went and spoke" (*wayyelek mosheh wayyedabber*). The deviating translation in the Septuagint must have been caused by the presence of a variant. According to the information in the concordance, the verb *synteleo* (finish) usually represents the Hebrew *klh* (finish); thus it may be assumed that the *Vorlage* of the Septuagint read *wayyekal* instead of *wayyelek* (i.e., metathesis of the last two consonants; see p. 187). The reconstruction of this variant is supported by an identical variant in a Qumran scroll (1Q5, frag. 13,2) and the similar expression in the Massoretic text of Deuteronomy 32:45. (The *Vorlage* of the ancient translations contained only consonants. Therefore in the reconstruction of this *Vorlage* vowels may be ignored.)

Very few elements in the versions can be retranslated with absolute certainty to specific Hebrew variants. In general, it is uncertain if a deviation in a translation is due to a Hebrew variant, or, for example, the result of a free translation or of exegesis (in choosing from the various possibilities, familiarity with the caliber of the translation of the various books is very important).

But even if it is certain that a detail in the translation can be translated back to a particular variant, this does not mean that that variant also existed in a Hebrew source. For it is possible that the translator misread a detail in his *Vorlage*, so that the variant existed only in his mind. Thus the Septuagint text of 1 Samuel 21:8 wrongly calls Doeg *ho Syros*, words that can be retranslated to *ha'arami*, "the Aramean," instead of *ha'adomi*, "the Edomite," as in the Massoretic text (and in other Old Testament references to Doeg). It is impossible to say whether the *Vorlage* of the Greek translation read *h'rmy* or the translator took *h'dmy* as *h'rmy* (for interchanges of *r* and *d* see p. 187). In both cases it is customary to say that the Septuagint reflects the "variant" *h'rmy*, even though this reading may never have existed in a Hebrew text.

Because of the different approaches in the reconstruction of the *Vorlagen* of the versions, many divergences in the versions are retranslated as Hebrew variants by some but regarded as stemming from translation technique, exegesis, etc., by others. Moreover, in the translation of the divergences back into Hebrew, the number of possibilities of retranslation appears to be almost unlimited.

## LITERATURE

J. Barr, *Comparative Philology and the Text of the Old Testament* (Oxford, 1968).

S. P. Brock, "Bibelübersetzungen I," *Theologische Realenzyklopädie* VI (Berlin/New York, 1981) 161–216.

S. R. Driver, *Notes on the Hebrew Text and the Topography of the Books of Samuel, with an Introduction on Hebrew Palaeography and the Ancient Versions* (Oxford, 1913²), pp. xxxiii-xxxviii.

M. H. Goshen-Gottstein, "Theory and Practice of Textual Criticism—The Text-Critical Use of the Septuagint," *Textus* 3 (1963) 130–58.

E. Tov, "The Use of Concordances in the Reconstruction of the *Vorlage* of the LXX," *Catholic Biblical Quarterly* 40 (1978) 29–36.

## (2) THE SEPTUAGINT

### (a) NAME AND ORIGIN

The most important Greek translation of the Old Testament, the Septuagint, received its name from the legend that seventy-two men translated the Pentateuch into Greek (in later tradition the number 72 was rounded off to 70). This tradition was expanded to cover all the translated books of the Alexandrian canon, eventually even including the books originally written in Greek.

The old traditions about the legendary origin of the Septuagint are recorded in various rabbinic sources (e.g., Babylonian Talmud *Megillah* 9a) and in greater detail in the *Letter of Aristeas*, one of the pseudepigraphal books. These old traditions were collected by P. Wendland, *Aristeae ad Philocratem epistula cum ceteris de origine versionis LXX interpretum testimoniis* (Leipzig,

1900), and translated by H. S. J. Thackeray, *The Letter of Aristeas* (London/New York, 1917).

According to the Letter of Aristeas, the Septuagint was translated at the time of Ptolemy Philadelphus (285–247 B.C.). Though the details of the story mentioned in this Letter may be questioned, it is certain that the translation was done at an early date because the grandson of Jesus Sirach (132 or 116 B.C.) knew the Septuagint text of many of the books. Moreover, several papyri of the Greek Pentateuch go back as far as the second century B.C.

The books of the Septuagint were translated in a period from the third to the first century B.C. The Septuagint canon also contains translations that are revisions of the original translation. Thus the Alexandrian canon comprises a heterogeneous collection of earlier and later translations, original translations as well as later revisions.

Opinions are divided about the origin and background of the Septuagint. Apart from the Egyptian-Jewish character of the technical vocabulary, the translation itself contains little evidence about its own background. The most significant source for the origins of the Septuagint is the above-mentioned Letter of Aristeas. The story told there is full of legendary details, which are even more pervasive in a still later version in Epiphanius's treatise on *Measures and Weights*. Nevertheless, the core of the story deserves credence: someone (perhaps the king himself) asked a group of Jewish men to prepare a Greek translation of the Pentateuch, and that translation was made in Egypt in the third century B.C.

Modern accounts of the origin of the Septuagint are based on purely theoretical arguments as well as on a particular view of the Letter of Aristeas and on early papyri of the Septuagint, many of which were discovered in our century (see Jellicoe, pp. 224–42).

According to de Lagarde, all manuscripts of the Septuagint are derived from one *Urtext* (hence the name *Urtext* theory). Consequently, in his judgment it is possible to reconstruct this *Urtext* on the basis of the three recensions (see p. 175) into which the original text of the Septuagint was split. This conception—based on purely theoretical considerations—implies that all extant Septuagint manuscripts represent only one trans-

lation (for de Lagarde's theory on the reconstruction of the *Urtext* of the *Hebrew* Bible, see p. 182).

Kahle's theories (the theory of many translations) were published between 1915 and 1959 in frequently contradictory formulations (see literature). The following points are of decisive significance in Kahle's reconstruction: (1) The heterogeneity of the textual witnesses of the Septuagint is the result of many different translations that, according to Kahle, can be likened to the multiplicity of the early targums (see section 4 below). The task of Septuagint textual criticism is therefore limited to a description of these divergent text traditions. There is no need to reconstruct an original text because such a text has never existed. (2) In the pre-Christian era none of these translations was regarded as authoritative.

Modern analyses of the origins of the Septuagint consider the opinions of de Lagarde and Kahle as being completely contradictory. One should not speak of a complete contradiction, however, because first, their respective theses do not deal with the same problems; second, they are of a completely different character; and third, they are based on different kinds of data. Thus according to de Lagarde every book of the Septuagint is based on one translation, while Kahle also believed that behind the multiplicity of translations lies one first translation.

Kahle's view is deficient on the following two points: (1) In contrast to other scholars he contended that the Letter of Aristeas does not describe a new translation of the Pentateuch but an official revision of earlier translations. This argument is based on a wrong interpretation of verse 30 in the Letter (a fine summary of the various interpretations of this verse is given by Gooding). (2) From the beginning of the twentieth century various papyri have been found whose text differs considerably from that of the most significant majuscule manuscripts of the Septuagint (i.e., A, B, and S). According to Kahle the new sources contain various Greek translations, whereas in reality most papyri contain revisions of one earlier form of the text.

Kahle's theories about the origin of the Septuagint have found few adherents. Especially problematic is his inclination to explain the development of the Hebrew, Greek, and Aramaic Bible with the use of the same principles. In our judgment Kahle's description of the background of the Septuagint is less justified than that of the Hebrew and Aramaic Bible (see pp. 182–83).

A third (synthetic) analysis of the development of the Septuagint is propounded by Tov ("Septuagint," see literature), who bases his theory partially on Bickerman. In his view, each individual book of the Septuagint was translated by one translator, but the original form of this translation did not remain unchanged for long, because in the second and first centuries B.C. copyists introduced changes into the various manuscripts, frequently with the intention of producing a translation that was more literally faithful to the Hebrew text.

Other theories about the origin of the Septuagint, in particular the "liturgical theory," which holds that the Septuagint originated in the reading of the Bible in the liturgy, and the so-called transcription theory, have few followers today (for descriptions see Jellicoe, pp. 64–73).

### (b) RECENSIONS OF THE SEPTUAGINT

The original text of the Septuagint was revised many times. Slight revisions are recognizable in corrections that have been inserted in most of the early papyri. Revisional work is more easily recognizable, however, in the sources that have undergone more systematic revision of the original translation. As a rule, such revisions aimed at a more accurate reproduction of the Hebrew text, but stylistic improvements of the Greek are also found. These revisions have only partially survived; they are found at various places, sometimes even within the canon of the Septuagint (see below).

With the exception of the Lucianic version, the recensions of the Septuagint are of little value for the textual history of the Hebrew Bible since their *Vorlage* was virtually identical with the Massoretic text.

The recensions can be subdivided into three groups, with the Hexapla having a central position.

Especially because of the account of Jerome (Introduction to Chronicles; J.-P. Migne, *Patrologia Latina*, XXVIII, 1324–25), the textual history of the Septuagint is often described as originating

from the transmission and contamination of three text-types: the recensions of Origen (Hexapla), Lucian, and Hesychius, current in Palestine, Syria, and Egypt, respectively. It is uncertain whether there ever was a Hesychian recension, and therefore all attempts to reconstruct this "threefold diversity" (*trifaria varietas*; the term is from Jerome) have met with little success.

### (i) The Pre-Hexaplaric Recensions

The pre-Hexaplaric recensions of the Septuagint have now become better known through the discovery of new papyri:

The significant *kaige*-Theodotion recension has become known in recent years through the discovery of a Greek scroll of the Minor Prophets at Nahal Heber in 1953. This scroll has been published in the pioneering book of D. Barthélemy, *Les devanciers d'Aquila* (Supplements to Vetus Testamentum 10; Leiden, 1963). The author describes a revision of the Septuagint that can be found in various books within the Septuagint canon (i.e., 2 Sam. 11:1—1 Kings 2:11, 1 Kings 21—2 Kings, Song of Songs, Ruth; probably also in other books) as well as outside it, namely, in the above-mentioned scroll of the Minor Prophets and in the sixth column of the Hexapla (Theodotion). Barthélemy called this recension *kaige* because one of its clearest characteristics is the translation of Hebrew *gam* (also) by Greek *kaige* (at least). In antiquity this anonymous recension, probably dating from the first century B.C., was ascribed to Theodotion, for which reason it was included in the Theodotion column of the Hexapla. Hence in current literature it is usually called *kaige*-Theodotion. It may be noted that the existence of a so-called Ur-Theodotion, frequently discussed in the literature of the last two centuries, may now be dismissed.

Aquila's recension (ca. A.D. 135), based on the *kaige*-Theodotion, contains the most literally accurate and etymologizing translation within the framework of the versions of the Old Testament.

Symmachus's recension (end of 2nd century A.D.), like the one of Aquila, is based on *kaige*-Theodotion and contains both literally accurate as well as free renderings.

In ancient sources, Aquila, Symmachus, and Theodotion (= *kaige*-Theodotion) are often cited as "the Three," because often they contain the same text. For editions of the text, see the following section on the Hexapla.

*(ii) The Hexapla*

The Hexapla, the "sixfold edition" of the biblical text compiled by Origen in the middle of the third century, contains the following six columns:

1. The Hebrew text
2. The Hebrew text transliterated into Greek
3. Aquila
4. Symmachus
5. Septuagint—this column also indicated the quantitative relationship between the Septuagint and Massoretic text (additions, omissions) with diacritical signs (asterisk, obelos)
6. Theodotion

The last four columns may also have appeared separately in the form of a "Tetrapla" (the fourfold edition). In some books, the Hexapla contains also a fifth (Quinta), sixth (Sexta), and seventh (Septima) column, following after the fourth column of the so-called Tetrapla.

In the beginning of the fourth century, the fifth column (Septuagint) was separately issued by Eusebius and Pamphilius. This edition soon dominated the textual transmission of the Septuagint in Palestine.

Fragments of all the columns of the Psalms have been published by G. Mercati, *Psalterii Hexapli reliquiae* I (Rome, 1958), and A. Schenker, *Hexaplarische Psalmenbruchstücke* (Freiburg/Göttingen, 1975).

Beyond that, many details from columns 3–6 of the Hexapla are cited by copyists in the margins of Septuagint manuscripts. Modern critical editions (see below) accurately reproduce these marginal notations. Furthermore, the older edition of F. Field, *Origenis Hexaplorum quae supersunt* I– II (Oxford, 1867–74; repr. Hildesheim, 1964), is still useful.

Though few fragments of the Hexapla have survived, a good idea of the Septuagint column can be obtained via the Syriac translation of the Hexapla (the so-called Syro-Hexapla) prepared by Paul of Tella (A.D. 616). Large parts of this translation have been translated over the years (see the bibliography of Brock). Special mention should also be made of a recent discovery: A. Vööbus, *The Pentateuch in the Version of the Syro-Hexapla. A Facsimile Edition of a Midyat MS. Discovered 1964* (CSC Or 369; Louvain, 1975).

*(iii) Post-Hexaplaric Recensions*

The most important post-Hexaplaric revision is that of Lucian (d. A.D. 312). In the nineteenth century Paul de Lagarde, among others, rediscovered the Lucianic text tradition and published an (inaccurate) edition of this text: *Librorum Veteris Testamenti canonicorum pars prior graece* (Göttingen, 1883). For careful research it is better to consult the variants in the Göttingen edition, indicated as L(ucianic), or various minuscule manuscripts (e.g., bo[r]c$_2$e$_2$ in the historical books) in the Cambridge edition. Presently it cannot be determined whether a Lucianic text of all the books of the Bible ever existed (doubts have been raised with respect to the Pentateuch).

In most books the Lucianic text gives a recension of the Hexapla, but in the historical books this text also contains many proto-Lucianic elements that are also known from pre-Lucianic sources, especially the biblical text of Flavius Josephus and the Hebrew Samuel scrolls from Cave 4 at Qumran. These proto-Lucianic elements, frequently described in the literature (see esp. Hooykaas), have been analyzed afresh in modern research, especially after the appearance of Barthélemy's book (see p. 175). There is no doubt that the Lucianic text contains a revisional layer, which may have derived from Lucian himself, though the nature of the substratum of this tradition must be further investigated. According to Barthélemy and Tov ("Lucian and Proto-Lucian," see literature) this substratum contains the original Greek translation (the "Old Greek"), but according to Cross it contains a proto-Lucianic recension of the Septuagint.

*(c) EDITIONS AND AUXILIARY TOOLS*

It is advisable that, of the many Septuagint editions available, especially the modern critical editions be used:

1. A diplomatic edition of Codex Vaticanus (B), supplied with an extensive critical apparatus: A. E. Brooke, N. McLean, and H. S. J. Thackeray, *The Old Testament in Greek* (Cambridge, 1906–40) (incomplete), and according to the

same system the edition of H. B. Swete, *The Old Testament in Greek according to the Septuagint* I–III (Cambridge, 1887–94).

2. An eclectic edition based on the principles of de Lagarde (see p. 174), prepared by the *Septuaginta-Unternehmen* in Göttingen: *Vetus Testamentum graecum auctoritate societatis litterarum gottingensis editum* (Göttingen, 1931– ) (incomplete); further, the edition of A. Rahlfs, *Septuaginta, id est Vetus Testamentum graece iuxta LXX* (Stuttgart, 1935).

The most frequently used concordance is E. Hatch and H. A. Redpath, *A Concordance to the Septuagint and the Other Greek Versions of the Old Testament (Including the Apocryphal Books)* I–II (Oxford, 1897; repr. Graz, 1954). This edition gives the formal equivalents of the Massoretic text and the Septuagint. For the use of concordances in the reconstruction of the Septuagint *Vorlage*, see Tov, *Text-critical Use*. A computerized concordance of all Hebrew-Greek equivalents is available on a data base prepared by R. A. Kraft and E. Tov: Computer Assisted Tools for Septuagint Studies.

### (d) TRANSLATIONS OF THE SEPTUAGINT

In antiquity, the Septuagint, the Bible of the Christians in the pre-Vulgate period, was translated into Latin (Vetus Latina), Syriac (the Syro-Palestinian translations), Coptic (Sahidic, Bohairic, and Akhmimic), Ethiopic, Armenian, Old Slavic, Gothic, and Arabic. An analysis of these versions is important for the history of the Septuagint in the various areas where these translations were used. But as a rule the so-called daughter translations are of lesser significance for the textual history of the Hebrew Bible. For a recent description of these translations, see Jellicoe, pp. 246–68.

### (e) TEXT-CRITICAL VALUE

The quality of the translation of the Septuagint varies from book to book, ranging from slavishly literal (e.g., Psalms and the revisions included in the Septuagint canon; see p. 175) to paraphrases (Isaiah, Proverbs, Job, Daniel). The analysis of this quality is very important for the text-critical analysis of the Septuagint, for one must determine

whether each variation between the Massoretic text and the Septuagint is due to a free translation or to a Hebrew *Vorlage* that deviated from the Massoretic text. See further pp. 173–75.

The Septuagint reflects a large number of Hebrew variants. Among the versions, the Septuagint is by far the most important source for textual criticism. Together with the Qumran scrolls and the Samaritan Pentateuch it constitutes the most important non-Massoretic textual witness, especially in Samuel, Kings, Ezekiel, and Jeremiah. Particularly important are those sections in which the Septuagint reflects a text which is recensionally different from the Massoretic text. In these passages the Septuagint usually represents a stage in the development of a biblical book that preceded the stage of development reflected in the Massoretic text. This holds especially for the Septuagint of Jeremiah (see p. 167), for the shorter Septuagint version of 1 Samuel 17–18, and for the chronological framework of the Septuagint in 1–2 Kings. In such instances the Septuagint offers data for the literary criticism of the Old Testament.

### LITERATURE

S. P. Brock, et al., *A Classified Bibliography of the Septuagint* (Leiden, 1973).

See further:

E. Bickerman, "Some Notes on the Transmission of the Septuagint," in *A. Marx Jubilee Volume* (New York, 1950), pp. 149–78.

S. P. Brock, "The Phenomenon of the Septuagint," *Oudtestamentische Studiën* 17 (1972) 11–36.

P. de Lagarde, *Anmerkungen zur griechischen Übersetzung der Proverbien* (Leipzig, 1863).

———, *Mitteilungen* I (Göttingen, 1884) 22–26.

N. Fernandez Marcos, *Introducción a las vérsiones griegas de la Biblia* (Madrid, 1979).

D. W. Gooding, "Aristeas and Septuagint Origins," *Vetus Testamentum* 13 (1963) 357–79.

I. Hooykaas, *Iets over de grieksche vertaling van het Oude Testament* (Rotterdam, 1888).

S. Jellicoe, *The Septuagint and Modern Study* (Oxford, 1968).

P. Kahle, *The Cairo Geniza* (Oxford, 1959[2]).

———, "Untersuchungen zur Geschichte des Pentateuchtextes," *Theologische Studien und Kritiken* 38 (1915) 399–439.

H. B. Swete, *An Introduction to the Old Testament in Greek* (Cambridge, 1914²).

E. Tov, "Lucian and Proto-Lucian—Toward a New Solution to the Problem," *Revue biblique* 79 (1972) 101–13.

———, "The Septuagint," in *Compendia Rerum Iudaicarum ad Novum Testamentum*, III, section 3b (forthcoming).

———, *The Text-Critical Use of the Septuagint* (Jerusalem Biblical Studies 3; Jerusalem, 1981).

## (3) THE PESHITTA

### (a) BACKGROUND AND EDITIONS

Little is known of the origin of the Syriac translation, the Peshitta (literally, "the simple [translation]," in distinction from the artificial language and the complicated apparatus of the Syro-Hexapla; see p. 176). For summaries see Roberts, pp. 214–28; and Vööbus, "Syriac Versions" (see literature). Some scholars emphasize the Christian background of the Peshitta while others stress its Jewish background.

A reevaluation of this translation needs to pay special attention to the following aspects:

1. The relationship between the Peshitta and rabbinic exegesis (elaborately described by Maori).

2. The close connection between the Peshitta and the Palestinian targums (see section [4] below), already emphasized by Vööbus.

3. The possibility that the Syriac Bible may have gone through several stages of development—traces of an earlier form of the Syriac Bible, the so-called *Vetus Syra*, can be found in the biblical quotations that deviate from the Peshitta, and in the commentaries of early Syrian church fathers (see Vööbus, *Peschitta*; cf. literature).

4. A reevaluation of the relationship between the Peshitta and the Septuagint (which also involves the targums). Also, through the research of Delekat it has become clear that the Peshitta is not based on the Septuagint, as is often said, but that it reflects oral "targum traditions" that were first included in the Septuagint and later made part of the Peshitta and the targums.

A critical edition of the Peshitta is being prepared by the Peshitta Institute of the University of Leiden: *The Old Testament in Syriac according to the Peshitta Version*. This project offers a diplomatic edition of Codex Ambrosianus (6th–7th century) with a critical apparatus of variants.

Noncritical but complete editions of the Peshitta include the edition of S. Lee (1823) and the editions published in Urmia (1852) and Mossul (1886–91).

There is no concordance to the whole Peshitta, but such a work is in preparation in Göttingen, with the use of a computer. Two parts have so far appeared (Ecclesiastes, 1973; Psalms, 1976). For a modern translation, see G. M. Lamsa, *The Holy Bible from Ancient Eastern Manuscripts* (Nashville, 1933).

### (b) TEXT-CRITICAL VALUE

The quality of the Peshitta translation varies from book to book, ranging from fairly accurate to paraphrastic.

The Hebrew *Vorlage* of the Peshitta was more or less identical with the Massoretic text. The Peshitta offers fewer variants than the Septuagint, but more than the targums and the Vulgate. See ill. 56.

## LITERATURE

L. Delekat, "Ein Septuagintatargum," *Vetus Testamentum* 8 (1958) 225–52.

M. H. Goshen-Gottstein, "Prolegomena to a Critical Edition of the Peshitta," *Scripta Hierosolymitana* 8 (1960) 26–68.

I. Maori, "The Peshitta Version of the Pentateuch in Its Relation to the Sources of Jewish Exegesis" (Ph.D. diss., Hebrew University, Jerusalem, 1975) (Hebrew).

B. J. Roberts, *The Old Testament Text and Versions* (Cardiff, 1951), pp. 214–27.

A. Vööbus, *Peschitta und Targumim des Pentateuchs. Neues Licht zur Frage der Herkunft der Peschitta aus dem altpälastinischen Targum* (Stockholm, 1958).

———, "Syriac Versions," in *Interpreter's Dictionary of the Bible, Supplementary Volume* (Nashville, 1976), pp. 848–54.

## (4) THE TARGUMS

### (a) BACKGROUND AND EDITIONS

During the period of the Second Temple, Aramaic was the lingua franca. Therefore the Old Testament, especially the Pentateuch, was several times translated into this language, both in Palestine and in Babylonia. At first these translations were made orally by a *meturgeman* (from *targum*, literally, "translation"; plural *targumin*). Later these targums were written down.

The existence of targums can be traced back to an early period:

1. Two early targums have been found at Qumran, the Job targum from Cave 11 (11QtgJob, dating from the 1st century B.C.), and the Leviticus targum from Cave 4 (4QtgLev, dating from the 2nd century B.C.). The Job targum may have been the same as the one known at the time of Rabban Gamaliel I (A.D. 25–50; see Babylonian Talmud *Shabbath* 115a). The Job targum has been published by J. P. M. van der Ploeg and A. S. van der woude, *Le targum de Job de la grotte XI de Qumran* (Leiden, 1971), and also by M. Sokoloff, *The Targum to Job from Qumran Cave XI* (Ramat Gan, 1974). The Leviticus targum is published in *Discoveries in the Judaean Desert* VI, 86–89.

2. The New Testament knows various exegetical traditions which elsewhere are known only from one of the targums, in particular from Codex Neofiti (see below). For detailed analyses of such traditions in the New Testament, see McNamara, and le Déaut, *La nuit pascale* (see literature).

Palestinian targums are known from texts from the geniza (see Kahle) and through Codex Neofiti, rediscovered in 1956 in the Vatican Library by A. Díez Macho. The "traditional" (printed) Palestinian targums are Pseudo-Jonathan (Jerusalem I, erroneously called Jonathan because of the abbreviation J[erusalem]) and the Fragment Targums, so called because of their fragmentary nature (Jerusalem II and III).

Critical editions of Pseudo-Jonathan have been published by M. Ginsburger (Berlin, 1903) and by D. Rieder (Jerusalem, 1974); editions of the Fragment Targums were published by M. Ginsburger (Berlin, 1893; repr. Jerusalem, 1967) and

M. Klein (Rome, 1980). Codex Neofiti has been published, with translation and description, by A. Díez Macho, *Neophyti I* I–V (Madrid/Barcelona, 1968–77), while a photomechanical edition appeared in *The Palestinian Targum to the Pentateuch* (Jerusalem, 1970).

The Babylonian targums are probably based on Palestinian targum traditions. Both Targum Onkelos on the Pentateuch and Targum Jonathan on the Prophets have been published in a diplomatic edition (based primarily on manuscripts B.M. Or. 2363, 2210, 2211) by A. Sperber, *The Bible in Aramaic* I–III (Leiden, 1959–62). Part IV.A of Sperber's edition (1968) contains the targums of (some of) the Writings (based on B.M. 2375 among others).

Modern translations of the targums are found in J. W. Etheridge, *The Targums of Onkelos and Jonathan Ben Uzziel on the Pentateuch with the Fragments of the Jerusalem Targum* I–II (London, 1862–65; repr. New York, 1968); J. Bowker, *The Targums and Rabbinic Literature* (Cambridge, 1969); and M. J. Mulder (see literature).

The following concordances have appeared: E. Brederek, *Konkordanz zum Targum Onkelos* (Beiheft zur Zeitschrift für die alttestamentliche Wissenschaft 9; Giessen, 1906); C. J. Kasowski, *Qonqordansiya le-Targum Onqelos* (Jerusalem, 1933–40); J. B. van Zijl, *A Concordance to the Targum of Isaiah* (SBL Aramaic Studies 3; Missoula, Montana, 1979).

### (b) TEXT-CRITICAL VALUE

The quality of the translation of the targums varies from targum to targum and from book to book (see especially Komlosh, Jongeling, and Mulder). As a rule, the targums from Palestine are more paraphrastic in character than the Babylonian targums. The more literal translations of 11QtgJob and 4QtgLev, though found in Palestine, are an exception to this rule. The connections among the various targums as well as their origins are elaborately discussed in modern research (on the origin of the targums see especially Díez Macho, Kasher, and Shinan).

The targums usually reflect the Massoretic text; deviations from the Massoretic text are mainly based on exegetical traditions, not on deviating texts. An exception must be made for 11QtgJob, which contains interesting variants and which (probably) lacks some verses of the Massoretic text (42:12–17), a fact which is significant for the literary criticism of the book. It may perhaps be assumed that other targums in an earlier stage of their development also contained more variants than in their present form.

Targum Onkelos as a rule contains more variants than the Palestinian targums. For a discussion and reconstruction of these variants, see Sperber, IV.B.

## LITERATURE

B. Grossfeld, *A Bibliography of Targum Literature* (Cincinnati/New York, 1972).

_____, *A Bibliography of Targum Literature* II (Cincinnati/New York, 1977).

See further:

A. Díez Macho, *El targum, introducción a las traducciones aramaicas de la Biblia* (Barcelona, 1972).

B. Grossfeld, *A Critical Commentary on Targum Neofiti I to Genesis* (New York, 1978).

B. Jongeling, *Een aramees boek Job* (Amsterdam, 1974).

P. Kahle, *Masoreten des Westens* II (Stuttgart, 1930).

M. Kasher, *Aramaic Versions of the Bible* (Torah Shelemah 24; Jerusalem, 1974) (Hebrew).

Y. Komlosh, *The Bible in the Light of the Aramaic Translations* (Tel Aviv, 1973) (Hebrew).

R. le Déaut, *La nuit pascale* (Rome, 1963).

_____, *Introduction à la littérature targumique* (Rome, 1966).

M. McNamara, "Targums," *Interpreter's Dictionary of the Bible, Supplementary Volume* (Nashville, 1976), pp. 856–61.

_____, *The New Testament and the Palestinian Targum to the Pentateuch* (Analecta Biblica 27; Rome, 1966).

M. J. Mulder, *De targum op het Hooglied* (Amsterdam, 1975).

A. Shinan, "The Form and Content of the Aggadah in the 'Palestinian' Targumim on the Pentateuch and Its Place within Rabbinic Literature" (Ph.D. diss., Hebrew University, Jerusalem, 1977) (Hebrew).

L. Smolar, et al., *Studies in Targum Jonathan to the Prophets* (New York, 1978).

A. Sperber, *The Bible in Aramaic, IV.B: The Targum and the Hebrew Bible* (Leiden, 1973).

## (5) THE VULGATE

### (a) BACKGROUND AND EDITIONS

In most of the biblical books the Vulgate (*Vulgata,* "common") is a Latin translation of the Hebrew Old Testament prepared between A.D. 390 and 406 by Jerome. It should be noted that in the case of some of the apocryphal books the Vulgate contains the *Vetus Latina* (see p. 177).

Jerome's experiences in Rome and Palestine have been described by Stummer, Roberts (pp. 247–65), and Kedar-Kopfstein (see literature). At the request of Pope Damasus (366–385), Jerome began with the revision of the text of the Psalms in the *Vetus Latina,* later called *Psalterium Romanum.* The second stage of his work was the revision, in Latin, of the Septuagint column of the Hexapla (*Psalterium Gallicanum*). After some time he began to realize the importance of the *hebraica veritas,* and with the help of Jewish scholars he translated the Old Testament from Hebrew into Latin. For a comparison of the various translations of the Psalms, see Allgeier.

The textual history of the Vulgate in the Middle Ages has been complicated by the various revisions that have been made of this translation, even after the invention of the art of printing.

The Benedictines prepared a modern critical edition entitled *Biblica Sacra iuxta latinam Vulgatam versionem* (Rome, 1926). This edition contains a great many—mainly orthographic—variants. But the eclectic text does not always evidence the correct insight, often preferring readings on account of their similarity with the Massoretic text or Septuagint. Containing fewer data but showing a keener insight is the editio minor of R. Weber, *Biblia Sacra iuxta Vulgatam versionem* (Stuttgart, 1969). A machine-readable (computer) text of the Vulgate is now available.

### (b) TEXT-CRITICAL VALUE AND IMPORTANCE

Though occasionally reflecting variants (see Nowack, Marks, and Kedar-Kopfstein), this transla-

XX. Qumran caves 4 and 5, which contained more than 40,000 fragments of biblical, pseud-epigraphal, and sectarian documents. (W. S. LaSor)

XXI. Column 10 of the Habakkuk commentary from Qumran (1QpHab), which quotes and interprets Hab. 2:13–14. The archaic script in lines 7 and 14 distinguishes YHWH (Yahweh) as a sacred name. (J. C. Trever, copyright 1964)

XXII. The Kenyon Excavations at Canaanite Tell es-Sultan (which she identified with OT Jericho) down to the Neolithic level, looking west to the Mount of Temptation. (J. C. Trever)

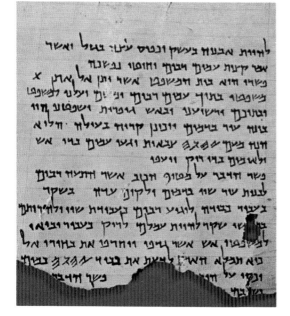

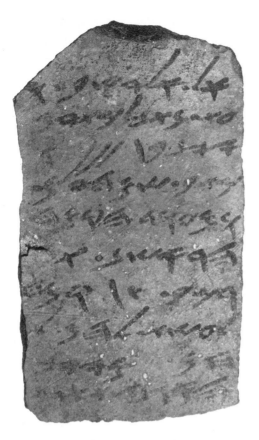

*52. The Greek inscription from the Jerusalem temple (ca. A.D. 30) forbidding Gentiles to enter the temple court. (Israel Department of Antiquities and Museums)*

*54. Chester Beatty papyrus P⁴⁶ (3rd century A.D.). showing the end of Rom. 16:23 and the beginning of Hebrews. Note the heading pros Hebraious, "to the Hebrews." (University of Michigan Library)*

*51. A Hebrew ostracon from Arad (ca. 600 B.C.) in which Eliashib (apparently the man in charge of supplies) is ordered to give wine and flour to the Kittim, who seem to have been mercenaries in the Judean army. (Israel Museum, Jerusalem)*

*53. The famous Theodotus inscription, which tells in Greek that he built a synagogue and a hostel for travelers. It is the oldest synagogue inscription found in Palestine, dating before A.D. 70. (Israel Department of Antiquities and Museums)*

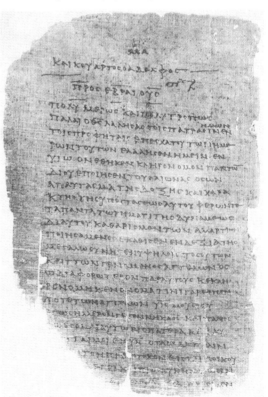

55. The Nash Papyrus, which contains the Decalogue and the Shema (Deut. 6:4). This is not a copy of the biblical text, however; it was perhaps a liturgical text. Until the discovery of the Dead Sea Scrolls, it was the oldest witness to the Hebrew text; it is dated variously between the 2nd century B.C. and the 2nd century A.D. (Biblical Archaeologist)

56. One of the oldest Peshitta (Syriac) manuscripts (A.D. 464), showing part of Exod. 13. The date is given in a colophon, a practice that Syriac scribes began. (British Library)

57. Part of the Samaritan Pentateuch of Deuteronomy (ca. 18th century A.D.). (Royal Ontario Museum, Toronto)

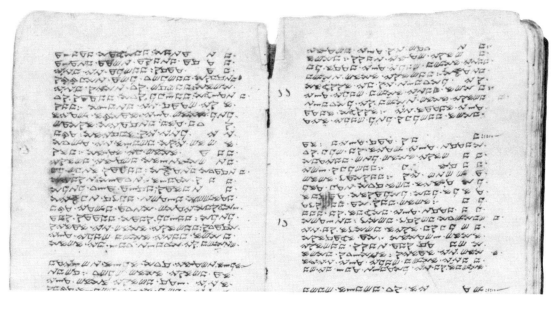

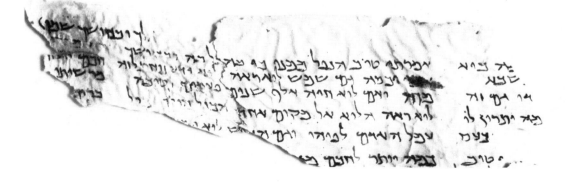

58. *A page from the renowned Aleppo Codex of the Hebrew Bible, ca.* A.D. *930. This manuscript was written by Shelomo ben Buya'a and provided with vowels by Aharon Ben Asher. The latter and his father Moshe Ben Asher did much for the fixation and spread of the Tiberian vocalized text of the Bible on which all modern editions of the Old Testament are based.*

59. *Part of a scroll of Ecclesiastes from Qumran, probably dating from the mid-second century* B.C. *(Israel Department of Antiquities and Museums)*

60. *A page from the Bodleian copy of the* Complutensian Polyglot *(the earliest known polyglot), here showing Gen. 21:28–22:3 in Septuagint (left, with interlinear Latin explanation), Vulgate (center), Hebrew (right), and Targum Onkelos (below left, with its Latin explanation, below right). Tyndale used this polyglot for his English translation of the Old Testament. (Bodleian Library, Oxford)*

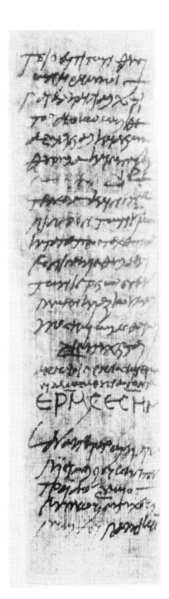

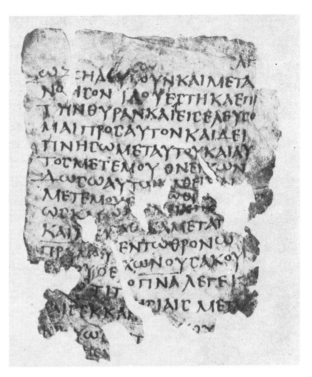

*62. Leaf from manuscript 0169 (4th century) with the text of Rev. 3:19–4:1. This is the only page surviving from what must have been one of the smallest vellum codices in antiquity: 9.5 by 7.3 cm. (3 ¾ by 2 ⅞ in.).*

*63. Assumed to be the oldest known papyrus of the New Testament, Papyrus Rylands Gr. 457, with the fragment of John 18:31–33 (recto), 37–38 (verso), now in the John Rylands Library in Manchester. See pp. 193ff.*

*61. A* libellus *from the time of the persecutions under Decius (A.D. 250) (Papyrus Hamb. 99).*

64. This Chester Beatty papyrus, P⁴⁶, is one of the earliest extant texts of Ephesians (ca. A.D. 200). Note that while the heading is pros Ephesious, "to the Ephesians," in v. 1 the en Epheso, "in Ephesus," of later manuscripts is missing. (University of Michigan Library)

65. A page from Codex Sinaiticus (4th century A.D.) showing part of John 21. (Trustees of the British Museum)

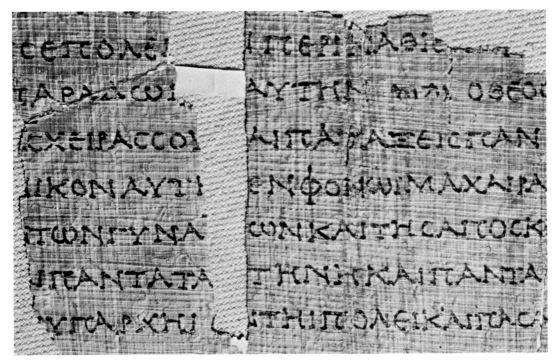

XXIII. A fragment of the Fouad papyrus, one of the oldest Greek texts of Deuteronomy (2nd-1st century B.C.). Note the use of Hebrew letters for the name Yahweh (upper right, line 2); this probably indicates that the scribe was Jewish. (Courtesy Société Egyptienne de Papyrologie. From The Interpreter's Bible, vol. 12; copyright 1957, Abingdon Press; used by permission)

XXIV. Core-formed glass vessels from the eastern Mediterranean area (5th-1st centuries B.C.). (Corning Museum of Glass)

tion almost always reproduces the Massoretic text.

The Vulgate is important for the history of the exegesis of the Old Testament, especially because the translation can be compared with Jerome's commentaries on the Minor Prophets, Isaiah, and Jeremiah, written between A.D. 406 and 420. These commentaries show (as the translation itself shows) that Jerome did not base himself exclusively on the Massoretic text but often was guided by the exegesis of the Septuagint, Symmachus, Aquila, and Theodotion (in this order).

---

### LITERATURE

A. Allgeier, *Die Psalmen der Vulgata* (Paderborn, 1940).

M. Johannessohn, "Hieronymus und die jüngeren griechischen Übersetzungen des Alten Testaments," *Theologische Literaturzeitung* 73 (1948) 148–52.

B. Kedar-Kopfstein, "The Vulgate as a Translation" (Ph.D. diss., Hebrew University, Jerusalem, 1968).

_____, "Textual Gleanings from the Vulgate to Jeremiah," *Textus* 7 (1969) 36–58.

J. H. Marks, *Der textkritische Wert des Psalterium Hieronymi juxta Hebraeos* (Winterthur, 1956).

W. Nowack, *Die Bedeutung des Hieronymus für die alttestamentliche Textkritik* (Göttingen, 1875).

B. J. Roberts, *The Old Testament Text and Versions* (Cardiff, 1951), pp. 247–65.

F. Stummer, *Einführung in die lateinische Bibel* (Paderborn, 1928).

---

### (6) THE ARABIC TRANSLATION OF SAADIA

The Arabic translation of Saadia (A.D. 882–942) is usually regarded as the last of the ancient translations. At the same time it is also the first medieval translation. It contains only some of the biblical books.

The older editions of this translation represent in one way or another the manuscript Arabe I of the Bibliothèque Nationale in Paris. Recent editions are also based on other manuscripts: P. de Lagarde (Leipzig, 1867; Göttingen, 1876), Derenbourg (Paris, 1893), P. Kahle (Leipzig, 1904).

The Hebrew parent text of the translation of Saadia is virtually identical with the Massoretic text.

## 3. TEXTUAL HISTORY

### a. Introduction

The history of the text from the second century A.D. is known in broad lines (see 2.a [1] above). But the history of the text before that time is in a sense prehistory about which we can only guess.

Theories about the history of the text were current already before the discovery of the Qumran scrolls, in other words, before one could have an idea of what ancient biblical scrolls looked like. In many respects these theories are now antiquated. Nevertheless, they are discussed here because of their influence on the development of the research and in particular on the terminology.

### b. The Relationship among the Textual Witnesses

The most important textual witnesses of the Old Testament are the Massoretic text, the Hebrew *Vorlage* of the Septuagint (in this chapter designated simply as Septuagint), several Qumran scrolls, and the Samaritan Pentateuch. All other sources (such as Peshitta, Vulgate, targums, and many Qumran scrolls) are less significant for the history of the Old Testament text because they are virtually identical with the Massoretic text.

During the last three centuries the idea has arisen that the Massoretic text, Samaritan Pentateuch, and Septuagint are the three main types of the text of the Pentateuch (the term comes from Kahle, "Untersuchungen" [see literature on p. 177], p. 436, who speaks of *"drei Haupttypen des Pentateuchtextes"*). This view has greatly benefited from the happenstance that the Massoretic text, Samaritan Pentateuch, and Septuagint have been preserved for posterity as the sacred writings of the Jewish, Samaritan, and Christian communities, respectively. Another influence was the analogy with the tripartite division of the manuscripts of the New Testament and of the Septuagint. This viewpoint developed gradually (before Kahle the term "recensions" was mainly used; after Kahle, "text-types") and the question was never really raised whether the three sources indeed represent different recensions or text-types, that is, texts that are *typologically* different. Only the recent research done in America has tried to ascertain the typological differences among these texts (see p. 183).

The problem with this approach has been expounded by Tov, "Nature" and "Modern Textual Outlook" (see literature). According to him, the Massoretic text, Samaritan Pentateuch, and Septuagint are to be regarded as three ancient *texts*, not as text-types. The complex of relationships among these texts is characteristic of the relationships among all early textual witnesses (see below, pp. 183–85). The relationship between the Septuagint and the Massoretic text is similar to that of any *early* source to another source (including recensional differences; see p. 177), but the relationship between the Massoretic text and the Samaritan Pentateuch is somewhat more complicated. The Samaritan Pentateuch reflects a number of typologically characteristic peculiarities, but it shares these with other sources (see p. 167), and therefore one cannot speak of a Samaritan text-type.

## c. The History of the Text in the Research before 1947

In 1915 Kahle gave the first fairly complete description of the textual history of the Hebrew Bible ("Untersuchungen"; see literature on p. 178). Prior to that there are only summary remarks and descriptions of the history of the text, of which the two most important are those of Rosenmüller and de Lagarde.

In 1797 Rosenmüller (see literature on p. 158) maintained that all the manuscripts of the Massoretic text belong to "one recension," which differs from the "recension" of the Septuagint (at that time the term "recension" was often used in the neutral meaning of "text"). Rosenmüller's remarks are an isolated opinion that, as far as we can tell, had no influence on the ideas of others.

By contrast, the brief theoretical remarks of de Lagarde (pp. 3–4; see literature on p. 177) in 1863 have until now been of great importance for the progress of the investigation. This scholar believed that all Massoretic manuscripts had certain characteristics in common (esp. the *puncta extraordinaria;* cf. p. 161) that are so specific that according to him all manuscripts would go back to "a single copy" (*ein einziges Exemplar*). This one copy he also regarded as "one recension" (the "Palestinian recension") that differed from the "Egyptian recension" (Septuagint), so that terminological confusion was unavoidable. According to de Lagarde, the text from which both recensions derive (the *Urtext*) can be reconstructed by way of an eclectic procedure (for de Lagarde's analogical theory on the reconstruction of the *Urtext* of the Septuagint, see p. 174). De Lagarde himself was not able to translate his theoretical arguments into practical applications, but subsequent generations have carried forward this line of argumentation in what became known as the *"Urtext* theory." It should not go unmentioned that in general more has been ascribed to de Lagarde than he himself had postulated. Another source of inaccuracy is the confusion in modern literature between the views of Rosenmüller and de Lagarde.

Kahle's views were especially influenced by the divergent text traditions that were known in his time: divergent biblical quotations in rabbinic literature (p. 159), the biblical fragments from the Cairo Geniza (p. 163), and the various Greek and Aramaic traditions (pp. 174, 179). Guided by these multiple text traditions Kahle sketched the history of the text as follows. Originally there was not one text of the Hebrew Bible, but a plurality of what Kahle called *Vulgärtexte* ("vulgar" texts). His model for this description was the development of the Aramaic targums, which, having come into existence as independent translations, were circulated in various forms. This multiplicity of text traditions disappeared during the first two centuries A.D., after the Massoretic text (ca. A.D. 100) had been "created" out of the recension of one of the *Vulgärtexte* into an accurate, official text which dislodged all other traditions. In this respect Kahle's description is directly opposed to that of de Lagarde: according to de Lagarde the history of the text began with one text which split into various texts, whereas for Kahle the history of the text began with a plurality of text-types out of which, later, one text emerged.

Kahle was correct in his assessment of some aspects of the textual history of the Hebrew Bible (for a discussion of Kahle's analogous idea on the development of the Septuagint, see pp. 174–75), but on several significant points his views need revision.

1. The textual variants on which Kahle's theories are based, like the variants in the rabbinic sources, are of much lesser significance than Kahle thought they were. Kahle was often impressed by lists of variants, whereas an accurate description of their nature should have led to other conclusions.

2. The Massoretic text was *not* created in the first or second century A.D., but it existed already before that time as one of many texts (see the Qumran scrolls).

3. Kahle's description of the contrast between *Vulgärtexte* and an official text is inaccurate and insufficiently elaborated.

4. For criticism of Kahle's description of the Massoretic text, the Septuagint, and the Samaritan Pentateuch as the three "main types" of the text of the Pentateuch, see p. 182.

Less well known than Kahle's theories are the following analyses, which develop further certain aspects of Kahle's insights.

A. Sperber further elaborated the difference between one official biblical text and many *Vulgärtexte*. He described especially the nature of these vulgar texts, in which group he also included the Samaritan Pentateuch and the Massoretic text of Chronicles.

On the analogy of the development of the Homeric writings, S. Lieberman introduced a qualitative difference between three kinds of manuscripts: *phaulotera,* "poor copies," in the possession of unschooled villagers; *koinotera,* or *vulgata,* the "generally accepted text," in the possession of city people, used especially for study purposes (e.g., in schools); and *ekribomena,* "accurate copies," in the possession of people connected with the temple.

Building on Lieberman, M. Greenberg suggested that at the time of the Hasmoneans two text-types were in circulation, the fuller, unofficial type (such as the Samaritan Pentateuch) and the shorter, official type (the Massoretic text).

Beginning with the 1950s, a new approach to the history of the text became current in American biblical scholarship. A theory of "local recensions/text-types/families" was set forth in broad lines by Albright and worked out by Cross. This theory reduces the multiplicity of textual witnesses to three text-types that were current in Palestine (inter alia, the Samaritan Pentateuch, the Massoretic text of Chronicles, several Qumran scrolls), in Babylonia (Massoretic text), and in Egypt (Septuagint). It is possible to give a general characterization of these text-types; for instance, "the Palestinian family is characterized by conflation, glosses, synoptic additions and other evidences of intense scribal activity, and can be defined as 'expansionistic'" (Cross, "Contribution," p. 86). The characteristics of the Babylonian and Egyptian text-types are described in the same way.

One of the great weaknesses of this theory is its lack of supportive material. Moreover, the terminology needs closer definition (see Gooding). The Qumran scrolls show that the boundaries between the three groups are not always clear. For instance, how must the relationship between 4QJer[b] (Palestine) and the *Vorlage* of the Septuagint (Egypt) be explained? How can it be determined that the Massoretic text is Babylonian and that the *Vorlage* of the Septuagint (thus not only the translation) is Egyptian? That scrolls of all three supposed text-types were found side by side at Qumran raises serious questions about the new theory.

Notwithstanding these objections, a central feature of the theory of local text traditions should be evaluated positively—there were undoubtedly geographical and social differences among the various text traditions. Only such an assumption can explain how altogether different forms of the text, in particular recensional differences (see p. 177), have been preserved, even after the Massoretic text had replaced the other text traditions.

## d. The History of the Text in Modern Research

The modern view of the history of the text is largely determined by the finds in the desert of Judea. It would be more accurate to say that the modern view *should* be determined by the new data, because all scholars have not yet realized how much the Qumran scrolls have done to alter the reconstruction of the history of the text. In this connection it should be said that the sectarian nature of the Qumran community in no way detracts from the great value of the Qumran scrolls for the description of the text's history, because the manuscripts of the Bible used by the Qumran community cannot be labeled sectarian. Undoubtedly many of these scrolls were "imports" at Qumran. Moreover, it can be stated that the various text forms found at Qumran (cf. pp. 167–68) provide a good reflection of the situation in the first two centuries B.C., even though the *proportion* in which certain text-forms occur at Qumran may differ from those outside this sectarian community.

In the analysis of the scrolls from the Judean desert, the following aspects should be noted:

1. The Qumran scrolls exhibit a multiplicity of texts that was characteristic of the last centuries B.C.

2. The scrolls from other places in the Judean desert (see p. 167) represent almost exclusively the Massoretic text. Because most of these scrolls are later than the Qumran writings (viz., A.D. 90–130), it is likely that already at that time the Massoretic text had replaced the other text traditions. According to another viewpoint, however, the nature of these scrolls depends on the kind of people that left them behind in the desert.

3. The Massoretic text was not created in the first two centuries A.D. (as postulated by Kahle; see p. 182), but this text existed already in the last two centuries B.C. This is demonstrated by the finding of so-called proto-Massoretic texts from that period.

Today it is not necessary to evaluate the correctness of the theories of de Largarde and Kahle because both theories were formulated before 1947 (Kahle's second edition of *Cairo Geniza* [1st ed. 1947] appeared in 1959, but the author had not essentially changed his earlier views). A modern description must start from the new data, not from old theories, even though elements of such theories may be incorporated in new descriptions. This is the methodology of the following attempt (cf. further Talmon, "Three Scrolls"; Greenberg; and Tov, "Nature").

As mentioned on p. 156, at the end of the period of literary growth there existed for each of the biblical books a finished literary form which constitutes the "original text" for the purpose of textual criticism. This original text cannot be reconstructed anymore in its entirety, but individual elements of the text are reconstructed.

The finished composition which was created after a period of literary growth also stood at the beginning of a new period, viz., that of the textual transmission. From now on the composition was copied in several copies and thus was transmitted from generation to generation. The situation was complicated in cases in which the textual transmission started—on a limited scale—at an earlier stage of the literary growth. In any event, also in such cases at one point a stage was reached when the literary process was completed. That point is the ultimate goal of textual criticism, but since this ideal cannot be reached, textual critics normally define their aims more modestly: the most textual critics can aim at is the text of the Old Testament current in a particular period (usually one thinks of the 4th or 3rd century B.C.). At that time the text of the different books had already developed in various directions, a great number of glosses and alterations had crept into the text, and the various texts had developed in different directions. Social and geographical factors (see p. 183) contributed to the long survival of earlier text forms.

In every period text forms were in circulation that differed qualitatively from each other (cf. the descriptions of Greenberg and Lieberman). The various kinds of Qumran scrolls (cf. p. 167) exhibit such a heterogeneity. There were less accurate biblical scrolls in which copyists introduced alterations without qualms, while the accurately transmitted temple scroll remained relatively free of such alterations. The existence of one or more temple scrolls is, to be sure, only an assumption, but it is supported by various references in rabbinic literature (see, e.g., the *sefer haazarah*, mentioned among others in the Palestinian Talmud *Taanit* 4:2, 68a; cf. Talmon, "Three Scrolls").

The carefully transmitted text of the temple scroll(s) is continued in the Massoretic text, which despite its corruptions (esp. in certain books, e.g., Samuel), is the best Hebrew representative of *one* of the texts that was current in the fourth–third century B.C. (Another representative of such a text is the Septuagint.) These texts can be considered "accurate" in the sense that after a certain point in time (4th–3rd century B.C.?) relatively few changes were introduced. By contrast, such changes were made in less accurately transmitted traditions that were open to changes, such as the Samaritan Pentateuch, several Qumran scrolls (e.g., 1QIsᵃ), and the Severus Scroll (see p. 159). The orthography of these texts is fuller than that of the Massoretic text to facilitate the reading by untrained people. For that same reason copyists of such texts were readily inclined to make minor grammatical and contextual alterations.

The above-mentioned distinction between the "conservative" traditions of the Massoretic text and the Septuagint on the one hand and the continually changing traditions on the other shows some similarity to the theories of Kahle. But Kahle should not be followed in all the details of his theory. The contrast in Kahle's description between the Massoretic text as the official biblical text and the so-called *Vulgärtexte* covers only part of the data. Moreover, typologically the Septuagint and several Qumran scrolls are closer to the Massoretic text than to the less accurate text traditions.

Influenced by the research of the last three centuries, scholars were readily inclined to reduce the multiplicity of texts at Qumran to three main types in the Pentateuch and to two or three in the other books. But as has already been pointed out, the Massoretic text, the Septuagint, and the Samaritan Pentateuch are not text-types but texts (see p. 182). Moreover, the description of the biblical text at Qumran should not start from conventional ideas that were formed before 1947; rather, the history of the text needs rewriting from the perspective of the situation as it existed at Qumran. This will quickly lead to a different picture. For instance, at Qumran a book such as Leviticus was not known in just three text forms (Massoretic text, Septuagint, Samaritan Pentateuch); one also finds there a fourth text (11QpaleoLev; see Tov, "Leviticus Scroll"), perhaps even a fifth and a sixth. The relationship among these four (five, six?) texts is characteristic of the relationship among all *early* textual witnesses. The relationship among all these textual witnesses is a complicated web of agreements, differences, and independent readings (e.g., 11Q = Massoretic text = Septuagint = Samaritan Pentateuch, etc.; cf. Tov, op. cit.) that cannot be reduced to a threefold relationship. The multiplicity of textual traditions at Qumran also elucidates the relationships between the texts that were known before 1947: the Massoretic text, Septuagint, and Samaritan Pentateuch do not represent the three main types of the Old Testament text but are three texts out of a larger number of texts (cf. Tov, "Modern Textual Outlook").

## LITERATURE

See Rosenmüller (p. 158), Aptowitzer (p. 165), de Lagarde (p. 177), Kahle (pp. 177–78), Lieberman (p. 166), and Gerleman (p. 172). See further:

W. F. Albright, "New Light on Early Recensions of the Hebrew Bible," *Bulletin of the American Schools of Oriental Research* 140 (1955) 27–33.

F. M. Cross, "The Contribution of the Qumran Discoveries to the Study of the Biblical Text," *Israel Exploration Journal* 16 (1966) 81–95 (repr. in Cross and Talmon, eds., *Qumran and the History of the Biblical Text*, pp. 278–92).

———, "The Evolution of a Theory of Local Texts," in Cross and Talmon, eds., *Qumran and the History of the Biblical Text*, pp. 306–20.

D. W. Gooding, "An Appeal for a Stricter Terminology in the Textual Criticism of the Old Testament," *Journal of Semitic Studies* 21 (1976) 15–25.

M. Greenberg, "The Stabilization of the Text of the Hebrew Bible in the Light of the Biblical Materials from Qumran," *Journal of the American Oriental Society* 76 (1956) 157–67.

A. Sperber, "New Testament and Septuagint," *Journal of Biblical Literature* 59 (1940) 193–293.

S. Talmon, "The Old Testament Text," in P. R. Ackroyd and C. F. Evans, eds., *The Cambridge History of the Bible, I: From the Beginnings to Jerome* (Cambridge, 1970), pp. 159–99.

———, "The Three Scrolls of the Law that Were Found in the Temple Court," *Textus* 4 (1962) 14–27.

E. Tov, "The Nature of the Hebrew Text Underlying the LXX," *Journal for the Study of the Old Testament* 7 (1978) 53–68.

_____, "The Textual Character of the Leviticus Scroll from Qumran Cave 11," *Shnaton* 3 (1979) 238–44 (Hebrew).

_____, "A Modern Textual Outlook Based on the Qumran Scrolls," *Hebrew Union College Annual* 53 (1982) 11–27.

## 4. TRANSMISSION OF THE TEXT

### a. Sources

The oldest biblical manuscripts from Qumran date from the end of the third century B.C. Together with the other biblical documents from the Judean desert these scrolls provide an idea of the transmission of the text in the period between the third century B.C. and the second century A.D. In accordance with what was said above (p. 184), the copying habits evident in the Qumran scrolls are generally accepted as representative for what was customary at that time.

The posttalmudic tractate *Soferim* (9th century) gives detailed instructions for writing biblical scrolls according to the tradition of the Masoretes. Many of the *halakhot* of this tractate represent old traditions. See the edition of M. Higger (New York, 1937; repr. Jerusalem, 1970).

### b. Outward Form

For many centuries the biblical books were written on scrolls (Hebrew *megillah*, plural *megillot*); only in the posttalmudic period did the codex also come to be used for the biblical texts. Still today scrolls are used in the synagogue for the reading of the Bible.

The text in the scrolls is written in columns. These columns are usually lined and the letters are written under the lines.

The script in which the Bible was originally written (the Old Hebrew script) was developed from the Canaanite script. Even when this script was no longer used, the Pentateuchal scrolls were often still written in the old script. This is also the case with one Qumran scroll of Job.

The transition from the Old Hebrew script to the so-called Aramaic or square script took place in the fifth century B.C. (tradition ascribed this change to Ezra).

The following elements that are often found in the printed text were not part of the old texts of the Bible:

1. In the old texts of the Bible the words were not separated by spaces—they were written in the so-called *scriptio continua*, as can still be seen in the *tefillin* and *mezuzzot* from Qumran and Masada. However, the biblical texts found in the desert of Judea do have spaces or marks between the words.

2. The scrolls from the desert of Judea contain neither vocalization nor accents (cf. p. 163).

3. The division into verses and chapters in the Hebrew manuscripts was not made until the Middle Ages. The old scrolls only had divisions into paragraphs, which were later carried over in the Massoretic manuscripts (cf. p. 160).

4. The letters *m, n, ṣ, p,* and *k* have two forms in the Aramaic script, one of which is used at the end of a word. The Qumran scrolls represent a transitional stage in which both forms of the letter are often used interchangeably.

The Qumran scrolls clarify various aspects of the procedure of *copying* (see especially Martin):

1. The similarity between various letters (cf. p. 187) explains interchanges of consonants as known from all the sources of the biblical text, including the Massoretic text.

2. The correction habits (crossing out, erasing, placing dots above or under the letters) are also known from contemporaneous Hellenistic sources and later Massoretic manuscripts (cf. pp. 160–61).

3. The addition of words in the margins or between the lines often created confusion for subsequent generations of copyists.

4. Some scrolls are systematically corrected according to other scrolls (sometimes following a text that is closely related to the Massoretic text).

5. The text and margins of the scrolls contain various diacritical signs. Some signs resemble the Alexandrian *antisigma* (cf. p. 161) and *korōnis* in form and function.

### c. Matres Lectionis

*Matres lectionis* (literally, "mothers of reading") are the letters *aleph, he, waw,* and *yod,* which are added to the basic form of Hebrew words to facilitate their reading. In principle the *matres lectionis* thus serve a function that was later taken over by the vocalization.

The textual witnesses differ considerably in their use of *matres lectionis*. This situation is the result of the development of Hebrew orthography. At first Hebrew did not use *matres lectionis*, but later they were added in several places to the basic form of the words: *yod* for *i* and *e*, *waw* for *u* and *o*, and *aleph* for *a, i, e*, and *o* (see Cross and Freedman). The increasing use of *matres lectionis* is reflected in the various kinds of biblical scrolls; older scrolls make less use of them than more recent ones. A spelling without a *mater lectionis* is called "defective"; those with a *mater* are called "full" (*plene*).

The orthography of the Massoretic text exhibits defective spelling to a certain degree. Therefore the Massoretic text represents a relatively early stage of the evolution of the biblical text (between the 4th and 2nd centuries B.C. according to Freedman). However, it is wrong to generalize about the books of the Massoretic text, for every book is different. The later biblical books (Daniel, Ezra, Nehemiah, Chronicles) reflect a fuller orthography than the earlier ones (cf., e.g., the spelling of the name David as *dwd* in Samuel and Kings with the preferred spelling *dwyd* in Chronicles). Also, within individual books different spellings are found side by side (e.g., Ezek. 32:23 *kbrtyh*, v. 25 *kbrth*, v. 26 *kbrwtyh*). For examples of the inconsistencies in the Massoretic spelling see especially Sperber, pp. 556–74.

Several Qumran scrolls contain a very full orthography, much fuller than the late books in the Massoretic text. Compare, for example, the spellings *ky'* and *r'ws* (also *rw's*) in 1QIs[a] (see the description of Kutscher). The background of these spellings is to be sought in the use of the scrolls by untrained readers.

## d. The Background of Textual Variations

The early biblical scrolls and the later manuscripts of the Massoretic text differ from each other in thousands of details regarding consonants, vocalization, verse division, etc. All these differences have arisen in the transmission of the text. A distinction is made between readings (variants) that were made in copying (i.e., unintentional variants) and those which reflect intentional alterations.

### (1) UNINTENTIONAL VARIANTS

Unintentional variants (for the most part mistakes) crept into the text for various reasons: the transition from the Old Hebrew script to the Aramaic script, the interpretation of the *scriptio continua* when the words were finally separated, and the misunderstanding and interchange of letters and words by the copyists.

The most common mistake is the confusion of consonants that look alike in the Old Hebrew and Aramaic scripts, especially *d/r*, *y/w*, *b/m/k*. This confusion is recognizable especially in the lists of names in parallel verses in the Massoretic text (e.g., Gen. 10:4 *Dodanim* // 1 Chron. 1:7 *Rodanim*; Gen. 10:3 *Riphat* // 1 Chron. 1:3 *Diphat*).

Other phenomena are:

*Dittography*, the repetition of letters or words (e.g., Jer. 51:3 *ydrk ydrk*; cf. the *Qere, ydrk*).

*Haplography*, the skipping of one or two (almost) identical letters or words (e.g., the erroneous omission of *whyh* in 2 Sam. 17:12 after *yhwh* in v. 11; the correct reading is found in the parallel text in 1 Chron. 17:10–11).

*Homoioteleuton*, the erroneous omission of a sequence of words caused by the fact that the eye of the copyist jumped directly from one word (or group of words) to another, identical word (or group of words) later in the sentence (e.g., the omission of Isa. 40:7b–8a in 1QIs[a]; in this case the omitted verses were subsequently inserted in the text and in the margin).

*Metathesis*, transposition of letters (e.g., 2 Sam. 23:31 *hbrhmy*, the Barhumite // 1 Chron. 11:33 *hbhrwmy*, the Baharumite).

Many examples of these phenomena have been collected by Sperber, pp. 476–90 (from parallel verses) and by Delitzsch.

### (2) INTENTIONAL ALTERATIONS

Copyists have made changes in and added glosses to all the textual witnesses, including the Massoretic text. A good example of this phenomenon is the tendency in the Massoretic text of Samuel to alter the component *Baal* in names.

Thus Gideon's second name *Jerubbaal* occurs thirteen times in Judges and in 1 Samuel 12:11, but was changed to *Jerubbosheth* in the Massoretic text of 2 Samuel 11:21, where the Septuagint still has the old name *Jerubbaal*. The name of Saul's fourth son was twice written *Eshbaal* in 1 Chronicles, but in 2 Samuel it was changed twelve times to *Ishbosheth* (see Ginsburg, pp. 399–404).

## LITERATURE

See Ginsburg (p. 165), Kutscher (p. 168).
See further:

F. M. Cross and D. N. Freedman, *Early Hebrew Orthography* (New Haven, 1952).

F. Delitzsch, *Die Lese- und Schreibfehler im Alten Testament* (Berlin/Leipzig, 1920).

D. N. Freedman, "The Massoretic Text and the Qumran Scrolls: A Study in Orthography," *Textus* 2 (1962) 87–102.

M. Martin, *The Scribal Character of the Dead Sea Scrolls* I–II (Louvain, 1958).

A. Sperber, *A Historical Grammar of Biblical Hebrew* (Leiden, 1966).

S. Talmon, "Aspects of the Textual Transmission of the Bible in the Light of Qumran Manuscripts," *Textus* 4 (1964) 95–132 (repr. in Cross and Talmon, eds., *Qumran and the History of the Biblical Text*, pp. 226–63).

## 5. THE PROCEDURE OF TEXTUAL CRITICISM

### a. Introduction

Old Testament textual criticism covers two areas. The first, the analysis of the biblical text as found in the Hebrew manuscripts and as reflected in the ancient versions, may be called textual criticism proper, while the second area, conjectural criticism, may be regarded as an appendix to textual criticism (see section d below). The task of textual criticism proper is further subdivided into two stages. The first stage is that of the collation (collection) and reconstruction of Hebrew variants (see section b below). The second stage deals with their evaluation (see section c below).

## b. The Collation and Reconstruction of Hebrew Variants

The evaluation of the textual witnesses can begin only after all the relevant data have been collected. For this purpose, variants have been collected and described in various kinds of monographs. Most of the information on variants is found in monographs which are devoted only to this issue, but much information can also be found in the scholarly commentaries on the Hebrew text, especially in the *International Critical Commentary* and in the *Biblischer Kommentar*. The usual course, however, is to turn to a modern critical edition of the Hebrew Bible that contains a selection of these variants. The modern editions are: R. Kittel and P. Kahle, eds., *Biblia Hebraica* (Stuttgart, 1927–37[3]; 1954[4]); K. Elliger and W. Rudolph, eds., *Biblia Hebraica Stuttgartensia* (Stuttgart, 1976–77); M. H. Goshen-Gottstein, *The Hebrew University Bible: The Book of Isaiah* I–II (Jerusalem, 1975–81).

These editions are necessarily subjective in character. Even if the subjective nature of such editions is fully recognized, it should not be overlooked that both *Biblia Hebraica* and *Biblia Hebraica Stuttgartensia* are incomplete and often inaccurate. Many important data have been omitted and much that is insignificant has been included; especially the work done with the versions leaves much to be desired (the latter edition is often more careful in its judgments than the former, but on the other hand the selection of the former often provides a better basis for further study than that of the latter). For a critical evaluation of *Biblia Hebraica* see especially Orlinsky. For the conjectures in these editions, see section d below. *The Hebrew University Bible* contains no conjectures and the selection of the data is much more complete than either edition of *Biblia Hebraica*. In four different apparatuses this edition includes variants from the versions (I), from the rabbinic sources and scrolls from the Judean desert (II), from medieval manuscripts: differences in consonants (III), and in vocalization and accents (IV).

## c. The Evaluation of Variants

After all the variants are collected from the Hebrew sources and reconstructed from the versions, they are compared with the parallel details in the *textus receptus* (the Massoretic text). For this purpose the Massoretic text is regarded as only one of the many textual witnesses of the Old Testament, *not* as the leading or best text. All the variants are indeed compared with the Massoretic text, but this is only a conventional procedure because the Massoretic text is the most complete and most accessible textual witness. In analyzing the readings, one should realize that all readings are in principle of equal value. Reconstructed variants are of just as much value as the Hebrew variants. The reconstruction itself may be subjective, but if it is faithfully done the reconstructed variants are equal in value for the analysis of the text to the readings that have been transmitted in Hebrew.

The goal of the comparison of Hebrew readings is to determine whether one of the transmitted readings is more "original" than the other, that is, whether this reading was a part of the "original" text of the Old Testament (as defined on p. 156). Often a decision is impossible. In some cases two variant readings are regarded as "synonymous" (see Talmon).

The readings are compared on the basis of their intrinsic value. This analysis is based on subjective considerations that are used as a guide to evaluate the reading in its context (for this purpose context is defined comprehensively, i.e., use is made of exegesis, language, literary criticism, and even of such disciplines as history and geography).

In view of the subjectivity of the evaluation of the readings, some have tried to draw up rules that would seemingly make this evaluation more objective (see, e.g., Klein, Thompson, Barthélemy, Payne, Tov [p. 178]). These rules, for example, pertain to such items as preferring shorter readings to longer ones, and "more difficult" readings to "easier" ones (*lectio difficilior*

*praevalet*). But these rules are so abstractly formulated and their use is so subjectively determined that the evaluation remains a subjective procedure. Common sense remains our main guide (see Tov).

## d. Conjectures

Conjectural criticism concerns itself with the correction of the biblical text. It is called in when neither Hebrew manuscripts nor ancient translations offer "satisfactory" readings that give the "original" text of the Bible. Conjectural criticism is one of the most subjective parts of biblical study because there are no objective criteria for determining the correctness of the transmitted readings. Conjectural criticism stems from exegesis and is only secondarily linked to text-critical criteria, for if a conjecture is proposed it must be acceptable text-critically. A conjecture must therefore be based on a kind of textual variation that is a frequent occurrence in the textual witnesses of the Old Testament, such as the interchange of the almost identically written consonants *d/r*, *y/w*.

The handbooks mentioned on p. 188 also list conjectures, especially those of *Biblia Hebraica* and *Biblia Hebraica Stuttgartensia*. There has been much criticism of the conjectures included in these editions (see Sperber, pp. 49–104 [p. 166], for criticisms of grammatical conjectures).

---

### LITERATURE

See Klein (p. 157), Margolis (p. 158), Sperber (p. 166), Tov, *Text-critical Use* (p. 178).

See further:

D. Barthélemy, et al., *Preliminary and Interim Report on the Hebrew Old Testament Text Project 1–4* (New York, 1979[2]).

———, *Critique textuelle de l'Ancien Testament* (Orbis biblicus et orientalis 50; Freiburg/Göttingen, 1982).

M. H. Goshen-Gottstein, "The Textual Criticism of the Old Testament: Rise, Decline, Rebirth," *Journal of Biblical Literature* 102 (1983) 365–99.

R. Kittel, *Über die Notwendigkeit und Möglich-*

*keit einer neuen Ausgabe der hebräischen Bibel* (Leipzig, 1901).

H. M. Orlinsky, "The Textual Criticism of the Old Testament," in G. E. Wright, ed., *The Bible and the Ancient Near East* (Festschrift W. F. Albright; New York, 1961), pp. 113–32.

D. F. Payne, "Old Testament Textual Criticism: Its Principles and Practice," *Tyndale Bulletin* 25 (1974) 99–112.

S. Talmon, "Synonymous Readings in the Textual Traditions of the Old Testament," *Scripta Hierosolymitana* 8 (1961) 335–83.

J. A. Thompson, "Textual Criticism, OT," *Interpreter's Dictionary of the Bible, Supplementary Volume* (Nashville, 1976), pp. 886–91.

E. Tov, "Criteria for Evaluating Textual Readings—The Limitations of Textual Rules," *Harvard Theological Review* 75 (1982) 429–48.

# B. Textual Witnesses and Textual History of the New Testament

*by J. Smit Sibinga*

Every written text that is being used by many readers requires reproduction, either by hand or by printing. Eventually the copies, whether handwritten or printed, will contain larger or smaller variations. This raises a question which, depending on the nature and use of the text, is variously formulated. Whatever the formulation, it always concerns the appraisal of the variants (i.e., of the differences among copies of the same text). Which of these variants is the correct and valid text and expresses the real intention of the author? Which variant is original and which from a later date? Is the later reading better or is it less correct? All such questions are closely connected to the meaning or to a particular aspect of the variants, and it is by no means always possible to answer definitely these questions.

Thus the existence of variants presents a problem to the reader. The investigation of that problem may focus on determining the correct text. Textual criticism is the science, one might also say the art, of choosing the one correct and original text out of the many variants. The investigation can also aim at obtaining insight into the origin and development of the various forms of a text. The purpose of textual history is, in principle, to study all the available variants and especially, though not exclusively, to try to recover the oldest text, which in many (perhaps most) cases is at the same time the original and correct text. It is obvious, however, that this last qualification— the correct text—is a value judgment whereas the first is only a (relative) dating. Critically appraised, the oldest ascertainable text may also be dubious or wrong. Therefore, from the point of view of method it is important to distinguish between textual criticism and textual history.

The study of the text as currently pursued is a relatively recent scholarly discipline, which in the course of the nineteenth and twentieth centuries has regularly resulted in new editions of the New Testament text.

## 1. EDITIONS OF THE GREEK NEW TESTAMENT

The first printed edition of the Greek New Testament to be generally circulated was the hastily prepared edition of Erasmus (1516). Since then numerous others have appeared, of which some must be mentioned.

The term *textus receptus* (the generally accepted text) serves as a global designation for the majority of printed editions from the sixteenth to the nineteenth century. The term is derived from the second edition of the Greek New Testament of the Elzeviers, published in Leiden in 1633. The author, Daniel Heinsius, calls the text of this edition, which had been prepared by Leiden professor Jeremias Hoelzlin (1583–1641), *nunc ab omnibus receptum* (the now by all accepted [text]). That designation, a suggestive hallmark of an undeserved monopoly, was to remain in vogue for a long time, too long in fact. Only in the twentieth century is there again a new, generally used, standard text in the editions of Eberhard and Erwin Nestle and Nestle-Aland. In contrast to the *textus receptus*, this text may with some justification be called a critical edition of the text. Nevertheless, nineteenth-century scholars such as Lachmann, Tischendorf, Tregelles, and Hort long before had laid the foundation for the setting aside of the traditional Greek New Testament text, and before that eighteenth-century experts such as Wetstein and Bengel clearly saw its untenability.

The printings of the *textus receptus* rely mainly on earlier printed editions, and ultimately on Erasmus. His selection of manuscripts happened to be arbitrary. Contrary to what he contended, they were fairly recent. In some other respects he was also not very fortunate. The one manuscript of the book of Revelation that was available to him was incomplete, making it necessary for him to complete the text by translating the missing passages back into Greek from the Latin Vulgate. Therefore the origin of the *textus receptus* offers no reason to suppose that it should be the careful reproduction of a reliable, old tradition, even though in principle the possibility is not excluded that an occasional reading of the *textus receptus* may be preferable to other readings.

As the starting point for the collection of manuscripts, that is, the determination and notation of divergent readings, the *textus receptus* is indispensable for many scholars. The Oxford 1873 edition is the accepted standard edition.

The just-mentioned Nestle edition, going back to Eberhard Nestle (1851–1913) and first published in 1898, is also based on printed editions of the Greek New Testament. But in this case the editions were the best critical editions that were available, while these in turn were based on direct and independent study of the oldest among the then known manuscripts. Eberhard Nestle's aim was to show both the similarities and the differences among the editions of Tischendorf (namely, his eighth, 1869–72), Westcott and Hort (1881), and Bernhard Weiss (1894, 1896, 1900). The edition of R. F. Weymouth (1886), which served as long as the one of B. Weiss remained incomplete, is of a different nature and offered already, like Nestle's, a "resultant text." In instances where the three first-mentioned editions, or any two of them, agree, their text is the one in Nestle; in the second case the deviant reading, in other words the reading of the minority, is separately mentioned in the critical apparatus at the bottom of the page with a reference to the edition that gives preference to this variant. In cases where Westcott and Hort indicate that they are in doubt about the correct reading by putting the

word(s) between square brackets, and if the other two editions disagree, the Nestle text has the same square brackets. This procedure demonstrated that one cannot, on the principle that is followed, reach a decision in such instances. Yet, the three basic texts are so much alike that generally the procedure is able to lead to the desired result, a critical text. Beginning with the seventeenth edition of Nestle (1941), in a very small number of passages (e.g., Rom. 5:1; 1 Cor. 15:49; Gal. 6:10) a "minority reading," that is, a reading supported by only one over against two editions, has been accepted into the text. Mainly, however, the text of this edition, even after 1941, represents the result of work done in the nineteenth century. It carries no other pretensions. By contrast, the critical apparatus—a marvel of conciseness—has regularly been brought up-to-date where newer findings made this possible and necessary.

Of even greater importance is that since the thirteenth edition (1927), edited by Erwin Nestle, the critical apparatus also indicates the basis of the printed text in some of the most significant manuscripts (e.g., in the Gospels, B, ℵ, C, D, θ). Wherever there are variants and the apparatus does not mention these manuscripts, they agree with the text. So unless the contrary is indicated, the text is based not only on the consensus of some prominent text critics from the previous century, but also on evidence from antiquity: the agreement between the old Egyptian text (e.g., in B) on the one hand, and on the other hand two prominent, so-called Western witnesses of altogether different origin, which in general are conspicuous because they diverge rather drastically from the Egyptian text. In this way one may recover a text that must be considerably older, go farther back in history, than each of its separate witnesses. This is how an idea for determining the correct text, which since Lachmann (1793–1851) has had a great influence, has been applied in the design of the critical apparatus. This is done in a very simple and practical way which was apparently first proposed by Hans Lietzmann.

The ambitious and impressive edition of Hermann von Soden (1852–1914), *Die Schriften des Neuen Testaments in ihrer ältesten Textgestalt hergestellt auf Grund ihrer Textgeschichte* I–IV (1902–13), is based on a comparable rule. The title of the work is significant. Out of the mass of manuscripts and other data von Soden reconstructed three textual recensions from the third or fourth century, possibly going back to Hesychius of Alexandria (therefore *H*), Pamphilus of Caesarea in Palestine (*I* for Jerusalem), and the martyr Lucian of Antioch (*K* from Koine, i.e., the text generally used by Greek-speaking Christians). Comparison of these three recensions yields an *Urtext* according to the following main rule: if the wording of the three recensions is sure, the variant that is found in two of them is accepted as the text. In part rightly so, von Soden's work has met with a great deal of criticism. Methodologically, however, it has great merit and so far it is undeniably the biggest achievement of the twentieth century for the text of the New Testament. For that reason it is proper that von Soden's decisions with respect to the text are included in Nestle's apparatus.

Recently a new textual edition has been prepared by an international team of scholars and it has appeared in two editions (the texts are largely identical; the notes differ). After the twenty-fifth printing of Nestle (1963), as well as some earlier printings prepared in cooperation with K. Aland and his helpers from the Institut für neutestamentliche Textforschung in Münster (Westfalen), the twenty-sixth edition (1979) offers a new text that is no longer based on the three nineteenth-century editions. True to the Nestle tradition, this edition is intended for scholarly use, such as university teaching and research, and the design of the apparatus is appropriate to that intention. The same text also appeared in the third edition of the *Greek New Testament* issued under the auspices of the United Bible Societies (1966[1], 1968[2], 1975[3]). This edition is meant for the use of Bible translators, who supposedly for a small number of passages need to have all the variants with full documentation—a strange starting point, with the result that in general this edition is less useful for study and research. On behalf of the editors, B. M. Metzger in the accompanying *Textual Commentary* (1971) offered a clarification and justification of the chosen text, which in many respects is very instructive and in any case would deserve imitation.

## 2. MANUSCRIPTS AND OTHER DATA

The manuscripts in which the Greek text of the New Testament has been transmitted are divided into certain traditional categories on the basis of several characteristics. The current numbering of the manuscripts, which goes back to C. R. Gregory (1846–1917), is so designed that there is a separate list for each of these categories, recognizable by a certain peculiarity of the number. Besides P[66] there is also 066, 66, and *l*66, that is, besides the papyrus (hence P), a manuscript in early script, and a lectionary (hence *l*). Part of the manuscripts from one of these groups, namely, the so-called uncials, are usually designated by a (Latin or Greek) capital letter, and a single one as a rule with the Hebrew letter *aleph* (א), though these manuscripts as well as the others from the same category have also received a number.

The various lists continue to grow; even now the research for unknown New Testament manuscripts still yields results. Thus from 1923 to 1963 the list of papyri with New Testament text has increased from thirty-two to seventy-six entries, and from 1963 to 1972 to eighty-five entries. In 1923 the list of uncials included 170 entries, but in 1976 had passed 270. The number of registered minuscules is well above 2800 (about 1800 of these are available on microfilm in Münster), and that of the lectionaries over 2200.

Lacking a colophon or other specific indication of the time of origin, the manuscripts as a rule must be dated on the basis of the script. The discipline which devotes itself to the study of the script of old documents is called paleography. The paleographer starts with those manuscripts whose date for one reason or another is known. Sometimes he can observe similarities or certain developments in a script, and so he is able to determine, by way of comparison, the origin of undated manuscripts more or less accurately.

### a. Papyri

The oldest manuscripts of the New Testament belong to the category of the papyri, designated with a P before the number. The earliest witness is P[52], a fragment of about 9 by 6 centimeters (3.5 by 2.4 in.) with a few lines from John 18, published in 1935 by C. H. Roberts and dated by him to the first half of the second century. In more recent years some scholars have dated this fragment to "the beginning of the second century." With respect to this and other datings, which in this essay are taken over from the current handbooks, it should be noted that it is easy, but wrong, to overestimate the accuracy and the certainty of the dating of a literary brand of writing as found in biblical manuscripts. Moreover, an expert such as E. G. Turner warns in general terms against the tendency, which he has observed in the last forty years, to date Christian codices too early.

Among the papyri of the New Testament, the Chester Beatty papyri, indicated as P[45] (Gospels and Acts, from the 3rd century) and P[46] (letters of Paul, ca. 200), published from 1933 to 1936, are very important. To the oldest documents of early Christendom belong also several of the Bodmer papyri, including P[66] (large parts of the Gospel of John from ca. 200, first published in 1956) and P[75] (extensive sections of Luke and John from the early 3rd century; published in 1961). These papyri carry the name of their owners. They are significant for their well-preserved condition, extent, early date, and the nature of their text. As with several uncials (for instance א, A, B), these papyri have been fully published in facsimile editions. See ill. 63, 64.

## b. Uncials

The *uncials* or *majuscules* constitute a second group of manuscripts, separate from the papyri. They are called *majuscules* (from the Latin *majusculus*, "somewhat larger") in distinction from the later *minuscule* manuscripts (from the Latin *minusculus*, "rather small") that are written in small cursive writing. The majuscule or *uncial* (from the Latin *uncia*, "one-twelfth," i.e., an inch) is a type of script that was used for literary texts. The letters look like our capitals: they are large and rounded and separate from each other, and as a rule are written between two imaginary

horizontal lines. In the classical period of this script they are placed within an imaginary square of fixed size. The traditional (but not at all logical) distinction between papyri and uncials does not lie in the script but in the material that was used: parchment instead of papyrus.

Some of the uncials contain the whole Greek Bible, the Septuagint as well as the New Testament. In several respects the text of the Old and of the New Testament has gone through the same history in the Christian church.

The Codex Sinaiticus (א or 01) is now in the British Museum in London; earlier it was in Leningrad, but with parts still in the university library of Leipzig and in the monastery at Sinai. It was discovered in the middle of the nineteenth century by Tischendorf in the monastery of St. Catherine at the foot of Mount Sinai (hence the name). The history of the discovery and acquisition of the manuscript has been a famous story for a century already, first told by Tischendorf and later retold by many others. Since 1960 another side of the story has also become known. In the library of the monastery is a letter, dated September 1859, in which Tischendorf promises to return the codex after completing his study of it.

In May 1975, as part of a much larger find of manuscripts, another nine whole pages as well as a large number of fragments of the manuscript were discovered in the Sinai monastery; but these have not yet been published. Besides the Old Testament (most of it) and the entire New Testament, Codex Sinaiticus also contains the *Epistle of Barnabas* and part of the *Shepherd of Hermas*—a reminder of the time when the Apostolic Fathers had not yet been strictly excluded from the canon. The manuscript is dated to the second half of the fourth century. The text is closely akin to that of Codex Vaticanus. See ill. 65.

The Codex Alexandrinus (A or 02) is also kept in the British Museum in London; it too is named after an earlier home (Alexandria) and originally contained the entire Greek Bible. Of the New Testament the bulk of Matthew and some other passages are now missing. Like Codex Sinaiticus, Alexandrinus contains some of the Apostolic Fathers, namely, *1 and 2 Clement*. It is usually dated to the fifth century. The text of the Gospels in

Alexandrinus is of a quite different type than that of the rest of the New Testament, which indicates that different parts of the same codex do not necessarily have the same origin. The Septuagint text of Vaticanus in the book of Isaiah is an example of the same phenomenon.

For centuries Codex Vaticanus (B or 03) has been in the Vatican Library in Rome, but for a long time it could be consulted only sporadically. This manuscript also originally contained all of the Old and New Testaments. Missing from the New Testament are now the last chapters of the letter to the Hebrews (from 9:14 on), the Pastoral epistles, the letter to Philemon, and the book of Revelation. The date of the manuscript is about the middle of the fourth century.

Sinaiticus has four narrow columns to a page, Vaticanus three, whereas other codices have two or one. Thus the reader of these two manuscripts is faced with six or eight columns at the same time. In an earlier period, text copies on scrolls must have presented a similar picture.

The appraisal of the text of Vaticanus (and Sinaiticus) as an unedited text is one of the key presuppositions of the nineteenth-century editions on which Nestle is based; thus it is also the presupposition of the Nestle text itself.

The Codex Ephraemi rescriptus (C or 04) is a fifth-century manuscript of the Greek Bible, of which remnants can be found in the Bibliotheque Nationale in Paris. In the thirteenth century, after the biblical text had been erased, it was used to write something else on it (hence *rescriptus*). The new text was a Greek translation of treatises by the fourth-century Syrian author Ephraem. Such a manuscript is called a *palimpsest* (from Greek and Latin *palimpsestos,* "erased, scraped again"). To recover the original text technical aids are needed. In 1843 Tischendorf published an edition which, page by page, reconstructs as well as possible the available parts of the New Testament in print.

The siglum D designates in the Gospels and Acts the Codex Bezae Cantabrigiensis (05) and in the letters of Paul a Parisian codex (06) that also once belonged to Theodore de Beze (1519–1605). The latter is called Claromontanus, after its earlier location at Clermont north of Paris. Both manuscripts are in two languages—the Greek text on the left page and the Latin on the right.

In Codex Bezae the order of the Gospels is Matthew, John, Luke, Mark—the names of the two apostles first. Already in the Gospels the text of Bezae has its own character. This is even more the case in Acts. The Western text, of which Bezae is the most important though not the only Greek witness, is regarded as particularly significant because of its age. From similarities with early Latin and Syrian data, one concludes that for the most part it must date from the second century. The date of Codex Bezae itself is difficult to estimate. In his *Kurzgefasste Liste* Aland mentions the sixth century as the time of origin. Elsewhere a wider time span is given (fifth or sixth century); a dating in the fourth century is also defensible.

Also in Codex Washingtonianus (W or 032), now in Washington, D.C., the order of the Gospels—which is all the manuscript contains—is Matthew, John, Luke, Mark. This manuscript, which dates from the fourth or fifth century, became known only in this century. It was bought in Egypt in 1907 by the American Charles L. Freer, and a facsimile edition has been published by the University of Michigan. Apart from a few verses in chapter 11, the text of Matthew is of the Byzantine type, designated by von Soden as *K*. The text of the Gospel of John, which in part was written by a different hand from the rest of the manuscript, is quite similar to the Egyptian text (von Soden's *H*). Thus in John 5:2 the name of the pool is not Bethesda or Bethzatha but Bethsaida, as in Vaticanus. Like Vaticanus, the text of Washingtonianus does not mention in 5:4 "an angel who would come down into the water and stir the water. . . ." Washingtonianus does mention, however, that the sick "waited for the stirring of the water" (5:3), words that are not found in the Egyptian text (P[66], P[75], B, ℵ, etc.). Although up to Luke 8 a great similarity with that type of text is observable, from Luke 8:12 on the manuscript gives again a Koine text, as in Matthew. Thus it is likely that Codex Washingtonianus, or one of its predecessors, was copied from parts of manuscripts of quite different origin—something which in principle is always possible but which in this case stands out clearly. A remarkable variant is the following conversation between Jesus and the disciples, which in Washingtonianus is found after Mark 16:14:

> And they excused themselves, saying, This age of lawlessness and unbelief is under Satan, who by the unclean spirits does not allow the truth (and) power of God to be understood. Therefore, reveal your righteousness now. Thus they spoke to Christ. And Christ answered them, The end of the years of Satan's power has come, but other terrible things are at hand. Let them, for whose sins I was delivered unto death, convert themselves to the truth and sin no longer, in order that they may obtain a share in the spiritual and imperishable glory of righteousness which is in heaven. Go . . . .

This passage, whose translation has to remain somewhat uncertain, is known as the Freer logion.

The Codex Koridethi of the Gospels (or 038) is named after its place of discovery in the Caucasus and is presently kept in Tiflis. It is probably from the ninth century. As in Washingtonianus, in this manuscript the text of the Gospel of Mark differs from that of the other Gospels. The relationship with the Western text and with quotations in Origen and Eusebius has provoked considerable interest.

## c. Minuscules

Unlike the majuscule manuscripts, some of the cursive manuscripts, also called minuscules, are written on paper. This material came into use gradually since the thirteenth century, without displacing the traditional parchment altogether. Also, among the minuscules a complete New Testament, in one volume, is fairly rare. See ill. 62.

As a whole this group of textual witnesses is of more recent date than many of the uncials. Manuscripts such as 33, 461, 565, 892, 1295, 2142, and 2224, which are dated to the ninth century, are early minuscules, while the Codex Boreelianus (F, 09), kept in Utrecht, also from the ninth or perhaps tenth century, is a rather late uncial, as is, for example, manuscript S (028) of the Gospels, dated in the year 949. It would be a mistake, however, to think that in the evaluation of the text of a manuscript or of individual readings the age of a manuscript should be a decisive factor. Certainly, if the origin of a manuscript can be determined, this goes to show that a reading found in it was known and used in a particular place at a particular time. But we are not told how long that has been the case. Nor do we know that another variant was not current then and there. In principle every reading is older than the manuscript containing the reading, though how much older we do not know. Therefore, that a manuscript is relatively old says little about the time of origin of its readings, and it says nothing at all about their value in comparison to other readings. For instance, it would be a blunder to contend that the problem of the brief Western text in various places in the last chapters of Luke (see, e.g., Luke 24:12, 40, 51), regarded as the correct text by Westcott and Hort, was virtually decided by the discovery of P[75]. Certainly, P[75] contains the long text and is earlier than any of the other manuscripts at issue. But it is a historical accident that this Egyptian manuscript has become known to us. It does not follow—in fact, it is highly unlikely—that in the second or third century, in Egypt or elsewhere, there were no manuscripts with the shorter text. Thus in the evaluation of variants, the date of the manuscripts is not a decisive argument. Naturally one looks for the oldest texts first of all in the oldest manuscripts, but that should not entail the disqualification of the text in other manuscripts.

For these reasons it would be a mistake to ignore or neglect the minuscule manuscripts because they are not very old, as has happened in the past. Meanwhile, the amount of extant material is so impressive that an adequate study of it will, for a long time to come, remain in its beginning stages. Presently the number of minuscules and lectionaries is about 5000 manuscripts.

Von Soden and his helpers grouped a great number of the minuscules, together with some uncials, into "types." This grouping goes back in part to earlier researchers such as Ferrar, Lake, and others. Among the later ones, the work of the American Jacob Geerlings deserves mention. Family[13] is an example.

The Irish scholar W. H. Ferrar discovered the relationship between the Gospel manuscripts 13, 69, 124, and 346. Later the minuscules 1689, 983,

788, 174, 826, 543, 230, 828, and 1709 were added to this list. The group is named the Ferrar group, or fam.[13]; the symbol in Nestle is ϕ. These manuscripts were for the most part written in the eleventh and twelfth centuries; 13 is from the thirteenth century, 69 from the fifteenth.

Together these manuscripts make it possible to reconstruct the text of a common ancestor of older date, namely, a manuscript that was extant in southern Italy or Sicily at the time of their origin. That does not mean that this lost manuscript itself is also from there, for it may have moved around. A much-discussed peculiarity of this group of manuscripts is that (with the exception of 1689, 174, and 230) they do not have the "pericope of the woman caught in adultery" after John 7:53, but in Luke, after 21:38.

## d. Lectionaries

All the manuscripts so far discussed have a more or less continuous text of one or more parts or books of the New Testament. The lectionaries contain a selection of Scripture passages to be read on certain days of the ecclesiastical year. Exhibiting a rich diversity, they reflect numerous details from the history of the liturgy. This somewhat separate area also has no dearth of materials. Though relatively late, the study of this particular category of manuscripts has developed into a specialty.

## e. Quotations in Ecclesiastical Writers

Along with the Greek manuscripts of the New Testament, which, as we have seen, are of diverse origin and have their own characteristics, the New Testament quotations in Greek ecclesiastical writers are another source for the history of the text. One reason why these data are important is that in most cases it is possible to determine the place and time of an author. This provides a valuable point of contact for the determination of time and place of the variants found in his New Testament text. One difficulty with these sources of information is that the determination of the text of the work of ecclesiastical writers is beset with all sorts of problems. Sometimes the reconstruction of the text is difficult because of the sheer size

of the manuscript material. In other, sometimes very important cases, it is the lack of sufficient material that makes the determination of a reliable text nearly impossible. Of the writings which we have of Justin Martyr (d. ca. 165), for example, our knowledge is uncertain and fragmentary; this is often forgotten when he is being quoted. Another difficulty is that it is not always evident whether a quotation in its entirety agrees literally with a then current biblical text or whether it is perhaps a free translation, an allusion, or an indication for the reader who knew what the writer wanted to say. As a rule and in principle a quotation should, however, first of all be regarded as a literal reproduction of an existing text.

If one assumes too soon or incorrectly that a quotation is a "free quotation," one blocks the road toward data that may differ from what is already known and is thus contrary to the intention of scientific investigation. There is a third difficulty that is connected to the ones just mentioned: particularly the biblical quotations may have been corrected in the transmission of the work of a church father, for instance by adapting them to the text of the milieu of the copyist and the new user. All this implies that patristic quotations require careful collection and detailed appraisal before they can contribute insights into the history of the texts.

The collection and study of quotations in Greek is less advanced than of those in the Latin area. This brings us to the early versions.

## f. Early Versions

The data mentioned so far have at least one thing in common with each other and also with the original text of the New Testament—the language. Together they constitute the Greek transmission. For the sake of completeness one might still add amulets and ostraca (potsherds with writing) and inscriptions, all of which have sometimes been ignored.

The early versions do not provide direct but only indirect data for the history of the Greek text. One reason why they are important is that, certainly in part, they go back to an early period from which Greek manuscripts are rare. For example—speaking first about the Old Latin Bible translations—we know much of the biblical text of the North African church father Cyprian (d. 258), that is, the Latin translation used in Carthage in his time, from the vast writings of this author. The lack of biblical manuscripts from that region in the first half of the third century makes Cyprian's writings a valuable source of information. If the quotations from this or another church father agree with an Old Latin text in a manuscript, this gives us an indication as to the origin of that text; it also offers possibilities to obtain from both the manuscript and the quotations a much more complete picture of a biblical text whose place and time have been determined in this manner. Comparison with other similarly recovered or reconstructed text-types, as they are called, provides insight into the diversity of the Old Latin material and into the developments that took place. The volumes of the comprehensive *Vetus Latina, Die Reste der altlateinischen Bibel . . .*, from the Vetus Latina Institut in Beuron (West Germany), present the collected material in an impressive manner. On the basis of a passage in Augustine, a schematic distinction used to be made between an Afra and an Itala, that is, translations deriving respectively from North Africa and northern Italy. Now it is possible to detect earlier and later north African text-types next to various European types, located for instance in certain parts of Spain and Italy.

There are few indications that stylistic demands were put on the Latin prose, though there are some. A continual change can be observed in the vocabulary. Old renderings, typical for the earliest strata (i.e., the North African texts), were gradually replaced by various new terms.

High demands of accuracy were made for the translation of the wording of the Greek text. Correction of a translation on the basis of a Greek manuscript is one of the regular causes of alterations in the text; at least in many cases that seems to be a satisfactory explanation. Being able by this route to detect in a change a correction, and in the correction the peculiarities of a Greek text known to us, we may gain from the Latin texts a contribution to the knowledge of the history of the Greek text. The question as to which other Greek reading in an earlier phase lay behind the Latin translation that apparently needed correcting is as a rule much more difficult to answer. The desire to reproduce a Greek text as accurately as possible became increasingly the norm. Earlier phases are characterized by a somewhat greater freedom, which implies that the original text can be detected behind the early Latin texts less clearly. Particularly in the oldest phase of the Latin versions, identification of a Latin expression with a Greek variant is very uncertain. For that reason the Old Latin evidence, normally included in the critical apparatus of a modern edition of the Greek New Testament, should be used with caution, if not a healthy measure of skepticism.

The result of the most recent correction of an Old Latin text of the New Testament on the basis of Greek manuscripts is found in the *Vulgate*, the ecclesiastical, officially authorized text of the Bible that Pope Damasus commissioned Jerome (d. 419 or 420) to prepare. In distinction from this translation, the earlier translations are designated as *Vetus Latina* (namely, *versio*, i.e., the Old Latin translation). It should be noted that in regard to the New Testament, in contrast to most of the Old Testament, the Vulgate was not a new translation. The reviser (on cogent grounds it has been doubted for a long time that it was indeed Jerome) prepared a careful, generally conservative revision of an existing translation, and he used material of different provenance for the various Bible books. Apparently his method was not consistent throughout. At any rate, historically the Vulgate of the New Testament is itself part of the Vetus Latina, being its final stage. The confusing multiplicity of biblical texts, to which Pope Damasus wished to put an end, continued nevertheless for a long time. Wherever the Vulgate was read and copied, words and expressions from the old and familiar tradition made their way into the manuscripts, starting almost as soon as the Vulgate had been published. So in its textual history the Vulgate shows something of the conqueror who was conquered.

Research into the origin of the Vetus Latina has to deal, among other things, with the Bible quotations in the writings of Tertullian (ca. 160–220).

The first phases of the translations into Syriac and Coptic are also very early. The function of the chief Syriac translation, the Peshitta (i.e., the "simple" translation), is comparable to that of the Latin Vulgate. The Peshitta was also supposed to end the confusing situation of having many deviating versions side by side in circulation. The date of the Peshitta is the end of the fourth or the beginning of the fifth century.

From the period before that, an old Syriac translation of the four Gospels has survived, in two famous manuscripts, both to be dated to the fifth century. The one is named after the first publisher, W. Cureton, the other after the place where it was discovered in 1892, Mount Sinai, where Mrs. Agnes Smith Lewis discovered and photographed it. The translation, found in Syrus Sinaiticus and Syrus Curetonianus, was called "the gospel of the separate" (namely, four books) in contrast to the Diatessaron, the harmony of the Gospels composed from the four Gospels. This work, ascribed to Tatian, which must be from the second half of the second century, initially played a large role in the Syrian church, and also elsewhere must have had considerable influence. But the original text is completely or just about completely lost; it is debated whether the original language was Greek or Syriac.

From a much later time are two other Syriac translations: the Philoxenian (named after Philoxenus of Mabbug), from the beginning of the sixth century, and the Harclean (named after Thomas of Heraclea), from the beginning of the seventh century. Of the first apparently only parts have been preserved—unless the second in its entirety or in part would be a revision or reissue of the first. The Harclean has marginal notes that are of special importance for the textual history of the book of Acts, being a source of our knowledge of the Western text.

A few words should also be said about the Coptic translations. Coptic is the final stage of the Egyptian language as it was spoken by the earliest Christians in Egypt. The script is the Greek alphabet, augmented with seven letters derived from Demotic, the late Egyptian script. In this connection the most important dialects are Sahidic, the language of Upper Egypt, and Bohairic, that of the Nile delta. The manuscripts of the Coptic Bible are numerous but most are fragmentary. Some are as early as the fourth or fifth century. Fragments

have also been preserved of bilingual manuscripts, in Greek and in Coptic.

Other early translations worthy of mention are the Gothic of Ulfilas (mid-4th century), the Armenian, and the Georgian. Together with the other ancient versions they reflect the many aspects of the spread of Christendom and the origin and growth of the different churches with which the history of the biblical text is closely interwoven.

## 3. TEXTUAL CRITICISM

The material of textual criticism indicates that the variations in the text go back as far as our earliest manuscripts, that is, to the second century A.D.

The goal of textual criticism, the reconstruction of the correct text, might be attainable if with every variant the cause or occasion for a change were clear. But such is by no means always the case. No explanation being available, one sometimes speaks of "accidental" variants, suggesting that one variant reading has an equally good chance of being original as another. However, the assumption of an "accidental" omission or an "involuntary" addition is the surest way to lead research into an impasse and to open the way for an arbitrary decision; though less time-consuming, the results are not convincing.

To be sure, involuntary mistakes, due to inaccuracy or tiredness, do happen. The omission of a small word is one of the most frequent errors. Often this happens without an obvious reason, but, for instance, in the case of a small word such as a negative, with serious consequences for the meaning of the text. In the case of larger parts of a sentence the omission is sometimes caused by a misleading similarity of a number of letters or sounds in places of close proximity in the text. The technical terms for it are *homoeoteleuton* (the end shows the resemblance) and *homoeoarchon* (the resemblance is at the beginning of a word or part of a sentence). Here is an example. The beginning of John 14:14, 15 and the end of John 14:13, 14 are so similar that the eye of a copyist could easily wander from the first *oean* to the second, so that in writing he would skip ten words, the whole of verse 14.

Wherever part of the text is skipped, whether it be one letter, ten words, or a number of pages, it is the longer variant that has preserved the original text. Yet an old text-critical rule says that the shorter of two readings deserves preference. For besides the unintentional or conscious abbreviation of a text, there were of course also stylistic alterations, elucidations, clarifications, or corrections by means of additions. For example, *asyndeton,* the omission of the conjunctions that ordinarily join coordinate words or clauses, may have appeared disturbing or stylistically graceless and for that reason have been removed. That is, conjunctions were added to the original text. It will be clear that the question whether a brief conjunction should be regarded as original or as an addition cannot be solved by systematically preferring the shorter or the longer variant, or by always following one particular manuscript or a certain combination of witnesses. Only knowledge of the language and of the style and idiom of the author in question, and in particular his use of conjunctions, can help in finding a solution. In more complicated cases insight into the intent and context of the problem passage is needed, as well as comparison with related passages and the like. But even then it is true that knowledge of the style of an author makes it possible to evaluate the variants in his text and to pick the right one. "But the core of practically every problem in textual criticism is a problem of *style* . . .', as P. Maas, an unquestionable authority, formulated it (*Textual Criticism* [Oxford, 1958], pp. 40–41). Textual criticism is not the application of one method, and certainly not the application of a series of general rules in the proper order. "A textual critic engaged upon his business is not at all like Newton investigating the motions of a planet: he is much more like a dog hunting for fleas. . . ." (A. E. Housman, "The Application of Thought to Textual Criticism," in J. Carter, ed., *A. E. Housman, Selected Prose* [Cambridge, 1961], p. 132).

Examples of the method of textual criticism are outside the scope of this handbook and therefore must be omitted.

Besides a proposal as to what may have been the original text, the editions of the text sometimes indicate another important result of textual investigation. The measure of certainty or uncertainty that exists with respect to various parts of the text may vary not only from book to book but also from word to word. Lachmann's edition of the New Testament (1842–50) illustrates a gradation on a scale from 1 to 6. The *Greek New Testament* of the United Bible Societies uses a system in which the letters A to D, noted in the critical apparatus, indicate the degree of certainty or uncertainty for the variant that has been chosen as the text. This is a meaningful procedure, for also in this branch of science the boundary between knowledge and ignorance is constantly shifting.

---

## LITERATURE

K. Aland, *Kurzgefasste Liste der Griechischen Handschriften des Neuen Testaments, I: Gesamtübersicht* (Arbeiten zur neutestamentlichen Textforschung 1; Berlin, 1963).

A. Dain, *Les manuscrits* (Paris, 1964).

J. K. Elliott, ed., *Studies in New Testament Language and Text: Essays in Honour of G. D. Kilpatrick* (Supplements to Novum Testamentum 44; Leiden, 1976).

J. Finegan, *Encountering New Testament Manuscripts: A Working Introduction to Textual Criticism* (Grand Rapids, 1974).

H. J. de Jonge, *Daniel Heinsius and the Textus Receptus of the New Testament* (Leiden, 1971).

B. M. Metzger, *The Early Versions of the New Testament* (Oxford, 1977).

_____, *Manuscripts of the Greek Bible: An Introduction to Greek Paleography* (New York/Oxford, 1981).

_____, *The Text of the New Testament: Its Transmission, Corruption, and Restoration* (Oxford, 1968[2]).

_____, *A Textual Commentary on the Greek New Testament* (London/New York, 1971).

H. J. Vogels, *Codicum Novi Testamenti Specimina* (Bonn, 1929).

_____, *Handbuch der Textkritik des Neuen Testaments* (Bonn, 1955[2]).

# V

# History of the Ancient Near East

*by K. R. Veenhof and M. A. Beek*

# A. History of the Ancient Near East to the Time of Alexander the Great

*by K. R. Veenhof*

## 1. INTRODUCTION

### a. Delimitation and Documentation

The word "history" in the title of this chapter is in the singular. This means that what follows is an attempt to draw a more or less comprehensive picture of the historical developments of the ancient world that constituted the geographical, cultural, and political framework in which the history of Palestine and Israel is to be placed.

This history covers a huge area both geographically and chronologically and is characterized by a great diversity in geography and cultural development. In central regions such as Mesopotamia and Egypt the transition from prehistory to history happened as early as approximately 3000 B.C.; the first written sources were composed around then and later historical traditions reach back to that time. Moreover, the oldest phase of the history of the entire area cannot be considered in isolation from the data of prehistory. As a matter of fact, the data of archeology continue to have a role in the reconstruction of the historical reality pretty much through the whole period, though they are specially important for the older periods and for phases and regions where written sources are scarce.

The end of the ancient Near East as a historical period is normally made to coincide with the collapse of the Persian empire and the rising influence of the West, personified in Alexander the Great and taking shape in the growing impact of Hellenism. We go along with that assumption, though it is obvious that political and cultural developments cannot be confined to precise chronological boundaries. Certainly in such matters as religion, law, language, and script, the changes happen very gradually, over a period of centuries.

Traditionally the ancient Near East extends from Asia Minor in the north, by way of Iran in the east, and the Persian Gulf to Egypt in the south. The Mediterranean Sea is usually taken as the western boundary, beyond which the later "classical" world begins. It is, however, a boundary that is frequently crossed, sometimes on a large scale, as is evident particularly in the many and varied cultural relations with Cyprus. From early on there were contacts with Crete and the Aegean world, especially through the Phoenicians, whose commercial and colonial enterprises were very much focused on the west. The best example of this Phoenician expansion is the Punic civilization of Carthage.

The geography of this area is enormously varied. Most striking are the large valleys, dominated by such rivers as the Nile, Euphrates, and Tigris. These rivers created the ancient irrigation cultures of Mesopotamia and Egypt and offered possibilities for large empires. Other areas were predominantly mountainous and hilly, covered with vegetation, receiving plenty of precipitation for agriculture. These areas were easily politically fragmented, though such was not the rule, as is shown from the Hittite empire. There were also the coastal plains with their narrow climbing hinterland, such as along the Syro-Palestinian coast and in Cilicia, providing good possibilities for commerce and shipping, and thereby for international contacts. The Syrian-Arabian inland is dominated by desert and steppe areas, with an annual rainfall of 150 to 300 millimeters (6 to 12 in.). The population consisted of both pastoral nomads and sedentary people who were keepers of small livestock. This varied natural terrain must have had a great impact on the cultural and political constellation, and it also helps to explain the tremendous internal differences in the area as a whole.

Numerous tribes and people inhabited the area, which in its long history was the home of a variety of states and empires, from small city-states to mighty realms, from short-lived power blocs to dynastic realms lasting for centuries, from tribally organized powers to urban militias. There were tribes consisting of keepers of small livestock and farming communities in rural villages beside cities or metropolises, with palace and temple, as centers of political power and of the cult.

Within the ancient Near East there were a great variety of languages and scripts. In the oldest period Mesopotamian cuneiform and the Egyptian hieroglyphic script were dominant. Both exercised a significant influence on the cultural development and therefore also on the historical documentation. The ancient Near East gave us the alphabet, which had a great influence from the first millennium B.C., via the Phoenician script and the variants derived from it, especially via the cursive Aramaic script (used, e.g., in the Persian empire). The diversity in writing traditions is the reason why the historical documentation in the ancient Near East assumed such widely different forms and is so unevenly preserved, not so much owing to the differences in languages as to the differences in scribal conventions that were used and the types of texts. In Egypt most inscriptions were on the stone walls of temples and tombs as well as on numerous steles, and (provided they are preserved, e.g., in graves) there are also inscriptions on papyri and ostraca. Besides nonliterary ostraca and papyri, mainly historical and religious ceremonial and literary texts are found in abundance. Most of the papyri that were written for utilitarian purposes have perished. In Mesopotamia the bulk of the hundreds of thousands of less perishable clay tablets consists of administrative, economic, or juridical documents and of letters. The volume of historical texts, especially building and display inscriptions and texts from schools and libraries, is in comparison considerably smaller. This remarkable difference explains why certain historical and cultural phenomena are much better known to us from the Egyptian documents than from the Mesopotamian. The above-mentioned difference in scribal conventions had an impact elsewhere too.

Where Mesopotamian influence gained the upper hand (especially through the Babylonian schools abroad during the 2nd millennium B.C.), as in Elam, among the Hittites, in northern Syria and Palestine (in the so-called Amarna Age, ca. 1400 B.C.), archives and sometimes whole libraries of clay tablets are found. These are written in Babylonian, which at that time was the vehicle for international diplomacy, or in the vernacular with the use of Babylonian cuneiform (Elamite and Hittite texts), or in a kind of cuneiform of their own (texts in the Ugaritic cuneiform alphabet). These texts are well preserved, owing to the durable material, and they contain information that is of considerable interest to the historian.

In places where the Egyptian tradition was dominant, especially in Palestine and southern Syria (e.g., in the city of Byblos), a limited number of ceremonial or dedicatory inscriptions are found, but the much more numerous hieratic papyri written for governmental and administrative purposes have for the most part been irretrievably lost due to the unfavorable climate. This probably also holds for papyri that were written in the so-called proto-Canaanite alphabet. In such cases the historian must labor with extremely scarce literary sources.

Following the Egyptian tradition, in the first millennium B.C. Phoenicians, Israelites, Arameans, and other peoples also made use of alphabet, papyrus, pen, and ink for their documentation. Virtually all their records and letters have perished. The few Aramaic papyri that have survived are from Egypt. Mesopotamia has yielded a few dozen clay tablets written in Aramaic. In such cases the historian must rely mainly on the scarce authentic ceremonial inscriptions on stone (from graves, on steles, and in buildings), on some ostraca and seals, on data preserved in the historical texts of foreign overlords and conquerors (for Syria and the Arameans, for instance, the Egyptian, Assyrian, Hittite, and Hebrew sources), on some fragmentary traditions indirectly passed on by later classical authors, and on archeological finds. Other nations do not have an uninterrupted body of literature such as the Old Testament. Imagine trying to write the history of Israel relying only on archeological and extrabiblical data!

The source material for a history of the ancient Near East is thus full of lacunae. For the oldest periods written sources are scarce for most areas and peoples, and they are usually fragmentary and very brief. Many data must be inferred from later historiographic texts whose reliability can be variously judged. Moreover, as is apparent from what has been said so far, the sources are unevenly distributed chronologically and geographically as well as culturally. The historian is highly dependent on the success of the spade and the chance find. If, to mention two examples, the palace archives at Mari had not been discovered and if the hundreds of Amarna Letters had not been preserved, much valuable information for the Old Testament as well as for the ancient Near East would have been lacking. Of course, huge gaps remain in our knowledge; only future discoveries can tell how serious and large such gaps are, as is clear from the recent finds at Tell Mardikh (Ebla) in northern Syria. Because these discoveries will continue—by archeologists in the field and sometimes also by philologists in the museums—it should be possible in the future to fill some of the gaps and to make some corrections; often new problems will have to be faced as well. Thus the historiography of the ancient Near East has a dynamic character; it is a developing and therefore fascinating and highly demanding discipline.

The art of writing did not spread evenly through the Near East. Many lands and nations lagged far behind Egypt and Mesopotamia. Barring exceptions such as Ebla and Byblos, the written documentation in Anatolia and Syria-Palestine began only in the second millennium B.C., those of other peoples such as the Israelites, Arameans, and South Arabians not until the first millennium B.C. Many so-called new peoples who entered the Fertile Crescent from the surrounding regions—such as the Guti, the Amorites, the Hyksos, the Kassites, the Sea Peoples, the Arameans, and the Nubians—were themselves without a script. In most cases after some time they adopted the script, the (written) language, and sometimes even the scribes of their new environment, but this process in which they adapted themselves so much to the older and higher culture often affected their own identity and recognizability. Moreover, the lack of a literary-historical tradition often prevented them from recording their own prehistory and the drastic changes their appearance brought to the countries they entered. Their presence was often accompanied by political and social revolutions and disturbances of the existing order, and thus also of the established bureaucracy and the historical documentation. There are several of these critical transition periods, usually called Intermediate Periods, in the history of the ancient Near East. Most familiar are the three in Egypt, though the term is also used for Mesopotamia. The designation "Dark Period" is used for the period around 1500 B.C. in Mesopotamia, and "Dark Ages" especially for the period around the eleventh century B.C. The lack of historical information is often the cause of uncertainties in the chronology, evident in changing dates.

## b. Historiography in the Ancient Near East

The sources that are available, especially the historiographical, should be used with caution, taking into consideration their own peculiar character. If there is no understanding of their origin, function, and literary form (aspects that are usually related), the danger is that they will be used uncritically and naively. Ancient historiographical compositions were as a rule not written out of pure scientific interest or to record the past objectively. They are not historiography in the modern sense of the word. In combination with an analysis of the peculiarities of ancient Near Eastern historiography, recent studies call attention to their *Sitz im Leben,* their literary genre, their political intent, and their religious or ideological background.

Many texts are politically or ideologically focused. The Sumerian King List aims to legitimate the last dynasty mentioned. Part of the function of a segment of the Assyrian King List was to conceal the foreign background of the usurper Shamshi-Adad I. Reports about campaigns and conquests serve to glorify the king who had triumphed in battle. The historical details in the prologues of the Hittite treaties are in part intended to remind the vassal of the prior history in order through encouragement or hidden threat to make him a loyal covenant partner. The frequently elaborate portrayal of corruption and evils in society and government is used as the foil for the contrasting highly beneficent rule of the present ruler. Familiar "reformers" such as Urukagina, Telepinus, and Horemheb used this method in their decrees, as did Kilamuwa (ca. 825 B.C.) from the north Syrian state Sam'al. It should also not be forgotten that the Amarna Letters from Palestine were written to convince the pharaoh of the loyalty and the good intentions of the sender and of the need for military aid. These examples can easily be multiplied.

A biased writing of history does not necessarily imply that the information is wrong or spurious: it does mean that the information is slanted, interpreted, and selected in order to achieve the intended goal. There were certainly "evils" that had to be set straight by the "reformers," and Urukagina was certainly also impelled by the desire for a better society and by compassion for the oppressed, but it is questionable whether the past was as black and the present as white as the decrees with their propagandistic and political slant suggest. The unbelievably favorable prices mentioned by some Mesopotamian rulers as prevailing during their rule present an idealized picture of the prosperity created by them. Such designs were not absent either from the origin of such texts as the "laws" of King Hammurabi; his regulations were intended to impress future generations with his insight and feeling for justice, for the sake of enhancing his own reputation. In general it can be said that court chroniclers often depicted the king as he wanted to be viewed. This is clear from the numerous royal hymns from Mesopotamia around 2000 B.C. and from Egyptian "propaganda literature," familiar particularly from the Twelfth Dynasty (the prophecies of Neferti, the Instruction of Amenemope, hymns to Sesostris III). It has correctly been observed that the vanishing genre of the royal hymns in Mesopotamia was taken over, especially in Assyria, by the later annals and display inscriptions that picture the successful conqueror as he liked to see himself. Traditional achievements, such as reaching the "upper and the lower sea" in Mesopotamia, are often claimed on insufficient grounds by kings who like to thrust through to "where no predecessor had yet set foot." In Egypt during the New Kingdom the long lists of places in Syria, Palestine, and elsewhere that were conquered by predecessors were copied. The temple reliefs of Ramses III at Medinet Habu, depicting the battles with the Nubians, Hittites, and Syrians, are taken over from his predecessor Ramses II, who did do battle with them. Lists and reliefs need therefore not be proof of contemporary conquests or campaigns.

The extent to which reality could be distorted is shown from cases where we have descriptions from both parties involved in a military conflict, such as the battle at Qadesh on the Orontes (ca. 1275 B.C.; Ramses II against the Hittites) and the siege of Jerusalem in 701 B.C. by Sennacherib (cf. the Old Testament and Assyrian annals). Defeats and failed operations are a sensitive spot in the reports, though there are instances of greater objectivity such as in the Hittite sources and the Babylonian Chronicles. Wherever control by checking parallel sources of information is impossible, caution is called for.

It is to be applauded that today greater attention is paid to a systematic analysis of ancient Near Eastern historiography, both its technical and literary aspects and its ideological backgrounds, in which questions concerning the relationship between history and myth, the presence of fixed motifs, and the view of history (*Geschichtsbild*) are considered. Hornung called attention to the essentially "ritual picture of history" of classical Egypt where history was experienced as "renewal of primal history" (*Erneuerung der Urgeschichte*), following more or less fixed schemes. Albrektson analyzed the idea of "historical events as manifestations of the deity" in the ancient Near East to compare the Old Testament view of history with that of Israel's neighbors. Though he discovered a far-reaching similarity on essential points, Lambert has correctly pointed out that the Mesopotamian texts do not know of a "divine plan in history," of a goal and an end toward which God works in history. Liverani has shown that historiography, in autobiographical compositions as well as in ceremonial, public texts, sometimes makes use of prefabricated schemes and structures such as of "the capture of the throne" (especially by usurpers), "the innocent sufferer" (Rib-Addi's letters of lamentation sent from Byblos to the pharaoh), and the "reformer" (who restores the old, sanctified order by abolishing the evils that had come about).

Of special significance for the Old Testament is the recent study of Hittite historiography, which occupies a separate place in the ancient Near East because, in the words of Goetze (1936), in the form of "a genuine historical report it breaks through the frames of the dry annals . . . bans myth and legend from historiography . . . and understands the art of summarizing events retrospectively, from uniform perspectives, and depicting situations in an impressive manner that remained unequalled until Israel's historical narratives." The great importance that the Hittite world ascribed to the knowledge of history is apparent, for example, from the presence of historical elements in various genres of literature, such as "laws" ("in the past . . . now"), rituals, and myths. Old Testament scholarship has rightly shown great interest in the historical introductions to the Hittite vassal treaties; for, as in the prophetic historiography of the Old Testament, they give historical motivation for the covenant relationship and the rules of conduct, and they use the earlier history as a pedagogical example and as the basis for the present relationship. Whether or to what extent Old Testament historiography was influenced by that of the Hittites is a question that is hard to answer. Because of the historical distance (several centuries) and the unlikelihood of direct contact, it seems more likely that there were only indirect influences via the—still largely unknown—Syrian-Canaanite culture, though of course aided by Israel's own creativity, and stimulated by the belief in a God who in history works with his people. Apart from the question of influence and origin, comparison of the more formal aspects of the historiography of the Hittites and that of the Old Testament, both sometimes characterized as *Handlungsdarstellung,* is fascinating and illuminating. It sheds light on composition technique (e.g., the use of earlier history and recapitulations, summarizing descriptions of concurrent events, the creation of larger historical reports as organic units around a theme), style (syntactic forms, logical schemes for indicating temporal or causal connections, introduction of concomitant circumstances), and the "use" of historical material in various contexts.

There are several clear reasons why the history of the ancient Near East may with some justification be regarded as a unity. A geographical relationship exists among the areas that belong to or adjoin the Fertile Crescent, as is evident from the numerous international contacts, going far back into history. These contacts were of a commercial, cultural, political-military, or diplomatic nature. They are the reason that despite the diversity, particularism, and difference in tempo and starting point, the cultural development in this large area shows unmistakable features of similarity, so that all sorts of literary, religious, social, technical, and military phenomena can be fruitfully compared and sometimes point to mutual influence. Particularly from the second millennium B.C., an increasing number of political and military confrontations can be noticed; wars were fought, treaties concluded, power blocs established, gifts, technicians, and princesses exchanged, all in the context of a fascinating complex of international diplomatic relations, made possible especially by the internationally used Babylonian language. The nations influenced each other's history. The increasing size of the nations and the range of the military campaigns, together with intensive international trade, highlight the geographical and political connections in the first millennium B.C. even more. Following the tremendous expansion of the Neo-Assyrian and the short-lived Neo-Babylonian empires, toward the end of the sixth century B.C. the Persian empire of the Achaemenids managed for the first time to unite the entire area under one rule and administrative system with Aramaic—an increasingly important language since the eighth century B.C.—as the linguistic medium (so-called Official Aramaic).

What has been said so far does not mean that it is easy to deal with this history as a unity. Despite similarities and mutual influences, the dominating picture is that of a series of nations, each with its own social structure, religion, language, literature, and history. This is particularly true of the "great" nations who, owing to their geographical position, power, or cultural superiority, were by nature large independent entities, such as Egypt, Mesopotamia, and to a lesser extent the Hittites. The smaller states, particularly those in the Syro-Palestinian area, were through the centuries exposed to foreign influences, and their history was greatly influenced by the activities of the large powers. In addition to internal developments, in these nations the international aspect played an important role. Treating the history of the ancient Near East as the history of Israel's *Umwelt* is a good starting point: it presupposes a particular focus and it has a point of departure in the international role of this disputed territory. On the other hand, it would be wrong to deal with the material too much from this perspective; it would distort that history and leave out significant backgrounds due to overconcentration on Palestine. In the framework of this handbook it will, however, be necessary to deal more extensively with phenomena and "peoples" (e.g., Amorites, Hapiru, Arameans) who play a significant role in the history or historiography of Israel.

The function of this section and the available space demand a rigid limitation and selection because of the enormous amount of material that has become available and the many difficult historical problems that have to be faced. The older history—in many ways a formative period—and the border areas (Elam, Urartu, Arabia) may not get the attention they deserve. Much material from the history of culture, such as socio-economic, art-historical, and religious matters, can at best be only briefly mentioned. Bibliographic references may do something to compensate for this lack.

### LITERATURE

The references here do not include the well-known handbooks and more general monographs, which are listed below under 10. "Supplementary Bibliography" (pp. 323–27).

Important recent literature published after the completion of the original Dutch edition of this survey and added for the benefit of the reader is marked by an asterisk.

B. Albrektson, *History and the Gods* (Lund, 1967); see the review by W. G. Lambert in *Orientalia* 39 (1970) 170–77.

H. Cancik, *Grundzüge der hethitischen und alttestamentlichen Geschichtsschreibung* (Wiesbaden, 1976).

R. C. Dentan, ed., *The Idea of History in the Ancient Near East* (New Haven/London, 1955).

*D. O. Edzard and J. Renger, "Königsinschriften," *Reallexikon der Assyriologie* VI (Berlin, 1980) 59–77.

A. K. Grayson, *Assyrian and Babylonian Chronicles* I (Locust Valley, 1975).

*_____, "Histories and Historians of the Ancient Near East: Assyria and Babylonia," *Orientalia* 49 (1980) 140–94.

*H. A. Hoffner, "Histories and Historians of the Ancient Near East: The Hittites," *Orientalia* 49 (1980) 283–332.

*H. Tadmor and M. Weinfeld, eds., *History, Historiography, and Interpretation: Studies in Biblical and Cuneiform Literatures* (Jerusalem, 1983).

*J. van Seters, "Histories and Historians of the Ancient Near East: The Israelites," *Orientalia* 50 (1981) 139–85.

*_____, *In Search of History* (New Haven, 1983).

## 2. CHRONOLOGY

### a. Problems

A historical survey without chronological framework (i.e., without dates) is an impossibility. However, the use of dates in ancient Near Eastern history requires caution and explanation. Only thus can one avoid unwarranted confidence in presumed absolute dates and an arbitrary moving of facts and kings over many centuries (Velikovsky). The main reason for the chronological problem, known especially from the changing dates ascribed to Hammurabi of Babylon, is the lack of one continuous time reckoning from a fixed starting point in the form of a specific era. In the course of the centuries there have been a few attempts in that direction, but the first genuine era, the so-called Selucid, does not begin until 312 B.C. (the recapture of Babylon by Seleucus I). Without a continuous time reckoning every lacuna or uncertainty about dates of reigns carries over backward into the preceding period. Attempts have been made to solve the chronological problems by the use of new technological methods, such as the radiocarbon method (applicable to organic remains containing carbon) or the investigation of thermoluminescence (applicable to baked pottery). Both are better suited for prehistory, however; the margin of uncertainty for the historical periods is still too great to provide any real solutions, and the value of the results obtained by these methods is debatable. For reasons insufficiently explained thus far, there is a great discrepancy between the carbon-14 datings (presently corrected by data from tree rings, especially of the *pinus arista*) for the Old Egyptian period (up to five centuries before the 3rd millennium B.C.) and the reasonably reliable data acquired in the "traditional" way.

Historians of the ancient Near East use two complementary methods to construct a chronology that is as accurate as possible. First, they use the "normal" historical sources (especially epigraphical, but also archeological) to construct a general framework in which the dated facts such as the reigns of kings are assigned a relative position (x years before or after y). For this purpose scholars use king lists, lists with names of years or eponyms, annals, chronicles, building inscriptions ("King A restored this temple x years after B had built it"), data about administrative careers or genealogies, and also dated documents, preferably those from archives. Then historians attempt to obtain absolute dates by means of astronomical data or through synchronisms. If this is still impossible, the least that can now be done is to calculate exactly how many years must have intervened between two widely separated events. In this way the general chronological framework becomes increasingly more reliable and the room for errors in the interim periods smaller. The result of this approach is that most dates from the first millennium B.C. may be regarded as being more or less definite (though particularly the Old Testament still has some seemingly insoluble problems). The margin of uncertainty for the second half of the first millennium ranges from ten to fifteen years. These uncertainties are carried over into the older periods where the margins are considerably greater because of the scarcity of the documentation.

Because it is impossible to present a full discussion of the present state of the problem, I limit myself here to a few main lines, both with respect to the methodology and to the facts.

The central role of the king in political history entails that in the chronology the length of his reign is of cardinal importance. Fortunately, precise information about the succession of the rulers and the years of their reigns can be extracted from the documents. Most important are the king lists, though substantive data can also be obtained from a combination of individual chronologies and chronicles (as in the Old Testament and in part for the Hittites). Series of names of kings, without years of reign, are found in extensive genealogies and especially in king lists used in the sacrificial cult. Such lists are known from Boghazköy and Ugarit, and they also played a role in Babylonia and Egypt. A disadvantage is that these lists are often without historical objectivity. For example, the list of seventy-five pharaohs in the mortuary temple of Seti I (at Abydos) omits several dynasties and a number of Seti's more immediate predecessors, among whom are the Amarna pharaohs. The greatest amount of information can be obtained from the more factual lists that mention the reign of each king and often total them for each dynasty.

It should be borne in mind, however, that such lists often have a long history behind them, which has resulted in corrupted figures and names. This corruption can sometimes be determined by comparing manuscripts (e.g., in the Sumerian King List). As was mentioned above, these lists do not always owe their origin to purely historical motivations. Political intentions and an idealistic vision of the past, sometimes coupled with defective historical information, repeatedly resulted in violence to the historical reality, for instance, by preserving the fiction that only one "lawful" king could reign at a time. Competing, partially overlapping dynasties could be enumerated after each other (e.g., the end of the Old Babylonian dynasty and the beginning of the Kassite dynasty; the 15th–17th Egyptian dynasties about the time of the Hyksos). Finer details such as temporary co-regencies and double counting of the beginning and final years of two successive kings also created problems. Moreover, these lists are almost always damaged. If these gaps—as often happens for Egypt—cannot be filled from duplicates and copies, one has to resort to estimates. The method involves starting from an average life span, the length of a generation, and the highest year of a reign mentioned in the documents.

## b. Egypt

We face this problem especially with Egypt. For the oldest periods lists are available, such as the fragmentary Canon of Turin, a manuscript from the New Kingdom that gives years of reign by ruler and by dynasty from Menes to the Fifteenth Dynasty, and the fragmentary Palermo Stone, an annal copied during the New Kingdom that enumerates years of reign and important events from predynastic times to the end of the Fifth Dynasty. On the basis of this information the beginning of the First Dynasty is put at around 3000 B.C. For the later periods there is the list of Manetho (3rd century B.C.), preserved in Greek extracts and resumes; he is responsible for the division into thirty (31) dynasties. For the New Kingdom his figures have proved to be unreliable. The uncertainty stemming from it is reflected in alternative dates for reigns and important events. A slight preference for later dates can be noticed. This preference is based on X-ray study of the mummies (control of estimated dates), analysis of the data of the jubilee of the pharaohs (*heb-sed* feast; apart from some exceptions—Hatshepsut and Akhenaten—always in the thirtieth year, with the years previous to that already involving preparations), and correlation with the dates for Mesopotamia in the fourteenth–thirteenth century. The data for the Twenty-first Dynasty have also been recalculated (ca. 1069–945 B.C.). There is no agreement yet.

Two kinds of data can lend Egyptian chronology a kind of absolute value. (1) Observations about the appearance of the new moon in a number of successive months of the year. For Thutmose III and Ramses II this yields a series of three alternatives as the beginning year: respectively, 1504, 1490, or 1479 B.C. and 1304, 1290, or 1279 B.C. Important, too, is that Baer's interpretation of a lunar phenomenon under Takelot II results in an accession to the throne in 860 B.C. (2) Notes about the appearance of the bright star Sothis (Sirius) on the day of the new year in the spring, after having been invisible on account of a conjunction with the sun. Assuming a calendar year of 365 days and a solar year of about 365 1/4 days, this so-called heliacal rise of Sothis did not happen again on the new year's day until after about 1460 years. The end of such a Sothis period came in A.D. 139, and there are notes about observations from about 1900 B.C. which, if they are clear and accurate (the position of Sothis relative to the sun changes gradually, and the place of observation also has a bearing on it), can produce absolute data. From this it has been deduced that the seventh year of Sesostris III was in 1872 B.C., the ninth year of Amenhotep in about 1542 B.C., and the first year of Seti I in 1316 B.C. A critical analysis of these data has, unfortunately, shown up uncertainties. The connection of particular observations with reigns of some kings is at times uncertain or indirect. The so-called era of Menophres, which according to the fourth-century astronomer Theon would begin about 1316 B.C. (1456 years before 139 A.D.) and be linked with Pharaoh Merneptah, Seti I, or Ramses I, is shown faulty by historical criticism. Using the defective king list (of Manetho?), Theon likely reckoned back from A.D. 139, without possessing authentic data. Despite the uncertainties, the Sothis data remain important in the chronological scheme because their incorrectness can also not be demonstrated.

Data from genealogies, biographies of government officials and priests, dated documents, notes about the life spans of Apis bulls, and the like help to refine the chronology. Particularly significant are the synchronisms with the Near East from the Amarna Age and that of the Ramesside kings recorded in exchanges of letters, in reports of battles, and in treaties. In this connection the more or less fixed Assyrian-Babylonian chronology serves an important function as a frame of reference, as does the occurrence of a solar eclipse in the tenth year of Murshilish II (1312 B.C.). Though problems and differences of opinion remain, leading to different dates for Akhenaten and the accession of Ramses II, for which, when one considers all the available data, the year 1279 B.C. remains the most likely. For the later periods Kitchen's study of the Third Intermediate Period (1100–650 B.C.) is very significant, though here, too, differences remain, as is indicated by Wente's discussion of Kitchen's work. For the Old Testament it is important that the beginning of the reign of Sheshonq I (Shishak), who invaded Judah in the fifth year of Rehoboam and who was already on the throne during Solomon's final years, must be around 945 B.C. (give or take about two years).

## c. Mesopotamia

The situation in Mesopotamia shows definite analogies to Egypt, but differences as well. In addition to various king lists, there are objective, administrative lists of names of years (Babylonia) and Eponyms (Assyria). The Sumerian King List (final revision in the 19th century B.C.) has proved of little use for the oldest periods (the period before the "deluge" and the first thirteen dynasties after that), though it contains valuable historical information. The kings of Lagash who are important for the chronology of the predynastic period are ignored. The internal chronology of the Akkad period (24th century) to the end of the Old Babylonian period (ca. 1600 B.C.) is, apart from the Guti period, fairly well known. We know all the rulers of the Ur III period, the Isin-Larsa period, and the first dynasty of Babylon (ca. 2100–1600 B.C.) from virtually complete lists with year-names. The chronology from then on causes problems, however. The Babylonian King List, of which some editions are carried into the time of the Seleucids, introduces after the first dynasty of Babylon a dynasty from the south ("Sealand") with 2 kings and 368 years, followed by that of the Kassites, with thirty-six rulers and over 576 years. According to the newest calculations this second dynasty ended about 1155 B.C. The 945 years in the list for the period between the end of the Old Babylonian era and the end of the Kassite dynasty is impossible. Clearly for important segments the end of the first dynasty of Babylon and the two following dynasties run parallel. But we do not know precisely for how many years this holds, despite the use of archeological data (e.g., from the Kassite capital Dur-Kurigalzu), information from documents, calculations of generations, and synchronisms with the Hittites (the end of the first dynasty of Babylon was sealed with a raid by the Hittite king Murshilish I), with Syria (especially with Alalakh), and with Assyria.

In some modern discussions, too, much attention has also been given to the Assyrian King List, which runs from the end of the third millennium to the seventh century B.C. Research has shown that the section covering the first half of the second millennium B.C. must be used with great caution, because in some cases the figures for the years of reigns of some kings are missing or are unclear and because the continuity immediately after the Old Assyrian period (after the fortieth king, Ishme-Dagan, son of Shamshi-Adad I, known from the Mari archives and a younger contemporary of Hammurabi of Babylon) is uncertain. Unfortunately, the real problem of Mesopotamian chronology remains without a clear solution here.

The different years indicated for Hammurabi are not based primarily on reconstruction and interpretation of the king lists, though these lists have furnished a general indication of the age in which he is to be placed. Also here the accurate years are based on an astronomical given: observations concerning periods of invisibility and reappearance of the planet Venus because of a conjunction with the sun during the first eight years of Ammi-Saduqa, the next to the last king of the first dynasty of Babylon. These observations are part of the sixty-third tablet of the large series of astrological omina *Enuma Anu Enlil*. Despite the inherent textual problems and some difficulties with the calculations, it can be determined that the first year of Ammi-Saduqa, in which the series of observations began, must have been in 1701 or 1645 or 1541 B.C. From this the years of Hammurabi's reign can be deduced as being 1848–1806, 1792–1750, or 1728–1686 B.C., called, respectively, the high, middle, and low chronology. Utilizing all possible data scholars have tried to make a definite choice. The preference has varied, but the majority today holds to the middle chronology (so, e.g., the *Cambridge Ancient History*), which fits rather well for Assyria and Syria. New, prosopographical research of texts from level VII at Alalakh (18th–17th century B.C.) has supported this choice. Advocates of the low chronology (e.g., Albright and Cornelius) can still be found, however. Particularly significant for a definite choice is the discussion concerning the reconstruction of the complete series of Hittite kings, known especially from sacrificial lists and genealogies. For example, the disputed question whether a Hattushilish II must be regarded as the father of Shuppiluliumash I (early 14th century B.C.) has consequences for calculations based on the number of generations and the average duration of a reign.

The situation with respect to the second half of the second millennium B.C. is more favorable. The Assyrian King List is the guide here (ill. 66). Certainty is still absent owing to some obscurities in the period from about 1500 to 1170 B.C., mainly due to textual variations in the various copies: differences concerning filiation, minor discrepancies (usually 1 year) in the numbers, and twice a variation of ten years. Even though these variations largely cancel out each other (the one copy assigns king no. 61 to 10 years less, the other no. 62 to 10 years more), until certainty has been obtained one must reckon with the possibility that dates before the middle of the twelfth century B.C. are about ten years too high. A recent study by Boese and Wilhelm has indeed made this almost certain (for details see below, pp. 251–52). Brinkman is now inclined to date the Kassite kings from the fourteenth-thirteenth century ten to fifteen years later, but still his figures might be too high. Similar redating in a period with many international contacts (e.g., the Amarna Age) entails consequences for the chronologies of the neighboring countries.

### d. The First Millennium B.C.

The chronology of this period exhibits far fewer problems, especially thanks to the Assyrian King List and the Assyrian list of eponyms. The chronology—also decisive for many other countries via numerous historical cross connections—is astronomically anchored because a more elaborate version of the second text, the so-called Eponym Chronicle, registers a solar eclipse in the year 763 B.C. From that time on, classical sources also become available, in particular the *Canon of Ptolemy* (2nd century A.D.). As an astronomer Ptolemy needed a fixed chronology, and for that purpose he constructed a list of Babylonian kings, starting with Nabonassar in 747 B.C., a starting point that is also found in Berossos's *Babyloniaca* or *Chaldaica* (3rd century B.C.). This is consistent with the fact that during Nabonassar's reign systematic astronomical observations began, recorded day by day (the so-called astronomical diaries), on which ultimately the reliable Babylonian Chronicle, which likewise starts with him, must also be based. The *Canon of Ptolemy* can be connected with the Assyrian King List because his list also contains those Assyrian kings who were king of Babylon. Three lunar eclipses in 721 B.C. mentioned in Ptolemy's *Almagest* for the rule of 'Mardokempados' (Merodak-Baladan) fix the Babylonian chronology.

Using astronomical calculations and taking into account the Babylonian time reckoning and calendar (certainly from the 6th century a nineteen-year cycle of fixed leap years), one can, by means of the tables of Parker-Dubberstein, convert the data in the Babylonian Chronicle and other Neo-Babylonian inscriptions into accurate dates on our calendar.

This state of affairs is significant for Syria-Palestine in the first millennium B.C. Notwithstanding the abundance of chronological notations in the Old Testament (length of reign of individual kings; synchronisms of Israel–Judah; dates of individual events) an exact time reckoning still involves problems there, including a few errors (Pekah's length of reign is too long), probable double counting of first and last years of reign, failure to take into account co-regencies or co-rule of two kings (especially in Judah under Amaziah, Azariah, Jotham), and the like. Exact synchronisms with Assyria provide the chronological framework and fixed points of reference: Ahab's battle with Shalmaneser III at Qarqar in 853 B.C.; Jehu's tribute to the same king in 841; Joash's tribute to Adad-nirari III in 796 (?); Menahem's tribute to Tiglath-pileser III in 738; the capture of Samaria by Shalmaneser V in 722; Sennacherib's siege of Jerusalem in 701 B.C. The precise date of the first capture of Jerusalem by Nebuchadrezzar on 16 March 597 B.C., mentioned in the Babylonian Chronicle, helps in dating the end of the Judean kingdom and Cyrus's edict (538 B.C.). Also for Syria—the Phoenician, Syro-Hittite, and Aramean states—the dated contacts with Assyria (and Babylonia) are chronologically very important, and may be supplemented by data from the Old Testament to a certain extent.

It is obvious that by no means all chronological questions have been solved. In particular the datings in the second millennium B.C., with the numerous international contacts, require refinement through continued research and discovery of new, especially written, material. The present margins of uncertainty are not so great, however, that they render a historical reconstruction impossible. The presence of these margins is relatively unimportant for the Old Testament and the history of Israel. There are enough sure dates and exact synchronisms for the tenth century B.C. (invasion of Shishak/Sheshonq in the fifth year of Rehoboam, ca. 925 B.C.), and the chronology of the time of the kings is reasonably certain. Shifts of one or more decades have little bearing on the time of the patriarchs, and even on that of the period of the judges. The facts from those periods can only be roughly dated anyway. The dating of the historical problems in connection with the exodus out of Egypt and the entrance into Canaan demand a more exact approach. But even an absolute chronology for Egypt would not be able to solve the problem because the Old Testament mentions no names of pharaohs in connection with Moses and Joseph. Only a combination of archeological, historical, and literary data can help.

## LITERATURE

J. von Beckerath, "Methode und Ergebnisse ägyptischer Chronologie," *Orientalische Literaturzeitung* 62 (1967) 5–13.

*J. Boese and G. Wilhelm, "Aššhur-dan I., Ninurta-apil-Ekur und die mittelassyrische Chronologie," *Wiener Zeitschrift für die Kunde des Morgenlandes* 71 (1979) 19–38.

J. A. Brinkman, *Materials and Studies in Kassite History* I (Chicago, 1976) 6–34.

———, "Comments on the Nassouhi Kinglist and the Assyrian Kinglist Tradition," *Orientalia* 42 (1972) 306–19.

S. M. Burnstein, *The Babyloniaca of Berossus* (Malibu, 1978).

*D. O. Edzard and A. K. Grayson, "Königslisten und Chroniken," *Reallexikon der Assyriologie* VI (Berlin, 1980) 77–135.

W. Ehrich, *Chronologies in Old World Archaeology* (Chicago, 1975).

P. Garelli, *Le Proche-Orient asiatique des origines aux invasions des peuples de la mer* (Paris, 1969), pp. 227–39.

O. R. Gurney, "The Hittite Line of Kings and Chronology," in *Anatolian Studies Presented to H. G. Güterbock* (Istanbul, 1974), pp. 105–11.

F. A. Hassan, "Radiocarbon Chronology of Archaic Egypt," *Journal of Near Eastern Studies* 39 (1980) 203–208.

W. C. Hayes, "Chronology. I. Egypt to the End of the Twentieth Dynasty," in *Cambridge Ancient History* I/1 (1970²) 173–93.

E. Hornung, *Untersuchungen zur Chronologie und Geschichte des Neuen Reiches* (Wiesbaden, 1964).

*P. J. Huber, *Astronomical Dating of Babylon I and Ur III* (Malibu, 1982). He argues for the "high chronology" (Hammurabi 1847–1795 B.C.) on the basis of attested lengths of months (29 or 30 days) during the Old Babylonian period.

A. Jepsen and R. Hanhart, *Untersuchungen zur israelitisch-jüdischen Chronologie* (Berlin, 1964).

J. O. D. Johnston, "The Problems of Radiocarbon Dating," *Palestine Exploration Quarterly* 105 (1973) 13–26.

K. A. Kitchen, *The Third Intermediate Period in Egypt (1100–650 B.C.)* (Warminster, 1973) (see the review by E. F. Wente in *Journal of Near Eastern Studies* 35 [1976] 275–78; and Kitchen's comments in *Journal of the Ancient Near Eastern Society of Columbia University* 5 [1974] 225–33).

B. Landsberger, "Assyrische Königsliste und 'Dunkles Zeitalter,'" *Journal of Cuneiform Studies* 8 (1954) 31ff.

R. D. Long, "A Re-examination of the Sothic Chronology of Egypt," *Orientalia* 43 (1974) 261–74.

N. Na'aman, "A New Look at the Chronology of Alalakh Level VII," *Anatolian Studies* 26 (1976) 129–43; 29 (1979) 103–13.

H. Otten, *Die hethitischen historischen Quellen und die altorientalische Chronologie* (Mainz, 1968).

R. A. Parker and W. H. Dubberstein, *Babylonian Chronology 626 B.C.–A.D. 75* (Providence, 1969³).

E. Reiner and D. Pingree, *The Venus Tablet of Ammiṣaduqa. Babylonian Planetary Omens* I (Malibu, 1975).

M. B. Rowton, "Chronology. II. Ancient Western Asia," *Cambridge Ancient History* I/1 (1970²) 193–239.

H. S. Smith, "Egypt and Carbon-14 Dating," *Antiquity* 38 (1964) 32–37.

H. Tadmor, "The Chronology of the Ancient Near East in the Second Millennium B.C.E.," in *The World History of the Jewish People* II (Jerusalem, 1970) 63–101, 260–69.

*_____, "The Chronology of the First Temple Period," *The World History of the Jewish People* IV/1 (Jerusalem, 1979) 44–60, 318–20.

E. F. Wente, "Thutmoses III's Accession and the Beginning of the New Kingdom," *Journal of Near Eastern Studies* 34 (1975) 265–72.

E. F. Wente and C. C. van Scilen III, "A Chronology of the New Kingdom," in *Studies in Honor of G. R. Hughes* (Chicago, 1977).

See also the literature below, p. 253.

---

# 3. THE THIRD MILLENNIUM B.C.

## a. Egypt under the Old Kingdom and the First Intermediate Period (1st–11th Dynasties)

After a long prehistory, to which in the final phases the names of (the cultures of) Badari and Nagada (Naqada) III are connected, Egypt entered historical time about 3000 B.C. According to tradition—coming from the New Kingdom period—Menes was the first king of the First Dynasty, the so-called Thinite dynasty, and he united Upper and Lower Egypt, as testified by his double crown. With him began the so-called *Protodynastic Period,* which includes the first two dynasties; according to Manetho this period lasted 550 years, but historians generally think in terms of four centuries. From inscribed steles in their tombs at Abydos and from gifts (including the famous stone palettes from the temple at Hierakonpolis) a group of rulers are known bearing the name Horus, of whom Scorpion is likely the oldest. Menes is usually identified with Narmer or Aha. Relatively little is known of the political and religious developments in this formative period. Beside the worship of Horus (at Abydos) developed a growing worship of Re and, under Peribsen, of Seth. Political and economic consolidation is evident, for example, from extensive commercial links; objects inscribed with names of pharaohs from the First Dynasty have been found in southern Palestine (Tel Gat; Arad) and in Nubia. As early as the twenty-seventh century B.C. (2nd Dynasty) there were relations with Byblos (inscription of Khasekhemui).

With the Third Dynasty (about 73 years) comes the *Old Kingdom,* also called the Pyramid Age after the most important monuments from that time. This period (3rd–6th Dynasties) is characterized by the classical shaping of Egyptian culture, politically, religiously, and artistically. The hierarchical structure of the realm is completely dominated by the divine king, who rules the land according to the principles of order, justice, and truth (*maat*). He is the sovereign, the chief priest, and the son of the sun-god Re; later he is also the king who in his death repeats the fate of Osiris and rules over the world of the dead. This kingly ideology was given monumental shape in the durable pyramids constructed of hewn stone, which regardless of their original religious symbolism—a form of the primordial hill, grave mound, or bridge to the sun—functioned as the king's final resting place and as the symbol of his power. The pyramids also pointed upward to Re, the sun-god of Heliopolis, who began to play a central role in this period, and beginning with the Fifth Dynasty was regularly given sun temples (especially at Abusir) with the obelisk as its main object.

The oldest more-or-less complete complex of pyramids—at the same time the first grave monument in stone—is the step pyramid of Djoser, the second king of the Third Dynasty, at Saqqara (545 by 280 m., 1790 by 920 ft.; height 60 m., 200 ft.). It was built by the architect Imhotep, who was later worshiped and deified as a wise man and a healer. Under this and the following dynasty, pyramids were built at Medum, Dashur, and Giza; during the Fifth Dynasty at Saqqara (by Userkaf), Abusir (e.g., by Sahure and Neuserre), and again Saqqara (by Unas), where the pyramids of the Sixth Dynasty (by Teti and Pepi I and II) are also found. The grand, presumably new, concept of Djoser and Imhotep was altered by the great pyramid builders of the Fourth Dynasty (Cheops, Chephren, and Mycerinus), after the first king of this dynasty, Snofru—of whom there are three pyramids—had already introduced changes. Important changes are the dropping of the "symbolic residence" and the functional changes in the temple of the dead, almost certainly due to developments in the ritual. Furthermore, they made their pyramids with smooth sidewalls, and higher (over 140 m., 460 ft.) than their predecessors. Besides the pyramid, the standard complex from the Fourth Dynasty consisted of a double temple of the dead (for sacrifices to the deceased and for the cult of the god-king; the temple was also used in the elaborate funeral ritual), while the whole was enclosed by a wall which by means of an incline was connected with a smaller temple in the valley and a mooring place for the procession boats (recovered at Cheops's pyramid). Around the complex, faithfully reflecting the power structures, were found the flat, rectangular tombs (*mastabas*) of the high officials. The Chephren complex boasts the royal sphinx—a human-headed lion—standing guard against hostile powers.

This architecture of the dead (very little has remained of the other temples and residences, especially at Memphis) underscores the dominant position of the king and speaks of great artistic and technological ability. Architecture, reliefs, sculpture, and painting show mastery of the material and a mature style, following rigid conventions. In later centuries these had for the most part a normative function. The many interesting reliefs with scenes from life, especially in the mastabas, also contain biographical inscriptions from officials with valuable historical information. In the pyramid of Unas (end of the 5th Dynasty; ca. 2355–2325 B.C.) are found for the first time, as wall reliefs, the so-called *Pyramid Texts* (were they heretofore written papyri that have since perished?). These are religious texts, magic spells that guarantee the well-being of the dead king and help him to occupy his deserved place among the gods. They live on, though transformed, in the later *Coffin Texts* from the First Intermediate Period—now also nondivine dead are provided with them—and later, from the time of the New Kingdom, in the *Book of the Dead*.

The large-scale building enterprises presuppose a centrally directed government, a common ideology, and economic prosperity. The king played the central role in the government. He was assisted by high officials, who were initially recruited from the royal family, and later, as bureaucracy grew, from other circles. The vizier appeared in the Third Dynasty; there were also the monarchs or district governors of the many Egyptian provinces—twenty-two in Upper Egypt, from Elephantine to below Memphis; and several (later 20) in Lower Egypt. In the course of time these district governors became more powerful, as is evident from the dynasties they formed and their independent choice of a tomb (especially after the 5th Dynasty). This was at the expense of the absolute power of the king, who increasingly had to reckon with their influence, and who therefore was brought down to a more human level. Another consequence was that his relations to his subjects acquired more personal and ethical aspects.

Egypt's prosperity was based on the fertility of the Nile Valley. The Palermo Stone records the Nile's high-water mark during the initial dynasties (ill. 67). The base of Egypt's prosperity was thus agriculture—made possible by the natural inundation of the land—and livestock, as is also shown by the reliefs from the mastabas. In the centrally and bureaucratically guided economy, the extensive building projects had an important place. They demanded an enormous amount of manpower, both in the quarries and at the building sites (performed perhaps in between the agricultural seasons with the assistance of prisoners of war?), huge payments for food rations, personnel, and materials (wood, granite, diorite), which sometimes had to be obtained from far away. Also, after their completion they remained an economic burden on the land because the large temple complexes and pyramids with their cultic apparatus could function only at government expense, by means of land donations, special allowances, and exemption from taxes. This could be accomplished only in periods of peace and prosperity, within a smoothly running administrative framework, conditions that were present during the flowering period of the Old Kingdom.

Inscriptions, objects with names of kings, and other finds testify to foreign relations. The shipping trade with Byblos provided wood; the mines in the Sinai (Serabit el-Khadim) turquoise and probably copper; Nubia, accessible since the Sixth

Dynasty by canals through the first cataract of the Nile, provided gold and hard stone. King Sahure (ca. 2450) is said to have been the first to reach the point of the land of incense (coast of Somaliland?), and he also sent a trade expedition to Syria. Objects with his cartouche have even been found at Troy (commerce via Crete in Early Minoan II?). Vases with inscriptions of the pharaohs Chephren and Pepi I were recently discovered in the royal palace of Ebla, where they may have arrived from Byblos.

Toward the end of the long and stable period of the Fourth–Sixth Dynasties (ca. 2575–2150 B.C.) signs of disintegration appeared; with remarkable speed, after the Seventh and Eighth Dynasties (together only 20 years with 15 rulers), the Old Kingdom collapsed. Though partially caused by infiltration and raids of "Asiatics" into the Delta and holdups of merchant caravans, the primary reasons for the decline were of an internal nature. They began to manifest themselves especially during the second half of the improbably long reign of Pepi II (a late-born son of Pepi I), who ruled more than ninety years. A number of closely related factors determined the developments. One important factor was the ecological crisis that began about 2250 B.C., caused by a series of unusually low floodings of the Nile. This meant a drastic lowering of agricultural productivity, and that implied food shortages, famine, death, and at the same time a decrease in state income (from taxes on produce), since there was a relationship between the level of the Nile floodings and the level of the state levies. The lack of means and of manpower, and the political and social unrest following in its wake—plunder, internal power struggles, local particularism—undermined the central government, resulting in a loss of power and prestige of the hierarchically organized structure of the state and of the monarchy. The loss of power in Memphis meant that the king became more and more dependent on the support of his powerful servants, especially the district governors who had formed local dynasties, among whom those of Elephantine, Coptos, and Abydos (to whom Pepi II had become related by marriage) occupied a dominant position. The many immunities granted them (of the 7th–8th Dynasties those of Coptos are known), and the impossi-

bly high costs connected with the construction and the maintenance of the pyramid complexes and temples, together with the economic problems, led to a crisis.

The biographical inscriptions of the high officials from this period mention the consequences of this crisis, as does the remarkable literature that is produced in this "crisis period" and the subsequent First Intermediate Period, which apparently experienced the collapse of the old, hallowed order as profoundly upsetting, as a *fin de siècle*. This "pessimistic literature" describes the misery and chaos and seeks to derive religious and social lessons from it (without ignoring ethical questions). It includes "The Conversation of a Man with His Ba," "The Counsels of Ipuwer," "The Instruction of King Merikare," "The Instruction of King Amenemope," "The Prophecy of Neferti," "The Complaint of the Farmer," and probably "The Song of the Harper." The flowering of this literature, which contains a new spiritual dimension, contrasts sharply with other expressions of art that are evidence of decline.

After the end of the Eighth Dynasty (ca. 2130 B.C.) new, at first local, rulers took over the government. They resided not in the three abovementioned cities but in new centers. In the north they were found in the twentieth district, in Herakleopolis (not far from Memphis), having become powerful through the control and the exploitation of the Faiyum. The local governors soon adopted the royal title and are known (thanks to Manetho) as the Ninth and Tenth Dynasties (ca. 2130–2040 B.C.). In the south, Thebes, with Mentuhotep I as the first "king," became a rival known as the Eleventh Dynasty. After a period of political and military maneuvering, in which Thebes could count on the support of the districts of Elephantine and Coptos, eventually the southern, Theban royal house got the upper hand. About 2040 B.C. Mentuhotep I completed the work of his predecessors (Intef I–III) by eliminating his northern rivals, Merikare and his successor, and conquering Herakleopolis. After a century of disunity Egypt in principle was again united under one scepter. In the procession of kings in the Ramesseum, Mentuhotep I appears later (in the New Kingdom), alongside the other two "uniters" of Egypt: Menes and Ahmose (who expelled the Hyksos). With Mentuhotep the Middle Kingdom begins.

---

## LITERATURE

*M. Antzler, *Untersuchungen zur Herausbildung von Herrschaftsformen in Ägypten* (Hildesheim, 1981).

W. Barta, "Die Erste Zwischenzeit im Spiegel der pessimistischen Literatur," *Jaarbericht Ex Oriente Lux* 24 (1976) 50–61.

J. von Beckerath, "Die Dynastie der Herakleopoliten," *Zeitschrift für Ägyptische Sprache und Altertumskunde* 93 (1966) 13–20.

I. E. S. Edwards, *The Pyramids of Egypt* (Harmondsworth, 1961²).

W. B. Emery, *Archaic Egypt* (Harmondsworth, 1961).

W. C. Hayes, *Most Ancient Egypt* (Chicago, 1964).

*A. Roccati, *La littérature historique sous l'ancien empire égyptien* (Paris, 1982).

---

## b. Mesopotamia to the End of the Third Millennium B.C.

The history of Mesopotamia during the third millennium B.C. is more difficult to describe than that of Egypt. Authentic written sources are scarce before about 2500 B.C.; the oldest clay tablets, to the extent that they are understandable, contain mainly economic information of a local nature. An exception is the word lists from the oldest schools that enumerate, among others, professions and place-names. Building and tomb inscriptions are lacking, as are historical reliefs. The first genuinely historical sources appear only about 2500 B.C.; these are texts from Lagash about Ur-Nanse and his successors, roughly contemporary with school texts and archives from Tell Farah (Shuruppak) and Abu Salabikh. Since it is a mixture of historical, legendary, and mythical data, the tradition embedded in the Sumerian King List is of little value for that early period; it does not even mention the best-known dynasty, that of Lagash.

Unlike Egypt, Mesopotamia did not have one dominating and lasting dynasty. It was instead fragmented into rival city-states, in which the common culture and especially the cult of the chief god Enlil in Nippur were the expression of a real bond that existed. Linguistically and ethnically the area was not a unity either. The sources are written in at least two languages (Sumerian and Akkadian), and various "peoples" are present in the land or invade it: Sumerians, Semitic Akkadians, Subarians or Hurrites (certainly from the 23rd century B.C.), and Amorites (about the same time). Some scholars believe that another, still older, pre-Sumerian indigenous population played an important cultural role. This diversity was mainly due to the lack of protective, natural boundaries; there were numerous political and economic contacts with the neighboring lands, giving the land a greater openness and a greater international orientation than Egypt.

### (1) THE URUK PERIOD

The transition to historical times happened toward the end of the fourth millennium B.C. in the final phase (layers V–VI) of the Uruk Period (which began about 3500 B.C.), to be dated in the thirty-third to the thirty-first centuries B.C. (earlier datings are based on disputed carbon-14 calculations). The oldest clay tablets, found in layer IVa, mark the transition and belong to a course of cultural developments that testify to a highly developed and mature civilization. The oldest architecture consists of monumental "low temples" (up to 50 by 80 m., 165 by 260 ft.), trisectional with a central T-shaped room, and smaller "high temples" on terraces, forerunners of the later ziqqurrats or tower temples. The alcove profiles of the outer walls, the use of limestone and geometrical burin mosaics on walls and pillars, and the dynamic-naturalistic style of sculpture, reliefs, and carvings (beginning at layer IV) betray artistic ability and mastery of the material. The script arose as a requirement of a growing economy, in which also the cylinder seals—rolled off, for example, on the clay stoppers of jars—had a function. Archeological investigation points to a growing number of agricultural settlements, in other words, to an increase in population and food, while the oldest lists of professions betray a highly stratified society, including a priest-king who was perhaps at the top (probably portrayed on seals). The gradual use of artificial irrigation supported the economic developments.

Traditionally the Uruk Period is followed, about 3000 B.C. (in Uruk layer III), by the Jemdet Nasr Period (named after the first site where the characteristic pottery was discovered). Archeologically this period, which probably overlapped with the end of the Uruk Period, is hard to grasp. In Uruk this period is associated with changes in temple construction (the first temples on high terraces) and the art of seal engraving. It plays a significant role in the discussions concerning the "Sumerian problem," that is, where and especially when the presumably nonautochthonous Sumerians invaded Mesopotamia. There are two opposing views. According to some the Sumerians came after the Uruk Period, and the changes of the Jemdet Nasr Period would be indications of a cultural break. This view, which assumes that the Sumerians adopted the cuneiform script and the high culture of an older indigenous population (which thus in fact put its ineradicable stamp on the culture of ancient Mesopotamia) argues, among others, that it has not been proven that the oldest texts are written in Sumerian, that phonetically the cuneiform script does not seem to have been devised for Sumerian, and that many of the old place-names and names of professions are non-Sumerian. Others, who underline the continuity between Uruk IV and Uruk III and interpret changes as internal developments, assume that the Sumerians entered Mesopotamia much earlier, for instance, about 3500, at the beginning of the Uruk Period, and that they were thus indeed the bearers of the oldest great civilization. So far this culturally and historically significant question cannot be answered with certainty. Answers may be expected from systematic attempts to read and understand the oldest texts from Uruk and from new archeological finds (made particularly in Syria along the western curve of the Euphrates), which show that the Uruk civilization was much more extensive than used to be thought.

## (2) THE EARLY DYNASTIC PERIOD

The Early Dynastic Period begins about 2900 B.C. It is subdivided into the following phases: I, about 2900–2750 B.C.; II, 2750–2600 B.C.; IIIa, 2600–2500 B.C.; IIIb, 2500–2350 B.C. This was Mesopotamia's formative period in which it developed its classical civilization and an agriculturally based economy, supported by much artificial irrigation and determined by the flow of the Euphrates and Tigris. Large-scale urbanization becomes evident in a number of cities that at the same time functioned as city-states, each with its own ruler, dynasty, temple, and pantheon. The most important are Eridu, Ur, Bad-tibira, Uruk, Larsa (state of Lagash), Umma, Shuruppak, Adab, Nippur, Akshak, Sippar, Kish, Eshnunna, and Mari. Slowly the historical documentation improves; in addition to the important archeological material from many places (Ur with its royal graves, Lagash, Nippur, Kish, Eshnunna), the first historical inscriptions with names of rulers begin to appear as well as larger groups of texts (economic documents, e.g., from Ur, ca. 2650 B.C.; economic and literary texts from Shuruppak and Abu Salabikh, ca. 2500 B.C., approximately simultaneous with the texts discovered in 1975 at Ebla in northern Syria). The cuneiform script was being standardized and became easier to read and understand.

Early Dynasty II is the period in which as a rule the legendary-epic traditions around the semidivine rulers of the earliest period are placed, such as Enmerkar, Lugalbanda, and Gilgamesh. Kramer called it the "heroic period" of ancient Mesopotamia. From the Sumerian King List we know these men as kings of Uruk (according to tradition, Gilgamesh built the walls of Uruk), who obtained the hegemony at the expense of the northern Kish. One of Kish's kings, Enmebaragesi, left behind the oldest known, original royal inscription, likely to be dated in the second half of the twenty-seventh century B.C. The later prestige enjoyed by Kish, which was expressed in the title "king of Kish," and which afterward came to designate a territorial power expansion in northern Babylonia, may go back to Enmebaragesi's dynasty. According to the King List, Ur followed Uruk, with the kings Mesanepada and Aanepada, from whom likewise inscriptions have survived (e.g., at Mari). Most of these rulers are mentioned in a literary chronicle recording the building history of a temple in Nippur (Tummal), though not always in the same sequence.

The mythical-legendary traditions from this time must be handled very cautiously, as is evident from the presence of mythical figures (Etana at Kish and Dumuzi at Uruk) and the fantastically long rules (900 years for Enmebaragesi). Documented rulers, such as Meskalamdug from Ur (where his opulent grave, dating from the 26th century B.C., was discovered) and Mesilim from Kish (because of his power and prestige acting as arbiter between Lagash and Umma), are not mentioned in it, according to some because they did not possess the cultically determined status of "great king," granted by the central sanctuary in Nippur.

The oldest part of the Sumerian King List, containing the dynasties before the great flood, is hardly suitable for historical reconstructions. This is also true of the notion of the flood itself, which concludes this part, a part that originally constituted an independent unit and was later joined to the list. A "deluge" at the beginning of the third millennium B.C. is historically and archeologically difficult to substantiate. The pure sediment layers detected in various cities, which some have tried to link with the deluge tradition, no longer fit one chronological pattern. It is better to connect the primary literary flood tradition, reflected in myth and in the King List, with the tradition of a primeval storm and a huge flood wreaking chaos in prehistoric times, and realistically described in the myths on the basis of floods experienced by inhabitants of the plain over the course of the centuries.

That the first "post-flood" dynasty consisted of a series of rulers with predominantly Semitic names in the fairly northern metropolis of Kish may also not be used to regard the flood as a metaphor for the large number of Semitic population groups who at that time established their center of power in the north of the plain. The true element in this vision is that already early in the third millennium there were Semites in Mesopotamia, not only as seminomadic invaders but as an element that quickly participated in the power struggle among the city-states and shared their culture. Already Queen Puabi from Ur (earlier called Shub-ad) had a Semitic name, and a remarkably high percentage of the learned writers, responsible for the school texts of Abu Salabikh from

around 2500 B.C., likewise bore Semitic names. Thus it is very difficult to distinguish the cultural (older?) Sumerian element from the (younger?) Akkadian. Already early on there was a symbiosis and a growing syncretism, resulting in a "Mesopotamian" civilization. Religious and literary compositions, written in Sumerian, and even Sumerian names of deities may not exclusively be regarded as exponents of the non-Semitic, Sumerian culture. Though the significance of the Sumerian component in many areas should not be underestimated, it was not the only culturally significant factor.

The later phases of the Early Dynastic Period are characterized by an increasing power buildup in several rival city-states. The epic, "heroic" tradition reflects the internal power struggle, and the King List testifies to it by telling how the (theoretically) single monarchy—originally descended from heaven—shifts from place to place through military superiority: "city A was hit with the weapons; its monarchy was brought to city B." Archeological discoveries (e.g., concentration of the population in cities surrounded by big walls) witness to it, as do a little later the oldest historical inscriptions from Lagash.

From this state—comprising the cities of Girsu, Lagash, and Nina—we know, starting from about 2500 B.C., a dynasty of eight rulers (about seven generations), beginning with Ur-Nanshe. Inscriptions from Lagash, which we owe to an extended conflict with the northern neighboring state Umma (see, e.g., the famous "vulture stele" of Eannatum, ca. 2450 B.C.), provide the oldest historical documentation, so that Lagash furnishes the chronological framework for Early Dynasty IIIb. After Lagash had acquired supremacy under Eannatum, who ruled over great parts of Mesopotamia and called himself "king of Kish," Umma recovered and eventually (ca. 2350 B.C.) defeated Lagash. That was the work of the conqueror Lugalzaggesi from Uruk and Umma, who was probably the first to aim at establishing a territorial state. After his victory he called himself "king of the four parts of the world, king of the Land [Sumer]," invested with the kingship by the chief god Enlil, who "has put all lands into his service and from east to west subjected them to him." In a short time he managed to establish a

Mesopotamian empire in which "peace ruled" and "the roads from the lower sea [Persian Gulf] to the upper sea [Mediterranean] were safe." His political aspirations were taken over and carried forward by the kings of Akkad.

Better known than the conqueror is his victim, Urukagina (now read as Uruinimgina), the last ruler of Lagash, famous for his "reform decrees," sometimes regarded as the oldest known social reforms. These fragmentary, difficult texts, which certainly played a significant role in national politics and which also served a propagandistic function, show that the ruler had various goals in mind. The power relationship between temple and palace, altered in favor of the latter (annexation of temple land, employment of temple personnel), was corrected; a halt was called to the arrogance of priests and officials (levying of taxes and services, payments for cultic activities); social evils were eradicated so as to guarantee justice and prosperity for the subjects (whose support the ruler needed in his military conflicts!). In whatever way one evaluates the measures, social concern and desire for reform (in the sense of the restoration of the proper relationships as they were in the past!) cannot be denied him. His decrees gained a following. Their influence can be detected in the prologue to Shulgi's later laws. By presenting himself as "the ruler who made a covenant with [the city god] Ningirsu that the rich and strong would no longer treat widow and orphan unjustly," he eloquently articulated the ideal of social justice for the entire ancient Near East (including Egypt).

In the Early Dynastic Period important developments took place in the areas of political, social, and religious life. Slowly the monarch took on a more distinct shape, though the course of development—not everywhere the same—is not easy to reconstruct, especially now that it has become apparent that the epic tradition and the old kingly titles (such as *en, ensi, lugal*) do not offer as much of a hold as used to be thought. There was probably a development from a more religious, eclectic leadership, with priestly functions, to a more autocratic, dynastic kingship, with a political-military aspect, brought about especially by the power struggles among rival city-states. This development was accompanied by increasing social stratification: a great number of dependent people, working for temple and palace for payment in goods ("rations"), were dominated by an upper class who often pulled the strings of power in temple and palace. Beside them there was, however, also a class of independent landowners of whom little is known. Jacobsen assumed that at the beginning of this development there was a "primitive democracy" in which a council or a meeting of the people exercised authority and in emergency situations could delegate plenary power to a military leader. The increasing number of military conflicts would later have given this leader an increasingly dynastic power position. The arguments for this reconstruction are mainly derived from epic-mythical sources. A reflection of it would supposedly be found in the world of the gods where an assembly of the gods under the leadership of An or Enlil possessed the power to make decisions, and in crisis situations could give plenary powers to one god; according to *Enuma elish,* the so-called epic of creation, Marduk received such powers before his combat with Tiamat, and after his victory he became the chief god in the pantheon.

On a more national level such a structure has been found in what is sometimes called the "Sumer confederation": a "confederation" of Sumerian city-states that had arisen around the central sanctuary of the chief god Enlil in Nippur, for which some have used the term "amphictyony" coined by Hallo. A reflex of it is found in the Ur III Period, when the council (*puhrum*), notwithstanding the almost despotic power of the kings, still played a role as a forum for discussion and political decisions. A comparison might be made with Old Assyria, where the autocratic kingship evolved much later and where the "City (gathering)" traditionally possessed great natural powers. To what extent the "Sumer confederation" in the Early Dynastic Period was not only a cultic but also a political reality, whose leadership might possibly be linked with the one kingship according to the King List, is a moot question.

Kingship retained its religious dimension, as is best demonstrated by the opulence of the royal graves of Ur (end of 26th century B.C.), in which the buried kings even in their death were accompanied by scores of subjects. The king felt himself called and mandated by the deity, as well as gifted with power and wisdom, to labor for the well-being of his city and for temples which he had to build and look after. The "theology" of this kingship is expressed in royal inscriptions and especially in the many royal hymns from the Ur III Period and the early Old Babylonian Period, in which the king is pictured as the son of the deity, born out of the union between king and high priestess—many compositions devoted to the *hieros gamos* deal with it—and suckled by a goddess. Often it is difficult to determine at what point the historical reality yields to theological perspective, court style, and literary form.

The rulers and cities of ancient Sumer felt their mutual ties especially in the political-religious center of Nippur, the city of the de facto chief god Enlil (the heavenly god An of Uruk was the titular chief god) with the temple Ekur, "mountain house." Providing for the maintenance and the worship in this central sanctuary in Nippur—itself never a power center with rulers of its own—was virtually a national duty, as is shown by the building records, votive gifts, and inscripturated monuments of many kings. The council meeting of Sumer was held in Nippur, which could grant and take away the kingship and thus, as it were, give shape to Enlil's will. Until the second millennium B.C. a new king sought legitimation by being crowned in Nippur, where Enlil's favorable decision as to his fate and blessing were of essential importance. Also, the gods of the various cities, in order to obtain that favorable fate for their city and king, traveled from time to time to Nippur, in acknowledgment of Nippur's status and power. As late as the Third Dynasty of Ur this concept was embodied in a system in which the *ensis* of the old cities—now as city governors dependent on the king of Ur—in turn provide for the material needs of Nippur's cult; this situation induced Hallo to propose the term "Sumerian amphictyony."

### (3) THE AKKAD PERIOD

With the rise to power of Sargon of Akkad (ca. 2340 B.C.), the history of Mesopotamia took a new turn. After a speedy career at the court of Kish he established his own power center in Akkad—not yet identified but presumably situated not far to the north of Kish—from where in "thirty-four battles" he subdued his rivals and, after having defeated Lugalzaggesi of Uruk, united all of Mesopotamia under one scepter. In a few large campaigns he won battles in Syria (Mari, Ebla, the Lebanon and "Silver" mountains) and in the north and the east (territory between the Balikh and the Habur [Subartu], the Zagros, and the Susiana). In a short time he created a vast realm, a territorial state centrally governed, with a powerful monarch at the head, whose garrisons and governors (*ensis*), recruited from the Akkadian upper class, controlled the conquered cities. The realm prospered, especially economically: the campaigns brought in booty and indispensable raw materials (wood, metals, stone), the commercial routes were controlled from strategic points, and foreign merchants from the area of the Persian Gulf and the Gulf of Oman moored with their cargo at the dock of Akkad.

Absolute authority (with which, e.g., *ensis* were appointed), unlimited power, and great administrative responsibilities in "the four parts of the world" elevated the Akkadian kingship far above the traditional level. In his creative, ordering, and ruling work the king fulfilled divine functions, in competition with the numerous city gods, as is also shown by the fact that now for the first time he is mentioned in the oath formulas of the legal documents, as the one who guarantees the upholding of justice. In Sargon's third successor this superhuman status results in a kind of deification (not only posthumous), as shown from the way the name is written and the picture of the person of Naram-Sin. By calling himself "god of Akkad" he underscored his great power, especially that he ruled and watched over his land "as a god"; this was also a political reality, and one that was also found in the Old Babylonian period in self-designations of the king as "god of humanity/of his land/of the kings."

The tensions that the Akkadian kingship in Sumer or Nippur entailed, described in literary compositions, should also be viewed in this light. Though Sargon was of Semitic descent and was the first to grant the Semitic Akkadian status as the written language for royal inscriptions and administrative documents, the conflict may not be ethnically or nationalistically loaded as a clash between Sumerians and Semites. Apart from the normal hostility toward a rising political rival, the authoritarian kingship and the central government that put itself above cities, city kings, and local pantheons played a role because it was difficult to harmonize with the traditions of the "Sumerian amphictyony." An additional factor was that the cult of Inanna of Akkad under Naram-Sin may have become a threat to that of Enlil in Nippur. The political-religious countermovement this threat inspired was unsuccessful, but in the "Curse of Akkad" it produced an important historiographical text. The desecration of Nippur by Akkad is described as the sin of Naram-Sin, the coming of the destroying Guti as the punishment by Enlil. To what degree this picture is true is difficult to determine. There are additional indications of the conflict (e.g., in the Ishtar hymn of Enheduanna), but it is also a fact that Sargon and Naram-Sin honored Nippur with their votive gifts and monuments. At stake also is a somewhat schematic, political-religious interpretation of the historical event that portrayed Naram-Sin as a godless, unfortunate king.

He was the opposite of the successful Sargon, who was favored by Ishtar and whose reputation is shown by Old Babylonian omina and the posthumous cult of his image. His person and career spoke powerfully to the imagination, as is evident from the legend of his birth (as a forbidden child abandoned in the Euphrates and so landing at the court of Kish) and from his role in legendary-heroic compositions, such as "King of the Battle," in which he penetrated into Anatolia. Two later Assyrian kings adopted his almost programmatic name, and a later text enumerates the sixty-five countries and cities of his immeasurable realm. He made his capital Akkad a center of power, which became the embodiment of the more northern, Semitic element, and lives on in the term "Sumer and Akkad" and in the generally used term "Akkadian" as a designation of linguistic and cultural phenomena.

After a rule of about thirty-seven years, when the decline of Akkad began, Sargon was succeeded by Rimush, Manishtushu, Naram-Sin (the most important ruler, ca. 2270–2215 B.C.), and Sharkalisharri. Historical sources are the royal inscriptions (mainly preserved in later copies of texts on monuments at Nippur) and the "year names" beginning already in the Pre-Akkadian period that record significant events in the previous year. These year names remained in vogue down to the fourteenth century B.C., when Kassite kings began to count the years of their reign.

Using strong military force, Akkad was compelled to defend its position in many directions: against the frequently rebelling Sumerian cities, against threats from the west (Ebla and Arman in Syria; later also the "Amorites"), the north (Subartu), and especially the east (peoples from the Zagros and from Elam). The large numbers of those killed and taken prisoner, mentioned especially in Rimush's texts (over 54,000 in his campaign in Sumer), show the scope and intensity of the conflicts. Eventually Naram-Sin entered into a treaty with Elam, which gave Akkad more freedom to wage the war against the mountain peoples of the Lullubu and Guti in the Zagros and the "Amorites" or "westerners" mentioned for the first time by Sharkalisharri.

Especially due to the pressure from the northeast, the realm collapsed shortly after 2200 B.C. After the sudden death of Sharkalisharri anarchy set in: "who was king? who was not king?" is the way the King List expressed it. Nevertheless, the last two (city) rulers managed to keep Akkad for about another thirty years. A confused period began, which did not end until about 2110 B.C. with the rise of Ur III; limited information is available about this period. Little is known about the hated Guti, who according to the King List usurped power. Not until the ninth ruler, Jarlagab (who like some of his successors appears to have a Semitic name, which may point to cultural assimilation in northern Babylonia), does the rule of the Guti become better known. For about fifty years, which according to the King List still remained for this period (a total of 21 kings with 91 years), there were two other competing states in the south.

The first is a relatively unknown dynasty of Uruk, the second is Lagash in the south, under a dynasty of six rulers who ruled fifty to sixty years (about three generations), of whom Gudea is the best known (ill. 68). This heyday of Lagash—the conventional name of the state; the capital is Tello = Girsu; Lagash = Al-Hiba is the old residence which lived on in the titles of the kings and misled the archeologists; the state also comprised cities such as Nina and Urukug—must be located in the second half of the twenty-second century B.C., largely before the rise of Ur III. Weak Uruk and the Guti, who were especially concentrated in the north, left Lagash (which also controlled Ur) so much room that for a number of decades it could maintain itself as a rich and prosperous political entity, known to us from building projects, sculpture (especially images of kings), and texts, including the important hymn of Gudea dedicated to the rebuilding of Eninnu, the temple of the god Ningirsu. It is one of the most important old Sumerian texts (originally written on three large clay cylinders) and a source of linguistic, literary, and religious-historical information. Lagash's prosperity had a broad base: besides irrigation agriculture it also had commercial relations with the east (Elam), the west (Syria and Lebanon), and the south, via shipping on the Persian Gulf.

Lagash's period of prosperity—sometimes, rather inexactly, designated as a "Sumerian renaissance"—waned and ended about 2120 B.C. due to the pressure of the Guti from Umma, the rise of Uruk, and the imperialism of Ur. Uruk was the first to regain its power, and King Utuhegal boasted a remarkable feat: the expulsion of the Guti and victory over their last king, Tirigan, elaborately told in an inscription in epic style. The "liberator of Sumer," who restored the kingship and assumed Naram-Sin's title "king of the four parts of the world," subdued Ur and appointed his brother Ur-Nammu as governor over it. Utuhegal's success was short-lived. Ur-Nammu soon made himself independent from his brother and started Ur's irresistible rise to power. After the disappearance of Utuhegal, the defeat of Nammahani (the last *ensi* of Lagash), and the subjection of the remaining cities of Sumer and Akkad (e.g., Shuruppak) who had briefly regained their independence, Ur-Nammu was already sole ruler by about 2105 B.C. He adopted the new title "king of Sumer and Akkad." The Akkadian north and Sumerian south were united as equal parts of the realm under one scepter.

## (4) THE THIRD DYNASTY OF UR

This new dynasty spanned a little over a hundred years (ca. 2112–2002 B.C.) and was politically and administratively most efficient. An effective, highly centralized government, with a well-developed bureaucracy under the sole direction of the virtually absolute ruler, was introduced. Under the king were the military governors of the "outlying provinces" and the governors of the administrative districts, again called *ensis*. In these districts the old city-states continued as territorial units, with nominal recognition of the old rights of the city gods. The lower governmental apparatus consisted of a series of services, offices (for the militia, corvee, labor supply for agriculture, irrigation, and building undertaking), including large depots (for storage and distribution of grain; for cattle; for materials), and nearly industrial workshops (for wool and textile industry, processing of leather, reed and metal industry). Some of these administrative centers have been excavated, yielding the remnants of extensive bookkeepings in the form of tens of thousands of clay tablets, an inexhaustible source of information for this period. Especially the sites of Ur, Lagash, Umma, and Puzurish-Dagan (the modern Drehem; founded in Shulgi's 39th year as a central cattle depot) have yielded important written materials. From Lagash we possess, moreover, an archive of the city courts containing a few hundred records of court proceedings (called *di.tila*, "completed lawsuit") and some recorded contracts. They are an important source of information about laws and legal procedures around 2000 B.C.

Ur-Nammu and Shulgi were very active in promoting unity in governmental matters, labor organization, administration of justice, militia, calendar, and measures and weights. This deliberate policy in an extensive realm, with a non-homogeneous population and old urban centers with their own traditions and drive for independence, got results. Even though after the fall of Ur particularism asserted itself again, a governmental and especially cultural (language, religion, laws) unity developed that was the core of what later could be characterized as "Babylonian." "Sumer and Akkad" blended into a successful symbiosis in which it was difficult to keep the Sumerian and Akkadian (Semitic) components apart, as is evident from the interchangeable use of Sumerian and Akkadian (with Akkadian already being the dominant spoken language) about

2000 B.C., even in the names of the members of the ruling dynasty. The result, called "Mesopotamian," can from now on be distinguished from other, new elements, such as the "Amorite." That does not alter the fact that in the outlying areas, such as Asshur, Eshnunna, and Mari, native traditions, including Old Akkadian elements, were preserved. At a later time Hammurabi would give further shape to the cultural unity of the specifically Babylonian region; however, the politically independent Assyria resisted total cultural assimilation.

Ur-Nammu (ca. 2112–2094 B.C.) laid the foundation for the empire through conquests, irrigation projects, reclamation of land in the Persian Gulf, and internal extension of the administration. He engaged in building activities (temples) in many cities, particularly in Ur (ill. 69), where the temple tower (ziqqurrat) obtained its classical three-level shape, which has permanently influenced the picture of the "tower of Babel." According to the latest interpretation by S. N. Kramer, Ur-Nammu's son and successor Shulgi (ca. 2093–2046 B.C.) was responsible for the "Codex Ur-Nammu," the oldest known "lawbook" to date: a composition, preserved only in fragments, consisting of a lengthy historical and programmatic introduction and the remnants of (presently) over thirty rules. The king presented himself as an active ruler who worked hard for the material well-being of his people and who saw himself as having been mandated by the sun-god to bring about "justice in the land." That goal was accomplished through such things as freeing the laboring population from oppressive taxes and levies, the standardization of measures and weights, and guaranteeing proper recourse to the courts, so that the orphan, the widow, and "the man of one shekel" were not being robbed of their rights by "the man of one mina [= 60 shekels]."

These legal procedures are spelled out concretely in a series of illustrative sentences, partially derived from precedents, partially from the judicial tradition, partially newly formulated and pertaining to such matters as marriage, bodily harm, false witness, and cultivation of the land. The regulations consist of a conditional opening sentence (protasis) that states the case, followed by an apodosis that formulates the sentence. This is the so-called casuistic formulation, which since that time was considered normative for such juridical-scientific compilations, and which is also known outside Mesopotamia (e.g., in the Old Testament, among the Hittites, and among the Romans). Shulgi, himself likely inspired by Uruinimgina's formulations and ideals, has put his stamp on the legal tradition of Mesopotamia, because his exemplary sentences influenced later compilations in contents and in form.

Having been designated as crown prince at a young age, Shulgi acceded to the throne after Ur-Nammu's sudden death, probably on a campaign against the Guti. A deified, absolute ruler—for whom now also temples and chapels with their own priests and feasts were built—who had imperial airs now governed the realm, whose sphere of influence extended from the Mediterranean Sea (the ruler of Byblos was considered an ensi) to Elam (especially the Susiana), to a kind of pax sumerica that continued under his successors. In about thirty hymns, some almost epic in character, Shulgi was extolled as the ideal king who also possessed special sportsmanlike (running), cultural (music), and scientific qualities (he was trained in a school; the founding of the "academy" of Nippur is linked with him). He spent the first half of his reign consolidating his realm internally. In his later years he launched several military campaigns, especially to the east. About 2064 B.C. he reached an agreement with Elam, sealed by giving one of his princesses (who increasingly became involved in political marriages) in marriage. The war against the Hurrite cities and the people in Kurdistan and near the Zagros mountains continued to demand much; particularly Simurrum and Urbillum (Erbil), both in the modern province of Kirkuk, and the Lullubu were difficult to subdue.

During Shulgi's reign a new threat comes from the northwest: the Amorites (Sumerian MAR.TU), with whom Sharkalisharri had already engaged in hostilities. How serious this threat was considered to be is shown by that fact that at Shulgi's initiative a "wall" or defense line 280 kilometers (185 mi.) long was being built. This line, strengthened by fortresses, ran in a northeastern-southwestern direction, probably between the point where the Diyala breaks through the Jebel Hamrin and the Euphrates near

Lake Habbaniya. Our knowledge of this tremendous defensive effort we owe to copies of letters that were exchanged between Shulgi and his successors and their high officials, relating to manpower, maintenance, and repair of this "wall which keeps the Tidnum nomads at a distance." As historically important correspondence they were later copied in the schools, and they document the beginning of a process that eventually resulted in a massive infiltration of Amorites into Babylonia, where at the beginning of the Old Babylonian period they managed to capture the thrones of many big cities.

After Shulgi's death (through murder?) the realm maintained itself in its full size under his successors Amar-Sin (earlier read as Bur-Sin) and Shu-Sin, extending in the northwest to the Cedar Mountains and Ebla. Resistance in the north was quelled, and the inhabitants of this region were deported "as booty" by Shu-Sin and carried to a settlement "for Enlil and Ninlil by the border of Nippur." This is one of the oldest known examples of mass deportation in which the prisoners were given as serfs to the temple, a practice later also known from Egypt.

Under Shulgi's third successor, Ibbi-Sin, the decline began. Beginning in the third year of his reign, this ruler, who came to the throne about 2026 B.C., saw the power over the border provinces of his realm slowly slip out of his hands, as we can infer from the disappearance of texts dated with his year names in such cities as Eshnunna, Susa, Umma, Lagash, and Nippur (3rd–8th year). This crumbling was particularly caused by military pressure from Elam, Amorite infiltration, worsening of the economy due to crop failures, and the halting of the supplies from the provinces, as well as the growing urge toward independence by the governors. Ishbi-Irra, hailing from Mari, *ensi* of Isin, played an important role in this process. After Ibbi-Sin's military failure against Elam in his ninth year, he carried through his claims to power and soon consolidated his position with the help of the Nippur priesthood, for Enlil by means of a favorable destiny oracle granted him the royal dignity. It is particularly the copies of the royal correspondence between Ibbi-Sin, Ishbi-Irra, and some other rulers, later studied as "classical texts" in the Babylonian school, that shed light on this critical phase.

After an initial restoration, Ur managed to maintain itself on a small territory for some ten years, but about 2002 B.C. the city succumbed to Elam and the "Su-people," living east of the Tigris and in the Zagros. Ibbi-Sin disappeared (with the image of the god Nannar) to Elam and the city was destroyed. The miserable fate of the population and the temples with their gods is vividly portrayed in the famous "Lament over the Destruction of Ur." It is a theological reflection on and description of the downfall of Ur, with a central lament put into the mouth of the city goddess Ningal and presumably later recited at the ritual rebuilding of cities and temples. It is a genre that has had many parallels, including Jeremiah's laments. Ur had received the monarchy, "but an everlasting dominion was not granted it." The decision of the divine council put an end to its hegemony; the kingship passed to Isin under Ishbi-Irra, introducing a transition period, sometimes designated as the "Isin-Larsa period" or "Second Interim Period," which issued in the Old Babylonian Period, a name rightly applied by some also to the entire time span between about 2000 and 1600 B.C.

## LITERATURE

R. M. Adams, *The Evolution of Urban Society* (Chicago, 1965).

*J. S. Cooper, *The Curse of Agade* (Baltimore, 1983).

*_____, *The Lagash-Umma Border Conflict* (Malibu, 1983).

J. S. Cooper and W. Heimpel, "The Sumerian Sargon Legend," *Journal of the American Oriental Society* 103 (1983) 67–82.

I. M. Diakanoff, *Structure of Society and State in Early Dynastic Sumer* (Malibu, 1974).

A. Falkenstein, *Die Inschriften Gudeas von Lagash* I (Rome, 1966).

_____, *The Sumerian Temple City* (Malibu, 1974).

J. J. Finkelstein, "The Laws of Urnammu," *Journal of Cuneiform Studies* 22 (1968) 66–82 (see S. N. Kramer, *Orientalia* 52 [1983] 453–56).

P. Garelli, ed., *Le palais et la royauté* (Paris, 1974), pp. 141–232.

I. J. Gelb, "The Ancient Mesopotamian Ration System," *Journal of Near Eastern Studies* 24 (1965) 230–43.

W. W. Hallo, "A Sumerian Amphictyony," *Journal of Cuneiform Studies* 14 (1960) 88–114.

T. Jacobsen, *The Sumerian King List* (Chicago, 1939).

*———, *Salinity and Irrigation. Agriculture in Antiquity* (Malibu, 1982).

———, *Toward the Image of Tammuz* (Cambridge, Mass., 1970).

T. B. Jones, *The Sumerian Problem* (New York, 1969).

*J. Klein, *The Royal Hymns of Shulgi, King of Ur* (Philadelphia, 1981).

S. N. Kramer, *The Sumerians* (Chicago, 1970).

B. Landsberger, *Three Essays on the Sumerians* (Malibu, 1974).

S. Liebermann, ed., *Sumerological Studies in Honor of T. Jacobsen* (Chicago, 1976).

D. and J. Oates, *The Rise of Civilization* (London, 1977).

A. Parrot, *Mari, capitale fabuleuse* (Paris, 1974).

———, *Tello* (Paris, 1948).

E. Sollberger and J. R. Kupper, *Inscriptions royales sumériennes et akkadiennes* (Paris, 1971).

*H. Steible, *Die altsumerischen Bau- und Weihinschriften, I: Inschriften aus 'Lagaš'* (Wiesbaden, 1982).

---

## c. The Near East outside Mesopotamia

Our knowledge of the rest of the Near East in the third millennium B.C. is limited. Despite many archeological discoveries, our historical picture is blurred due to the lack of written sources.

In the east *Elam* entered the light of history already about 3000 B.C. with its Proto- and Old Elamite culture, which at an early date led to the development of its own script, the building of cities, commerce, and industry, as discovered at Tepe Sialk, Susa, and Tepe Yahya. Elam—and Iran in general—entered history by means of a limited number of its own inscriptions in cuneiform (the Proto-Elamite script soon disappeared again) and by means of Mesopotamian influence. During the whole millennium there were economic relations with Mesopotamia: goods not found in the alluvial plain (in particular stones and minerals) were imported from the east, either by way of the southern route through the Susiana or by way of the caravan route along the Diyala, Kermanshah, and Hamadan, with connections as far as Baluchistan and Afghanistan. In addition there were political-military contacts to protect the commercial routes and the movement of goods and to safeguard the area against threats from the neighboring countries. In this process Susiana was the most vulnerable because the plain was geographically connected with and open to Mesopotamia. It was repeatedly conquered, plundered, or dominated, but from its side it could also fight back, and even put an end to the power of Ur III (ca. 2000 B.C.). The northern border territory—Kurdistan, the Zagros, Luristan—harbored a number of cities and mountain peoples, such as the Guti, the Lullubu, and the Shu, who were a constant potential threat to the plain.

According to tradition, Gilgamesh had already traveled along the Karun and Enmebaragesi of Kish had made war on Elam, while Enmerkar of Uruk clashed with the Iranian city of Aratta. According to the Sumerian King List, about 2550 B.C. Awan took the royal power from the First Dynasty of Ur. During the Old Akkadian times we get firmer ground under our feet. Sargon subdued Elam about 2325 B.C., under the eighth king of the Second Dynasty of Awan (in the north of Elam), which introduced a period of increasing Akkadianization, as is evident from the inscriptions. Rimush mentioned his war with cities such as Barahshe and Anshan (recently identified with Tall-i-Malyan west of Persepolis; city and countryside play an important role to the 6th century, Cyrus calling himself "king of Anshan") and the spoil taken from these cities. Naram-Sin, also in order to free his hands against other enemies, made an agreement with King Hita (?) of Awan; the elaborate text of the treaty, written in Old Elamite, was rediscovered in Susa in the temple of the chief god Inshushinak ("Lord of Susa"). The treaty contained for the first time the formula, known from many later treaties: "Naram-Sin's enemy is my enemy, Naram-Sin's ally my ally." A marriage sealed the political relationship. From Puzur-Inshushinak, governor of Naram-Sin in Susa, we have a number of (Akkadian and Elamite) inscriptions, in which he mentioned conquests and battles, among others against Guta (the Guti?) and Simashki, which result in the independence of Awan, with the use of the Akkadian royal titles. Awan's hegemony was later taken over by Simashki (in Luristan), of which little is known.

In the following centuries Mesopotamian domination became an increasingly heavier yoke on Elam, Gudea having military successes as far as Anshan. Later Elam fell into the hands of Ur III, though faraway Anshan managed to maintain a measure of independence. Shulgi built a temple for Inshushinak in Susa. The contacts with southern Mesopotamia were numerous, involving intensive traffic of messengers and goods. Many Elamite mercenaries were in the employ of Ur, with a concentration in the boundary territory of Lagash, where they were under the command of a *sukkalmah*, a term which later evolved into an almost royal title. When Ur's power began to wane, resistance flared up in Elam. Around 2020 B.C. Ibbi-Sin was still able to quell it, but about ten years later Elam gained its independence and became a serious threat, eventually leading to the capture of Ur about 2000 B.C. by Elam under King Kindattu and the Su-people. Ibbi-Sin was taken prisoner and disappeared with the image of the moon-god Nannar to Anshan. Elam withdrew itself for good from the hegemony of Mesopotamia, whose culture, however, had put an ineradicable stamp on the land.

During the third millennium B.C. *Asia Minor* was still in the scriptless prehistoric times, though already during the Early Bronze II and III periods (ca. 27th–21st centuries B.C.) important cities were centers of power and economic development, such as Troy (I–IV), Alishar (8–6), Alaça Hüyük, Kanish (Kültepe), Mersin, Tarsus, Beycesultan, and Tilmen Hüyük. The royal graves of Alaça Hüyük (ca. 24th century B.C.) testify to the status and power of the rulers, and with the architecture they afford insight into the cultural development; especially striking is the highly developed metal industry (copper, bronze, gold, silver, electrum). Relations with the south (as far as Palestine) can be inferred from merchandise and especially from the widespread Khirbet Kerak ware, a black and red, very shiny pottery with

relief decorations. Especially Cilicia, the Amuq (in northern Syria), and the Euphrates were important connecting links. As early as the twenty-fifth century B.C. Ebla may have had trade connections with Anatolia; a century later the kings of Akkad penetrated to "the silver mountains" (the Taurus), and legend has it that Sargon in Burushkhanda (central Anatolia) came to the aid of Mesopotamian merchants. Among Naram-Sin's enemies were kings of Kanish and Hatti. The population of this area comprised specifically the (Proto-) Hatti, users of a non-Indo-European, agglutinative language, after whom this area was later called Hattum (from which the city name Hattush/Hattushash is derived). Not long before 2000 B.C. the Indo-European Hittites (origin debated) must have penetrated into this territory, whereby the city of Neshas (Kanish) must have played a central role as is shown by the fact that the Hittites themselves called their language "Nesian" (*nesili*). Not until the Middle Bronze Age, in the twentieth century B.C., did Anatolia enter the light of history, in the archives of Old Assyrian merchants who had settled near Kanish. Also the oldest proto-Hittite historical traditions go back to that time.

Until very recently hardly any written sources for the early history of *Syria and Palestine*—together also designated as the *Levant*—originated from these countries themselves, though some information came from inscriptions in Egypt and Mesopotamia. Discoveries at Ebla (Tell Mardikh, about 60 km. or 40 mi. southwest of Aleppo) since 1974 have changed all this. The extensive, now partially published textual material (about 7,000 cuneiform tablets, some of which are exceptionally large and well preserved) gives us a better insight into the material culture, religion, economy, administration, and politics of northern Syria and adjoining areas in the twenty-fifth–twenty-fourth centuries B.C. The texts reveal a highly developed urban civilization, earlier disclosed in its material aspects by archeological discoveries from Early Bronze III at cities like Ugarit, Byblos, and Hama. This urban culture may have had still older precursors, such as the extensive urban settlement at Habuba Kabira and adjoining Jebel Aruda (walled and with a temple complex), discovered north of Meskene on the

Euphrates, which betrays close contacts with southern Mesopotamia around 3000 B.C. (late Uruk Period). Also at Ebla there are, according to the excavators, indications of very old cultural influences from the south.

Ebla itself was the heavily populated, prosperous capital of an extended city-state with a flourishing industry (textiles, metals, agriculture, handcrafts). The zenith of its power seems to have been under Ar-Ennum, Ebr(i)um, and Ibbi-Zikir (the second, third, and fourth kings). The prosperity depended also on trade and the arrival of many goods, including great quantities of silver and gold as tribute, taxes, or gifts from vassals and dependent towns in northern Syria. There existed rather close political and economic relations with Mari on the Middle Euphrates, itself an important city in the Pre-Sargonic Period, whose dynasty—some rulers of which are attested in documents from Ebla—is included in the Sumerian King List. The nature of the relations between Mari and Ebla still requires further analysis, but it is not even excluded that Mari temporarily enjoyed a nominal supremacy over Ebla.

The end of early Ebla is usually associated with the rise and conquests of Akkad, some of whose rulers reached Ebla. Naram-Sin boasts of having reached and destroyed Ebla, and this would date the destruction to about the middle of the twenty-third century. This historical connection is not generally accepted, however. Not only are references to the kings of Akkad missing in the texts of Ebla, but also the paleographic and textual evidence, when compared with Mesopotamia, seem to point to a date about a century earlier. After all, several contemporary rulers and powers may have attacked this rich city.

The importance of the discoveries at Ebla, which still will require many years of patient analysis, is that they have shown that already in the third millennium B.C. Syria had a well-developed urban civilization that produced extensive written documentation. The script of Ebla is the Mesopotamian cuneiform of around 2400 B.C., and the lists of signs and words studied at Ebla to master the Sumerian writing system compare well with similar texts known from southern Mesopotamia and dating to around the twenty-fifth century B.C. Eblaite scribes recorded the in-

formation they wished to preserve in the mixed logographic-syllabographic Sumerian writing system. But the texts most likely were meant to be read in their own "Eblaite" language, as the many native words and Eblaite morphological elements reveal. Gelb has pointed out that the scribal tradition they embody links up with that of the Old Akkadian inscriptions from Mari and Akkad and in general with early texts from northern Mesopotamia. He assumes that this points to a common, non-Sumerian tradition, which may have radiated from the old royal city of Kish, whose influence apparently penetrated as far as Mari and northern Syria. It was used to write non-Sumerian texts, employed a series of logograms not attested in "native" Sumerian, and favored a far more syllabic way of writing.

Ebla's own language, Eblaite, is an old North Semitic language, related to later languages such as Ugaritic and Hebrew, but certainly not their direct or main precursor. Eblaite has remarkable affinities with "Amorite" and in particular with Old Akkadian, though it is not warranted to qualify it simply as an Old Akkadian dialect. We know the language from the many Eblaite words and elements which occur in the administrative texts, from a limited number of texts written mainly in Eblaite (letters, contracts, incantations), and especially from the many extensive bilingual word lists. These were based on unilingual Sumerian prototypes and were provided with Eblaite glosses, giving the Eblaite equivalent of the Sumerian words listed. They provide us with about one thousand Eblaite words, complete with vowels, as is customary in cuneiform writing.

Apart from the texts and handbooks used for mastering the cuneiform script, the archives from Ebla contain numerous administrative documents, lists and records concerning trade, industry, tribute, taxes, gifts, disbursements, personnel, etc. They will in due time add considerably to our knowledge of the history of early Syria and prove to be very important for linguists studying ancient Semitic languages and Sumerian. Their value for biblical studies, stressed in many early reports, has been exaggerated. There are, not surprisingly, similarities in vocabulary and in personal names. But "Eblaite" cannot simply be identified as "Proto-Canaanite." Even their impact on our understanding of the oldest parts of the Old Testament, the patriarchal stories, will be limited. The chronological distance is considerable (perhaps 500–700 years), and Syria cannot simply be equated with Palestine. Even though Harran, where Abraham lived and where his clan perhaps originated, may have been within Ebla's political and cultural horizon, we cannot assume close relations between a pastoral nomad and a highly developed urban culture (disregarding for the moment the temporal gap). The discoveries of Ebla will no doubt enlarge our knowledge of the language, religion, material culture, and institutions of ancient Syria, from which biblical studies are bound to profit, but we should not expect revolutionary results. Much depends on the question how much cultural continuity there was in the Levant in the areas of language, institutions, literary traditions, and religion. Some elements later attested at Ugarit or in Canaan may prove to have Eblaite precursors (such as the cult center of the moon-god Larugatu, attested in Eblaite records and, a thousand years later, in an Ugaritic incantation against snake bites), but they have to be carefully established and should not be assumed at the outset.

Apart from information from "abroad" and now from Ebla, historical data about southern Syria and Palestine during this period are largely lacking. The important archeological discoveries from the Early Bronze period, with its high degree of urbanization, do provide insight into cultural history, but they do not make the writing of a history possible—for that we need written data. Thanks to the excavations of Dunand and Montet and the Egyptian inscriptions they discovered, we are somewhat better informed about the history of Byblos. Egypt and Byblos (indicated as *Kpn*, in which the later name Gebal/Gubla comes through, modern Jubail) maintained close, though fluctuating, relations in the "land of Negau" between the Second and Sixth Dynasties, as is shown by dozens of inscriptions on artifacts (found particularly in the two temples known from that early period: the temple of the "Lady of Byblos" and the "L-shaped temple," later partially included in the "Obelisk temple"). The relations were especially of an economic character. From Byblos Egypt obtained

fine types of wood and resins (especially cedar but also pine trees) and some copper. Egypt's exports to Byblos included decorative objects of metal and stone, grain, linen, papyrus, ivory, and gold, for which use was made of *kbnwt*, "Byblos ships," a name for seaworthy ships. Byblos and Egypt also had religious ties. The casket with the body of the murdered Osiris was believed to have floated across the sea to Byblos, where at the coast it was enclosed by a growing cedar. Isis discovered it, cut down the tree, and brought her beloved back to Egypt. The myth shows similarities with that of Adonis, connected with the brook just north of Byblos, for whom Astarte wept, and for whom there was a central shrine in Afqa farther away. The city of Byblos, which existed already at the beginning of the third millennium B.C., was thoroughly destroyed about 2200 B.C.

## LITERATURE

U. Bahadir Alkim, *Anatolien* I (Munich, 1968).

P. Amiet, *Elam* (Auvers-sur-Oise, 1966).

A. Archi, "The Epigraphic Evidence from Ebla and the Old Testament," *Biblica* 60 (1979) 556–66.

*R. D. Biggs, "The Ebla Talbets. A 1981 Perspective," *Bulletin of the Society of Mesopotamian Studies* 2 (1982) 9–24.

*L. Cagni, ed., *La Lingua di Ebla* (Naples, 1981).

J. A. Callaway and J. M. Weinstein, "Radiocarbon Dating of Palestine in the Early Bronze Age," *Bulletin of the American Schools of Oriental Research* 225 (1977) 1–16.

I. J. Gelb, *Thoughts about Ibla: A Preliminary Evaluation* (Malibu, 1980).

W. Hinz, *Das Reich Elam* (Stuttgart, 1964).

N. Jidejian, *Byblos through the Ages* (Beirut, 1968).

S. Lloyd, *Early Anatolia* (London, 1956).

P. Matthiae, "Ebla in the Late Early Syrian Period: The Royal Palace and the State Archives," *Biblical Archaeologist* 39 (1976) 94–113.

_____, *Ebla: An Empire Rediscovered* (Garden City, 1981).

_____, "Fouilles à Tell Mardikh-Ebla, 1980: Le palais occidental de l'époque amorrhéenne," *Akkadica* 28 (1982) 41–87.

G. Pettinato, "The Royal Archives of Tell Mardikh-Ebla," *Biblical Archaeologist* 39 (1976) 44–52.

———, *The Archives of Ebla: An Empire Inscribed in Clay* (Garden City, 1981).

*———, *Testi Lessicali Bilingui della Bibliotheca L.2769* (Naples, 1982).

*M. W. Stolper, "On the Dynasty of Shimashki and the Early Sukkalmahs," *Zeitschrift für Assyriologie* 72 (1982) 42–67.

*E. Strommenger, *Habuba Kabira. Eine Stadt vor 5000 Jahren* (Mainz, 1980).

O. Tuffnell and W. A. Ward, "Relations between Byblos, Egypt, and Mesopotamia at the End of the Third Millennium," *Syria* 43 (1966) 165–241.

W. A. Ward, "Egypt and the East Mediterranean from Pre-Dynastic Times to the End of the Old Kingdom," *Journal of Economic and Social History of the Orient* 6 (1963) 1–57.

---

## 4. THE MIDDLE BRONZE AGE (20TH–16TH CENTURIES B.C.)

### a. Egypt during the Middle Kingdom (12th Dynasty; 20th–18th Centuries B.C.)

Just before 2000 B.C. Egypt was united under one scepter by Mentuhotep. It stood at the beginning of a new period of prosperity, the so-called Middle Kingdom, virtually coinciding with the two hundred years (ca. 1990 to 1785 B.C.) of the Twelfth Dynasty, which had eight rulers. Under a line of long-reigning, powerful pharaohs, political stability, an effective administration, and economic prosperity, in which also foreign trade played an important role, were the pillars of the realm. The dynasty soon developed its own character. A new residence was built south of the strategically located Memphis, near the present el-Lisht, also the site of some pyramids. The system of nomes and nomarchs was reorganized. Their office was practically hereditary and their power great until they were drastically curtailed by Sesostris III (ca. 1875–1841 B.C.), the most imposing monarch of the dynasty. From now on the nomes were centrally governed from three "departments." Finally, already under the first pharaoh, Amenemhet I (ca. 1991–1962), the system of a co-regency of the crown prince was introduced, promoting a smooth succession and training for the future king.

The crises of the "First Intermediate Period" gave a new relief to the monarchy. The nearly superhuman, idealistic aspect was overshadowed by the awareness of administrative responsibility and the care for the realm and the subjects, which demanded strength and vigilance. This awareness is reflected in the royal statues and in the literature, which has an apologetic element. In almost programmatic fashion, "The Instruction of King Amenemhet" (from the time of Sesostris I, ca. 1971–1926 B.C.) describes the duties of the monarch, from the perspective of the assassinated Amenemhet. His death is also the starting point of "The Story of Sinuhe." Sinuhe forsook his duty by fleeing to Palestine, but was finally received back into favor by Sesostris, who quelled the crisis. Sinuhe spent his remaining years in Egypt and was given a fitting burial. The ode to Sesostris's wisdom and forgiveness that introduces the last part of the text underscores the propagandistic aspect of this type of literature, an aspect also clearly present in "The Prophecy of Neferti" and "The Loyalist Instruction."

In conjunction with a different evaluation of the monarchy, a growing emphasis on worship can be noticed, evident, for example, in impressive temple-building programs of the kings and the growing number of statues of kings and high officials erected in the temples.

Central in the worship are Amon, with his temple at Karnak near Thebes; Ptah, whose shrine was in Memphis and who from there gained in importance; and Re, whose temple at Heliopolis received the special attention of Sesostris I. Beside this triad of great, almost national, gods, the cult of Osiris in his sanctuary at Abydos retained its important place as the symbol of the belief in the hereafter. The memorial stones, erected by many Egyptians along the road to the place where the "mysteries" of his death and resurrection were annually performed, bear witness to it.

The prosperity was based on agriculture, handicraft, and foreign trade. Agriculturally the partial reclaiming of the Faiyum, the large oasis west of the Nile in a depression in the Libyan desert, was very important. This reclaiming also resulted in greater worship of the crocodile-god Sobek. Information about life and activities can be found in biographical inscriptions, in some papyrus archives (the varied archive of Illahun), pictures in tombs, and since the Eleventh Dynasty also in the miniature images, "models of daily life," that accompanied the dead as a substitute for the detailed tomb reliefs of the Old Kingdom. Tomb construction in general and the large building projects of the kings demanded much manpower, organizational talent, and investments. We are informed of that by the Reissner papyri, as well as by the inscriptions of nomarchs and leaders of expeditions to the quarries, particularly that of Wadi Hammamat (east of Thebes). A text from the time of Sesostris I mentions an expedition of 17,000 men to get sixty sphinxes and 150 images. Together with the new pyramids at el-Lisht and Dashur, the predilection for the sphinx betrays a desire to tie in with the traditions of the Old Kingdom. During the Middle Kingdom, Egyptian art again reached a height of artistry and form.

Trade and foreign expeditions were indispensable for the economy. Important in that connection was Nubia, which supplied gold, copper, ivory, gems, and stones, and therefore became a target for annexation. The northern part of it was annexed to Egypt, as is shown by the border steles at the second cataract, erected under Sesostris III. Militarily the domination became visible in the building of fortresses at the borders, of which the most familiar are Buhen, Mirgissa, and Semna/Kumma. Egypt's influence in the south extended to Kerma near the third cataract, where it came into contact with the people called Kush. In the Eleventh Dynasty mention is again made of trade expeditions to Punt, probably the present Somalia.

The events of the First Intermediate Period as well as the presence of many "Asiatics," especially in the Delta area, made Egypt more receptive to contacts with the east: the Sinai, Palestine, and southern Syria. The trade connections, already existing during the Old Kingdom, were renewed. The interest in these regions is shown by the fascinating "Story of Sinuhe" (Sinuhe lives among the nomads, rises to the position of sheik, and experiences many adventures),

though the story is more a literary representation of the ideas current in Egypt about Retenu (Palestine) and its inhabitants than a real autobiography and eyewitness report. The bitter experiences of the First Intermediate Period also made Egypt aware of the latent threat from the east. Because of this threat Amenemhet I constructed the "Royal Wall" (also mentioned in Sinuhe), a line of border fortifications to stop the "Asiatics" and "to crush the 'sand dwellers'" (Sinuhe). The potential enemies are here indicated as *st. tyw* (Setyu, Asiatics) and the *hryw. š‘* (sand dwellers, bedouin) terms that together with the frequently used "Amu" designate the inhabitants of the eastern desert, the Sinai, and Palestine, though the precise distinction is not always clear.

The interest in the east was especially of an economic and commercial character. Though occasionally military operations are mentioned—Sesostris III made a raid into central Palestine, in which he reached Shechem (*skmm*)—there is no military subjugation or administrative domination. Only in the Sinai was the Egyptian presence more permanent, as is shown by inscriptions and reliefs at Serabit el-Khadim, because of the turquoise and copper mines. Clear traces of contacts with Egypt in this period have been found at Ugarit and Byblos in the form of inscribed objects, especially statuettes and royal sphinxes, presented by pharaohs to city rulers and temples. From early times both cities played an important role in Egyptian trade, for example, in the import of wood from the Lebanon. Egyptian statuettes and scarabs from this period have also been uncovered in scattered locations in Palestine, including Gezer, Megiddo, and Tell el-Ajjul. But such objects may no longer be interpreted as signs of Egyptian domination or permanent presence. Recent investigation (by Weinstein and Helck) has made clear that these objects came to Palestine through trade, especially in the Hyksos period; such objects have also been discovered in Palestine in more recent archeological settings. The persons mentioned are usually not military people, traders, or diplomats who could have lived and died in Palestine, but native Egyptian officials.

Egyptian domination of Palestine cannot be derived either from another important source from this period, the so-called Execration Texts. These are three groups of texts of diverse origin, inscribed on earthenware bowls and statuettes (depicting bound men), in which numerous princes and tribal chiefs with their cities are mentioned. Bowls and statuettes were ceremonially broken in an execration ritual as a way of magically breaking the power of these potential enemies. The texts are from the end of the nineteenth and the beginning of the eighteenth century B.C. The cities that are mentioned—Byblos, Ullaza, Apu (Damascus and surroundings), Hazor, Aksaf, Megiddo, Jerusalem, Ashkelon; many are still unidentified—were not primarily a threat to Egypt's presumed supremacy but for the trade that went by way of the *via maris* and the plain of Jezreel to Syria. See ill. 70.

After the death of Amenemhet III (ca. 1844–1797 B.C.) and of the first female pharaoh (Sebekneferu, ca. 1789–1786 B.C.), the Twelfth Dynasty came to an end. It was a period in which, under good government and economic prosperity, art, literature, and science (e.g., mathematics and medicine) reached heights.

## b. The Hyksos Period

The Thirteenth Dynasty, officially listed as having over fifty rulers who reigned a total of 154 years, forms the transition to the "Second Intermediate Period," the Hyksos Period. Changes in ruling monarchs and internal difficulties gradually weakened the monarchy and the central government, while in the Delta, where the "Royal Wall" was no longer equal to its task, numerous "Asiatics" entered Egypt. Also, in the south the border moved northward, to the first cataract (Elephantine). Initially, especially due to the powerful, almost hereditary, vizier system, the rulers of this dynasty who reigned in el-Lisht managed to maintain their power, as is shown by the inscriptions of Neferhotep I (who had contact with Yantin-Hammu of Byblos) and Sebekhotep III. The developments in the Delta, where independent rulers made their appearance (14th Dynasty) and the infiltrating Asiatics (sometimes because of their influential positions in the army and the gov-

ernment apparatus) gained more and more influence, limited the power of the dynasty, which after 1700 B.C. was pushed back to the south, with Thebes as its center.

It is in particular the Fifteenth Dynasty—which comprised six monarchs and from about 1670 B.C. usurped the power in the Delta and Memphis—that began to determine the historical picture and to which the name Hyksos is linked. The Hyksos have received a lot of attention, owing to their somewhat mysterious background, their Palestine connections, and the fact that Joseph's career and the arrival of Jacob's sons are often placed in the Hyksos period. Their name is a reproduction of the Egyptian *ḥq3ḥ3swt* (*hekau chasut*), "rulers of foreign lands," used already in the Twelfth Dynasty to designate Asiatic and Nubian princes and tribal chiefs, and now (e.g., in the Canon of Turin) applied to rulers who invaded Egypt from the east and usurped the throne in Memphis. Their name may also be related to the historically enigmatic Fourteenth Dynasty of "Xois" (*h3sww*), which apparently does not refer to the city by that name (modern Sakha), but is a name formed from *h3swt*, which indicates that it concerns here non-Egyptian rulers, probably for the most part independent Asiatic princes or vassals of the "great" Hyksos, and not so much their predecessors and contemporaries. Of the great Hyksos kings four are known from their own monuments. The names of the others we know from the tradition of Manetho. The best known are Salitis (no. 1), Apophis (no. 4, but also the name of two others), and Iannas (= Khiyan).

Who the Hyksos were and how they acquired power continue to be subjects of discussion. Scholars have proposed two opposite views of their identity. According to one view, especially defended by Helck, the Hyksos were not a "people" but a Hurrian *Herrenschicht* (ruling class), who through newer and superior weaponry and war methods (especially the war chariot and the composite bow) acquired dominion over the tribes and cities in Syria and Palestine and from that position overran the Delta, and thus established a new dynasty at Avaris around 1670 B.C. A link with the rulers and leaders with Semitic names who since the end of the Middle Kingdom operated especially in the Delta is denied. Opposed to that is the view, especially advanced by Van Seters, that essentially the Hyksos were invading Amorite groups, part of the highly urbanized culture of Phoenicia-Palestine (Middle Bronze II.B-C) who, in part supported by the Semitic element residing in the Delta, there assumed power.

The second view has more adherents and is based on better arguments. Hurrian elements in the onomasticon of the Hyksos Period are hard to identify, whereas names with the clearly Semitic etymology are not lacking, including names of the type Yaqub-Addu (especially on scarabs), which belong to the linguistic milieu that for Palestine was documented over a hundred years earlier in the Execration Texts. Also, archeology has uncovered a cultural link between Hyksos settlements in the Delta and Middle Bronze II.B-C in Palestine, especially with respect to tombs, weapons, and pottery. Generally speaking, Hurrian penetration and rule over Palestine did not happen until the sixteenth–fifteenth century, that is, after the actual time of the Hyksos, though Hurrian penetration in northern Syria may have occasioned shifts in Palestine.

Much uncertainty remains about the takeover of power itself. Helck's view of a military invasion, which ties in with the report of Manetho, stands in contrast to Van Seters's Amorite coup d'etat, carried out with the support of Asiatic elements in the Delta and dissatisfied groups of Egyptians (deprived of their power by the centralization of the government during the 12th Dynasty). Internal developments in the Delta through erosion of the central authority and infiltration of Asiatics had undoubtedly paved the way for the Hyksos and likely supported their takeover of power. But that did not happen without military violence, in which forces from the east may have played a role. Recent Austrian excavations at Tell el-Dab'a, the ruins of the Hyksos capital Avaris (not to be identified with Tanis, situated 25 km. or 15 mi. to the north), have uncovered a large burn-layer that separates the habitation in the Middle Kingdom from the Hyksos settlement. A similar observation has been made at Bubastis. That precisely at Avaris and at Tell el-Yahudiya (30 km., 18 mi., northeast of Cairo) evidence for the presence of the Hyksos has been discovered can be explained because they controlled the big connecting roads between the Delta and Palestine. Their material culture also points to relations with Palestine and Syria. Flinders Petrie named the large square earthen wall with the outward slanting glacis of the second city "Hyksos camp." This wall has been connected with comparable walls from the Middle Bronze Period II.B-C in Syria and Palestine, where similar fortifications have been found in cities such as Ebla, Qatna, Hazor, Dan, and Gezer. It should be noted, however, that newer investigation explains the construction at Yahudiya as an artificial terrace of a sanctuary (?), while the pre-Asiatic "Hyksos fortifications" should not be associated with the use of war chariots. The earthen walls did not enclose chariot or nomad camps, but the inhabited lower cities.

The Hyksos dynasty, comprising a total of six rulers with 108 years of reign according to the Turin Papyrus, managed to extend its influence over large parts of Egypt. The rulers living in Lower and Middle Egypt, sometimes with complete royal titles, were known in historiography as the "little Hyksos" of the Sixteenth Dynasty and were presumably local rulers and Hyksos vassals, partly Semitic in origin. This is also true of the princes of the Fourteenth Dynasty of Xois, and the indigenous Seventeenth Dynasty of Thebes also had to acknowledge the nominal supremacy of the Hyksos. With some exceptions (Khiyan, Apophis), the Hyksos kings themselves are historically hard to grasp, mainly due to a dearth of sources. That the later, hostile Egyptian tradition (especially Hatshepsut) regarded them as barbarians and violators of temples is not surprising. In reality, as is evident for example from their throne names composed with Re, they adjusted quite well to Egyptian traditions. It cannot be proven that they introduced the war chariot and the horse into Egypt, though it is possible (the oldest mention of it comes immediately after the Hyksos Period). The introduction of the fast rotating disk and the composite bow is also sometimes put in their era. In the Hyksos princes Egypt came into contact with a new kind of "Asiatic," not sheiks, tribal chiefs, or local princes, but militarily powerful representatives of the highly developed urban culture of the later Middle Bronze Period. This contact led to a growing receptivity for cultural influences from Syria and Palestine. At the same time it made Egypt aware of the need for an aggressive, military "Asia policy" for the defense of the eastern frontier and for the control of Palestine and Syria. These matters had a great impact on the military efforts of the New Kingdom.

The indigenous Theban monarchs of the Seventeenth Dynasty tried from about 1580 B.C. to extend their influence at the expense of the Hyksos king Apophis. Sekenenre II failed; apparently he was killed in battle, as can be inferred from his mummy. Later a tale was written about his dispute with Apophis. Kamose was more successful. As shown by the report of his exploits—the story of the "liberation war" recorded on two steles in the temple of Amon—he renounced the Hyksos sovereignty and conquered the Hyksos strongholds south of the Delta (e.g., Hermopolis). He did not manage, however, to take Avaris. That was done by his brother Ahmose who, after a struggle of ten years (ca. 1560 B.C.), ended the rule of the last Hyksos monarch, Khamudi, and pursued the remaining Hyksos who sought refuge in Palestine. After a siege of three years (as much an indication of the strength of the Hyksos fortifications as of the still underdeveloped art of subduing cities) the fortress city of Sharuhen was captured. After Nubia, which maintained friendly relations with the Hyksos and nominally acknowledged their supremacy, was subdued, the basis was laid for a new expansion of Egypt's power: the New Kingdom that begins with Ahmose.

## LITERATURE

J. von Beckerath, *Untersuchungen zur politischen Geschichte der zweiten Zwischenzeit in Ägypten* (Glückstadt, 1965).

M. Bietak, "Hyksos," *Lexikon der Ägyptologie* (Wiesbaden, 1977).

W. Helck, "Ägyptische Statuen im Ausland—ein chronologisches Problem," *Ugarit-Forschungen* 8 (1976) 101–15.

———, *Die Beziehungen Ägyptens zu Vorderasien im 3. und 2. Jahrtausend v. Chr.* (Wiesbaden, 1962).

G. Posener, *Littérature et politique dans l'Égypte de la XIIe dynastie* (Paris, 1956).

———, *Princes et Pays d'Asie et de Nubie* (Paris, 1940).

D. B. Redford, "The Hyksos Invasion in Tradition and History," *Orientalia* 39 (1970) 1–51.

T. L. Thompson, *The Historicity of the Patriarchal Narratives* (Berlin/New York, 1974).

J. Van Seters, *The Hyksos: A New Investigation* (New Haven, 1966).

J. Weinstein, "Egyptian Relations with Palestine in the Middle Kingdom," *Bulletin of the American Schools of Oriental Research* 217 (1975) 1–16 (see 213 [1974] 49ff.).

### c. The Hurrians

Especially from about 2000 B.C. some peoples and population groups, though already present in the Near East for centuries, became more prominent in history and in the sources: Hurrians, Amorites, and nomads.

The Hurrians are clearly recognizable by their agglutinous language, which is neither Indo-European nor Semitic. They were already present in northern Mesopotamia in the twenty-third century B.C., from where a few reached the south. We know them from brief inscriptions and personal names. Nothing is known of their prehistory, though it is usually assumed that they are from the northeast (the Caucasus region). Some want to identify them with the Subarians who lived in northern Mesopotamia in this early period. Apparently the latter were an old, northern Mesopotamian indigenous population, whose name was derived from Subar (later Subartu; the name lived on in such terms as *shubur* and *subrum*, which stand for a kind of slave). Sumerian texts refer to them as inhabitants of the north with a language of their own, Subarian. In the opinion of some scholars, in some of the known Subarian texts—old incantations—linguistic Hurrian elements can be detected; others, however, see links with the language of Elam. Though geographically Subar/Subartu and the central Hurrian territory largely overlap, it is a moot question whether the Subarians may be identified with the oldest layer of the Hurrians.

How the Hurrians called themselves in this early period is not known. Old inscriptions from Hurrian rulers use only terms such as "ruler [*lugal;* Hurrian *endan?*] of place x" and do not mention nationality. The current designation is based on the root *hur-*, which does not appear until about 1500 B.C. Idrimi of Alalakh spoke of the king of the *sabe Hurri*, "troops of the *Hurru*," and the Egyptians also started using this designation, which in the Old Testament continues as *hori*. It is likely that the Hurrians, arriving in northern Mesopotamia, assimilated elements of the older indigenous culture (perhaps also Subarian elements). This might explain why "Hurrian" elements (e.g., names of gods) are found already in the Ebla tablets.

Around 2000 B.C., in northern and eastern Mesopotamia, from the Zagros to the Habur, the Hurrians became a significant power that the kings of Ur III could not ignore. Known by name are some (or only one) rulers called Tishatal, who ruled over Urkish and Nawar, Nineveh and Qarqar. The kings of Ur III established relations with and undertook numerous campaigns against cities and city-states that bore the names (from east to west) Karkhar, Kimash, Shashrum, Urbillum (Erbil), Simurrum, Nineveh, Simanum, and Mardaman. From these positions they also infiltrated the south and west, so that in the Old Babylonian Period we also find them, for example, in Dilbat and Mari, but northern Mesopotamia remained their center. We know of at least twenty cities with Hurrian names from the time of the Mari archives. The Turukku, in the east near Shusharra, were probably also Hurrians. In the eighteenth century B.C., after Yamhad and Mari had disappeared as political powers, the penetration into northern Syria began, in which cities such as Urshu, Hashshu, and Aleppo played an important role. This infiltration process becomes clear from the personal names at Alalakh. In layer VII (17th century B.C.) they are already very much present, but in layer IV (15th century B.C.) they constitute a dominant element in the population.

From about 1550 B.C. the development runs parallel with the growth of a Hurrian state in northern Mesopotamia, called Mitanni (also designated as Hanigalbat). It was a power with international importance that in the fifteenth century B.C. stretched from Nuzi, east of the Tigris, to Syria, where Alalakh was a Mitanni vassal-city. Many Hurrians were in Ugarit in the fourteenth century B.C.; Hurrian texts, including a "dictionary," have been found there. In the more southern Syria and in Palestine princes with Hurrian names have been found in scattered places. This is, however, no more than an administrative and military upper layer; there is nothing like a thorough "Hurrianization" of the country. The old, western Semitic population always remained dominant, which is one reason why the identification of the Hyksos with the Hurrians is unlikely.

In the north, from the fifteenth century, the Hittite empire betrayed a growing Hurrian influence, extending especially from southeast Anatolia, where Kizzuwatna and Ishuwa were greatly influenced by the Hurrians. Hittite royal names as well as the many literary texts (particularly rituals) discovered at Boghazköy witness to "Hurrianization." Here and elsewhere it is clear that the Hurrians played a significant cultural-historical role. On the one hand they made their own contribution, and on the other hand they served as the link between Mesopotamia and its northern and western neighbors, especially in the transmission of writing traditions, literature, and religion (e.g., Hurrian translations of Babylonian compositions such as the Gilgamesh Epic have been found). In scattered localities, including Mari, Ugarit, and Emar, remains of collections of scientific and literary-religious Hurrian texts have been found, even in areas where Hurrian was probably not spoken, and from a period when the power of the Mitanni was not yet or no longer dominant.

## LITERATURE

I. J. Gelb, *Hurrians and Subarians* (Chicago, 1944).

"Hurriter," *Reallexikon der Assyriologie* IV (Berlin, 1972–75) 507–19.

E. A. Speiser, "The Hurrian Participation in the Civilisation of Mesopotamia, Syria and Palestine," in J. J. Finkelstein and M. Greenberg, eds., *Oriental and Biblical Studies* (Philadelphia, 1967), pp. 244–69 (overview with a focus on the Hurrians in Palestine and the Old Testament).

R. M. Whiting, "Tish-atal of Nineveh," *Journal of Cuneiform Studies* 28 (1976) 173–82.

*G. Wilhelm, *Grundzüge der Geschichte und Kultur der Hurriter* (Darmstadt, 1982).

## d. The Amorites

"Amorites" appear in the second half of the third millennium B.C. in texts from Mesopotamia, especially from the Akkad period (24th century B.C.). They are persons and later groups, called MAR.TU, a Sumerian logogram reproduced in Akkadian as *Amurrum,* from which the gentilic "Amorite" derives, with the use of the vocalization (*'emori*) used in the Old Testament. *Amurrum,* which almost immediately evokes "west," probably designated originally a people or tribal group (with the territory they lived in) who must have lived west of the Euphrates, in the Syrian steppe between the Orontes and the Middle Euphrates, having as its center the Bishri mountains (formerly Basar) and Tadmor/Palmyra. Gudea had already called this territory the "MAR.TU-mountains," and here, a little before 2200 B.C., Sharkalisharri defeated the Amorites. After that the frequency with which Amorites are mentioned increases greatly, especially after the Ur III Period, because of contacts with their territory through emissaries and trade and by references to Amorites penetrating middle and southern Babylonia. We find them as separate individuals who render services and as tribal groups living in the steppe between the cities. They are mentioned in ration lists, as suppliers, and as buyers of livestock and leather products. These Amorites, who for the most part had non-Akkadian names and initially were identified by the addition MAR.TU, were regarded as foreigners (there were "Amorite interpreters"). To the extent that they lived as nomads in tribal groups, they were distinguished by their manners and customs, which some literary Sumerian texts arrogantly and almost hostilely enumerated: they live in tents, do not know about homes, cities, agriculture, and burial of the dead, and are destructive and beastly.

Ur III experienced the massive infiltration more and more as a threat, and Shulgi's successors built the "Amorite wall" to stop them. When Ur III collapsed, especially people with Amorite names—generals and officials of Ur III, sometimes also tribal heads—started conquering the thrones in various cities, such as Isin, Larsa, Eshnunna, Babylon, Uruk, and Mari. They had such names as Sumuabum, Naplanum, and Yaggid-Lim. Therefore old sources and modern historians quite correctly speak of "Amorite dynasties," even though these princes soon assimilated the Babylonian culture by taking over names (Hammurabi's father had an Akkadian name though he himself had an Amorite name!), court traditions, and the Akkadian written language. There are no texts in Amorite, though a number of Amorite words are found in the Mari Texts, especially those connected with tribal structure and animal husbandry. It is even difficult to find Amorite elements back in the contemporary Babylonian culture. The *ius talionis,* expressed in the Code of Hammurabi, has been interpreted as such. On the other hand, the cult of the god Amurru is not in the least typical of the "Amorites." But the awareness of their "Amorite" origin long remained, as is shown by the "genealogy of the Hammurabi dynasty" and a number of composite royal titles.

The presence of "Amorite" rulers caused a complicated situation in the city-states of Mesopotamia. The state comprised the sedentary, urban, predominantly Akkadian element as well as the element originally related to the ruler, still living in a tribal context and in part sometimes nomadic in character. Rowton coined for this the concept "dimorphic state"; examples of it he finds in Eshnunna, Larsa (Yamutbal), Uruk, and especially Mari, whose kings not only called themselves "king of Larsa" (etc.), but also chief (*abu; rabianum*) of a tribe or tribal group. The latter can have a more general name, such as "Amorites" in Eshnunna, or be more specific, such as Yamutbal (Larsa), Haneans (Mari), or Amnanum-Yahrurum (Uruk). City and tribe were subsumed under one state. Culture, social structures, and political and economic interests of both groups sometimes diverged, but they were also complementary. Only slowly and only in part did they become integrated. Zimri-Lim of Mari—in connection with the question whether he will ride on a horse or on a mule—was reminded that he was not only "king of the Akkadians" but also "tribal head of the Haneans." As late as Ammi-saduqa's edict (ca. 1650 B.C.) Akkadians and Amorites were nominally distinguished, though the differences gradually faded. In this period the "Amorites" were no longer being distinguished by the addition of MAR.TU to their names (as they were especially ca. 2000 B.C.) and were often only recognizable by their non-Akkadian names, insofar at least as they had not taken on Akkadian names, something that happened early in some dynasties.

"Amorites" penetrated not only Mesopotamia from the steppe, but also Syria. How this happened is difficult to reconstruct due to the lack of written sources. From the time of the nineteenth century B.C. we know more names of rulers (from the Mari Texts; through data from Aleppo, Alalakh, Ebla, Byblos, and Hazor; from the Egyptian Execration Texts); but it is not possible to identify two linguistic groups, the native West Semitic rulers and the invading "Amorite" newcomers, perhaps due to the fact that by then "Amorite" infiltration had become an established fact in Syria. But the lack of differences also indicates that the linguistic, and probably also the ethnic, differences were much smaller in that area. There is reason to assume that in that region the "Amorites" had become sedentary much earlier and were no longer clearly distinguishable from the native population. Landsberger, who spoke of "East and West Canaanites," distinguished the "Amorites" of Mesopotamia from the inhabitants of Syria-Palestine, but his terminology also implied relationship because linguistically two related dialects would be involved.

An earlier "Amorite" infiltration of Syria-Palestine is very well possible, but for the time being it cannot be clearly demonstrated archeologically, linguistically, or historically. Perhaps the Ebla texts will shed light on this question. It has been rightly pointed out that in Syria one must reckon with the presence of an old, non-Semitic population element. The mixture between this element and the (Western) Semites happened at an early date, as is now apparent from religious data and the linguistically nonuniform royal names from ancient Ebla (ca. 2400 B.C.). The absence of such a non-Semitic element in Palestine proper and the impossibility of distinguishing linguistically the possibly younger "Amorite" invaders from the indigenous "proto-Canaanite" element are remarkable facts. This has induced some to conclude that this area was in fact the cradle of the West Semitic population, which need not per se have had a nomadic origin in the Syrian-Arabian desert. In that case the "Amorites" would be linguistically and ethnically related to this old population, though the possibility remains that younger phases and groups can be distinguished historically and linguistically.

One of these younger, nomadic groups of "Amorites," living in a tribal setting, is often given an important role in the history of Palestine. They would mark the transition between the highly urban Early Bronze III period (to ca. 2300 B.C.) and the subsequent Middle Bronze Age (ca. 2100 B.C.). The destruction of the cities would be due to an "Amorite invasion," and the perpetrators might be traced by means of the material remains in the large "cemeteries" that can hardly be associated with the nearby urban settlements. Included in these "Amorite invaders," who then gradually became sedentary and the bearers of the urban culture of Middle Bronze II.B-C (from ca. 1800 B.C.), would then also be the Hebrew patriarchs. This historical reconstruction is, however, being questioned more and more. As indicated above, it is impossible to identify these "Amorites" linguistically. Also, archeologically the situation is not as clear as is sometimes suggested, because the material culture of the non-urban invaders is not uniform, and because there are more and more indications that the transition from Early Bronze to Middle Bronze was more gradual and that the city population did not cease to exist. Moreover, it is striking that a similar destructive invasion in Syria is archeologically difficult to determine. In general there is a growing reserve against assuming such a massive invasion, and it seems more likely that the process was one of a gradual infiltration, though violent conflicts cannot be ruled out. The historic-ethnic equation of these nomadic infiltrants in Palestine with the "Amorites" coming from the Syrian steppe and who are to be distinguished from the indigenous, urbanized "Canaanites" is not impossible, but it is difficult to prove. If, as indicated above, one wants to keep open the possibility of the presence of "Amorites" in Palestine as a part of the older indigenous population, one may also suspect internal developments behind the transition from Early Bronze to Middle Bronze. It is the task of Palestinian archeology to introduce greater clarity into this historical process by means of careful analysis. For the time being it is better to avoid ethnically and historically determined names and qualifications.

## LITERATURE

G. Buccelatti, *The Amorites of the Ur III Period* (Naples, 1966) (see C. Wilcke, *Welt des Orients* 5 [1969] 1–31).

C. H. J. de Geus, "The Amorites in the Archaeology of Palestine," *Ugarit-Forschungen* 3 (1971) 41–60.

J. J. Finkelstein, "The Genealogy of the Hammurapi Dynasty," *Journal of Cuneiform Studies* 20 (1966) 95–118.

I. J. Gelb, "The Early History of the West Semitic Peoples," *Journal of Cuneiform Studies* 15 (1961) 27–47.

*P. Gerstenblith, *The Levant at the Beginning of the Middle Bronze Age* (Cambridge, Mass., 1984).

H. B. Huffmon, *Amorite Personal Names in the Mari Texts* (Baltimore, 1965).

*K. A. Kamp and N. Yoffee, "Ethnicity in Ancient Western Asia During the Early Second Millennium B.C.," *Bulletin of the American Schools of Oriental Research* 237 (1980) 85–104.

K. M. Kenyon, *Amorites and Canaanites* (London, 1966).

M. Liverani, "The Amorites," in D. J. Wiseman, ed., *Peoples of Old Testament Times* (Oxford, 1973), pp. 100–133.

A. F. Rainey, "The World of Sinuhe," *Israel Oriental Studies* 2 (1972) 369–408.

T. L. Thompson, *The Historicity of the Patriarchal Narratives* (Berlin/New York, 1974).

## e. Nomads

The nomads were another population element, though present in the Near East for two millennia already, who acquire greater historical relief only in the beginning of the second millennium B.C. Data from Babylonia (the "Amorite" dynasties) and especially from the Mari archives—from a city on the edge of the Syrian desert and with a "dimorphic" political structure—shed light on nomadism, which as a rule in documentation deriving from urban societies played a very subordinate role. It is important to be aware of the fact that "nomads" in this period (before the domestication of the camel) and in this area (not a desert land with oases, but a steppe area between civilized land with rivers on the one side and desert on the other) exhibited a number of unique characteristics. They were not the "classical" camel nomads from the Sahara, the Arabian peninsula, and Central Asia, who were less dependent on water supply and pasturelands, and therefore were much freer to roam over a wide area and were socially and politically independent. Nomads in the ancient Near East had small livestock, lived in the steppe and pasture areas with 100 to 250 millimeters (4 to 10 in.) precipitation per year (at that time with much more vegetation than now), moved from pasture to pasture in seasonal migrations that covered a limited territory (200 to 500 km. or 125 to 300 mi. per year), and maintained numerous contacts with the people of the civilized land. Their social structure was that of tribes ruled by sheiks or elders, but their manner of living exhibited an enormous variety. Besides "pure" nomads who lived in tents in the steppe, there were nomads who settled in the open areas in the cultivated land (e.g., between the Babylonian cities—"enclosed nomadism"), and tribes of whom part still lived nomadically while another part had become sedentary and lived in villages, engaged in farming. This diversity carried through to the social and political level. Besides autochthonous tribes and groups of tribes, who could be an important military factor, there were tribes that were integrated into a state (such as the Haneans at Mari), whose movements were controlled and who were subject to census and military service. In such a situation, the king of the city could at the same time be the sheik of the tribal group, but it was also possible that the more or less autochthonous tribe would be controlled by royal officials (*hazannu, merhu*), who had their seat in the main territory of the tribe, often in the city or village, where the part of the tribe that had become sedentary had its power center under its tribal head (sometimes called "king"). In such cases the political relationship was sometimes sealed by contracts or by the swearing of oaths, resulting in a kind of vassal relationship, often guaranteed by marriages or the keeping of hostages. There were also in-between forms, depending on the extent to which city and tribe needed each other for a good symbiosis and the extent to which the population of both was ethnically related.

Especially the political and economic relations with tribes and tribal groups are well documented in the Mari Texts. They show the administrative problems the king of Mari and his governors had with this element of the population, ranging from the highly integrated Haneans to the still largely nomadic and independent Yaminites. The texts mention the names of various tribes and of some larger tribal groups such as the Haneans, whose later center was Terqa in the "land of Hana," north of Mari on the Euphrates; the Yaminites, which included, for example, the tribes of the Ubrabu, Yahurru or Yahruru, Amnanu, Yarihu, and Ya'ilanu; and the Sutu, more often appearing in the first millennium B.C. Probably related to the Yaminites (originally meaning "from the right," i.e. the south, but found especially in the "Upperland," northern Mesopotamia between the Habur and Euphrates) are the Simalites ("those from the left," i.e., the north) and the Rabbu. Many tribes were spread over a wide area. Haneans were found from Assyria to Syria; tribal groups of the Yaminites, such as the Amnan-Yahruru (one example of the more often occurring double names), also settled in Babylonia, between Sippar and Uruk. Sippar was especially important, owing to its strategic location on the Euphrates, whereby transmigration, trade, and cult must have played a role. Suburbs or parts of a city (originally probably large encampments) reflected that meaning in their names: Sippar-Amnanum and Sippar-Yahrurum. The Yamutbal were found in northern Mesopotamia and in Larsa, as well as east of the Tigris.

The Mari Texts provide us with all kinds of valuable information about social structure, life-style, religious customs, and language of these tribal groups. Their language, especially known from their names, belongs to the West Semitic group and is usually called "Amorite." It is not possible to differentiate solely on a linguistic basis among the members of the various tribal groups. The Mari Texts also contain a number of words derived from their language, particularly relative to social structure and keeping of livestock: *gayum*, "clan, tribe" (cf. Hebrew *goy*); *hibrum*, "tribal group" (cf. Hebrew *heber*); *nawum*, a group connected with changing of pastures in the steppe, and a collective designation for flocks and camps (Hebrew *naweh*); *sugagum*, "sheik"; *q/kasum*, "steppe"; *hamqum*, "valley" (Hebrew *emeq*); *hasarum*, "corral, camp" (Hebrew *haser*); *hayarum*, "foal of an ass" (Hebrew *ayir*); *higlum*, "calf" (Hebrew *egel*); *hazzum*, "goat" (Hebrew *ez*); *behrum*, "(elite) soldier" (Hebrew *bahur*); *nahalum*, "to inherit" (Hebrew *nahal*), etc.

In this connection one cannot avoid the frequently asked question, Before the entrance into Canaan, was ancient Israel nomadic? The question is often answered positively, with a reference to Abraham's extensive journeys (Ur-Haran-Palestine-Egypt), his wanderings (*sahar;* not to be interpreted as traveling as a caravaneer), his great possessions in livestock, and his dwelling in tents. Moreover, the "nomadic" stay in the Sinai plays a role in this view. More recent investigation makes it clear that we have to be careful speaking about Israel's "nomadism." If it did exist, it was especially in the oldest phase of the time of the patriarchs, and in the historical and geographical sense as described above. In Palestine increasing contacts with the sedentary population can be observed, with more fixed places of abode (with changes in pasture, Gen. 37:12) and even changeover to agriculture, as is significantly told of Isaac in Genesis 26. A nomadic existence in Egypt does not agree with the account in Genesis. Therefore it is certainly not permissible to ascribe the profound changes that happened to Israel after the entrance into Canaan to the changeover from a nomadic to a sedentary form of life. What is true is that the keeping of livestock (with transmigration, pastoralism) and the tribal structure play an important role in that ancient history; the terminological similarity with Mari lies especially in this area. But these phenomena do not necessarily point to genuine nomadism; they are also found at Mari in politically integrated and sometimes sedentary tribal groups.

## LITERATURE

C. H. J. de Geus, *The Tribes of Israel* (Assen, 1976) (especially chapter III).

H. Klengel, *Zwischen Zelt und Palast: Die Begegnung von Nomaden und Sesshaften im alten Vorderasien* (Vienna, 1972).

J.-R. Kupper, *Les nomades en Mesopotomie au temps des rois de Mari* (Paris, 1957).

A. Malamat, "Aspects of Tribal Societies in Mari and Israel," in J.-R. Kupper, ed., *La civilisation de Mari* (Liège, 1967), pp. 129–38.

V. H. Matthews, *Pastoral Nomadism in the Mari Kingdom* (Missoula, Montana, 1978).

M. B. Rowton, "Autonomy and Nomadism in Western Asia," *Orientalia* 42 (1973) 247–59.

———, "Dimorphic Structures and Topology," *Oriens Antiquus* 15 (1976) 17–31.

———, "Enclosed Nomadism," *Journal of the Economic and Social History of the Orient* 17 (1974) 1–30.

See also the literature under "Amorites" and "Apiru."

## f. The Old Babylonian Period Generally

Important changes happened in Mesopotamia after 2000 B.C. The ripened symbiosis between the Sumerian and the Akkadian elements during the Ur III Period led to a fairly uniform "Mesopotamian" culture in middle and southern Babylonia. Sumerian disappeared as a spoken, and soon also as a written, language, though remaining in use as the language of science, tradition, magic, and cult. The schools aimed to preserve the knowledge of Sumerian among the writers and to record the literary legacy; especially the schools of Nippur and Ur were important in this respect. Old Babylonian gained the field as the common written language as far as Susa, Eshnunna, and Mari. Though the influence and traditions of the local pantheons and temples

remained strong, there was a growing supraregional religion, with corresponding religious practices, a number of almost national deities (Shamash, Sin, Nabu, Aya, Adad, Ishtar, later Marduk), and a constantly growing religious literature. Besides prayers and hymns, that literature also includes mythical-epic texts, such as the Atrahasis Epic and the Gilgamesh Epic, as well as incantations. In this period divination began to play an important role, especially that based on the inspection of the liver, as is apparent from the increasing role of the *baru* (diviner), the number of his reports, and especially the growth of systematic collections of *omina*. A more personal relationship to the deity developed, manifesting itself in new types of prayers (including penitential psalms and prayers in the form of a letter), in components of personal names (with expressions of confidence, desires, and gratitude), and in the role the "lesser deities" and especially the personal god come to have: they can intercede with the main deities and be more directly involved in the life of their devotees. Development in the conception of the gods gave rise to questions concerning the cause of suffering, to inquiries after the often unknown will of the gods, and to inquiries after human sins. In addition there are urgent supplications and expressions of confidence, especially on the personal level, based on the conviction that god as his father is genuinely interested in man.

The demise of the absolute bureaucratic authority of the state, coupled with the decline of the economic significance of the temples, resulted in greater prominence of private persons and families, with their possessions, rights, duties, and written heritage. From this period there are thousands of private letters, records, memoranda, and legal documents, relating to virtually all aspects of life: family (marriage, adoption, inheritance), possessions (purchase, selling, hiring out and pledging of slaves, movable and immovable goods), work (livestock breeding, agriculture, trade, commerce, profession), and society (within the civil, military, and religious frameworks, entailing rights and obligations). They afford a unique insight into the many-faceted life, especially of the economy, social conditions, and common law. There was a slowly growing but never total uniformity, promoted by inter-local contacts and a growing administrative unity, which reached a climax under Hammurabi.

There was economic interaction between the private sector and the palace, while the economic role of the temples decreased. To handle its governmental tasks in the areas of administration, army, irrigation, agriculture, commerce, farming, and textile production, the state possessed a well-organized and well-guided group of officials, renters, conscripts (invested with home and land), and other workers and dependents, whose rights and duties were protected by the ruler, as we can read in letters and "law collections." Private life and business also flourished, however, as we know from the contracts. The rights of the citizens were guaranteed by local law courts with the possibility of appealing to the palace, which considered the upholding of justice its task and which gradually extended its influence over the local scene. The various collections of ordinances ("laws") and the numerous records of legal proceedings afford us insight into the functioning of law.

The base of the prosperity was agriculture, farming, trade, and commerce. For the sake of agriculture many canals were dug (preserved in the year names) and new land was opened up. The canals were necessary because of changes in the water level. Apparently the quantity of water had decreased and the water was collected in a number of great watercourses, along which the population was concentrated. Moreover, the increasing salinization of the old arable grounds as well as the retreat of the western branches of the Euphrates forced a reorientation that required much effort. Trade among the cities and with foreign countries (Persian Gulf countries, Iran, Syria) flourished, due to private initiative and also through the mediation of state traders, acting as agents, whose duty it was to sell the surpluses of the palace and to exchange them for indispensable raw materials.

The monarchs, reduced to human proportions, were conscientious administrators, intent on safety, prosperity, and legal security, as we know from the large letter archives of Shamshi-Adad of Assyria, Hammurabi of Babylon, and Zimri-Lim of Mari. The social-economic situation as well as the political rivalry among the cities and between cities and nomadic tribal groups demanded watchfulness, and the control of the water also played a role. The military potential of the monarchs, especially the more prominent ones, was considerable, as we know from the letters. Movements of tens of thousands of soldiers over considerable distances were not rare. The technique of laying siege to cities was perfected by means of siege entrenchments, battering rams, attack towers, and tunnels. In the internal struggle for power diplomacy assumed an increasingly important role; support troops, royal weddings, diplomats, and spies, as well as solemn oaths and contracts sealed with sacrificial ceremonies, were of great influence, as we learn especially from the Mari Letters.

The kings were conscious of the social responsibility which they possessed as judge, landowner, and employer of the people who were dependent on the palace. In this period the kings also made attempts to help the disadvantaged, who in spite of everything threatened to become the victims of the shaky economy and social inequality. From time to time by royal decree overdue rent, taxes, and debts to governments, landowners, and moneylenders were cancelled (though also the temples, especially those of Shamash, the god of justice, tried to help by means of interest-free loans). For what they tried to do the rulers used such terms as "bringing freedom" and "effecting justice," but their measures were essentially ad hoc, purely retroactive solutions, which from time to time were unavoidable in crisis situations that might also be dangerous for the palace. The social-economic order was not essentially changed, not even by the so-called "laws," which were much more in the nature of codification, jurisprudence, and royal idealism than genuine reforms.

---

## LITERATURE

J. Bottero, "Symptômes, signes, écritures en Mésopotamie ancienne," in J. P. Vernant, ed., *Divination et rationalité* (Paris, 1974), pp. 70–197.

G. R. Driver and J. C. Miles, *The Babylonian Laws* (London, 1952).

T. Jacobsen, *The Treasures of Darkness* (New

Haven/London, 1976) (see especially Chapter 5, "Rise of Personal Religion").

*F. R. Kraus, *Königliche Verfügungen in altbabylonischer Zeit* (Leiden, 1984).

_____, *Vom mesopotamischen Menschen der altbabylonischen Zeit und seiner Welt* (Amsterdam, 1973).

W. F. Leemans, *Foreign Trade in the Old Babylonian Period* (Leiden, 1960).

_____, *The Old-Babylonian Merchant* (Leiden, 1950).

J. M. Munn-Rankin, "Diplomacy in Western Asia in the Early Second Millennium B.C.," *Iraq* 18 (1956) 68–110.

J. M. Sasson, *The Military Establishments at Mari* (Rome, 1969).

W. von Soden, "Das Fragen nach der Gerechtigkeit Gottes im alten Orient," *Mitteilungen der Deutschen Orientgesellschaft* 95 (1965) 41–59.

## g. The Old Assyrian Period

Though these developments did not bypass Assyria, between the twentieth and eighteenth centuries Asshur had its own political and cultural makeup. It is not clear whether this is connected with its early history, because little is known of that history. Influence from the south was strong in the second half of the third millennium, as shown, for example, by the prayer statuettes discovered in the "archaic Ishtar temple" (25th–24th century B.C.). Kings of Akkad left behind some inscriptions, proof of their supremacy in that locality. An important question is how the oldest traditions, preserved in the Assyrian King List, should be evaluated historically. This question is still unanswerable. That the names in the first group of "seventeen kings who lived in tents" bear strong resemblance to the list of forefathers of the Hammurabi dynasty, known from elsewhere, suggests that the list was taken over on the basis of a common prehistory, perhaps anchored in the figure of the Amorite usurper Shamshi-Adad I. The kings numbered 18–26, listed as "forefathers," were in fact the forefathers of this usurper, who sought to legitimize himself by means of the King List.

A period of independence followed the Akkad age. That is probably the period in which the rulers Ushpia, builder of the Asshur temple, and Kikkia, builder of the city wall, both known from the historical tradition, are to be placed. Later the city belonged to the jurisdiction of Ur III and was ruled by a military governor (*shagina/shakkanakku*). After the fall of Ur Asshur also became independent (ca. 2000 B.C.). In the period to about 1940 B.C. kings 30–32 of the King List ruled: Puzur-Ashur I, Shalimahum, and Ilushuma. Particularly under Ilushuma, Asshur's greatness and prosperity began, marked by the building of temples and a city wall and a governmental policy purposely directed to the strengthening of the role of the city in international trade. According to his inscriptions, Ilushuma lowered taxes or abolished monopolies to lure traders from Babylonia and the region east of the Tigris (to which he probably undertook a campaign) to Asshur. This is the basis for the important economic role that the city began to play in the next century under his successors Erishum (40 years), Ikunum, Sargon I, and Puzur-Asshur II, a role with which we have become familiar through the archives discovered at Kanish (now Kültepe) in central Anatolia, the administrative center of a network of Assyrian trade settlements in this area.

Old Assyrian trade is known from about three thousand texts in the *karum* (quay, harbor district, also trade district) of Kanish, discovered in the homes of the traders (10,000 texts, unearthed by Turkish excavators since 1948, are still unpublished). For the first time one sees here large groups of traders settled in trade colonies abroad. Their trading, predominantly the import into Anatolia of tin (for making bronze) and woollen textiles (from Asshur and Babylonia) and the export of silver and gold, was no exponent of military domination. Trade was possible because of contracts, "oaths," made by the Assyrian government—in Anatolia represented by "Envoys of the City" (of Asshur) and the administration of the core colony at Kanish—with the Anatolian city rulers. In the contracts the rights and duties of both parties were stipulated; foreign traders were allowed to live and work in special districts, sometimes outside the walls. Trading exhibited all kinds of facets, testifying to commercial and juridical savvy, sometimes resembling modern trade. There was an elaborate system of levies, tolls, custom duties for imports and transfers; promissory notes (transferable) and accounts of the traders in the *"karum* house" that could be used for "deposits," so that this institution almost functioned as a trading bank. Also, the rules regulating the relations among shareholders, merchants, agents, and commissioners, and the economic and juridical powers of the meeting (plenary or not) of the merchants (of which fragmentary statutes have been recovered) show how highly this system of trade was developed.

Thus during about 1920–1850 B.C. (in Kültepe-Kanish level II) Asshur was a flourishing trade city, serving as an international staple town, with a population of rich merchants and moneylenders. Probably because of this prosperity the governmental institutions of the city differed from those in the south. The "king" was not an absolute ruler, but first of all priest and vicar of the god Ashur (the "king" called himself *ishshiakkum*—the old *ensi* title—or *waklum*, avoiding *sharrum*, "king") and leader of the autonomous "city (council)," which possessed great powers and whose decisions he had to execute, giving him also military obligations. His power was, furthermore, limited by the eponyms, called *limmum*, annually appointed by lot from the prominent families, after which the year was named. The *limmum* probably had a religious function, and at the same time influence on the city finances, governed by "city hall."

Little is known of Asshur's foreign policy. The economic prosperity was disturbed around 1850 B.C. by the violent destruction of Kanish, while slightly later Puzur-Ashur II was ousted from the throne by Naram-Sin of Eshnunna, who for some time had Asshur in his power.

Following the brief rule of Erishum II, the usurper Shamshi-Adad I conquered the throne around 1810 B.C. He was of Amorite origin, son of Ilakabkabu(hu) who resided in Terqa (north of Mari), though originally he may have come from the Habur region, where he had his base in the city of Shubat-Enlil. According to tradition, from northern Babylonia he thrust through to Assyria, where after some years, from Ekallatum, he conquered the throne of Asshur. He was a capable and energetic ruler, quite familiar to us from the Mari archives and texts from Shusharra east of the Tigris. His activities brought new greatness and prosperity for Assyria, but at the same time meant a break with the traditions of the past. Assyrian "democracy" could not cope with this potentate, who took the royal title and turned the city-state into a territorial state with a more centralized government. He acquired greater control over the trade and appointed his crown prince as an eponym. During his time the temple of Asshur acquired its standard form, but he also worshiped the southern god Enlil with a temple and *ziqqurrat*. It is remarkable that his inscriptions were written in Babylonian and not in the Assyrian dialect.

Through conquests Shamshi-Adad extended his power to include the largest part of northern Mesopotamia, from Shusharra in the east to Carchemish and Mari in the west. His younger son Yasmah-Addu received the throne of Mari. Assyria itself was ruled by his oldest son, Ishme-Dagan, from Ekallatum. The eastern flank of the empire he had to defend against Eshnunna and the dangerous Turukku, a Hurrian (?) threat from the Zagros. In the west the territory of the state of Aleppo, ruled by Yarim-Lim, was the political border, while in the south the rising power of Babylon kept his aspirations in check. It was a period of military tensions; the sources mention armies of tens of thousands of soldiers. Trade flourished from Mari (along the Euphrates) as well as from Asshur. The commercial ties with Anatolia were renewed, as is shown by the finds at Kanish I.B and elsewhere in Anatolia (bullae with Shamshi-Adad's name have been found at Açemhüyük). By about 1800 Assyria had evolved into one of the most powerful nations in the Near East.

## LITERATURE

M. Anbar, "Le début du règne de Shamshi-Addu Ier," *Israel Oriental Studies* 3 (1974) 1–33.

P. Garelli, *Les Assyriens en Capppadoce* (Paris, 1963).

A. K. Grayson, *Assyrian Royal Inscriptions* I (Wiesbaden, 1972), 1–28.

———, "The Early Development of Assyrian Monarchy," *Ugarit-Forschungen* 3 (1971) 311–20.

J. Laessoe, *People of Ancient Assyria* (London, 1963).

M. Trolle Larsen, *The Old Assyrian City-State and Its Colonies* (Copenhagen, 1976).

## h. The "Isin-Larsa" Period (ca. 2000–1800 B.C.)

Under Ishbi-Erra, Isin proclaimed itself the sure successor of Ur shortly before 2000 B.C. Forms and traditions of Ur were maintained: royal titles, royal hymns, ceremonies (*hieros gamos*; crowning at Nippur), building and irrigation works, also inscriptions in Sumerian, such as the "Laws of Lipit-Ishtar," of which fragments remain. Though having a limited territory, Isin under Idin-Dagan (ca. 1960 B.C.), Ishme-Dagan (ca. 1940 B.C.), and Lipit-Ishtar (ca. 1930 B.C.)—all known from inscriptions, year names, and royal hymns—managed to maintain its supremacy at least to the final quarter of the twentieth century B.C. Then its rival Larsa in southern Babylonia (according to its king list it had become independent ca. 2000 B.C. under the Amorite Naplanum) became a serious threat under Gungunum (ca. 1930–1905 B.C.). Larsa developed itself through irrigation projects and also derived its prosperity from the sea trade on the Persian Gulf, which had been secured by Gungunum's conquest of Ur. About 1900 B.C. his successor Abisare defeated Ur-Ninurta of Isin, which resulted in a protracted power struggle in which Isin attempted to underscore its claims to the "kingship of Sumer and Akkad" by means of a final recension of the Sumerian King List that now ends with the dynasty of Isin. This was the beginning of a century of political fragmentation and struggle between rival city-states. Numerous small city-states arose in the military and politico-ideological power vacuum (especially in northern Babylonia), mainly ruled over by kings with Amorite names. Worthy of mention are Uruk, Kisurra, Der, Tutub, Kish, Marad, Kazallu, Malgium, and Sippar.

In the northeast, Eshnunna under Ituriya had gained its independence already before 2000 B.C.

To the end of the nineteenth century we know by name twenty rulers from that region, who initially called themselves "city prince of Eshnunna," avoiding the royal title reserved for the city god Tishpak, "king of (the land) Warum." Ipiq-Adad (ca. 1860 B.C.) became the first to take on the royal title. Historical data are scarce; the thorough American excavations have unearthed virtually no historical inscriptions of significant length, while most of the letters and records are still unpublished. Only the many year names give information about the history of the state, which about 1920 B.C. lost much of its power when Tutub (modern Khafaji, known for its temple to the moon-god Sin) became independent under a line of rulers with Amorite names. About 1840 B.C. an expansion of power began to which the names of Naram-Sin (ca. 1820 B.C.) and Dadusha (ca. 1800 B.C.) are linked. The former penetrated to the Euphrates near Rapiqum (strategic on the trade route along the Euphrates) and probably also conquered Asshur. The latter took Mankisum and Ekallatum, both strategically situated on the Tigris. Dadusha is known especially for the "Laws of Eshnunna," stemming from the time of his reign, a collection of tariffs and legal regulations (60 sections) written in Akkadian, and in places substantively related to Hammurabi's laws.

Shortly after 1900 B.C. Babylon (Babylonian *bab-ilim*, "gate of the god," a prestigious popular etymology of a name appearing under Ur III as Pabila) appeared on the scene as an independent state. Until about 1800 B.C. not much is known about the history of city and state, especially due to the lack of royal inscriptions (the Old Babylonian layers of Babylon lie on a branch of the Euphrates below the water level). Year names—virtually all of them known—are the most important source. They show that Babylon's gradual rise began under its second ruler, Sumulael (ca. 1880–1845 B.C., successor of Sumuabum, ca. 1894–1880), regarded by the later kings as founder of the dynasty. Through varying military successes and cautious maneuvering Babylon gradually, to about 1800 B.C., extended its power to large parts of northern Babylonia. Cities such as Dilbat, Kutha, Sippar, Kish, and Kazallu, which earlier still had rulers of their own or other rulers in between, were conquered. Sabium (ca. 1844–1830 B.C.) and Apil-Sin (ca. 1830–1812 B.C.) advanced the realm, which through the building of fortresses was consolidated by Sin-muballit (ca. 1812–1792 B.C.). His attempts to extend the territory to the south met with little success. A coalition among him, Isin, and Uruk was defeated by Rim-Sin of Larsa. A conquest of Isin had no permanent result. For the time being Babylon was forced to acknowledge Larsa as its superior.

In the south, Uruk associated with the tribal group of the Amnanum, managed under Sin-kashid to break away from Isin about 1865 B.C. Living on a limited territory the city was able to withstand the pressure of Larsa until 1802 B.C., when it was conquered. It was often supported by Babylon, because both city-states, as King "Anam" wrote in a letter to Sin-muballit, were "one house." This points to genealogical relationships with the same Amorite tribal group and to marriage ties, established when Sin-kashid married Sumulael's daughter.

In the center of Babylonia, the old rivals Larsa and Isin kept each other at bay for the time being, especially because Larsa went through a military and economic crisis under Nur-Adad (ca. 1865–1849 B.C.) and Isin lost its power over Uruk. Neither managed to come out on top. Within the space of two decades the ownership of the cultic center Nippur changed hands six times. A real shift in power took place around 1835 B.C. when the presumably Amorite tribal chief with an Elamite name, Kudur-mabuk, conquered the city of Larsa, together with its territory called Yamutbal. His son Warad-Sin took the throne and ruled till about 1822 B.C. Larsa's power crisis was slowly overcome, especially under Warad-Sin's brother and successor Rim-Sin, whose long reign (ca. 1822–1763 B.C.) was a period of prosperity, marked by a flourishing trade, a policy of land reclamation, and irrigation projects, made necessary by changes in the water level of the eastern branch of the Euphrates and because part of the old cultivated land had become salinated. Around 1794 B.C. he conquered Isin decisively, an event to which he ascribed great importance as is evident from the fact that he named the next thirty years of his reign after this military feat (thereby also depriving us of the historical information that is normally contained in year names!).

In the east, Susa managed to break free from Ur already before 2000 B.C. The realm, whose boundaries are not precisely known, was ruled by a dynasty that hailed from Simash, who called themselves *sukkalmah*, using the official title stemming from the Ur III Period (other dignitaries were the *sukkal*, "vizier of Elam and Simalh," a younger brother of the ruler, and the *sukkal* of Susa, the son of the ruler). The family structure was apparently fratriarchal, for the ruler was succeeded by his brother. We know the rulers of this dynasty and its successor (ca. 1850 B.C.) from a series of brief Akkadian votive inscriptions, which, like a few hundred legal documents and letters, testify to the depth of Mesopotamian influence, both in the language and in the legal system. It was not until centuries later that the Elamite language was again written (in cuneiform). In this period Elam established a position of power, whose influence could sometimes be felt as far as northern Mesopotamia, as is shown by the Mari archives and the texts from Shusharra.

In the far west, Mari began to flourish. This city, with a long history and a rich culture reaching back to the pre-Sargonic era, had belonged to the realm of Ur III, being ruled as a border province by a military governor, called *shagina* (Akkadian *shakkanakku*). Even after the downfall of Ur the by then presumably independent ruler continued to have this title. We know some of these rulers from the period 2000–1850 B.C. by name, thanks to brief votive and seal inscriptions: Isi-Dagan, Tura-Dagan, and Puzur-Ishtar. Their names reflect the great veneration of the old West Semitic god Dagan, whose cultic center was at Tuttul (where the Balikh enters the Euphrates) and who at Mari and Terqa was regarded as the "god of the land." According to the royal names, the dynasty of Isin also venerated this god, thus having a tie with traditions from the Akkad period, a tie suggested also by the fact that Isin's first king, Ishbi-Erra, hailed from Mari.

Around 1840 B.C. a new dynasty, Amorite as indicated by the names, came to the throne; its second ruler, Yahdun-Lim (ca. 1825–1810 B.C.), contributed especially to Mari's prosperity. Two long inscriptions from Yahdun-Lim mention his great deeds and military campaigns (to the "cedar mountains" and the "Great Sea") and the territorial expansion to the north, especially at the

78. *A drawing of a relief from the mortuary temple of Ramses III at Medinet Habu with a reproduction of a naval battle with the Sea Peoples (ca. 1185 B.C.; see pp. 277–79). The Sea Peoples, in boats with a large sail, armed with long swords and round shields, and having horned helmets (Sherden?) or a hairdo supported by a head band (Philistines?) are defeated by the Egyptians.*

79. *A drawing of a Hittite relief from the rock sanctuary Yazilikaya at Boghazköy: King Tudhaliash IV (?) in cultic garments in the protective embrace of the god Sharruma (13th century B.C.). See pp. 275–76.*

80. *An anthropoid clay sarcophagus from Beth-shean (ca. 12th century B.C.). The hairdo shown in relief resembles that of the "Philistines"; it is possible that the relief concerns an Egyptian-style interment of someone of the Egyptian garrison there who was one of the "Sea Peoples." See pp. 277–78.*

81. *A Babylonian* kudurru *or boundary stone, with the text of a land gift by Nebuchadrezzar I (end of the 12th century B.C.) to his officer Sitti-Marduk. The facet pictured here shows the symbols of the gods, who in the imprecatory formula are called upon as guarantors of the gift. See pp. 280–81.* (Trustees of the British Museum)

82. *An engraved ivory lid from Megiddo with a representation of a Palestinian king from the 13th(?) century B.C. Seated on his throne he celebrates his victory by receiving his triumphal army commander (with prisoners), preceded by a (royal) lady, who offers him a drink and a lotus flower, and a lyre player. (Oriental Institute, University of Chicago)*

74. *Conquered kings from Syria, Libya, and Nubia on a relief from the tomb of Horemheb (ca. 1320 B.C.; Leiden, National Museum of Antiquities). See pp. 259–60.*

75. *An Ugaritic clay tablet with the Akkadian text of an agreement between Ini-Teshub of Carchemish (with imprint of his bilingual seal) and the "men of Ugarit" concerning compensations to be paid in case of the murder of a citizen of one of the two states inside the territory of the other (RS 17.230; cf. C. F. A. Schaeffer,* Le Palais royal d'Ugarit, *IV, 153–54; 13th century B.C.).*

77. *The acropolis or fortress of Boghazköy, Buyukkale, in the 13th century B.C.*

76. *Ramses II cutting down his Asiatic prisoners (relief from the large temple at Abu Simbel). See p. 275.*

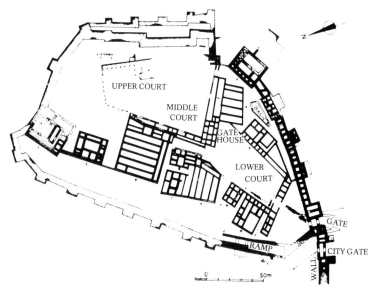

70. A terra-cotta figure of an Egyptian imprecatory text from the Middle Kingdom (12th Dynasty; ca. 1800 B.C.; see G. Posener, Princes et Pays d'Asie et de Nubie [1940], no. 2; Brussels E 7442). See pp. 230–31.

71. The central panel (redrawn) of the murals in the court 106 of the palace at Mari (see ill.72), with a reproduction of the investiture of a king (Zimri-Lim?) by the goddess Ishtar, who hands him a ring and staff, the symbols of kingship. See p. 245.

72. The monumental palace of Zimri-Lim at Mari (18th century B.C.) in a perspectival reconstruction; in the center is court 106 with the mural of the investiture. See p. 245 and ill.71.

73. A statue of King Idrimi of Alalakh (ca. 1500 B.C.) with the text of his unique life history (photo Trustees of the British Museum). See pp. 260–61.

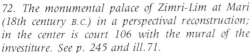

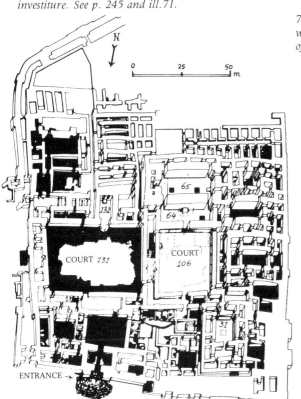

66. A copy of the Assyrian King List owned by the Seventh Day Adventist Theological Seminary in Washington (front: the list can be turned over like a calendar); it enumerates the kings up to and including Shalmaneser V (727–722 B.C.). See p. 211.

67. A copy of the Palermo Stone (front) with the royal names and events during the Pre-Dynastic period and the first Egyptian dynasties. See p. 209.

69. Aerial photo of excavations at Ur, with the view of the temenos; the dark spot, upper left, is the tower temple or ziqqurat; to the right of it is the large temple court.

68. Statue of Gudea of Lagash (Louvre, Paris, AO 2), holding on his knees a stone slab with the ground plan of a temple to be built by him. See pp. 221–22.

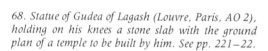

expense of the seminomadic Haneans in the Euphrates and Balikh valley and by means of irrigation works along the Euphrates. His great rival in a serious power struggle for the supremacy over northern Mesopotamia was Shamshi-Adad I of Assyria. Already at that time Mari, strategically located, must have profited from the receipts from the international transit-trade along the Euphrates route, which connected Mesopotamia, the Persian Gulf, and Elam with Syria, Anatolia, and the Mediterranean Sea region. After Yahdun-Lim's death (ca. 1800 B.C.) and the obscure Sumuyamam, Mari was seized by Shamshi-Adad I, who made it a province of his realm, soon ruled over by his son Yasmah-Addu, who had the throne for about ten years. Zimri-Lim lived as a fugitive at the court of Aleppo, where King Yarim-Lim offered him asylum and through marriage with his daughter made him an ally, in anticipation of better times. Those broke shortly after 1780 B.C. when Zimri-Lim, with the aid of Aleppo, managed to overthrow the Assyrian rule, which had been weakened by Shamshi-Adad's death and the attack by Eshnunna (ill. 71, 72).

## LITERATURE

*D. Arnaud, et al., "Larsa," *Reallexikon der Assyriologie* VI (Berlin, 1983) 496–506.

D. O. Ezward, *Die 'Zweite Zwischenzeit' Babyloniens* (Wiesbaden, 1957).

J. J. Finkelstein, "The Genealogy of the Hammurapi Dynasty," *Journal of Cuneiform Studies* 20 (1966) 95–118.

W. H. Ph. Römer, *Sumerische 'Königshymnen' der Isin-Zeit* (Leiden, 1965).

E. Sollberger and J. R. Kupper, *Inscriptions royales sumériennes et akkadiennes* (Paris, 1971).

## i. Hammurabi and His Dynasty; the Coming of the Kassites (ca. 1800–1500 B.C.)

The beginning of the eighteenth century B.C. was for Mesopotamia a period of a power equilibrium. The nations mentioned in the previous section governed the political scene, each with its vassals and large army. The situation is stated to the point in a letter to Zimri-Lim of Mari: "No king is powerful by himself; ten to twenty kings follow Hammurabi of Babylon, just as many Rim-Sin of Larsa, just as many Ibalpiel of Eshnunna, just as many Amutpiel of Qatna, and twenty follow Yarim-Lim of Yamhad [Aleppo]." To this series belongs also Zimri-Lim, who from his impressive palace at Mari (over 260 rooms; famous also in his day) ruled over a realm extending to the north as far as the basin area of the Balikh and Habur. A mural in the inner court before the throne room depicts his investiture by the goddess Ishtar. The archives discovered in the palace are our most important historical source. A letter underscores the power of Yarim-Lim of Yamhad. In this document, found at Mari, he prides himself on having come to the aid of Babylon by means of a military campaign and at the same time of having saved the throne of the king of Der (east of the Tigris, about 1000 km., 600 mi., from Mari). That made it possible for him to curtail the power of Eshnunna and probably also that of Larsa. Asshur is missing from the series of powers. From other sources we know that this state lost a lot of power after the death of Shamshi-Adad I (ca. 1780 B.C., after Hammurabi's tenth year), even though his successor Ishme-Dagan, despite the threat of Eshnunna and the conquests of Hammurabi, managed to retain the throne till the end of his forty-year reign (ca. 1760 B.C.?), according to the Assyrian King List. Eshnunna and Mari and soon also Babylon claimed the political legacy of Asshur. In the south, Larsa and Babylon, though initially getting along with each other, became rivals in the struggle for control over "Sumer and Akkad." In that struggle Mari was Babylon's faithful ally, among others in the war against Eshnunna, which sometimes received help from Elam.

Hammurabi's political successes came toward the end of his reign. Military operations between his seventh and eleventh years made clear his aspirations, though success was limited. Between his twenty-ninth and thirty-seventh years he gained supremacy over all of Mesopotamia. In his thirty-first year he conquered Larsa with the help of Mari and Eshnunna; Rim-Sin was dethroned. In the following years he attacked his former allies unscrupulously: in his thirty-second year Eshnunna, Asshur, and the territory east of the Tigris (called Gutium); in his thirty-third year

Mari, penetrating far into northern Mesopotamia. Two years later Mari was totally destroyed, never to be rebuilt again. Some years after that he engaged in a hard, decisive battle against Eshnunna, Asshur (called Subartu), and the Turukku. After his successes he could rightly claim to have brought Sumer and Akkad under his scepter, while the conquest of cities such as Mari and Malgium entitled him to be called "king of all Amorites." In the final revision of the prologue to his famed "laws," probably from his thirty-ninth year, he enumerated all the cities whose temples and gods he had honored in the wake of his military successes. His laws, divided in modern editions into 282 paragraphs, with prologue and epilogue, present him as being almost the ideal king, who "as the sun(god) rises over the nations and illumines the land," as the "god of the kings," who with his wise, "righteous judgments" (that is how he himself spoke of his "laws") wants to guarantee the "justice of the land" for the benefit of his subjects. His letters make him known as a good ruler, who preserves justice, safety, and prosperity, for example, through the digging of canals. His capital Babylon became the governmental, ceremonial, and increasingly also the religious center of the land, whose culture from now on more and more deserves the name "Babylonian." Marduk, the initially unimportant city-god of Babylon, gained greater influence and became more and more an almost national god. His career was literarily sealed a few centuries later in the so-called creation epic *Enuma elish* ("When on high . . ."), in which he overcomes the powers of chaos in exchange for the kingship over the gods. His position was "genealogically" founded through identification with Asalluhi, a god of purification and exorcism, son of the great god Enki of Eridu.

The empire built by Hammurabi did not last long after his death. Already under his son and successor Samsu-iluna (ca. 1749–1712 B.C.) rebellions and threats from many sides caused disintegration. In his eighth year the south rebelled; a usurper, who called himself Rim-Sin (II), held out for two years and temporarily controlled Uruk, Larsa, Nippur, and Ur, before the king eliminated him. In the north Eshnunna rebelled, while in the west in later years the Euphrates front required strengthening. In the course of Samsu-iluna's reign the south was definitely lost to the so-called "dynasty of Sealand," which had come to power under Ilamuila shortly after Hammurabi's death. The dynasty incorporated the anti-Babylonian southern element, which according to the names of the later rulers had a high regard for the Sumerian tradition. Isin apparently was one of the instigators (the third ruler of the dynasty bore the same name as Isin's last king) and hence was dismantled by Samsu-iluna. Despite repeated campaigns by Samsu-iluna and his successor Abi-eshuh (ca. 1711–1684 B.C.), the southern dynasty managed to maintain itself in its residence Urukug (site unknown), where till the end of the fifteenth century (when the Kassites managed to extend their power to the south) a dozen kings ruled.

As early as Samsu-iluna's eighth year mention is made of a military confrontation with the *Kassites*—the oldest mention of a new population element that would eventually succeed Hammurabi's dynasty and for about four and a half centuries would nominally have supremacy over Babylonia. The earliest history of the Kassites is unknown. From the king lists we know only the names of the oldest rulers, beginning with Gandash, Agum I, and Kashtiliash. The center of their power in this period has not yet been located. Traditionally they are connected with the territories northeast of Babylonia, the Zagros, and the east Tigris area where Hammurabi had to wage pitched battles on his last campaigns, without decisive success. One may probably also link them with the land of Hana, on the Middle Euphrates, around Terqa. Some documents tell us about rulers from an indigenous dynasty, which probably arose there about 1740 B.C. They bore Amorite names, with the exception of one, called Kashtiliash. It is not certain, however, whether he was a forefather or the third ruler of the Kassite dynasty or an isolated Kassite tribal chief who managed to obtain a local throne.

After the death of Abi-eshuh it still took ninety years before the last descendant of Hammurabi, Samsu-Ditana (ca. 1629–1595 B.C.; successor of Ammi-Saduqa, ca. 1647–1625 B.C.), lost his throne in the raid of the Hittite Murshilish I. It is likely that the Kassite dynasty, which according to the king list lasted for 576 years, made its history begin long before the fall of Babylon, so that there must be considerable overlap of both in the

Babylonian King List. The precise extent of the overlapping cannot be determined because very little is known of the first fifteen Kassite kings; most of the dates of the reigns have also disappeared from the list. It is, for example, entirely unclear how one can fit into the dynasty a king by the name of Agum II (Kakrime), who (ca. 1570 B.C.) according to a later inscription (supported by a "Marduk prophecy") returned the statue of Marduk carried off by the Hittites twenty-four years earlier.

The year names of the last kings of Babylon indicate that the realm crumbled down to a small area with such cities as Babylon, Sippar, Kish, and Borsippa, and temporary extensions. Military undertakings are hardly mentioned anymore; rather, all the more pious deeds, such as the dedication of temples, cultic objects, and images of gods and kings, are recorded in their year names. The extant texts show that the economic activity of the palace, officials, and private individuals continued on a reduced scale. Especially the bureaucracy increased; the many royal officials eventually managed to strengthen their position and in some cases even made it hereditary. Traditional forms were maintained, such as the periodic proclamation of royal decrees, to lighten the burden of the people. Also the literary activity, concentrated in the schools, maintained itself. Classical Summerian and Akkadian texts were copied, such as the so-called Atrahasis Epic, the myth of creation and deluge, which we know especially from a beautiful copy on three large tablets, dating from the middle of Ammi-Saduqa's reign. From his time is also the only virtually intact copy of a royal decree, already mentioned above.

Babylon collapsed in 1595 B.C., but there are no contemporary texts that describe this as an epochal event, such as happened four hundred years earlier with Ur. Babylon's fall did not mean that politically and culturally it disappeared from the scene; far from it. For the time being, however, a "dark period" began, because we know very little of the history of the next two centuries.

## LITERATURE

J. A. Brinkman, *Materials and Studies for Kassite History* I (Chicago, 1976).

A. Finet, *Le Code de Hammurapi* (Paris, 1973).

H. Klengel, *Hammurapi von Babylon und seine Zeit* (Berlin, 1976).

F. R. Kraus, et al., *Altbabylonische Briefe in Umschrift und Übersetzung* I–X (Leiden, 1964–85).

———, *Königliche Verfügungen in altbabylonischer Zeit* (Leiden, 1984).

The history of Assyria after the death of Ishme-Dagan (ca. 1760 B.C.?) cannot yet be written. Through the King List we know only the names of a series of kings (nos. 41–60), with a deviating tradition for the numbers 41–53. A puzzling text of Puzur-Sin (not included in the King List) records that he expelled the dynasty of Shamshi-Adad, whom he characterized as a non-Assyrian usurper, under his grandson. Starting from king number 57, Adasi, we possess a source, unfortunately very fragmentary at the beginning, in the "Synchronistic History," a chronicle-like text describing the relations between kings of Asshur and Babylon in historical sequence, perhaps the historical introduction to a pact of friendship. We have again a few texts from the time of Puzur-Ashur II (no. 61, ca. 1500 B.C.)—brief building inscriptions offering little information—but we lack them again for nos. 63–68. That must have been the period, in the fifteenth century, when Asshur was dominated by the Mitanni, and its kings were probably vassals.

## LITERATURE

A. K. Grayson, *Assyrian Royal Inscriptions* I (Wiesbaden, 1972).

B. Landsberger, "Assyrische Königsliste und 'dunkles Zeitalter,'" *Journal of Cuneiform Studies* 8 (1954) 31ff.

## j. Syria and Palestine in the First Half of the Second Millennium B.C.

The knowledge of Syria and Palestine in the period between about 2000 and 1500 B.C. is rather limited. Textual material is scarce; only after 1500 B.C. does it become more voluminous and useful for the historian. Besides the data from the neighboring countries—from Mari, Boghazköy, and Egypt (the Execration Texts; see above, p. 232)—we have so far only the cuneiform texts from layer VII (end of the 18th to the mid-17th century B.C.) from Alalakh (Tell Atshanah), a city on the upper course of the Orontes in the plain of Amuq. The city, excavated by Sir Leonard Woolley, was in this period the governmental center of a city-state with its own rulers, under the supremacy of the "great king" of the state of Yamhad, who had his seat at Aleppo (Halab), center of the worship of "Adad (Haddu) of Aleppo," an important weather-god worshiped by the Hittites as the hypostasis of Teshub.

In the nineteenth century B.C. Yamhad had developed into an important political power, reaching its peak under Yarim-Lim I (ca. 1800–1775 B.C.). Precisely how far the boundaries of his realm reached is difficult to determine (in the south to Qatna in the plain of Homs, in the east to Carchemish, and in the southeast to the territory of Mari). The status of cities such as Ebla and Emar is unclear in this period. At the time of Shamshi-Adad I of Asshur, Yamhad experienced a difficult period, menaced by Asshur, Mari, and the rulers of Carchemish, Urshu, and Hashshu (the last two with Hurrian names). After Shamshi-Adad's death and the accession to the throne of the friendly Zimri-Lim at Mari, there was a change for the better. Relations were normalized with the other Syrian states, including Carchemish under Aplakhanda and Yatarami. Mari mediated between Yamhad and Qatna. In spite of Hammurabi's extension of power, even far into northern Mesopotamia (after the conquest of Mari ca. 1760 B.C.), Yamhad managed to maintain itself under the rulers Abbael, Yarim-Lim II, Niqmepa, and others. Under Abbael, Alalakh acquired a great autonomy with a dynasty of its own; important rulers were Yarim-Lim and Ammitaqum, whose testament, approved by his "lord" (belum), has been preserved. He maintained relations with Ebla among others. After about 1640 B.C. the military operations of the Old Hittite kings Hattushilish I and Murshilish I put an end to the power of Yamhad and the other north-Syrian city-states.

Information about the other city-states is even scarcer. Something can be derived from the Mari correspondence, which shows that there was considerable movement of messengers between east and west, by which Mari and Mesopotamia had contact with Syria and Palestine, via the Euphrates route by way of Emar and Aleppo or through the desert from Mari by way of Tadmur (Palmyra) to Qatna (on this route waterbags were taken along). In this Qatna played an important role. The state tried to maintain its independence from Yamhad, first in coalition with Asshur (Ishi-Adad gave his daughter in marriage to Yasmah-Adad of Mari), later in coalition with Mari, which served as the mediator with Yamhad. The Mari Texts show that at that time the area south of Qatna was called Amurru and had at least four rulers. South of it lay the region Apum, having as its center the city of Damascus (not mentioned by this name in the texts). Via these regions Mari even maintained political and commercial contacts with Palestinian city-states, such as Hazor (of which a king Ibni-Adad is known) and Laish. There were even contacts with Cyprus (Alashiya) and Crete (Kaptara; cf. Old Testament Kaphtor).

A number of familiar coastal cities also occur in the Mari Texts, such as Ugarit and Byblos, which apparently were autonomous, ruled by their own "Amorite" dynasties. Despite commercial and diplomatic contacts, being separated from the inland by mountains they were more independent and commercially were just as much oriented to the Mediterranean territory and Egypt. Egypt's influence is clearly shown by the numerous, sometimes inscribed, Egyptian objects uncovered in excavations, particularly at the time of the Twelfth Dynasty (till ca. 1780 B.C.). In Ugarit a dynasty ruled that went back to Yaqarum, son of Niqmaddu, whose seal was also later still used as the dynastic seal. To this dynasty belonged furthermore such rulers as Niqmaddu and Hammurapi, known from a still unpublished list of (posthumously) deified rulers of Ugarit.

Still farther south at Byblos, from ancient times connected with Egypt, ruled such kings as Abishemuabi, Abishemu, and later Yantinhammu (probably identical with a ruler of Byblos known from Egyptian texts as Inten). Their names as well as abundant evidence of their contacts with Egypt under the pharaohs Amenemhet II–IV came to light in the graves of the royal necropolis (especially tombs 1–4) and in the "Obelisk temple," which in addition to many obelisks yielded numerous buried ex-voto gifts: decorative weapons, and statuettes of people and animals in gold, copper, stone, and faience. Especially the cult of the Lady of Byblos, worshiped by the Egyptians as a form of Hathor, was very prominent. Egyptian influence at Ugarit and Byblos survived the crises of the Hyksos period, and from the end of the sixteenth century B.C. we find again evidence of contacts with and the presence of Egyptians (e.g., in inscriptions of Amenhotep II and Thutmose III).

## LITERATURE

*J.-M. Durand and J. Margueron, eds., *MARI, Annales de recherches interdisciplinaires* 1– (Paris, 1982– ).

*P. Gerstenblith, *The Levant at the Beginning of the Middle Bronze Age* (Cambridge, Mass., 1984).

R. Giveon, "The XIIIth Dynasty in Asia," *Revue d'Egyptologie* 30 (1978) 163–67.

N. Jidejian, *Byblos through the Ages* (Beirut, 1968).

K. A. Kitchen, "The King List of Ugarit," *Ugarit-Forschungen* 9 (1977) 131–42.

H. Klengel, *Geschichte Syriens im 2. Jahrtausend v.u.Z* I–III (Berlin, 1965–70).

A. Malamat, "Northern Canaan and the Mari Texts," in J. A. Sanders, ed., *Near Eastern Archaeology in the Twentieth Century* (Festschrift N. Glueck; Garden City, 1970), pp. 164–77.

*J. M. Weinstein, "The Egyptian Empire in Palestine: A Reassessment," *Bulletin of the American Schools of Oriental Research* 241 (1981) 1–28.

L. Woolley, *A Forgotten Kingdom* (London, 1953).

## k. The Old Hittite Empire (till ca. 1500 B.C.)

About 1650 B.C. the Old Hittite empire entered the light of history with its own historical texts. A prince from Kushshara (not yet located) with the (dynastic?) name L/Tabarnas, rounding off the work of his predecessors, seized the supremacy over central Anatolia in a surprisingly short time. He also annexed Hattushash (near Boghazköy), an important event, which made him change his name to Hattushilish. He became "suzerain of Hatti.

Before his time Anatolia consisted of a conglomerate of city-states with groups of vassals around a suzerain. As we know from Old Assyrian commercial texts, discovered at Kanish-Kültepe and dating from the first half of the nineteenth century B.C., the ruler of the old city of Buruskhanda (perhaps present Açemhöyük near Aksaray) was initially such a suzerain. His position was taken over by Anittas, son of Pithanas, ruler of Kushshara. We know him from the later Old Assyrian texts (ca. 1800?) and especially from the so-called Anittas Text, a historiographical document kept in the Hittite archives in Hattushash that reports on the rise and political significance of Neshas under the kingship of Anittas. The historical developments are hard to follow. There was certainly an Anatolian power struggle; traces of it have been found in the destructions experienced by the *karum* of Kanish-Kültepe (= Neshas) at the end of layer II (ca. 1840 B.C.) and layer I.B (ca. 1750 B.C.), and the Anittas Text also mentions it. Hattushilish and his son Murshilish I (end of the 17th century B.C.) made Hattushash their residence, though after its conquest by Anittas the city had been sown with weeds, with the invocation of the curse of the gods upon whoever would rebuild it (but already ca. 1800 B.C., at the time of Shamshi-Aad I, the city is mentioned as an important center of commerce).

Under its first two kings the Old Hittite empire quickly expanded its power. It extended its influence to northern Syria: the power of Yamhad (Aleppo) was curtailed, Alalakh was destroyed by Hattushilish I; cities such as Carchemish, Urshu, and Ebla encountered the power of the Hittites, which was also directed against Hahhum in the southeast, a representative of the rising power of the Hurrians. Attacking them, Hattushilish crossed the Euphrates. The climax came under Murshilish I, who eliminated Yamhad and pushing on via the Euphrates, perhaps with the support of the Kassites (in the land Hana = Terqa), took Babylon in 1595 B.C. This raid, which except for giving the Hittites some booty had little permanent result, meant the end of the Old Babylonian realm of Hammurabi's dynasty.

Until about 1500 B.C., the throne of Hattushash was occupied by such kings as Hantilish, Zidantash, Ammunash, Huzziash, and Telepinush. It is a period increasingly characterized by a power struggle for the throne, whereby the realm gradually shrank to its core territory. An external cause was the growing power of the Hurrians, which in northern Mesopotamia took shape in the Mitanni kingdom (the texts also speak of Hanigalbat) with the capital Washshukkanni (in the east of the Habur region). From there they penetrated into southeast Anatolia, where the states of Kizzuwatna (the heart of Cilicia) and Ishuwa (area of Elazığ) arose. Telepinush entered into a parity treaty with Kizzuwatna, the oldest known state treaty of a long series of such Hittite documents. Also, northern Syria rid itself of Hittite overlordship and entered the power sphere of Mitanni, as we know from the textual materials from Alalakh (layer V; 15th century B.C.), which betray the presence of a substantial Hurrian population component.

Knowledge of the oldest Hittite history can be gained from a number of remarkable texts: historical and legendary compositions about pristine times, such as the Anittas Text and the story about the city of Zalpa, with legendary elements of a saga. Furthermore, there are texts of Hattushilish himself: his "political testament," a bilingual text in which he addresses his successor Murshilish I, and his annalistic *res gestae*, discovered in 1957. In addition to a court chronicle and records of land grants, very important is especially the Decree of Telepinush, which regulated the succession to the throne of a monarchy that certainly initially was less absolutistic and despotic than anywhere else in the Near East, in part due to the important role played by the *pankus*, the council of nobles or prominent people. The decree describes the earlier history elaborately and contrasts "earlier" with "now," in order by means of the pressure of a historic example to put an end to the power struggle for the throne within the royal family. From then on, after the sons in first and second degrees, also the king's son-in-law was a poten-

tial heir to the throne. This textual material illustrates for this early period the peculiar nature and functionality of Hittite historiography, which occupies a special place within the historiography of the ancient Near East. Also, the oldest version of the "Hittite laws" goes back to this formative period.

---

## LITERATURE

P. Garelli, *Le Proche-Orient asiatique* (Paris, 1969), pp. 302ff.

*H. A. Hoffner, "Histories and Historians of the Ancient Near East: The Hittites," *Orientalia* 49 (1980) 283–332.

E. Neu, *Der Anitta-Text* (Wiesbaden, 1974).

H. Otten, "Der Weg des hethitischen Staates zum Grossreich," *Saeculum* 15 (1964) 115–24.

K. K. Riemschneider, "Die Thronfolge im althethitischen Reich," in *Beiträge zur sozialen Struktur des Alten Vorderasien* (Berlin, 1971).

F. Starke, "Halmashuit im Anitta-Text und die hethitische Ideologie vom Königtum," *Zeitschrift für Assyriologie* 69 (1979) 47–120.

---

## 5. THE LATE BRONZE AGE (16TH–12TH CENTURIES B.C.)

### a. Introduction

From the middle of the second millennium B.C. important historical developments took place. Through an imperialistic policy, first of Egypt, later also of other states, the political and military theater of operations was enlarged. The great powers of this period, to which since about 1500 B.C. the north Mesopotamian kingdom of Mitanni also belonged, later joined by the Hittites, Babylonia, and Assyria, began to clash with each other. This led to great military conflicts (in which from now on the horse-drawn war chariot played an important role) and to intensive diplomatic contacts, resulting in international treaties, political marriages, exchange of gifts and specialists (particularly in the medical field), and trade. These contacts were facilitated by administrative control over large areas and by the widespread (from Anatolia to Egypt) use of Babylonian as the *lingua franca*, which in many places could be learned in schools and was used for diplomatic correspondence, as demonstrated by the archives of Tell el-Amarna, Ugarit, and Boghazköy. Moreover, historical documentation benefits from the fact that Babylonian was also used for internal purposes, particularly in Syria and Palestine.

In these historical developments Syria played a central role, being the territory where the powers and interests clashed and where decisive battles were fought, such as that between the Egyptians and Hittites at Qadesh by the Orontes. These conflicts marked off the spheres of influence and determined the fate of the small Syrian states as vassals of this or that power. Moreover, these conflicts occasionally resulted in essential changes: the liquidation of Mitanni gave the Hittites their chance, and it enabled Assyria to recover in the fourteenth century and reenter the political arena. When in the thirteenth century a temporary status quo was reached, it was soon disturbed by external factors. From the Syrian-Arabian steppe Aramean tribes increasingly infiltrated the civilized world of Syria and Mesopotamia. A century later the Sea Peoples contributed to the political collapse, especially of Syria and Anatolia, in ways not yet fully understood. The power vacuum created by them was filled in Anatolia in particular by the Phrygians, who probably administered the death blow to the Hittite empire, and in Syria and northern Mesopotamia by the Arameans, who, in spite of fierce and initially successful Assyrian resistance, settled in large areas on both sides of the Euphrates. This transition period toward the end of the Late Bronze Age was probably also the time when the tribes of Israel entered Canaan, where they encountered or acquired as neighbors the Philistines (belonging to the Sea Peoples), Edomites, Moabites, and Ammonites, people who at the same time settled there or consolidated themselves. Only the Phoenician city-states Tyre, Sidon, and Byblos (Ugarit disappeared once and for all) and the small so-called Neo-Hittite states in northern Syria and southern Anatolia survived the drastic changes that archeologically mark the transition from the Late Bronze to the Early Iron Age.

## b. Chronological Problems

Unfortunately, the chronological problems of this period have not yet been fully solved; the margins still amount to ten to twelve years. It is very difficult to arrange the dates from various countries in one closed chronological scheme. The prime reason is that the sources are often insufficient. For Egypt and the Hittites, trustworthy king lists are lacking (Manetho is unreliable), making it necessary to take as starting point the highest number of regnal years (which only yield a minimal length of reign!) mentioned in the records, and estimated ages and generations. Relative to the Hittites there is a difference of opinion about the number of generations in connection with the question who was the father and/or predecessor of Shuppiluliumash I (Hattushilish II, Arnuwandash, or Tudhaliyash I [or II]). In Egypt there is uncertainty about the length and the inclusion of the years of co-regencies; an earlier assumed eleven- or eight-year co-regency between Amenhotep III and IV is now seriously questioned. The uncertainty about Egyptian chronology is disturbing because in the reconstructions the synchronisms from the Amarna correspondence play an important role, as well as the contacts between Ramses II and the Hittites.

Thus Burnaburiash II of Babylonia, who according to the latest calculations of Brinkman came to the throne about 1359 B.C., was a contemporary of Ashuruballit I of Assyria and maintained correspondence with the pharaohs Amenhotep III (?), IV (Akhenaten), and Tutankhamon. It is also clear that there were relations with the Hittites. Shuppiluliumash I belongs in this period, with a reign of at least thirty-five years, perhaps beginning as co-regent with his predecessor. His great Syrian campaign, which drastically changed the political constellation (e.g., it changed Ugarit from an Egyptian vassal into a Hittite vassal), happened about the middle of this century.

The Egyptologist Hornung, who assumed the low Babylonian chronology (fall of Babylon ca. 1531 B.C.), put Amenhotep III's ascension to the throne around 1400 B.C., Amenhotep IV's (Akhenaten) reign about 1364–1347, Tutankhamon about 1347–1339, Horemheb about

1334–1306, and Seti I about 1304–1290 (presumably Ramses II came to the throne in Seti's last year; see p. 209). Wente and Siclen proposed other dates on the basis of an analysis both of dated texts and of data about anniversaries of pharaonic reigns and of pharaonic mummies. There are significant differences with respect to the length of Thutmose IV's reign: Hornung proposed about 1412–1402, while Wente proposed 1419–1384. One of the consequences is that Hornung has the New Kindgom begin under Ahmose in about 1550, but Wente in about 1570. Wente also arrived at 1279 for the beginning of the reign of Ramses II. Though his dates are lower than those of Brinkman, the data of the Babylonian-Assyrian chronology as analyzed by Brinkman play a role in his dating. According to Brinkman, Burnaburiash II ruled about 1359–1333, which means that he can hardly have corresponded with Tutankhamon, who according to Wente came to the throne about 1334. There are also problems in connection with Hittite chronology, because a solar eclipse in the tenth year of Murshilish II, if put at March 13, 1335, would fix the end of Shuppiluliumash's reign at about 1345. Since a widow of a pharaoh asked Shuppiluliumash I toward the end of his reign for a Hittite prince as a husband, according to this scheme the pharaoh could not even have been Akhenaten.

Wente proposed his dating on the assumption of a ten-year margin of uncertainty for the Mesopotamian dates, caused by the presence of variants for the regnal years of two Assyrian kings about the middle of the twelfth century B.C. (see p. 211). Brinkman had opted for the high alternative. In a recent study Boese and Wilhelm have shown that the low alternative is correct, which means that the beginning of the reign of Burnaburiash II (probably about the 30th regnal year of Amenhotep III) has been fixed at 1349 (± 5 years). This low dating provides independent support for the low date of the beginning of the reign of Ramses II: 1279. It also provides a solution for the problem with the Hittite data. For the solar eclipse in the tenth year of Murshilish II can be shifted to the next most likely astronomical date, June 24, 1312 (magnitude 0.97), enabling us to put the beginning of his reign and the death of Shuppiluliumash at about 1323/22. The widow of the pharaoh, who shortly afterward asked for a prince, is then almost certainly the widow of Tutankhamon, who died young in 1324.

Other synchronisms can be connected with this one. During the famed battle at Qadesh, which must now be dated in 1275 B.C., Muwatallish was still king of the Hittites. He was succeeded by Urhi-Teshub (7 years) and Hattushilish III, who still corresponded with Ramses II in his forty-second regnal year (1238), but was also still a contemporary of Adad-nirari I of Assyria, who must have died in 1266/63. The next Hittite king, Tudhaliyash IV (after 1238), engaged in correspondence with Shalmaneser I of Assyria, which is possible with the new and later dates, because the latter now reigned between about 1265/63 and 1234/33.

All this has provided much more certainty about the end of this period. Considerable divergences in the reconstruction of the beginning of this period, before the Amarna Age, still remain, because the data are less numerous and also because there are differences in interpretation. Hornung is critical of the regnal years that have been reconstructed on the basis of anniversaries (which were desired rather than actually experienced), particularly with respect to Thutmose IV. Moreover, there is no unanimity about the beginning date of the New Kingdom, which is in part derived from a Sothis date in the ninth year of Amenhotep I (see p. 209). The calculation of the exact date of this event is also dependent on the question where the Sothis observations took place during the New Kingdom. If it was not Thebes, but the more southern Elephantine, and that appears very likely, seven to nine years have to be deducted from the dates, which would mean that the beginning of the New Kingdom can be put at about 1542/40, the accession of Amenhotep I at about 1517, and that of Thutmose III at about 1479. These dates, which are lower than those proposed by Wente, can only be maintained if one is willing to assume a brief reign for Thutmose IV; if not, the synchronisms accepted above for the Amarna Age become impossible, and Ramses II's accession to the throne would have to be still later.

In the historical overview below, we follow for Egypt the dates of Wente, while for the rest of the Near East we accept those of Brinkman, decreased by ten (always with a margin of uncertainty of a number of years); sometimes alternative dates are mentioned.

## LITERATURE

W. Barta, "Die ägyptischen Sothisdaten und ihre Bezugsorte," *Jaarbericht Ex Oriente Lux* 26 (1979–80) 26–34.

*J. Boese and G. Wilhelm, "Aššur-dan I., Ninurta-apil-Ekur und die mittelassyrische Chronologie," *Wiener Zeitschrift für die Kunde des Morgenlandes* 71 (1979) 19–38.

E. Hornung and E. Staehelin, *Studien zum Sedfest* (Basel, 1974).

K. A. Kitchen, *Suppiluliuma and the Amarna Pharaohs* (Liverpool, 1962) (cf. the discussion of Ph. H. J. Houwink ten Cate in *Bibliotheca Orientalis* 20 [1963] 270–76).

C. Kuhne, *Die Chronologie der internationalen Korrespondenz von El-Amarna* (Kevelaer/Neukirchen-Vluyn, 1973).

See also the literature above, pp. 212–13.

## c. Egypt during the New Kingdom

With Ahmose of the Eighteenth Dynasty, the Egyptian New Kingdom began a period of great prosperity. In the fifteenth century, especially under Thutmose III, the empire took shape, eventually including also Upper and Lower Nubia to the fourth cataract (Wawat and Cush), and in Asia extending to central Syria, where Ugarit, Amurru, and Qadesh mark the boundary. Graphic arts and craft work reached great heights, as is demonstrated by sculptures, murals, and many art objects such as have come to light in Tutankhamon's tomb. We know the architecture from Akhenaten's new capital Akhetaton, from the Ramesside residence Pi-Ramessu (Raamses in the Old Testament; now Qantir) in the Delta, from fortresses built in Nubia (in particular the fortress Buhen), and from the building of temples. Most of the building was done to the imperial temple of Amon at Karnak, where new pillar-flanked halls, pylons, and obelisks were constructed. Important temples were also constructed at Luxor, Soleb, and Abu Simbel. The kings built their mortuary temples, of which the one of Hatshepsut at Deir el-Bahri is the best known. Of the temple of Amenhotep III in Thebes, virtually all that remains are the colosses of Memnon. These temples were clearly separated from the rock tombs in an isolated valley, the "Valley of the Kings," and were intended to remain closed and hidden forever, though that hope was hardly fulfilled.

Religiously the changes brought about by the Aten-cult of Amenhotep IV (Akhenaten) have the greatest interest. Important, too, is that the Book of the Dead obtained its classical form, and written on papyrus, often illustrated, was deposited with the dead in their graves. Many rituals acquired their own form. Influenced by royal funerals, the "writing of the hidden space" (Amduat) appeared and became the model for the "guide to the hereafter" that now came into vogue. Familiar, among others, is the "Book of the Gates," which has as its theme the nocturnal journey of the sun through the underworld and its rising again. A familiar hymn is the "Hymn to the Sun," in which gods are depicted as forms in which Re appears. There are also numerous other hymns to the sun and hymns and prayers to Osiris, who was thought of as the nocturnal underworld appearance of the sun. Along with this religious literature, which was written in classical Middle Egyptian, profane literature developed, especially in the Ramesside times. This literature contained, among others, love songs and stories, written in the Late Egyptian colloquial language.

The large kingdom demanded an efficient government, which was centralized in Thebes, where the most important person after the pharaoh, the vizier, had his official seat. Here resided also the influential high priest of Amon-Re, the chief steward of the wealthiest temple of the land, and numerous lower officials who supervised finances, grain, building activities, and the like. Nubia was ruled by a vice-king; "royal son of Cush" was his title. From their graves in Thebes and Sawwara we get an impression of the prosperity, importance, and loyalty of the officials, who were often strongly attached to the person of the king.

Besides the governmental class, the military

gained in power during the New Kingdom, concentrated in the south, against Nubia, and in the north, where Memphis became the military headquarters. There princes were trained in the use of weapons and, as stated in the texts, were made familiar with "the work of (the martial god) Montu." The sanctuaries of this god at Medamud and Tod received special attention, especially since Thutmose III. With Horemheb, toward the end of the fourteenth century, a general came to the throne, probably succeeded by his former adjutant, Ramses I.

The vastness of the empire and increasing international contacts made Egypt more and more accessible · to foreign influences. Merchandise, military people, emissaries, and princesses came to Egypt from abroad. Prisoners of war, including groups of Apiru, were carried off from Palestine and given to the temples. Asiatics also penetrated the official ranks, especially under Hatshepsut. Interest in foreign lands was on the increase, graphically expressed by the murals depicting the trade expedition to the distant Punt (Somalia) in Hatshepsut's mortuary temple. Religious influences from abroad are noticeable too; numerous Syro-Palestinian gods were worshiped in Egypt: Baal (equated with Seth, already during the Hyksos), Astarte/Anat (especially as goddess of war), Resheph (first under Amenhotep II as god of war, later especially as god of medicine, together with Qadshu), Horon (on the basis of his name connected with the great sphinx in the cult of Harmakhis-Horon), Koshar (god of artistry, equated with Ptah of Memphis), Asherah (as Qadshu and fertility goddess), and Ishtar (of Nineveh).

The numerous stele of kings and officials, "annals" written and illustrated on temple walls (especially at Karnak), murals and texts in tombs of high officials and military people, and papyrus documents (letters, reports, records) are our sources for this time. In addition there are Amarna Tablets, the international correspondence of the pharaohs Amenhotep III and IV and Tutankhamon. Ostraca and papyri from Deir el-Medineh, the village opposite Thebes, on the western bank of the Nile, where the craftsmen and artists lived who during the Eighteenth–Twentieth Dynasties had to construct the tombs of the Theban necropolis and look after their interior, inform us about daily life and social, economic, and juridical situations.

---

## LITERATURE

M. Bierbrier, *The Tomb-builders of the Pharaohs* (London, 1978).

W. Helck, *Die Beziehungen Ägyptens zu Vorderasien im 3. und 2. Jahrtausend v. Chr.* (Wiesbaden, 1962).

E. Hornung, *Untersuchungen zur Chronologie und Geschichte des Neuen Reiches* (Wiesbaden, 1964) (cf. E. Hornung, *Zeitschrift der deutschen Morgenländischen Gesellschaft* 117 [1967] 11–16).

*P. H. Newby, *Warrior Pharaohs: The Rise and Fall of the Egyptian Empire* (London, 1980).

C. F. Nims, *Thebes of the Pharaohs: Pattern for Every City* (London, 1965).

D. B. Redford, *History and Chronology of the Eighteenth Dynasty of Egypt: Seven Studies* (Toronto, 1967).

*J. Romer, *Valley of the Kings* (London, 1982).

A. R. Schulman, *Military Rank, Title and Organization in the Egyptian New Kingdom* (Berlin, 1964).

G. Steindorff and K. C. Sethe, *When Egypt Ruled the East* (Chicago, 1957²).

K. Sethe and W. Helck, *Urkunden der 18. Dynastie* (= Urkunden des ägyptischen Altertums IV), Parts 1–22 (Leipzig/Berlin, 1906–1968).

---

## d. From the Eighteenth Dynasty to Amenhotep III (1550–1350 B.C.)

Shortly after 1550 B.C. Ahmose, the founder of the New Kingdom who consolidated the boundaries in the south (Nubia) and east (Sinai, southern Palestine), was succeeded by Amenhotep I, who ruled over twenty years, after having been coregent for six years. During his reign Nubia was subdued to the second cataract. The border was made secure through fortresses at Semna, Kumma, and Uronarti. His building projects at the Amon temple at Karnak and his preference for a rock tomb near Thebes were the model for the entire dynasty. During his predominantly peaceful reign culture flourished; a significant witness is the medical Papyrus Ebers.

About 1520 B.C. he was succeeded by Thutmose I, born from a secondary branch of the royal family, under whom Egypt's military expansion became very evident. In the south he thrust through to the fourth cataract, in the east his expeditionary army moved through Syria and Palestine, reaching the Euphrates at Carchemish, where the king left his stele. The confrontation with Mitanni, the rulers of northern Syria, began. He was the first pharaoh who had his rock tomb made in the famed "Valley of the Kings" near Thebes, in the necropolis, which in the course of time was put under the protection of the deified Amenhotep I.

After a reign of some ten (?) years he was succeeded by his son Thutmose II, who, reared at the military headquarters in Memphis, followed in the footsteps of his father, but without penetrating so far into Syria. He died after less than ten years, and because his son (by a concubine) Thutmose III was not yet of age, his wife Hatshepsut became regent (1500 B.C.). This remarkable queen, daughter of Thutmose I—whose activities are an example of the important role queens and queen-mothers began to play during the New Kingdom—not satisfied with her role as regent, presented herself after some years as pharaoh. For the first time a woman bore Egypt's double crown, thereby making use of male-oriented names, titles, and symbolic representations, but without denying her femininity in her images and epithets: she was at once "female Horus" and male sphinx. She secured the support of two dignitaries of the Amon Temple, especially of Senenmut. Her reign was a time of peaceful development, in which the new national consciousness expressed itself in taking distance from the Hyksos tradition, and the material culture was refined, partly under the influence of fruitful contacts with Asia and the late Minoan Crete. The dominant monument of her reign is her fairly well-preserved mortuary temple at Deir el-Bahri, having as its high point the "Punt hall," a pictorial report in relief of a trade expedition to Punt, the exotic coast of Somaliland. Here as well as in the "birth hall," she emphasized her divine provenance and birth as legitimate successor to the throne.

After some fifteen years, about 1485 B.C., Hatshepsut's influence began to wane; her confidants were purged, and after her death, a few years later, Thutmose in his twenty-second year became sole ruler. In course of time a reaction began: Hatshepsut's images and name fell victim to an iconoclasm and in official king lists she was ignored.

The neglect of the Near Eastern empire in the meantime had had serious consequences. Mitanni had established itself in Syria, where many prominent city princes probably acknowledged Mitanni's sovereignty, such as the rulers of Qadesh, Qatna, Tunip (east of the Orontes against the Lebanon), Nuhashshe (east of Ugarit), and Mukish and Alalakh. From now on this entire area appears in Egyptian sources as *Huru*, in view of Hurrian infiltrations. Later the term was applied to Syria and Palestine as a whole (the older "Retenu" fell into disuse). The southern Palestinian rulers also freed themselves from Egypt. Already in his twenty-second year Thutmose III (ca. 1500–1450 B.C.), who after this reigned for another thirty-two years, undertook a major campaign into Palestine. A large coalition under the leadership of Qadesh was defeated at Megiddo; the city itself was taken after a seven-month siege, as were other cities in the wider surroundings. The names, prisoners of war, and booty, as well as detailed battle reports, are found in the annals inscribed on the temple walls of Karnak, while conquered cities are listed on the sixth and seventh pylons of the temple.

Egypt's position as a major power was especially established between Thutmose's twenty-ninth and thirty-third years, on his fifth to eighth campaigns. These campaigns brought him as far as northern Syria, made him do battle with Mitanni near Aleppo, and after crossing the Euphrates led him into the interior of the Mitanni, called *Naharin(a)*—a name that continued in the Old Testament as "Aram-Naharaim" and the later "Mesopotamia," the territory in and behind the large curve of the Euphrates. Though Thutmose marched along the Euphrates, via Carchemish and Emar, Mitanni avoided a decisive confrontation and remained unbeaten. Returning, Thutmose did take Qadesh with its territory (Takhsi in the Biqa). Though Egypt had strengthened its position, compelled international recognition—witness the delegations from Hattushash, Assyria, and Babylon—and obtained much booty and tribute, Syria beyond Qadesh remained an uncertain possession. Regularly in later years rebellions had to be quelled and later on Qadesh even held again a Mitanni garrison.

The conquered territory was administratively organized under a "governor of the northern foreign lands." Military points of support with garrisons, harbors along the coast (in particular Byblos, where the king built a Hathor temple for Baalat) for bringing in material and troops, royal hostages (at the same time future, "Egyptianized" claimants to the throne), vassals bound by oaths of allegiance, and warning punitive expeditions had to maintain Egypt's supremacy.

In Egypt Amon's temple at Karnak benefited from the successes, through land grants and donations in booty and slaves. In the far south, Thutmose established his rule as far as the territory of Napata, the fourth cataract.

Amenhotep II (ca. 1450–1420 B.C.), co-regent for some years already, was a worthy successor of his father. Already in his first year he marched to Syria, where he later also undertook campaigns. His major goals were Qadesh, Niya, and Tunip, places that had rebelled after his father's death. This military-oriented king, whose actions and vengeance were harsh, had nevertheless to realize that northern Syria and the Euphrates were beyond his grasp, because of the power of Mitanni and the actions of the Hittite Tudhaliyash. Egypt's northern boundary was consolidated on the line from Ugarit to the middle course of the Orontes. Under that line he maintained his authority with harsh hands, as is evident from the many deported prisoners-of-war (including *Maryannu* and *Apiru*) and public execution of Syrian rebels.

Under Thutmose IV (Wente: ca. 1419–1386 B.C.; Hornung: 1412–1402 B.C.) the political front began to move. Slowly relations with Mitanni began to relax, due to the threat of the Hittites and the awareness that both had reached the limits of their power. A daughter of Artatama I was married to the Egyptian pharaoh. In Palestine—at Gezer and Sidon—the king still made his influence felt, but in general it was a rather peaceful period, marked by building on the temple at Karnak; later Thutmose's monumental obelisk was carried from there to Rome.

His successor was Amenhotep III, "the Magnificent," who held the throne for more than thirty-eight years (ca. 1386–1349 B.C.). He ruled with oriental splendor; witness his impressive, in some cases colossal, building structures (e.g., the temple at Karnak, Soleb, and Luxor), his numerous ceremonial scarabs (on which memorable events were recorded), and his extensive harem with many princesses, including the daughters of the Mitanni kings Shutarna II and Tushratta, the first with her retinue of over three hundred persons. Art and commerce flourished, as shown by the tombs of high officials, such as Ramose and Cheruef, and especially the mortuary temple (!) of the wise architect Amenhotep, son of Hapu, the king's favorite, later worshiped as god of wisdom. Military activity was limited to Nubia (years 5 and 6), especially to maintain the flow of tribute, particularly gold. This gold played a significant role in the international diplomatic relations with many lands and courts; good relations were maintained and in some cases support and peace bought through an almost ritual exchange of gifts, letters, envoys, and harem princesses. The extensive contacts, commercial as well as political, are evident from the international correspondence and from the names of places inscribed on socles of images in the pharaoh's mortuary temple (e.g., Asshur, Babylon, Carchemish, Damascus, Knossos [on Keftiu = Crete], Mycene, Nauplia, and Cythera; the last three classified as Tanayu = Danaoi?).

Egyptian authority in Syria-Palestine was threatened by the lack of military activity—the pharaoh never showed himself there—and by the Hittite recovery of power, while from the inside it was undermined by independent actions of some vassals, particularly Amurru, who with the help of the Apiru carried on a power politics of their own.

## LITERATURE

F. J. Schmidt, *Amenophis I* (Hildesheim, 1978).

## e. The Amarna Age in the Fourteenth Century B.C.

The above-mentioned developments are easy to follow, particularly during the Amarna Age. This is the period of about twenty-five years (ca. 1353–1328 B.C.) between the final years of Amenhotep III and the early years of Tutankhamon, covered by international correspondence of the pharaohs, discovered in the residence of Akhenaten, modern Tell el-Amarna. It concerns a collection of about 380 cuneiform texts, mostly letters, the (considerable) remainder of a clandestine discovery made at the site in 1887. Together with the (for the most part) somewhat later texts from Hattushash and the archives from Ugarit, they offer a unique insight into the complexities of the political situation of those days. They are also very important linguistically; for example, the Tushratta letter is by far the longest Hurrian text known to us. Through the letters of the vassals from Canaan, who write officially in Babylonian but lace it with glosses in their own language and numerous hybrid grammatical forms, we get an idea of the "language of Canaan" before the entry of Israel.

The correspondence consists mainly of two parts. First are extensive letters of "great kings" who regard themselves as the equal of the pharaoh and address him as "brother": those of Arzawa (southern coast of Asia Minor; letters in Luwian), Hattushash, Alashia (Cyprus), Mitanni, Assyria (only later), Babylon (letters nos. 1–42 in the edition of Knudtzon). Second are letters from the vassals in Syria-Palestine; represented in particular are Qatna, Amurru, Damascus, Byblos (under Rib-Addi; 60 letters), Beirut, Sidon, Tyre, Qadesh, Kumidi, Hazor, Ashtaroth, Akko, Megiddo, Akshaf, Shechem, Jerusalem, Gezer, Lachish, and Ashkelon, besides a number of places and some rulers whose city-states are still unidentified. There are also a few copies of letters, written by the pharaohs to their allies and vassals (nos. 162–63). One might expect more of such replies—for which the senders sometimes, according to their letters, had to wait in vain for a long time—but thus far the result is disappointing, though new excavations, such as at Tell Nebi Mend or Qatna, may change that. The only real

Amarna Letters from Syria are those recently discovered at Kamid el-Loz or Kumidi. From Tell el-Hesi in southern Canaan is a letter, addressed to an Egyptian functionary, dating from this period and dealing with the actions of the rulers of Lachish, known from other letters. Older (15th century?) are the thirteen cuneiform texts discovered at Taanach; two cuneiform texts from Shechem are likely from the fourteenth century, but present no substantive points of contact with the Amarna correspondence.

Egyptian rule over these territories was concentrated in three centers: the south and the Phoenician coast were administered from Gaza; the northwest, the territory of Amurru, from Sumur; the area around Damascus (Upe) from Kumidi. Here resided the governors, called *rabisu* or *sokinu*, who had the supervision over the city princes, designated as *hazannu* or "man of . . . ." Government officials in various cities and small garrisons maintained Egyptian authority, in emergency cases buttressed by an expeditionary army. Egyptian influence was particularly strong in the coastal plain and the Phoenician cities, but also in the plain of Jezreel, with fortresses such as Megiddo, Taanach, and Beth-shean.

The signs of the disintegration of the empire can be read in the letters. Egypt gradually lost territory, so that eventually north of Palestine only the Phoenician cities and Damascus still acknowledged Egypt's sovereignty. Here and farther south internal rivalry flourished in an atmosphere of conspiracy and suspicion, in which irregular elements such as the Apiru assumed a large role (see below) and supported local powers, sometimes in a nationalistic anti-Egyptian movement. Surprise attacks, murder, and unsafety of caravan roads are mentioned, while pleas for military help from Egypt (at times limited to a few dozen soldiers!) often remained unanswered. Within the nominally still prevailing vassal system, charges of rebellion, betrayal, and hostility toward the pharaoh, beside moving asseverations of faithfulness (particularly from Rib-Addi of Byblos, who went through rough times and presented himself as a "righteous sufferer"), were a common occurrence.

In the north, especially Amurru, under Abdi-Ashirta and Aziru, was a source of unrest. With the help of the Apiru, Abdi-Ashirta succeeded in expanding his power to the entire coastal strip between Ugarit and Byblos, and eventually also temporarily annexed Byblos. Later Aziru crossed over to the Hittite camp and became a vassal of Shuppiluliumash, who gradually extended his power to the Lebanon. That was also the fate of Qatna, ally of Egypt, especially through the instrumentality of Qadesh under Aitagama. Farther south, Hazor, the only one of the vassals with a ruler who dared to carry the kingly title (*sharru*), had ambitions of territorial expansion, which threatened Tyre and Sidon. In the central Palestinian highlands, Shechem under Labaya was a center of anti-Egyptian activity. With the help of the Apiru even Megiddo was attacked, while in the south, with help from Gezer, Jerusalem under Abdi-Hepa was pressured. Jerusalem, together with Shuwardatta (of Hebron?), received a contingent of war chariots as help from Akko and Akshaf to keep the Apiru at bay. Immediate Egyptian help was usually too long in coming, or was not given at all, particularly when under Amenhotep IV all the attention was concentrated on internal Egyptian affairs.

---

## LITERATURE

E. F. Campbell, *The Chronology of the Amarna Letters* (Baltimore, 1964).

*B. Cumming, *Egyptian Historical Records of the Later Eighteenth Dynasty* (Warminster, 1982–83).

J. A. Knudtzon, *Die El-Amarna Tafeln* (Leipzig, 1915; repr. 1964) (letters nos. 1–358).

C. Kuhne, *Die Chronologie der internationalen Korrespondenz von El-Amarna* (Kevelaer/Neukirchen-Vluyn, 1973).

M. Liverani, *Three Amarna Essays* (Malibu, 1979).

A. F. Rainey, *El Amarna Tablets 359–379* (Kevelaer/Neukirchen-Vluyn, 1970).

A. R. Schulman, "Some Remarks on the Military Background of the Amarna Period," *Journal of the Egyptian Research Center in Egypt* 3 (1964) 51–69.

## f. Akhenaten and the End of the Eighteenth Dynasty (1350–1300 B.C.)

After Amenhotep III died, despite the sending of a medicinal statue of Ishtar from Mitanni, he was succeeded by his second son, Amenhotep IV, a child of the remarkable queen Tiy (whose mummy has recently been identified). As sole ruler (a co-regency is highly dubious) he ruled 1349–1334 B.C. His kingship heralded a radical change in Egypt's religious history, which earned him—viewed from the traditional Egyptian standpoint—the title "heretic king." Changing the traditional worship of the national sun-god Amon-Re or Re-Harakhti, he gave central place to one specific aspect of Re in cult and theology: the solar disk with its light, warmth, and life-giving rays, often depicted on his monuments from Karnak and el-Amarna. He changed his birth name to Akhenaten (Ikhnaton), built a temple for Aten at Karnak, and in his sixth year constructed an entirely new residence on new soil, halfway between Thebes and Memphis. This residence, called Akhetaten, was situated on the eastern bank of the Nile opposite Hermopolis; now called el-Amarna after a Bedouin tribe living there, it has provided the greatest measure of insight into Akhenaten's renewal through its monuments and the content of the rock tombs of its high officials.

The background and motives of his revolutionary action are unknown. It has been conjectured that he was influenced by his mother Tiy or his wife Nefertiti, but this is hard to prove. Both genuine religious motivations—the urge to worship one creator of the universe, experienced as a good and life-giving god, as he is prayed to and described in the hymns preserved in the tombs, which in places manifest a substantive similarity with some psalms of David (e.g., Psalm 104)—and political motivations seem to have been at work. For the Amon cult had evolved into a more secularized religious, political, and economic complex that could overshadow the monarchy. The removal of Amon's name, even on monuments in Nubia, indicates the sharpness of the contrast; later there was a partial restoration, which particularly affected his Aten temple at Karnak (his residence was abandoned soon after his death and the building materials were later used for different purposes by his successors). Thousands of its limestone blocks, decorated with reliefs, have been discovered in the foundations of buildings of Horemheb, in particular as the stone core of the second pylon of the Amon temple.

These reliefs, now with difficulty being restored, depict some of the theology of the Aten cult. The king with his wife and daughter appear in the aureole of Aten (the rays end in blessing hands) while they worship him. But Akhenaten and Nefertiti also appear together with Aten as object of adoration and worship; from universal mediators they have become like gods. Some of the reliefs, as well as the way in which Nefertiti's Aten name is written, underscore her special relation to the solar disk: she alone prays to him. Elsewhere she appears as god-king, who defeats the enemies, or even beside three goddesses on one of the corners of Ay's sarcophagus.

Art clearly reflects the renewal of the Amarna Age. The Aten temple differed from the traditional temples in its lack of a closed sanctuary with an image of the gods looked after by the priests. The temple was open to the rays of the sun, and its center was a high altar surrounded by numerous sacrificial tables. In sculptures the private life of the royal family was depicted idyllically, perhaps as a conscious manifestation of life in the warmth of Aten's love. The portraits witness to expressionism and exaggerated realism, in which also the individuality of the artists (some known by name, also with proofs from their workrooms) could express itself. Divergent conclusions about the nature of the king have been drawn from pictures of the king—depicted as deformed, effeminate, bisexual, or overly expressive—conclusions which, considering also that the beautiful Nefertiti had herself pictured in that style, seem exaggerated. Some see the king as god of fertility (Hapi) and as "father and mother" of the people (and therefore almost androgynous). It is clear that a person who introduced such a drastic religious change and was able to carry it out organizationally cannot have been a weakling, but was a strong, aggressive, creative personality.

The resistance which he encountered, despite his relative isolation in his new residence, induced him (probably after Nefertiti had fallen into disgrace) about his twelfth or thirteenth year to be more moderate. During the last years of his reign, besides Aten, Amon was also again worshiped. The appointment of his son-in-law Smenkhkare (in the absence of a son of his own) as co-regent and crown prince—married to Akhenaten's daughter Meritaten—may be another indication of compromise (according to some, however, Smenkhkare is no one else but Nefertiti represented as a man!), for Smenkhkare restored Amon-worship fully after Akhenaten's death.

After the seventeenth year of his reign the king died, outlived only briefly by Smenkhkare. The crown passed to Tutankhamon (ca. 1333–1324 B.C.), who was married to one of Akhenaten's daughters. In the third year of his reign the young ruler, for whom Ay acted as regent, abandoned Akhetaten as his residence and went to Memphis, from which a peaceful restoration began. The king was especially known for his fabulously rich grave, found in nearly perfect condition in 1922 in the Valley of the Kings—a tomb which probably was not originally intended as his grave, but one with which the pharaoh had to be content because his own tomb, as yet incomplete, and mortuary temple were annexed by his successor Ay. When Tutankhamon died at the age of eighteen, Ay assumed the throne, supported by Horemheb. After Ay's brief reign (only five years), General Horemheb mounted the throne, for which he had been selected by the childless Ay. He restored some of Egypt's military prestige, which he had already started under Tutankhamon with an expedition to Qadesh and a campaign to Nubia. In the beginning of his reign an Egyptian army appeared twice in southern Syria, not so much to attack Hittite positions, which were competently consolidated by Shuppiluliumash's successor Murshilish II, as to restore Egypt's sovereignty over its own territories. Horemheb, who reigned twenty-eight years (ca. 1321–1293 B.C.), made his own contribution to the peaceful restoration of the Amarna Age, for example, by construction on the Amon temple at Karnak (erection of three new pylons and a colonnade). Here, in the Theban necropolis (which despite the transfer of the residence to Memphis remained in use for a few more centuries) he was buried, after having abandoned his monumental tomb in Saqqara—the burial place of the dignitaries from the Amarna Age. Already before his death he appointed a ranking military person, Peramesse, his vizier and "deputy of his majesty in Upper and Lower Egypt," as his successor. Ruling only two years as Ramses I, he founded the Nineteenth Dynasty. See ill. 74.

## LITERATURE

C. Aldred, *Akhenaten and Nefertari* (New York, 1973).

———, *Akhenaten, Pharaoh of Egypt: A New Study* (London, 1968).

Ch. Desroches-Noblecourt, *Tutankhamen: Life and Death of a Pharaoh* (New York, 1963).

R. Krauss, *Das Ende der Amarnazeit* (Hildesheim, 1978).

A. Malamat, "Campaigns of Amenhotep II and Thutmose IV to Canaan," *Scripta Hierosolymitana* 8 (Jerusalem, 1961) 218–31.

D. B. Redford, *History and Chronology of the Eighteenth Dynasty of Egypt* (Toronto, 1967).

*H. A. Schlögl, *Echnaton-Tutanchamon. Fakten und Texte* (Wiesbaden, 1983).

J. A. Wilson, "Akh-en-aton and Nefert-iti," *Journal of Near Eastern Studies* 32 (1973) 235–41.

## g. The Hurrians and Mitanni (16th–13th Centuries B.C.)

From the sixteenth century the Hurrian element evolved gradually into a powerful factor in the area where the boundaries of Mesopotamia, northern Syria, and Anatolia come together. After the death of Murshilish I, they penetrated farther into Anatolia, especially in Kizzuwatna and Ishuwa; Hurrian elements also surfaced in northern Syria, though without a specific urban center. Not until 1500 B.C. can one speak of a real Mitanni state in northern Mesopotamia, from which it made its influence felt in the north and west. We know the oldest rulers only from the dynastic seal, later used by Shaustatar, that names

"Shuttarna, son of Kirta, king of *Ma-i-ta-ni-i,* and must be from about 1550 B.C. Historically these rulers are unidentifiable, in particular now that it has become clear that the dynastic ancestor Kirta may not be identified with King Krt, known from an Ugaritic legendary-mythical text. Already about 1500 B.C. we encounter Parattarna as suzerain of Idrimi of Alalakh, who speaks of him as "powerful king, king of the Hurrian troops." Mitanni became very prominent from the time of Shaustatar (ca. 1470 B.C.), who is mentioned in the texts from Alalakh (layer IV) and Nuzi carrying the old title "king of Mitanni." He was the antagonist of Thutmose III, and he plundered Asshur and was recognized as suzerain from northern Syria as far as the area east of the Tigris (Nuzi, with the kingdom of Arrapkha).

The terminology used for the Hurrian kingdom is somewhat confusing. Initially, though the kings themselves carry the title "king of Mitanni" (name of the people or the territory?), sources from Syria and Boghazköy only speak of "Hurrians" or "Hurrian troops." To indicate the territory of the state, Mitanni's rivals speak mainly of Hanigalbat, a name later also used a great deal in Asshur, and again by Assyrians and Hittites in the fourteenth century when the kingdom had become a powerless vassal state. From the end of the fifteenth century, especially in Syria and Hattushash, the term Mitanni is used for the realm in its heyday (occasionally also "land of the Hurrians/of Mitanni" is still used). The Egyptians as a rule spoke of the territory east of the Euphrates as Naharin(a), in effect "Mesopotamia" in a broader sense: the territory in and east of the great Euphrates curve.

The designation "Hurrian" is applicable to Mitanni on the basis of the linguistic character of many personal names (also familiar from Nuzi), names of gods (Nubadig, Teshshub, Shauska, Kushukh, Hepa[t], Adammu, Kumarbi, Kubaba, Ashtabi, Shimegi, et al.), and place-names. The written and spoken language was Hurrian, as is shown by the Amarna Letters and the many Hurrian terms in Akkadian texts from Nuzi. There is nothing like an "Indo-Arian" kingdom and a large penetration of Indo-Arians into northern Mesopotamia, as is sometimes suggested in older historical treatments. Linguistically considered, Mitanni does have some Indo-Arian elements that exhibit relationship with Vedic. In the curses of Shattiwaza's treaty with Shuppiluliumash, "the gods belonging to Mitra, Varuna, Indra," and Nasatya are mentioned. Some names of Mitanni rulers are Indo-Arian, such as Shuttarna, Parsasatar, Artatamar, and Tushratta, and also elsewhere where the Hurrians penetrated such names occur: Aitagama (Carchemish), Biryawaza (Damascus), Indaruta (Akshaf), Biridya (Megiddo). Also some terms relating to war chariots and the training of horses, such as *maryannu* (prominent charioteers), are Indo-Arian. However, all these elements appear in a context which historically and culturally is Hurrian; the names of the deities mentioned have Hurrian grammatical endings. The most plausible explanation is that in an early time a group of Indo-Arian "nobles," who at that time were already experienced in the use of the (originally not Indo-Arian) war chariot, probably in the vicinity of the Caucasus, came in contact with Hurrians and became part of them, while maintaining their own types of names and pantheon. Their origin and qualities enabled them to play a leading role among the Hurrians.

Information about Mitanni is limited, mainly because the capital Washshukanni with its archives (in the Habur area?) has not yet been discovered. Historical data can be gleaned from the Mitanni letters discovered at el-Amarna, from Hittite sources (especially the prologues to more recent treaties), from some Egyptian texts, and from material from Syria. This last-named material is predominantly from Alalakh, which in the fifteenth century B.C. was under the suzerainty of Mitanni.

Idrimi of Alalakh had conquered the throne shortly after 1500 B.C. when Mitanni's political influence was still minor. He recognized the Mitanni king Paratarna, but also independently made a treaty with Kizzuwatna and undertook raids against Hittite cities. Idrimi is especially known from his historically interesting and literarily remarkable autobiography, inscribed on a large statue of the king enthroned (now in the British Museum). As the youngest son of the king of Aleppo (with the Semitic name Ilimilimma), he fled with his brothers to Emar during a rebellion (instigated by Mitanni?). Preferring there the life of a freebooter, in the steppe he came in contact with the Sutu-nomads and ended up in the city of Ammia in Canaan (*Kinanum*). Together with fugitives from Mukish, Aleppo, and other cities he formed a commando unit and lived seven years among the *Apiru*. Finally, after landing at the coast near Mons Casius, he managed to capture Mukish and the city of Alalakh; there he became king and after "seven years" was recognized by the Mitanni ruler. He consolidated his position by palace building and control over the nomads. He mentioned two heirs to the throne: Niqmepa and Ilimilimma II. This historiographically unique document, a story about the uphill attempts by a lawful pretender to take the throne, shows that Syria possessed a remarkable literary creativity, probably influenced by Hittite historiography. It also gives us a view of the unstable situation in Syria prior to the supremacy of Mitanni and the campaigns of Thutmose III. See ill. 73.

We can obtain some idea of Hurrian society from the profusion of textual material dug up at Nuzi, a small city east of the Tigris in the vicinity of Kirkuk (now to be supplemented with textual material dug up at Kurrukhanni = Tell al-Fachar in the same region). In the fifteenth century, Nuzi was part of the kingdom of Arrapkha (now Kirkuk), which itself was under the suzerainty of Mitanni. Written in Akkadian, these texts are increasingly (over five generations) laced with Hurrian terms. They deal with family law (marriage, adoption, estate laws, testament), agriculture, landownership, feudal system, conscription, trade, industry, palace administration, and administration of justice. The Hurrian character of this more "feudally" organized society is also evident from the personal names, which are for the most part Hurrian, though there is the aftereffect of Babylonian influences, for example, in the formulation of contracts and common law. This fascinating material has often been uncritically used as a parallel and illustration of customs described in the patriarchal narratives of the Old Testament, and for dating these. The similarities are no more than relative, however, and, moreover, cannot be explained on the ground of precise contemporaneity or even the taking over of Hurrian common law by the patriarchs (as suggested by Speiser). Certain customs and legal practices were widespread in the second millennium, also due to Mesopotamian scribal traditions; the crystallization of it is found both in the Nuzi material and in the Genesis stories, which by themselves are not dependent on each other and have illustrative value of their own.

Despite the campaigns of Thutmose, around 1460 B.C. Mitanni could maintain itself as a large power. The last ten years of the pharaoh were without further conflicts; also under his successor Amenhotep II, who penetrated no farther than Ugarit and Qadesh, clashes are absent. In fact, under Shaustatar's successor, Artatamar I, even Mitanni and Egypt established an alliance sealed by a marriage. Artatamar's son and successor Shuttarna II was assassinated after a relatively short reign and succeeded by a younger brother Tushratta, bypassing Artatamar II, who went to the Hittites for help. According to the Amarna correspondence (e.g., letter no. 24, almost 500 lines long, in Hurrian, the most extensive Hurrian document we possess), Tushratta maintained diplomatic contact with Amenhotep III (ca. 1350 B.C.), whereby their pact was directed against their common threat: the powerful Shuppiluliumash of Hatti. His campaigns and Assyria's recovery in the east led to Mitanni's collapse after the death of Tushratta. The increasingly weakening Mitanni was divided into two parts in the second half of the fourteenth century: the west under Shattiwaza, vassal and son-in-law of Shuppiluliumash, was actually a Hittite protectorate; the east had to pay tribute to Assyria. Later Shattiwaza disappeared from the scene without an obvious successor. The last two kings whom we know are Shattuara and his son Wasashatta, shortly after 1300 B.C. Their relations with Hatti are not clear, but it appears likely that under Murshilish II Mitanni regained some of its influence; at any rate, according to the Egyptian sources Mitanni, under the name Naharina, participated in the great battle between Hatti (under Muwatallish) and Egypt (under Ramses II) at Qadesh on the Orontes in 1275 B.C.. Following Ashuruballit (ca. 1340 B.C.), Adad-nirari I (ca. 1295–1264 B.C.) sealed Mitanni's fate. Rebellions by Shattuara and Wasashatta were cruelly suppressed, Washshukanni was captured, and the last Mitanni king was deported. The help expected from the Hittites was not forthcoming. After the death of Adad-nirari I, Mitanni, perhaps with Hittite help, only briefly became independent once more, but soon Shalmaneser I recaptured the territory, thrusting through to the Euphrates (ca. 1260 B.C.). The area between the Euphrates and the Habur lost its political identity. First it was ruled by Asshur; shortly afterward it became a bone of contention between Asshur and the advancing Arameans, who settled there in the eleventh century.

---

## LITERATURE

M. Dietrich and H. Klengel, "Die Inschrift der Statue des Königs Idrimi von Alalah," *Ugarit-Forschungen* 13 (1981) 199–278.

P. Garelli, ed., *Le palais et la royauté* (Paris, 1974), pp. 359–94 (Nuzi).

A. Kammenhuber, *Die Arier im Vorderen Orient* (Heidelberg, 1968) (see I. M. Diakonoff, *Orientalia* 41 [1972] 91–120).

H. Klengel, *Geschichte Syriens im 2. Jahrtausend v.u. Z.* III (Berlin, 1970), 156–217.

*M. A. Morrison and D. I. Owen, eds., *Studies on the Civilization and Culture of Nuzi and the Hurrians* (Winona Lake, 1981).

T. L. Thompson, *The Historicity of the Patriarchal Narratives* (Berlin/New York, 1974), ch. 10: "Nuzi and the Patriarchal Narratives."

R. de Vaux, *The Early History of Israel* (Philadelphia, 1978), pp. 83–89.

*G. Wilhelm, *Grundzüge der Geschichte und Kultur der Hurriter* (Darmstadt, 1982).

L. Woolley, *A Forgotten Kingdom* (London, 1953).

---

## h. The Hittite "New Kingdom" in the 15th–13th Centuries B.C.

After Telepinush, the Hittite empire passed through difficult times due to the invasion of the Gasga tribes from the north and the growing power of Mitanni in the south. Restoration happened around the end of the fifteenth century B.C. under Tudhaliyash II (or I). He extended his power from far in the west of Asia Minor (e.g., Lukka and Arzawa) all the way to the upper course of the Euphrates (Malatya, Ishuwa, Suhma) in the east. There, and in Kizzuwatna (Cilicia; center Kummanni) which he had annexed, he clashed with the Hurrian element, which was allied with Mitanni. In this period the southeast part of Anatolia became increasingly important. Hurrian influences are evident from royal names and from the cultural mediation between Mesopotamia and Hatti. Luwian influence is shown by the personal names of the population and the many Luwian rituals. The international contact can be determined from the rituals enumerating the foreign lands and cities whose gods "have been attracted by Hatti land."

This period of prosperity was short-lived. Under Arnuwandash rebellions broke out everywhere. The enemies pressed forward, and even Hattushash was burned, except for its "hesti-house" (mausoleum?). The crisis climaxed just before Shuppiluliumash's accession to the throne. Our knowledge of this period in history has increased by the redating to about 1400 B.C. of a group of texts that used to be placed in the last decades of the Hittite empire (end of the 13th century B.C.). These texts mention a series of kings called Tudhaliyash, Arnuwandash, and Shuppiluliumash. Linguistic, philological, and historical arguments have made this redating possible.

Shuppiluliumash used the first twenty years of his reign (from ca. 1360 B.C.[?]) to beat back the ememies, to consolidate the empire, and to build up the army. We are able to reconstruct the history on the basis of the (fragmentary) "Deeds of Shuppiluliumash," written by his son Murshilish II, and from the historical prologues to later vassal treaties. In the south and east (Kizzuwatna and Ishuwa) he clashed with Tushratta of Mitanni, suffering a defeat east of the Euphrates, near Ishuwa (Tushratta proudly reported this to Amenhotep III in an Amarna Letter). This confrontation was the beginning of a bitter struggle over the hegemony in northern Syria, which Shuppiluliumash ultimately won. After his defeat of Ishuwa, crossing the Euphrates from the east he entered Syria, where Aleppo and Mukish (in the Amuq valley with Alalakh) were forced to surrender. At Alalakh other small kingdoms, former Mitanni vassals such as Nuhashshe and Nii, surrendered. Also Ugarit, ruled by Ammishtamru

and later Niqmaddu, thus far linked with Egypt, became a vassal, but enjoyed preferential status because under Niqmaddu it had not aligned itself with the anti-Hittite coalition. Likewise Tunip, Qatna (plain of Homs), and Qadesh (Kinza), also belonging to the Egyptian sphere of influence, were forced to submit. At Qadesh the anti-Hittite king was replaced by his son Aitagama. Amurru (west of Qadesh) under Aziru remained for the time being nominally the vassal of Egypt. During a second campaign, evoked by military actions of Egypt and Mitanni, the Mitanni fortress of Carchemish was captured. Shuppiluliumash also gained territory in the south; Aziru of Amurru likewise became a vassal. The Hittite empire had reached the Lebanon.

Soon afterward the power of Mitanni was broken. Tushratta had been assassinated, and after an internal power struggle, in which his son Shattiwaza was forced to flee, he was succeeded by his brother Artatama and his son Shuttarna III. When Mitanni came under the influence of Asshur, Shuppiluliumash helped Shattiwaza to reconquer the throne from Carchemish. Through a treaty, an oath of allegiance, and a marriage with Shuppiluliumash's daughter he was closely linked with the Hittite empire. Mitanni, reduced in size and supervised by the Hittites, was allowed to function as a buffer between Hatti and Asshur.

In the end Shuppiluliumash ruled over a vast empire. His vassals were part of a more or less federally organized empire, in which they, while keeping a measure of independence, were as "vassal kings" personally tied to the Hittite state and king. Not only those who voluntarily submitted were treated like that; also conquered cities were given this status after a pro-Hittite member of the royal family had been put on the throne. By this policy fragmented Syria was kept under control, while apparently it was also simpler and more acceptable to the population of the highly developed, strongly Hurrian Syria to be ruled by indigenous kings under Hittite suzerainty. Also, that the kings of Carchemish, who were Hittite and who were responsible for the governmental control over the Syrian vassals, often assumed Hurrian throne-names points in that direction. Finally, it was also in Hatti's interest to give a measure of freedom to the Syrian trade cities, in particular Ugarit, so that they could continue to play their important commercial role (connections with Egypt and Cyprus), important also for the Hittite empire. That freedom could only be profitable for Hatti, also in the form of higher tribute.

The vassal treaty began with a preamble, in which the "great king" of Hatti, "the sun," presented himself. This was followed by a parenetically intended survey of the history of the relations between the two partners, after which the stipulations of the treaty were stated. The keeping of the treaty was solemnly sworn to by extensive curses and (briefer) formulas of blessings. Such "oaths of allegiance" are not new; they are also known from the Old Babyonian period. Mitanni also used this instrument in northern Syria, as we know from Alalakh. The Hittite treaties, more elaborate in form and better preserved (so far almost 40 texts), were systematically used in the upbuilding of the empire, with later treaties referring back to earlier ones. The great king was the feudal lord who invested his vassal with city and kingdom and thereby—barring unforeseen circumstances—guaranteed the heredity of the royal dignity. When there was a change in ruler the treaty was reenacted or renewed. The text was recorded in detail, usually in two languages, Hittite and Akkadian, the diplomatic language of that time. Sometimes local translations were made, for example, at Ugarit. The stipulation that the text was regularly to be read publicly demonstrates the importance of such local translations. The texts were carefully kept in the chief temples of both partners.

The great king guaranteed the status of his vassal and offered him protection and help. The large remainder of the stipulations concerned the obligations of the vassal: allegiance, payment of tribute, military support. The vassal relinquished his independent, foreign military relations: Hatti's enemy was the vassal's enemy, Hatti's friend the vassal's friend. Rebellion and resistance had to be reported and put down. Fugitives and enemies had to be handed over. A treaty once made remained valid, but in its details (tribute, boundaries) it could be updated to fit newer conditions, for instance, after war, rebellion, or territorial changes.

The relative freedom of the vassals was counterbalanced by the efficient control exercised by the suzerain. Besides traveling officials, the above-mentioned king of Carchemish, a kind of viceroy of Hatti, helped control the vassals. From that city Hatti could, if necessary, interfere in their mutual relations and internal affairs. Records and decrees about border conflicts, dynastic connections, military obligations, throne succession, and business affairs witness to it. Aleppo, too, was the seat of a Hittite prince; perhaps it was his task in this old royal city, cultic center of the important "weather-god of Syria," to supply the ideological basis for the system.

After his death (ca. 1325 B.C.) Shuppiluliumash was briefly succeeded by Arnuwandash. He soon died, probably from the plague brought in from Syria by Hittite troops; in the "plague prayers" of Murshilish II this plague is viewed as divine punishment for the violation of the Egyptian territory in Amqa, the valley between Lebanon and Anti-Lebanon. Murshilish II (ca. 1323–1295 B.C. [?]) found himself confronted with insurrections everywhere after the death of Shuppiluliumash; in his annals he reported that within ten years he had quelled these rebellions. In Asia Minor, Arzawa and Kizzuwatna were again brought in line and the Gasga punished, while in the east he recorded triumphs against Azzi-Hayasa. In the south, where after the weakening of Mitanni the Assyrians under Adad-nirari had occasionally threatened, he strengthened the Euphrates front. Carchemish, under Prince Piyassilish (Hurrian name Sharrikushush), remained the most important point of support, together with Aleppo, where Talmisharrumash came to the throne. Qadesh, ruled by Aitagama, and Nuhashshe, ruled by Tette, were subdued; Ugarit, which under (the usurper?) Arhalba had taken an anti-Hittite stance, was forced to toe the line, and Niqmepa, son of Niqmaddu, was made king. The loyalty of Aziru of Amurru, soon succeeded by his son Duppiteshub, strengthened the Hittite position relative to Egypt, which under Horemheb appeared twice in southern Syria, but did not contest the status quo. Assyria, kept occupied in the south by conflicts with Babylonia, became less dangerous; the grip on western Mitanni could be reinforced.

## LITERATURE

A. Goetze, *Die Annalen des Mursilis* (Leipzig, 1938; repr. Darmstadt, 1967) (see P. H. J. Houwink ten Cate, *Journal of Near Eastern Studies* 25 [1966] 162–91; and *Anatolica* 1 [1967] 44–61).

*H. G. Güterbock, "The Ahhiyawa Problem Reconsidered," *American Journal of Archaeology* 83 (1983) 133–38.

————, "The Deeds of Suppiluliuma as Told by His Son Mursili II," *Journal of Cuneiform Studies* 10 (1956) 41–68, 75–98, 107–30.

P. H. J. Houwink ten Cate, *Records of the Early Hittite Empire (ca. 1430–1370 B.C.)* (Istanbul, 1970).

K. A. Kitchen, *Suppiluliuma and the Amarna Pharaohs* (Liverpool, 1962).

V. Korošec, *Hethitische Staatsverträge* (Leipzig, 1931).

D. J. McCarthy, *Treaty and Covenant* (Rome, 1978²).

*E. von Schuler, "Hethitische Rechtsbücher," in O. Kaiser, ed., *Texte aus der Umwelt des Alten Testaments* I/1 (Gütersloh, 1982) 96–125.

*I. Singer, "Western Anatolia in the 13th Century B.C. according to Hittite Sources," *Anatolian Studies* 33 (1983) 205–17.

E. F. Weidner, *Politische Dokumente aus Klein-Asien* (Leipzig, 1923; repr. Hildesheim/New York, 1970).

## i. Apiru and Shosu

During the second millennium B.C. the Apiru were found throughout the entire Near East (from Asia Minor to Egypt). Early on scholars attempted to identify them with the Hebrews (*ibrim*) in the Old Testament: phonetically the names *Apiru* and *ibrim* are considerably similar, while according to the Amarna Texts the Apiru played a significant role in Palestine during the fourteenth century B.C., a fact which has been associated with the invasion of the Israelite tribes.

According to its Babylonian equivalents (*shaggashum* or sa.gaz, and *habbatum*) the term *Apiru*—perhaps of Amorite origin—designates "robbers, highwaymen," then also "displaced persons, outlaws." The etymology is uncertain;

none of the proposed derivations—'*br*, "to cross; '*pr*, "to forage; '*afar*, "dust(y)—is clearly demonstrated. Ugaritic modes of writing show clearly that '*apiru* is the correct spelling, of which the Babylonian *ḫapiru* is an approximation. Apparently already early the word was a kind of technical term. In Akkadian there is a derived verb *ḫpr*, "become Apiru," used for fugitive debtors and slaves.

As to its origin, the term is probably not an ethnic or tribal name (ethnicon), but a social appellative with an unfavorable meaning. Apiru came into existence through disintegration of sedentary (village, city) and nomadic societies, in which individuals or groups were cast out or fled, due to political or social conflicts: crimes, persecution, debts, poverty, slavery, famine. On the fringes of the civilized world or elsewhere in sedentary society they tried to find a new existence. They are found as independent people, as groups of robbers or guerrillas (favored by the landscape, which was much more wooded than now), or as mercenaries in the service of a ruler (in the Amarna Age the king of Damascus possessed Apiru and *Sutu* troops). Others served as individuals, as personnel, or as clients. When they consolidated themselves into a group they could become a powerful force. In the fragmented Syro-Palestinian territory they could become a threat to the political status quo and support national and rebellious movements. That could lead to armed conflict, and sometimes also to treaties with groups of Apiru.

The relationship between Apiru and *ibri* is a moot question, because it is related to one's view of Israel's prehistory and of the history of the origin of a book such as Genesis, which calls Abram an *ibri*. In the Old Testament, particularly in Samuel, *ibri* is predominantly ethnic in meaning; it distinguishes the Israelites from other ethnic entities, especially as used by non-Israelites. Yet the term also appears to have social implications, especially in a judicial context. Newer research has shown that the two options are not necessarily mutually exclusive. Rowton has pointed out that often in history social appellatives become names of tribes and peoples and vice versa: Kazak/Kozak, Mawali, Turk, etc.

From a historical perspective the stay in Egypt

cannot have turned the tribes of Israel into *ibrim*. Apiru do not come into existence there; on the contrary, they are imported as prisoners of war from Syria-Palestine, sometimes in large numbers. Also, one may not equate the *ibrim* simply with the Apiru in general, since in space and time the Apiru were widespread. There was no process in which the Apiru became united and developed into a tribe or people. If there is a connection between *ibri* and Apiru, it is to be found in a particular historical and social context, probably in a specific region. Two possibilities suggest themselves: either the Middle Bronze Age (the "Amorite" milieu of the patriarchs), or the later developments in Canaan in the fourteenth–thirteenth centuries B.C.

Albright in particular held that the Middle Bronze Age was the most likely time because in Genesis Abraham is called an *ibri*. That was an apt name for him because he represented a clan that had become detached from his tribe and family in Haran, and which was not indigenous to Canaan. Therefore his descendants were automatically *ibrim*. This line of thought also attaches great significance to Abraham's military pursuits (with allies) in Genesis 14, comparable to the activities of Apiru as robbers or mercenary soldiers. In his last publications Albright pictured Abraham as a merchant plying his trade with donkey caravans, and presumably owing his name to the denigrating term "dusty," which was applied to such wayfarers. This idea has found little support; the etymology behind "dusty" is quite unconvincing.

If one takes as the starting point the fourteenth–thirteenth centuries, the data from the Amarna Age becomes very important. It is obvious that in these texts the Apiru were not primarily an invading, foreign population element, but a part of the native population—to which even city princes belong—that was anti-Egypt, nationalistic in orientation, and disturbing the peace. In this view, the tribes invading from Egypt could hardly have been Apiru. To find a connection it is necessary to associate the tribes of Israel with the native population of Canaan. That is usually done by assuming that not all tribes of Israel were in Egypt, and that the entry into Canaan was a process in which a number of tribes reunited themselves with their autochthonous relatives in

Canaan, who had lived there since the Middle Bronze period, in the "Amorite" milieu, as farmers and shepherds. In one way or another they would have acquired the name Apiru, which was then applied to the entire tribe.

How did they acquire this name? One reconstruction is as follows. The native "Israelites" were presumably a part of the nucleus of an anti-Egyptian, nationalistic movement, eventually reinforced by support from tribal relatives who had fled Egypt and who were labeled as "outlaws" by authorities and pro-Egyptian elements. Nationalistic opposition transformed the designation "rebel," "outlaw," into an ethnicon (*ibri*).

Others, particularly Mendenhall, who reject this political-nationalistic view as well as that of sedentarization of nomads, assume a revolution on the part of the rural population of farmers and shepherds who were exploited by the feudal city-states and their agents, a revolution which was aimed at the Canaanite as well as the Egyptian forces. This farmers' revolution was made possible by the crises of the Late Bronze Age, which diminished the influence of the city-states, and it was sparked by originally Canaanite groups who had escaped to Egypt and who, under Moses, inspired the rebellion from the other side of the Jordan, where they overran the kingdoms of Heshbon and Bashan. These groups gave the rebellion its religious foundation, on the basis of a covenant with Yahweh in which the notions of social justice and brotherhood played a central role. Weippert has noted that the image of the Apiru that comes through in the Amarna Letters does not agree with this view. He also objected to the equation of *ibrim* with "Israelites" as they play a central role in exodus and conquest; *ibrim* is used only in certain contexts.

Rowton assigned a lot of weight to the Apiru as a disintegrated tribal element which he discovered in northern Mesopotamia, as we are familiar with it from the Mari Letters. Such tribal elements constituted the nucleus of groups who were joined by urban Apiru, gradually assuming a tribal structure. The *ibrim* who presented themselves as indeed belonging to Israel (Yahweh, the god of the *ibrim*, is interchangeable with "Yahweh, the god of Israel") presumably constituted the nucleus of such a new tribe, which included especially the detribalized element of one particular people, Israel, and so acquired ethnic significance.

Choosing among these various views is almost impossible. The connection between Apiru and *ibrim*, undeniable linguistically and sociologically, does not imply that exact identifications are possible. It is not possible to equate the *ibrim* with the Apiru who worked as forced laborers in Egypt in the Ramesside time (mid-13th century B.C.), nor with the Apiru who were found in Canaan in the fourteenth century and who aligned themselves, for instance, with Labaya of Shechem. Knowledge of the old tribal history of Israel is still limited, while the social and political developments in the Late Bronze Age are highly complicated. Moreover, information in the historical sources is widespread and fragmentary about such a "fringe phenomenon" as the Apiru; on the whole, little is known about their earliest phase. The necessary unity in outlook on Israel's oldest history and tribal traditions is not there either. Furthermore, so far unknown elements such as the Shosu may also have played a role in the history.

The *Shosu*, too, appear in this period, particularly in Egyptian sources from the fifteenth to the twelfth centuries B.C., as a population element in Syria-Palestine (from Aleppo in the north to the Sinai and the Negeb). They are found especially on the edges of the civilized world, in the Lebanon as well as in Transjordan and southern Palestine. Even as they did with the Apiru, the Egyptians viewed the Shosu as a hostile, disturbing element, threatening the trade routes and Egypt's eastern border (including the important mining in the Wadi Arabah [Timna] and the Sinai). They were repeatedly fought and defeated, with prisoners sometimes being deported to Egypt. They are also found as helpers of the Hittites in the battle at Qadesh on the Orontes.

In southern Palestine they appear as tent-dwelling nomads with small livestock, living tribally and ruled by tribal chiefs, restricted to places where water was to be found. Besides a "Shosu source" and a "Shosu district" in Syria, under Ramses II and III especially Seir and Edom are linked with them, where in a sense they are Egypt's immediate neighbors.

As with the term Apiru, the word Shosu was apparently applied to widely spread groups, particularly nomads. Therefore it is probably not (no longer?) the name of a tribe of people, but a social appellative, perhaps "nomad, bedouin." As such the term is hard to detach from *Sutu (Shutu)*, the name of an important nomadic element along the entire middle Euphrates, occurring as late as the first millennium B.C. (see above, p. 237). Sutu and Apiru are used side by side a few times in a manner that suggests that they are comparable entities. The king of Damascus assured the pharaoh that he would strengthen the Egyptian army with all his troops, including "my Apiru and my Sutu"; another Palestinian king pleaded with the pharaoh to save him from the power of "Apiru, robbers [*habbatu*], and Shutu." Both cases concern apparently nomadic elements, either recruited as mercenary soldiers or acting as enemies. Forced to flee, Idrimi of Alalakh lived for a while among the Sutu in east Syria and later integrated these nomadic elements into his government.

Similar nomadic elements, called Shosu by the Egyptians, are also found in Palestine, especially in the fringe areas not inhabited and controlled by the Canaanites, where also the Israelites at first settled. In view of the social and territorial overlapping, the inevitable question is, what is the relationship, if any, between Israel and Shosu? A decisive answer cannot be given, but it seems quite possible that Israelites, for instance, living in Kadesh-barnea and apparently related to the Kenites, were included in the term Shosu by the Egyptians, before they adopted a more sedentary life in Palestine. In this connection it is noteworthy that according to the Old Testament there were ancient ties between Edom and Seir—a Shosu area—and Israel: Edom is a kinspeople and Israel knows "Yahweh who comes from Seir." It is difficult to make definite identifications in this period, in which specific names of people, such as Israel, Moab, and Edom, are hardly mentioned in the sources. Moreover, in the search for ethnic entities, "peoples" such as the Kenites and Amalekites should not be forgotten.

---

## LITERATURE

J. R. Bartlett, "The Brotherhood of Edom," *Journal for the Study of the Old Testament* 4 (1977) 2–27 (see M. Rose, "Yahweh in Israel—Qaus in Edom?" ibid., 28–34).

J. Bottero, "Hapiru," in *Reallexikon der Assyriologie* IV (Berlin, 1971) 14–27.

_____, *Le problème des habiru à la 4e Rencontre Assyriologique Internationale* (Paris, 1954).

F. M. Cross, ed., *Symposia* (Cambridge, Mass., 1979); see especially the contributions of H. Tadmor, M. Weippert, A. Malamat, and Y. Yadin.

R. Giveon, *Les bédouins Shosou des documents égyptiens* (Leiden, 1971).

*O. Loretz, *Habiru-Hebräer* (Berlin, 1984).

G. E. Mendenhall, "The Hebrew Conquest of Palestine," *Biblical Archaeologist* 25 (1962) 66–87.

M. B. Rowton, "Dimorphic Society and the Problem of the *apiru-ibrim,*" *Journal of Near Eastern Studies* 35 (1976) 13–20.

M. Weippert, "Abraham der Hebräer?" *Biblica* 52 (1971) 407–26.

_____, "Semitische Nomaden des zweiten Jahrtausends. Über die *Šʾśw* der ägyptischen Quellen," *Biblica* 55 (1974) 265–80.

_____, *The Settlement of the Israelite Tribes in Palestine: A Critical Survey of Recent Scholarly Debate* (Naperville, IL, 1971), pp. 63–102.

See also *Journal for the Study of the Old Testament* 7 (1978), which has various articles on the problem of Israel's conquest.

---

## j. Assyrians and Kassites: Mesopotamia in the 15th–12th Centuries B.C.

The history of Mesopotamia in the fifteenth century is poorly known due to the lack of sources. Asshur was greatly pressed by Mitanni, though according to the King List it kept its own rulers (temporarily as vassals of Mitanni?). The names, order, and length of reign of the Kassite kings nos. 11–14 are disputed. Only toward the end of the fourteenth century do the data increase. Asshur's recovery is evident from increasing building activity from the time of Ashurbelnisheshu (king no. 69), who about 1405 B.C. "builds the great wall of the new city." Shortly after 1400 B.C. the Kassite Kurigalzu I founded the new capital Dur-Kurigalzu, now the impressive ruin Aqarquf, about 20 kilometers (12 mi.) west of Baghdad, for a long time thought to be the tower of Babel.

From now on there is also military contact between Asshur and Babel, especially east of the Tigris, resulting about 1400 B.C. in a border agreement between Ashurbelnisheshu and Karaindash.

This contact was the beginning of a rivalry lasting two centuries, in which Asshur often was the stronger, as we can learn from notes in chronicles, in the "Synchronistic History," and in historical-epic compositions about the conflict written by both sides. From Asshur we possess a story about Adad-nirari I (ca. 1295–1264 B.C.) and especially the extensive "Tukulti-Ninurta Epic." From Babylon come (fragments of) a "Kurigalzu (II) epic" and epic stories about Adad-shumusur (ca. 1200 B.C.) and Nebuchadrezzar I (end of the 12th century B.C.). These compositions betray an obvious political and religious ideology. In the Babylonian texts the theme of Marduk's supremacy over the gods and his curse on every king who ignores his cult is dominant. Thus it is thought that these texts were composed during the reign of Nebuchadrezzar I, according to Lambert "a turning point in the history of Mesopotamian religion," because the supremacy of Marduk was at that time climaxed by his official recognition as "king of the gods."

From the Amarna Texts we know that the Babylonian king Kadashman-Enlil I (ca. 1365 [?]–1350 B.C.) maintained correspondence with Pharaoh Amenhotep III (Ni[b]muwaria). Little is known about his activities, because it is still impossible to distinguish his building inscriptions from those of his namesake, who reigned about 100 years later (a problem encountered also with other Kassite kings, particularly Kurigalzu I and II). His son is the well-known Burnaburiash II (ca. 1349–1323 B.C.), one of the most notable Kassite kings, who in one of his numerous building inscriptions—found in many cities of southern Mesopotamia, such as Ur, Larsa, Uruk, and Nippur—calls himself king of "Sumer and Akkad." He maintained diplomatic relations with Amenhotep III (?) and IV (Niphuriria) of Egypt. Asshur now presented itself as a new superpower. After Tushratta's death, under Ashuruballit I (ca. 1353–1318), it threw off the yoke of Mitanni, made Artatama a tributary, and annexed parts of its kingdom. According to Amarna

Letter no. 16, the self-assured Assyrian king took up diplomatic contacts with Egypt, referring to earlier relations under his grandfather. This gesture, in which he presented himself as "great king" and "brother" of the pharaoh, evoked an indignant reaction from Burnaburiash of Babylon, who according to Amarna Letter no. 9 still regarded himself as Egypt's suzerain. Soon he became aware of the political realities; he acknowledged Asshur's claims and entered into friendly relations by means of a marriage.

Such diplomatic contacts consisted in the sending of emissaries, in an almost prescribed exchange of expensive gifts—gold, war chariots, horses, precious stones, decorative objects, weapons—and in a back-and-forth giving in marriage of princesses. It happened, too, that specialists (especially doctors) were put at each other's disposal. The diplomatic marriages are well documented in the accompanying correspondence, in the dowries recorded in writing, and in the provisions made in case of later difficulties, such as neglect of a princess, "inheritance" of a widow, and unfaithfulness. Such agreements were not only made by representatives of large powers (Burnaburiash allied himself by marriage with Ashuruballit, while his daughter was given to the harem of the pharaoh; intermarriage also occurred among Egyptians, Hittites, and Mitanni), but also among the vassals, for instance, between Ugarit and Amurru.

Such marriage practices presuppose the existence of harems in which the many wives and concubines could find a place. Their existence, already inferred for Mari in the eighteenth century B.C., is demonstrated by a collection of "Court and harem decrees" from Assyria, made at the time of Ashuruballit and his successors. These decrees lay down strict rules for the behavior and the treatment of courtiers, harem wives, and eunuchs. Failure to observe the prescriptions could result in corporal punishment and mutilation. Similar rules may also have been in force elsewhere, though the Assyrian rules are characterized by harsh punishments, such as are also found in the Middle Assyrian Laws that must also have originated in these centuries.

Asshur's power became really evident when Burnaburiash's son and successor was murdered.

Ashuruballit interfered militarily, deposed the usurper Nazibugash, and put his grandson Kurigalzu II (ca. 1323–1300 B.C.) on the throne. He is one of the best-known Kassite kings, who engaged in extensive building projects and also was successful militarily. Despite his background, he made war on Asshur. A battle was fought by Sugagu on the Tigris and by Arbela (Erbil) not far from the Assyrian heartland, in which battle he was certainly not on the losing end. In the south he gained successes against Elam, which after centuries again made its appearance on the political scene.

The conflicts between Asshur and Babylon were the beginning of a century of almost constant war, alternated with military operations of each against its own enemies. Asshur was forced to take action against the hostile mountain tribes in the north and east, in the Zagros and southeast Anatolia—where old names such as Turukku and Guti surface again and Urartu now also appears—and in the territory between the Habur and the Euphrates. Babylonia more and more had its hands full with Elam, and was also forced to reckon with the nomadic Sutu along the Middle Euphrates, where now also the first Aramean groups, the Ahlamu-Aramu, appeared.

Asshur regained the initiative under Adadnirari I (ca. 1295–1264 B.C.). We can follow the course of events quite well, because, starting with his reign, for the first time more elaborate annalistic *res gestae* are available, a textual genre probably inspired by Hittite historiography. Mitanni (Hanigalbat) became tributary, and the Assyrian armies, to the dismay of the Hittites, reached the Euphrates at Carchemish. In the south Nazimaruttash of Babylonia (after ca. 1300 B.C.) was defeated at Kirkuk, resulting in an agreement in which the border ran from Jebel Hamrin in a northeasterly direction. Moreover, Babylonia was threatened by Elam, which recaptured Susa and under Untashnapirisha (ca. 1250 B.C.) penetrated as far as Eshnunna. Asshur's power asserted itself even more under Shalmaneser I (ca. 1263–1234 B.C.), who won battles against Urartu and conquered all the territory east of the Euphrates. Despite Hittite support from Hattushilish III, what remained of Mitanni was defeated, and in the battle many were taken captive.

Asshur's power reached its apex under Tukulti-Ninurta I (ca. 1233–1197 B.C.). He brought peace to the northeast flank of the realm by defeating the peoples of the Zagros and intimidating them by mass executions (he "fills the ravines with corpses," pours the lives of the troops out like water," "butchers armies like sheep," and "blinds prisoners"). Asshur's militarism now clearly shows itself in the inscriptions of kings who describe themselves as "the valiant hero, competent in battles, who crushes the enemies, who in the battle with the enemies makes the battle cry sound, whose attack shoots out like a flame and whose weapons strike like a ruthless scepter [variant: trap] of death" (see Grayson, *Inscriptions*, p. 80 no. 256). Two things catch the attention: on the one hand Asshur's ruthless manner accompanied by intimidating cruelty, on the other hand its eagerness for booty in the form of materials, utensils, horses, and the like. In subsequent centuries these two traits continued to characterize Asshur, though not all kings were the same. The first element—less exceptional for that time than it may seem, though it contrasts with the military behavior of the Hittites—has been variously explained. It is important to note that Asshur was able to defeat the surrounding hostile tribes and people, but could not permanently subdue them through military occupation. Military intimidation was a means to repress repeated rebellions; Asshur's ruthless actions were specifically against rebels. It seems likely that later also the war against the evasive Aramaic tribes contributed to Asshur's brutality. Asshur was small, possessing limited means and manpower, and the economic profit derived from the war was of vital importance to it and became more and more so through the centuries as the military campaigns and building projects required it. The deportations of the conquered peoples must also be seen in this light. They were not only intended to break the resistance of the vanquished, but also to maintain or to raise the Assyrian population level, the size of the army, and the number of craftsmen and forced laborers. Already Shalmaneser I had incorporated a "selection from the young men" of Urartu into his army.

In the north, the Assyrian war machine put its sights on the areas of Tur Abdin (Kashiari Mountains) and the kingdom of Alshe/Alzi, north of Diyarbekir. More to the east there were heavy battles with the "Nairi countries," a territory of small kingdoms around Lake Van. In the west the armies again reached the Euphrates, where they defeated the Hittites (almost 29,000 prisoners-of-war). These campaigns gave Asshur control over the important trade routes to the west and to the Iranian plateau, and also gave it access to the rich copper mines of Ergani Maden.

About 1220 B.C. war broke out with Babylonia. Kashtiliash IV had advanced to Kirkuk but was decisively defeated and taken captive. Babylon was captured and dismantled, and many of its inhabitants were deported along with the image of Marduk. Advancing along the Euphrates and penetrating to Mari, Tukulti-Ninurta I could boast that he controlled "Sumer and Akkad" and made the "lower sea" his border. His praise was sung in the nationalistic "Tukulti-Ninurta epic," and he himself immortalized it in a new residence built opposite Asshur, Kar-Tukulti-Ninurta.

The Assyrian successes were not permanent, however. In Babylon, which for a while was governed by Assyrian governors, a resistance movement put Adad-shumusur on the throne. Elamite invasions also undermined Assyrian authority. Around 1200 B.C. the Assyrians were forced to leave Babylonia, while in his own country Tukulti-Ninurta was murdered by his own son, indicative of the opposition against the headstrong king. In the space of fifteen years three kings came to the throne; meanwhile, Babylonia recovered. Only under Ninurta-apalekur (ca. 1180 B.C.) did the situation in Assyria become stabilized, likely under the influence of the south, because according to the King List this king "from Karduniash" (Babylonia) conquered the throne. The stabilization continued under Ashurdan I (ca. 1178/1168–1133), but the historical texts do not mention much that is important.

Babylonia went through a quiet period under Adad-shumusur, Melishipak (ca. 1186–1172 B.C.), and Marduk-apaliddina I (ca. 1171–1159 B.C.). Construction went on at various temples while according to the numerous land-grant documents (*kudurrus*) the government functioned efficiently. In 1158 B.C. a crisis suddenly arose. In Elam, operating from his capital Susa, Shutruk-

Nahhunte strengthened his power through a nationalistic and centralistic policy. In that year, reacting to a military campaign of Ashurdan I, he marched against Babylonia, conquering many cities, capturing booty, and imposing tribute (as shown by stele fragments). Babylon was captured and Shutruk-Nahhunte's son, Kuttir-Nahhunte, was made governor. The sudden death of the Elamite left his work unfinished. On the stele with the laws of Hammurabi that he had carried off to Susa—one of the many great Babylonian monuments found in Susa; other important finds are a statue of Manishtushu from Eshnunna and the victory stele of Naram-Sin from Sippar—he had part of the original text erased for a victory inscription of his own, which, however, was never engraved. Within three years his son subdued the Babylonian uprising that had flared up. Finally, Babylon was razed and the last Kassite king (Enlil-nadinakhi) disappeared from the scene about 1155 B.C. Together with many Babylonians, the images of Marduk and Nanaya went into exile.

The Kassite period is poorly known. There are few texts from the older phase; many texts from later centuries, especially coming from Nippur—which occupied an important position and was governed by a hereditary governor, called *guenna*—are still unpublished. The records show that there was no break with bureaucratic traditions (e.g., as regards the legal system, irrigation undertakings, and agriculture). The scores of *kudurru*s or land-grants that occur starting from the fourteenth century are remarkable. These are ceremonial inscriptions on hard stone, in the shape of steles and rounded pillars, on which the kings often make considerable donations of land, accompanied by various immunities, to their favorites and high officials. The elaborate texts conclude with extensive curse formulas; the gods appealed to in these curses are as a rule pictured on top of the monument by means of their symbols, which makes the *kudurru*s important for iconography. The texts betray a feudal structure of the state and landownership, in which possessions and villages (for which the term *bitum*, "house," is used), arranged according to family or clan, play an important role.

The Kassites soon adapted themselves to the higher Babylonian culture, probably also due to the takeover of the administrative officials, including the writers. They distinguished themselves for some centuries by their Kassite names. The meaning of some of them we know from bilingual word lists, in which seventy names of persons, gods, and objects are "translated." Beyond that, Kassite is poorly known, because (apart from some "horse-texts") no texts are extant. The kings were energetic builders who restored or built many temples; following tradition they made known their efforts by means of building inscriptions, often in Sumerian (especially on bricks). Original features are found in the cylinder seals, in the palaces and temple of Dur-Kurigalzu, and in the brick friezes of the Inanna temple, built by Kuraindash in Uruk (ca. 1400 B.C.).

The Kassite period was not intellectually stagnant, even though there was much interest in tradition. The activity of writers and scholars was significant. During that time a process of "canonization" of Babylonian literature took place, in which an almost normative selection was made from the tradition, a selection which in many cases also included a revised *textus receptus*. A number of scribal families, some going back to the fourteenth century, occupied themselves with this task and also handled the preservation and the processing of the tradition. To this period belongs, among others, the standard edition of the Gilgamesh Epic, credited to Sinleqeunninni. For such texts, and also for new creations, a literary language developed that we call "standard literary Babylonian." The literary works of the Kassite period include important hymns to deities, for example, the great Shamash hymn. Kassite cylinder seals contain many benedictions and prayers. In this period also some writings exploring the problems of human suffering, guilt, and divine justice were produced, in particular *Ludlul bel nemeqi* ("I will praise the lord of wisdom") and the "Babylonian Theodicy." There was interest in Sumerian, as can be gathered from bilingual texts and word lists in two languages, which in some cases lend an impression of (artificial) erudition to the activities. So in many ways the Kassite period, in regard to intellectual development, constituted a not-to-be-underestimated transition from the Old Babylonian Period to the later periods, in which the traditions were continued despite real changes.

## LITERATURE

K. Balkan, *Kassitenstudien, I: Die Sprache der Kassiten* (New Haven, 1954).

J. Brinkman, *Materials and Studies for Kassite History* I (Chicago, 1976).

———, "Kassiten," in *Reallexikon der Assyriologie* IV (Berlin, 1978) 464–73.

G. Cardascia, *Les lois assyriennes* (Paris, 1969).

A. K. Grayson, *Assyrian and Babylonian Chronicles* (Locust Valley, 1975).

———, *Assyrian Royal Inscriptions* I (Wiesbaden, 1972).

C. Kühne, *Die Chronologie der internationalen Korrespondenz von El-Amarna* (Kevelaer/Neukirchen-Vluyn, 1973).

W. G. Lambert, *Babylonian Wisdom Literature* (Oxford, 1960).

H. Limet, *Les légendes des sceaux cassites* (Brussels, 1971).

U. Seidl, "Die babylonischen Kudurru-reliefs," *Baghdader Mitteilungen* 4 (1968) 1–220.

F. X. Steinmetzer, *Die babylonischen Kudurru (Grenzsteine) als Urkundenform untersucht* (Padenborn, 1922).

## k. Ugarit in the Fourteenth–Thirteenth Centuries B.C.

Ugarit deserves closer attention here, because the city is fairly well known from the extensive excavations and the archives discovered in the process. Its history and structure can serve somewhat as a model of a Syro-Palestinian city- and vassal-state in these tumultuous centuries. Moreover, from Ugarit come important literary-religious, especially mythical, texts that shed light on religion and are still unique for the Syria-Palestine of that time.

The history before 1350 B.C. is barely known, due to the absence of older archival material, certainly not primarily due to an earthquake and fire at the palace, mentioned in an Amarna Letter of the king of Tyre (no. 151). Ammishtamru I (to ca. 1350 B.C., writer of Amarna Letter no. 45) was an Egyptian vassal. His son and successor, Niqmaddu II (Niqmaddu I is known from an old dynastic seal), continued this policy (Amarna Letter no. 48; cf. Egyptian vases discovered at Ugarit, one of which probably depicts the king with his consort, an Egyptian princess), but about 1340 B.C., during Shuppiluliumash's first Syrian campaign, he passed over to the Hittite camp; during a later Syrian rebellion he remained loyal. After the brief reign of the usurper Arhalba (ca. 1320 B.C.; pro-Mitanni?), Niqmepa began to reign in year 9 of Murshilish II (ca. 1315–1265 B.C.?). Ugarit later supported the Hittites in the battle at Qadesh and profited from the peaceful times that followed upon the Egyptian-Hittite treaty. Niqmepa's successor was Ammishtamru II (ca. 1265–1230 B.C.?; began to reign shortly after the accession of Hattushilish III), under whose rule took place the developments surrounding the "great sin" of the princess of Amurru, who became queen of Ugarit. After the brief reigns of Ibiranu and Niqmaddu III, Ugarit's history ended with Ammurapi. Of his time more is known, due, among others, to the find of some seventy texts in an oven of the palace, from which they could not be removed when the palace was suddenly destroyed. The correspondence between Ugarit and Cyprus (still ruled by Shuppiluliumash II of Hatti) is important for the insight it gives into the catastrophe shortly after 1200 B.C. that caused the demise of Ugarit and the Hittite empire. The king of Alashia (part of Cyprus?) reported about enemies in ships who made surprise attacks and who were difficult to locate, but against whom Ugarit had to defend itself with its troops, chariots, and walls. Like a final cry of distress we hear in a letter from Ammurapi: "My father, see, the ships of the enemies are coming! My cities and villages they have burned with fire and wreaked havoc in the land. Does my father not know that all the troops of (my) lord, my father, stay in Hatti and all my ships are in Lukka [south coast of Asia Minor]?" Shortly thereafter Ugarit fell, presumably under the attacks of the Sea Peoples, to which these lines refer. According to Egyptian indications this happened in the eighth year of Ramses III (ca. 1180 B.C.).

Ugarit was a cosmopolitan trade city with relations in all directions. Even after it went over to the Hittite camp (ca. 1340 B.C.) the commercial contacts with Egypt remained. Besides Semites, its population included a sizable Hurrian component. Furthermore, there was an Aegean-Mycenean trade colony, according to finds in tombs in the harbor and necropolis Minet el-Beida, the Greek Leukos Limen. The policy of the city was aimed at a flourishing trade, which demanded that war be avoided, though the city did have an army which included war charioteers and a fleet that was sometimes used by the Hittites. According to one document (*Le Palais royal d'Ugarit*, IV, 150; mid-13th century B.C.), Ugarit could buy itself out of participating in the war against Assyria with the payment of 50 minas of gold. Commerce is quite prominent in the texts; some relate also to murder and plunder of merchants. A treaty between Ugarit and Hattushilish III regulated the trade rights of merchants from Ura, an important Hittite harbor in Cilicia, who were in Ugarit.

Being a Hittite vassal, Ugarit was under the king of Hatti, with whom the city concluded vassal treaties, which among other things stipulated the payment of sizable tribute. After the intermezzo of Arhalba, the treaty was renewed by Murshilish II, whereby Ugarit lost territory in the south at the expense of Siyannu, but also had its tribute lowered accordingly. In the course of daily life most of the contacts were with the Hittite viceroys of Carchemish, Ini-Teshub and Talmi-Teshub, who began to play a dominant role in the thirteenth century. They are mentioned in numerous documents and records relating to military and nonmilitary matters, including mutual differences among the vassals (ill. 75).

According to the international correspondence—discovered in the "central archive"; six different archives are distinguished in the palace—Ugarit maintained contact with many neighboring cities and with Cyprus. Particularly the relations with southern Amurru were close. Niqmepa was married to a daughter of the king of Amurru, Ahatmilku, and his son Ammishtamru II followed this example by marrying a daughter of Benteshina. A "great sin" she had committed resulted in all kinds of political complications, which were dealt with by Carchemish and ultimately resolved by the Hittite king himself (as we know from an extensive dossier).

The king of Ugarit had a firm grip on the populace, both as titular head of the land owned by the state and as head of the "men of the king" (*bunushu malki*), who were administratively organized according to professions and services. The latter served in agriculture, craft, trade, government, and the army. Depending on rank, they received remuneration in goods and silver from the treasury; many also possessed a piece of crown land given to them in exchange for service obligations (*pilku; unushshu*). The king also exercised similar rights with respect to the village communities, whose members were obligated to military service and levies in silver and goods. Special privileges in this more or less feudally organized society were enjoyed by the direct servants of the king, such as the vizier (*sakinu*), the "friends of the king" (*mudu sharri*), and the war charioteers living on estates; these privileges consisted of immunities and rights to local levies. At the bottom of the social ladder were found the *hupshu* and the slaves.

Being at the head of the palace organization, the king had a firm grip on society: he looked after the division of his subjects into service categories and could assign and expropriate lands, while he controlled transactions in immovable property (linked to service and levies) as well as inheritance of land. He had command over the centrally equipped army, recruited from the villages, augmented by mercenary soldiers and the *maryannu*. The king was likewise the highest judge, a function he also has in the legendary-mythical texts *Aqht* and *Krt*, where he is pictured as dispensing justice in front of the gate on the threshing floor as protector of orphan and widow. In these literary texts these kings appear as heroic, superhuman figures, who stand in close relation to the gods and whose well-being is connected with the fertility of the land. The altogether different documentation of the administrative archives contains virtually nothing that elucidates this aspect of the kingship. Consequently it seems likely that it is nothing else than a literary representation of a heroic-mythical past. The ritual texts do show that as the head of the community the king had a role in the cult, for example, in a repentance liturgy and at sacrifices, including those concerned with the fertility of the soil. There is nothing like a "deified king," though it is known that the dynastic forefathers were honored by means of sacrifices to their "shades" and though there exists a list of "deified" (deceased) kings (some, however, think that it refers to the personal gods of the kings). Despite the sacral traits inherent in the kingship, daily reality consisted of being head of a small state and vassal of a suzerain who presented himself as "sun(god)."

The mythological and ritual texts that have been found in Ugarit are very important. These texts have given us for the first time a direct acquaintance with the mythology pertaining to such gods as El, Baal, Mot, Yam, Shapsh, Ashera, Anat, Ashtart, Horon, Koshar, and many others, as well as with many aspects of the cult. They come from the palace (where ca. 1340 B.C. important literary texts were recorded by the scholar Ilimilku to be given to the Baal temple by King Niqmaddu II, who besides calling himself king of Ugarit also speaks of himself as "prince of *Yrgb* and lord of *Trmn*") and from the collections of some learned priests. They are highly significant for the knowledge of the "Canaanite" religion (it should be noted here that geographically Ugarit lay north of Canaan and that the language of Ugarit may not be simply equated with the Canaanite language) and for the study of the religious and literary background of the Old Testament. Within the scope of this contribution it is not possible to dwell on their content.

---

## LITERATURE

A. Caquot, M. Sznycer, and A. Herdner, *Textes ougaritiques, I: Mythes et legendes* (Paris, 1974).

*J.-C. Courtois, et al., "Ras Shamra," in *Supplément au Dictionnaire de la Bible* (Paris, 1979), cols. 1124–1466.

H. Gese, M. Höfner, and K. Rudolph, *Die Religionen Altsyriens, Altarabiens und der Mandäer* (Stuttgart, 1970), pp. 50–181.

M. Heltzer, *The Rural Community in Ancient Ugarit* (Wiesbaden, 1976).

H. Klengel, *Geschichte Syriens im 2. Jahrtausend v.u.Z.* II (Berlin, 1969) 326–421.

M. Liverani, "La royauté syrienne de l'âge du Bronze Récent," in P. Garelli, ed., *Le palais et la royauté* (Paris, 1974).

M. Liverani, ed., *La Siria nel Tardo Bronzo* (Rome, 1969).

J. Nougayrol, *Le palais royal d'Ugarit* III–V (Paris, 1955–70).

A. F. Rainey, "The Kingdom of Ugarit," *Biblical Archaeologist* 28 (1965) 102–25.

*Ugarit-Forschungen* (1969– ).

*Ugaritica* V–VII (Paris, 1968–79).

*G. D. Young, ed., *Ugarit in Retrospect: Fifty Years of Ugarit and Ugaritic* (Winona Lake, 1981).

---

## l. Egypt and the Hittite Realm in the Thirteenth Century B.C.

Seti I (ca. 1301–1279 B.C.) introduced a new era, the Nineteenth Dynasty. The political point of gravity shifted to the Delta in connection with the interests of the Asiatic empire and the threat from Libya and the Mediterranean Sea. Instead of Memphis, Pi-Ramesse became the new capital (now the ruins of Qantir near the ancient Avaris, on the Pelusiac branch of the Nile). Already in the beginning of his reign Seti undertook a campaign to Syria and Palestine, where he had set his sights on Qadesh and Amurru. In Palestine, according to steles found at Beth-shean, the king strengthened his grip on the strategic plain of Jezreel, and he also reestablished his authority in Tyre and Acco. On the way back he appeared in the Hauran (east of the Jordan), where Pella was punished and a stele was erected at Tell es-Sihab. In the south Egypt maintained its grip on the copper mines at Timna, where Seti I, like the later Ramses III, left his cartouche behind in the local Hathor sanctuary. In Egypt, Asiatic influences increased, especially in religion, in particular through the incorporation of many Asiatics living in the Delta, in army and government. The god Seth—already in the Hyksos period identified with Baal—was restored to honor; the army companies were named after him and the three chief gods, Amon, Re, and Ptah. The king had a remarkable cenotaph constructed at Abydos, but had himself buried in his rock tomb at Thebes, where many important religious texts have been found on the walls.

Meanwhile in Hattushash, Murshilish II had been succeeded by Muwatallish (ca. 1295–1273 B.C.?), about whose reign little is known; the most important source is the apology of his later successor Hattushilish III, a work that is certainly not always objective. After the serious threat from the north—from the Gasga, who even induced the king to abandon Hattushash in favor of his more southern residence Datassa—had been averted by Hattushilish, and Kizzuwatna and Arzawa had been pacified, all attention was focused on Syria. A treaty made between Seti I and Muwatallish was not able to prevent the increase of Egypt's power and influence under Ramses II (ca. 1279–1212 B.C.), which induced Amurru under Benteshina to choose the side of the pharaoh and posed a serious threat to Qadesh. In Ramses' fifth year (1275 B.C.) the famous battle on the Orontes was fought, well known from Ramses' temple reliefs and descriptions and from Hittite reports. Ramses, who was ahead of his main army and under the impression that the Hittites were still at Aleppo, was taken by surprise by Muwatallish's large army (35,000 men and 3,500 chariots; contingents from all parts of the realm, including Mitanni, Ugarit, Lukka, and Dardana) and almost defeated. Heroically he managed to break through the encirclement and so avert inminent defeat. The battle ended indecisively, but the consequences—Amurru became Hittite again, Qadesh remained Hittite, and the Hittite army penetrated in the direction of Damascus—point to a Hittite success. Expeditions by Ramses in his eighth and tenth years were unable to alter the situation. Egypt did maintain its firm grip on Canaan, ruled from Gaza. A rebellion of Ashkelon was put down in 1269 B.C. Ashdod, Jaffa, and Beth-shean remained Egyptian strongholds, according to inscriptions found there.

In Hattushash, Muwatallish had in the meantime been succeeded by Urhi-Teshub. After seven years he had to yield to the strong Hattushilish III, who, initially remaining loyal, refused to play a

secondary role. Urhi-Teshub was banished to Syria. Hattushilish III (ca. 1267–1235 B.C.) was confronted with the Assyrian expansion, which brought about the downfall of Mitanni, and by which Asshur approached the Euphrates. While formally maintaining relations with Adad-nirari and Shalmaneser I, he entered into friendly relations with Babylonia (Kadashmanturgu, ca. 1260 B.C.) and especially with Egypt. In 1259 B.C., likely awed by Shalmaneser's actions, he made a treaty with Ramses II that included the agreement that the allies would refrain from aggression and support each other; the treaty also established legitimate throne succession and provided for the extradition of fugitives. The boundary was not fixed, but the status quo was continued: the spheres of influence of both empires touched each other along a line running from the north side of the Anti-Lebanon to above Byblos. Amurru (under Benteshina, who had been pardoned by Hattushilish) and Qadesh were definitely lost to Egypt. Egyptian territory now comprised Canaan (Palestine, with the Phoenician coastal strip) and the area of Damascus (Upe). In 1245 B.C. Ramses II and a Hittite princess were married amid great splendor. We know of this event from Egyptian steles and the detailed correspondence between Ramses II with his court and Hattushilish III with his consort Puduhepa, in which not only this marriage alliance but also the peace agreement and the sending of Egyptian medicines and doctors to Hattushash are mentioned.

After having built fortifications to protect the Delta against the Libyans, Ramses could now devote himself to internal affairs: ambitious building programs, traces of which can be found throughout Egypt, ranged from Abu-Sumbel (ill. 76) in Nubia to his new residence, "Ramses city," in the eastern Delta. Austrian excavations have brought to light its extent and identified the ruins of it at Qantir: residential areas, temples, and a large palace, with a "palace lake" as harbor, linked with the Pelusiac branch of the Nile by means of a canal. This city is to be identified with the biblical Raamses, on which also the Hebrews worked as forced laborers (not the more northern Tanis or the more southern Bubastis). The strategically situated city seems also a good starting point for an "exodus" along the most important connecting road with southern Palestine, the *via maris*. It has strengthened the conviction that the Exodus of the Israelites under Moses happened during the reign of Ramses II, while also the locale of Raamses can shed light on the route of the Exodus. According to the excavator Bietak, the Israelites moved along the Pelusiac Nile to Tell Defneh—to be identified as Baal-Zephon, and Daphnae—from where, in order to avoid the border fortification Sile, they trekked in a southeasterly direction to cross Lake Ballah, the "Red Sea" north of Ismailya.

Around 1235 B.C. Hattushilish was succeeded by Tudhaliyash IV (ill. 79). He soon had a serious confrontation with Tukulti-Ninurta I of Asshur, who had penetrated to the Euphrates, taken many Hittite captives, and violated Hittite territory. Self-restraint on both sides prevented the outbreak of war, though contacts were broken off and the Hittites attempted to blockade Asshur.

We are but poorly informed about the last decades of the Hittite empire, all the more so now that it has become apparent that the historical texts, which used to be dated in this century, are from the end of the fifteenth century (when kings with similar names reigned). There were the usual problems with the vassals in east and west and with the Gasga, but nothing indicated the threatening end. Under Tudhaliyash even Cyprus was conquered, a feat that had to be repeated under Shuppiluliumash II and was crowned with success. It is difficult to determine what precisely caused the downfall of Hattushash and the Hittite realm. Simple explanations (an earthquake, which also struck Ugarit [Schaeffer]; conquest by the Phrygians; purely internal problems that erupted) are given alongside complicated constructions in which a connection is attempted with the incursions of the Sea Peoples. In the latter case one might think of certain "Sea Peoples" penetrating to the heart of Anatolia, or assume that the population movements in the Aegean Sea and in western Asia Minor, which caused the movements of the Sea Peoples, had repercussions in Central Anatolia, so that the Hittite empire became disabled, from which the Phrygians—who in that region were the *Mushke* or *Moschoi* known from other sources—profited eventually.

A definite connection with the actions of the "Sea Peoples" is evident from the correspondence between Ugarit and Alashia (= Cyprus?; see p. 272) discovered at Ugarit, which mentions hostile ships at sea and landings on the north Syrian coast. But it is not sure that these kinds of exploits extended deep into Anatolia. The end of Hattushash, recognizable from a destruction layer also observable in other Anatolian ruins, came shortly after 1190 B.C. (ill. 77).

After a long reign, Ramses II was succeeded by Merneptah in 1212 B.C.; he reigned ten to fifteen years. During his reign there was a clash, about 1208 B.C., with Libyan tribes, under the leadership of prince Meryey, who allied themselves with groups such as the Sherden, Shek(e)lesh, Tursha, Ekwesh, and Lukka, which, except for the last two, are later also found among the "Sea Peoples" of Ramses III. The enemies were dealt a shattering defeat. The contacts with Asia were continued: Egypt helped Hatti with shipments of grain, the eastern border was controlled by means of fortified border posts (mentioned in Papyrus Anastasi III–V), and the sovereignty in Palestine was maintained. The pharaoh was called "subduer of Gezer" and described the quiet in the realm in the so-called "Israel stele"—actually a supplement to a victory hymn celebrating his conquest of the Libyans—as follows: "Now Tehenu is destroyed, Hatti is pacified; Canaan is plundered . . . ; Ashkelon carried off; Gezer captured; Yanoam destroyed; Israel is laid waste, it has no seed; Hurru has become a widow for Egypt. All lands are pacified." The mention of Israel in connection with a campaign to Palestine (for which historical proof seems to be available, particularly in connection with the capture of Gezer; but cf. Weippert, *Settlement*, pp. 61–62 n. 24) supports the hypothesis of an Exodus under Ramses II, while the fact that Israel is the only name not written with the determinative for land, but with that used for people or tribe—assuming that it is intentional—may be an indication that it was not yet regarded a political entity as (a part of the) sedentary population.

After Merneptah, the Nineteenth Dynasty ended with some kings whose brief reigns partly overlapped each other: Seti II—simultaneous with Amenmose—, Siptah, and Queen Tausret, consort of Seti, who became regent for his successor, but eventually became pharaoh herself and was a remarkable personality. Her cartouche had been found, for example, on a votive vase at Deir Alla in Jordan, an indication that even then Egypt had relations with Canaan.

---

## LITERATURE

J. von Beckenrath, *Tanis und Theben* (Glückstadt, 1951).

M. L. Bierbrier, *The Late New Kingdom in Egypt* (Liverpool, 1975).

M. Bietak, *Tell el-Dab'a* II (Vienna, 1975) 23ff., 217ff.

E. Edel, *Ägyptische Ärzte und ägyptische Medizin am hethitischen Königshof* (Opladen, 1976).

A. H. Gardiner, *The Kadesh Inscriptions of Ramesses II* (1960).

*K. A. Kitchen, *Pharaoh Triumphant: The Life and Times of Ramesses II* (Warminster, 1982).

A. Kuschke, "Das Terrain der Schlacht bei Qadeš," *Zeitschrift des Deutschen Palästinavereins* 95 (1979) 7–35.

G. A. Lehmann, "Der Untergang des hethitischen Grossreiches und die neuen Texte aus Ugarit," *Ugarit-Forschungen* 2 (1970) 39–74.

*H. Otten, *Die Apologie Hattusilis III* (Wiesbaden, 1981).

*E. Otto, "Erwägungen zum Palästina-Abschnitt der 'Israel-Stele,'" *Zeitschrift der Deutschen Morgenländischen Gesellschaft*, Supplement IV (1980) 131–33.

E. P. Uphill, "Pithon and Raamses: Their Location and Significance," *Journal of Near Eastern Studies* 28 (1969) 15–39.

---

## 6. THE NEAR EAST AND EGYPT FROM THE TWELFTH TO THE NINTH CENTURIES B.C.

### a. Sea Peoples and Philistines

The most important event in the eastern part of the Mediterranean Sea around 1200 B.C. was the exploits of the "Sea Peoples," a conglomerate of tribes and groups of people, so called because in some Egyptian inscriptions certain people such as the Sherden, Weshesh, and Tursha are supplied with the addition "from the sea [*ym*]." The great confrontation came in the eighth year of Ramses III (ca. 1180 B.C.) in the Nile Delta. He was able to deal the massive invasions of Peleset, Tjeker, Shekelesh, Deyen, and Weshesh a destructive blow, after already in his fifth year some "Sea Peoples" had joined the Libyan invasions. The impressive report of this confrontation is preserved on the walls of Medinet-Habu, the king's mortuary temple near Thebes, excavated by Americans. Later the monument served as a fortress and Coptic church, for which reason it has been better preserved than would normally have been the case. Brief captions, beside some longer, comprehensive texts, elucidate the scene. Also the famous Papyrus Harris—almost 40 meters (120 ft.) long, containing a survey of all land grants of the pharaoh to the temples, in particular the Amon temple at Thebes; at the end there is also historical information—describes the event. The reliefs depict battles with troops in boats and with invaders seated in ox-drawn carts. Their headdress enables us to identify certain groups, in particular the Sherden with their horned helmets, and other groups (e.g., the Peleset) with their typical hairdo (the hair is held straight up by means of a band), described by some as a "crown of feathers." See ill. 78.

The invasion was the culmination of a population movement that had been going on for some decades. Sherden had been in Egypt for some time already. Also under Merneptah (ca. 1208 B.C.) there was an invasion of Sea Peoples and Libyans. On the basis of texts that speak of enemies from northern lands and of a "conspiracy on their islands," it is generally thought that the "Sea Peoples" come from the northeast of the Mediterranean Sea: the Aegean Islands and the west of Asia Minor, regions known by the Egyptians, as shown by the topographical list of Amenhotep III, who mentioned cities from *Keftiu* (Crete) and *Tanaya/u* (Danaoi; e.g., Mycene, Nauplia, and Cythera; others assume that Tanaya is a name for Cyprus, connected with the later Yadnana). The origin of the population movement is regarded as due to the crisis in the late-Mycenean world (end of the 13th century B.C.), to the loss of Hittite hegemony over western Asia Minor (where, e.g., the *Ahhiy/va/[wa]*, not to be isolated from the Ekwesh/Aqay(a)wash and the Acheans, and the Lukka dwelt), the subsequent power struggle, and the prolonged famines found then and there. Some detect even more roots, such as the Dorian invasion of Greece or the coming of the Phrygians from the Balkan, events viewed by others more as consequences of the vacuum caused by the actions of the Sea Peoples there.

Whatever the case may be, it is clear that the "Sea Peoples," with names such as Lukka, Aqay(a)wash, Sherden, Peleset, Tjeker, Weshesh, Shekelesh, Tursha, and Denyen, represent for the most part a new population element; only in the west of Asia Minor does it have older roots. It has been suggested that the names of some of these peoples—after the example of the Peleset, who gave their name to Philistia/Palestine—in the wake of their migrations are reflected in ethnic or geographical names: Sherden/Sardana—Sardinia, Tursha—Etruskes, Shekelesh—Sicily. The identifications are not always convincing, however.

This new element, arriving massively on the scene between 1210 and 1180 B.C., was not new in every respect. Some of these "peoples," such as Lukka, Shardana, and Danuna (= Denyen; in Cicily) were already mentioned a few times in the fourteenth century in the Amarna Letters, Ugaritic texts, and Hittite sources. In the battle of Qadesh (1275 B.C.) Lukka and Kelekesh were on the side of the Hittites, while the Egyptian army also included Shardana. Such groups were apparently in one way or another integrated into the large nations, either as subdued or captured enemies who had been reorganized into military contingents, or as mercenary soldiers recruited from the population of annexed territories, particularly from Syria and southwestern Anatolia. They may also have settled as groups of military colonists or garrisons at strategic points of the realm.

In the great clashes between Ramses III and the Sea Peoples—especially the Peleset, Tjeker, Shekelesh, Denyen, and Weshesh—two major groups can be observed. Some groups apparently came from overseas by boat and fought in naval battles on the branches of the Nile Delta; others with their families came by land in wagons and fought at the "border in/by Djahi," the east side of the Delta. Papyrus Harris records that these "enemies from the north" first attacked areas in southern Anatolia, Syria, and Cyprus—mentioned are Hatti, Qadi, Carchemish, Arzawa, and Alashia—and after that pitched their camp in Amor (= Amurru, south of Byblos). Apparently from there, by land and sailing past the coast, presumably with reinforcements from Cyprus, they came to Egypt. There are archeological and historical indications that Cyprus was reached by the Sea Peoples and probably served as temporary bases. The Old Testament also mentions Kaphtor (to be linked with Keftiu = Crete) as their place of origin. Ugaritic texts mention naval battles near Cyprus. Archeological traces of Sea Peoples—perhaps in a later phase also crossing over from Syria—have been found on Cyprus, especially in the period after 1200 B.C., where they would mark the transition from Late Cyprian II.C to III.A, B through destruction, rebuilding, and new cultural expressions, for example, in architecture, weapons, and ceramics.

Sea Peoples may have arrived in Palestine by land from the north, by sea from the Aegean world via Crete and Cyprus, or both ways after they had been beaten back in the Egyptian Delta. Their presence in the Egyptian military organization may also be explained by regarding them as colonists or garrison soldiers. The Shardana were already used as such by Egypt in the thirteenth century, and they fought with Ramses III against the Sea Peoples, while this pharaoh himself forced captured Sea Peoples to serve as soldiers in his army. According to the reliefs, soldiers with a "Philistine" hairdo fought with Egypt against the Nubians.

When the Egyptian realm collapsed, such military colonists, together with newcomers, may have freed themselves and become independent. The "Philistines" and the Tjeker (near Dor) were concentrated in the former Egyptian strongholds of Gaza, Ashdod, and Ashkelon in the Shephelah (later also Gath and Ekron), Lachish and Sharuhen in the southern highlands, and Beth-shean in the strategic plain of Jezreel. In most of these places the literarily or archeologically determined presence of Sea Peoples can be combined with clear traces of Egyptian culture, such as steles at Beth-shean (Seti I, Ramses II, III) and the Ptah temple at Ashkelon (cf. also 1 Sam. 31:10). Archeologically their presence has been deduced from the characteristic pottery with Cypriotic-Mycenean and local Canaanite motifs (which was also traded, however) and from clay coffins in Egyptian style, which in relief depict a face with a hairdo that looks "Philistine" (ill. 80). Philistine, local Canaanite, and Egyptian traits, however, are not always easily distinguished. In many respects they quickly adapted themselves to their Canaanite environment. Not only are the names of their kings in the first millennium B.C. Semitic, but also their chief god Dagon is an old West Semitic deity. Nothing is known of their language; inscriptions have not been found. The hypothesis that the few clay tablets discovered in the sanctuary of Deir Alla in Jordan (beginning of the 12th century B.C.) and inscribed with an unknown script resembling Cypriotic and Linear B may be Philistine has not yet been proven.

Strategically located in the coastal plain and the valley of Jezreel, they controlled the important trade route, the *via maris*. Also, being familiar with the sea and having good harbors such as Gaza, Ashkelon, Ashdod, and Tell Qasile (north of Tel Aviv), they were no doubt also a trading power, probably to the detriment of the Phoenician cities. With Israel, which was militarily inferior to them and lived pushed back in the highlands, a life-and-death clash ensued, a confrontation that was at last decided by David and Solomon, but without the Philistines altogether disappearing from the political scene. In the eighth to sixth centuries they still played a significant role in the relations between Assyria and Palestine and in the opposition against Sargon II, Sennacherib, and Nebuchadrezzar.

## LITERATURE

R. A. Crossland and A. Birchall, *Bronze Age Migrations in the Aegean* (London/Park Ridge, 1974).

*T. Dothan, *The Philistines and Their Material Culture* (New Haven, 1982).

R. Hestrin, *The Philistines and the Other Sea Peoples* (Jerusalem, 1970).

K. A. Kitchen, "The Philistines," in D. J. Wiseman, ed., *Peoples of Old Testament Times* (Oxford, 1973), pp. 53–78.

B. Mazar, *The Philistines and the Rise of Israel and Tyre* (Jerusalem, 1964).

N. Nibbi, *The Sea Peoples in Egypt* (Park Ridge, 1975) (cf. D. Lorton, *Journal of Near Eastern Studies* 36 [1977] 315ff.).

N. K. Sandars, *The Sea Peoples: Warriors of the Ancient Mediterranean* (London, 1978).

A. Strobel, *Der spätbronzezeitliche Seevölkersturm* (Berlin/New York, 1976).

G. E. Wright and H. Tadmor, *Biblical Archaeologist* 29 (1966) 70–102.

## b. Egypt under the Twentieth Dynasty (ca. 1185–1080 B.C.)

The military successes during the first years of Ramses III (ca. 1185–1155 B.C.), the most important prince of the dynasty, brought once more a brief period of prosperity, characterized by great building activity from Soleb in Nubia all the way to the Delta, the construction of tombs in Thebes, and expeditions to the stone quarries of the Wadi Hammamat. Egypt's influence and a measure of power in Canaan and the Sinai were certainly continued until about 1170 B.C., as shown by the stele from Beth-shean, a royal statue from Megiddo, a cartouche of Ramses III from Lachish, and inscriptions in the copper mines of Timna and the turquoise mines of Serabit el-Khadim. Also, Ramses IV was still mentioned in some texts, but this period was definitely the end of Egyptian supremacy, though the trade relations continued: by land on the *via maris* along the Palestinian coastal plain and by sea through shipping to the coasts of Canaan and Phoenicia. In the south all the rulers of the dynasty managed to hold on to their influence in Nubia.

Around the middle of the twelfth century the internal problems increased due to corruption, arbitrariness by officials, rivalry and power struggles between leaders and claimants to the throne, criminality, and poor economic conditions (low inundations of the Nile, resulting in enormous inflation and famine). It is remarkable that particularly from this period many written data have been preserved in papyri and ostraca that afford an idea of the situation. In addition to the above-mentioned Papyrus Harris, there is the Papyrus Wilbour, which offers a unique overview of land-ownership, harvest yields, and taxes in a district of central Egypt. Furthermore, many texts from the village of the workers in the necropolis, Deir el-Medineh, provide an idea of daily life and religion, as well as of the economic crises leading to price hikes and the loss of wages and new supplies, which twice caused protests (ca. 1155 and ca. 1100 B.C.) and strikes.

Ramses III was assassinated about 1155 B.C., the result of a palace conspiracy with the support of Queen Tiye. This conspiracy failed in that the rightful claimant, Ramses IV, ascended the throne and had the conspirators tried. The legal protocols are an important source of information as are those (shortly after 1100 B.C.) that relate to judicial investigation and the execution of the grave robbers of the royal necropolis. The power of the kings gradually diminished, especially because of the competition of the two "mighty men," the "viceroy of Nubia" and the powerful high priest of Amon in Thebes, whose office had become nearly hereditary. Shortly after 1100 B.C., in a period of unrest and famine, a crisis occurred in Thebes. The viceroy of Nubia, Pinhasi, invaded Upper Egypt with his army and wielded power there for some years. He was compelled to leave, however, when Herihor, the new high priest of Amon, came to power. He introduced the new "renaissance era," acted as commander and governor of Nubia, and with his titles and cartouches presented himself as the de facto king, though nominally the long-reigning Ramses XI (ca. 1098–1069 B.C.) remained on the throne. Also in the north this last of the Ramessides had to content himself with a subordinate position; the royal family of Djede (Mendes), governing from Tanis, became the de facto ruler in the Delta, especially after the accession of Smendes I in about 1080 B.C. He was the one who about 1069 B.C. took over the double crown from Ramses XI. That Egypt's authority in Canaan had greatly waned at this time we learn from the famous "Story of Wen-Amon," an officer who by order of the Amon temple in Thebes and with the approval of Smendes in Tanis was sent to obtain wood in Byblos for the procession boat of the god (ca. 1075 B.C.). His experiences in Dor and Byblos—where King Zakar-Baal ruled and a prophet was active—are informative for the situation in Canaan and the position of Egypt.

## LITERATURE

M. Bierbrier, *The Tomb-builders of the Pharaohs* (London, 1978).

H. Goedicke, *The Report of Wenamun* (Baltimore/London, 1975).

J. J. Janssen, *Commodity Prices from the Ramesside Period: An Economic Study of the Village of the Necropolis Workmen at Thebes* (Leiden, 1975).

## c. Assyria and Babylonia from the Twelfth to the Tenth Centuries B.C.

In Babylonia, about 1155 B.C., the Second Dynasty of Isin came to power. It was destined for the next century to occupy the throne, which would soon be in Babylon. The first decades offer little that is noteworthy. There were border clashes with Assyria, where Ashurreshishi (ca. 1133–1116 B.C.) was able to hold out as Ashurdan I's successor, and the country suffered from the attacks of Elam under King Shilhak-Inshushinak. Elam experienced again, temporarily and for the last time, a period of prosperity, in which it controlled the entire eastern border zone of Mesopotamia and made raids inland, also against Assyria. Ninurta-nadinshumi, who clashed militarily with Assyria, was about 1126 B.C. succeeded by the best-known king of the dynasty, Nebuchadrezzar I, in later tradition a heroic figure, whose programmatic name would become even more important 500 years later. He liberated Babylonia from Elamite pressure by decisively defeating Elam on the shores of the Eulaeus. The report of the battle is found in the land-grant document with which his cavalry officer, Sitti-Marduk, was rewarded for saving the king's life (ill. 81). Marduk's statue was brought back from Elam, which probably was the occasion to proclaim this god now officially as the head of the pantheon. Nebuchadrezzar did much building and under this "pious monarch" literature flourished. His empire extended from Elam to the Diyala and the Middle Euphrates near Hit, where some border conflicts with Assyria were resolved through military force. Both countries, however, left each other alone for the time being. Only under Nebuchadrezzar's second successor, Marduk-nadinahhe (ca. 1100–1083 B.C.), did the war really break out. Initially the Babylonians succeeded, advancing as far as the Lower Zab, but eventually the Assyrian chariot armies seized Babylon and burned down the palace. The realm of Nebuchadrezzar again shrank down to the heartland of Babylonia.

These Asyrian successes were achieved by the great king Tiglath-pileser I (ca. 1115–1077 B.C.). We are reasonably well informed about his reign, thanks to inscriptions, including the formal annals now being published. He was a man of many talents and interests who through a library in Asshur promoted the literary-scientific tradition. In this library have been discovered the definitive texts of the "Assyrian Laws" and the "Court and Harem decrees" in addition to many literary texts, which later in part were incorporated into Ashurbanipal's library. The king did a lot of building in Asshur, including the Anu-Adad temple, his own palace, and the city wall, presumably more out of bitter necessity than for the sake of prestige. Tiglath-pileser was king in a critical period, and his great energy likely preserved Assyria from destruction. In the east he undertook many campaigns against the mountain people of the Zagros, and in the north against southeastern Anatolia, for example, against the "Nairi lands." He was especially successful against the dangerous Mushki, who had followed the path of the Phrygians and penetrated into Anatolia, settling north of Assyria in Katmuhi, on the southeast side of Lake Van. Defeating them, he assumed control of Katmuhi and the upper course of the Tigris.

An even greater threat, this one from the west and southwest, were the advancing Arameans. Tiglath-pileser battled them fiercely, chasing them at times across the Euphrates (in no less than 28 expeditions, sometimes two per year). Initially he was successful in that he managed to prevent further penetration into Assyria. Once he even thrust through to the Mediterranean Sea to receive tribute from Byblos and Sidon in Arvad. The fights with the Arameans took place along the Middle Euphrates, from Rapiqu via Anat in Suhu and Tadmur (Palmyra) in Amurru to Carchemish. Even so the raiding bands of Arameans were elusive and could not be decisively defeated. After about 1085 B.C. drought, poor harvests, and depopulation of the countryside brought Assyria into trouble, and the Arameans advanced irresistibly. The roads became dangerous, the rural population fled, the king was forced to withdraw to Katmuhi, and the invaders appeared under the walls of Nineveh.

Nevertheless, Asshur withstood this crisis. Under Ashurbelkala (ca. 1074–1057 B.C.) it resumed the initiative. A treaty with the Babylonian Marduk-shapikzeri allowed him greater freedom of movement, enabling him to attack the Arameans (according to the "broken obelisk," to be attributed to him) in the Kashiari Mountains and the Habur area. Though occasionally the Euphrates was reached, the war was mainly fought on Asshur's immediate borders. This situation did not change under his successors Ashurnasirpal I (ca. 1050–1032 B.C.; the "white obelisk" is likely from him), Shalmaneser II (ca. 1031–1021), Ashurrabi II (ca. 1012–972 B.C.), and Tiglath-pileser II (ca. 967–935), from whom we have few inscriptions. According to later witnesses, under Ashurrabi the Arameans penetrated even farther to the west: they conquered Pitru (Petor, known as the residence of Bileam, on the Euphrates north of Carchemish) and settled in the Habur area in such cities as Nasibina and Guzana. This situation continued under Ashurdan II (ca. 934–912), though under him Asshur became stronger and more militarily active in the north and east.

### d. Arameans and Chaldeans

In the beginning of the tenth century, the Aramean presence consolidated itself in a number of small states and political alliances with a fairly fixed territory. We are acquainted with: Bit-Zamani (capital Amedi, in the area around Diyarbekir); south of it, Bit-Bahian (capital Guzana [Gozan; Tell Halaf in the reign of Kapara]); Bit-

Halupe, along the lower course of the Habur; Suhu, along the Middle Euphrates south of the mouth of the Habur, where from of old the Sutu also lived; north of Mari the Hindanu; around the mouth of the Habur the Laqe; in the large curve of the Euphrates, the heart of "Aram Naharaim," Bit-Adini (Beth-eden; cf. Amos 1:5) with the capital Til Barsip, to which also Harran belongs. The eastern outpost was Nasibina (Nisibis) with its own prince, a "Temanite." The occurrence of *bit*, "house," indicates that according to tradition these states go back to a particular tribe, after whose ancestor or leader the state was named (cf. the Assyrian designation *Bit-Humri* for Israel/Samaria, regarded as founded by Omri; the inhabitant or prince of such a small state is called— omitting *bit*—*mar Humri*, etc., to be translated as "Omride" [e.g., Ahab] or "inhabitant of *Bit-Humri*").

After 1100 B.C. the Arameans were a permanent element in Assyrian history. From 900 B.C. there was intensifying war against the Aramean states, first at the Euphrates, then in Syria, ending with Tiglath-pileser's capture of Damascus (732 B.C.). When Aram's political-military role was over, however, its cultural importance increased. Through Aramean infiltrations and Assyrian deportations (whole populations, soldiers, artisans, royal persons), Aramean elements became part of Assyria. Especially the Aramaic language became popular, and in the seventh century it competed strongly with the indigenous Assyrian. Proof for this—in the absence of all Aramaic papyri, which have perished—is found in the Aramaic loanwords, names of persons, grammatical influences, some Aramaic ostraca and clay tablets, Aramaic captions on cuneiform texts, and pictures of official writers: one with stylus and clay tablet, one with pen and papyrus. Because of the important position of Aramaic (also elsewhere; cf. 2 Kings 18:26) it became later, in the Achaemenid realm, the *lingua franca*; Aramaic texts from Persepolis, the Elephantine Papyri from Egypt, the Aramaic documents in Ezra, and Aramaic inscriptions in Asia Minor are indicative of this position of Aramaic. Also elements of Aramaic art and religion spread through the Near East; the Aramean Ahiqar became Esarhaddon's wise counsellor. Who were these Arameans? Where did they come from? What is their earlier history?

These questions are difficult to answer because the Arameans have left no traditions about their prehistory and because, barring a few exceptions, Aramaic inscriptions do not begin until the ninth century, and then only in limited numbers (exception: a text from Tell Halaf [= Guzana] from the 10th century). We are dependent on information from neighbors and enemies, especially Assyria and Israel. The name "Arameans" (*Aramu, mat Arime, Ar[a]maya*) is seldom used before 1100 B.C. (personal names such as Aram[u] are difficult to use; at Ugarit someone is called *bn. army* and mention is made of "fields of *a-ara-mi-me*"). One very important question concerns the relationship between the Ahlamu and the Arameans, in view of their pairing in a text from Tiglath-pileser. The Ahlamu appear already in the fourteenth century (e.g., Amarna Letter no. 200) and as individuals in a variety of Middle Babylonian texts. They were responsible for the stagnation in the interchange of messengers between the Hittites and Babylonia around 1250 B.C. in the curve of the Euphrates, and in Hanigalbat they fought with the Hittites against Shalmaneser I. Some decades later, Tukulti-Ninurta I marched victoriously along the Middle Euphrates and through the "mountains of the Ahlamu" (*shadan ahlami*). Some (e.g., Malamat) regard the combination Ahlamu-Aramaya in references from Tiglath-pileser I and later Assyrian kings as an indication that two nomadic groups or tribes had joined each other (after the example of earlier association such as the Amnan-Yahruru; see above, p. 238) without, however, being identical. Others assume that the concepts greatly overlap, and that at an early stage "Ahlamu" became a kind of generic designation, an appellative for (a particular type of) nomads. (A text from Uruk, ca. 1800 B.C., already mentions *ahlamayu*-messengers; see *Ugarit-Forschungen* 10 [1975], 129 no. 20.) It is remarkable that in the combination Ahlamu-Aramaya the determinative for countries and peoples and the determinative for the plural is applied only once, to the second term (which thereby becomes a genuine gentilic), which requires the translation: "Aramaic Ahlamu." With respect to time and area in which they were active, both groups greatly overlap, so that there must be a close connection. In later Neo-Assyrian texts Ahlamu is used as gentilic for "Aramaic," as a designation of tribes, and of Aramaic words in lists. Ahiqar was an Ahlamu, and still later slaveowners' names were written on the hands of slaves in Akkadian and "Ahlamite." It must be granted that it is not clear why already with Tiglath-pileser I the singular *Aramu/mat Arime* changes to the dual designation, but that does not mean that we may regard Ahlamu and Aramu as separate entities.

The Arameans infiltrated Mesopotamia by way of the Middle Euphrates, from Carchemish to Rapiqu, which suggests that in the thirteenth–twelfth century they forced their way in from the Syrian-Arabian desert, especially in northeasterly and northwesterly directions. Northern Babylonia was then also confronted with them, though the situation is less clear there. In the eleventh–tenth century there were repeated attacks by Arameans and Sutu-nomads, two entities that are hard to distinguish. The Sutu, known already from the Old Babylonian Period, were also found at the Middle Euphrates; with respect to their actions, areas of residence, and language they sometimes resemble the Arameans closely, though it seems reckless simply to equate the two. King Adad-apaliddina, who came to the throne in Babylon about 1069 B.C. and ruled for twenty-two years, was called an "Aramean usurper." His coup was probably connected to the above-mentioned harvest failures and famine that forced the Arameans (with their flocks) into the civilized areas. Proofs for settlement in Babylonia in this period are lacking, however. The same is true for the tenth century B.C., though there are references to a combined Babylonian-Aramean military action against Assyria at Suhu (Middle Euphrates). Only from about 900 B.C. do we find indications of Aramean groups settling in Babylonia, a process that appears to have come to an end in the eighth century B.C., when Tiglath-pileser III in southeast Babylonia found and made war with more than thirty different Aramean tribal groups. Their presence in such large numbers is still difficult to explain. Brinkman mentioned three possibilities: (1) they were presumably distant descendants from the Amorites, who were equally widespread and who, in regard to names, exhibit some affinity; (2) they penetrated—though there is no indisputable proof—already in the eleventh–tenth century; (3) they did not get there

until about 800 B.C. from northern Babylonia, where one tribe (the *I/Utu*) was found earlier. A combination of (2) and (3) seems most likely.

Finally, a problem concerning Babylonia is the relationship between Arameans and Chaldeans. Already in the ninth century B.C. Chaldean tribes were present in Babylonia; at that time we also find the term *mat Kaldu* in Assyrian inscriptions. Three large tribes came especially to the fore: the Yakin, in the far south near the Great Lagune (the area is also sometimes designated "southern Sealand"); the Amukanu northwest of it, roughly between Uruk and Isin; and the Dakkuru south of Babylon. The Chaldeans were seminomadic, living at times in cities and villages. They were engaged in agriculture (e.g., growing dates) and animal farming and carried on trade, including exotic products coming from the Persian Gulf area and Arabia. They lived in a strategic zone along the Euphrates and were de facto independent of the Babylonian kings. Sometimes, however, they supported the Babylonians against the Assyrians. In the eighth century some Chaldean princes conquered the throne of Babylon; the first one was Mardukapalusur (ca. 775 B.C.); the best known is Mardukapaliddina (Old Testament Merodak-Baladan; beginning in 722 B.C.). Gradually, however, the Babylonian and the urban Chaldean elements merged, while the difference between Aramean and Chaldean also diminished. Toward the end of the seventh century a "Chaldean" dynasty came to the throne in Nabopolassar and his son Nebuchadrezzar, symbolizing Babylonian nationalism, and the old distinctions became mainly a matter of the past. In an earlier phase those distinctions were certainly there. Historical sources clearly distinguish the Chaldean from the Aramean territory; the latter lay more in the east of Babylonia, along the Tigris, the former especially along the lower course of the Euphrates and in the south called "Sealand." During Tiglath-pileser III's reign there were a few large Chaldean tribes, but these were matched by no less than thirty-six Aramean tribes and groups, of which the only large ones were the Gambulu and Puqudu along the lower course of the Tigris. The Aramean tribal chiefs were called *nasiku* (*nasih*), the Chaldean *rasanu*, "heads." Some inscriptions on bricks, pottery, and tablets in a kind of script that seems to have been derived from the Old South Arabian script have been connected with the Chaldeans. The languages of both groups are certainly related, though the limited number of names that have survived make it difficult to draw specific conclusions; many Chaldeans assimilated into Babylonian culture at an early stage and had Babylonian names.

## LITERATURE

J. A. Brinkman, *A Political History of Post-Kassite Babylonia* (Rome, 1968), pp. 260–88.

M. Dietrich, *Die Aramäer Südbabyloniens in der Sargonindenzeit* (Kevelaer/Neukirchen-Vluyn, 1970) (cf. the critical review of J. A. Brinkman in *Orientalia* 46 [1977] 304–25).

A. Dupont-Sommer, *Les Araméens* (Paris, 1949).

J. C. L. Gibson, *Textbook of Syrian Semitic Inscriptions, II: Aramaic Inscriptions* (Oxford, 1975).

J. R. Kupper, *Les nomades en Mésopotamie* (Brussels, 1957), pp. 83–146 (Sutu, Ahlamu).

A. Malamat, "The Arameans," in D. J. Wiseman, ed., *Peoples of Old Testament Times* (Oxford, 1973), pp. 134–55.

## e. Syria between "Syro-Hittites" and Arameans (11th–9th Centuries B.C.)

The inroads of the Sea Peoples also changed the face of Syria-Palestine. The demise of Egyptian and Hittite sovereignty resulted in new political developments, though these were not uniform. We must distinguish Syria and the adjoining southern Anatolia from the Phoenician coast and Palestine. Except in the Phoenician coastland where the old trade cities maintained their position, new small states came into being throughout the area, most of them city-states but some of them expanding into larger territorial units (e.g., Aram-Damascus) and in some cases national states (Israel). From north to south the most important political entities were: Tabal, a conglomerate of principalities between the Halys River and the Anti-Taurus Mountains (Cappadocia); Hilakku, the territory southwest of the central course of the Seyhan; Melid, the area around Malatiya; Gurgum, the area around

Maraş; Que (Qume), Cilicia Campestris with Adana and Tarsus; Samal or Yadiya (Yaudi), the area around Zenjirli, south of Gurgum; Kummuhu, Commagene, the region south of Malatiya; Carchemish on the Euphrates; Bit-Adini, south of it on both sides of the river (capital Til Barsip); Unqi ('*mq*) or Patina (formerly read Hattina), the Amuq valley on the lower course of the Orontes, with, among others, the city of Kinalua/Kullani/Kalne (cf. Amos 6:2); Arpad (Tell Rifaat), just north of Aleppo, the area of Bit-Agushi; Luash or Luhuti, with its capital Had/zrak or Hatarikka, north of Hamat; Hamat on the Orontes; Aram-Damascus; the Phoenician trade cities Arvad, Byblos, Sidon, and Tyre; Israel with its neighbors Ammon, Moab, Edom, and the Philistine pentapolis in southwestern Palestine. Older states such as Amurru, Nuhashshe, and Ugarit, and important cities such as Alalakh and Ugarit, disappeared.

As the foundation and legacy of Hittite domination, a strong Anatolian influence continued in the northern part of this region, particularly in Tabal, Melid, Kummuhu, Gurgum, Carchemish, and Unqi. This remained so, though it was increasingly mixed with Semitic—especially Aramaic—elements present in Que, Samal, and Hamat. The extent of the Anatolian influence is indicated by the many monuments inscribed with Hittite hieroglyphs, written in Luwian, and the fact that names of the kings were as a rule non-Semitic and sometimes exhibited a preference for Old Hittite kingly names such as Muwatallish, Arnuwantash, Shuppiluliumash, and Lubarnash. In the area of religion and art, too, Anatolian forms are found, sometimes influenced by Phoenician, Aramaic, or northern Mesopotamian traits. They are known from stone plates with reliefs (along walls) in palaces, from monumental gate lions, and from steles at such sites as Tell Halaf, Zenjirli, Karatepe, Malatiya, and Carchemish. From this perspective it is understandable that neighboring countries called this northern Syrian and southern Anatolian territory Hatti. That Tiglath-pileser (ca. 1100 B.C.) came into contact first with the ruler of Carchemish, Ini-Teshub, called "king of Hatti," promoted this usage. Though it is not true, as has been presumed, that this ruler of Carchemish acted as the sovereign ruler of "Great Hatti" (this term is based on a faulty reading), by way of Carchemish the name Hatti did become applicable to northern Syria and later even to the entire Syro-Palestinian area (cf. the use of Huru by the Egyptians in the Amarna Age). In the interest of clarity modern historians prefer "Syro-Hittite."

The history of these small states before the ninth century—when Assyria appeared on the scene—is poorly known. We know a number of royal names, while actually only from Carchemish are we familiar with a line of kings, especially the dynasty of Suhis from the tenth century B.C.

Aramean influence in Syria greatly increased after the end of the eleventh century. Assyrian sources mention the intruding Arameans under Ashurrabi (ca. 1000 B.C.) who reached the Habur, where the state Bit-Bahian (Tell Halaf, Guzana) and the principality of Nisibis came into existence. The expansion westward turned Samal and Arpad into Aramean states as early as 900 B.C., besides the older Bit-Adini along the Euphrates. For a long time Hamat remained the most southern Syro-Hittite stronghold, but about 800 B.C. it became Aramean. A fact of importance was the Aramean expansion toward southern Syria, about which we know from the Old Testament (2 Samuel 8 and 10; 1 Chronicles 18). Around 1000 B.C. the territory west and north of Damascus was ruled by Hadadezer (I), who controlled Soba (the later Assyrian province Subatu), northeast of the Anti-Lebanon, and Bet-Rehob, southwest of the Lebanon. When the Ammonites appealed to Hadadezer against Israel, he defended himself with the help of vassals and allies, such as Maacha and Tob (both in northern Transjordan, Bashan), with supporting troops from the Euphrates area (with which he thus still maintained contact), and with the support of the Arameans from Damascus (no king is mentioned). In a series of battles he was defeated; in these battles David apparently captured Damascus and extended his power far into the north and also maintained good contacts with the anti-Aramean Hamat under Toi. Solomon's territory reached to Tadmur (Palmyra) and Lebo-Hamath, north of Lebanon. Hadadezer's former vassals now joined Israel and paid tribute.

Already before the end of Solomon's reign,

however, a new Aramean state appeared on the scene, Aram-Damascus, which managed to become independent under Rezon (Aramaic *Radyan*, also the name of the last king of Damascus, ca. 730 B.C.), a former vassal or officer of Hadadezer. Damascus soon became the most important Aramean state in southern Syria, and both in the Old Testament and in some Aramean inscriptions (e.g., those of Zak[k]ur and Hamat) it is simply called "Aram." From 1 Kings 15:18–19 we know that Tabrimmon (or Tabramman; Ramman is a name for the weather-god Hadad), son of Hezion, as king of Damascus had a covenant with Abijah of Judah (ca. 910 B.C.) and his son Benhadad (I; Aramaic Barhadad), with Baasha, and later with Asa. It is possible that the founder of the dynasty, Rezon (ca. 940 B.C.), is to be identified with the above Hezion, one generation before 910 B.C. (the conjectured restoration of Tabrimmon and Hezion in an Old Aramaic inscription, the so-called Barhadad inscription [see Donner-Röllig, no. 201] has little basis). Aram-Damascus grew into a powerful state and a great threat to Israel, as far as the "threat from the north" (Assyria) in the coming centuries allowed these states an independent military policy.

### f. Phoenicia from 1100 to 900 B.C.

Archeological traces indicate that the Phoenician trade cities also suffered from the Sea Peoples. Apparently they soon managed to recover, though there are only scant data from the twelfth century. Around 1100 B.C. Byblos, Sidon, and Tyre flourished again. Tiglath-pileser I, who reached the sea at the most northern Phoenician port, Arvad, received their "tribute" from Byblos and Sidon. In his report, Wen-Amon mentions all three cities and makes it clear that there is a fair amount of commercial activity, in particular by means of the fleets of Byblos and Sidon. Trade connections were maintained with Egypt under Smendes I (ca. 1075 B.C.). Byblos had its own king (Zakar-Baal), as did Sidon. Though the Phoenicians lost competition through the downfall of such harbor cities as Ugarit and Ura (Cilicia), the maritime activity of the new Philistine cities in southern Palestine (Ashkelon and Gaza, and farther to the north, Dor) was a factor to be reckoned with, as is also evident from Wen-Amon's story. In Sidon, ships traded "in company" (*hbr*) with *Wrktr*, perhaps a Philistine. Mazar has suggested that the new prosperity of Phoenicia from 1000 B.C. was due to the fact that under David and Solomon the Philistines gradually lost power, though they remained in control of the *via maris* running through the plain. In his judgment, the treaty between Hiram and David/Solomon had a strong commercial and anti-Philistine focus.

The mutual relations among the Phoenician cities are not very clear. According to later traditions Tyre was reestablished by people from Sidon in the twelfth century; it is believed by some that the city was initially ruled by Sidon. To substantiate that, reference is sometimes made to Genesis 10:15 (Sidon is Canaan's firstborn), to the fact that Tiglath-pileser I did not mention Tyre, and that in the Old Testament (1 Kings 5:20) as well in Homer "Sidonians" means Phoenicians. These arguments are not altogether convincing. Tiglath-pileser did not penetrate so far to the south, and the mention of Sidonians may also reflect the situation in the ninth century when Tyre indeed outstripped Sidon and a Tyrian king by the name of Itto-Baal (Old Testament Ethbaal, the father of Jezebel; ca. 875 B.C.) was called "king of the Sidonians."

Inscriptions from Tyre itself are almost totally lacking; the oldest from Sidon are from the end of the sixth century B.C. Therefore we are dependent on other information: the Old Testament and the material transmitted by late classical authors. Of particular significance are the traditions concerning the "royal annals" of Tyre, especially known from Josephus's *Contra Apionem*, in which he, presumably by way of Alexander Polyhistor (1st century B.C.), cites from Dius's "History of Phoenicia" and Menander of Efeze's Greek translation of the Tyrian annals. The existence of such annals for such an early period is quite possible, considering the old writing traditions of Phoenicia, where as early as the eleventh century the standard alphabet had obtained its definite shape and in subsequent centuries spread throughout all of Syria and Palestine, while according to legend Cadmus introduced it

into Greece. It is also quite conceivable that in the period of David and Solomon the Tyrian writing of annals had an impact on Israelite historiography. As a matter of fact, Phoenician influence on Israel in the area of culture and technique was great in that century, as we learn from the story of the building of the temple.

Though initially Tyre and Israel were rivals in northern Canaan, the Phoenician territory, which ideally belonged to Canaan, was never conquered. The tribes living close to it, such as Asher and Dan, became paid Tyrian workers, and were later even pushed back, according to Genesis 49:13; Judges 1:31; 5:16–17. Under David the two formed a relationship of close cooperation, issuing in a treaty between Hiram I and David and Solomon, sealed by Solomon's marriage with "Sidonian princesses" (1 Kings 11:1). The two nations were equals, with Tyre keeping the coastal area north of Carmel (the "ladder of Tyre"). In addition to cooperating in the building of the temple, there was also cooperation in the area of trade. At the time of Solomon the joint fleet of "seaworthy merchant vessels" ("Tarshish ships") left from Elath to obtain gold and other exotic articles from Ophir (likely the coast of Somaliland, the "Punt" of the Egyptians). Tyre must also have played a role in Solomon's trade in chariot horses (from Musri [!] and Que in Cilicia) and war chariots (from Egypt; 1 Kings 10:28–29). From the commercial aspect, Israel's control of the major land routes and Tyre's fleet complemented each other. Israel's military power (Solomon's chariot cities) was important for Tyre because of the competition from Philistines and Aram-Damascus.

According to tradition and the interpretation of information in Josephus, Phoenician colonization in the Mediterranean Sea region would have begun under Hiram I ("the Great"), who reigned thirty-four years (ca. 970–936 B.C.). According to classical authors, one of the first colonies was Utica (near Carthage), probably established about 1100 B.C. Some historians maintain that there was already a Tyrian settlement at Kition (Larnaka, on the east coast of the island) at the beginning of the tenth century B.C. Two old inscriptions from the ninth century B.C., one from Kition and one of unknown origin, presumably furnish epigraphical proof. But further investigation has shown that one must be very skeptical about these conclusions. There is a growing consensus that the beginning of the colonization happened no earlier than the end of the ninth century, but probably after 800 B.C. Josephus writes about a Tyrian expedition under Hiram I to put a vassal, who refused to pay tribute, back in line, but that is not the same as colonization. Nor do the two inscriptions prove settlement on Cyprus. It is quite possible that they stem from Late Bronze Age Syrian settlements, which in the ninth century—like other non-Phoenician states, for example, Samal—made use of Phoenician, which functioned as the *lingua franca* and written language, without being themselves of Phoenician origin. Archeological and epigraphical data—such as the Nora inscription (Donner-Röllig, no. 46) from Sardinia and the inscription on bronze bowls found north of Limasol (mentioning "Baal of the Lebanon," King Hiram II of Tyre from ca. 730 B.C., and the existence of a Qarthadasht, "Carthage" ["new city"], as settlement)—almost always point to the period from about 800 B.C. That agrees with the data that yield roughly 814 B.C. as the date of Carthage's founding by Elissa-Dido, fleeing from Tyre to escape from her brother and King Pygmalion (Pumyaton).

According to the annals tradition, Hiram I was succeeded by Baal-Azor (ca. 935–919 B.C.) and subsequently by four other kings. The last one, Phelles, had murdered his brother and within a year experienced the same fate himself. The perpetrator and successor to the throne was Itto-Baal (I), of royal blood and at the same time priest of Astarte. With him a new dynasty came to power. His kingship, lasting thirty-two years according to the annals (ca. 887–856 B.C.), brought great prosperity to Tyre. It surpassed Sidon, and good relations were established with the neighbor to the south, Israel, that were sealed by a marriage between his daughter Jezebel and Ahab, about 875 B.C.

The history of Byblos in the north in the tenth century B.C. is slightly better known owing to five royal inscriptions (tomb, building, and dedicatory inscriptions; Donner-Röllig, nos. 1, 4–7) that give us the names of the kings Ahiram (actu-

ally Ahirom; Hiram is an abbreviation) (ca. 1000 B.C.), Itto-Baal (ca. 975 B.C.; he had Ahiram's sarcophagus made, the lid of which contains the oldest monumental Phoenician inscription; it was discovered in grave 5 of the biblical necropolis), Yehimilk (ca. 950 B.C.), Ahibaal (ca. 935 B.C.), Elibaal, son of Yehimilk (ca. 910 B.C.), and his son Shipitbaal (ca. 900 B.C.). The inscriptions provide little historical information, but show that the city was an independent kingdom and continued to play its commercial role, demonstrated by Wen-Amon for the time around 1075 B.C. The relations with Egypt remained very important. It is interesting that Abibaal's inscription is engraved on an image of Pharaoh Shoshenq I (ca. 945–915 B.C.) that the king "brought up from Egypt," while Elibaal's text is found on a statue of Shoshenq's successor Osorkon I (ca. 915–905 B.C.?). Both statues are indicative of the pharaonic adoration of the two great gods, Baalat Gebal, "Lady of Byblos," and Baal-Shamem, the increasingly more prominent "Lord of Heaven" from Tyre, and of the desire for commercial connections with Byblos.

In Palestine itself, after the critical period of the judges and the kingship of Saul, during whose reign the Philistines became the masters of a great part of Palestine, David's accession to the throne and his military activities brought a remarkable recovery, which Solomon continued at first. Damascus, Ammon, Moab, and Edom were defeated, forced to pay tribute, and kept subdued in part by garrisons. There were also victories over the Philistines. Though reducing their military power and capturing their strongholds in the north—Dor, Beth-shean—he did not conquer their central territory, the pentapolis. The military skirmishes happened along the southwestern border of Judah. This area remained a vulnerable spot, where as late as about 965 B.C. Pharaoh Siamun could still capture the city of Gezer (from the Philistines?) and where political fugitives could find asylum with the independent king Achish of Gath. Gaza was later the city from which Shoshenq (Shishak) made his campaign against Israel. During Solomon's and Rehoboam's reigns the situation changed for the better. The Philistines were pushed back farther and farther, the army was strengthened by contingents of war chariots, and fortifications protected the border: Hazor in the north against Aram, Megiddo in the strategic plain of Jezreel, Gezer against Philistia, and Tamar in the southeast against Edom. But the first great military confrontation with Shoshenq (Shishak) in about 925 B.C. proved that these defensive measures were not sufficiently effective.

## LITERATURE

D. R. Ap-Thomas, "The Phoenicians," in D. J. Wiseman, ed., *Peoples of Old Testament Times* (Oxford, 1973), pp. 259–86.

*H. W. Attridge and R. A. Oded, *Philo of Byblos: The Phoenician History* (Washington, 1981).

G. Buccellati, *Cities and Nations of Ancient Syria* (Rome, 1967).

*J. Elays, "Les cités phéniciennes et l'empire assyrien," *Revue d'Assyriologie* 77 (1983) 45–58.

K. Galling, "Der Weg der Phöniker nach Tarsis in literarischer und archäologischer Sicht," *Zeitschrift des Deutschen Palästinavereins* 88 (1972) 1–18, 140–81.

J. D. Hawkins, "Assyrians and Hittites," *Iraq* 35 (1974) 67–83.

H. J. Katzenstein, *The History of Tyre* (Jerusalem, 1973).

B. Landsberger, *Sam'al* (Anakara, 1948).

A. Malamat, "Aspects of the Foreign Policies of David and Solomon," *Journal of Near Eastern Studies* 22 (1963) 1–17.

O. Masson and M. Sznycer, *Recherches sur les Phéniciens à Chypre* (Geneva/Paris, 1972).

B. Mazar, "The Aramean Empire and its Relations with Israel," *Biblical Archaeologist* 25 (1962) 98–120.

———, *The Philistines and the Rise of Israel and Tyre* (Jerusalem, 1964).

S. Moscati, *The World of the Phoenicians* (London, 1968).

J. D. Muhly, "Homer and the Phoenicians," *Berytus* 19 (1970) 19–64.

M. von Oppenheim, *Tell Halaf. Une civilisation retrouvée en Mésopotamie* (Paris, 1939).

W. Orthmann, *Untersuchungen zur späthethitischen Kunst* (Bonn, 1971).

## g. Egypt under the Twenty-first–Twenty-fourth Dynasties (11th–9th Centuries B.C.)

The Twenty-first Dynasty, which began in 1080 B.C. with the "renaissance era," is difficult to grasp historically, due to the lack of good sources. During this period the main focus in the land was on internal problems. Nubia and Canaan were lost and in Egypt there were in reality two governing royal houses: the official kings at Tanis in the Delta, and the high priests of Amon at Thebes who behaved as rulers and sometimes (e.g., Penudjem I, ca. 1055 B.C.) proclaimed themselves king. Moreover, from the outset there were Libyan princes, "great chief of the Ma(shwash)," in Bubastis, in the south of the Delta, whose power grew and who intermarried with the ruling dynasty and the powerful high priest of Ptah in Memphis. They became the Twenty-second Dynasty. It was not a period of civil war, only of political rivalry, in which the ruling families in various ways became related by marriage and shared the offices and prebends (especially within the hierarchy of the Amon temple in Thebes that was also economically powerful). In addition to the high priest of Amon and his "second-fourth prophet," especially the rank of "divine spouse of Amon," continued by adoption, was important, whereby often a daughter of the ruling king was advanced. The importance of Amon and its high priest turned Thebes and Upper Egypt into a kind of theocracy, in which the Amon oracle (the moving of his statue) played an important role in juridical and political decisions. This official cult of the upper class was contrasted by a more popular religiosity that developed, expressing itself, for example, in prayers that evidenced a deep personal piety.

The most important kings were Smendes I (ca. 1080–1043 B.C.), Psusennes I (ca. 1039–991), Siamun (ca. 978–959), and Psusennes II (perhaps identical with the Theban high priest Psusennes "III"; ca. 959–945; all according to the chronology preferred by Kitchen). Though Memphis, being the governmental center of Lower Egypt, still played a role and though the kings were building there at the Ptah temple, the harbor city of Tanis was the residence, favorably situated for trade with Canaan, as mentioned in Wen-Amon's story (ca. 1075 B.C.). Building there was done especially by Psusennes I and Siamun, for example, on the temple domain of Amon, which also contained the royal tomb recovered by Montet. For the work of building many stones and bricks from the more southern Avaris and Pi-Ramesse were used, which has led to wrongly identifying Tanis with the old Hyksos capital. More and more the powerful high priests of Thebes took care of the reburial of the great pharaohs of the New Kingdom whose tombs had been robbed. Eventually the royal mummies were collected in two large groups in secret graves. Those of Amenhotep II, Ramses I and II, and Seti I were eventually entombed in the grave of Penudjem II (ca. 980 B.C.), who himself made use of the adapted sarcophagus of Thutmose I.

Siamun directed his attention again to Canaan. He received crown prince Hadad, who had fled from David out of Edom, at his court, where he married an Egyptian princess. Siamun also undertook a raid against Philistia in which Gezer was seized and destroyed. The city was then given as the dowry of his daughter to Solomon (1 Kings 9:16), to seal the political alliance of both countries. These actions were likely motivated by political-economic considerations: Egypt was interested in protecting the valuable trade links with Phoenicia, which were probably threatened, or at least made difficult by the militant Philistines along the *via maris* and from their harbor cities. Therefore he also allied himself with Israel, the powerful eastern neighbor which itself was allied with Tyre.

Around 945 B.C. (with a margin of about 2 years), with Shoshenq I (pronunciation based on the Babylonian reproduction *Susinqu;* Old Testament Shishak) the Twenty-second or Libyan Dynasty came to power. He was the son of the Libyan prince of Bubastis who had made his way to the throne by means of an impressive career under Pharaoh Psusennes II—himself without a son—whose daughter he married. He was an energetic ruler who presented himself as a new Smendes; he started a new era, and after some years even extended his power to Thebes. Egypt's power was again extended to Nubia

while the economic ties with Byblos were tightened; at the time of Abibaal, the king devoted his statue to the "Lady of Byblos." His most important military feat was an extensive campaign to Palestine in Rehoboam's fifth year (ca. 925 B.C.). The division of the realm and the weakening of Judah and Israel offered an opportunity which Egypt did not pass up. The cause was apparently a border incident, after which the pharaoh, reneging on his earlier contacts with Jeroboam—who had been given asylum in Egypt—entered Palestine with his Libyan and Nubian supportive troops by way of Gaza, conquering, plundering, and destroying large parts of Judah and Israel. We are able to follow his exploits to a certain extent from the elaborate topographical list in the temple at Karnak, where there is also a relief depicting the king as triumphing over his Palestinian enemies (the terms *Retenu* and *Huru* are still being used). At Megiddo a piece of a monumental statue of Shoshenq I was discovered that probably goes back to this campaign. From the strategic plain of Jezreel he also penetrated into Transjordan as far as Peniel (cf. Kitchen, Excursus E, 432–47). Laden with booty he returned to Egypt, where he devoted himself to extensive building activities, particularly at Karnak. After celebrating his government jubilee (according to Wente) he died (ca. 913 B.C.).

His successor was Osorkon I (ca. 916–904 B.C.), who continued the policies of his father, as is evident from his statue discovered at Byblos. He was succeeded by Takelot I (ca. 904–890 B.C.), about whom next to nothing is known. The Nubian Zera, who about 897 B.C. attacked Judah under Asa, was likely a Nubian general of this pharaoh. In about 890 B.C. (according to the chronology of Baer and Wente) he was succeeded by Osorkon II, who distinguished himself as a builder in Tanis, Bubastis, and Thebes. In Thebes he was more and more confronted with the southern drive for independence, personified in the high priest of Amon-Re, Harsiese, who had royal ambitions. Osorkon was able to preserve the central government by, among other things, the appointment of his own son in Thebes, but the conflicts remained and eventually, after an internal struggle between 845 and 835 B.C., led to a schism: Thebes chose the side of the new dynasty of Leontopolis, founded by Pedubast I in about 828 B.C.

Osorkon kept up the relations with Canaan: a statue of him was discovered at Byblos, and an alabaster jar with his name on it in the ruins of Samaria. Was it a sign of political affiliation and was the oil, which the jar likely contained, meant for a ceremony as described in Hosea 12:1? Similar vases (later?) also reached Asshur by way of Phoenicia (as part of the spoil) and even Al-muñécar in Spain by way of Phoenician trade. During Osorkon's reign begins the chronologically important continuous series of dated and mummified Apis bulls, whose steles with chronological data—year of installation, age, and date of death—were recovered in the Serapeum in Memphis.

Around this time Assyrian expansion began to assume threatening forms. Egypt, having vested interests in Syria, could not ignore that. Takelot II (ca. 860–835 B.C.) was aware of it, as is evident from the Egyptian contingent of one thousand soldiers that at Qarqar on the Orontes fought on the side of the "coalition" against Shalmaneser III of Asshur (853 B.C.). On his black obelisk this Assyrian king mentioned for 841 B.C. a gift (he called it "tribute") consisting of exotic animals, which must have come from Takelot II. That pharaoh was succeeded by Shoshenq II (ca. 835–783 B.C.) during a period of rapidly increasing internal tensions in Egypt, when the rival Twenty-third Dynasty manifested itself.

## LITERATURE

K. Kitchen, *The Third Intermediate Period in Egypt (1100–650 B.C.)* (Warminster, 1973) (cf. the review by E. F. Wente, *Journal of Near Eastern Studies* 35 [1976] 275ff.; and that of K. Baer, *Journal of Near Eastern Studies* 32 [1973] 4–25).

J. Leclant, "Les Relations entre l'Egypte et la Phénicie du voyage d'Ounamon a l'expédition d'Alexandre," in W. W. Ward, ed., *The Role of the Phoenicians in the Interaction of Mediterranean Civilizations* (Beirut, 1968), pp. 9–31.

D. B. Redford, "Studies in Relations between Palestine and Egypt during the First Millennium B.C.: II, The Twenty-Second Dynasty," *Journal of the American Oriental Society* 93 (1973) 3–17.

# 7. THE NEAR EAST AND EGYPT DURING THE NEO-ASSYRIAN EMPIRE (9TH–7TH CENTURIES B.C.)

## a. Sources and Assyrian Policy

Under Adad-nirari II (911–891 B.C.), who waged war against the Arameans, Asshur's new expansion began (ca. 900 B.C.), which in the seventh century would make it into a world empire stretching from Anatolia and Iran to Egypt. The copious source material of all kinds enables us to obtain a good picture of this development, its methods, and its political motives.

Of the written sources, the *annals* are particularly significant. They are ceremonial inscriptions, usually on stone plates, which year by year contain the standard report of the great deeds of the king. In a sense they replace the older royal hymns, as is also evident from the pompous introductions in which the king glorifies himself with dozens of epithets. Complete editions of the annals from various years are very valuable, because the report of the early years was later abbreviated and sometimes also subjected to editorial revision that combined facts. In addition there are many nonannalistic inscriptions, in particular the "summary inscriptions," with an overview of defeated cities and rulers, sometimes geographically arranged. Shorter texts on statues, steles, and throne bases provide selective information, sometimes about one event (e.g., the inauguration of Kalhu). There are also excerpt texts. Very important are the building inscriptions, especially the Assyrian prisms placed in the foundations of temples and palaces. The building report is preceded by an elaborate historical report (originally the temporal protasis of the building report: "When I had . . . , then I built . . .") about the military feats of the king, arranged according to years of reign (*palu*) and later according to campaigns (*gerru*). This historical report, too, grew year by year, so that of various kings we possess a successive series of prisms (e.g., of Ashurbanipal), with the development being analogous to that of the annals. Furthermore, from the royal chancelleries we possess numerous records, letters, and lists, particularly from Kalhu and Nineveh (8th–7th century B.C.), including census lists and records of tribute; oracle requests (and answers) and prophetic messages (from the temple of Ishtar of Arbela, the Assyrian war-goddess) that "charge" and encourage the kings; fragments of vassal treaties with defeated rulers (with Arpad, ca. 740; Tyre, ca. 676; Median rulers, 672), in part corresponding to the "oaths of allegiance" (ade, an Aramaic loanword; cf. Hebrew edo/ut; 'dym in Isa. 33:8 [1QIsᵃ]) sworn by the court and high officials. Letters and reports afford insight into the Assyrian information service, the movement of messengers, taxation, forage, conscription, militia, and many religious matters.

Also important are the "letters to the god," detailed and highly literary reports about the annual(?) campaign, written to the god Ashur and his city (population) by whom the king had been mandated to enlarge the territory of the realm. They were probably recited in a public ceremony, in which also spoil and prisoners were divided. We possess copies from Sargon II (undamaged, 430 lines, against Urartu; 714 B.C.), Sennacherib (fragment of campaign against Palestine, 701 B.C.), Esarhaddon, and Ashurbanipal. A continuously dated overview of the most important campaigns is found in the *Eponym Chronicle*. It is an extensive version of the eponym list, containing in a separate column brief reports about military activities, except when, as shown by notations such as "rebellion," epidemic," "(the king remained) in the land," it was left out or had to yield to notations about cultic events (e.g., dedication of a temple). The notations—preserved, with lacunae, for the period 816–700 B.C.—as a rule indicate only the purpose of the yearly campaign ("to city/country x"), but occasionally are more detailed (e.g., 743 B.C.: "Urartu defeated at Arpad"), especially in later years. Occasionally, when it is said "in place/land x" the reference may be to the place where the king and army were at the beginning of the year, when the eponym (*limmu*) was designated. Besides this text there are also other *chronicles* of various kinds

(now available in Grayson's edition) that as a rule offer a selective and politically and ideologically colored picture of history, such as the pro-Assyrian "Synchronistic Chronicle" (Asshur/Babylonia) or the Esarhaddon Chronicle. Alongside of it since 747 B.C. there is the objective "Babylonian Chronicle," which describes, for example, the collapse of Assyria and the rise of the New Babylonian kingdom of Nabopolassar and Nebuchadrezzar.

Besides the epigraphical material—often only partially and unsatisfactorily published; frequently also fragmentary—there is since the ninth century B.C. pictorial material from the Assyrian palaces. Initially the palaces probably had only fresco decorations; in addition, there were also some sculptured stone monuments, which certainly from the eleventh century also contained historical scenes: in particular the Assyrian "obelisks" of Ashurbelkala (mid-11th century B.C.) to Shalmaneser III (2nd half of the 9th century B.C.). From the time of Ashurnasirpal II there also appear (besides the frescoes, which as shown by a discovery in Til Barsip continued to be used, but are now mostly lost) relief plates, bull colosses, and other monuments. These were apparently inspired by the Syro-Hittite world, where already in the tenth century B.C. (Tell Halaf, Carchemish) orthostats with reliefs were used in palace architecture, as well as full reliefs of statues of bulls, lions, sphinxes, and other hybrid figures flanking the entrance. This type of decoration, together with the palace entrance—a wide portico with supporting columns, flanked by the above-mentioned statues; the whole structure was called *bit hilani*—was taken over by the Assyrians. We have Assyrian reliefs, decorating corridors and certain rooms, from Kalhu (Ashurnasirpal II and Tiglath-pileser III), Dur-Sharrukin (Khorsabad, the new residence of Sargon II), and Nineveh (palaces of Sennacherib, Esarhaddon, Ashurbanipal). Besides court scenes, religious and magic-symbolic pictures, building scenes (transport of bull colosses), and hunting tableaus, many "historical" reliefs preserve moments from the king's campaign: the army camp, the army on the march, later also battles and especially attacks, conquests, plundering, deportation, and destruction of cities, often identified in brief captions. These pictures are as it were the illustrations accompanying the annals (sometimes written under it) that deal with the same moments and, in view of their ideological function, like the reliefs never show failures. See ill. 83.

The situation with respect to the reliefs is far from ideal. As a result of inexpert excavations around the middle of the nineteenth century, accidents in transport (by way of the Tigris on rafts and by means of the quay of Bombay), division and cutting of the pieces, poor publication, and of course the destruction of the palaces at the end of the seventh century B.C., much has become lost so that now it is no longer possible, or only with difficulty, to determine how large series of reliefs fit together and to ascertain their original function and locale. The Assyrians themselves, too, have contributed to that. The reliefs from Tiglath-pileser's unfinished palace in Kalhu were broken up for use in Esarhaddon's palace in Nineveh, but that, too, remained an unfinished project. Still, whatever is left—in part only in good, old drawings—is artistically and historically very important, because of the extensive scope of Asshur's operations, which extended from Elam to southern Anatolia and southern Palestine.

Important reliefs have also been uncovered in the palace and temple of the city of Imgur-Enlil (Balawat, southeast of Kalhu), in the form of bronze bands covering the large gates, coming from Ashurnasirpal II and Shalmaneser III. Especially the large, well-preserved bands of the last king (16 pieces, each 2.25 m. or over 7 ft. long and containing two friezes) are important, because there are no reliefs in stone from him, except for a beautiful throne base from Kalhu. This material gives us an idea of Asshur's military, political, and economic aims and strategy. The military developments include further development of the war chariot, which in many battles was decisive and for which the many horses, enumerated in tribute lists, were indispensable. The art of "forcing cities" was also perfected; besides starving a city by erecting barriers around it (from the time of Adad-nirari II), also the attack on the wall by means of improved battering rams (hauled to the walls over dams), undermining, and scaling ladders was given a great deal of attention; not

even city moats proved an insuperable obstacle. This military technique was used on the one hand during long campaigns in enemy territory, especially from the ninth century B.C. on; the land was plundered, and local rulers, defeated or intimidated, came to subject themselves with "gifts," after which they were reduced to vassals and obligated to pay tribute. On the other hand there was a more systematic conquering of territory, whereby cities were besieged and taken, thus enlarging Asshur's territory. Already in the ninth century B.C. this latter strategy brought Asshur to the Euphrates, where Shalmaneser III conquered Bit-Adini's capital and changed Til Barsip to Kar-Shulmannashared. Further conquering of territory and annexing it to Asshur happened from about 745 B.C. when Tiglath-pileser III mounted the throne. In many cases he broke with the vassal system and, like his successors, turned conquered territory into Assyrian provinces ruled by Assyrian governors, who were supported by garrisons, an efficient interchange of messengers, and an information service. Exceptions were almost always the Phoenician cities Tyre and Sidon, as well as Judah and Philistia. That was apparently due principally to economic considerations, because the coastal cities also functioned as harbor and trade cities for the Assyrian empire, for which they needed a measure of freedom of movement, even though taxes were levied and the movement of goods controlled (including the shipping of wood from the Lebanon to the enemies).

Asshur's expansion was very economically motivated. Already Adad-nirari II declared that he was chosen king by the great gods "to plunder the possessions of the lands." The acquisition of booty and the collecting of tribute and gifts—to be distinguished from the fixed yearly tribute of the vassals (*mandattu*) and the often much larger "spectacular gifts" (*tamartu* or *namurtu*), with which enemies subjected themselves or bought Asshur's favor at the coming of the army—became almost institutional and are often referred to in texts and reliefs. The army became a large, goods-collecting caravan, returning home laden with spoils. Commercial traffic had to yield increasingly to a militarily forced one-way traffic, destination Asshur. The booty of the army contained cattle, small livestock, donkeys, horses, all kinds of metals (copper, bronze, iron, gold, and silver), stones, wood, wool and textiles, and a great variety of utensils. All those goods and materials served to strengthen Asshur's limited economic potential and made the military effort possible, while stimulating it at the same time in a vicious circle.

Increasingly the booty of the army also began to include deported subdued people, especially under Tiglath-pileser III (who deported more than a half million people), in order that as soldiers, farmers, artisans, laborers, and city dwellers (especially of the new cities and residences) they might augment the manpower of Asshur's heartland or fill in the gaps elsewhere caused by deportations. Following in their wake all kinds of elements, especially from the culture of Syria-Palestine, streamed into Asshur, where, despite a measure of assimilation of the deported people into Assyrian life, they changed Assyrian culture from the inside. Especially noticeable is a growing "Aramaization," which from the eighth century B.C. constituted the basis for an increasing use of the Aramaic language, challenging the Assyrian language and becoming the international medium, resulting at last, during the Achaemenids, in "Official Aramaic" becoming the *lingua franca* of the entire Near East. On the other hand, due to the deportation of Babylonian-Chaldean and Elamite populations, and as a result of Assyrian rule, the west was also penetrated by foreign elements.

To reach their goal, Assyria, in addition to military means and deportations, increasingly used cruelty and intimidation. Texts and reliefs document not only the destruction of harvests, orchards, and irrigation works and the levying of ransoms, but also the merciless heaping up of piles of cut-off heads, and the impaling, skinning, burning, and mutilating of conquered enemies. This treatment—in those days considered less gruesome than today, though the detailed descriptions and pictures are striking—was especially given to revolting rebels. These tactics had a calculated effect: the inclination to revolt was suppressed and adversaries already in advance "overwhelmed by the fear for Asshur's weapon" subjected themselves with rich "gifts." Even so, Asshur's imperialism and cruelty were not able to prevent revolts from flaring up regularly; in fact, they may even have evoked them. These facts have put a permanent stamp on Asshur's image in contemporary (cf. Isa. 10:13–14; 14:16–17) and later historiography. They also strengthened the expectation of a realm of peace, set forth by the Israelite prophets as the ideal precisely at the time of Asshur's brutal acts, an ideal that could not be satisfied by the *pax assyriaca*, mentioned, for example, in 2 Kings 18:31ff. and in a famous Assyrian royal letter (Oppenheim, *Letters from Ancient Mesopotamia*, no. 86), and that was approached especially in the seventh century.

Though the Assyrian kings were appointed by their god Ashur, and according to the coronation ritual called upon to enlarge Asshur's territory, and though Ashur ordered them to engage in campaigns (supporting them through oracles, prophecies, and omens), they hardly engaged in religious imperialism. Though the recognition of Asshur's supremacy included at the same time the recognition of the power and the "weapon of the god Ashur" (also as divine symbol)—god, city, and people cannot be separated—that did not mean that the cult of their own gods was in any way suppressed. What is found is a theological view on and a justification of Assyria's behavior. The other gods were thought to have abandoned their city and people and to have surrendered them to Asshur's power, in fact even to have mandated Asshur to punish their people—a vision in the Old Testament not only expressed by the Assyrian field commander (2 Kings 18:25) but also acknowledged by Isaiah (10:5ff.), though in its pride and brutality Asshur went too far. This conception was actualized in the carrying off of the (images of the) gods of the subdued peoples, who after surrender to Asshur were allowed to return. In the vassal treaties or oaths of allegiance (*ade*) made between Asshur and the defeated kings, the vassals also had to swear by their own gods, who in case they should become disloyal would punish them with their curses. Therefore Assyria's harsh actions against revolting vassals were explained in the inscriptions as an execution of the curses which the insurgents had invoked upon themselves, also by involving their own gods. This viewpoint in the Assyrian annals (even verbalized in question and answer: "Why did all this . . . happen? Because . . .") is endorsed by the Old Testament as is evident from Deuteronomy and especially from Ezekiel 17:12–21, where Yahweh in verse 19 speaks of "my curse/covenant" violated by the king of Judah.

## LITERATURE

R. D. Barnett, *Sculptures from the North Palace of Ashurbanipal at Nineveh* (London, 1976).

R. D. Barnett and M. Falkner, *The Sculptures of Assurnasirapli II, Tiglath-pileser III and Esarhaddon from the Central and South-West Palaces at Nimrud* (London, 1962).

M. Cogan, *Imperialism and Religion: Assyria, Judah and Israel in the 8th and 7th Centuries B.C.* (Missoula, Montana, 1974).

R. Ellis, *Foundation Deposits in Ancient Mesopotamia* (New Haven/London, 1968).

*F. M. Fales, *Assyrian Royal Inscriptions: New Horizons in Literary, Ideological, and Historical Analysis* (Rome, 1981).

R. Frankena, "The Vassal-Treaties of Esarhaddon and the Dating of Deuteronomy," *Oudtestamentische Studiën* 14 (1965) 122–54.

*P. Garelli, "La propaganda royale assyrienne," *Akkadiaca* 27 (1982) 16–29.

B. Hrouda, *Die Kulturgeschichte des assyrischen Flachbildes* (Saarbrücken, 1965).

*S. Lackenbacher, *Le roi bâtisseur* (Paris, 1982).

D. D. Luckenbill, *Ancient Records of Assyria and Babylonia* I–II (Chicago, 1926–27) (cf. also the translations in J. B. Pritchard, ed., *Ancient Near Eastern Texts* [Princeton, 1969³]).

D. J. McCarthy, *Treaty and Covenant* (Rome, 1978²).

*F. Malbran-Labat, *L'Armée et l'organisation militaire de l'Assyrie* (Geneva, 1982).

W. Martin, *Tribut und Tributleistungen bei den Assyrern* (Helsingforsiae, 1936).

*B. Menzel, *Assyrische Tempel* I–II (Rome, 1981).

B. Oded, *Mass Deportations and Deportees in the Neo-Assyrian Empire* (Wiesbaden, 1979).

A. T. Olmstead, *Assyrian Historiography: A Source Study* (Columbia, 1916).

S. Parpola, *Letters from Assyrian Scholars to the Kings Esarhaddon and Assurbanipal* (Kevelaer/Neukirchen-Vluyn, 1970).

A. Parrot, *Assur. Mesopotamische Kunst von XII. vorchristlichen Jahrhundert bis zum Tode Alexanders des Grossen* (Munich, 1972²).

A. Paterson, *Assyrian Sculptures: Palace of Senacherib* (The Hague, 1915).

N. J. Postgate, *Taxation and Conscription in the Assyrian Empire* (Rome, 1974).

J. B. Pritchard, ed., *Ancient Near Eastern Texts* (Princeton, 1969³), pp. 532–41 (translation of Assyrian vassal treaties by E. Reiner), 659–61 (Aramaic vassal treaties, by F. Rosenthal).

W. Schramm, *Einleitung in die assyrischen Königsinschriften* II (934–722 B.C.) (Leiden, 1973).

J. B. Stearns, *Reliefs from the Palace of Ashurnasirapli II* (Graz, 1961).

H. Tadmor, "Assyria and the West," in H. Goedicke and J. J. M. Roberts, eds., *Unity and Diversity* (Baltimore, 1975), pp. 36–48.

*_____, "Treaty and Oath in the Ancient Near East," in G. Tucker and D. Knight, eds., *Humanizing America's Iconic Book* (Chico, 1982).

M. Weinfeld, "The Loyalty Oath in the Ancient Near East," *Ugarit-Forschungen* 8 (1976) 379–414.

M. Weippert, " 'Heiliger Krieg' in Israel und Assyrien," *Zeitschrift für die alttestamentliche Wissenschaft* 84 (1972) 460–93.

Y. Yadin, *The Art of Warfare in Biblical Lands* (Jerusalem, 1963).

## b. Asshur and Its Neighbors in the Ninth Century B.C.

The foundation for Asshur's new expansion under Ashurnasirpal II (883–859 B.C.) was laid by Ashurdan II (934–912), Adad-nirari II (911–891), and Tukulti-Ninurta II (890–884). They made Asshur internally strong, cautiously moved up its frontiers, and enlarged the economic base of the empire, particularly through an ever increasing influx of tribute and "gifts" (especially all sorts of metals, flocks, donkeys, horses, and chariots). Their efforts were directed to the north and east—the arch between the Zagros and the upper course of the Tigris—and, from the time of Adad-nirari II, also to the west: the southern part of Anatolia and the Habur territory, once ruled by Mitanni and still called Hanigalbat. The conquered and plundered territories include Katmuhi, Alzi, and Nairi. In the west the Arameans were attacked. After a long and bitter struggle, first Nisibis (Nasibina) and Guzana (Bit-Bahiana under Abisalamu) were conquered and Ammebaal (of Bit-Zamani) subdued. Tukulti-Ninurta II again reached the Middle Euphrates during a large campaign by way of Wadi Tarthar, the east Tigris area (where the Aramean Utu lived), northern Babylonia (Dur-Kurigalzu, Sippar, Rapiqu), Hit and Suhu, and finally the Habur. Babylon placed no obstacles in the way of the Assyrians. Under Adad-nirari II there had still been a military conflict with Shamashmudammiq (ca. 900 B.C.), but under his successor Nabushumukin (ca. 899–888)—who was able to force the Assyrians back to Arrapha (Kirkuk)—a peace agreement, sealed by a marriage, had been reached in 891 B.C.

Assyria's power grew under Ashurnasirpal II (883–859 B.C.), a self-assured ruler, hard and cruel. In the east, he penetrated farther into Kurdistan, near the upper course of the Lower Zab (Zamua, Babite), on the route to Iran. In the north, he reached the springs of the Tigris (Bit-Zamani), where at the Subnat he left his rock relief (beside that of his Middle Assyrian predecessors) and annexed the city of Tushha as an advanced military base. He was harsh toward the Arameans in the triangle between the Middle Euphrates (Suhu, Hindanu, Laqe), Habur, and the Euphrates. About his tenth year, Bit-Adini under Ahuni and Carchemish under Sangara submitted themselves with gifts, but without having been conquered. Later in his reign the king even engaged in a march to the Lebanon and the Mediterranean Sea in "the land Amurru." Many princes brought him homage with "gifts": Lubarna from Kunulua (Old Testament Kalne) in Patina, Luhutu (Luash), Tyre, Sidon, Byblos, and Arvad. After "having washed his weapons in the Great Sea" and having cut down cedars on the Amanus—traditional climaxes of the westward expansion—the army returned with hostages and an immense quantity of spoil. The desire for the riches of Syria has once and for all been aroused. In the future Asshur would go for it through conquest and tribute; for the present time it had to be content with "gifts," because large powers such as Carchemish, Samal, Hamat, and Damascus were still unbroken. Commerce and economic infiltration determined Asshur's interest; as the counterpart of Tushha in Anatolia it annexed Aribua in Patina/Unqu as an outlying post.

The wealth of this "crowned robber" not only benefited the military, it also supported his immense building projects. First in importance was his new residence Kalhu, now the ruin Nimrud (in part excavated ca. 1850 by Layard, and from 1950 by Mallowan), which from his fifth year was gradually occupied by Ashurnasirpal. About 865 B.C. it was inaugurated with great festivities, including a banquet for 70,000 people, among whom envoys of all subdued and friendly nations and the 16,000 future inhabitants, taken "from the lands over which I had gained dominion." The city, which until about 720 B.C. remained the residence, betrays in its population and in its botanical garden, with all the "trees and seeds of the lands and mountains I passed through," the cosmopolitan and imperialistic character of Asshur, a character that would later become even more pronounced. Ashurnasirpal's large northwestern palace with its halls, bull colosses, and monumental reliefs gives us an idea of Asshur's new vigor and drive.

Under Shalmaneser III (858–824 B.C.) the actual confrontation with and subjection of Syria and southern Anatolia began. Already in his first year following a northern route, he marched through Commagene (Kummuhu) and Gurgum (Maraş), which subjected themselves. At Lutibu he encountered the troops of a north Syrian coalition, composed of Bit-Adini (Ahuni), Samal (Hayani), Patina (Sapalulma), and Carchemish (Sangara), which were now and again later defeated, a defeat also including Que (Cilicia Campestris). Asshur's ruler penetrated to the Amanus and the Mediterranean Sea. Resistance had, however, increased and the Phoenician cities did not come forward to do homage to the conqueror. Further military activity was necessary, but this could not be done until first the hinterland had been subdued. After a struggle of three years, the obstinate Ahuni of Bit-Adini was forced to surrender. Under the name "Fortress of Shalmaneser" his capital Til Barsip became Asshur's outlying post on the Euphrates; the territory east of the Euphrates was annexed.

The fall of Bit-Adini had a dual effect. When Asshur reappeared in 853 B.C. the north Syrian and southern Anatolian rulers submitted themselves with tribute: Commagene, Melid (Malatiya), Carchemish, Samal (under Hayani),

Patina, Gurgum, and Aleppo (Halman). In the south, however, an anti-Assyrian coalition was formed, led by the seriously threatened Irhuleni of Hamat and Benhadad (II; called Hadadezer by the Assyrians) of Damascus, who received great help from "Ahab the Israelite" (*Ahabbu Sir'ilaya*) and contingents from Que, Egypt, Arabia (the last two probably for reasons of trade interests in Syria), and the north Phoenician cities (among others, Arvad). According to the (somewhat exaggerated?) Assyrian numbers, the total strength of the troops of the coalition amounted to about 45,000 foot soldiers, 4,000 chariots (including 2,000 from Ahab), and 3,000 cavalry soldiers, among whom were 1,000 camel troops. Ahab and Benhadad ceased their mutual battle for Gilead. Probably owing to its superior number of chariots, the coalition was able to stop Asshur at Qarqar on the Orontes. When Shalmaneser returned after four years (849–848 B.C.) and again in 845 B.C., the coalition functioned effectively; the Assyrian inscriptions mention only conquests of rural areas; an invasion of the south did not happen. Asshur had no success until 841 B.C., when Hamat was weakened and the rivalry between Damascus and Israel had flared up again. Hazael, who around 842 B.C. captured the throne of Damascus in a coup (cf. 2 Kings 8:7ff.), became a threat to Israel, which itself was weakened through the loss of Moab under Mesha (mentioned on his stele) and where Jehu, likewise through a military coup, had taken over from Joram. In his first year (841 B.C.) Jehu paid tribute to Shalmaneser, as depicted on the "Black Obelisk," where he is called *Ja-u-a mar Humri* (a reproduction of "Ja[w]hu[a] of Bit Omri; cf. M. Weippert, *Vetus Testamentum* 28 [1978] 113ff.). Presumably he looked upon Asshur as a "deliverer who would free him from Aram's grip" (even as Jehoahaz did later; cf. 2 Kings 13:5). Hazael, left to battle Assyria by himself, was shut up in Damascus, which held out though the land was laid waste and plundered. Thereupon, by way of Hauran (and likely Gilead), Shalmaneser marched through the north of Israel to the coast near Tyre where he collected tribute from the Phoenician cities. Until 833 B.C. the king regularly appeared in the west, where he strengthened his grip on the metal-rich Que (Cilicia), maintained friendly relations with the north Phoenician harbor city Arvad (under Mat-

tinbaal), and received "gifts" elsewhere. Damascus, however, was able to hold out, even after 833 B.C. when General (*turtanu*) Daian-Ashur was in charge of the expeditions.

Besides the usual activities in the north and east, the king became active in Babylonia. There Nabuapaliddina (888–855 B.C.), who had forcefully rid the land of the Sutu, had been succeeded by Mardukzakirshumi I (854–819 B.C.). Soon a civil war erupted there between the king and his brother. Called in for help, Shalmaneser intervened and supported the king; they made a treaty with each other as depicted on a throne base from Kalhu. The Assyrian ruler worshiped the Babylonian gods of Babylon, Kutha, and Borsippa—an example that would be followed by many of his successors—and in southeast Babylonia attacked the Chaldean tribes of the Amukanu, Dakuru, and Yakin, an action yielding him immense booty. The finds in the great palace (attached to the military headquarters) of Kalhu, usually called "Fort Shalmaneser," give an idea of the tremendous wealth that streamed into Asshur in the wake of the military campaigns. The quantity of carved ivory—used as inlay work for furniture—is especially impressive and of great variety.

Shalmaneser's final years were without military activity. Since 827 B.C. Asshur had been involved in an internal power struggle, presumably between the old nobility and aristocracy in the cities in the heartland and the new military class and governors of the frontier provinces as representatives of Asshur's imperialism. The battle favored the latter, not coming to an end until Shamshi-Adad V (823–811 B.C.) eliminated his (half?) brother with the support of Mardukzakirshumi, who in this way got his revenge. Under such conditions military actions in the west were impossible, even when the Syrian vassals failed to pay homage to the new king. Asshur fought closer to home, in the north and south of Lake Urmia, where now for the first time the peoples of the Manneans (Manai) and Medes (Matai) are mentioned. In 814 B.C. relations with Babylonia were normalized. Mardukbalassuiqbi (818–810 B.C.) was defeated with his mercenary army consisting of Chaldeans, Elamites, Kassites(!), and Arameans, and even taken captive the next year. Shamshi-Adad V marched through northern Babylonia, plundering as he went along, called himself "king of Sumer and Akkad," and worshiped the gods of the great cultic centers. Babylonia entered a chaotic period, lasting about forty years, in which the political center of gravity gradually moved to the south ("Sealand"), where the Chaldean tribes, made prosperous by trade, became an important political power.

Shamshi-Adad died in 811 B.C. He was succeeded by the very young Adad-nirari III, who was initially overshadowed by the queen-mother Sammuramat—the Semiramis of the legend, but who was never queen or regent. Asshur recovered and was ready for an attempt to restore the damage done in the west.

In Syria most vassals had thrown off Asshur's yoke by stopping the payment of tribute. In the north, Arpad under Athtarshumki had become very powerful. In Hamat an Aramean dynasty had come to power shortly before 805 B.C.; Zak(k)ur was now the ruler there and his realm also included Luash and Hatarikka (Hazrak). In the Phoenician cites, which had profited from the freedom, trade flourished; they also served as harbors for Damascus and Hamat. Tyre retained its supremacy under Baalazor II, succeeded by Mattan in 830 B.C. Civil disturbances erupted when Pygmalion (Pumyaton) about 820 B.C. took the throne. The losing party fled led by his sister Elissa (Dido), whose husband, the high priest of Melqart, had been murdered. By way of Cyprus—where Idalion was a Tyrian colony—she and her retinue reached the north African coast, where in 814 B.C. Carthage ("new city"; *Qarthadasht*) was founded. According to tradition Pygmalion ruled from about 820 to 774 B.C. Damascus had recuperated from the Assyrian war and regained a powerful position, especially at the expense of Israel under Jehoahaz (ca. 814–799). Hazael reduced Israel to the city-state of Samaria (2 Kings 13:1–7), while the Arameans even penetrated as far as Gath and threatened Jerusalem under Joash. The attack was, however, averted by the payment of rich gifts (2 Kings 12:17–18).

In this situation Adad-nirari III (810–783 B.C.) appeared in 805 for the first time on the Syrian scene. Arpad was the chief opponent. The Assyrian actions continued till 802 B.C., with troops penetrating far south along the coast. Mention is made of subjection and tribute, but there are no decisive victories. It did, however, lead to a weakening of Damascus, where Hazael before 805 B.C. had been succeeded by "Benhadad" III (in Aramaic inscriptions Barhadad; with the Assyrians *Mari*, "my lord," presumably an abbreviated name with the omission of the theophoric element). The Assyrian intervention spelled "deliverance" for hard-pressed Samaria (2 Kings 13:5) and enabled Jehoahaz to reconquer the lost territory (vv. 22–25). After 800 B.C. Aram-Damascus recovered and tried to form an (anti-Assyrian?) coalition. The allied "Aram" (= Damascus), Arpad, Que, Unqi, Gurgum, Samal, and Melid now apparently tried to compel Zak(k)ur (often called Zakir) of Hamat and Luash to join by besieging his residence (cf. Zak[k]ur's inscription, Donner-Röllig, no. 202). Zak(k)ur, however, was able to repel the common attack. His god Baalshamem, "Lord of Heaven," delivered him after having encouraged him by seers and prophets in words that remind us of the Old Testament: "Fear not. For I have made you king and I will help you and deliver you from all these kings who have besieged you!" This "deliverance" was probably the intervention in 796 B.C. by the Assyrian Adad-nirari III (called for help by Zak[k]ur?). The Assyrian armies penetrated to the Beqa (Mansuate) and seized Damascus. In that city Adad-nirari received submission and tribute, also from Tyre, Sidon, "Joash, the man of Samaria" (*Jaasu Samerinaya*), Edom, and Philistia (*Palashtu*). Judah under Amaziah remained out of range. [The dating of the events is disputed. Some maintain that the events mentioned by Zak[k]ur happened before 805 B.C. or even after 796 B.C.; Joash's tribute is sometimes differently dated too, especially because Adad-nirari's summary inscription does not give an exact date. However, a dating in 802 B.C. causes chronological problems, because at that time Jehoahaz was still king and because it is difficult to link his name with the Assyrian *Jaasu*.]

---

## LITERATURE

*J. A. Brinkman, "Babylonia c. 1000–748 B.C.," in *Cambridge Ancient History* III/1 (Cambridge, 1982) 282–313.

M. Elat, "The Campaigns of Shalmaneser III against Aram and Israel," *Israel Exploration Journal* 25 (1975) 25–35.

W. de Filippi, "The Royal Inscriptions of Assur-Nasir-Apli (883–859)," *Assur* I (1977) 123–69.

J. C. L. Gibson, *Textbook of Syrian Semitic Inscriptions, II: Aramaic Inscriptions* (Oxford, 1975).

H. J. Katzenstein, *The History of Tyre* (Jerusalem, 1973).

W. G. Lambert, "The Reigns of Assurnasirpal II and Salmaneser II: An Interpretation," *Iraq* 36 (1974) 103–10.

*E. Lipiński, "Aram et Israël du X<sup>e</sup> au VIII<sup>e</sup> siècle av.n.è.," *Acta Antiqua* 27 (Budapest, 1979) 49–102.

B. Mazar, "The Aramean Empire and its Relations with Israel," *Biblical Archaeologist* 25 (1962) 98–120.

A. R. Millard and H. Tadmor, "Adad-Nirari III in Syria," *Iraq* 35 (1973) 57–64.

W. Schramm, "Die Annalen des assyrischen Königs Tukulti-Ninurta II," *Bibliotheca Orientalis* 27 (1970) 147–60.

## c. Between Adad-nirari III and Tiglath-pileser III (800–745 B.C.)

For the time being Adad-nirari's victory was the last great Assyrian military feat in the west. For the next fifty years Assyria was hardly able to assert itself. The expeditions in the years between 773 and 754 B.C. mentioned in the Eponym Chronicle (to Damascus, Hazrak, and Arpad) were little more than military raids without permanent effect. For now Syria and Palestine enjoyed a measure of rest. Asshur was being weakened by internal power struggles, epidemics (for 765 and 759 B.C. mentioned in the Eponym Chronicle), and by the threat from Urartu.

Adad-nirari was able to make a reasonable accord with Babylonia. Later, after battles at Der, a border agreement was reached. The king worshiped the great gods of Babylon, Kutha, and Borsippa (Nabu, who in this period was immensely popular), and allowed prisoners to return. Only conflicts with Chaldean tribes and with the Aramean U/Itu are worth mentioning. He was succeeded by three sons, successively Shalmaneser IV (782–773), Ashurdan III (772–755), and Ash-

urnirari V (754–745). Of these kings we possess no annals; our historical information is limited, pointing to internal difficulties, something that is confirmed by the Eponym Chronicle.

Internally there were problems with the powerful and pretentious high officials, who acquired great power as military or provincial governors, sometimes by means of a cumulation of functions. They resided in their own palaces, engaged in building activities of their own, and produced decorative inscriptions. Under the young kings they got their chance, such as the governor of Rasappa and the general Shamshi-ilu, who resided in Kar-Shulmanuashared and three times became an eponym. For 762–759 B.C. the Eponym Chronicle mentions revolts in Asshur, Arrapha, and Guzana. The king (with his army) was compelled to remain in the land. The threats from abroad were especially from the east and the north. Already Adad-nirari III between 800 and 788 B.C. had to undertake six campaigns against the Medes southeast of Lake Urmia. His successor battled Urartu, Asshur's great rival in the eighth century B.C., for six years; Asshur was only able to hold out by constantly being on the defense, aided in particular by the military efforts of Shamshi-ilu.

From about 840 B.C., Urartu, headed by King Sarduri I, grew into an important territorial state. The name Urartu is associated with that of the dominating Ararat mountain range (it is not sure whether a tribal name or a geographical name came first). The Urarteans called themselves and their central territory Biainili, which likely reflects the name Van—the center of their kingdom (in Urartian the city of Van is called Tu[u]pa). Natural resources, organizational ability, and technical competency explain Urartu's rise. Agriculture, trade, irrigation, metal industry, rock architecture (especially for the building of fortifications), military technique, and horsebreeding played an important role. The realm developed more or less along Assyrian lines, using royal titles (in which the kingship over the Nairi lands is mentioned), the vassal system, and provinces, controlled by garrisons in strategically located fortresses. The oldest inscriptions use Assyrian cuneiform and are written in Assyrian, though already from about 800 B.C. there are texts written in Urartian, a language distantly related to Hurrian. The expansion happens particularly under Menua (810–781), Argisti I (780–756), and Sarduri II (755–735). In the north the fertile Araxus valley was annexed. In the south Urartu penetrated to the Lake Urmia region and came in contact with Medes and Persians (Parsua). In the west it reached the great Euphrates curve: Malatiya and Kummuhu. Especially along the upper course of the Euphrates and Tigris the situation became critical for Asshur. It threatened to become surrounded when Urartu, allied with Arpad and perhaps also Carchemish, asserted itself militarily in northern Syria. Asshur was completely on the defensive, though it engaged in some battles in the west and east (against the Medes and Namri). Fortunately the relationship with Babylonia caused no severe problems. Generally speaking, the status quo was maintained, though there were some difficulties with the Chaldean Eriba-Marduk (from Yakin), who conquered the throne of Babylon (769 B.C.), in a period in which there were constant conflicts between Aramean tribes and the Babylonian cities, with the Chaldean kings trying to act as mediators. The end of the "Synchronistic History" expresses Assyrian suspicion against Babylonia.

The Assyrian absence from the west offered it opportunities for political and economic growth, but at the same time deprives us of our most important source of information: the Assyrian royal inscriptions. We must try to reconstruct the history from the scarce native inscriptions, from some Old Testament data, and from the picture of the situation given by Tiglath-pileser III when he appeared on the scene in 743 B.C. In the northeast the influence of Urartu around 750 B.C. was on the increase, especially in Milid (Malatiya) and Kummuhu (Commagene). The other states of southern Anatolia, such as Que, Tabal, Tyana, Hubishna, Gurgum, and Samal, had regained their independence. We are only somewhat better informed about Samal (which also called itself Y'dy, perhaps Yaudi) through some monumental inscriptions, for the most part votive or building inscriptions. Samal's self-assurance was shown by the fact that the inscriptions were no longer written in the traditional, literary Phoenician, but in the native (spoken) language, sometimes called

the Yaudian dialect of Samal. Not until after 730 B.C. was the increasingly popular Old Aramaic also used in Samal. We know some rulers of Samal from about 800 to just before 700 B.C.: *Qrl*, Panammu I, Barsur, Panammu II, and Barrakkab. Panamu I recorded on his statue dedicated to Hadad how he came to the throne with the help of the gods Hadad, El, Resheph, Shemesh, and the dynastic god Rakkabel, and he appealed to future kings not to neglect his tomb and veneration after death, in order that "his soul may (continue) to eat and drink with Hadad." Panammu II mounted the throne in a period of civil war and scarcity, in which his father was murdered. But the "gods of Yaudi rescued him from destruction on account of his righteousness," after which there was a change for the better.

In northern Syria, Arpad assumed an increasingly dominant position. In 754 B.C. this development was disturbed by a raid of Ashurnirari V, who by means of a treaty made a vassal of Arpad's ruler Mati-ilu (the fragments of the treaty are translated in Pritchard, ed., *Ancient Near Eastern Texts*, pp. 532–33). The vassal was obligated to help his suzerain on his campaigns with chariots and troops. The oaths of allegiance were sworn by numerous gods, while the curse, resting upon transgression in symbolic-magical fashion, was actualized by taking a lamb from the flock and beheading it: "this head is not the head of the lamb; it is the head of Mati-ilu; if he sins against this treaty he will likewise . . . (etc.)." This solemn oath of loyalty had little effect, for after only a few years he made a new pact, this time with an Aramean ruler who called himself "son" (descendant) of *G'yh* (perhaps *Ga'uni*), and "king" of KTK, presumabley to be read *Kittika* and perhaps the ancient name of Til Barsip on the Euphrates. A recent interpretation equates him with the Assyrian general (*turtanu*) Shamshi-ilu, a descendant of an older native dynasty that became an Assyrian vassal (with an Assyrian name). It is possible that behind this alliance should be seen the influence of Urartu, which militarily infiltrated northern Syria and according to a note in the Assyrian Eponym Chronicle had troops at Arpad. The Aramaic treaty, engraved on three stelae discovered at Sefire, is an important literary and political document that shows how widespread the conception and the literary form of the oath of loyalty and the vassal treaty were at the time. The Aramaic name for it (*adin*) was taken over in Assyrian and is also reflected in the Hebrew *edu/ot*. The covenant stipulations in Deuteronomy cannot be understood apart from these conceptions.

Farther to the south Hamat strengthened its position. Around 740 B.C. it controlled many cities, as far as the coast. There was great building activity in Carchemish on the Euphrates, to which the names of the kings Yariris and Kamanis are linked. The Phoenician cities could freely expand their trade; particularly Tyre occupied a dominating position and ruled Sidon, which had no kings of its own. The trade relations overseas increased in scope and intensity and led to increasing colonization. Damascus likewise recovered, but we have no name of a king from that period (we do not know the length of Barhadad III's reign). His aspirations were, however, curbed by Israel, which under Jeroboam II (ca. 783–743 B.C.) had its final period of bloom, expanding its territory or at least its military influence to Damascus and north of the Lebanon (*Lebo Hamat*). (He also controlled the Gulf of Aqabah.) Judah's recovery is shown by a victory of Amaziah over Edom (ca. 790 B.C.), but after that he was beaten by Israel. Under Azariah/Uzziah there was a peaceful development, undisturbed by outside influences. The idea that around 740 Azariah played an important role in northern Syria in an anti-Assyrian coalition with Hamat has recently been shown to be incorrect (apart from the chronological difficulties such an assumption would cause). The text on which this was based appears to refer to Hezekiah of Judah and his war with Sennacherib. Another text which indeed mentions a King Azriyau (but does not indicate him as a Judean) must refer to an (unknown) north Syrian king who with Hamat rebelled against Asshur around 740 B.C. Until the rule of Sargon II, Judah remained outside the sphere of Assyria's influence.

---

## LITERATURE

J. C. L. Gibson, *Textbook of Syrian Semitic Inscriptions, II: Aramaic Inscriptions* (Oxford, 1975).

*A. Lemaire and J.-M. Durand, *Les inscriptions araméennes de Sfiré et l'Assyrie de Shamshi-ilu* (Geneva, 1984).

M. N. van Loon, *Urartian Art* (Istanbul, 1966).

M. E. L. Mallowan, *Nimrud and Its Remains* I–II (London, 1966).

N. Na'aman, "Sennacherib's 'Letter to God' and His Campaign to Judah," *Bulletin of the American Schools of Oriental Research* 214 (1974) 25–39 (cf. J. D. Hawkins in *Reallexikon der Assyriologie*, V, 227).

M. Noth, "Der historische Hintergrund der Inschriften von Sefire," *Zeitschrift des Deutschen Palästinavereins* 77 (1961) 118–72.

B. B. Piotrovskii, *Urartu: The Kingdom of Van and Its Art* (London, 1967).

---

## d. Egypt during the Eighth Century B.C. (22nd–25th Dynasties)

About 828 B.C., under Pedubast I (ca. 828–803 B.C.), the Twenty-third Dynasty began to reign at Leontopolis, soon afterward also gaining recognition in Thebes. Together with the older Twenty-second (Libyan) Dynasty it maintained itself in the Delta until 715 B.C. The political fragmentation of which these competing dynasties were the expression increased even more in the eighth century B.C. Beside the dynasties of Bubastis and Leontopolis we find in the western Delta the "great chiefs of Libu," who had their residence in Mendes, Busiris, and Sebennytos, and a more or less independent principality of Athribis-Heliopolis. Farther south the rulers of Heracleopolis and Hermopolis had acquired independence and presented themselves as "kings."

After 750 B.C. the movement of events began to accelerate. In the Delta the monarchy of Sais (*So* in 2 Kings 17:4) under Osorkon "C" and his successor Tefnakht (ca. 740–720 B.C.)—later counted as the Twenty-fourth Dynasty—gradually extended its power over the western Delta. Via recognition by Memphis and an alliance with Hermopolis, Sais pushed forward against Lower Egypt, where siege was laid to Heracleopolis and a penetration to Thebes seemed possible. At that moment a powerful reaction from the Nubian south arose.

Since the beginning of the century an independent principality had arisen in the south, and under Kashta (ca. 760 B.C.) it advanced to the north. King Piye (formerly read Piankhy), who reigned roughly 747–716 B.C. and introduced the Twenty-fifth or Nubian Dynasty, became the rival of Tefnakht. First Piye gained nominal recognition in Thebes, where his daughter was consecrated "divine consort of Amon." In 735 B.C. he led an expedition to the north, directed against Tefnakht's aspirations, in which all of the Delta dynasties came to him to express their submission. Tefnakht also acknowledged Piye's hegemony, after having been driven out of Lower Egypt. In his northern residence at Sais he was able to hold out without great loss of power, and after the departure of the Nubian army to the south, he presented himself, being the most powerful king of the Delta, as pharaoh: the Twenty-fourth Dynasty. In 720 B.C. he was succeeded by Bakenrenef, the Bochchoris of Manetho, who ruled till about 715 B.C. and controlled Memphis; according to Diodrus he was a great lawgiver.

Besides the rulers of Sais there were the likewise independent last rulers of the dynasty of Tanis-Babastis, Shoshenq V and Osorkon IV (ca. 735–715 B.C.; the Shilkanni of the inscriptions of Sargon II of Asshur), and the rulers of Leontopolis. When in 716 B.C. Piye was succeeded by his energetic brother Shabaka, things changed. Already in 715 B.C. he came with his army to the north to put an end to the claims to power of all the dynasties still in power, so effectively obtaining absolute sovereignty for the Twenty-fifth Nubian Dynasty.

---

## LITERATURE

M. Elat, "The Economic Relations of the Neo-Assyrian Empire with Egypt," *Journal of the American Oriental Society* 98 (1978) 20–34.

W. B. Emery, *Egypt in Nubia* (London, 1965), ch. viii.

K. Kitchen, *The Third Intermediate Period in Egypt (1100–650 B.C.)* (Warminster, 1973).

---

## e. From Tiglath-pileser III to Sargon II (745–705 B.C.)

The accession to the throne of Tiglath-pileser III (745–727 B.C.) in Asshur heralded important political changes in the Near East. His energetic military exploits and accompanying administrative reorganizations laid the foundation for the Neo-Assyrian empire of the seventh century B.C. His name—appearing in later sources and in the Old Testament also as Pulu (meaning and function unknown)—inspired dread, even in Israel and Judah, which were now directly threatened by Asshur. He restored Assyria's power and influence in Babylonia, in the east (against the Medes and Urarteans), in southern Anatolia, and in large parts of Syria-Palestine. Increasingly Tiglath-pileser broke with the system of putting or leaving members of the native dynasty, bound to him by oaths of loyalty, on the throne of nominally independent states. Cities and territories that had revolted or were conquered now became provinces of the Assyrian empire, governed directly by Assyrians. Large-scale deportations, including ever more people (it is estimated that under Tiglath-pileser's rule alone over half a million people were deported on nearly forty different occasions), became part of the system. These deportations also served to break national resistance and to repopulate depopulated cities. An example of what happened to a city that was seized for the second time is Samaria in 722–720 B.C., as this is described by Sargon II: "I rebuilt the city of Samaria and made it greater than ever before and brought into it people from the lands I had conquered. I appointed my functionary as prefect over them, imposed levies and tribute on them as if they were Assyrians [variant: I counted them among the people of Assyria] and showed them how to conduct themselves" (cf. Cogan, pp. 50–51). Places whose princes submitted themselves without offering resistance (Samal under Panammu II) or who called for Assyrian help (Ahaz of Judah), border regions (Judah at a later time), and cities that were politically and economically of special importance to the Assyrian empire, such as the Phoenician trade cities (needing a measure of freedom for trading, but being controlled in their trade and subject to paying taxes), retained for the most part their own rulers, who were bound to Asshur by oaths of loyalty. According to the inscription of Barrakkab (Donner-Röllig, no. 215; ill. 84), Panammu II of Samal "seized the tail of the garment [*knp*] of his master, the great king of Asshur . . . and he [ran] at the wheel of his master Tiglath-pileser, king of Asshur, on campaigns from east to west" (lines 11–13).

In 745 B.C. affairs in Babylonia were set in order: the Babylonian king Nabunassar—known especially because the Babylonian Chronicle and the Canon of Ptolemy begin with him; see above, p. 291—was supported and a campaign undertaken against Aramean and Chaldean tribal groups as far as the Persian Gulf. Captives from these tribes, mentioned in large numbers in the inscriptions, were deported by the thousands to Asshur. After operations against the Medes and Persians had covered the eastern flank in 744 B.C., Tiglath-pileser turned his sights to the west in 743 B.C. His actions were directed against the allies of Urartu in southern Anatolia and northern Syria. A northern coalition, led by Sarduri II (with Arpad, Melid, Gurgum, and Kummuhu), was defeated. Arpad, the seat of the resistance in northern Syria, fell after three years, in 741, after which, in 740, peace was restored to this area (cf. 2 Kings 18:34). It is not clear to what extent other northern Syrian states in this phase were involved in the hostilities or came to pay tribute.

Following a campaign in the east in 739 B.C., Asshur reappeared in 738 B.C. The anti-Assyrian coalition was then led by Eniil of Hamat and Azriyau. Large areas of the nineteen districts of Hamat were conquered, in addition to Kullani(a)/ Kilanua (Kalne, Amos 6:2), the capital of Unqi. Three Assyrian provinces were formed in northern Syria, having as their centers Kullani, Hazrak, and Simirra. Hamat itself was not subdued, nor Carchemish under Pisiris. The rulers of these areas, together with cities from southern Anatolia (Panammu II of Samal and Urik/Awariku of Que), did come to pay tribute, an example that was followed by Byblos, Tyre (under Tubail = Ittobaal), Damascus (under Rah/qianu-Radyan; Old Testament Rezin), and Israel under Menahem (*Minihimmu* ^*mat*^*Samerinaya*). The names of those paying tribute were recorded in the later annals

and on a stele recently discovered in Iran, erected during the campaigns against the Medes (737–736 B.C.), on which the Assyrians penetrated far into the east, presumably to the Elbourz. An attempted attack on Urartu's heartland at Lake Van and its capital Tushpa failed in 735 B.C.

Meanwhile the resistance in the west had spread again: the main stimulus came from Radyan of Aram, who received support from King Pekah of Israel (*Pa-qa-ha* of *Bit-Humri*) and from Edom. Together they also tried to compel Ahaz of Judah to participate through the so-called Syro-Ephraimite war (2 Kings 16:5ff.; cf. B. Oded, *Catholic Biblical Quarterly* 34 [1972] 153–65). Despite all the warnings of Isaiah (7:1–8:8), Ahaz appealed for help to Assyria, presenting himself with rich gifts as a vassal. The consequences were not long in coming. In 734 B.C. Tiglath-pileser undertook a campaign along the coast to Philistia (*mat Pilishta*) as far as Gaza (to make Egyptian help impossible?). On the way home he attacked Israel, which lost much territory, and many were deported (2 Kings 15:29). Pekah fell victim to a coup that put the pro-Assyrian Hoshea (*A-u-si-i* = *Hawshi*) on the throne. Damascus was able to hold out for another two years, but in 732 B.C. it was captured and left the political map for good. All the southern cities and states rushed to acknowledge Asshur's power and to pay tribute: Ammon (*Bit-Amman*), Moab (*Maab*), Ashkelon, Edom (*Udum* under King Qaushmalaka), Gaza (*Hazat* under *Hanunu*), and Judah (under Ahaz: *Ya-u-ha-zi* ^*mat*^*Ya-u-da-a-a;* his full name with the theophoric element Yau). For the time being Judah had escaped, but all buffers had disappeared.

Already during the siege of Damascus political unrest started in Babylonia: Nabunassar's successor was killed in a civil war and Mukinzeri, a Chaldean prince of the Amukanu tribe, conquered the throne of Babylon. In 731 B.C. the Assyrian armies appeared in politically divided Babylonia. Using military actions, negotiations, and diplomatic exchanges they managed to isolate Mukinzeri. He was defeated in 729 B.C., and with the help of pro-Assyrian elements Tiglath-pileser had himself proclaimed king of Babylon; according to the Eponym Chronicle "he seized the hands of Bel (Marduk)." The earlier-used prestigious title of "King of Sumer and Akkad" now obtained substance through a personal union between Asshur and Babylon. Babylon was spared the status of province.

Due to the lack of inscriptions little is known of the briefly reigning Shalmaneser V (727–722 B.C.), also known as Ululayu. About 725 B.C. he was confronted with independence movements in the west that he was able to put down. The destruction of Samal, where Barrakkab, son of Panammu II, had revolted, was one of his deeds. He also wiped the city-state of Samaria off the map after, perhaps already in 732 B.C., the northern and eastern parts were turned into three Assyrian provinces: Megiddo, Dor, and Gilead. Rebellious Hoshea was carried away captive, after which siege was laid to Samaria (2 Kings 17:4–5). Left in the lurch by Egypt, the city was forced to capitulate after a siege of about two years (724–722). While the Babylonian Chronicle and the Old Testament rightly ascribe this military feat to Shalmaneser V ("he broke *Samarain*"), it was soon claimed by his successor, Sargon II, who otherwise could not claim military achievements in the first full year of his reign.

Sargon II (722–705 B.C.) was a very ambitious ruler who consistently carried forward the policy of Tiglath-pileser, added new provinces to the empire, and consolidated the borders. With him the so-called Sargonid period began, when Assyria had its greatest success. His aspirations received concrete shape in his monumental new capital Dur-Sharrukin ("Sargon Fortress," now called Khorsabad), officially dedicated in 706 B.C. It was a square city of about 300 hectares (740 acres) northeast of Nineveh with an impressive citadel, temples, and the palace, from which came Sargon's historic reliefs. Due to his sudden death this new residence remained unfinished; his successor abandoned it in favor of the old Nineveh.

The sudden departure of the Assyrian army at the changing of the throne in 722 B.C. had resulted in a renewed flaring of the rebellion in the west and in leaving the capture of Samaria incomplete. In 720 B.C. Sargon appeared in Syria. At Qarqar he defeated a coalition of the rebellious Assyrian provinces (including such cities as Arpad, Hazrak, and Damascus; cf. Zech. 9:1–8,

which some connect with these happenings), a coalition that was supported by Yaubidi of Hamat. Hamat was captured and annexed to Assyria; Yaubidi (also called Ilubidi) was executed. Samaria, which together with Gaza under Hanun(u) had revolted, experienced the Assyrian revenge: 27,290 inhabitants were deported (with "the gods in whom they trusted!") and the territory reorganized into an Assyrian province. The city was being populated with deportees from Babylon, Kutha, and Haat, to which in 716/715 were added groups of Arabians, and under Esarhaddon and Ashurbanipal (cf. Ezra 4:9) still other Babylonians and Elamites. Sargon was honored as lord by Elulaeus of Tyre and Sidon and also by Hezekiah, and left behind his victory steles (a fragment was recovered at excavations in Samaria). Gaza was captured and an Egyptian army that had come to help was defeated at the border. Pharaoh Tefnakht of Sais (*So* from 2 Kings 17:4), who was behind this action, saw his border fortress Rafia destroyed and Assyria's power reaching Egypt's borders. Within fifty years Asshur would penetrate far into Egypt.

Also between 717 and 712 B.C. Assyria concerned itself with the west. In 717 B.C. Carchemish, which under Pisiris with the help of Midas the Phrygian (Mita of the Mushki) had rebelled, was conquered and annexed. The following year an Assyrian army arrived in southern Palestine. Judah and Philistia acknowledged Asshur's power and permitted it to pass through unhindered to the Egyptian border. Assyrian colonists settled near the "River of Egypt" (the Wadi el-Arish), especially for economic reasons: "I opened the sealed harbor of Egypt, mixed Assyrians and Egyptians and had them trade with each other." Pharaoh Shilkanni (= Osorkon IV), ruler in the Delta over Tanis and Bubastis, "greeted" the Assyrians with a gift of twelve horses. Shortly afterward he had to step aside, as did Bochchoris (Bakenrenef) of Sais, Tefnakht's successor, when Shabako, successor of "Piankhy" (Piye), of the Twenty-fifth or Nubian Dynasty, included the Delta in his rule in the second year of his reign (715 B.C.).

Supported by Egypt, resistance flared again in Palestine, probably already as early as 714 B.C. The instigator was Ashdod, where Yamani seized power after a change of the throne engineered by the Assyrians (Azuri was replaced by Ahimeti). This resistance, aided by Edom, Moab, Cyprus (?), and presumably initially also by Judah under Hezekiah—which, however, soon withdrew especially at the urging of Isaiah—threatened Asshur's position. The reaction followed in 712 B.C. Sargon sent his general, the *turtanu*, to the south, where Gibbethon, Gath, Ashdod, and Ashdod-yam (the harbor) were conquered and made into an Assyrian province. Excavations in Ashdod have uncovered part of Sargon's victory stele (see *Eretz Israel* 8 [1967] 241–42). Judah paid tribute while Yamani, having fled to Egypt, was handed over to Asshur. Resistance in southern Palestine had been quelled for good and the relations with Egypt were improved. It would take ten years before Asshur came again. Meanwhile Sargon's military actions left a deep impression on Judah, reflected especially in the book of Isaiah (cf. ch. 20).

Sargon's reign abounded with military activities on many fronts. In the south he clashed with Babylonia, where Mardukapaliddina (Merodak-Baladan), the Chaldean ruler from Bit-Yakin, in 722 B.C. conquered the throne with the help of rejuvenated Elam, ruled by Humbanigash (d. 717 B.C.). The first clash with Elam in 720 at Der brought no advantage to Assyria. Occupied on other fronts, Sargon had to leave Babylonia alone for ten years. In 710 accounts were squared. Elam, now under Shutruk-Nahhunte (711–699), was defeated and Merodak-Baladan fled first to the south, where he was driven from his stronghold Dur-Athara, and then to Elam. In 709 Sargon officially proclaimed himself king of Babylon. A renewed action by Merodak-Baladan in his home territory ("Sealand") failed; his city Dur-Yakin was captured, after which, carrying with him the gods and the bones of his forefathers, he fled to the Elam border, waiting for a new opportunity, which he would seize in 703.

The eastern part of the realm continued to demand attention. There Asshur had to maintain its grip on the Zagros, begun under Tiglath-pileser, and reinforce it against local resistance and the encroaching of Urartu. Many battles were fought after 719 B.C.; Asshur, however, maintained the upper hand in a strategically important territory, through which the big Khorasan Road ran and an area from which many horses came. The apex came during Sargon's famed eighth campaign in 714 B.C.—in details described in his letter to the gods—when he penetrated to the heart of the Zagros, restored his authority over Parsua (north of Kermanshah), Mannea (south of Lake Urmia), and the Medes (Deioces was deported), and repulsed the Urartean threat of Rusa I (ca. 735–713 B.C.). In this campaign he penetrated the region west of Lake Urmia and on his return conquered the city of Musasir (north of Rowandiz) and plundered the temple of the Urartean chief god Haldi (after whom earlier Urartu was sometimes wrongly designated as Haldia/Chaldia).

Fierce battles also took place in southern and southeastern Anatolia, where, among others, the Phrygians under Midas (Mita of the Mushki) were troublesome and where the power of Urartu was unbroken. In the east, Tabal, Kummuhu, and Que (Cilicia) became Assyrian provinces; Melid and Gurgum were captured. The unrest was also due to the invasion of the Cimmerians (from the Caucasus?), for which reason Midas in 709 B.C. sought peace with Asshur. In 707, Rusa's successor Argishti II (713–685) suffered a defeat against the Cimmerians. In 705 fate struck Sargon himself: he was killed in a campaign in Tabal during a surprise attack on the Assyrian army by "Eshpai the Kulummean" (probably a Cimmerian). Sargon's violent death (even his body could not be recovered) induced his successor Sennacherib to inquire of the gods after "the sin of Sargon" that caused his death, an event that also left an impression elsewhere (cf. Isa. 14:4ff.).

## LITERATURE

J. A. Brinkman, *A Political History of Post-Kassite Babylonia 1158–722 B.C.* (Rome, 1968).

——, "Merodach-Baladan II," in *Studies Presented to A. Leo Oppenheim* (Chicago, 1964), pp. 6–53 (cf. J. Brinkman, *Journal of Near Eastern Studies* 24 [1965] 161–66).

M. Elat, "The Economic Relations of the Neo-Assyrian Empire with Egypt," *Journal of the American Oriental Society* 98 (1978) 20–34.

H. J. Katzenstein, *The History of Tyre* (Jerusalem, 1973).

N. Na'aman, "The Brook of Egypt and Assyrian Policy on the Border of Egypt," *Tel Aviv* 6 (1979) 68–90.

B. Oded, "The Phoenician Cities and the Assyrian Empire in the Time of Tiglathpileser III," *Zeitschrift des Deutschen Palästinavereins* 90 (1974) 38–49 (cf. Cogan, *Journal of Cuneiform Studies* 25 [1973] 96–99).

A. L. Oppenheim, "The City of Assur in 714 B.C.," *Journal of Near Eastern Studies* 19 (1960) 133–47.

N. Postgate, "Sargon's Letter Referring to Midas," *Iraq* 35 (1973) 21–34.

H. Tadmor, "The Campaigns of Sargon II of Assur," *Journal of Cuneiform Studies* 12 (1958) 22–44, 77–100 (cf. M. Ford, *Journal of Cuneiform Studies* 22 [1968] 83–84).

———, "Philistia under Assyrian Rule," *Biblical Archaeologist* 29 (1966) 86–102.

H. Tadmor and M. Cogan, "Ahaz and Tiglath-Pileser in the Book of Kings," *Biblica* 60 (1979) 491–508.

## f. Egypt from Shabako to Psammetichus I (715–610 B.C.)

Shabako's move to the Delta in 715 B.C. and his abandonment of his Nubian residence Napata in favor of Tanis marked the nominal end of the Twenty-third and Twenty-fourth Dynasties with Osorkon IV and Bochchoris. However, the numerous local principalities in the Delta and in Lower Egypt continued to exist, as shown, for example, by their enumeration by Ashurbanipal at his conquest of Egypt (cf. Pritchard, ed., *Ancient Near Eastern Texts*, p. 294). The dynasty of Sais and later Memphis continued to play an important role in the Delta. In the south Shabako was acknowledged in Thebes, where his sister became "divine spouse" and his son high priest of Amon. In 712 B.C. he faced Assyrian aggression: after subduing southern Palestine, Sargon's army appeared on the border with "Egypt that belongs to Meluhha [= Kush]." Shabako prevented a clash by delivering up Yamani of Ashdod, who had fled to Egypt. Egypt and Assyria probably continued diplomatic contact, as shown by a clay bulla of the pharaoh discovered at Nineveh.

In 702 B.C. Shabako was succeeded by Shebit-ku (702–690 B.C.), who immediately summoned his brothers to the Delta, particularly Taharqa—later appointed his successor—who according to his steles in the Amon-Re temple at Kawa (between the third and fourth cataracts) must have been already about twenty years old at the time. The motivation for this summons was presumably the desire to strengthen the Nubian grip on the Delta as well as to respond to the threat of Asshur. Supported by Egypt, in Palestine Judah and Philistia had revolted against the new king Sennacherib, who undoubtedly would not put up with it. When he appeared in 701 B.C. a Nubian army under Taharqa marched to Judah, where at Elteqe it was defeated by the Assyrians. This failure had no consequences for the Egyptian throne since Asshur was unable to take Jerusalem and Sennacherib had other worries at the time. Taharqa's reign was the apex of the Nubian Dynasty. He engaged in enormous building activities, particularly in the Amon temples at Thebes (Karnak) and Napata, activities marked by great interest in Old Egyptian forms and traditions: the last three rulers of the dynasty preferred to choose first names of famous predecessors.

In 677 B.C. Sidon (supported by Taharqa?) revolted. Asshur brutally quelled the rebellion. In 674 B.C. Esarhaddon marched with his army to the Egyptian border (Arsa, el-Arish), but the Assyrian army suffered a defeat against Taharqa. In 671 B.C. Asshur appeared again; this time Taharqa was defeated and the Assyrians captured Memphis. Esarhaddon, the conqueror of "*Musur, Paturisi,* and *Kusu*" (Lower Egypt, Upper Egypt [Old Testament Patros], and Nubia), accepted the submission of some twenty rulers mentioned by name, whom he left as vassals on the throne. Taharqa soon returned, however, and recaptured Memphis. Esarhaddon hastened to Egypt but died on the way. In 667 B.C. his successor Ashurbanipal came to finish the work of his father: Taharqa was defeated and Thebes (*Ni;* Old Testament No-Ammon) captured. The Egyptian princes who were not involved in the "revolt" of the Nubian were left in place. But when shortly after there was another revolt against Asshur, the king set an example: the princes of, among others, Sais and Tanis were humiliated and carried off to Asshur; inhabitants of the rebellious places were publicly executed. It did not take long, however, before "Neco of Sais and Memphis" (*Niku* of *Saa* and *Mempi*) was absolved and, bound to Asshur by an oath of loyalty, solemnly put on the throne as prince of the Delta. Thus Asshur skilfully created a valuable, anti-Nubian ally. Garrisons and Assyrian administrators were used to keep the country under control. In the south, at Thebes, ruled the "fourth prophet of Amon," Montuemhat (*Mantimankhe*), first as Nubian governor, then as a virtually independent Assyrian vassal, under whom Thebes had a final boom period, shown impressively by his tomb.

Taharqa died in 664 B.C. in Napata and was entombed in his pyramid grave at Nuri (the older pyramid graves of the dynasty are found in Kuru). His successor to the throne was Tanutamon (*Tantamani*), who immediately undertook an anti-Assyrian offensive. He captured Thebes and Heliopolis (On) and laid siege to Memphis. Neco I of Sais (674–664 B.C.) opposed him, but was killed in battle. Ashurbanipal returned again to Egypt and with the help of Sais, where Psammetichus had succeeded his father, defeated Tantamani. Thebes was captured and sacked (cf. Nahum 3:8–10), but Montuemhat retained his "throne." Egypt was securely in Asshur's power, in part owing to the loyalty of Psammetichus, prince in the Delta and in reality Asshur's viceroy. In subsequent years, when Asshur was kept occupied with internal problems with Babylonia and war with Elam, he was able to become more and more independent and with the use of Ionian and Carian mercenary soldiers ("men of bronze") he could extend his hegemony over large parts of Egypt. When Heracleopolis took his side, he aimed at Thebes. Maneuvering cautiously he obtained the recognition of Thebes and managed to have his daughter, Nitocris, adopted as future "divine spouse of Amon." Gradually important positions were filled by members of his family. So, though nominally still an Assyrian vassal, by 658 B.C. he had united all Egypt under one scepter again. Thus with Psammetichus I (664–610 B.C.) the Twenty-sixth or Saite Dynasty began about 658 B.C. He made himself also formally independent of Asshur by stopping the payment of tribute and by entering into a treaty with Gyges of Lydia. The relationship with Assyria was normalized,

though it is uncertain whether Psammetichus's prolonged siege and subsequent capture of Ashdod may have been seen as an anti-Assyrian operation, since it concerned here a city that was strategically situated for Egypt on the route to Syria. Following that route, Egypt around 610 B.C. (in vain) sought to give help to Asshur in its final days, so at the same time presenting itself as heir of Asshur's Syro-Palestinian empire.

Psammetichus's military power was based heavily on foreign mercenaries from Greece, Caria, Lydia, Libya, Nubia, Judah, and Phoenicia. Garrisons and colonies manned by foreigners included those at Daphne/Takhpanes in the eastern Delta and at Syene and Elephantine (Yeb) at Aswan and the first cataract (as outpost against Nubia). Probably this was also the genesis of the Jewish military colony at Elephantine, about which, for the fifth century B.C., we are well informed from the papyri. The mercenary soldiers (Greek marine units and foreign merchants from the area of the Mediterranean) gave particularly the Delta a cosmopolitan character. Naucratis soon grew into a center of Greek trade and culture. Beside it there was a great interest in Egypt's cultural heritage under the Saite Dynasty, especially that of the Old Kingdom, for which reason it is sometimes called the "Saite renaissance." In the area of art this interest in the old heritage was seen in the many polished, freestone statues and in the beautiful bronze figurines of gods and animals that were sometimes given to the temple as votive gifts. Religiously there was a growing worship of Osiris and Abydos, whereas by contrast Amon and Thebes, whose political role had come to an end, lost significance. During the reign of Psammetichus, Demotic, both script and idiom, also gained an importance in the royal chancellery and for use in recording legal documents from which we become aware of new elements in Egypt's common law.

The expulsion of the Nubians from Egypt became final in the seventh century B.C. The Nubian Dynasty held out on its own territory in the old residence of Napata. The Nubian campaigns of Psammetichus II (591 B.C.) and Cambyses (shortly after 525 B.C.) forced the "Kingdom of Cush" to abandon the residence of Napata and to move to the much more southern (between the fifth and the sixth cataract) Meroe, which definitely became the center of the Meroite kingdom when, around 295 B.C., the royal tombs were also moved there. Meroite civilization and the kingdom of Meroe continued to the fourth century A.D.

---

## LITERATURE

M. F. Gyles, *Pharaonic Policies and Administration 663–323 B.C.* (Chapel Hill, 1959).

F. K. Kienitz, *Die politische Geschichte Ägyptens vom 7. bis zum 4. Jahrhundert vor der Zeitwende* (Berlin, 1953).

H. de Meulenaere, *Herodotus over de 26e dynastie* (Leuven, 1951).

A. Spalinger, "Assurbanipal and Egypt," *Journal of the American Oriental Society* 94 (1974) 316–28.

———, "Esarhaddon and Egypt," *Orientalia* 43 (1974) 295–326.

See also the literature above under section 7.d.

---

## g. Asshur from Sennacherib to the Collapse of the Assyrian Empire (705–610 B.C.)

As happened regularly, resistance flared again among the peoples subdued by the Assyrians when *Sennacherib* (705–681 B.C.) succeeded his father. But the situation was changing: in many areas Asshur's authority and military superiority were so evident that revolts became more limited and sporadic. The almost institutional, yearly campaign became superfluous. In Sennacherib's twenty-four-year reign there were only ten campaigns, most of which were directed against the south. There the "Babylonian problem" required most of Asshur's attention, which in 689 B.C. led to a dramatic unravelling. Asshur's policy was marked on the one hand by a tie with and deep respect for the Babylonian gods and culture—with which Asshur itself was permeated—and on the other hand by the political determination of military control of this important territory with its wealth and connections. The latter was difficult to achieve due to the inner division among the Babylonian cities (some of which were quite pro-Assyrian), the Chaldean tribal heads, and the Aramean tribes, who apparently were easily drawn together in an anti-Assyrian politics in which Chaldeans such as Merodak-Baladan became champions of Babylonian nationalism. The problem became acute through the new power display of Elam that strongly supported anti-Assyrian movements and gave a new course to history.

The first revolt, led by Merodak-Baladan, who had returned and for nine months was able to conquer and hold the throne of Babylon, was put down by Sennacherib in 703 B.C. Merodak-Baladan fled to his native land in the south and Asshur's protégé Belibni was put on the throne. In 700 B.C. the Chaldean appeared once again, this time with the help of Elam. Sennacherib routed him as far as his native land Bit-Yakin in "Sealand," and he disappeared to Elam, ending his career. Sennacherib's son Ashurnadinshumi took the throne of Babylon until 694 B.C. Then resistance broke loose anew, supported by Elam's new king Hallushu-Inshushinak (699–693 B.C.). When Sennacherib with his army and fleet—built by Phoenicians and manned by westerners—penetrated deep into the south, Elam invaded northern Babylonia, where the Babylonian nationalists captured Sennacherib's son and handed him over to the Elamite ruler. The following year Sennacherib got to them, but he could not prevent Mushezib-Marduk (as Shuzubu his enemy already in 700 B.C.) from temporarily conquering the throne and forging an anti-Assyrian coalition of Babylonians, Chaldeans, Arameans, and Elamites, thereby using the funds of the Marduk temple. Commanded by the Elamite Humbannimena (693–689 B.C.), who only a short while before had captured the throne, the army, which included troops from Parsua and Anshan under the command of *Hachamanish* (= Achaemenes), the patriarch of the Achaemenids, encountered the Assyrians at Halule on the Tigris, but the battle remained indecisive (691 B.C.). However, in 690 Asshur turned toward Babylon; the city was besieged and surrendered after more than a year and a half (689 B.C.). Sennacherib vented his rage on the city by plundering and destroying it. Not even Marduk's temple was spared; Marduk's statue was carried "into exile" to Asshur. Finally, the water of the Euphrates was directed to flow over the ruins. Esarhaddon's inscriptions betray some of the pain later experienced on account of Sennacherib's merciless devastation of the city. Babylon's fall was described as a divine judgment, announced by signs from heaven, in which the Arakhtu (the branch of the Euphrates on which the city was situated) flooded the city like a deluge, which "had incurred Marduk's wrath by its gross injustice and cultic abuses."

Besides the necessary campaigns to the north and east—Sennacherib's second and fifth campaigns and two campaigns by generals in 696–695 B.C.; there were battles in the Zagros against the Medes (under Cyaxares I = *Uwaksatar*), the Manneans, and the "Kassites," while in Anatolia order was established in Commagene, Melid, and Que—particularly the west had Asshur's attention during the large campaign in 701 B.C. Stimulated by a legation of Merodak-Baladan (2 Kings 20:12ff.) and with moral support from Egypt the west had revolted about 704 B.C. At Sennacherib's appearance many states and cities—perhaps in part co-revolters—surrendered immediately: Byblos, Ashdod, Ammon, Moab, and Edom. The city-state of Sidon (including both Tyre and Sidon) succumbed when Elulaeus (Lullu) fled by way of the sea (to Cyprus?). All the cities of the empire, as far as Akko, submitted themselves. The port city of Tyre remained impregnable, but the inland city of Usu fell. Perhaps Isaiah 23:1–14 reflects these events. Sidon now became an independent state under King Tubalu (Itto-Baal), while in Tyre Elulaeus nominally retained the throne, later to be succeeded or replaced by Balu. Perhaps at that time also Hezekiah of Judah, one of the leaders of the revolt, acknowledging his "sin"—that is, reneging on his oath of loyalty to Sargon II (cf. 2 Kings 18:14ff.)—submitted himself with gifts and tribute.

First the rebellious Philistine cities were punished: Sidqa of Ashkelon and his cities Yaffo, Asor (Hazor), Bit-Dagan, and Banaibarqa were defeated and deported. Siege was laid to Ekron, which had delivered the pro-Assyrian king Padi to Hezekiah. From the coastal plain Sennacherib approached the Judean hill country, where Azeka and Gath (taken from the Philistines by Hezekiah and fortified) were the next victims, as

shown by Sennacherib's "letter to the gods" (Na'aman). Probably at this time an Egyptian army under the command of Prince Taharqa showed up to give aid, forcing the Assyrians to interrupt the siege of Jerusalem and Lachish. The Egyptians were defeated in the coastal plain near Elteqe (north of Ashdod); Egypt proved again to be "a reed piercing the hand of whoever leans on it." Ekron and Lachish were captured. The taking of Lachish was impressively depicted on a relief from Nineveh showing the capture, sacking, and deportation of the city (ill. 85). It was one of forty-six Judean cities that, according to Sennacherib, met this fate in which 200,150 people (according to some, 2,150; see *Zeitschrift für alttestamentliche Wissenschaft* 59 [1947] 199ff.) were deported. Hezekiah (Hazaqyahu) was shut up "like a bird in a cage" in his capital *Ursalimmu*. Using all the technical means at his disposal and with demoralizing addresses, Sennacherib's general tried to break the resistance (cf. Isaiah 36–37). The city was spared by a miracle, and with great losses—God sent a sickness into the army—Sennacherib was forced to withdraw, by which also Egypt was spared from the consequences of his defeat. In Sennacherib's version of the event Hezekiah later sent him a rich tribute in Nineveh. Parts of Judah's western territory were given to the Philistine vassals that had remained loyal to Asshur (Ashdod, Ekron under Padi, and Gaza), following the principle of the divide-and-rule policy. The resistance in Syria-Palestine was now definitely broken; in later years there were only sporadic revolts, mainly in Phoenicia, all unsuccessful.

Sennacherib's campaign against Judah in 701 B.C. is a chronological point of reference for the history of Judah, especially now that Egyptian data (see above, section 7.f) have shown that in that year Taharqa was old enough to be a general and because there is not a single indication pointing to a later, second campaign of Asshur against Judah. This does entail problems for Old Testament chronology, for if Hezekiah began to reign in Hoshea's third year (2 Kings 18:9; ca. 729 B.C.), he must have died after a reign of twenty-nine years (2 Kings 18:2), shortly after Sennacherib's retreat, which therefore cannot be in his fourteenth year (so 2 Kings 18:13). After a

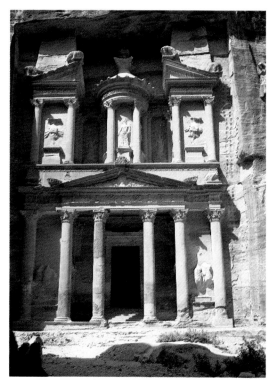

XXV. Petra, the rock-carved city of the Nabateans. The grave ed-Deir (shown here) is entirely hewn out of the rock (it does not have one man-made stone!). (C. H. J. de Geus)

XXVI. The Khazneh Farun, the most magnificent monument at Petra. (W. S. LaSor)

XXVII. Petra, looking out at the east wall of the valley at numerous grave monuments. (C. H. J. de Geus)

*83. A relief from the palace of Ashurbanipal at Nineveh showing Arabs mounted on camels battling Assyrian forces. (Trustees of the British Museum)*

84. King Barrakkab of Samal (Zenjirli), seated on the throne before his scribe (ca. 730 B.C.; see p. 302). The inscription reads: "(For) my Lord, Baal of Harran. I am Barrakkab son of Panamu[wa]" (cf. H. Donner and W. Röllig, Kanaanäische und Aramäische Inschriften, no. 218). (Vorderasiatisches Museum, Berlin)

85. An Assyrian relief from the palace of Sennacherib in Nineveh, representing the capture of Lachish (701 B.C.; see pp. 308–309). Moving across siege barriers thrown up against the wall, soldiers with ladders, spears, bows and arrows, and mobile battering rams storm the wall, braving a hail of stones and torches; archers positioned behind shields try to provide covering fire. In the center, fugitives leave the city and prisoners are impaled. (Trustees of the British Museum).

86. The stele of King Esarhaddon of Assyria (ca. 675 B.C.) found at Samal in which he "holds on the line" his vanquished enemies (an Egyptian prince and a Syrian ruler). (Vorderasiatisches Museum, Berlin)

87. The grave stele of a priest of Shahar at Nerab (near Aleppo) from the 7th century B.C., with an Aramaic inscription (see Donner and Röllig, Kanaanäische und Aramäische Inschriften, no. 225). (Louvre)

88. The Cyrus Cylinder records the Persian king's bloodless capture of Babylon and his program of religious tolerance, including the release of the Jewish exiles and restoration of the temple (ca. 538 B.C.). (Trustees of the British Museum)

XXVIII. Looking west toward the three main heights at Petra: Sela, Robinson's High Place, and ed-Deir. Note the rugged terrain. (L. T. Geraty)

XXIX. The outer wall of the temple tomb of Ramses III at Medinet Habu, depicting this pharaoh's victory over the Sea Peoples. In earlier centuries the picture was painted in vivid colors, but now it is completely faded from the hot Egyptian sun. (C. H. J. de Geus)

XXX. The stone head of a woman and a terra-cotta figurine of a naked goddess from the Israelite period. The head is also from a figurine. Because such statuettes and figurines were believed to promote fertility, they are usually called ''Astarte figurines.'' (Collectie Instituut voor Semitstiek en Archeologie van het Nabije Oosten, Gronigen)

XXXI. This stone lion in bas relief was part of the outer decoration of the Hellenistic structure (palace? temple?) which goes back to a building of the Tobiads. From Araq el-Emir, Jordan. (C. H. J. de Geus)

89. King Darius I on his throne; behind him is crown prince Xerxes, receiving the Median commander of the bodyguard. This relief was originally made on Darius's "palace" at Persepolis (end of the 6th century B.C.). (Oriental Institute, University of Chicago)

90. The ground plan of Persepolis.

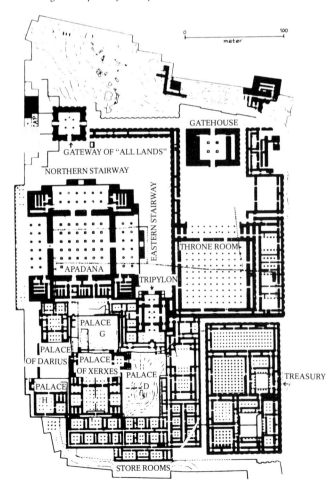

GATEHOUSE

GATEWAY OF "ALL LANDS"

NORTHERN STAIRWAY

EASTERN STAIRWAY

THRONE ROOM

APADANA

TRIPYLON

PALACE G

PALACE OF DARIUS

PALACE OF XERXES

PALACE D

PALACE H

TREASURY

STORE ROOMS

91. A glazed brick relief from Darius's palace at Susa, showing an Elamite archer. (Louvre)

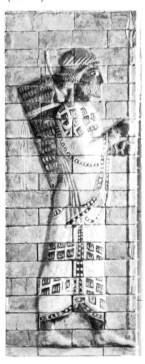

93. A silver tetradrachma of Antiochus IV Epiphanes (168 B.C.). (From the collection of G. L. Archer; picture W. S. LaSor)

92. A bust of Alexander the Great now in the Capitoline Museum, Rome. (P.I.P. Photos by Radio Times Hulton Picture Library)

94. A silver denarius of Tiberius, a common coin in New Testament times and referred to as a penny in Luke 20:24. (Ewing Galloway)

95. Ruins of a street in Pompeii with Mount Vesuvius in the background. (B. K. Condit)

XXXII. A reconstruction of a fortified gate and wall at Hazor, which was an important Amorite city in the 19th-18th centuries B.C., a Hyksos stronghold in the 17th-16th centuries, a major city-state in the Amarna period, and one of Solomon's chief fortified cities. (Institute of Archaeology, Hebrew University of Jerusalem)

XXXIII. A reconstruction of the throne room of the pharaoh Merneptah (ca. 1212–1200 B.C.). (University Museum, University of Pennsylvania; picture W. S. LaSor)

brief interval, in about 697 B.C. he was succeeded by the young Manasseh as Assyria's vassal.

In 701 B.C. the ambitious and talented Sennacherib made Nineveh his residence (with its tremendous palace adorned with bull colosses and reliefs), and for its water supply he redirected a river by means of a large aqueduct (which was also used to water the gardens with the cotton plants he had imported). In 681 B.C. he was assassinated by his son Arda-mulishshi (Isa. 37:38 speaks of two sons, including Adrammelech, a garbled rendering of the unfamiliar name of the Assyrian prince only recently discovered).

After a few months of civil war *Esarhaddon* (681–669 B.C.) succeeded him, having been designated by oracles and pushed forward by his mother, the Aramean princess Zakutu/Naqia. During his reign Asshur's hegemony was no longer seriously threatened, though here and there problems presented themselves. Initially there was unrest in southern Babylonia, in "Sealand," where Merodak-Baladan's son was active, and around the cities of Ur, Uruk, and Nippur, while in 675 B.C. Elam under Humban-Haltash II (ca. 680–675) again invaded northern Babylonia. The situation changed after his sudden death (his successor was Urtaki) and especially through Esarhaddon's rebuilding of Babylon (Marduk had pity on his city and in his grace turned the two figures of the announced exile of 70 years [60 + 10] around and read them as 11 years!).

In the east watchfulness remained important. In the Zagros the Scythians (A/*Ishguzai*) now appeared on the scene, and around 673 B.C. together with the Medes and Manneans opposed Asshur. In the north the Cimmerians—not clearly distinguishable from the Scythians and sometimes designated as "West Scythians"—made their presence felt after having defeated Rusa I and Argishti II of Urartu (among others, in 707). Around 695 (after the death of Midas) they were responsible for the disintegration of the Phrygian realm. In 697 Esarhaddon defeated them under Teushpa. Yet in that same year his army showed up in the west, where he pushed through to Philistia and the Egyptian border. Nevertheless, shortly afterward Sidon under Abdi-Milkutti, supported (morally) by Egypt under Taharqa, revolted. The revolt, directed against Asshur's interference in

Sidon's trade, was stamped out brutally. Sidon ceased being an independent state. After its northern cities had been given to Tyre, the rest were reorganized into an Assyrian province, having as its new administrative center the port city of Kar-Esarhaddon, which made it possible for the Assyrians to take the trade into their own hands. The city was built quickly with compulsory labor service of "the twenty-two kings of Hatti" who recognized Asshur's suzerainty: ten princes of Cyprus (*Yadnana*) with predominantly Greek names (including the cities of Idalion, Salamis, Tamassos, and Carthage), and twelve kings of the mainland, led by Balu of Tyre and Manasseh (*Me-na-si-i*) of Judah, and furthermore those of Ammon, Moab, Edom, Byblos, and the Philistine cities (cf. Borger, *Asarhaddon*, p. 60). Around 676 B.C. Esarhaddon concluded a vassal treaty with Balu of Tyre (Borger, pp. 107ff.; Katzenstein, pp. 268–77) that regulated such matters as shipping and trade (Asshur's right to stranded ships; Tyre's right to harbor facilities and transit trade from Arvad to Dor). It was sealed by solemn oaths, among others by Tyre's own gods Baal-shameme, Baal-malage, Baal-Zaphon, Melqart, Eshmun, and Astarte (see Pritchard, ed., *Ancient Near Eastern Texts*, pp. 533–34).

Apparently Asshur's control over Tyre's trade and urge for an embargo of Egypt evoked opposition. After Esarhaddon's failure to invade Egypt in 674 B.C., when the battle at the border was won by Taharqa, Tyre again revolted with the support of Egypt. In 671 the Assyrian king showed up again. After having laid siege to Tyre, he marched by way of Ashkelon to Egypt where he defeated Taharqa (see above, section 7.f). Now that Asshur also controlled Egypt, Tyre, holding out against the siege, deemed it expedient to submit: Balu asked for and received mercy. The city lost its territory on the mainland; later, under Ashurbanipal, it became an Assyrian province. When Taharqa rebelled the following year, Esarhaddon marched to Egypt but died on the way (669 B.C.). See ill. 86.

Without attendant internal problems he was succeeded by his son *Ashurbanipal* (669–ca. 630 B.C.). His father, conscious of the problems accompanying his own succession to the throne, had prepared him well by an early, official appointment as crown prince of Assyria (and his brother Shamashshumukin as crown prince of Babylonia) and having this nomination sworn to with elaborate and solemn oaths of allegiance (*ade*) by princes, members of his court, high officials, and vassals. The eloquent proof of it is found in the extensive "vassal treaties," discovered at the excavation of Kalhu, imposed in 672 B.C.—the date of the ceremony—upon a number of Median vassals. The entire text of the treaty is directed at the loyalty of the vassal toward the reigning king and the crown prince designate, whose accession to the throne the vassal must support in whatever way possible (see Pritchard, ed., *Ancient Near Eastern Texts*, pp. 534ff.). The particular orientation of these "treaties" implies that caution is demanded in using them as a model of "the" Assyrian vassal treaty; as such the—unfortunately heavily damaged—treaty with Tyre is even more significant, even though there is great similarity in the structure of both texts.

First Ashurbanipal completed the interrupted conquest of Egypt. Between 667 and 664 B.C. he managed to establish his supremacy as far as Thebes, with which his realm had reached its largest extent. About 660, however, Asshur began to lose its grip on Egypt. About 658 Psammetichus I made himself formally independent (see above, section 7.f). In the north and east the developments were more favorable for Asshur. There the Scythians and Medes played an important role, while also the Cimmerians were a significant factor. After first having fought them, the Scythians around 670 joined up with the Assyrians, which also meant that a halt was called to the aspirations of the Medes and Manneans (south of Lake Urmia). In 653 Asshur defeated the Medes, who under Phraortes (*Kashtarite*, ca. 675–653) had allied themselves with the Cimmerians, in which battle Phraortes was killed. The Persians under Cyprus (from the Achaemenids) benefited from this development, for until 625 B.C. they had the rule over Media. In that year Cyaxares II (*Uwakishtar*, whose namesake was the contemporary of Sargon II and Sennacherib) freed his land, with eventually disastrous consequences for Asshur. The actions of the Cimmerians in Asia Minor induced Gyges of Lydia around 664 to seek the help of Asshur, an

example later followed by Rusa III of Urartu (ca. 660–645). However, when Gyges around 658 exchanged Asshur for Egypt as his ally and the Cimmerians entered into a nonaggression pact with Asshur, the situation became critical for Lydia. About 645 Sardis was captured by the Cimmerians under Tugdamme (Lygdamis), in which battle Gyges was killed. The Cimmerians pushed through to Ephesus. Later they clashed again with Asshur, which now had an ally in Gyges's son. About 640 Ashurbanipal once and for all averted the Cimmerian threat. In that year Tugdamme's son Sandahshatru even asked Asshur for help, an example followed by Sarduri III of Urartu (644–625). All the problems in the north and east appeared to have been solved shortly after 640 B.C.

Ashurbanipal experienced many difficulties in the south between 653 and 648 B.C., where, as arranged by Esarhaddon, Shamashshumukin ruled over Babylonia. In 653 Elamite aggression, led by the new king, the usurper Teumman, disturbed the equilibrium. Asshur reacted swiftly and defeated him at the Karun. Elamite princes, who had been repelled by Teumman and fled to Asshur, now secured the power. But after some years they aligned themselves with a large-scale anti-Assyrian movement, led by Babylonia, "Sealand," and Arabian tribes and supported among others by the Persians under Cyrus I. Nationalistic sentiments, opposition to Asshur's yoke, and the frustrations of Shamashshumukin resulted in a large coalition. Through military intervention in southern Babylonia and Elam and through diplomatic maneuvers, Ashurbanipal was able to isolate Babylon; it was besieged in 650 and captured in 648, and Shamashshumukin was killed. Ashurbanipal himself now became king of Babylon, assuming the throne name Kandalanu.

A campaign against Elam followed, where Humban-Haltash III capitulated in 648 B.C. The area became an Assyrian province; even Cyrus I came to indicate his submission by sending his son Arukku (Aryavaka) to Nineveh. Finally, in the west Balu of Tyre revolted once more, in 663, but without success. After a siege, without being captured, the city submitted. According to some, Manasseh of Judah (*Mi-in-se-e*) participated in this revolt, for which reason he was deported, while later, being a faithful vassal, he was given back his throne (cf. 2 Chron. 33:11–12). A final revolt in this area broke out in 643 but again without success.

Hardly anything is known of Ashurbanipal's final years (he died between 629 and 627 B.C.), because the Eponym canon stopped in 648 B.C. He has become famous through his cultural achievements: the building of his palace at Nineveh, decorated with numerous wall reliefs (with historical events and hunting scenes), where also his extensive library was discovered already early in the nineteenth century. The king, who claimed to be able to read and write, as shown by his beautiful literary inscriptions, as if sensing the end of the Assyrian era, made a successful attempt to collect all the traditional "canonical" literature—*belles lettres*, religious and scientific texts. This was done by including older collections, by confiscation (particularly after the conquest of Babylonia), and by having traveling scholars in Nineveh and Babylonia copy everything of significance. The total collection, estimated to be about 1,500 large clay tablets (with, in addition, many duplicates), now known as the K(uyunjik) Collection in the British Museum, is the most important source of our knowledge of classical Babylonian culture, and is still not fully exhausted.

After Ashurbanipal's death a struggle for succession ensued involving the princes Ashuretililani and Sinsharishkun and the strong man, General Sinshumlishir. So far there is no consensus about the details and the chronology of this period of civil war, which was fought especially in Babylonia with its Assyrian garrisons and generals, with shifting frontiers, and in which also the Chaldean Nabopolassar was heavily involved. We do know that Nabopolassar became king of Babylon in 626 (his crowning is also described in an epic text), and that after the death of his competitors (ca. 623), Sinsharishkun remained as the only king of Assyria (623–612). The battles around the cities of Uruk and Nippur (with Assyrian garrisons and sometimes pro-Assyrian) turned into a power struggle between Nabopolassar and Sinsharishkun, which after shifting positions resulted in Babylonian supremacy around 620. Important documents from Nippur, dated "when the city gate was closed," present a vivid image of the need in the embattled city.

In addition to documents dated after certain kings, these events can particularly be followed with the use of the Babylonian Chronicle. This text has, however, a gap for the fourth–ninth years of Nabopolassar. When the story resumes in 616 B.C., he ruled over all Babylonia and began the attack. Despite successes, an advance along the Euphrates was at first, in 616, stopped by combined Assyrian-Egyptian action. In the east, Nabopolassar in 615 advanced by way of Kirkuk to the city of Asshur, but was thrown back. However, in that year, after the Medes appeared on the scene under Cyaxares II (*Umakishtar*; Uvarkhashatra), who about 625 had thrown off the Scythian yoke, Asshur's fate was sealed. The Medes conquered Asshur in 614; the Babylonians who arrived too late concluded a treaty with the Medes. Nineveh succumbed to their combined attack in 612. The city was razed, its role in history finished. Sinsharishkun was killed, but Ashuruballit II (612–609), who fled, was able to hold out a few more years in Haran. Despite Egyptian help for Asshur, the Babylonians and Medes captured that city in 610 and the following year also overcame the final counterattacks.

A great empire disappeared that during its final century (often indicated as a period of *pax assyriaca*) paired political and military successes with cultural development, paralleled by a constantly growing Aramaization. In the sphere of religion, besides an increasing syncretism, in particular on the part of some Assyrian kings (notably Esarhaddon), we note a search for divine guidance, fear of evil powers and influence, superstition, and uncertainty about the future. This is reflected in the constant stream of alarming or quieting information about all kinds of signs (especially in the sky) given to the court by scholars, and the the ritual-magic trappings to which the king often for a long time had to submit. It consisted of apotropaic ceremonies, cumbersome purification rites, white magic, and prayers of incantation, culminating in the institution of the substitute king (*shar puhi*) in case of a total lunar eclipse, when the king lived incognito for one hundred days. We know of numerous oracle requests (especially to Shamash), prayers, oracles, and prophecies (especially of the Assyrian war-goddess Ishtar of Arbela), in which the king sought certainty and was encouraged and comforted. This uncertainty was fed by such matters as awareness of wrong deeds, inferred from the fate of such kings as Sargon II and Sennacherib, by the constant fear of intrigues, conspiracies (still in 670 B.C. against Esarhaddon), and threat of revolt. The court—often inwardly divided in connection with the dynastic succession and the policy toward Babylon—was kept informed about these things by the king's intelligence service ("the eyes of the king") and the officials and vassals, who were solemnly obligated by their oaths of loyalty (as verbalized in Esarhaddon's vassal treaties) to provide information. Also, the appearance on the borders of the realm of new and hard-to-control peoples such as Scythians, Cimmerians, and Medes would have fueled this uncertainty. The texts that speak of this mentality and mood belong to the most significant period, that of the Sargonids.

## LITERATURE

R. Borger, "Der Aufstieg des neubabylonischen Reiches," *Journal of Cuneiform Studies* 19 (1965) 59–78 (for a different view of the development of the dating between 630 and 620, cf. W. von Soden, *Zeitschrift für Assyriologie* 58 [1967] 241ff.; J. Oates, *Iraq* 28 [1965] 135ff.; J. Reade, *Journal of Cuneiform Studies* 23 [1970] 1ff.).

_____, *Die Inschriften Asarhaddons, Königs von Assyrien* (Graz, 1956).

J. A. Brinkman, "Sennacherib's Babylonian Problem," *Journal of Cuneiform Studies* 25 (1973) 89–95.

*_____, "Through a Glass Darkly: Esarhaddon's Retrospects on the Downfall of Babylon," *Journal of the American Oriental Society* 103 (1983) 35–42.

*_____, "Babylonia under the Assyrian Empire, 745–627 B.C.," in M. T. Larsen, ed., *Power and Propaganda* (Copenhagen, 1979), pp. 223–50.

A. K. Grayson, *Assyrian and Babylonian Chronicles* (Locust Valley, 1975).

*L. D. Levine, "Sennacherib's Southern Front: 704–689 B.C.," *Journal of Cuneiform Studies* 34 (1982) 28–58.

D. D. Luckenbill, *The Annals of Sennacherib* (Chicago, 1924).

N. Na'aman, "Sennacherib's Campaign to Judah and the Date of the LMLK Stamps," *Vetus Testamentum* 29 (1979) 61–86.

*_____, "The Chronology of the Reign of Ashurbanipal," *Zeitschrift für Assyriologie* 70 (1981) 226–45.

A. L. Oppenheim, "Divination and Celestial Observation in the Last Assyrian Empire," *Centaurus* 14 (1969) 97–135.

S. Parpola, *Letters from Assyrian Scholars to the Kings Esarhaddon and Assurbanipal, I: Texts* (Kevelaer/Neukirchen-Vluyn, 1970); *II: Commentary and Appendices* (1983).

*_____, "Assyrian Library Records," *Journal of Near Eastern Studies* 42 (1983) 1–30.

A. J. Spalinger, "The Date of the Death of Gyges and Its Historical Implications," *Journal of the American Oriental Society* 98 (1978) 400ff.

M. Streck, *Assurbanipal und die letzten assyrischen Könige. . . I–III* (Leipzig, 1916) (see also T. Bauer, *Das Inschriftenwerk Assurbanipals vervollständigt und neu bearbeitet I–II* [Leipzig, 1933]).

D. J. Wiseman, *Chronicles of Chaldaean Kings (626–556 B.C.) in the British Museum* (London, 1956; repr. 1961).

## 8. THE NEO-BABYLONIAN EMPIRE AND ITS CONTEMPORARIES (625–539 B.C.)

*Nabopolassar* (626–605 B.C.) lived only a few more years after his military feats described in the previous section. In campaigns with his son and later successor, he consolidated the boundaries to the north (Urartu) and west (Middle Euphrates). He died just at the moment that his rival in the west, Egypt, had been decisively beaten back. Except for building inscriptions from Babylon, Borsippa, and Sippar, little is known of his other deeds. This is due to a situation that is true of the whole dynasty, namely, that the Babylonians apparently did not write official annals or feel the need to include historical and political information in their numerous and extensive building inscriptions. In that respect they were different from their Assyrian predecessors, as well as in the fact that they did not decorate their palaces with historical reliefs. Since no royal correspondence has come down from their reign, we are very much dependent on a limited number of (fragmentary) sources, of which the reliable—based on astronomical diaries—data of the Babylonian Chronicle are the most important. Of some rulers we possess a few historically significant texts (especially of Nabonidus). Beyond that we are dependent on data from other sources (Old Testament, Herodotus, and the like).

The dissolution of the Assyrian realm did not offer new chances only to Babylonia and the Zagros (the Medes). That was also true of the west in Syria-Palestine, where Asshur's power, which until about 630 B.C. was still fairly effective (cf. the Assyrian documents from Gezer and Samaria coming from the years 650–649; the governor of that province was still eponym in 646–645), began to wane. Judah (under Josiah; cf. 2 Chron. 34:6), the Phoenician cities, Damascus, Hamat, et al., must have profited from it. Soon, however, a new candidate for the supremacy presented itself: Egypt under Psammetichus I, who already around 635 B.C. strengthened his position by the capture of Ashdod. Presumably shortly after 620 the Egyptian armies marched to Syria, where Ribla, Hamat, and Carchemish became their strongholds. In 616 Egypt fought at the Euphrates as an ally of Assyria. A stele from 612 points to contacts with Phoenicia, which reestablished its old trade connections with Egypt that had been disrupted by the Assyrians. According to Herodotus there existed at that time in Memphis a "camp of the Tyrians," presumably a trade colony. Egypt was particularly active in Syria around 610, during Asshur's final years, after having effectively repulsed the threat by the Scythians on the eastern border. In 609 the new pharaoh, Neco II (609–594), hurried to the north to support Asshur in the fight for Harran and especially to announce himself as the heir of Asshur's western empire. Josiah of Judah tried to stop him—understandably, considering his own aspirations, which also included the former province of Samaria, though it has not been demonstrated that he annexed northern territory—but was defeated at Megiddo (a military stronghold of Neco; *bet milhamti* in 2 Chron. 35:21?) and lost his life.

Between 608 and 605 B.C. fierce battles raged on the Euphrates, where the Egyptian troops, operating from their base at Carchemish, initially were successful; in 606 the Babylonians were forced to pull back at Kimuhu. But in 605 *Nebuchadrezzar* (605–562) defeated them totally, pursuing them as far as Hamath. Princes of "Hatti" submitted themselves to him (cf. Jer. 46:2). Nabopolassar died that same year and his son briefly visited Babylon to assume the throne. In the following years he strengthened his grip on Syria-Palestine, "moving about triumphantly." Ashkelon (and Gaza?) were taken and Neco II could forget about his aspirations (cf. 2 Kings 24:7). Judah, where in 609 Neco II had replaced Jehoahaz by the pro-Egyptian Eliakim/Joiakim, became a Babylonian vassal state in 604 or shortly after that. In 601 the Babylonians marched out to Egypt. The reports about their coming traveled ahead of them, as we know from an Aramaic letter discovered at Saqqara, in which the (Phoenician or Philistine) king Adon informed the pharaoh that the Babylonians had already gone as far as Aphek (Donner-Röllig, no. 266); also Jeremiah 46:13 belongs to this time. Nebuchadrezzar suffered defeat at the Egyptian border, however, requiring more than a year to recover militarily. That must also be the period in which Judah rebelled. In 598 Nebuchadrezzar advanced on "the city of Judah" (*al Yahudu*), which fell on March 16, 597 B.C. Jehoiachin, who had succeeded Joiakim the year before, was exiled to Babylonia, where together with other Palestinian and Phoenician princes he was mentioned in a document from 593/592 and released in 561 when Evilmerodach became king.

Egypt, where *Psammetichus II* (594–588) ruled, left Nebuchadrezzar undisturbed in Palestine. The pharaoh himself was occupied with a campaign against Nubia. On the campaign extending past the third cataract, the Greek, Phoenician, and Jewish mercenary soldiers of General Amasis's army chiseled their names on the rocks of Abu Simbel. The situation changed under his successor Hophra or Apries (588–568), as we can tell from the few sources. Herodotus is now the chief source of information, supplemented with data from Egypt itself, the Old Testament, and some classical authors. Unfortunately, the residence of the Twenty-sixth Dynasty, Sais, with its necropolis and Neith temple, has not yet been found, so that royal inscriptions are virtually lacking. Aided with a fleet built by Greeks and Phoenicians, Hophra engaged in an expedition to Sidon and Tyre as early as 588. From the south he also penetrated on land. Presumably, in the setting of intensive diplomatic consultation (according to Jer. 27:3-4 there were foreign envoys in Jerusalem) and in spite of his vassal oath sworn to Yahweh (2 Chron. 36:13; Ezek. 17:16-17), that move induced Zedekiah of Judah to rebel. Already on January 15, 588 B.C., Nebuchadrezzar besieged Jerusalem. Military intervention on the part of Hophra resulted in a temporary interruption of the siege but failed to save the city (Jer. 37:5; Ezek. 17:17). In July, 586 B.C., the city capitulated to the generals Negalsharusur and Nabushezibanni. Zedekiah fled but was seized and brought to Nebuchadrezzar, who had his headquarters at Ribla, like Neco II earlier. Between August 14 and 17, 586, Jerusalem was destroyed and sacked, and several thousand Jews were deported into exile. The following year the Babylonians lay siege to Tyre, which after thirteen years surrendered (cf. Ezekiel 26ff.). Itto-Baal III (ca. 590-572) was dethroned and replaced by Balu II (till 564). This was for the time being the end of the Tyrian monarchy; the region was placed under Babylonian administration and governed by "judges." In 582/581 there was again a campaign against Judah, where the situation remained restless (murder of Gedaliah; exodus to Egypt). Nabuzeriddin (Nebuzaradan) carried a few more thousand Judeans into exile (Jer. 52:30).

In 568 B.C. Nebuchadrezzar, benefiting from the unrest in Egypt, where Hophrah had been replaced by his general *Amasis* (568-526), subdued Egypt. The damaged texts are not able to tell us much about the size of the expedition (cf. also Jer. 43:8ff.; Ezek. 29:19). Apparently Babylonian domination was of a passing nature. Amasis lost his throne and was unable to cope with the problems, including those in connection with his attempt to extend his power: an abortive

expedition to Libya to fight the powerful Greek colony of Cyrene, with which he finally made a treaty. The controversial (for the Egyptians) relations with the Greeks and Greek culture were resolved by assigning Naucratis to the Greek colonists and traders in the Delta and by good political and cultural relations with Greece itself (the source of the pharaoh's valuable mercenary soldiers). At home in Egypt Amasis was an energetic restorer and builder of temples, while he also introduced administrative and legal reforms. His long reign was for the time being Egypt's final period of independence.

In the meantime, Babylonia reaped the fruits of its political power over the west through receipt of tribute, taxes, and income from trade. Nebuchadrezzar engaged in intensive building activity, especially in Babylon and Borsippa (the city of Nabu with the temple Ezida, which played a very important role in the 1st millennium B.C.). The construction of a wall and the digging of a kind of water line north and east of Babylon protected the residence. It was enclosed by a double wall, 19 kilometers (12 mi.) in length, stretching over both shores of the arm of the Euphrates. Far in the north was the summer residence (*Babil*), and on the north side near the inner wall the large palace (about 6 ha. or 15 acres). East of it rose the large Ishtar gate with accompanying procession road (*Ayiburshabu*), decorated with glazed bricks with pictures of mythical animals on a blue background. This is the route followed by the gods, led by Bel/Marduk, during the New Year festival in the month Nisan. The gods were carried from the temple *Esagila* (with its "cella" where the fate is decided) to the ziqqurrat complex (*Etemenanki*, 92 by 92 m. or 300 by 300 ft.; now destroyed) and to the *Akitu* house. Here Marduk's triumph over Tiamat was symbolically enacted and the *Enuma elish,* which describes his triumph and ordering of the cosmos, recited in his honor before his image. The city—known from a detailed Babylonian description and from data in Herodotus—had fifty-three temples, almost 1,000 chapels, and many street altars in roomy and systematically laid out residential districts. Even today the ruins still give a good indication of the "great Babylon."

In 562 B.C. Nebuchadrezzar was succeeded by

*Awil-Marduk* (Evil-merodach; 562–560) and after that by the general Neriglissar (559–556), whose activities included a campaign to Cilicia to restore his influence in this strategic and ore-rich territory. That was the limit of Babylon's sphere of influence and there began the territories of the new powers: Lydia under Alyattes and the Medes under Cyaxares, who had eliminated Urartu and the Cimmerians. After initial conflicts they had made peace in 585, with the use of Babylonian mediation (Labynetos = Nebuchadrezzar?), with Halys as the boundary. The Medes, soon under Astyages (*Ishtuwegu; Arshtivaiga*), continued to control large parts of northern Mesopotamia, including Assyria and Harran, until around 550 they had to bow to the Persians.

Babylon's last king, *Nabonidus* (556–539 B.C.), succeeded Labashi-Marduk, who was assassinated after three months. At first Nabonidus's reign proceeded normally, with campaigns to Cilicia (Hume), Syria (Hamat), and even Edom in the first three years. Then the king suddenly marched to northern Arabia, where he penetrated to Dedan and even Yathrib (the later Medina), in order finally to make Tema his temporary residence. His ten-year stay there had two consequences: the New Year festival of Marduk could not be held in Babylon, because he "did not grasp the hand of Bel" (in the procession), and the crown prince Belshazzar (Belsharusur) looked after the administrative and military affairs. About 540 B.C. Nabonidus returned to Babylon, presumably due to the threatening advance of the Persians.

These events betray a drastic change in the religious outlook of the king, with serious consequences. Tradition, too, mentions it; fragments of an Aramaic prayer of Nabonidus, discovered at Qumran, mention Tema. It has been assumed that the event described in Daniel 4 originally related to that king and not to Nebuchadrezzar (it is more often said that Daniel contains a general blending of the figures of both kings; cf. Berger, listed in the literature following section 9). Information from Babylon itself sheds further light on the background. According to two steles discovered in Harran—one of Nabonidus and one of his Aramaic mother, a fervent devotee of Sin of Harran—

the king, in part through a vision in a dream at his accession, was gripped by the cult of the moon-god Sin and the urge to restore his temple and cult, which had seriously suffered as a result of the capture of Harran in 610 B.C. His devotion to Sin was so great that the state cult of Marduk began to suffer, to the great displeasure of its priests. This occasioned a serious controversy, as is evident from a Babylonian "defamatory poem" on Nabonidus (see Pritchard, ed., *Ancient Near Eastern Texts*, pp. 312–15) and from the welcome given to Cyrus in 539 B.C. According to the Babylonian Chronicle, Cyrus even made sure that there was "no interruption of the cult in the Esagil" and the other temples during and immediately after the capture of Babylon. Returning after ten years, Nabonidus could once more (?) take Marduk's hand and lead the procession.

But Babylon's days were already numbered; the writing on the wall of Daniel 5 (drawings of symbolic representations of weights, interpreted as root-related verbs and names) had already appeared! Cyrus defeated the Babylonian troops at Opis on the Tigris (opposite the later Seleucia) and captured Babylon (according to Herodotus by making the water defense line useless through diverting the waters of the Euphrates). When Cyrus's troops under Ugbaru (probably not identical with Gubaru/Gobryas, later appointed as governor by Cyrus) were in control of the city, Cyrus himself appeared on October 29, 539 B.C., "to speak friendly to the population while there is peace in the city." Nabonidus, who had first fled, returned and was taken prisoner. The "great Babylon," renowned and feared for its power, riches, and violence, had fallen (cf. Jeremiah 50–51). But via the New Testament its name would remain as a symbol, while the city and tower (Gen. 11:1–9) remained as embodiments of the drive for power and the negative aspects of urbanism, of which Babylon was indeed a prototype.

---

## LITERATURE

W. Baumgartner, "Herodots babylonische und assyrische Nachrichten," *Zum Alten Testament und seiner Umwelt* (Leiden, 1959), pp. 282–331.

P. R. Berger, *Die neubabylonischen Königsinschriften* (Kevelaer/Neukirchen-Vluyn, 1973).

C. J. Gadd, "The Harran Inscriptions of Nabonidus," *Anatolian Studies* 7 (1958) 35–92.

A. K. Grayson, *Assyrian and Babylonian Chronicles* (Locust Valley, 1975).

G. F. Hasel, "The First and Third Year of Belshazzar," *Andrews University Seminary Studies* 15 (1977) 153–68.

R. Koldewey, *Das wieder erstehende Babylon* (Leipzig, 1925⁴).

W. G. Lambert, "Nabonidus in Arabia," *Proceedings of the 5th Seminar for Arabian Studies* (Oxford, 1972), pp. 53–64.

S. H. Langdon, *Die neubabylonischen Königsinschriften* (Leipzig, 1912).

A. Malamat, "Josiah's Bid for Armageddon," *Journal of the Ancient Near Eastern Society of Columbia University* 5 (1973) 267–79.

S. Smith, *Babylonian Historical Texts Relating to the Capture and Downfall of Babylon* (London, 1924; repr. 1975).

E. Unger, *Babylon, die heilige Stadt, nach der Beschreibung der Babylonier* (Berlin/Leipzig, 1931; rev. ed. 1970).

---

## 9. THE PERSIAN REALM OF THE ACHAEMENIDS (550–330 B.C.)

For Cyrus (*Kurush*), the conquest of Babylon was the culmination of his large-scale policy of conquest, making him, with his scepter now also over the Neo-Babylonian empire, the mightiest ruler of his time. He was descended from a dynasty which toward the end of the eighth century B.C. had been established by Achaemenes (*Hahamanish*) and continued by Teispes (*Caishpish*), Cyrus I, and his father Cambyses (*Kanbuziya;* married to Astyages's daughter Mandane). A legend soon afterward about "Cyrus the Great" speaks of his birth and rescue after he had been abandoned. The dynasty ruled over the Persian tribes who since the ninth century B.C., under the pressure of Urartu, the Medes, and the Scythians, had slowly moved to the south, so that eventually they came to live in the area of Shiraz: the province of Fars (Persis), where later Pasargadae and Persepolis would

arise. Here was also located the old Elamite city of Anshan, after which the princes called themselves "great king, king of Anshan," thereby underlining—even as they did at first in their use of Elamite as their written language—that they carried on the tradition of ancient Elam.

In 558 B.C., Cyrus (ca. 560–530) had revolted against the Medes under Astyages, which in 550 led to the capture of Ecbatana (*Agmatana*, near Hamadan), after the Median army under Harpagus had run over to his side. From now on Persians and Medes, with equal rights governmentally and militarily, formed the core of the realm. This was soon followed by subjugation of the Median provinces, such as Parthia and Hyrcania. Already in 547, according to the Babylonian Chronicle, Cyrus crossed the Tigris to subdue Asia Minor. Yet in that same year Croesus of Lydia was defeated and Sardis captured after a brief siege (Croesus had sent home his army too early at the end of autumn). Soon also the Greek trade cities on the west coast of Asia Minor had to acknowledge Persian sovereignty, willingly (Miletus) or unwillingly (most of the others). The following years were used for the conquest of the territories east of Persia; Cyrus advanced to the Indus and the Oxus, placing Gandara, Sogdia, and Chorasmia under his authority. Here in 530 he was killed in a battle against the Massagetes or Sakes, and then buried in his monumental tomb at Pasargadae, where he also had his palace.

Cyrus was a ruler who spoke to the imagination. He was regarded as a ruler who practiced tolerance and who was devoutly religious, both qualities that were considered characteristic of the Achaemenids in their attitude toward conquered peoples and their cults. Especially Cyrus's decree that made possible the rebuilding of the temple in Jerusalem by the Judean prince (?) Sheshbazzar (Babylonian *Shashshabausur*) and regulated the return of the temple utensils (Ezra 6:3–5) has greatly contributed to this image. In the prophetic vision of Deutero-Isaiah (ch. 41; 44:26ff.; ch. 45), Cyrus appears as Yahweh's anointed, divinely mandated to rebuild city and temple and to free the captives. Newer investigation has shown that it is wrong to regard this "tolerance," "religiosity," and this sparing of religious-national feelings as a distinctive characteristic of the Achaemenids. There are no clear indications of a special honoring of Israel's "God of heaven"—as Yahweh is usually called in the Aramaic documents in Ezra—for instance, on the basis of a kind of essential kinship with the chief Persian god Ahuramazda. Nor can Cyrus's policy be explained as due to his Zoroastrian religion, because there are no proofs that the (first?) Achaemenids were devotees of Zarathustra and his ideas. In most cases their policies can be explained as motivated by political considerations which dictated the wisdom of leaving subdued nations free in their religion (the Assyrians did the same!) and to spare their national-religious feelings in order to avoid unnecessary conflicts. On the other hand it is very obvious that the economic power of the great temples in various lands was curtailed: instead of receiving aid from the state treasury, now in most cases they had to pay taxes and levies in goods, and perform services, and were controlled by a royal commissary. It should be added, however, that in general the Jerusalem temple occupied a very favorable position, because not only was the cost of rebuilding paid out of the royal treasury but also the sacrificial cult (Ezra 6:9–10; 7:20ff.) and its maintenance were financed, while the priests were exempt from taxation (Ezra 7:24).

That the Achaemenids were interested in avoiding conflicts in their large empire with its many ethnic and national entities by respecting old traditions and feelings is evident from various measures. After their conquest, Media, Babylonia, and Egypt were not simply annexed; instead the Persian king in a personal union also became king of those countries and had himself crowned king following local traditions and with the use of native titles. At first the local government was left intact as much as possible; the governor of the province of Babylonia remained in function for many years and also elsewhere local self-government continued. Politically and theologically Cyrus and his successors adapted to the prevailing modes and also made use of them. The "Cyrus Cylinder" from Babylon (ill. 88) depicts him as a ruler chosen by Marduk, who delivered city and population from oppression (by Nabonidus), who avoids the plundering of temples and disruption of the cult at his conquest and

receives Marduk's blessing, almost being welcomed by the inhabitants. Cyrus allowed the statues of the gods that Nabonidus (for security reasons?) had carried off to Babylon from many cities, together with their deported worshipers, to return to their homes, because he wanted to be assured of their unceasing intercession with Marduk and Nabu on his behalf and that of the crown prince. This last aspect was an important motive of his "religious policy"; in Ezra 6:10 it is mentioned as the purpose. About 410 B.C. the Jews at Elephantine used the same argument (see Pritchard, ed., *Ancient Near Eastern Texts*, p. 492, lines 25–26) to obtain permission from Bagoas, the Persian governor of Judah, to rebuild the destroyed Yahu temple of their colony.

What happened in Egypt is illustrative in this respect. Cyrus's successor *Cambyses* (530–522 B.C.), earlier already designated as co-regent, was able to extend Persian authority to include Syria (Phoenici) and Palestine, and in 525, with the aid of Polycrate of Samos, successfully attacked Egypt, where Pharaoh Amasis had just died and been succeeded by Psammetichus III. After having broken the military resistance at Pelusium and Memphis, Cambyses became king of Egypt; general Udjahorresne, who had helped him obtain Sais and who later presented him as a pharaoh to Egypt with full Egytian titles, played an important role in this. When revolt started in Egypt after an abortive campaign against Nubia, it was harshly suppressed; especially the temples— rightly feared by the Persians as centers of anti-Persian feelings and significant economic powers—became the target. Though the facts bear out that the stories of Greek historians about Cambyses's reign of terror are exaggerated (for instance, the sacred Apis bull was not killed but died in Cambyses's sixth year and was entombed in the Serapeum in a beautiful sarcophagus given by the king), there was undoubtedly destruction and the theft of property. The traditional pharaonic gifts to the temples ceased; from now on they had to raise their own levies, and the personnel of the priestly offices was checked by the Persian satrap Aryandes. Three important temples, including those of Memphis and Hermopolis, retained their income, while also the Neith temple at Sais was given preferential treatment on account of the political behavior of Udjahorresne. Also the Persian attitude toward the Yahu temple at Elephantine was political in nature. The Jewish military colony, which had been here for a considerable length of time already (its origin is about the middle of the 7th or the beginning of the 6th century B.C.) and had served Apries and Amasis, was apparently taken over by the Persians as a reliable, non-Egyptian garrison on the strategic border with Nubia. The above-mentioned letter of Bagoas, pleading for restoration of the Yahu temple, also mentions that "when Cambyses came to Egypt, he found this temple intact. They [the Persians] demolished all the temples of Egyptian gods, but no one damaged this temple."

In 522 B.C. a crisis broke out in the realm, aggravated by the sudden death of Cambyses as he rushed from Egypt to Persia. The magician Gautama—a member of the old Median priestly caste of the *magi*—revolted and after Cambyses's death captured the throne. He gained a following by social measures such as exemption from military service, a three-year exemption from taxes, and curtailment of the privileges of the Persian noble families. According to the official version of the later victor Darius, Gautama strengthened his position by presenting himself as Cambyses's younger brother Bardya (who in reality was secretly killed by Cambyses in 526 for fear of a conspiracy), for which reason the text speaks of the "false Bardya (Smerdis)." Revolts also erupted in other parts of the realm: in Media a Phraortes presented himself, aided by Parthia and Hyrcania; Armenia seceded; in Babylonia usurpers with the significant name Nebuchadrezzar (III and IV) temporarily captured the throne (Oct.– Dec. 522; Aug.–Nov. 521). Many satrapies, among others those of Egypt, acted quite independently.

*Darius I* (522–486 B.C.; Darayavaush), son of the powerful satrap of Persis and Parthia Hystaspes (Vishtaspa), member of a younger branch of the Achaemenids, saved the throne. Together with six nobles he murdered Gautama in 522 at Ecbatana, after which he was proclaimed king. Supported by his father, his guard, and small army units he was miraculously able to quell all revolts in a few years and establish his sovereignty, and in 518 the satrapies of Lydia-Ionia and Egypt that

had regained independence also acknowledged his supremacy. On the expedition to Egypt in 519–518 the army also passed by Judah. The rebuilding of the temple, begun under Sheshbazzar but stopped soon afterward, had been resumed in 520 by the arrival of Zerubbabel—grandson of Jehoiachin—and thousands of exiles (Ezra 2), presumably ordered by Darius, who was interested in maintaining good relations with Jerusalem, since it was strategically located relative to the border with Egypt. Inspired by the prophet Haggai (Ezra 5) the work was taken in hand; a Samaritan complaint sent to Darius by the satrap Tatenai had no effect because of an old decree of Cyrus and the policy of Darius. The temple was completed in 515, whereupon Zerubbabel presumably returned to Babylonia.

Under Darius (the Great), an unusually competent ruler and general, the empire had its first period of great prosperity. The realm now comprised the areas conquered by Cyrus, to which Cambyses added Egypt, Cyrene, Libya, and Cyprus, while Darius even before 512 incorporated the northwest of India, Thrace, and Macedonia. This last conquest happened during the famed campaign against the Scythians, when the Bosporus was bridged and the Persian troops pushed through to the Danube, including also the Black Sea in the Persian sphere of influence. Prosperity and relative quiet prevailed throughout the whole empire. This lasted until the confrontation with Greece led to a climax toward the end of Darius's reign, first in the Ionian revolt of 500– 494 B.C., ending with the capture and destruction of Miletus, after that in the unsuccessful landing on the Greek mainland where the Persian invasion army was defeated in 490 at Marathon by the Athenians under Callimachus.

Persepolis was Darius's new capital of Persis. It also had an important ceremonial function, for example, at the New Year festival (Susa was the capital of the realm), and it stood as the symbol of Darius's world empire, which was comprised of numerous peoples and ethnic entities and which has been characterized as a "commonwealth." The facade of the magnificent northern stairway depicts the twenty-three peoples who brought tribute, and the almost international character of the city is underscored by the architecture and sculpture, betraying Egyptian, Assyrian, Median, and Greek elements which are a (conscious?) synthesis of the input of artists from many countries who were put to work here. See ill. 89–91.

The history of the Achaemenian realm is less well known than one might wish. The native sources—though not yet utilized to the full—contain limited information and are often only of local interest; beyond that one is dependent especially on information passed on by Greek historians such as Herodotus, Thucydides, and Ktesias. An adequate description of the realm from within is lacking.

One of the most important texts is the inscription accompanying the great rock relief of Behistun (Bisitun; east of Kermanshah): in three languages (Elamite, Babylonian, and Old Persian—the inscriptions are cut in this order and exhibit some variations in connection with a retouching of the story), Darius recounts his victory over the "false Smerdis" and the "deceptive kings." The monument, copied with great difficulty, not only offered the key to the decipherment of the cuneiform script but is also the oldest inscription in the syllabic, Old Persian cuneiform script, devised (supposedly) by Darius I about 520 B.C. and used especially for ceremonial inscriptions (building inscriptions, tomb inscriptions, rock inscriptions). From ancient times Elamite functioned as the written language in the realm; already from about 650 B.C. there are several hundred Elamite cuneiform texts of an administrative nature from the armory at Susa. Very significant, moreover, are the more than one hundred texts on tablets from the treasury of Persepolis and the more than two thousand texts from the walls of this city ("fortification tablets"). They provide insight into all kinds of governmental affairs and give us the names and titles of many functionaries.

From Babylonia are many Akkadian texts: some ceremonial and historiographical texts (Cyrus Cylinder, late king lists, Babylonian Chronicle) and thousands of administrative and juridical documents from these centuries that provide insight into the local government, the system of landownership, taxes, levies, commerce, and the monetary system. Particularly the archives of the merchant house of Murashu and the banking

house Egibi are enlightening in this respect and provide insight into the social structure and economy of a part of the realm.

Finally there are the texts in Aramaic, the language employed for quite some time already in the west by the Assyrians as the "governmental language," and now, especially through the governmental reforms of Darius, also introduced in the east, enabling the chancelleries throughout the whole empire to maintain contact with each other. From the governmental centers official documents in so-called Official Aramaic were sent to all parts of the realm, as is shown, for instance, by the Aramaic decrees and letters in the book of Ezra. Alongside it the vernacular remained in use in many areas: Elamite in Persepolis (till ca. 460), Phoenician in Phoenicia, and Demotic in Egypt. As a consequence many officials and "writers" were bilingual and there were numerous documents to be translated. The Aramaic texts from Persepolis consist of a few hundred inscriptions on ceremonial pottery, used with the Hauma rites. From many parts of the realm are ceremonial inscriptions on tombs, steles, and boundary stones in Aramaic. From Egypt we possess documents on perishable material such as leather and papyrus. The last category includes over one hundred Aramaic papyri from the Jewish military colony at Elephantine covering the entire fifth century B.C., in addition to a number of Aramaic letters found at Hermopolis and sent from the Aramaic colony of Syene (Aswan). Furthermore, there are documents from or intended for the chancellery of the Persian satrap of Egypt, Arsames, written when he was temporarily in Susa (ca. 410 B.C.).

In addition to the international linguistic medium, the contacts among the parts of the realm were promoted by good connections along famed (post) roads, such as the road from Sardis in Lydia through Asia Minor to Babylon and from there to Susa and Persepolis, and the caravan road that linked Babylon and Ecbatana with Bactria and the borders of India. These roads were of strategic military importance as well, while they also benefited the trade for which Darius dug the canal—earlier begun by Neco (but left incomplete?)—from the Nile to Suez that linked the Mediterranean Sea with the Red Sea. In these centuries international trade took great strides, profiting from the fact that the most important eastern states were governmentally under one scepter as well as from the protection enjoyed by the caravans and shipping traffic. The evolution of the currency and coinage system, started already in the second half of the seventh century B.C. in Lydia and later taken over by Greeks and Phoenicians, contributed to the profit. In 517 Darius I introduced the gold *dareikos* or daric (weighing 8.4 grams or 0.3 oz.) and the silver shekel (5.6 grams or 0.2 oz.; worth 1/20 of the *dareikos*) as legal currency. Alongside these the many local coins remained in circulation, while many satrapies also had their own coins.

The Phoenician trade cities, which appear to have passed into Persian supremacy without problems, benefited particularly from this situation. On the whole, until the fourth century B.C. they remained loyal to the Persian kings and enjoyed self-government and commercial freedom in exchange for the payment of tribute and taxes and giving support by their naval units, which were indeed a powerful factor in wars with Egypt and Greece and in the preparation of invasions. In this period Tyre, Sidon, and Byblos had again their own kings, some of whom we know by name from building and tomb inscriptions and from texts on statues. Sidon seems to have played the most important role. Of the many kings from the fifth century that are known to us by name, Eshmunazar II deserves special mention; he was given an expansion of his territory by the "lord of kings": "Dor and Yaffa, the beautiful cornlands [or lands of Dagon] in the field of Sharon" (for the texts cf. Donner-Röllig, nos. 9–10, 13–16; and W. Röllig, *Welt des Orients* 5 [1969] 121ff.).

The Persian governmental system was based on a division of the realm into large provinces (often identical with former national or political units), called satrapies, a term derived from the name of its governor: *khshatrapavan*, Aramaic *'ḥshdrpn*, "satrap." Originally the number of satrapies was about twenty (so, e.g., in Darius's Behistun Inscription), but it did not remain the same as a result of conquests and redivisions (Herodotus's list in iii.89ff. is something else and of more recent date). Thus in 535 B.C. Cyrus created a satrapy comprising Babylonia and its for-

mer territory in Syria and Palestine, governed by Gubaru/Gobryas, who after 525 was succeeded by Ushtani. Shocked by the crisis at the beginning of his reign, Darius began a policy of making changes and split this territory into Babylonia proper and a satrapy *Ebirnari*, "across the river," the area west of the Euphrates, governed by Tattenai, who was under Ushtani. Under the satraps were the chief of the chancellery (the *beeltem*); the chief of the "treasury" (*ganzabara*), charged with the collection of tribute and levies and with making payments; the herald (*azdakara*); inquisitors (*frasaka;* Aramaic *'prstk'*); bookkeepers (*hamarakara*); and scribes. Most of these functions occur in the Aramaic parts of Ezra. The (smaller) provinces belonging to the satrapy (such as Samaria) were ruled by a governor, who (even as sometimes the satrap) bore the Aramaic title *peha;* because this title is also used in another context for royal commissaries, it is not always clear which territorial units were genuine provinces under a satrap. This problem is also encountered with respect to Judah and Jerusalem, which despite the use of this title for Sheshbazzar did not become an independent province until late in the fifth century B.C. (certainly under Nehemiah). Such provinces occasionally enjoyed a great measure of self-government, sometimes under their own princes or chiefs, who were often recruited from the native population; this was, for example, the case with Nehemiah and the governors from the period after 400 B.C. (we know this from coins from the province of Yehud and jar stamps from Ramat Rahel). Bagoas, who ruled at the end of the fifth century B.C., was probably an exception.

Darius's governmental reforms involved, among other things, that from now on the satraps were preferably chosen from the Persian nobility, that governmental and military authority remained separate, and that an accumulation of functions was to be avoided. This last-mentioned rule was no doubt to prevent political aspirations of satraps, but that was not always successful, owing to a later relaxing of these norms. We know of several revolts of satraps, in particular the failed attempt of Cyrus the Younger, operating from his base in Asia Minor and with the aid of his 10,000 Greeks, to dethrone his brother Artaxerxes. Included in the restructurings, pertaining among others to the army and taxes, was the re-writing of laws. The laws and regulations of various peoples were studied and sometimes codified, including Egyptian law, as this was in force till Amasis's death, having been brought to Susa by Egyptian scholars (495 B.C.). An attempt was made to create a more general system of law above and beside local legal customs; the term "the right [data] of the king," refers to this general system. Promulgated by the king on the authority of Ahuramazda, the laws were an important factor in the central government of the kingdom. They were based on traditional Medo-Persian law. Attention was given to the administration of justice, in which royal judges and satraps played a significant role beside local agencies (assembly of the people, temples). In the area of private law, Assyrian-Babylonian laws occupied an important place, especially in the west, through the use of the forms employed for contracts and the frequently used clauses, also in their Aramaized form as we know this from the Elephantine documents. The ministry of Ezra, priest and lawyer, with his special interest in laws and justice (including codification), also fits into this historical framework.

*Xerxes* (485–465 B.C.) was Darius's successor. After having put down the revolts that broke out in Egypt and Babylon between 486 and 484 at the changing of the throne, he prepared a great expedition against Greece to make up for the defeat at Marathon and at the same time to punish Athens for its aid to the Egyptian insurgents. After extensive preparations the army departed from Sardis, accompanied by a large fleet, manned by Ionians, Phoenicians, and Egyptians, in addition to Persians. After the battle at Thermopylae and the capture of Athens, the Persians suffered a big defeat in 480 B.C. in the sea battle of Salamis, followed in 479 by the defeat on land of General Mardonius; in this last battle Artabazos was, however, able to retreat with a large part of his army to Asia Minor. While the war dragged on and Xerxes' government decreased in effectiveness (according to Greek sources he spent more and more time on his harem—the story of Esther would fit here; the building at Persepolis, identified as a harem by Herzfeld, is probably not a harem but an annex to the treasury house), he was assassinated by Artabanus in 465 and succeeded by *Artaxerxes I* (465–424).

In 460 Artaxerxes was confronted with a serious revolt in Egypt, which lasted until 455 with the help of Greece. Also in Syria the situation was troublesome; only with difficulty could the powerful general and satrap Megabyzos be held in line. Therefore in this period (ca. 450 B.C.) the Persian court was open to a complaint from Samaria under governor Rehum (Ezra 4:8ff.) against the building of the walls of Jerusalem, which was regarded as the center of opposition and rebellion (an earlier complaint, when Mithredath was governor of Samaria, to which Ezra 4:7 refers, was without success). The building of the wall was interrupted for about five years, until the king's cupbearer, Nehemiah, as the king's plenipotentiary and governor of the now autonomous province of Judah (*Yehud,* later also occurring on coins and official stamps), arrived from Susa in 445. During his stay, lasting till 433, the wall was completed, despite the opposition of Samaria, where Sanballat (*Sinuballit*) had succeeded Rehum. Artaxerxes died in 423; his memory lives on in his rock tomb at Persepolis and in the magnificent throne room (or "room of 100 pillars"), according to the building inscription started by Xerxes and finished by Artaxerxes.

His successor *Darius II* (423–404 B.C.) came to the throne when Greece was being torn apart by the Peloponnesian War. In the province of Judah, Nehemiah had meanwhile (directly?) been succeeded by the Persian Bagoas. Tensions increased in the Jewish colony at Elephantine, particularly through the arrival of Hananiah, who handed a royal decree to satrap Arsames (to leave the colony alone?) and gave instructions about the celebration of Pesach (Passover?) (419 B.C.). The tense relationship with the Egyptian priesthood of Khnum, the ram-god, whose temple bordered on the Jewish colony, exploded in 410, when the Egyptians—no doubt also provoked by the bloody sacrifices of small livestock in the Yahu temple—aided by the Persian prefect (*frataraka*) Vidranga destroyed the temple. Though the perpetrators were punished, the Jews had to wait a long time for permission to rebuild, as is shown by their repeated petitions. One of these (Cowley, no. 30; see Pritchard, *Ancient Near Eastern Texts,* p. 492), found in the archive of Yedoniah, the priest and leader of the Jewish community, was directed to Bagoas, the governor of Judah; it was parallel with a similar request to Delaiah and Shelemiah, sons and successors of Sanballat. It also acquaints us with the details of the history, as well as the fact that an earlier request for support, directed to the Jewish high priest Johanan and the leader of the Jewish "nobility" Ostanes, was without success (due to their dislike of a sacrificial cult outside Jerusalem or out of political considerations?). Finally the request was granted, just before the end of Darius's reign or already under Artaxerxes II, perhaps to assure himself of the support of the Jewish garrison in the worsening situation in Egypt, where rebellion had broken out. A memorandum sent by both Bagoas and Delaiah (Cowley, no. 32), to be brought to the satrap Arsames, mentions the (royal?) permission to rebuild the temple and to resume the sacrificial cult, though with the stipulation that bloody sacrifices were not permitted (out of consideration for the objections from the Khnum priests and/or the priesthood of Jerusalem?). It is very questionable whether reconstruction could be realized, because the revolt of 400 B.C. under the leadership of Amyrtaeus put an end to Persian supremacy, thereby also sealing the fate of the Elephantine colony.

The time of Darius's successor *Artaxerxes II* (404–359 B.C.) was perhaps also the time when Ezra came from Babylon to Judah, that is, if the date mentioned in Ezra 7:8 refers to this reign. A later dating might help to explain how after Nehemiah, under Bagoas, all kinds of evils arose. The date would be sure if "Jehohanan son of Eliashib," who had a room in the temple (Ezra 10:6), would be identical with the priest Jehohanan, grandson of Eliashib, on the one hand, and with the high priest J(eh)ohanan, who according to the Elephantine letter to Bagoas about 407 was in office in Jerusalem, on the other hand. Others place Ezra's coming during the reign of Artaxerxes I, that is, in 458; at least thirteen years later he would then have worked together with Nehemiah (Nehemiah 8). Beyond that little is known about the history of Judah and Samaria of the fourth century when they were under Persian rule, though we know the names of a number of governors (presumably recruited from the native population) from both provinces. There is no unanimity about the dating of those of Judah (known from inscriptions on coins, jar stamps, *bullae,* and seals); Avigad places Elnatan, Jehoezer, and Achzai before Nehemiah and assumes that Judah was already an autonomous Persian province before the sixth century B.C. Thanks to the "Samaria Papyri" there is more certainty with respect to those of Samaria: Delaiah was succeeded by (his son?) Sanballat II (ca. 375), Hananiah (ca. 355), and Sanballat III (ca. 335). Both provinces, of course, sustained the influences of the political developments, which were particularly turbulent in Syria-Palestine about the middle of the fourth century.

For sixty years (till 342 B.C.) Egypt under the Twenty-eighth–Thirtieth Dynasties was able to maintain its independence under such kings as Nepherites (398–393), Achoris (390–378), and Nectanebo I (378–360) and II (359–342). It involved itself actively in the anti-Persian politics in the eastern Mediterranean Sea basin through numerous contacts with Sparta, Athens, and Cyprus and rebellious movements in Syria and Palestine. The situation became dangerous for Egypt after Persia had obtained quiet on the Greek front through the great "royal peace" of Antialkidas in 386. In 373 the Persian army, commanded by Pharnabazus and with the help of Athens, undertook a massive assault on Egypt from Pelusium. Nectanebo I (with whom the 30th Dynasty begins) was able to stop the Persians through a strong line of defense, water works, and the flood-waters of the Nile. Its support to rebellious movements in Syria, already begun on a large scale by Pharaoh Teos (without success) in 360, proved ultimately fatal for Egypt. Nectanebo II, who in 351 had repelled an attack on Egypt by *Artaxerxes III Ochus* (359–338), after that energetically supported the revolt in Phoenicia (Sidon, under King Tennes; Tripolis; aid from Cyprus). After Artaxerxes had put down Sidon and the other Phoenician cities (Sidon was betrayed and destroyed) in 343, he concentrated his attack on Egypt. From Pelusium, with the aid of betrayal, Bagoas cut through the strong defense line at Mendes in the Delta, whereupon Nectanebo II fled to Egypt. This was the end of Egypt's independence, which during the Thirtieth Dynasty had again briefly flourished, as attested by the many remains of buildings and statues of the two Nectanebo's. For more than ten years the country was again under a harsh Persian government—the Thirty-first Dynasty—before Alexander the Great appeared there in 332 B.C., honored the Egyptian temples, visited the oracle of Amon in the Siwah oasis, and was acknowledged as ruler and liberator.

In 338 B.C. Artaxerxes III was murdered by Bagoas, his vizier and eunuch. Following the brief reign of Arses, *Darius III Codomannus* (336–330 B.C.) came to the throne as the last Persian king. He faced the difficult task of holding together the disintegrating empire and at the same time heading off the new threat, personified in Alexander of Macedonia. In the first he was successful initially, especially in the east; in the second he failed, being confronted with the greatest general of his time. After the conquest of Asia Minor, after the battle at the Granicus River in 334, both rulers met each other for the first time at Issus. Here, at the Gulf of Iskenderun, and two years later at Gaugamela (in the old Assyria), the Persians were decisively defeated. Babylon, Susa, and Persepolis were taken. With his own hands Alexander the Great threw the burning torch into the palace of Xerxes, avenging the desecration of the Greek temples. Darius himself, having fled from Ecbatana to the east, fell into the power of Bessos, the satrap of Bactria, who eventually killed him so that he would not fall alive into the hands of the Macedonians (330 B.C.). After more than two hundred years the Persian empire had come to an end. It lived on in the stories of the Greek historians, in the monuments that withstood the ravages of time, such as the tomb of Cyrus restored by Alexander, in the magnificent, relief-decorated rock tombs of the Achaemenids at Naqsh-i-Rustam, and in what archeology has uncovered of Persian culture, especially at Persepolis.

## LITERATURE

P. R. Berger, "Der Kyros-Zylinder . . . ," *Zeitschrift für Assyriologie* 64 (1975) 192–234.

*E. J. Bickerman and H. Tadmor, "Darius I, Pseudo-Smerdis, and the Magi," *Athaenaeum* 56 (1978) 239–61.

W. Culican, *Imperial Cities of Persia: Persepolis, Susa and Pasargadae* (London, 1970).

*J. Elayi, "The Phoenician Cities in the Persian Period," *Journal of the Ancient Near Eastern Society of Columbia University* 12 (1980) 13–28 (see also 13 [1981] 15–30).

K. Galling, *Studien zur Geschichte Israels im persischen Zeitalter* (Tübingen, 1964).

R. Ghirshman, *Iran* (Harmondsworth, 1954).

*W. Hinz, *Darius und die Perser. Eine Kulturgeschichte der Achämeniden* (Baden-Baden, 1976).

A. T. Olmstead, *History of the Persian Empire* (Chicago, 1948).

B. Porten, *Archives from Elephantine: The Life of an Ancient Jewish Military Colony* (Berkeley/Los Angeles, 1968).

G. Posener, *La première domination perse en Egypte* (Cairo, 1936).

G. Walser, *Die Völkerschaften auf den Reliefs von Persepolis* (Berlin, 1966).

———, ed., *Beiträge zur Achämenidengeschichte* (Wiesbaden, 1972).

J. Wieschöfer, *Der Aufstand Gaumatas und die Anfänge Darios I* (Bonn, 1978).

D. N. Wilber, *Persepolis. The Archaeology of Parsa, Seat of the Persian Kings* (London, 1969).

## 10. SUPPLEMENTARY BIBLIOGRAPHY

Some important recent books have been added in the interest of the reader, even though they appeared after the original Dutch version of this survey was completed and the author could not take them into account. They are marked by an asterisk.

### a. History

#### (1) ANCIENT NEAR EAST

*The Cambridge Ancient History* (3rd ed.), I/1–2; II/1–2; III/1 (Cambridge, 1970–82).

*Fischer Weltgeschichte* II–IV (= *Die altorientalischen Reiche* I–III); V (= *Griechen und Perser*) (Frankfurt, 1965–67).

W. W. Hallo and W. K. Simpson, *The Ancient Near East: A History* (New York, 1971).

*W. Helck, *Die Beziehungen Ägyptens und Vorderasiens zur Ägäis bis ins 7. Jahrhundert v. Chr.* (Darmstadt, 1979).

M. T. Larsen, ed., *Power and Propaganda: A Symposium on Ancient Empires* (Copenhagen, 1979).

*H. J. Nissen, *Grundzüge einer Geschichte der Frühzeit des Vorderen Orients* (Darmstadt, 1983).

D. J. Wiseman, ed., *Peoples of Old Testament Times* (Oxford, 1973).

## (2) NEAR EAST (ASIA)

P. Garelli, *Le Proche-Orient asiatique, I: Des origines aux invasions des peuples de la mer* (Paris, 1969); II (with V. Nikiprowetzky): *Les empires mésopotamiens, Israel* (Paris, 1974).

*J. H. Hayes and J. M. Miller, eds., *Israelite and Judaean History* (Philadelphia, 1977).

H. Klengel, *Geschichte Syriens im 2 Jahrtausend v.u.Z.* I–III (Berlin, 1965–70).

N. Postgate, *The First Empires* (London, 1977).

H. Schmökel, *Geschichte des alten Vorderasien* (Leiden, 1957).

## (3) EGYPT

*J. Baines and J. Málek, *Atlas of Ancient Egypt* (Oxford, 1980).

J. von Beckerath, *Abriss der Geschichte des alten Ägypten* (Munich, 1971).

A. Gardiner, *Egypt of the Pharaohs* (Oxford, 1961).

W. Helck, *Die Beziehungen Ägyptens zu Vorderasien im 3. und 2. Jahrtausend v. Chr.* (Wiesbaden, 1971²).

*M. A. Hoffman, *Egypt Before the Pharaohs: The Prehistoric Foundation of Egyptian Civilization* (New York, 1979).

E. Hornung, *Geschichte als Fest* (Darmstadt, 1966).

———, *Grundzüge der ägyptischen Geschichte* (Darmstadt, 1965, 1978²).

E. Otto, *Ägypten. Der Weg des Pharaonenreiches* (Stuttgart, 1955²).

*B. G. Trigger, et al., *Ancient Egypt: A Social History* (Cambridge, 1983).

# b. Cultural History

## (1) NEAR EAST

R. McC. Adams, *The Evolution of Urban Society* (Chicago, 1966).

J. P. Asmussen, J. Laessoe, and C. Colpe, *Handbuch der Religionsgeschichte* I (Göttingen, 1971).

C. J. Bleeker and G. Widengren, eds., *Historia Religionum I: Religions of the Past* (Leiden, 1969).

H. Frankfort, *The Birth of Civilization in the Near East* (London, 1951).

———, *Kingship and the Gods* (Chicago, 1948; repr. 1978).

H. Frankfort, et al., *The Intellectual Adventure of Ancient Man* (Chicago, 1946) (= *Before Philosophy* [Harmondsworth, 1949]).

H. Hodges, *Technology in the Ancient World* (Harmondsworth, 1971).

D. and J. Oates, *The Rise of Civilization* (London, 1977).

H. Ringgren, *Religions of the Ancient Near East* (Philadelphia, 1973).

*W. Röllig, ed., *Altorientalische Literaturen* (Wiesbaden, 1978).

H. Schmökel, *Kulturgeschichte des Alten Orient* (Stuttgart, 1961).

Y. Yadin, *The Art of Warfare in Biblical Lands* I–II (Jerusalem, 1963).

## (2) MESOPOTAMIA

*E. Heinrich, *Tempel und Heiligtümer im Alten Mesopotamien* I–II (Berlin, 1982).

T. Jacobsen, *The Treasures of Darkness: A History of Mesopotamian Religion* (Chicago, 1976).

S. N. Kramer, *The Sumerians* (Chicago, 1963).

*J. Margueron, *Recherches sur les palais mésopotamiens de l'âge du bronze* I–II (Paris, 1982).

B. Meissner, *Babylonien und Assyrien* I–II (Heidelberg, 1920–25).

*H. J. Nissen and J. Renger, *Mesopotamien und seine Nachbarn* I–II (Berlin, 1982).

A. L. Oppenheim, *Ancient Mesopotamia* (Chicago, 1964, 1977²).

———, *Letters from Mesopotamia* (Chicago, 1967).

H. W. F. Saggs, *The Greatness that was Babylon* (London, 1962).

## (3) EGYPT

H. Brunner, *Grundzüge einer Geschichte der altägyptischen Literatur* (Darmstadt, 1966).

K. W. Butzer, *Early Hydraulic Civilization in Egypt* (Chicago, 1977).

A. R. David, *The Egyptian Kingdoms* (London, 1977).

*_____, The Ancient Egyptians: Religious Beliefs and Practices* (London, 1982).

R. Giveon, *The Impact of Egypt on Canaan* (Göttingen, 1978).

J. R. Harris, *The Legacy of Egypt* (London, 1971²).

W. C. Hayes, *The Sceptre of Egypt* I–II (New York, 1953–59).

*E. Hornung, *Conceptions of God in Ancient Egypt: The One and the Many* (London, 1982).

*T. G. H. James, *An Introduction to Ancient Egypt* (London, 1979²).

H. Kees, *Das alte Ägypten. Eine kleine Landeskunde* (Vienna, 1977³).

A. Lucas, *Ancient Egyptian Materials and Industries* (London, 1962⁴).

S. Morenz, *Ägyptische Religion* (Stuttgart, 1977²).

J. Pirenne, *Histoire de la civilisation de l'Égypte ancienne* I–III (Neuchâtel, 1961–63).

J. A. Wilson, *The Culture of Ancient Egypt* (Chicago, 1951).

W. Wolf, *Kulturgeschichte des alten Ägypten* (Stuttgart, 1962).

### (4) OTHER AREAS

P. Amiet, *Élam* (Auvers-sur-Oise, 1966).

K. Bittel, *Hattusha, the Capital of the Hittites* (New York, 1970).

H. Th. Bossert, *Altsyrien* (Heidelberg, 1951).

R. Collins, *The Medes and Persians* (London, 1974).

R. N. Frye, *The Heritage of Persia* (New York, 1963).

H. Gese, M. Höfner, and K. Rudolph, *Die Religionen Altsyriens, Altarabiens und der Mandäer* (Stuttgart, 1970).

A. Goetze, *Kleinasien* (Munich, 1957).

O. R. Gurney, *The Hittites* (Harmondsworth, 1961²).

_____, *Some Aspects of Hittite Religion* (Oxford, 1977).

*V. Haas, *Hethitische Berggötter und hurritische Steindämonen. Riten, Kulte und Mythen* (Mainz, 1982).

W. Hinz, *Das Reich Elam* (Stuttgart, 1964).

H. Klengel, *Geschichte und Kultur Altsyriens* (Heidelberg, 1966).

_____, *Zwischen Zelt und Palast. Die Begegnung von Nomaden und Sesshaften im alten Vorderasien* (Vienna, 1972).

S. Moscati, *The World of the Phoenicians* (London, 1968).

H. H. von der Osten, *Die Welt der Perser* (Stuttgart, 1966⁵).

A. Parrot, M. H. Chehab, and S. Moscati, *Die Phönizer* (Munich, 1978).

*F. Vallat, *Suse et l'Elam* (Paris, 1980).

G. Walser, ed., *Neuere Hethitherforschung* (Wiesbaden, 1964).

## c. Art History and Archeology

### (1) NEAR EAST

*R. McC. Adams, *Heartland of Cities* (Chicago, 1981).

P. Amiet, *Die Kunst des Alten Orient* (Freiburg, 1978).

C. Burney, *From Village to Empire. Introduction to Near Eastern Archaeology* (Oxford, 1977).

G. Contenau, *Manuel d'archéologie orientale* I–IV (Paris, 1927–47).

H. Frankfort, *The Art and Architecture of the Ancient Orient* (Harmondsworth, 1970⁴).

_____, *Cylinder Seals. A Documentary Essay on the Art and Religion of the Ancient Near East* (London, 1939; repr. 1965).

B. Hrouda, *Handbuch der Archäologie. Vorderasien* I (Munich, 1971).

*S. Lloyd, *The Archaeology of Mesopotamia* (London, 1983²).

K. R. Maxwell-Hyslop, *Western Asiatic Jewellery (c. 3000–612 B.C.)* (London, 1971).

A. Mootgat, *The Art of Ancient Mesopotamia* (London, 1969).

_____, *Einführung in die vorderasiatische Archäologie* (Darmstadt, 1971).

W. Orthmann, *Der Alte Orient* (Berlin, 1975).

A. Parrot, *Archéologie mésopotamienne* I–II (Paris, 1946–53).

_____, *Assur* (Munich, 1961).

_____, *Sumer* (Munich, 1960).

E. Strommenger and M. Hirmer, *Funf Jahrtausende Mesopotamien* (Munich, 1962).

### (2) EGYPT

H. Kayser, *Ägyptisches Kunsthandwerk* (Braunschweig, 1969).

K. Lange and M. Hirmer, *Egypt. Architecture, Sculpture, Painting in 3000 Years* (London/New York, 1968⁴).

J. Leclant, "Fouilles et Travaux en Égypte" (annual overview in the journal *Orientalia*).

K. Michalowski, *Ägypten Kunst und Kultur* (Freiburg, 1969).

C. Desroches Noblecourt, *Tutankhamen* (Harmondsworth, 1971).

H. Schäfer, *Principles of Egyptian Art* (Oxford, 1974).

W. S. Smith, *The Art and Architecture of Ancient Egypt* (Harmondsworth, 1981³; rev. W. K. Simpson).

J. Vandier, *Manuel d'archéologie égyptienne* (Paris, 1952ff.).

C. Vandersleyen, *Das Alte Ägypten* (Berlin, 1977).

### (3) OTHER CULTURES

U. Bahadir Alkim, *Anatolien* I (Genf, 1968).

E. Akurgal, *Die Kunst der Hethiter* (Munich, 1961).

B. Doe, *Southern Arabia* (London, 1971).

R. Ghirshman, *Perse (Proto-Iraniens, Mèdes, Achéménides)* (Paris, 1963).

A. Grohmann, *Arabien* (Munich, 1963).

A. Kempinski and M. Avi-Yonah, *Syrien-Palästina, II: Von der mittleren Bronzezeit bis zum Ende der Klassik (2200 v. Chr.-324 n. Chr.)* (Genf, 1978).

J. Mellaart, *The Neolithic of the Near East* (London, 1975).

W. Orthmann, *Untersuchungen zur späthethitischen Kunst* (Munich, 1971).

I. Perrot, *Syrien-Palästina I: von den Ursprungen bis zur Bronzezeit* (Genf, 1978).

E. Porada, *Ancient Iran* (London, 1965).

N. Robertson, *The Archeology of Cyprus: Recent Developments* (Park Ridge, 1975).

L. Vandenberghe, *Archéologie de l'Iran ancien* (Leiden, 1959).

## d. Reference Works, Text Editions, Bibliographies

### (1) REFERENCE WORKS

H. Bonnet, *Reallexikon der ägyptischen Religionsgeschichte* (Berlin, 1971²).

R. Borger, *Handbuch der Keilschriftliteratur* I–III (Berlin, 1967–75).

H. W. Haussig, ed., *Wörterbuch der Mythologie, I: Götter und Mythen im Vorderen Orient* (Stuttgart, 1965).

J. Hawkes, *Atlas of Ancient Archaeology* (London, 1974).

E. Hornung, *Einführung in die Ägyptologie* (Darmstadt, 1967).

O. Keel, *The Symbolism of the Biblical World: Ancient Near Eastern Iconography and the Biblical Psalms* (New York, 1978).

E. Laroche, *Catalogue des textes hittites* (Paris, 1971).

*Lexikon der Ägyptologie* (Wiesbaden, 1972– ).

G. Posener, *A Dictionary of Egyptian Civilization* (London, 1962).

J. B. Pritchard, ed., *The Ancient Near East in Pictures Relating to the Old Testament* (Princeton, 1969², with supplement).

*Reallexikon der Assyriologie* (Berlin, 1928ff.) (completed through vol. VI [L]).

W. Röllig, ed., *Répertoire géographique des textes cunéiformes* (Wiesbaden, 1974ff.).

### (2) LITERATURE OF TEXTS IN TRANSLATION

*A. Barucq and F. Daumas, *Hymnes et prières de l'Égypte ancienne* (Paris, 1980).

W. Beyerlin, ed., *Near Eastern Religious Texts Relating to the Old Testament* (Philadelphia, 1978).

J. H. Breasted, *Ancient Records of Egypt* I–V (Chicago, repr. 1962).

A. Caquot, et al., *Textes ougaritiques, I: Mythes et légendes* (Paris, 1974).

H. Donner and W. Röllig, *Kanaanäische und aramäische Inschriften* I–III (Wiesbaden, 1976³).

J. C. L. Gibson, *Textbook of Syrian Semitic Inscriptions, I: Hebrew and Moabite Inscriptions* (Oxford, 1971); *II: Aramaic Inscriptions* (Oxford, 1975); *III: Phoenician Inscriptions* (Oxford, 1982).

A. K. Grayson, *Assyrian Royal Inscriptions* I–II (Wiesbaden, 1972–76).

*O. Kaiser, ed., *Texte aus der Umwelt des Alten Testaments* I– (Gütersloh, 1982– ).

S. N. Kramer, ed., *Mythologies of the Ancient World* (Garden City, 1961).

*R. Lebrun, *Hymnes et prières hittites* (Louvain, 1980).

M. Lichteim, *Ancient Egyptian Literature* I–III (Berkeley, 1973–80).

*Littératures anciennes du Proche-Orient* (Paris, 1967ff.).

J. B. Pritchard, ed., *Ancient Near Eastern Texts Relating to the Old Testament* (Princeton, 1969³, with supplement).

M.-J. Seux, *Hymnes et prières aux dieux de Babylonie et d'Assyrie* (Paris, 1976).

W. K. Simpson, ed., *The Literature of Ancient Egypt* (New Haven/London, 1972).

### (3) BIBLIOGRAPHIES

*Annual Egyptological Bibliography* (Leiden, 1947ff.).

"Bibliographie" (in *Archiv für Orientforschung* 25–26 [1978–79]).

J. H. Hospers, ed., *A Basic Bibliography for the Study of the Semitic Languages* I– (Leiden, 1973– ).

"Keilschriftbibliographie" (annual review in the journal *Orientalia*).

# B. History of the Ancient Near East from the Time of Alexander the Great to the Beginning of the Second Century A.D.

*by M. A. Beek*

## 1. ALEXANDER THE GREAT

In the second century B.C., a Jewish writer gave expression to the impression Alexander the Great's campaign of conquest had made on his contemporaries and on those who shortly after had heard about it. In apocalyptic style, looking back as a visionary, he conjured up the moving image of a he-goat who had come from the west "across the face of the whole earth, without touching the ground" (Dan. 8:5). From a distance of about a century and a half in time, he saw the rushing speed with which the world conqueror had moved over the nations of Asia. A chronicle writer tells that Alexander III of Macedonia, standing on his ship as it approached the coast of Asia Minor, threw his spear into the ground of the part of the world he wanted to castigate and conquer. This happened in 334 B.C., and after only seven years he had crossed the Indus with his soldiers. With that he had reached what in the mind of the writer of Daniel 8 had to be "the whole earth." See ill. 92.

That this "earth" and in particular the structure of the immense empire of the Medes and Persians had not remained untouched the writer knew just as well as we who are able to follow the events between 334 and 327 B.C. in detail from a greater distance. The scars of slaughtered people and destructive war have remained visible. Even today the so-called pan-Hellenic retaliation against Persepolis in 331/330 reveals the mercilessness with which the Greeks avenged the misery and shame that Xerxes' invasion of Europe had brought upon their land and people. The desire to settle old scores was one of the impelling motives of Alexander the Great's actions against the Persians, and

apparently this ambition enjoyed the support and sympathy of many Greeks. When Alexander died on June 13, 323, at the age of thirty-two, he left behind him a world whose structure had been widely disrupted. The new societal structure, whose contours were becoming visible, would be altogether different; certainly externally there would be no similarity with what used to be.

One could ask to what extent this power of an unusually strong personality was determinative for the course of history. It is undeniable that situations such as the inner decay of the realm of the Medes and Persians, which had announced itself long before Darius III's downfall, favored Alexander. However, not everyone is capable of using and taking full advantage of circumstances. Alexander's contemporaries experienced his great deeds as an eruption of superhuman, volcanic forces. His erudition demonstrated that he had been taught by Aristotle, his military ability that before his eyes he had the ideal of Achilles. Physically and spiritually he was tireless; he possessed the vision of both the strategist and the politician. He could be alternatingly magnanimous and cruel. In a bout of drunkenness he killed the friend who had saved his life in a precarious situation. His behavior and actions were as arbitrary as those of the powerful gods his subjects worshiped. So Alexander could obtain a place in the world of the gods, who with impunity do what they want, having no regard for good and evil.

We do not know what new society Alexander had in mind in the last days of his life. Did he dream of a world empire, having as its center ancient Babylon, the city where he was staying when he was struck by a fatal illness? In any case he ordered the city that had been destroyed by Cyrus to be restored to glory. We are better informed from direct information about the results of Alexander's actions than about his intentions. Contemporary written sources are scarce and shed little light. Whatever the contemporaries perceived and recorded is only fragmentarily preserved and used by history writers of later generations. We are dependent on information provided by Diodorus in *Bibliotheca,* book 17, Curtius Rufus in *Historiae Alexandri,* Plutarch in *Vita Alexandri,* Arrianus in *Anabasis* and *Indica,* and Justinus in an excerpt from Pompeius Trogus. It is certain that Alexander aimed at an empire that would include many nations and cultures, not only in a peaceful coexistence, but also and especially through integration. His marriage with the Bactrian princess Roxanne set an example that was shortly followed by thousands of Macedonians. So a process of syncretism and assimilation was started, but with Greek culture setting the pace, at least in the cities and among people of rank and intellectuals. We should not be misled by the information of those and about those who were able to make themselves heard. We may assume that in the countryside life continued as if little had changed in the world. Here people kept speaking their own tongue and continued to hold on to their own traditions. To others, such as the Jews, hellenization became a challenge, the concern being to maintain one's own identity in the dress of the new culture. We shall see below how this became the occasion for sharp confrontation and fruitful reflection.

Alexander was without successor. A few months after he died, the child he had conceived by Roxanne was born. Thirteen years later the child and his mother were murdered by Cassander to ensure that the child would never play a role. There were those who presented themselves as successor, high military officers who quarreled about the power and who went down in history under the name "diadochi." The writer of Daniel 8 saw them as "four conspicuous horns toward the four winds of heaven," who took the place of the great horn of the he-goat. He must have been thinking of the situation after the battle of Ipsus in 301 that had resulted in a temporary stabilization. The territories were divided among the four. Ptolemy maintained himself in Egypt, Lysimachus in Asia Minor and Europe, Cassander in Macedonia, and Seleucus was able to add the territory of Syria to the realm he had ruled over from Babylonia.

---

## LITERATURE

P. Cloche, *La dislocation d'un empire. Les premiers successeurs d'Alexandre le Grand (323–281/280 avant J.-C.)* (Paris, 1959).

F. Schachermeyer, *Alexander der Grosse. Das Problem seiner Persönlichkeit und seines Wirkens* (Vienna, 1973).

---

## 2. THE PTOLEMIES

We shall now focus our attention on the Ptolemies and the Seleucids. Already in 281 B.C. Lysimachus was crushingly defeated by Seleucus I and all of Asia Minor passed to the Seleucids. Cassander's dynasty came to an end just four years after his death. His realm did not play a politically significant role. Palestine's fate was for a long time determined by its position as buffer state between two large powers, who waged war for the possession of this, in many respects, desirable territory, with the "beautiful land" and its population suffering under these wars.

From a distance, Egypt gave the impression of being a stable society, neither disturbed by wars within its own borders nor by rebellions. Alexander had been greeted as a liberator of the Persian yoke that had more and more been felt as a burden. After the founding of the city which he called Alexandria, he went to the oasis of Siwah to consult the oracle of Amon. He was addressed by the priest as son of Amon, which was very significant, not the least for Alexander himself, on account of the identification of this Egyptian god with Zeus. He left Ptolemy, the son of Lagua, behind as governor of the satrapy of Egypt. After Alexander's death, Ptolemy consolidated his position and began to rule as a pharaoh who appeared to continue the traditions of an independent Egypt. He tied this to the glory of the deified Alexander by having his body entombed at Memphis from where his son later brought it to Alexandria. The tomb became a pilgrimage shrine. He did not found new cities, except Ptolemais, which was named after him, on the western bank of the Nile in Upper Egypt. Ptolemais, Alexandria, and the old Naucratis in the Delta had their own governments; the other cities, though given the title "polis" in combination with divine names, were dependent on the Greek district governor.

The first Ptolemaic pharaohs, with the added names of Soter (305–282), Philadelphus (282–246), and Euergetes I (246–222), were good rulers interested in the welfare and the power of the realm entrusted to their care and guided by the interests of the people and not by forcing an ideology upon the population. They ruled as pharaohs, but did not know the language of their subjects. They spoke exclusively the Greek based on Attic, called Koine, and this remained so until Cleopatra, the last pharaoh of Egypt. Therefore they needed interpreters, but also interpretation of the religious ideas which since time immemorial had lived among the Egyptians and were recorded in the hieroglyphic scripts that were not accessible to them.

So a high priest of Heliopolis, known as Manetho, was commissioned by Ptolemy I Soter to write a history of Egypt. This work, entitled *Aigyptiaka*, has perished, but Josephus has preserved fragments of it in his apology of Judaism, *Contra Apionem*, and an excerpt of it with the list of the dynasties has survived. Manetho's division into thirty or thirty-one dynasties and his mode of transcription of the royal names were generally accepted, giving him a permanent influence. For the rest we know little of this man who was prepared to divulge to the Greek king what the priest-scholars might have preferred to keep as a secret science.

The question has been raised whether the Greek translation of the Old Testament may not likewise have been made by order of the king of Egypt, as is stated in the Letter of Aristeas. The letter seems to have been written by Aristeas, a courtier of Ptolemy II Philadelphus, to his brother Philokrates. In brief the contents are as follows: librarian Demetrius of Phaleron brought to the king's attention that the library of Alexandria

had only poor quality translations of the Jewish law. After negotiations, which concerned the freeing of slaves among other things, the high priest at Jerusalem was found willing to send seventy-two scholars to prepare a new translation of the Law from Hebrew into Greek. In Alexandria they were treated to a meal at which they gave evidence of their sharp intellect and wisdom. After that they completed their work in seven days and it was admired both by the king and by the representatives of the Jewish community.

The purpose of Aristeas's letter was to make propaganda for a translation that had been preceded by many other translations. The historical value of the document is very limited. But one item of information is to be taken seriously. The execution of the translation was apparently not due to needs existing within a Jewish community that was no longer able to handle Hebrew, but to a government order. The Jewish community in Alexandria was numerous, and, moreover, for centuries there had been Jewish colonies in Egypt, even with their own temple. Together they were a part of the population whose presence had to be reckoned with. It was in line with the policy of the Ptolemies that they had to overcome a lot of resistance on the part of Jews, because a translation also implied a betrayal since it meant the disclosure of secrets to the outside world.

In one respect Ptolemy I tried to realize an ideal of Alexander, namely, the institution of the worship of Serapis (or Sarapis). Opinions vary about the origin of this name. Most likely it is a combination of Osiris and Apis. The deity, depicted as a bearded Zeus with a corn measure on his head, was worshiped in the Serapeion at Alexandria, a temple long regarded as one of the seven wonders of the world. But elsewhere in Egypt temples were also made for him, and later the Serapis cult spread far into Greece and Italy. In conjunction with a story about the visit of Vespasian to Alexandria, Tacitus relates in his *Historiae* (4.81–84) what he had heard about the origin of a religion that found greater acceptance among the Greeks and Romans than among the native population of Egypt. According to Tacitus, legend has it that Ptolemy was divinely ordered to obtain the image of the deity from Sinope on the south coast of the Black Sea, an expedition that entailed a lot of trouble and time. The story does not fit the picture of a pragmatic ruler such as Ptolemy. But it does agree with his syncretistic goals: in Serapis the Egyptians were able to recognize their own Osiris and the Apis bull who had became immortal in Osiris, while for the Greeks he exhibited the features of Zeus, a sun-god, a healer, and the sovereign chief god of the pantheon.

Already under the first Ptolemy, Alexandria must have evolved into a center of culture, with its museum that had grown from being a temple of the Muses to a university with scholars living there and enjoying board and privileges, especially the large library. As to the library, Ptolemy was similar to Ashurbanipal, the great collector. Instead of collecting clay tablets, Ptolemy collected scrolls of books, preferably the originals. The story goes that from Athens he obtained the works of Aeschylus, Sophocles, and Euripides in order to have copies made. However, so the story goes, he sent back the copies and kept the originals for a collection that was later judged to contain a half million scrolls. He was more than willing to forfeit the large sum of money which he had had to post as bond with the Greek state librarian.

The Greeks behaved on the throne as if they were pharaohs. Not only did they adopt the cultic titles of the deified rulers, but they also practiced intermarriage with close relatives. Ptolemy II repudiated his wife and married his sister Arsinoe, who was given the title "philadelphos," meaning "lover of the brother." After her death and acceptance into the world of the gods, she and her husband were honored as *theoi adelphoi*, brother gods.

During the reign of this Ptolemy, an event happened whose significance must have eluded the contemporaries. In the year 273 a delegation from Rome arrived in Egypt. On that occasion a trade agreement was made, and with that the first step had been taken in a course toward Roman interference in the affairs of the Near East. It was the beginning of a patient, persistent, and originally peaceful penetration, which after two and a half centuries would lead to the total Roman domination of Egypt.

## LITERATURE

H. I. Bell, *Egypt from Alexander the Great to the Arab Conquest. A Study in the Diffusion and Decay of Hellenism* (Oxford, 1948).

E. R. Bevan, *A History of Egypt under the Ptolemaic Dynasty* (London, 1927).

_____, *The House of Ptolemy* (London, repr. 1968).

A. Bouclé-Leclercq, *Histoire des Lagides* (Paris, 1903–1907; repr. 1963).

P. M. Fraser, *Ptolemaic Alexandria* I–III (Oxford, 1972).

P. E. Kahle, *The Cairo Geniza* (Oxford, 1959$^2$), pp. 209–264.

G. J. F. Kater-Sibbes and M. J. Vermaseren, *Apis, I: The Monuments of the Hellenistic-Roman Period from Egypt. II: Monuments from ouside Egypt* (Leiden, 1975).

B. H. Stricker, *De Brief van Aristeas* (Amsterdam, 1956).

E. Van 't Dack, *Reizen, expedities en emigratie uit Italië naar Ptolemaeïsch Egypte* (Brussels, 1980).

C. E. Visser, *Götter und Kulte im ptolemäischen Alexandrien* (Amsterdam, 1938).

## 3. THE SELEUCIDS

We cannot continue the history of Egypt without first focusing our attention on the developments within and around the neighboring realm of the Seleucids. A striking difference from the actions of the Ptolemies is that they literally made a name for themselves by the founding of new cities. On the east bank of the Tigris, about 40 kilometers (25 mi.) from modern Baghdad, Seleucus I founded the residence Seleucia ("the city belonging to Seleucus") in 312 B.C. The plan of making Babylon a new center was abandoned, perhaps because the worsening salinization of the ground had made living there less attractive. Excavation has shown, however, that Seleucus used the bricks of the dismantled temple tower of Babylon for the construction of an amphitheater. Of enduring significance was the establishment of Antioch, named after the father of Seleucus. This city on the Orontes became the great residence of the Seleucid kingdom. Outstripping Alexandria in glory, it remained until A.D. 500 the most important city of the east.

Seleucus I, surnamed Nicator, was succeeded by his son Antiochus, who ruled 281–261. He had established a reputation as the commander of the cavalry in the battle of Ipsus. On account of his victory over the Galatians in 275 he received the honorary title Soter (savior). This particular battle has become famous for its use of elephants. But this Antiochus made his impact through the founding of cities, several of which were named after him, rather than from military exploits.

The first Seleucids faced the same problems as the first Ptolemies. They had subjects whose language they did not understand. The literature and the history of the country were recorded, at least for the most part, in a cuneiform script they were unable to read. So they too needed the help of interpreters and native scholars to become acquainted with the traditions and culture of Mesopotamia. Antiochus I found Berossus, a priest of Marduk-Bel, willing to provide the desired information in a great work, the *Babyloniaka*, which comprises the history from the beginning to Alexander the Great, a period of 468,215 years according to the time reckoning of Berossus. Like that of Manetho, Berossus's work has survived only in fragments, which can be found in Josephus and Eusebius. The Seleucids not only had to deal with the spiritual heirs of the Mesopotamian and Persian culture; their realm was a conglomerate of many peoples, all of whom had been able to maintain their own culture and religion under the tolerant regime of the Achaemenids. The spiritual situation in Jerusalem, about which, comparatively speaking, we are best informed, is a clear example. Though continuing this policy, the Seleucids, as we shall see below, were forced by circumstances to become intolerant.

For the Seleucids themselves and also for the Jewish historiographers, a new era started with Seleucus I. The Seleucid calendar, also adopted by the writer of 2 Maccabees, begins in the fall of 312. For a long time this calendar has been determinative for the chronology, in some parts of the Middle East even until the modern age.

The Seleucid kings were Greeks who were conscious that they had taken over a world empire such as that of the Assyrians and Babylonians. This realm was enormously vast, stretching from the coast of the Mediterranean to the Indus and from the Caspian Sea to the Persian Gulf. Attempts to invade Europe and to bring even parts of Egypt under their scepter failed, not only weakening the empire but also contributing to its collapse. The waging of extremely expensive wars seemed to be the first and most important duty of the king. Between 312 and 129 fourteen Seleucid kings ruled; of these two were assassinated, ten lost their life in battle or during a campaign, and only two died a natural death.

The king owed his throne to heredity, but he was expected to show his mettle by his military achievements. For that he mustered a large and mobile army. It is told of Seleucus I that in one of his battles he commanded 20,000 foot soldiers, 12,000 horsemen, 480 elephants, and 100 chariots; there is no reason to regard these figures as exaggerated. Such an army consisted not only of trained professional military men and mercenaries, but also of soldiers conscripted from subjected nations and cities, whose governments were obligated to provide such soldiers, in addition to paying the customary tribute. Such a government was formed from the native population, but the Seleucid king kept the final authority for himself. His preference was determined by the size of the tribute the people were willing to pay. This policy resulted in all kinds of intrigues. Again we are indebted to information about the tensions in Jerusalem as an indication of how much fighting and suffering there was also elsewhere. The Seleucid king was dependent on the loyalty of the regional or local governments. They had to make sure, by collecting and paying the "phoros" (tribute), that the treasury of the kings was always full. Their loyalty promoted the hellenization process considerably.

Skipping many battles and attempts to enlarge the territory and to maintain the status quo by means of marriages, we now come to the rule of a king whose actions caused a turnabout in the fate of Palestine and indirectly caused the Maccabean war of 167–164. In 223 Antiochus II succeeded his brother Seleucus II, taking over a realm that was inwardly weakened and threatened at its borders. He came to be called "The Great" after several successful military campaigns between 212 and 205 that had brought him to the Indus as a second Alexander.

The historiographer who assesses his deeds regards him as far from great, but in the eyes of his contemporaries he was a king-general par excellence. In the exercise of his sovereignty he recognized no restrictions, acting according to the principle already formulated by Seleucus I: "a royal decision is always just." So he decided all matters of war and peace, without being responsible to anyone. He surrounded himself with a court of "friends" who were arbitrarily taken in or sent away. He could promote or demote them in rank. Outward signs of dignity, such as a purple robe, a gold crown, a gold buckle, showed the degree of dignity the "friends" enjoyed. They gave advice and it was up to the king to accept or ignore it.

Antiochus III availed himself of a weakening Egypt under Ptolemy IV Philopator (222–205) that continued under Ptolemy V Epiphanes, who had come to the throne as a child. To be sure, in the year 217 the Egyptians still won a significant victory over Antiochus III in the battle at Raphia, but ultimately that victory made no difference. Availing himself of politically favorable factors, in about 200 B.C. Antiochus was able to bring all of Palestine under his rule, including Jerusalem. On that occasion he allowed Jerusalem certain privileges that are recorded in a letter to a certain Ptolemy, a man who had defected from the Egyptian side to Antiochus. The letter is in reality a decree of far-reaching importance, which is one of the reasons Josephus entered it verbatim in his *Jewish Antiquities* (12.3.3). For Jerusalem this was absolutely the end of the period of Egyptian dominance, though that dominance had not been oppressive. From now on they had to deal with the rulers who held sway and waged war from Antioch and were willing to support the spiritual authority of the high priest as long as this agreed with their own interests.

For a more distant future, Antiochus III's defeat against the Romans was of decisive importance. Not even the counsel of Hannibal, who in 196 had

sought refuge with him, could protect him against Rome. In 190 Antiochus was dealt a crushing defeat at Magnesia on the Sipylus, and from that time on the Seleucid realm ceased to be a threat to the west. In the peace of Apamea in 188 Seleucia lost all of Asia Minor west of the Taurus, was compelled to destroy its fleet, and was forced to pay a war indemnity of 15,000 talents. This amount was so massive that it could not be paid out of the normal taxes, however high they were, and thus resulted in a chronic lack of money. Therefore the Seleucids resorted to means that added to the unrest among the population. It is known that in antiquity many entrusted their savings to the temple, considering it a safe place. Especially widows deposited their money there, as it were under the protection of the deity: robbing a temple was regarded as inexcusable sacrilege. Antiochus III was murdered while robbing a Baal temple in the vicinity of Susa. His successor, Seleucus IV Philopator (187–175), sent Heliodorus to the temple in Jerusalem to find out about the treasures it contained. The writer of 2 Maccabees 3 has left us a vivid account of the failure of this mission, which for the time being foiled a raid on the temple treasury.

Antiochus IV Epiphanes (175–164) knew that the Romans stayed put and refused to be driven from wherever they had gained a foothold. Ancient historiographers are ambivalent in their judgment of him. Jewish historiography sees him as the enemy of the religion of the fathers, but Tacitus calls him a man who attempted to teach sound morals to a terrible people, but who unfortunately did not succeed in that attempt. It will always remain difficult to present fairly this whimsical ruler whose image seems forever based on his role in the desecration of the temple of Jerusalem in 167. See ill. 93.

He was a son of Antiochus III, who in 189 was forced to send him as a hostage to Rome. His stay in the world center of the future failed to give him a sound awareness of the balance of powers. Only a little insight into Roman ambitions would have kept him from interfering in Egypt. In the years 170–168 he was able to occupy much of the weakened empire of Ptolemy VI Philometor (180–145). When after the battle of Pydna he threatened even Alexandria, however, the Romans had had enough. An envoy of the Romans appeared in the army camp of Antiochus, ordering him summarily on behalf of the senate to leave Egypt. According to the chronicler this confused the king, who asked time to think it over. Then the Roman, Popilius Laenas, with his staff drew a circle around the king and demanded that he decide on the spot. All that Antiochus could do was give in. From now on Rome would not tolerate a disruption of the power equilibrium, but wait patiently until both Egypt and the Near East would fall into its lap like ripe apples.

Antiochus's deeds will be discussed elsewhere. It is enough to mention that the king once more would prove to be a capable general. He went to war against the Parthians, but during that campaign succumbed to an illness. After his death there was a measure of stabilization, and it is appropriate to ask which spiritual developments in the countries around Palestine had come to a close or were still going on.

---

## LITERATURE

E. R. Bevan, *The House of Seleucus* I–II (London, 1902; repr. 1966).

E. Bi(c)kerman(n), *Institutions des Séleucides* (Paris, 1938).

A. Bouclé-Leclercq, *Histoire des Séleucides* (Paris, 1913; repr. 1963).

L. Casson, *Travel in the Ancient World* (London, 1974).

P. Klose, *Die völkerrechtliche Ordnung der hellenistischen Staatenwelt in der Zeit von 280–168 v. Chr.* (Munich, 1972).

M. I. Rostovcev (= Rostovtzeff), *The Social and Economic History of the Hellenistic World* I–III (Oxford, 1941; rev. P. M. Fraser, Oxford, 1972).

R. Schubert, *Die Quellen zur Geschichte der Diadochenzeit* (Leipzig, 1964²).

---

## 4. RELIGION AND CULTURE

Under the Ptolemies, Egypt remained what it always had been: a land whose western border was protected by the desert and which only from the east, from Palestine, had to fear an invasion. Guarded by natural borders it preserved its own character. The papyri offer a unique and rich source of information about daily life in the time of the Ptolemies. Since 1778, when the first written sheet of papyrus appeared on the market, papyrology has evolved into a formidable auxiliary science for historians and philologists.

The dry desert sand was an ideal storage place for the papyri. They are not found in humid places, unless they have been preserved through accidental circumstances, such as partial combustion (which changed the structure of the material and made it more resistant against decay). They have been found in garbage dumps, ruins, graves, and wrapped around the mummies of holy crocodiles—wherever they could not be affected by moisture. Today, if we speak of papyrology, we think of texts in Greek and Latin, but papyri texts written in Demotic, Coptic, and hieroglyphics have likewise been preserved. They accompany Egypt's history from 311 B.C. to the middle of the eighth century A.D.

The data from the period of the first Ptolemies are still relatively scarce; after that they become more numerous, in number as well as in content. There is no facet of the daily life of the ordinary citizen, from important to unimportant, that is not represented. The many texts containing fragments of the classical Greek writers are an indication that the erudite inhabitants occupied themselves with the tragedians, with Pindar, Sappho, Plato, and Aristotle.

These papyri are of inestimable value for our knowledge of the social and economic circumstances in which people lived. Historiographers as a rule limited themselves to writing about events that happened in the upper classes, uninterested in the life of the ordinary person. Their interest was focused on what they regarded as permanently significant. The writer who jotted down a note on his papyrus sheet, recorded an appointment, wrote down a complaint or a declaration of love, has thus, unawares, given later generations a glimpse of the life of his time, ordinary life with the thousand and one things that are of passing significance. Spontaneously an official kept a diary or an administrator drew conclusions from regulations, thinking of irrigation or land distribution.

These texts and fragments of texts enable us to put the pieces together so that they constitute a faithful representation of life in Egypt under the Ptolemies. Counting all the fragments, we come to at least tens of thousands of papyri, and the number would have been much larger if Alexandria, owing to its humid location, had not been unsuitable as a storage place for this vulnerable material. That does not mean that we are not extensively informed about cultural and religious life in Alexandria. However, the sources of this information are from outside this city, in which so many temples of Egyptian and Greek gods had promoted syncretism.

The general impression created by the extant material is that the Greeks had no difficulty accepting the cult of the deified gods, perhaps because for them the boundaries between people and gods had already for the most part been obliterated. The native population continued worshiping the gods as they had done from ancient times, and one cannot say that the hesitant beginnings of Hellenism appeared to them as a reformation. Rather, the worship of Sarapis and Isis fascinated the Greeks, leading to the introduction of the cult of Egyptian gods into Europe. So about 200 B.C. Egypt and Greece had a lively exchange of each other's spiritual possessions.

As to life in the realm of the Seleucids, we must do without information from papyri and rely more on chroniclers and—in view of the important place of the Maccabean war in Jewish history—on the indirect light that is shed from Jerusalem on the actions of the Syrians. It is obvious that there was no less writing in the realm of the Seleucids: the ponderous bureaucratic apparatus made correspondence necessary. The clay tablet had yielded to parchment, leather, wood, and potsherds. This process had started already during the reign of the first Achaemenids, when Aramaic had become the medium of diplomacy, and this language required the use of the writing material that was doomed to perish in moist ground. Yet enough data remain that we are able, though in less detail, to follow the development of ideas and religious conceptions.

During the entire second century B.C., cities, territories, and states were able to maintain a measure of independence, though at the price of a heavy tribute. Numerous inscriptions on monuments and coins, which are supplemented by reliefs and murals, steles and symbols, attest to the fact that the various peoples were able to preserve their own culture, religion, and language. Not all writing systems have been deciphered, but whatever has become legible contributes to the formation of the multicolored mosaic of religions and legal customs in the Seleucid kingdom. Fragments occasionally enable us to reconstruct a local history, and it may be assumed that similar developments happened in places about which we lack such evidence.

Aramaic is the most important linguistic medium for providing information. It is a very old language that in the kingdom of the Medes and Persians became the language of diplomacy. After the conquests of Alexander it continued to be spoken and written from Asia Minor to the Red Sea and in the east as far as the Euphrates and Tigris. Numerous sites where texts have been uncovered attest to it. It is highly unlikely that the native population of these places would have spoken another language and only have used Aramaic for writing, as has sometimes been suggested. The language exhibits regional dialects. Presumably in the course of time it was also subject to changes. Yet despite the hellenization, Aramaic remained a language that was used in all corners of the empire.

Extremely important are the data derived from places at the intersections of caravan routes. These roads were used by trade caravans and in their wake followed diplomatic couriers, pilgrims, and tourists. There was a great deal of travel, in part out of curiosity, in order, after the manner of Herodotus, to obtain knowledge about the land and its peoples. But it was especially trading that did not stop at national boundaries, not being held back either by tolls that had to be paid along the routes. So staple towns with agencies came into being, and these evolved into trade colonies. Believers in various gods took up their residence around them, worshiping the gods of the places they came from, and often receiving permission from the city government to build a shrine, preferably on the outside against the city wall or outside the wall. This did not mean that the various religions were isolated from each other. There was an awareness that under different names the same gods were worshiped. Even as in Egypt, the gods were identified with each other.

Bilingual inscriptions from the famed trade center Palmyra demonstrate that the most important god of the Palmyrene pantheon, Bel, was identified with the Greek Zeus. Bel, however, was the same as Marduk, who was worshiped in Babylon. A transportation of types of worships took place, peacefully and gradually through commercial traffic, less peacefully through movement of troops and encamping of garrisons. It happened that two gods bore the same name and yet were not regarded as the same by their devotees. In such cases their name and the geographical origin of their worship are explicitly mentioned, a phenomenon also found in the Old Testament.

Religiously the Seleucid regime characterized itself by tolerance, continuing the policy of the Achaemenids. Under Antiochus I, Buddhism was active in a mission effort that was in no way hindered. The worship of the Egyptian gods made its entry without any objections; the Seleucid kings were prepared to support every local shrine. As a matter of course they worshiped their own gods first and built temples for them. Daphne south of Antioch became the special center for the worship of Apollo, and feasts and games were organized there, as much in honor of the Seleucids as of the deity. The Greek rulers showed respect for the gods of Mesopotamia and had a high regard for the astrologers of Babylon. They sought their counsel in setting the date for important events, such as the founding of a new city. The kings received titles indicating their apotheosis, being called "epiphanes" and "theos," yet the people were not compelled to worship them as gods; every local community was left to follow its own discretion. There was no such thing as a state religion.

The competitive worship of gods rarely led to serious conflicts. If these did occur within the groups themselves and the government became involved, it might seem as if there was intolerance. In the ancient world the worship of one deity did not exclude that of an other. Often a devotee, in order to be certain, sought the aid of a number of gods at the same time.

From the standpoint of religious history the inscriptions from Hatra are significant in more than one respect. The impressive ruins of this city, still only partially excavated, lie now desolate in the steppe between the Tigris and Euphrates, about 100 kilometers (60 mi.) southwest of Mosul. Until shortly before the destruction of Hatra by the Sassanids in A.D. 241, Eastern Aramaic was still in vogue as the language of inscriptions. The inscriptions are to be dated in the first centuries after Christ, but the information they give about the worship of deities must be considerably older. In addition to names of gods, we find here the phenomenon of a triad of gods. It occurs also at Palmyra, where there was the triad of Bel, Yarchi-bol, and Agli-bol. Of these, Bel is the most powerful, ruling over cosmos and vegetation; he is creature- and nature-god at the same time. Yarchi-bol was thought of as the sun-god, and Agli-bol— whose name is related to the Hebrew word for bull calf—as the moon-god. It is remarkable in Hatra that a goddess was part of the triad, so that one could almost speak of Our Lady, Our Lord, and the Son of Our Lord.

Recent decipherments and investigations have also turned languages other than Aramaic and Greek into rich sources of information. One such language, spoken and written along the south coast of Asia Minor, is Luwian. It is the oldest language of that territory, recorded in various writing systems, of which the last is derived from a Greek example. It was spoken in Lycia and Cilicia, districts that had already felt the impact of Hellenism before the coming of Alexander the Great. Inscriptions and numismatic data demonstrate that this area successfully defended the considerable independence it possessed, until in A.D. 43 the area was joined with Pamphylia and made into a Roman province. Arrianus, who between A.D. 130 and 138 ruled the province of Cappadocia as *legatus Augusti pro praetore*, wrote about this history. Without embellishment, in pure Attic, he wrote about what he had heard and seen—which was not a little. Through him we know that from 295 to 197 B.C. Lycia was still under the Egyptians, but Antiochus III then annexed it to his realm. The situation of this territory was for a long time comparable to that of Palestine. While Egypt defended its trade interests on the south coast of Asia Minor, Mesopotamia from ancient times possessed trade colonies in Cappadocia. So Cilicia functioned as border, meeting place, and battle ground until Roman authority was established.

The inscriptions in Luwian confirm for the most part the reports of Arrianus and add authentic data to it. Here too we see that despite the changes in rulers the same institutions continued. New rulers took over the existing administration without making drastic changes. Also in religion conservative forces remained operative. A list of priests from Corycus on the south coast opposite Cyprus contains Luwian names which demonstrate that especially the god Runt was worshiped (between 250 and 175 B.C.). This god was later identified with Hermes. In the western heartland around Lycia the moon-god Arma was worshiped. The proper names in the inscriptions indicate that the chief deity was called Tarchunt; next to it in Cilicia and surroundings the deity Shantra was mentioned.

Luwian is related to Lydian and must be reckoned among the Anatolian subgroup of the Indo-European languages. At first Lydia was under the sovereignty of the Seleucids. From 190 it belonged to Pergamum and from 133 to the Roman province of Asia. Lycaonian was the language of a territory in the center of Asia Minor, with the cities Iconium, Derbe, and Lystra located along the great trade route to Syria. Paul traveled this road, and the travel report in Acts 14:11 mentions Lycaonian, of which so far we know nothing. Archeological discoveries have, however, increasingly elucidated what could be surmised from other evidence, namely, that in the first centuries B.C. Asia Minor served a unique function in the cultural exchanges among the three parts of the world. The presence of a great number of nationalists, who despite foreign domination were able to preserve their own character, did not hinder this bridging function.

The Seleucids had to reckon with this reality. The order in their realm was dependent on the integrity of the Greek rulers and the loyalty of the elite of the native people they were able to involve in the government. The enormously vast realm could not be kept intact without a bureaucracy and the apparatus of officials that went

with it. What is remarkable is that the high officials and the intellectuals, including the priestly class, proved receptive to Greek culture, more than might have been expected. Proper names were given a Greek form; even institutions that were uniquely national in character were given Greek names. The terms "synagogue" and "sanhedrin" that came in vogue among the Jews are an astounding example of this Grecization.

## LITERATURE

U. Bianchi, *The Greek Mysteries* (Leiden, 1976).

F. Dunand, *Le culte d'Isis dans le bassin oriental de la Méditerranée, I: Le culte d'Isis et les Ptolemées; II: Le culte d'Isis en Grèce; III: Le culte d'Isis en Asie Mineure* (Leiden, 1973).

P. C. Hammond, *The Nabataeans: Their History, Culture and Archaeology* (Gothenburg, 1973).

J. Hoftijzer, *Religio Aramaica: Godsdienstige verschijneselen in Arameese teksten* (Leiden, 1968).

Ph. H. J. Houwink ten Cate, *The Luwian Population Groups of Lycia and Cilicia Aspera during the Hellenistic Period* (Leiden, 1961).

L. Vidman, *Sylloge inscriptionum religionis Isiacae et Sarapiacae* (Berlin, 1969).

## 5. THE END OF EGYPT

Having provided a bird's-eye view of tenacious traditions and renewals that slowly took over, we now return to the facade of the happenings as they are recorded in the equally necessary as well as misleading table of dates. For behind these events hide the forces of which only posterity is aware that they have determined the future. The chronicle writer was interested in events that later served no purpose except as crutches for the memory. He enlightens us about conflicts that from within weakened both the kingdom of the Ptolemies and that of the Seleucids. We shall not trace this development in detail, but only illustrate it with the use of some examples.

In the dynasty of the Ptolemies women began to play a dominant role. Almost without exception they were called Cleopatra, and they ruled alone or together with their spouse, who in that case was a close relative, a brother or a cousin. In 175 B.C. Cleopatra II married her brother Ptolemy VI, and after his death contracted a second marriage with her other brother Ptolemy VIII Euergetes II. He in turn, in 142, took his cousin Cleopatra III to wife. Together the three of them took the reins of government, an adventure that ended in failure.

In the middle of the second century B.C. rebellious movements arose. Among the officials, the Egyptians had become more influential and the Greeks often felt themselves passed by. The papyri speak clearly in that respect. Prophets articulated the voice of the people and announced that foreigners would be driven out and Alexandria destroyed. In 131 B.C. there was indeed a serious revolt, inducing Ptolemy to flee with his cousin to Cyprus. Cleopatra II remained behind, governed for some time by herself, but then also fled after she had learned that her husband had returned. Meanwhile her son had been assassinated on orders from her husband. After five years (in 124) reconciliation was effected, and the triad—husband, sister, and cousin—ruled again over Egypt. Cleopatra III proved the strongest; from 116 to 107 she ruled together with Ptolemy IX Soter II, and from 107 to 101 with Ptolemy X Alexander I. Both men were her own sons by blood; reportedly, the latter had her assassinated.

The family life of the Seleucids was equally unsavory. A brief episode during which a marital alliance between the two royal families of Egypt and Syria seemed to be able to promote the peace in the center of the realm is enough to demonstrate this. Cleopatra III had a daughter Cleopatra IV by Ptolemy VIII. This daughter married her brother Ptolemy IX, but was repudiated by him, of all things at the insistence of his mother. Cleopatra IV did not accept that rejection; mustering an army on Cyprus, she took it to Syria to aid Antiochus IX in his war with his brother Antiochus VIII. She offered at the same time to marry him; both the military aid and the proposal were accepted. The undertaking came to a bad end for her. Antiochus VIII, married to her sister Cleopatra Tryphaena, was able to defeat his brother by capturing Antioch. On that occasion Cleopatra IV was gruesomely killed in a temple

by order of her vengeful sister. The same fate awaited her sister a few months later, by order of Antiochus IX. These complicated events, hard to tell in a few words but offering a wealth of material to writers of tragedies, took place in the very highest circles of the two kingdoms that had dominated the Near East after Alexander the Great.

The amazing thing is that the life of the ordinary citizens continued without much disruption, only because of a reasonably functioning apparatus of officials. Less amazing is the mounting influence and power of the Romans, also without military intervention.

Internal struggle eventually led to the total collapse of the kingdom of the Seleucids. Typical of the degree of disintegration was the campaign of Tigranes, king of the Armenians, who even threatened Jerusalem. Armenia, inhabited by Indo-Germans related to the Phrygians, had already in 190 B.C. thrown off the yoke of the Seleucids. Though checked by neighbors, it was an autonomous nation, which under Tigranes I (94–55) had annexed the final remnants of the Seleucid world empire. That Tigranes was unable to realize his ambitious plans was due to the Roman legions which under Lucullus had appeared at his borders. But in 64 B.C. the Roman Pompey, without striking a blow, was able to unseat the next to the last Seleucid king Antiochus XIII Asiaticus together with his successor Philippus II. He established the province of Syria, starting a new chapter in Western Asia's history. The period that now followed, lasting several centuries, was dominated by the Romans.

Egypt's downfall will be forever connected with the name of the last Cleopatra, the seventh, the most famous and the most notorious. The life of this woman has been told and dramatized many times, and therefore need not be related in detail here. Her relationship with Julius Caesar, with whom she lived as his mistress in Rome for a while, is well known. After Caesar's murder in 44, she fled to Egypt, but only two years later she became the paramour of Marcus Antonius, and thus the most powerful woman in the Roman empire. She was also feared. One story relates that Herod the Great had his casemate palace built on the inaccessible rock of Masada near the Dead

Sea, not only because he was afraid of his subjects but also to entrench himself against possible attacks by Cleopatra. There is also a statement by a historian to the effect that in its history Rome has really been afraid of only two people—Hannibal and a woman. This woman was Cleopatra, whose historical image has become distorted due to Roman propaganda against her. Undoubtedly she had in mind the interests of an independent Egypt. She also wished to secure her dynasty. To reach her goals she used Caesar and Antonius, and they were willing instruments.

During her reign Egypt briefly became politically important again. In the generation preceding her, Egypt had suffered a period of great decline caused by civil wars. A persistent revolt had ended in 85 B.C. with the destruction of Thebes, the famous and beautiful city, of which only the ruins have remained. Cleopatra's actions and her diplomatic successes were greeted by the Egyptians as harbingers of a better future.

In the summer of 36 B.C. she accompanied Antonius on his campaign against the Parthians. She had become his spouse according to the laws of Egypt and had several children by him, including the twins Alexander Helios and Cleopatra Selene. From Antonius she could get what she wanted. Returning home from the Euphrates to Egypt she received as a wedding gift Jericho and Transjordan. In 34 Antonius celebrated his victory over the Armenians in Alexandria and on that occasion divided Egypt among Cleopatra and her children. Roman areas were also given to her. Between 34 and 32 Antonius and Cleopatra visited Ephesus, Samos, and Athens. But that was also the end of Roman patience with Antonius. Octavius declared war. The decisive naval battle for Egypt took place at Actium on December 2, 31 B.C., and from Syria Alexandria was conquered by Octavius. Having no way out, Antonius committed suicide, while Cleopatra preferred death from a poisonous snake to humiliation in Roman captivity. It was a symbolic deed of the last pharaoh of Egypt who had borne the serpent crown. The bite of this serpent meant immortality and acceptance into the world of the gods. Her land was joined to the Roman empire but retained its own character.

Rome treated Egypt as a conquered country, tolerating no rebellion there. Augustus put three garrisons in the land, a comparatively large occupational force (later Tiberius recalled one of these legions). Rome had a twofold interest in the possession of Egypt. The first was economic. Since Italy suffered from a chronic trade deficit, Rome made Egypt its granary, while giving little in compensation. Furthermore, the sea route between the center of the Roman empire and the east had become increasingly important. Rome therefore could not tolerate disruptions in the connections and had to be able to rely on loyal governors in the newly acquired territory.

The priesthood was always a mainstay of rebellious nationalistic movements. It was placed under the supervision of the high priest of Alexandria and of all Egypt, a high Roman official who administered temples, priestly organizations, and religious services. A clear distinction was made between Roman citizens and Egyptians who were not given citizens' rights. Only the hellenized population of the three Greek cities and inhabitants of the Faiyum were privileged, with the exception of the Jews. A sharp social division between the civilized, hellenized elite and the rural dwellers was the consequence.

A census was introduced, a house-to-house registration held every fourteen years, but in the interim kept up to date by adding and subtracting birth and death figures. This census was for the purpose of collecting taxes, which, judging by the many complaints in the papyri, must have been heavy. In addition to the taxes, later also the "liturgy" was introduced, which meant in practice that the inhabitants could be drafted for all sorts of activities, including administration. A specialist in the history of Egypt under Roman rule has used the description "shortsighted exploitation which eventually had to lead to economic and social decline."

It cannot be said that Egypt was Romanized. In practice Romanization meant hellenization. Military power never implied a cultural preponderance. The manner in which Greek culture put its stamp on that of Italy during the heyday of the Roman empire is an illustration. The *pax romana* offered some advantages, such as the curbing of piracy in the area of the Mediterranean Sea, but the papyri teach us that the Roman yoke was hard for the nonprivileged Egyptian. Rome raided Egypt and the Roman government was politically experienced enough to act as if old times were continued. Augustus conducted himself as successor of the last pharaoh and was depicted on monuments as the Lord of the Two Lands and provided with attributes that had also been used for the deified pharaohs.

What made Egypt significant from the biblical perspective during Roman domination was the presence of a numerous and spiritually strong Jewish population group. From ancient times there had been communities in Egypt that, because of their origin and relation to Jerusalem, felt a common bond. Some of these had started as military colonies in order that in the service of a foreign government they might protect the borders of the land. The new cities founded by the Greeks had exerted a tremendous attraction, most of all Alexandria. We possess few figures that might be used to estimate the total number of Jews in Egypt, but Philo Judaeus—to whom we shall return—speaks of a million, already in Alexandria alone. It sounds incredible, and it is possible that he exaggerated or was thinking of the entire Nile Delta and included the proselytes, quite a sizable group.

The Jews possessed synagogues, and even possessed, as if there were no centralization of the cult in Jerusalem, a temple in Leontopolis. This so-called Onias temple was not closed until A.D. 73, by Titus, for fear of Jewish uprisings. The Jews lived in the diaspora, which was experienced as a punishment, but at the same time they were compelled to reflect on their own spiritual heritage by accepting the challenge of living in a foreign land. They felt themselves strangers in a pagan world; what this meant for them—and on a comparable level later for the Christian community—can best be seen in the religious life in Rome.

## LITERATURE

H. Bengston, *Herrschergestalten des Hellenismus* (Munich, 1975).

M. Grant, *Cleopatra* (London, 1972).

E. Olshausen, *Rom und Ägypten von 116 bis 51 v. Chr.* (Erlangen/Nürnberg, 1963).

J. Seibert, *Historische Beiträge zu den dynastischen Verbindungen in hellenistischer Zeit* (Wiesbaden, 1967).

E. Seidl, *Rechtsgeschichte Ägyptens als römischer Provinz* (Sankt Augustin, 1973).

## 6. EASTERN RELIGIONS IN ROME

Among the Romans there must have arisen a need for a religious life that could not be satisfied by the rigid forms of the old religion. The gods and their priests had lost their authority in a period of political uncertainty. Toward the end of the second Punic War spiritual depression and a feeling of unsafety prevailed. Because the ancient rites had not provided visible help, aid was sought elsewhere. The Old Testament offers a parallel example in Jeremiah 44:15–19. The people of Jerusalem turned their backs on the God in whose name Jeremiah had preached and started sacrificing to the Canaanite goddess of heaven, because, since they had stopped doing that, they had suffered a scarcity of everything. Here there was a falling back to something repudiated by the prophet; in Rome something new was added to the old, something very drastic, as would be seen later.

Poor conditions in Italy and alarm about a bad omen, such as the shower of stones that occurred at Hannibal's last stand, had made the senate decide to consult the Sibylline books. These oracle books advised acquisition of the statue of the *Magna Mater Idea* from Phrygia, the mythical homeland of the Romans. A delegation went to friendly Pergamum and returned with a black meteoric stone. That the deity was worshiped in a stone as a symbol of power and indestructibility is not a strange thing in religion. The worship of Jupiter Lapis offers a classic example. Dusares was the chief god of the Nabateans, an Aramaic-speaking people flourishing from 50 B.C. to A.D. 100 in the south of Palestine, and he, too, was worshiped in Petra in the form of a stone. Precisely the nonhuman form of the stone, the so-called bethel, indicated that the worshipers were confronted with what was more than human. The translators of the Septuagint were so afraid that Israel might be suspected of a similar kind of stone worship that they consistently omitted the words for "rock" whenever it was used in their Hebrew text as an image of the stability of God.

Thanks to Livy we are sure that the meteorite introduced the worship of the Phrygian Cybele into Rome. It happened on April 4, A.D. 204. According to reports, political circumstances and warning signs (*omina*) were the direct occasion. But that does not yet explain the influence of the worship of Cybele. The focal point of her worship was the city of Pessinus in Asia Minor, and she was always mentioned in conjunction with the spring-god Attis. Around this divine pair myths had sprung up that are irrelevant in this connection. What is significant is that the festival days of mourning and joy, which were celebrated in the spring in honor of these gods, were characterized by a licentiousness that was repugnant to the conservative Romans and evoked ambivalent feelings in them. They observed the orgiastic debauchery with revulsion and fear. Therefore the citizens of Rome were at first not permitted to participate in the rites; the celebrations had to remain restricted to the priest of Cybele. These priests, called *galli*, in drunkenness and ecstasy had castrated themselves, an offensive act to the Romans.

Even so, despite hesitation and opposition, the worship of the mother-goddess, which is what Cybele really was, spread to all parts of the Roman empire: to Spain and northern Africa, to France, and along the Rhine to the Lowlands. In Greece she had been known for a long time already and temples had been erected for the virgin-mother, who was identified with Demeter or Artemis. Though having her own identity, Cybele was nevertheless one of the many manifestations in which the *Magna Mater* was worshiped in the ancient world. In reality she was the same as Ishtar of the Mesopotamians and Anahita of the Persians.

She was generally represented flanked by lions and with a horn of plenty. She was mother and virgin at the same time, being able to do what people were not, namely, to create spontaneously by herself. Processions in her honor were accompanied by frenzy-inducing music. In the mountains of Phrygia she was invoked with such primitive cries as Ma, Amma, and Nanna.

Her devotees could be initiated into her mysteries and so share in her divine life. The greatest appeal, however, must have been the possibility of transcending the limitations of humanity and rising above oneself in a holy frenzy. Sexuality played an important role. It was experienced as terrifying power that could be restrained on the one hand by the indulgence in orgiastic feasts and on the other hand by self-castration. Despite strenuous opposition, the worship of Cybele-Attis received public recognition in Rome under emperor Claudius (A.D. 41–54). We are extensively informed about the games, the *Ludi Megalenses*, that were held in the spring. They were highly fascinating because of the symbolism and the exotic involved. It is difficult to determine what they meant for people for whom religion was primarily an emotional experience. Of course, ecstatic phenomena also occurred in the early Christian churches.

What was said about Cybele can in part be repeated in connection with the earlier-mentioned spread of the worship of Isis. This worship of a goddess imported from another country also evoked revulsion on the part of the conservative Romans. In Italy Isis sanctuaries were destroyed a few times, but eventually this form of religion was also ineradicable. In 105 B.C. a so-called Iseum stood in Pompeii, and frescoes from the excavated Herculaneum illustrate the worship as it was celebrated in such a shrine. See ill. 95.

It was possible to be initiated into mysteries whose secrets might not be divulged. In the Iseum there was, however, also a worship that was open to everyone, and this added considerably to its popularity. For outsiders this created a holy place where in prayer and meditation they experienced a comfort that was hard to find elsewhere. The possession of an esoteric truth obtained through initiations was fascinating to many.

Details of the initiation into the Isis mysteries were bound to be scarce on account of the obligation of secrecy. Here and there, however, the veil was lifted just a little. Apuleius, a philosopher and writer from the beginning of the second century A.D., tells us something of these mysteries in his rightly famous story *Asinus aureus* (The Golden Ass). It is the comical story of a certain Lucius, who through the use of magic ointment was changed into an ass, retaining, however, his human mental capacities. During an Isis celebration he got back his human form through the eating of roses. Then there follows an account of his initiation into the Isis mysteries, in all probability based on his own experiences. He may not tell everything, but he does reveal: "I came to the boundary of death and after having stepped onto the threshold of Proserpina, I rode through all the elements and returned. In the middle of the night I saw the sun shining with a bright light; I approached to the subterranean and supraterrestrial gods and prayed to them from nearby. . . ."

This impressive text shows the true concern of a mystery. The initiated began to share in the invisible reality of the gods and to experience their eternity already in their earthly life. There were degrees of initiation and there were also high moral demands. The theology of the garment is important in these mysteries: many garments are extensions of the body, outwardly expressing what has happened in the soul. For five centuries the Isis mysteries added an aspect of Eastern religious life in Rome-controlled Europe.

Only much later do we hear of the advent of Mithras worship in Italy. According to some reports it began with the arrival of captive pirates after Pompey (ca. 70 B.C.) had successively combated piracy. This seems quite probable because the light-god Mithras, who hailed from Persia, was worshiped by mariners, soldiers, and slaves, generally by those who practiced an occupation requiring courage and contempt of death. In a short time the spread of Mithraism reached the area of Roman influence, as the following example illustrates. During excavations in the winter of 1955/56 a sanctuary was uncovered in an early civilization layer at Uruk (in southern Mesopotamia) that was difficult to identify. The solution to the problem came from London, where, due to bombardments during World War II, it was possible to engage in fruitful archeological investigation in the heart of the city. A shrine was unearthed exhibiting similarity with that of Uruk, and this time it was evident that it concerned a Mithraeum. In Uruk there were no garrisons of legionnaires, yet Mithras temples were erected along the roads of the Roman empire and even farther than that, from London to Uruk.

Wherever possible the sanctuaries were hewn out of rock, but where such was not possible, as in London and Uruk, they were built above the ground. They were limited in size, allowing room for only small groups ranging from twenty to one hundred participants. The advantage was that the members of the Mithras community became familiar with each other and were relieved of their loneliness. The large number of shrines discovered, the one under the Santa Prisca in Rome being the most famous, is an indication how many felt attracted to the worship of Mithras. They united themselves around the statue of the godhead in human form, who killed the bull, while vegetation shot up out of the flowing blood. The light-god, later identified by the Romans with Sol Invictus, was thus especially the god of the unconquerable life rising again from the earth.

The men who were initiated into the Mithras mysteries had to sustain tough physical tests. Despite the obligation of silence imposed on them, much has become known. There were seven degrees of initiation, corresponding to the seven planets, a strict hierarchy. Though only men were admitted, and they had to submit to an iron discipline, Mithraism attracted numerous followers. In a world in which one as it were walked constantly hand in hand with death, the initiated felt themselves conquerors, reborn people sharing in Mithras's immortality. For Christianity on the rise this worship was a formidable rival; therefore it is not surprising that the Christian apologists provide information in their polemic writings that otherwise we would not have. Not until Constantine the Great elevated Christianity to the state religion did persuasion cease to be the only reason for people to abandon Mithraism.

It is obvious that in a world that had become so large, traveling preachers found a ready hearing. The report of Paul's experience in Athens, as recorded in Acts 17, offers a typical example of what proclaimers of strange religions and philosophical systems might expect in the way of an interested audience. In addition to curiosity, there was a diligent search for certainty in an outwardly changed environment. A preacher often compared with Jesus is Apollonius of Tyana, who labored between about A.D. 3 and 97. We possess a biography of him, written by Philostratus about A.D. 220.

This Apollonius drew attention not only through the contents of his preaching, but also through the miracles he performed. His preaching was that of a Neopythagorean philosopher who emphasized virtuous conduct. He is also reckoned among the representatives of the cynics in their third period, when they had softened their criticism of the state and traditional religious conceptions and tried to help people in their religious need. Apollonius is also described as a parapsychologically gifted man, who, for example, was distracted in a speech because he observed the murder of the emperor in Rome some days before it happened, and reported this to his hearers as if he followed the events on the spot. This evidence of telesthesia was later confirmed by couriers. This explains why he received almost divine adoration. Alexander Severus (208–235) put his statue in a house chapel beside that of Abraham, Orpheus, and Christ.

Despite repeated attempts to assure the unity of the state and the loyalty of the citizens through submission to a state religion, religious life remained pluralistic. Generally the government accepted this, to the extent that it felt that its authority was left untouched. What did happen was a process observed earlier in the kingdom of the Seleucids and of the Ptolemies: the identification of gods worshiped locally with the gods of the Greeks and Romans.

Now and then an accidental find through a detail yields needed elucidation. On Mount Carmel a large foot, hewn out of stone and resting on a plinth with an inscription in Greek, was discovered. The inscription indicated that at the end of the second century A.D. the foot had been given by a citizen from Caesarea, mentioned by name, to the deity worshiped locally on the mountain. More of such foot-gifts have been discovered; their intention was to put one's own footsteps into the triumphal advance of the deity. In the case mentioned here this godhead was called Zeus Heliopolis Carmel. It so happens that Tacitus reports (*History* 2.78.3) that a local numen was

worshiped on the mountain, named after the mountain, without image or temple, but having an altar, a report that makes one think of the events recorded in 1 Kings 18. Locally a deity was worshiped, the name survived in combinations, but there was identification. When the citizen from Caesarea brought his gift to Carmel, the deity was identified with Zeus Heliopolis.

---

## LITERATURE

C. J. Bleeker, *De moedergodin in de oudheid* (The Hague, 1960).

F. Cumont, *The Oriental Religions in Roman Paganism* (New York, repr. 1956).

S. L. Guterman, *Religious Toleration and Persecution in Ancient Rome* (London, 1951).

S. K. Heyob, *The Cult of Isis among Women in the Graeco-Roman World* (Leiden, 1976).

Z. Kádár, *Die klein-asiatischen-syrischen Kulte zur Römerzeit in Ungarn* (Leiden, 1962).

H. W. Obbink, *Cybele, Isis, Mithras. Oosterse godsdiensten in het Romeinse Rijk* (Haarlem, 1965).

H. Temporin and W. Haase, eds., *Aufstieg und Niedergang der römischen Welt. Geschichte und Kultur Roms im Spiegel der neueren Forschung* II (Berlin/New York, 1979).

M. J. Vermaseren, *Mithras, de geheimzinnige god* (Amsterdam, 1959).

M. J. Vermaseren and C. C. van Essen, *The Excavations in the Mithraeum of the Church of Santa Prisca in Rome* (Leiden, 1965).

_____, *The Mithraeum at Ponza* (Leiden, 1974).

_____, *The Mithraeum at Santa Maria Capua Vetere* (Leiden, 1971).

---

## 7. THE JEWS IN THE DIASPORA AND IN ROME

An addition to the book of Esther, in a so-called copy of the order of the king of the Medes and Persians, contains Haman's complaint "that among all the nations in the world there is scattered a certain hostile people, who have laws contrary to those of every nation and continually disregard the ordinances of the kings." In these words the Jewish author, writing in excellent Greek, captured the thinking in Alexandria and generally in the Roman empire about his people. He appended the complaint to the book of Esther so as to have an opportunity for a defense against the "Macedonian" Haman in the counter-order of the king, who had come to the conclusion that the Jews were not evildoers but "are governed by most righteous laws and are sons of the Most High, the most mighty living God."

The writer of these fictional pieces lived in what we call "the diaspora," and he knew how vulnerable he could be as a Jew in that situation. Yet diaspora is not the same as exile, since for the great majority the dispersion was due to voluntary emigration from the homeland. The difficulties they became embroiled in were the result of their persistent refusal to become assimilated or to admit even the slightest element of syncretism into their religion. That made them conspicuous, and therefore they drew the attention of ancient writers, though this attention expressed itself negatively toward the Jews.

There are familiar statements about the extent of the Jewish diaspora. The Sibyl says: "Every land is full of you, and every sea" (*Sibylline Oracles* 3:270). Strabo, cited by Josephus, observed that there was no land where the Jews had not penetrated. The perspective of these spokespeople was limited to the Roman empire, but they may have known that there were also flourishing Jewish settlements beyond the borders of the realm, such as in Babylonia and in the land of the Parthians. In these last-mentioned areas Jewry had an opportunity to develop itself independent of Hellenistic influence on its culture. This enabled it to make its own contribution to the shaping of Jewish morality in later times.

There are no traces of a central organization of the Jews, not in the Egypt of the Ptolemies nor in the Roman empire. There was, however, a center, namely, Jerusalem. It acted as the binding influence till the destruction of city and temple in A.D. 70, as attested by the collection of the temple tax and the pilgrimages during the chief festivals. The temple tax of half a shekel was faithfully paid. In the kingdom of the Parthians the money was collected in the cities of Nehardea and Nisibis and from there transported to Jerusalem by heav-

ily guarded caravans. After the fall of Jerusalem this tax was changed into a compulsory contribution of two drachmas for Jupiter Capitolinus, something that was regarded as a terrible indignity. Yet it cannot be said that the status of the Jews in the realm changed greatly after A.D. 70.

It was the policy of the emperors to try as much as possible not to violate acquired rights. They allowed the Jewish communities the independence of a *politeuma*. What this meant in practice is elucidated by authentic information from the papyri. A Jewish community had the right to govern itself by chosen leaders. Such a community might be headed by an ethnarch or a college of archons. They were responsible for collecting taxes and turning them over to the government. On their own initiative they built synagogues and schools, and they administered their own justice in civil matters. They did not live in cultural isolation; especially the better schooled among them knew what was going on in philosophy and literature in the world on which Hellenism had put its stamp. It may be assumed as certain that in the days of the Roman emperors every Jew could understand some Greek, and that many were also able to write it, though not flawlessly. Especially archeology has come up with authentic evidence, in particular the discoveries near the Dead Sea, confirming that Greek was the general language in the diaspora, not only in the cities but also in the country.

If they had received instruction in it, the Jews knew Hebrew, Aramaic, and Latin. Others took pains to get to know Greek so well that they could write it fluently. For generations they had to deal with Greek officials who issued laws in Greek, used it in the courts, and made announcements in it. Hence this general familiarity with Greek is not all that surprising. Apparently there was no objection either to using Greek names; even some ordinary thieves of grapes who were arraigned bore names such as Theophilus, Philistion, and Timaios. The document in which the names occur is to be dated 210 B.C.!

This explains why in Alexandria most Jews could read Homer but not the Torah in the original language. For this reason the grandson of Jesus Sirach, in about 125 B.C., saw it as his task to translate the wisdom book of his grandfather into

Greek, and in his prologue he explains that he went to considerable trouble doing it. But he was willing to do it, as he says, "for those living abroad who wished to gain learning." Translators were also cautious, aware of the diligence with which the outside world read Jewish literature. They knew, especially where it concerned translations of wisdom books, which idioms were greatly liked by the Jews, and by slight nuances they attempted to show that the noble teachings of Greek philosophy, in particular of the Stoics, were already present in the ancient wisdom of Israel. The Greek translation of the book of Proverbs is an example of it.

The most prominent of the Jewish philosophers in the first century A.D., Philo of Alexandria (ca. 25 B.C.–A.D. 45), tried tirelessly in his many books to express the basic ideas of Judaism in the philosophy of his time, but it is more than likely that he knew the Law and the Prophets only in Greek translation. This Philo was personally involved in a number of events in Alexandria that are sometimes called the first Jewish pogrom. Also in 145 and 38 B.C. there were attacks on Jews in Egypt, but in intensity they were not comparable to what happened during the reign of Caligula (A.D. 37–41). There was murdering and plundering, synagogues were destroyed, and the economic life of the Jewish community, primarily centered in the Delta district of Alexandria, was totally disrupted. This lasted till the intervention of Claudius (A.D. 41–54) who was favorably disposed to the Jews. A copy of his decree, which speaks out harshly against both parties but nevertheless restores the Jews' rights, is one of the most significant papyri discoveries from that time. It has gradually become evident that the leaders of the anti-Jewish movements and sentiments were Greeks, and not, as used to be thought, from the native Egyptian population.

The most important question that comes up in this respect, and often asked as well as answered, concerns the cause of what in the nineteenth century was wrongly called "anti-Semitism." The answers that were given are not free from the prejudices of the researchers. It is therefore all the more fortunate with respect to objectivity that the papyri provide so much information about which the party-tied literature is silent.

Gradually the causes of the persecution of the Jews in Alexandria have become clear, for the papyri contradict several established ideas. The offense created by the Jews was due to their being different, in regard to both their religion and the morals and customs that went with it. The Jews certainly did not distinguish themselves through status or power. There were a few rich Jewish families, but most Jews were poor or belonged to the category of merchants and artisans, who did little more than make a living. There was no reason to be envious of their prosperity. Politically they were not influential either, and if some of them did achieve status, it was at the expense of denying their traditions. Only all-out hellenization gave access to politically important offices. Racist prejudices were unknown in the ancient world; at least no written testimonies of racism have come down to us. In ordinary life Jews and non-Jews had normal contacts with each other, though there were obstacles.

After what we have said it is now possible to obtain a clear idea of the isolation of the Jews in their environment. In antiquity religion had a bearing on everything; there is hardly an area in public life one can think of in which the gods were not involved. Every game, each festival began with a sacrifice, making it impossible for the Jew who rejected the idols to participate. The dietary regulations of the law of Moses made it impossible for Jews to eat with their non-Jewish neighbors. They kept the sabbath; what was so special about it was not only the keeping of a day of rest, but also that manservant and maidservant were obligated to cease all labor. The Romans had more days of rest than the Jews, but these were reserved for the higher social classes who could afford to rest while their slaves worked. So the Jewish people obtained a reputation of being work-shy. By law the Jews were exempted from honoring deified kings or emperors, and in return they made a sacrifice for the well-being of the emperor in their temple. However, this attitude could easily be regarded as a lack of loyalty, as happened more than once. For the Jews it was impossible to worship any other god than the God of Israel. His place could not be taken by any other power. This exclusivism, foreign to other religions, resulted in conflicts as well as persecutions. This religious stance was more than once used by leaders to incite a population group that felt itself disadvantaged against the Jews. This was not hard to do, since the Jews were a defenseless minority, as long as the government condoned it.

The persecutions were incidental and locally restricted. What happened in Alexandria was not typical of what happened to the many Jewish communities in the Roman empire. Also, after the unsuccessful revolt that ended with the fall of Jerusalem in A.D. 70, the Jews were able to develop in relative quiet, while their spiritual center had been transferred to the academic center established by Johanan ben Zakkai in Jabneh (Jamnia) on the coast of Palestine. Even in Palestine it was possible to establish schools and synagogues, centers of a spiritual character and outlook that would survive all empires. The synagogue of Capernaum, whose excavated remains are today visited by tourists, is tangible proof of how Jewish spiritual life could flourish in Galilee after the suppressed revolt of Bar Kochba in the second century A.D.

In Rome itself a Jewish congregation had been established that has been called the oldest in Europe, because despite many ups and downs it has managed to survive to the present time. Envoys of Judas Maccabeus, coming to Rome in 161 B.C. to further the interests of their people, discovered there a Jewish congregation. In the eyes of the Romans, Judaism was one of the eastern religions, possessing an enormous attraction while at the same time being viewed with suspicion by conservative citizens. Judaism's power to attract converts must have been great, for reports indicate that the number of Jews increased not only through immigration but also and especially through the joining of proselytes. Cicero, in 59 B.C. defending his client against a Jewish complaint, called the Jewish religion a superstition, while at the same time objecting to the large number of Jews who obstructed his defense by their presence. Julius Caesar and Augustus protected the congregations in Italy and in the diaspora, which certainly advanced their growth and spread.

Difficulties arose as a result of the increasing number of proselytes. One familiar case is that of a prominent lady, named Fulvia, who had adopted the Jewish faith and professed new faith by sending expensive gifts to Jerusalem. On route these treasures were stolen by confidantes, leading her husband to register a complaint with the government. That resulted in an unexpected consequence. For Tiberius, after he had been informed about the matter, banned all Jews from Rome. This was no more than an isolated incident, for shortly afterward the community reestablished itself in the city. The Jews did, however, remain dependent on the whims of the emperor and on the political gain he thought he could expect from the sympathy of the Jews. Caligula was outspokenly anti-Jewish, especially on account of his obsession to be worshiped as a divine emperor. Claudius on the other hand was favorably disposed to his Jewish subjects; in that respect his friendly relationship with Agrippa must have been a significant factor. This lends a puzzling aspect to the report that about 49 or 50 he ordered the Jews to leave Rome. The report about that in Acts 18:2 is confirmed elsewhere. It seems that a clash between the Jews and a growing Christian community and the accompanying disturbances may have been the cause of what was no more than an isolated measure that did not affect all Jews.

The destruction of the temple in Jerusalem in A.D. 70 did the congregation more good than harm. One of the first consequences was that captive Jews, entering Rome as slaves, strengthened the Jewish community, if not in prosperity, at least in number. Jewish beggars and street vendors became part of the Roman street scene. Well-to-do Romans looked down on them and did not understand what could move their fellow citizens to convert to the faith of these easterners. Poets such as Juvenal (50–127) and Martial (40–104) demonstrated in their satire that they were well acquainted with Jewish customs and habits. Their derision was especially directed against the proselytes, who submitted to circumcision, kept the sabbath, lighted lamps for the deity they worshiped, refused to eat pork, and by their manners and customs distinguished themselves from their milieu.

The feeling of community among the Jews increased proportionally to the opposition they endured from the authorities. For instance, the introduction of the *fiscus judaicus* had the opposite result from what was intended. This tax was to be paid to the government and replaced the two drachmas temple tax that until A.D. 70 had been paid voluntarily by the diaspora. Now children from the age of three, men and women till their sixty-second year, Jews as well as proselytes, were compelled to pay the tax, which had always been sacred to them, to a pagan government. Especially under Domitian (81–96) the tax collectors acted roughly when they collected the tax. However, it seems that the entire *fiscus judaicus* was abolished under his successor Nerva (96–98). Inscriptions on coins at least say that this chicanery against the Jews was abolished. But in contrast the papyri in Egypt give evidence that for a long time the *fiscus judaicus* was continued. This strengthened the bond among the Jews throughout the empire.

The extant inscriptions give an impression of the economic life of the Jews in Rome and its immediate surroundings. Particularly the texts that have been preserved in six catacombs are enlightening. These indicate that a few became people of importance, but that by far the majority earned a living as small shopkeepers or artisans. Of the about five hundred inscriptions that have survived, three-fourths are written in Greek, a ratio similar to that in the synagogue of the port city of Ostia, excavated in 1961. Here the ratio between Latin and Greek is one to eight. Hebrew and Aramaic as written languages are sparsely represented. Estimates vary as to the number of Jews relative to the total population. A cautious estimate would be about ten thousand, including Jews by birth and proselytes.

---

## LITERATURE

S. W. Baron, *A Social and Religious History of the Jews* I (New York/London, 1952).

H. I. Bell, *Juden und Griechen im römischen Alexandrien* (Leipzig, 1927).

J.-B. Frey, *Corpus Inscriptionum Judaicarum: Jewish Inscriptions from the Third Century B.C. to the Seventh Century A.D., I: Europe* (Rome, 1936; repr. New York, 1975, with a Prolegomena by B. Lifshitz, pp. 21–107).

H. Fuchs, *Der geistige Widerstand gegen Rom* (Berlin, 1964).

M. Grant, *The Jews in the Roman World* (London, 1973).

M. Hengel, *Die Zeloten* (Leiden, 1976²).

H. J. Leon, *The Jews of Ancient Rome* (Philadelphia, 1960).

C. Münchow, *Ethik und Eschatologie. Ein Beitrag zum Verständnis der frühjüdischen Apokalyptik mit einem Ausblick auf das Neue Testament* (Göttingen, 1980).

Th. Reinach, *Textes d'auteurs grecs et romains relatifs au Judaisme* (Paris, 1895; repr. Hildesheim, 1963).

S. Safrai and M. Stern, eds., *Compendium Rerum Iudaicarum ad Novum Testamentum, I: The Jewish People in the First Century* (Assen, 1974), pp. 117–215, 420–503.

J. N. Sevenster, *Do You Know Greek? How Much Greek Could the First Jewish Christians Have Known?* (Leiden, 1968).

————, *The Roots of Pagan Anti-Semitism in the Ancient World* (Leiden, 1975).

E. M. Smallwood, *The Years under Roman Rule: From Pompey to Diocletian* (Leiden, 1976).

H. Stadelmann, *Ben Sira als Schriftgelehrter* (Tübingen, 1980).

V. Tcherikover, *Hellenistic Civilisation and the Jews* (Philadelphia, 1966).

V. Tcherikover and A. Fuks, eds., *Corpus Papyrorum Iudaicarum* I–III (Cambridge, Mass., 1957–64).

---

## 8. THE PAVED ROAD

Briefly surveying the political and spiritual developments of the four centuries after Christ, one perceives the paved roads along which the faith of the Christians reached the heart of the Roman empire and with surprising speed established a congregation there. First, there was the possibility of safe travel from Jerusalem to Rome. The roads were controlled, shipping was not threatened by pirates. In 2 Corinthians (11:23–28) Paul mentions the many misfortunes he encountered in his travels, but the many dangers to which he was exposed do not include banditry. He complains especially about persecution by Jews who did not care for his preaching. Nevertheless, the synagogue with its great number of non-Jewish adherents was the institution that provided the people who were interested in Paul's preaching. For a large number the road to the first Christian congregation went by way of the synagogue. So Diaspora Judaism despite itself has served a mediating role without which the rise and establishment of the Christian church would have been unthinkable.

We have also noted that there was no language problem. The proclamation of the gospel could not be stopped by language barriers—at most only slowed down. Paul could use his Greek everywhere; his letters were just as readable in the church of Rome as in that of Corinth. We cannot overestimate the importance of needing only one language in one large empire without boundaries. This was the language into which the Holy Scripture, on which the missionaries of the Chris-

tian faith based themselves, had been translated. So there was, in addition to one realm and one language, also one Book, which could be used for citation and argumentation, while observing the rules that had been adopted by the rabbis.

Finally, there was the way that led directly to the heart of searching and inquiring people. What is said of the Athenians in Acts 17:21 with a touch of irony was certainly true of the population of Rome. We noted how receptive they were to the message of strange, eastern religions. The proclaimer of the gospel of Jesus and of the resurrection found a soil that was well prepared. Of the people who listened with surprise, responded positively, and were prepared to endure for the sake of the confession, "not many . . . were wise according to worldly standards, not many were powerful, not many were of noble birth" (1 Cor. 1:26).

# VI

# Biblical Institutions

## by K. Roubos

The life of people in biblical times exhibited a variety of societal structures. Within these structures prevailed behavior patterns sanctioned by tradition and fixed by laws. This concerns both ordinary, daily life and religious life. These two areas cannot be separated from each other, certainly not in Israel. Yet in the interest of clarity it is necessary to distinguish between profane and religious institutions. Cultic affairs require most of the attention. However, in order to understand the biblical message it is just as necessary to observe how people conducted themselves in their daily environment. A brief description of some *realia* (utensils and the like) is therefore necessary.

### LITERATURE

G. A. Barrois, *Manuel d'Archéologie biblique* I–II (Paris, 1939–53).

A. Ben-David, *Talmudische Ökonomie* I (Hildesheim/New York, 1974).

I. Benzinger, *Hebräische Archäologie* (Leipzig, 1927²).

G. Dalman, *Arbeit und Sitte in Palästina* I–VII (Gütersloh, 1928–42; repr. Hildesheim, 1964–71).

K. Galling, ed., *Biblisches Reallexikon* (Tübingen, 1977²).

W. H. Gispen, "Bijbelsche archaeologie," in F. W. Grosheide, ed., *Bijbelsch Handboek* (Kampen, 1935), pp. 237–95.

E. W. Heaton, *Everyday Life in Old Testament Times* (London, 1957²).

J. Jeremias, *Jerusalem in the Time of Jesus* (Philadelphia, 1969; repr. 1975).

S. Krauss, *Synagogale Altertümer* (Berlin/Vienna, 1922).

———, *Talmudische Archäologie* I–III (Leipzig, 1910–12; repr. Hildesheim, 1966).

M. Noth, *The Old Testament World* (London, 1966).

F. Nötscher, *Biblische Altertumskunde* (Bonn, 1940).

Sh. Paul and W. G. Dever, *Biblical Archaeology* (Jerusalem, 1973).

J. Pedersen, *Israel: Its Life and Culture* I–II, III–IV (London/Copenhagen, 1926–40).

R. de Vaux, *Ancient Israel* I–II (New York, 1961; repr. 1965).

P. Volz, *Die biblischen Altertümer* (Stuttgart, 1925²).

G. E. Wright, *Biblical Archaeology* (New York, rev. 1962).

See also:

G. W. Bromiley, et al., eds., *The International Standard Bible Encyclopedia* I–II (Grand Rapids, 1979–82; vols. III and IV in preparation).

G. Buttrick, et al., eds., *The Interpreter's Dictionary of the Bible* I–IV (Nashville, 1962); *Supplementary Volume* (ed. K. Crim, et al.; Nashville, 1976).

B. Reicke and L. Rost, eds., *Biblisch-Historiches Handwörterbuch* (Göttingen, 1962–66).

Th. Schlatter, ed., *Calwer Bibellexikon* (Stuttgart, 1967²).

# A. Institutions of Ordinary Life

## 1. REGULAR LIFE: HOUSING AND CLOTHING

a. The Old Testament relates of the patriarchs that they lived in tents (see the stories in the book of Genesis; cf. Heb. 11:9). According to the biblical narratives such was also the case with the first generations (cf. Gen. 4:20; 9:21, 27). In later times the Rechabites elevated living in tents to a religious ideal (cf. Jer. 35:9). After Israel had settled in Canaan the tent continued in use, for instance as a shelter for herdsmen (cf. 2 Chron. 14:15). Also in times of war the tent served a function. The expression "to your tents!" still reminds us of that (cf. Jdgs. 7:8, et al.). The tent of nomads was probably pointed and made from canvasses of black goatskins. With ropes these covers were fastened to one or more pegs (cf. Jdgs. 4:21; see also section B.7 below). Sometimes there were separate tents for the women and guests (Gen. 27:15; 30:16; 31:33). Besides the tent there was also the tabernacle (see section B.9.d below).

The houses built in Palestine after the conquest were made of mud bricks and wood; a solid foundation of stone or rock was necessary (cf. Matt. 7:24–27). Part of the time, at least in the coolness of the evening, was spent on the flat roof, reachable from the outside by means of stairs (cf. Josh. 2:6; Isa. 22:1). Sometimes it was possible to walk over the roofs from one house to another (cf. Matt. 24:17). The houses of humble folk consisted of one room, in which the animals also lived (2 Sam. 12:3). Sometimes partitions were added to make separate rooms (2 Sam. 13:10). With larger homes the rooms were built around a courtyard (Neh. 8:17). Sometimes there was an upper room on the roof (1 Kings 17:19; etc.) The houses were dark inside. Only the door or at most one window opening let in light. Little furniture was used. 2 Kings 4:10 mentions a bed, a table, a chair, and a lamp. Sleeping was done on the ground. A bed was only for an honored guest. The prophet Amos spoke of the wealth of some people who sleep on beds of ivory (Amos 3:12; 6:4; cf. Prov. 7:16–17). See ill. 96, 97.

### LITERATURE

H. S. Baker, *Furniture in the Ancient World: Origins and Evolution, 3100–475 B.C.* (London, 1966).

H. K. Beebe, "Ancient Palestinian Dwellings," *Biblical Archaeologist* 31 (1968) 38–58.

_____, "Domestic Architecture and the New Testament," *Biblical Archaeologist* 38 (1975) 89–104.

V. Fritz, "Bestimmung und Herkunft des Pfeilerhauses in Israel," *Zeitschrift des Deutschen Palästinavereins* 93 (1977) 30–45.

Y. Shiloh, "The Four-Room House: Its Situation and Function in the Israelite City," *Israel Exploration Journal* 20 (1970) 180–90.

_____, "The Four-Room House—The Israelite Type House?" *Eretz Israel* 11 (1973) 277–85 (Hebrew).

See also the works cited above:

Barrois, I, 244–85; Dalman, VII, 1–175; Galling, pp. 138–41, 228–31.

b. Clothing was very simple. Regular dress was a long shirt or garment (a kind of tunic) with long or elbow-length sleeves. It could be tucked into the belt (Exod. 12:11; 2 Kings 4:29; Acts 12:8).

This "girding" made it possible to work (cf. Luke 12:35). Sometimes a waist cloth was worn under the garment. Other underwear was unknown. Over the shirt one usually wore a mantle or cloak, a large cloth with holes for the arms. For poor people this served at the same time as a blanket, which in case it had been given in pledge had to be returned before the night (Exod. 22:26–27; Deut. 24:13). This was taken off for working (Matt. 24:18), and in case one wanted to run fast (Mark 10:50). There was also the festival clothing and the clothing for nobles, priests, and prophets (Gen. 37:3; 2 Sam. 13:18; 1 Kings 19:13; Zech. 13:4; Matt. 3:4 and parallels; see also section B.5 below; ill. 98). Even the simplest clothing was costly for the ordinary person, all the more so fancy clothing (cf. Josh. 7:21; Jdgs. 14:12). It happened, too, that items of clothing were exchanged to indicate a close bond and friendship. Thus one, as it were, got inside the skin of the other (cf. 1 Sam. 18:4; Rom. 13:14; Eph. 4:24). Transvestism was forbidden (Deut. 22:5); yet as far as we know women's clothing did not differ that much from men's clothing. For the people of that time the difference must have been clear enough (other colors, perhaps different length). In New Testament times women wore a hanging head cloth (1 Cor. 11:5–15). In Isaiah's days the "haughty daughters of Zion" wore many ornaments (Isa. 3:18–23). Wearing idolatrous objects was forbidden (cf. 2 Macc. 12:40).

## LITERATURE

S. Bertman, "Tasseled Garments in the Ancient East Mediterranean," *Biblical Archaeologist* 24 (1961) 119–28.

J. C. de Moor, "Some Garments," *Journal of Near Eastern Studies* 24 (1965) 361.

J. Ruppert, *Le costume juif depuis les temps patriarchaux jusqu'à la dispersion* (Paris, 1939).

G. E. Wright, "Israelite Daily Life," *Biblical Archaeologist* 18 (1955) 61–70.

See also the works cited above:

Galling, pp. 185–88; Dalman, V, 199–362; *Interpreter's Dictionary of the Bible* I, 650–55, 869–71; *International Standard Bible Encyclopedia* II, 401–407.

## 2. MARRIAGE

A man wanting to marry a woman had to give a marriage present (*mohar*) to the father of the bride (Gen. 34:12; Exod. 22:16; 1 Sam. 18:25). Sometimes the amount of the price was left up to the family of the bride (cf. Gen. 34:12), but generally in Israelite marriage law there was a fixed agreement. However, because this might be regarded as generally known, it is nowhere mentioned. From comparisons it can be concluded that the amount was from thirty to fifty silver shekels (cf. Deut. 22:29; Lev. 27:1–8). Instead of paying with money, the bride could also be obtained by performing certain services (cf. Gen. 29:15–30; 1 Sam. 18:25). When the price had been paid, the engagement became effective and legally binding. The woman was then regarded as already married, though until the actual wedding she remained subject to the authority of her father.

Some men in the Old Testament had several wives (e.g., Abraham, Jacob, Gideon, David, and especially Solomon). The Old Testament contains no prohibition of polygamy, though at the beginning of the Bible there stands Genesis 2:24. The creation intent professed by Israel, as mentioned in that text, has not failed to leave its mark. Note the apocryphal book of Tobit and what Jesus and the disciples said about marriage (Matt. 19:5; Mark 10:6–9; 1 Cor. 7:1–8; etc.). In Israel polygamy belonged to the permitted exceptions, at least in the Old Testament. It was due to political considerations (e.g., among the kings) or to prestige and "status." It was often connected with childlessness. Then the husband "received" or "took" a concubine (Gen. 16:1–4; 30:1–13; 1 Sam. 1:2). But marriage with "the wife of your youth" was praised as being the normal thing (Prov. 5:18; cf. Isa. 54:6; Mal. 2:14). God is the protector of marriage.

The wedding followed upon the betrothal as a legal "taking" of the woman. From the Bible one can infer some customs that were part of the wedding feast (a separate word for "wedding feast" occurs only in Cant. 3:11; the Old Testament has no special word for "wedding," but the New Testament does). Already in ancient times a great banquet was part of the wedding feast (Jdgs. 14:10ff.). Psalm 45 (a song for the wedding feast of a king) mentions festive occasions, which also must have formed a part (though on a more modest scale) of the wedding of an ordinary man and woman from the people: the bride was beautifully dressed and escorted by bridesmaids to the house (of the family) of the bridegroom (1 Sam. 25:42; Ps. 45:15–16; cf. Genesis 24). Friends of the bridegroom served as his helpers and companions (cf. Jdgs. 14:11; Matt. 9:15; Mark 2:19; Luke 5:34). "The friend of the bridegroom" had a special, official task (cf. the figurative language in John 3:29; 2 Cor. 11:2). Bridesmaids could also accompany the bridegroom, as shown by the parable in Matthew 25:1–13 (cf. Ps. 45:10; Cant. 3:11). The wedding dinner must have been sumptuous, with wine (John 2:1–11) and meat (Matt. 22:1–13). The easterner seldom ate meat at ordinary meals. Songs were sung at the wedding feast (cf. Canticles) and riddles told (Jdgs. 14:12–14). The wedding festivities lasted for days (according to later Jewish custom a whole week). Often God's covenant with his people was compared to a marriage (cf. Jer. 2:2; Hos. 2:18).

Adultery was strictly condemned (Exod. 20:14; Deut. 5:18). By adultery is meant the sexual union of a man with an engaged or married woman (Lev. 20:10). In the New Testament Jesus put the adultery of both man and woman under the same judgment (Mark 10:2–12). Sinful lust also falls under that judgment (Matt. 5:27–32). "Let marriage be held in honor among all" (1 Cor. 6:10; Heb. 13:4). Divorce was permitted in the Old Testament in certain situations; in that case the man had to give his wife a letter of divorce (Deut. 24:1–5). Various regulations and customs were used to protect the marital institution (Deut. 22:13–19, 29), for God hates adultery (Mal. 2:10–16). Jesus viewed marriage as a union for life (Matt. 19:1–12; cf. Matt. 5:32; 1 Cor. 7:10, 39).

## LITERATURE

G. Beer, *Die soziale und religiöse Stellung der Frau im israelitischen Altertum* (Tübingen, 1919).

M. Burrows, *The Basis of Israelite Marriage* (New Haven, 1938).

W. G. Cole, *Sex and Love in the Bible* (New York, 1959).

M. David, *Vorm en wezen van de huwelijkssluiting naar de oudoosterse rechtspleging* (Leiden, 1934).

G. Delling, *Paulus' Stellung zur Frau und Ehe* (Stuttgart, 1931).

J. Doller, *Das Weib im Alten Testament* (Münster, 1920).

K. Dronkert, *Het huwelijk in het Oude Testament* (Leiden, 1957).

L. M. Epstein, *Marriage Laws in the Bible and the Talmud* (Cambridge, Mass., 1942).

B. Maarsingh, *Het huwelijk in het Oude Testament* (Baarn, 1963).

D. R. Mace, *Hebrew Marriage* (London, 1953).

E. Neufeld, *Ancient Hebrew Marriage Laws* (London, 1944).

R. Patai, *Sex and Family in the Bible and the Middle East* (New York, 1959).

A. van Selms, *Marriage and Family Life in Ugaritic Literature* (London, 1954).

See also the works cited above:

*Interpreter's Dictionary of the Bible* III, 278–87; de Vaux, I, 24–38.

## 3. CHILDREN: NAMING AND NURTURING

In a long history, especially that described in the Old Testament, personal names are a very constant factor. M. Noth has said: "A people sooner changes its language than its personal names" (Noth, *Personennamen*, p. 41). The naming of the child was regarded as highly important. Names sometimes contained wishes and promises in which God's name was used, but newborn children were also named after certain animals (on account of special characteristics). Sometimes there was a later change of name; familiar are the examples Abram-Abraham, Jacob-Israel, Simon-Peter. Israel was forbidden to use names for magical purposes. In 1 Chronicles 4:9–10 a certain Jabez is mentioned. The sound of the name in Hebrew is similar to the Hebrew word for "pain" (though the etymology is not clear). This Jabez prayed to God because his own name made him fearful; he prayed for removal of the fear and the pain. "Then God granted what he asked." But God did not give him another name! In the New Testament it is assumed that the naming of a child occurs together with circumcision on the eighth day (see section B.2 below), but this custom was not known in earlier days. According to 1 Samuel 4:21 the child Ichabod received his name immediately after his birth. The naming of the child after the (grand)father occurred in Israel only after the Exile (the so-called patronymy; cf. Luke 1:59–60).

Especially in the Old Testament sons were seen as a blessing of the Lord, because they continued the name of the family (Ps. 127:3; 128:3). This is not to be understood in the modern sense, for a surname or family name did not exist in biblical times. That made it all the more important to know to which family one belonged and who one's ancestors were. If only daughters were born from a marriage, and at the marriage of those daughters the hereditary property threatened to pass to another tribe or even another people, the possibility existed that a son-in-law would drop his own name and assume that of his father-in-law. He was then considered to be his son (cf. Numbers 36; Ezra 2:61). 1 Chronicles 2:34–41 contains an example of giving a daughter in marriage to a slave.

In general a great number of children was seen as a blessing. The deeds of the Lord and the stories of his dealings with Israel and the world were to be told to the children (cf. Ps. 78:4). With small children the mother was mainly responsible for this teaching. At a later stage in life the training by the mother was also considered very important (cf. Prov. 31:1–9). To those outside the family the father was responsible for the behavior of his children (1 Sam. 2:18–25; cf. 1:1–3). The Old Testament speaks often of "the sins of the fathers." This is an indication of the great responsibility that was given to the fathers. In the "home" (family, extended family) it had to be shown that a man was serious about the commandments of the Lord. A case such as that mentioned in Deuteronomy 21:18–21 (an obstinate son was brought before the elders of the city by his parents) is clearly an exception. The disintegration of the family would affect the roots of society. In the end-time the hearts of the fathers and of the sons will again be turned to each other (Mal. 4:6; cf. Luke 1:17).

## LITERATURE

M. David, *Adoptie in het oude Israël* (Amsterdam, 1955).

L. Dürr, *Das Erziehungswesen im Alten Testament und im Antiken Orient* (Leipzig, 1922).

I. Mendelsohn, "The Family in the Ancient Near East," *Biblical Archaeologist* 11 (1948) 24–40.

M. Noth, *Die israelitischen Personennamen im Rahmen der gemeinsemitischen Namengebung* (Stuttgart, 1928; repr. Hildesheim, 1966).

## 4. DEATH AND BURIAL

Every person is destined to go "the way of all the earth" (Josh. 23:14; 1 Kings 2:2). The words of a dying person are often given special attention (Moses, Joshua, Samuel, David). In this connection we can think, too, of the great care with which the Evangelists have passed on to us the final words Jesus spoke. Dying at an advanced age was seen as a gift of God, recalling the death of Abraham and Isaac ("old and full of days"). A premature death was experienced as a terror and a judgment (cf. Ps. 102:24–25; Eccl. 7:17; Isa. 38:10). In the so-called royal documentation (the brief survey of the life and works of a deceased king), it is often said that the king "slept with his fathers." This expression does not say more than that the king died on his bed and was buried in the family grave. Especially in the Pentateuch it is said of some that they "were gathered to their fathers" (cf. Gen. 25:8, 17; 49:29, 33; etc.). A deceased person was to be properly buried (cf. 2 Sam. 21:13–14). Burning was practiced only with the corpses of certain criminals. The prophet Jeremiah said concerning King Jehoiakim that no one would mourn for him and that he would be buried with the "burial of an ass," that is, his dead body would be discarded like a carcass (Jer. 22:19; 36:30; cf., however, 2 Kings 24:6). Though it was to be regarded as an exception, a deceased person could be buried in his own house (cf. 1 Sam. 25:1). Tombs were often dug out of the soft limestone. Natural caves were also used. In the Kidron Valley there was a common burial place for condemned criminals and other rejected persons. According to 2 Kings 23:6 there was a burial place "of the common people" (the parallel text 2 Chron. 34:4 speaks of "the graves of those who had sacrificed to them [i.e., idols]"; cf. Jer. 26:23). Often it was unnoticeable that a dead person lay buried somewhere (Luke 11:44). During the Passover, in order to avoid cultic uncleanness, such a grave was marked with lime (cf. Matt. 23:27).

Worshiping the dead and sacrificing on the graves (as was done by the Canaanites) was forbidden in Israel. No special power was to be attributed to the dead or the spirits of the dead (Isa. 8:19–20). Saul's desperate attempt to consult the dead shows the total darkness of this king (1 Samuel 28). Help was to be expected from no one, except from God and his word (1 Sam. 28:15–20; Luke 16:29–31). Everything that related to the dead was unclean (Lev. 11:32–35; Num. 19:1–22; Deut. 14:1–3).

In Old Testament times embalming of the body was not practiced in Israel (the embalming of Jacob and Joseph is explicitly related to Egyptian custom, Gen. 50:2–3; cf., however, Mark 16:1; Luke 24:1; John 12:1–8; 19:38–42). Burial usually took place on the day of death. In Old Testament times the deceased was buried in his own clothes. See ill. 99.

It was the duty of the surviving relatives to "lament" the dead. Originally this was done with a simple lamentation shout, later with a lamentation song performed by mourners, men and women (cf. 2 Sam. 3:33–35; 2 Chron. 35:25; Amos 5:16; Mark 5:38).

In the older parts of the Old Testament, death was viewed as being in the underworld (*sheol*), where the dead lead a kind of shadowy existence and where God's praise is not sung. "Grave" and "realm of the dead" are sometimes identical (Gen. 37:35; 47:30). Yet Israel also believed that the realm of the dead was not beyond God's power (cf. Ps. 139:8), for YHWH is sovereign over life and death (Deut. 32:29). Job asked God to hide him in Sheol until his anger had passed

(Job 14:13). Someday death will be swallowed up forever (Isa. 25:8). In the later part of the Old Testament the belief in resurrection emerged (Isa. 26:19; Dan. 12:2). Already in the old narratives that speak of "taking away" (Gen. 5:24; 2 Kings 2:12) it becomes evident that God's hand is stronger than death. Jesus was not spared from death but delivered up to death, in order to be raised as the "firstborn from the dead."

## LITERATURE

A. Bertholet, *Die israelitischen Vorstellungen vom Zustand nach dem Tode* (Tübingen, 1914²).

P. Heinisch, *Die Totenklage im Alten Testament* (Münster, 1931).

_____, *Die Trauergebräuche bei den Israeliten* (Münster, 1931).

R. Martin-Achard, *De la mort à la résurrection* (Neuchâtel/Paris, 1956).

E. M. Meyers, *Jewish Ossuaries: Reburial and Rebirth* (Rome, 1971).

G. Quell, *Die Auffassung des Todes in Israel* (Leipzig, 1925).

L. Rahmani, "Ancient Jerusalem's Funerary Customs and Tombs," *Biblical Archaeologist* 44 (1981) 171–77, 229–35; 45 (1982) 43–53, 109–19.

N. Tromp, *Primitive Conceptions of Death and the Nether World in the Old Testament* (Rome, 1969).

L. Wächter, *Der Tod im Alten Testament* (Stuttgart, 1967).

## 5. FAMILY, GENERATION, TRIBE

Household and family were inseparable in the Old Testament (also in later times there was no clear demarcation). One could speak of family if there was a common ancestor three to four generations back. A clan was then an extended family, in which blood relationship in the direct sense still formed the link; yet here, too, there was no difference in the terms employed. The Old Testament used "flesh" or "bones" for what we call blood relationship, not the word "blood" (Gen. 29:14; 37:27; Jdgs. 9:2; 2 Sam. 5:1; 19:13–14;

cf. Gen. 2:23). Due to Greek influence a different word usage is found in the New Testament (cf. John 1:13 and the reading of Acts 17:26 in some manuscripts; see the Authorized Version). Household and family as well as clan were designated in the Old Testament as "father's house" (compare Exod. 12:3; 1 Chron. 7:2 with Num. 3:24; 17:2). In ancient times every clan had its annual sacrificial feast, for which even a royal invitation could be turned down (1 Sam. 20:6, 29).

A tribe consisted of a number of clans. In the story of the defeat at Ai and the sin of Achan first the tribe was indicated, then the clan, next the family (the house), and finally the guilty person (Josh. 7:14–18). According to Old Testament sources the sons of Jacob-Israel were the eponyms (name-givers) of the tribes. In all genealogical lists there are twelve. This figure is not clear in the "blessing of Moses" (Deuteronomy 33) and in the lists in Chronicles (1 Chronicles 2–8; 12:25–38; 27:16–22), though particularly in these last passages copying errors may have crept into the text. The figure twelve remains significant throughout the whole Bible as a designation of the fulness of the people of God. With two exceptions the names (also in their order) are virtually identical (Noth, *System*). These exceptions to the rule are:

a. In such pericopes as Genesis 29:31–30:23 and Genesis 49:1–27 (the blessing of Jacob), Levi is mentioned third and the Joseph tribe is mentioned as one. The same names are also found in Genesis 35:23–26; 46:8–25; Exodus 1:2–4; Deuteronomy 27:12–13; 1 Chronicles 2:1–2; Ezekiel 48:31–35. This is also the sequence on the postage stamps issued by the state of Israel in 1956: Reuben, Simeon, Levi, Judah, Dan, Naphtali, Gad, Asher, Issachar, Zebulun, Joseph, Benjamin. The following texts successively list their names: Deuteronomy 33:6; Genesis 49:5; Deuteronomy 33:8; Genesis 49:9, 16, 21, 19, 20; 1 Chronicles 12:32; Genesis 49:13; Deuteronomy 33:13; Genesis 49:27. Compare also the Chagall windows in Jerusalem (also depicted on postage stamps). In the Old Testament the name-givers of the tribes were divided into four groups as sons of Jacob-Israel, after the two wives and the two concubines. There were Leah tribes: Reuben, Simeon, Levi, Judah, Issachar,

Zebulun; Bilhah tribes: Dan, Naphtali; Zilpah tribes: Gad, Asher; and Rachel tribes: Joseph, Benjamin. The Old Testament lends no support to the idea that there may have been a Dinah tribe, nor to the idea that the names Leah, Rachel, Bilhah, and Zilpah might designate ur-tribes.

b. Besides these lists there are others (used especially to designate the tribes and not referring as much to the eponyms) in which Levi is missing (section B.5 below), in which Gad is usually in third place, and in which the two tribes descended from Joseph, Manasseh and Ephraim, are mentioned. The primary pericope is Numbers 26:5–51 (compare further Num. 1:5–15, 20–43; 2:3–31; 7:12–83; 10:14–28; 13:4–15; 34:18–29; Joshua 13–19; Ezek. 48:1–29). The list in Revelation 7:1–8 should be mentioned separately. Here Dan is missing (perhaps because many early Christian writers thought of him as the ancestor of the antichrist), as is Ephraim (Joseph is mentioned instead); Levi, however, is mentioned.

Joshua 24 speaks of a "national gathering" at Shechem, to which Joshua summoned "all the tribes of Israel" to renew the covenant with YHWH. Perhaps we should think of it as a regularly recurring event in antiquity. During the time of the monarchy every tribe had its own "prince." The daily government and the administration of justice must have been done by those princes. Judges 10:1–5; 12:7–15 mentions the names of some men who were called the "minor judges." Unlike the "major judges," who were more like charismatic leaders in time of need, these men administered justice (on the basis of the Mosaic laws). The "elders" were charged with the administration of justice in cities. See further section A.7 below.

## LITERATURE

A. Causse, *Du groupe ethnique à la communauté religieuse* (Strasbourg, 1937).

E. B. Cross, *The Hebrew Family* (Chicago, 1937).

C. H. J. de Geus, *The Tribes of Israel* (Assen, 1976).

N. Gottwald, *The Tribes of Yahweh* (Maryknoll, NY, 1979).

D. Jacobson, *The Social Background of the Old Testament* (Cincinnati, 1942).

I. Mendelsohn, "The Family in the Ancient Near East," *Biblical Archaeologist* 11 (1948) 24–40.

M. Noth, *Das System der zwölf Stämme Israels* (Stuttgart, 1930; repr. Darmstadt, 1966).

S. Nyström, *Beduinentum und Jahwismus* (Lund, 1946).

R. Patai, *Sex and Family in the Bible and the Middle East* (New York, 1959).

M. S. Seale, *The Desert Bible: Nomadic Tribal Culture and Old Testament Interpretation* (London, 1974).

---

## 6. MONARCHY AND STATE

Considered historically, the Philistine threat evoked the desire for a king in Israel. The surrounding nations had had kings for a long time already. Even before the time of Saul there was in Israel the desire for a stronger authority and a hereditary ruler. But in Judges 8:23 Gideon enunciated what was to be the rule in Israel: "YHWH shall rule over you" (the word "king" is not used there). Abimelech (Judges 9) was an imitation of Canaanite monarchy. 1 Kings 21 (the story of Naboth and vineyard) shows clearly the clash between the legitimate Israelite conception of freedom and hereditary property and the pagan view of the king having absolute power (1 Kings 21:7). The so-called royal law (Deut. 17:14–20) severely limited the power of the king. All Israelite kings were subject to prophetic critique (cf. 1 Sam. 13:13; 2 Sam. 12:10; 24:11–12; 1 Chron. 21:9–10). Saul's kingship was a debacle due to his clash with the law of God, as represented by Samuel, and therefore, according to the Old Testament history writer, he was rejected by God (1 Sam. 15:23; 16:14).

Around 1000 B.C. the Philistines controlled a large part of the territory of the Israelite tribes. The Israelites were not even allowed to have their own smiths, making it impossible for them to manufacture their own weapons (1 Sam. 13:19–22). Other nations also suppressed Israel in those days (cf. 1 Sam. 11:1–3). It was then that "the Spirit of God came mightily upon Saul" (1 Sam. 11:6). According to 1 Samuel 9:15–16, this event was preceded by a divine revelation in a vision to Samuel about the coming "prince." In 1 Samuel 10:18–21 Saul was designated king by divine lot. Saul was anointed to be Israel's first king, which meant that he was not just a charismatic leader but occupied an office. The people shouted, "Long live the king!" (1 Sam. 10:24). This event made Israel into a people of status for the first time. Yet they were not allowed to be a people like other nations. Here, too, the prophetic voice issued a warning (cf. 1 Sam. 8:10–18).

Under Saul's successor, David, the monarchy really developed. He can be called the first king of the state of Israel. The men of Judah anointed him in Hebron (2 Sam. 2:4). This must have meant that the men proclaimed him king and that a priest anointed him. For a short while Ishbaal or Ishbosheth (son of Saul) still was king over the northern part of Israel. After that the northern tribes also acknowledged David as king, so that he was thus king over Judah and Israel. On the basis of Old Testament data it is generally thought that the union of north and south into one kingdom was more of a "personal union," which continued till Solomon. David broke completely the power of the Philistines and took Jerusalem from the Jebusites (2 Sam. 5:5–10; 1 Chron. 11:4–9), after which he made it the capital of his realm and brought the ark there. Not much is known of the set-up of David's kingship over the land. To be sure, 1 Chronicles speaks in detail about the division of the army and about all kinds of offices (1 Chronicles 23–27), but here we should remember that the writer of Chronicles projected all sorts of things from a later age back into the time of David. Moreover, the figures which he mentions often have another purpose, for instance, to portray David's glory. So it is impossible to imagine that David would have had a standing army of twelve times twenty-four thousand men (1 Chron. 27:1).

Solomon benefited from David's conquests, but he himself was not a soldier. He is called "a man of peace." His chief and best-known undertaking was the building of the temple (see section B.8 below) and of his palaces. Of course, David too had a palace, but little is said about it (2 Sam. 5:11; 1 Chron. 14:1). 1 Kings 7:1–12 writes about the much larger and richer palace of Solomon. From the report it can be gathered that the building complex consisted of three parts, namely, the House of the Forest of Lebanon, the Hall of the Throne, and the actual palace. The name "House of the Forest of Lebanon" was likely given to it because of the many cedars that were used as pillars (there are also other explanations). This house alone was larger than the temple Solomon had built. It was used for representative purposes. According to 1 Kings 10:17, it was also used for storage of the golden shields and later even for all kinds of weapons (assuming that the "House of the Forest" in Isa. 22:8 refers to the same building). It is also mentioned in 2 Chronicles 9:16, 20, but Chronicles says nothing about the other parts of the palace complex.

Solomon gave a well-organized government to the land (in part extending what had already been under David). 1 Kings 4:8–19 mentions the division into twelve districts. In part the old tribes and tribal areas are still recognizable in them: Ephraim, Naphtali, Asher, Issachar, Benjamin, Gad (in verse 19 that name was later altered to Gilead). The areas subdued by David were also fitted into the system of (still twelve) provinces. It is striking that Judah is not mentioned as a district, unless, following the Greek translation, the end of verse 19 and the beginning of verse 20 are to be read as if there was one governor for all of Judah. Even then Judah retained a place of its own. That Judah was likewise divided into twelve districts (as assumed by some) has not been proven. For that one refers to Joshua 15 and 18. According to de Vaux, those chapters reflect the situation at the time of Jehoshaphat (cf. 2 Chron. 17:2, 12); according to Noth, the time of Josiah. Each of the twelve districts was responsible, for one month per year, to supply the provisions of the royal court (1 Kings 4:7). Every district was headed by a governor, a commissary of the king. 1 Kings 4:2–6 enumerates the "high officials," the aids or ministers of the king. The priest Azariah, son of Zadok (see section B.5.c below), heads the list. There are two secretaries, charged with handling the royal correspondence and taking care of the archives. Then follows a chancellor, whose title is also rendered as "interpreter" or "public prosecutor." Next a man in charge of the district officers, and one who is called the "king's friend."

This last-mentioned title had become an official title under Solomon (designating the man in charge of secret affairs), but in earlier and later times it was an honorary title (cf. 1 Chron. 27:33; John 19:12). The last persons mentioned are a man in charge of the palace and a functionary who was in charge of forced labor. From 1 Kings 5:13 it might be inferred that Solomon also conscripted native Israelites for forced labor. That would make it even easier to explain the opposition against Solomon's son Rehoboam (1 Kings 12:4, 18; 2 Chron. 10:4, 18). According to 1 Kings 9:20–21 and 2 Chronicles 2:17–18, which omits the above 1 Kings 5:13, the Israelites were excluded from forced labor; at least they were not reduced to slaves. Nevertheless, it seems plausible that they were compelled to perform *labor* services. See ill. 100.

## LITERATURE

A. Alt, "Das Königtum in den Reichen Israel und Juda," *Kleine Schriften* II (Munich, 1953) 116–34.

K. H. Bernhardt, *Das Problem der altorientalischen Königsideologie im Alten Testament* (Leiden, 1961).

M. Buber, *Kingship of God* (New York, 1967, 1973³).

H. Donner, *Herrschergestalten in Israel* (Berlin/Heidelberg/New York, 1970).

J. de Fraine, *L'aspect religieux de la royauté israélite* (Rome, 1954).

T. Ishida, *The Royal Dynasties in Ancient Israel* (Berlin/New York, 1977).

G. Ch. Macholz, "Die Stellung des Königs in der israelitischen Gerichtsverfassung," *Zeitschrift für die alttestamentliche Wissenschaft* 84 (1972) 157–82.

A. Malamat, "Organs of Statecraft in the Israelite Monarchy," *Biblical Archaeologist* 28 (1965) 34–65.

T. N. D. Mettinger, *Solomonic State Officials* (Lund, 1971).

J. A. Soggin, *Das Königtum in Israel: Ursprung, Spannungen, Entwicklung* (Berlin, 1967).

## 7. ADMINISTRATION OF JUSTICE AND LAWS OF ASYLUM

a. In Israel justice was grounded in the Mosaic laws, collected in the Pentateuch. We can make a distinction between casuistic and apodictic laws (the terms are from A. Alt). The first kind refers to laws such as are also found in the Mesopotamian law codes (see the survey in the book of H. A. Brongers), which start from a particular hypothetical case. The second kind refers to laws embodying a direct categorical command or prohibition (the clearest example is found in the Decalogue). The latter are typically Israelite, though there are parallels in the terminology of the Hittite covenants (vassal treaties).

b. The elders "in the gate" were in charge of pronouncing justice. During the monarchy, one could appeal to the king as the highest authority in a variety of cases, as attested by the story of Solomon's judgment (1 Kings 3). King Jehoshaphat (his name means "YHWH is judge") introduced district courts and a high court (in Jerusalem) (2 Chron. 19:4–11). According to 1 Chronicles 23:4–5, David had already assigned a judicial responsibility to the Levites. A death sentence could be pronounced only if there were at least two accusing witnesses (cf. Matt. 26:61), who in the death by stoning had to cast the first stone (Deut. 17:6–7; 1 Kings 21:1–16; John 8:7). For death penalties see, for example, Exodus 21:12; Leviticus 24:17; Deuteronomy 13:6–19; 17:2–7; 21:18–21; Matthew 26:59–60; Hebrews 10:28. For the "ordeal" see section B.3.e below.

c. Israel had six cities of refuge (see section B.1 below) to which anyone could flee who unintentionally had killed another (Num. 35:9–34; Deut. 4:41–43; 19:1–13; Josh. 20:1–9). In Joshua 20:9 the cities are designated with a term that is found only there and is usually rendered "the cities designated" (RSV). Others, including Noth, have argued that an old technical term is used there, meaning something like "cities of the agreement" or "of getting together." They are included among the "Levitical cities" at a time that is hard to date (cf. Joshua 21; 1 Chron. 6:54–81; see section B.5.b below). Perhaps the institution of the cities of refuge was substituted for a custom, also later still occurring, to seek divine protection at

the altar (cf. 1 Kings 1:50–51; 2:28–35). It is interesting and significant that according to the laws of Numbers 35 a person who had killed someone could return from the city in which he had found refuge to his own town only after the death of the high priest in function at the time. By his death the high priest as it were atoned for the blood shed by the killer (Num. 35:25).

---

### LITERATURE

A. Alt, "Die Ursprünge des israelitischen Rechts," *Kleine Schriften* I (Munich, 1953) 278–332.

H. J. Boecker, *Redeformen des Rechtslebens im Alten Testament* (Neukirchen-Vluyn, 1964).

———, *Law and Administration of Justice in the Old Testament* (Minneapolis, 1980).

H. A. Brongers, *Oud-oosters en bijbels recht* (Nijkerk, 1960).

D. Daube, *Studies in Biblical Law* (Cambridge, 1947).

F. Horst, *Gottes Recht* (Munich, 1961).

B. van Oeveren, *De vrijsteden in het Oude Testament* (Kampen, 1968).

---

## 8. MONEY, WEIGHTS, MEASURES

a. In ancient times payment was made in goods. Already at the time of the patriarchs, however, a measured quantity of silver was used as a form of currency. Both methods continued to exist side by side, certainly in the Old Testament (compare 1 Kings 5:11 with Gen. 20:16). Not until the late Old Testament period do we find mention of coins, the Persian daric and the drachmas (1 Chron. 29:7; Ezra 2:69; 8:27; Neh. 7:70–71). They are of equal value (twenty shekels). Ezra and Nehemiah mentioned minas, which weighed fifty shekels. Matthew 22:20, Mark 12:16, and Luke 20:32 mention the silver denarius or shekel containing the image of the emperor. Various coins from the Maccabean age are known (cf. 1 Macc. 15:6). In New Testament times many foreign coins were in circulation (cf. Matt. 21:12). A shekel was originally a weight of about 11.5 grams (0.4 oz.; in discussing weights a wide margin should be allowed). From ancient times a quantity of silver was weighed, as Jeremiah did to purchase a field (Jer. 32:9). Gold was used as currency, its relative value to silver being one to sixty. Solomon's treasure of silver and gold was proverbial (cf. 1 Kings 10:27; 2 Chron. 1:15).

It is difficult to translate the value of biblical money and coins into modern values. For the Old Testament the account in 2 Kings 7 offers some clues. There it is said (2 Kings 7:1) that after the inflation prices will again come down to somewhat the normal level: a measure of fine flour for a shekel or two measures of barley for the same price. Since a measure was twelve to thirteen liters (3.1 to 3.4 gals.), one can make a comparison with our modern systems of measurement. In the Old Testament, some of the weights used were the shekel (ill. 101), the mina (fifty shekels, about 570 grams or 20 oz.), and the talent, usually in the shape of a round disk, equivalent to three thousand shekels and weighing about thirty-four kilograms (75 lbs.; Exod. 38:25–26). For the New Testament the note in Matthew 20:2 offers some basis for comparison: the (Roman) denarius, about similar to the (Greek) drachma, was worth the fourth part of an Israelite silver shekel (ill. 102). According to that text, this was the daily wage of a laborer. The Greek monetary weights and coins mentioned in the New Testament are the talent (probably about 41 kgs. or 90 lbs., thus heavier than in Old Testament days; Matt. 25:15), the pound (about 328 grams or 12 oz.; Luke 19:16), the stater (piece of silver; Matt. 17:27), the double drachma (personal tax; Matt. 17:24), the drachma (shekel; Luke 15:8), and the copper coin (Mark 12:42). The Roman coins are the denarius (shekel; Matt. 18:28; 20:2), the asarion (Matt. 10:29), and the penny, having a value of two copper pieces (Matt. 5:26).

b. The weights of the various measures can also be stated only approximately. First something about the measures of capacity. For the Old Testament the homer estimates (Strobel, p. 303) vary from 220 to 450 liters (58 to 120 gals.). According to others (de Vaux, I, 199) even the lowest estimate is too high. A tenth part of it is called the ephah, bath, or *metrete*. The tenth part of an ephah is an omer (Exod. 16:36; see section B.9.c below).

It has been said that there is difference between the ordinary and the royal bath (see section B.8.b below). The log was only used for liquids and was about half a liter (0.1 gal.). In the New Testament the bushel is used, measuring a little over 12 liters (3 gals.; in Rev. 6:6 another measure of a little more than a liter or a quart is meant). The Roman bushel (corn measure) was almost 9 liters (2.4 gals.). A bath (Luke 16:6) held about 36 liters (9.5 gals.), a *metrete* or jar (John 2:6) almost 40 liters (10.6 gals.). Finally there is the cor or bag (Luke 16:7) of about 360 liters (95 gals.).

As regards linear measure, the cubit is about half a meter (18 in.; going by the measurements of the temple). Actually the Old Testament mentions two kinds of cubits, the large and the ordinary cubit, with a ratio of seven to six (cf. 2 Chron. 3:3; Ezek. 40:5; 43:13). A span is half a cubit (9 in.; Isa. 40:12), a palm (four fingers) is eight centimeters (3 in.). A rod or reed (e.g., Ezek. 40:5) could measure six large cubits. In the New Testament the Roman cubit (over 44 cm. or 17 in.) is used (John 21:8; Rev. 21:17). The Roman mile (Matt. 5:41) is about 1,500 meters (5,000 ft.), a stadium (Lk. 24:13) about 200 meters (650 ft.), the step (not used in the Bible as a measure) about a meter (3 ft.), the double step or fathom (Acts 27:28) two meters (6 ft.). A foot is two-thirds of a cubit.

## LITERATURE

F. Banks, *Coins of Bible Days* (New York, 1955).

A. G. Barrois, "La métrologie dans la Bible," *Revue biblique* 40 (1931) 185–213; 41 (1931) 50–76.

A. Reifenberg, *Ancient Jewish Coins* (Jerusalem, 1947²).

———, *Israel's History in Coins from the Maccabees to the Roman Conquest* (London, 1953).

R. B. Y. Scott, "Weights and Measures of the Bible," *Biblical Archaeologist* 22 (1959) 22–40.

D. Sperber, *Roman Palestine 200–400. Money and Prices* (Ramat-Gan, 1974).

See also the works cited above:

Barrois, II, 258–73; *Biblisch-Historisches Handwörterbuch* II, cols. 1159–1168 (A. Strobel); *Interpreter's Dictionary of the Bible* III, 423–35 (H. Hamburger); IV, 829–39 (O. R. Sellers); *Dictionnaire de la Bible, Supplément* V (Paris, 1957), cols. 1212–1250.

## 9. UTENSILS AND WEAPONS; THE ARMY

a. In ancient times there was no essential difference between utensils (used in the house, for working the fields, and for hunting) and weapons. Ax and knife were useful for both. In later times Israel also had its special weapons (Isa. 2:4–5; Micah 4:3; also Joel 3:10). The bow was not used in Israel in the army until the time of David (cf. 1 Chron. 12:2). The camel nomads were already famous archers in ancient times (Gen. 21:20). The Benjaminites were not only (left-handed) stone slingers (Jdgs. 3:15; 20:16) but also experts in using bow and arrow, with either hand (1 Chron. 12:2). The bow was strung (stretched taut) with the foot to be ready for use (Isa. 5:28). The arrows, made of wood, with a point of iron, were kept in a quiver. Incendiary arrows were used in later times (Eph. 6:16), though mentioned already in Psalm 7:13. A hole was made in the tip and combustible material inserted (*hennep tow*). The sling was known in primitive times (cf. the story of David and Goliath), but also later. According to 2 Chronicles 26:14–15, Uzziah provided his entire army with shields, spears, helmets, coats of armor, bows, and sling stones. Moreover, he made "ingeniously constructed weapons" to shoot arrows and large stones or (according to others) to protect archers and stone throwers. Probably large catapults are meant. For dagger and sword the Old Testament had only one word. We distinguish them according to length. It is better to translate Judges 3:16, 31 with "dagger." According to 2 Samuel 20:8 Joab had a sword or dagger (according to some, both) in a sheath. Also in the New Testament the same word could designate a knife, dagger, or sword (Matt. 26:51). "To put the sword into the sheath" is the general description of "to stop fighting" (1 Chron. 21:27; Matt. 26:52). Paul speaks of "the sword of the Spirit." The New Testament contains still another term for a (large) sword that is wide and two-edged (cf. Rev. 1:16). The club was also used; originally it was specifically the royal weapon (cf. Ps. 2:9). There were also various spears, javelins, and lances. A short javelin for cutting or throwing is mentioned, for instance, in 2 Chronicles 23:10, a long spear in Judges 5:8. The lance could be of varied sizes. In the story in 1 Samuel 17 such a lance is carried by Goliath; the expression "like a weaver's beam" need not refer to the measurements (de Vaux, I, 242), but rather to the fact that the lance was wrapped around with a leather belt for use as a throw weapon.

As to shields, there was the large and the small shield. Both were found (as status symbols) in Solomon's house, the "Forest of the Lebanon" (1 Kings 10:16–17; 2 Chron. 9:15–16) (see also section A.6 above). Metal shields such as those of Solomon or Rehoboam (1 Kings 14:27; 2 Chron. 12:10) were hardly in regular use; the shields normally employed were made of wood or wickerwork, overlaid with leather. The large shield covered the whole body and in battle was the defensive weapon of the "heavy infantry." The small round shield (*magen*) belonged to the light weapons (cf. 2 Chron. 14:8). Other equipment included a helmet (1 Sam. 17:5, 38; Goliath, Saul) and armor (1 Kings 22:34). Most of these arms were in use from very ancient times; in the Bible they are again mentioned with the Roman armor (Ephesians 6).

b. In the premonarchical era Israel did not have a professional army. The warriors went out on foot, in "thousands" (to be read as a technical term, not as indicating a figure, for sometimes it is used as a designation of the "clans"; cf. Micah 5:2) or in smaller units, for instance "fifties" (1 Sam. 8:12). The professional army was formed in the days of Saul. The earlier "people's army" was not enough for this king; he needed trained fighters as other kings had (cf. 1 Sam. 13:2, 15; 14:2). The king had a bodyguard. Thus at the time of David and Solomon there were "the Crethi and the Plethi," "the Cherethites and Pelethites." Some interpret this expression as "Cretans and Philistines," others as "Cretans and similar people" (2 Sam. 8:18; 20:33; 1 Kings 1:38, 44). In ancient times when all capable men bearing arms went to war, each tribe had its own banner or standard (Num. 2:1–31), perhaps with pictures after the symbolism of Genesis 49. In Old Testament times the Egyptians and (especially) the Assyrians were experts in the arts of war. Already in David's days, however, Israel was also familiar with the method of laying siege to a city by means of construction of a wall (2 Sam. 20:15). Compare also what is said about Uzziah's time in 2 Chronicles 26:15 (see above) and note especially the "siege law" given in Deuteronomy 20:10 (verses 19–20 speak of a palisade wall). Important at every siege was the water supply of a surrounded city. Famous is the so-called Shiloah (Siloam) tunnel, dug at the time of Hezekiah in view of a threatened Assyrian attack on Jerusalem. This tunnel provided continued access to the spring Gihon (ill. 103; cf. 2 Kings 20:20; 2 Chron. 32:30). From the time of Solomon the kings had chariot cities. These cities, built or fortified (that is, surrounded by a wall) by Solomon, are summed up in 1 Kings 9:15–19. In his own time the prophet Hosea saw the building of "fortified cities" as a sign that the people did not trust in God (Hos. 8:14).

---

## LITERATURE

H. Bonnet, *Die Waffen der Völker des Alten Orients* (Leipzig, 1926).

O. Keel, *Wirkungsmächtige Siegeszeichen im Alten Testament* (Freiburg/Göttingen, 1974).

Y. Yadin, *The Art of Warfare in Biblical Lands* I–II (Jerusalem, 1963).

———, *The Scroll of the War of the Sons of Light Against the Sons of Darkness* (Oxford, 1962).

---

## 10. SLAVERY

In biblical times (and long after it!) slavery was a common phenomenon. A person could be deprived of his freedom (mostly due to wars or captivity) or, pressed by circumstances, he could sell himself to another. Slavery was known in Israel too, but the laws in the Old Testament warn against and set limits to the abuse of power. Particularly in Solomon's time many foreign slaves were used in the building of temple and palaces, in mines and workshops (1 Kings 9:20–22, 26–28; 2 Chron. 2:17–18). Their descendants were still mentioned in Ezra 2:55–58; Nehemiah 7:57–

60; 11:3, together with the temple servants (Neh. 11:21), who at a certain time were the servants of the Levites (Ezra 8:20; for the "service" of the Israelites see the end of section A.6 above).

Already in ancient times Israel was also familiar with the custom of having "house slaves." The Decalogue in Exodus 20 includes under not desiring the neighbor's house, in addition to the wife, also the manservant and the maidservant. They represented a person's capital. The remarkable laws in the Book of the Covenant (Exodus 21–23) deal with the treatment of such a slave. The last sentence in Exodus 21:18–21 says: "for the slave is his money." From Exodus 21:32 we know that at the time the value of a slave was thirty shekels (cf. Matt. 26:15). In 2 Maccabees 8:11 it is said that Nicanor wanted to sell ninety Jews for a talent, that is, for about three thousand shekels. This would amount to only a slightly higher price per slave. De Vaux, however, points out that this was far below the market value of the slave at the time. The men- and maidservants are also mentioned in Deuteronomy 20:10–18; 21:10–14.

In the case of slaves of Israelite extraction (usually called "Hebrew slaves"), the law of Leviticus 25:46 was basic; it stipulated that one might not rule over one's brethren, the Israelites, with harshness, that is, they might not be mistreated. The slave had to be regarded as a member of the family (cf. Gen. 17:13, 27; see also B.2, on circumcision). Israel also had to remember that it had been delivered from (Egyptian) slavery. It entered history as a people freed from slavery! In 2 Chronicles 28:10 the prophet Oded lambasts the plan of the (northern) Israelites who wanted to make the inhabitants of Judah and Jerusalem their slaves. Something like that could thus happen, but it was condemned. However, in case an Israelite had to sell himself into slavery, on account of his debts, or because he saw no other opportunity to make a living, Leviticus 25:39–43 stipulates that he had to be treated as a "hired servant" and not as a slave. In the sabbatical year he could regain his freedom (cf. Exod. 21:1–6), or he could voluntarily remain in slavery for life (cf. Deut. 15:12–18; Jer. 34:14; see also section B.10.e below, "Year of Jubilee"). Separate rules obtained for female slaves. In ancient times they were sometimes taken or given as concubines (Abraham, Jacob). A slave who had fled could not be extradited if he had found asylum somewhere. We must realize that when the translations read "servant," the original often reads "slave," in both the Old and New Testaments. Often it had become an honorary title for someone who had dedicated himself with heart and soul and who considered himself as having been bought by a king, or even by God. So the second part of the book of Isaiah speaks of the mysterious "servant of the Lord," who through the ages has been viewed as the embodiment of the messiah. Paul calls himself a slave of Christ. In the New Testament the abolishment of slavery is not commanded by law (cf. Eph. 6:5 and the letter to Philemon), but the direction is indicated (cf. Gal. 3:28; Col. 3:11; and already Job 31:13–15).

## LITERATURE

M. David, "The Manumission of Slaves under Zedekiah," *Oudtestamentische Studiën* 5 (1948) 63–79.

P. Heinisch, "Das Sklavenrecht in Israel und im Alten Orient," *Studia Catholica* 11 (1934/35) 201–18.

I. Mendelsohn, *Slavery in the Ancient Near East* (New York, 1949).

_____, "State Slavery in Ancient Israel," *Bulletin of the American Schools of Oriental Research* 85 (1942) 14–17.

J. P. M. van der Ploeg, "Slavery in the Old Testament," *Congress Volume Uppsala 1971* (Supplements to Vetus Testamentum 22; Leiden, 1972), pp. 72–87.

# B. Religious Institutions

## 1. LEVIRATE AND REDEMPTION

Genesis 38:6–11, 26 and Deuteronomy 25:5–10 speak about levirate marriage. Both the late Latin word *levir* and the Hebrew word *yabam* mean "brother-in-law." According to ancient law the brother of a man who had died young and whose widow was still childless was obligated to marry the widow, in order, if possible, to raise a son by her, so that the name of the deceased would not be wiped out. The background of this custom lies in the great importance of the "family" or the "father's house," in which several brothers lived together under the authority of the father. In Mark 12:18–27 and parallels, the Sadducees went back to this Mosaic law to present the hypothetical case of a woman who successively was married to seven brothers. The stipulations of the law, according to Deuteronomy 25:10, included the "removal of the sandal" in case someone declined the levirate obligation.

The "redeemer marriage" resembled levirate marriage, but apparently it concerned a wider circle (see below). The *goel* (redeemer) was the closest relative, who had to protect the rights of someone who through circumstances was in danger of losing his property. He was obligated to "redeem" the property that otherwise would pass into strange hands (outside the family). So Israel was familiar with the redemption of a piece of land and of the house of the nearest relative (Lev. 25:23–34). An example is found in Jeremiah 32:6ff. There the story is told of a cousin of Jeremiah who asks the prophet if he is willing to buy the land of his father in Anathoth. Being hard-pressed (siege of the city of Jerusalem), the family was apparently no longer interested in the property. So this is not a case of buying back property. Jeremiah fulfills the redeemer obligation. His deed is at the same time a message which on behalf of God he is to give to the people: YHWH has given the land to Israel (Jer. 32:22)! In Israel redemption was thus religiously determined, unlike other nations that had customs and laws about similar matters but not with that same background; for that matter, the root *g'l* has not been found in any other language. From Ruth 4:5, 10 it might be inferred that the redemption obligation toward a widow also included a marriage, making it a particular form of levirate marriage (see above). It is, however, the only example of it in the Bible. The duty of redemption also pertained to the member of the people who had become a slave, but only in case he was forced to sell himself as a slave to an alien (*ger*) or a sojourner (*toshab*) (Lev. 25:47–49). Redemption did not pertain to an impoverished person who had to sell himself to a member of his own people. In that case the relevant legislation was to set the person free in the year of Jubilee (Lev. 25:39–46) or—according to other laws—in the sabbatical year (Exod. 21:2–6; Deut. 15:12–18; see section B.10.e below). The last-mentioned regulations are the reason that redemption was practiced in the Old Testament only in cases that concerned property or a member of the people who had been killed. In the latter case the closest relative acted as "avenger" (Num. 35:12, 19–27; Deut. 19:6, 12; Josh. 20:2, 5, 9; cf. 2 Sam. 24:11). The killer could seek refuge in one of the six cities of asylum or refuge; in Transjordan: Bezer, Ramoth-Gilead, and Golan (Deut. 4:43; Josh. 20:8); on the western side of the Jordan: Kedesh, Shechem, and Kiriath-arba or Hebron (Josh. 20:7).

In the cultic laws of the Old Testament the word for "redemption" is also used with the meaning of "buying back of sacrificial gifts" (Lev. 27:13, 15, 19, 31). According to Numbers 5:8 a redeemer is also the person who as the head of the family receives the redemption or atonement money. The beneficial impact which the word had on Israel's national life explains why the term "redeemer" was given not only to the king as the guardian of Israel's rights (cf. Ps. 72:14a), but also to YHWH, for example, in reference to the redemption from Egypt (Exod. 6:5; 15:13; Ps. 74:2; 77:16; 78:35; 106:10; Isa. 63:9). It expresses that YHWH already at the exodus from Egypt redeemed his people from slavery as his legal possession. Especially in the second part of the book of Isaiah the term is frequently used to announce the coming new redemption.

---

## LITERATURE

H. A. Brongers, "Enkele opmerkingen over het verband tussen lossing en leviraat in Ruth IV," *Nederlands Theologisch Tijdschrift* 2 (1947/48) 1–7.

M. Burrows, "The Ancient Oriental Background of Hebrew Levirate Marriage," *Bulletin of the American Schools of Oriental Research* 77 (1940) 2–15.

D. A. Leggett, *The Levirate and Goel Institutions in the Old Testament* (Cherry Hills, 1974).

J. Mittelmann, *Das altisraelitische Levirat* (Leipzig, 1934).

E. Neufeld, *Ancient Hebrew Marriage Laws* (London, 1944), pp. 23–55.

J. Schoneveld, *De betekenis van de lossing in het boek Ruth* (Gravenhage/Brussels, 1956).

---

## 2. CIRCUMCISION

Circumcision (Hebrew *mulah;* Greek *peritome*) is a surgical operation that according to the law (Lev. 12:3) was to be performed on the eighth day after the birth of a male child. A comparable operation on girls is found among other people, but not in the Bible. The "foreskin" of the male organ had to be removed. In ancient times this was done with a flint knife (Exod. 4:25; Josh. 5:2–3). The origin of the rite is obscure; it is found among many nations (ill. 104). Israel took it over and incorporated it into its own beliefs. That the Old Testament says relatively little about it is an indication that everyone was apparently familiar with it. Slaves, too, were to be circumcised (Exod. 12:44). At Gilgal there was even a "hill of foreskins" (Josh. 5:3). Exodus 4:24–26 and Joshua 5:2–9 intimate that circumcision originally contained the idea of a substitutionary sacrifice (pars pro toto). It is certain that there was a connection with cultic cleanness, and that it belonged to the many purification regulations. In that respect being circumcised was a *conditio sine qua non* for the Israelite. In Esther 8:17 the Hebrew text contains the verb "to become a Jew," but the Septuagint adds circumcision to it. During and after the Exile there was increasing emphasis on circumcision as the sign of the covenant. The ground for that was the covenant with Abram-Abraham, Genesis 17 (cf. Gen. 21:4). The idea that being circumcised and being saved were the same was attacked by the prophets (Jer. 4:4; cf. Deut. 10:16). They began to spiritualize the sign (cf. Ezek. 44:6–7) and to use it figuratively of "uncircumcised in heart" (Jer. 4:4; 9:26; Deut. 30:6; Lev. 26:41) and of "uncircumcised lips and ears" (Exod. 6:11; Jer. 6:10). Especially Jeremiah's figurative use points in the direction that continues to Paul. Later Judaism has, however, banned that "spiritual circumcision" from its official theology.

In the New Testament, in Luke 1:59; 2:21, the emphasis is especially on the name giving (see section A.3 above). John 7:22 shows that according to the scribes of that time even the sabbath commandment was of lesser significance than the prescription regarding circumcision, which had to be performed even if the eighth day was a sabbath. Paul mentions circumcision several times (Rom. 2:28–29; 1 Cor. 7:18–19; Gal. 2:3, 7; 5:6; Phil. 3:3; Col. 2:11–12). He continued the line of the prophets (see above) by speaking of "the circumcision of the heart" and by positing that faith and conversion are of greater value than circumcision or uncircumcision. The pagan who accepted Christ in faith did not have to be circumcised. Apart from some exceptions (Copts and Abyssinians), the Christian church has dropped circumcision as an outward sign. However, already early a connection was made between infant baptism and circumcision. Circumcision of the heart, the circumcision of Christ, and baptism were all viewed from one perspective (cf. Col. 2:11–12).

## LITERATURE

W. H. Gispen, "De besnijdenis," *Gereformeerd Theologisch Tijdschrift* 54 (1954) 148–57, 174–82; 55 (1955) 9–16.

J. de Groot, "The Story of the Bloody Husband," *Oudtestamentische Studiën* 2 (1943) 10–17.

H. Kosmala, "The 'Bloody Husband'," *Vetus Testamentum* 12 (1962) 14–28.

R. Meyer, "*peritemno*," in G. Kittel and G. Friedrich, eds., *Theological Dictionary of the New Testament* VI (Grand Rapids, 1968) 72–84.

P. Romualdus, "De besnijdenis bij St. Paulus," *Studia Catholica* 22 (1947) 216–66.

J. Soep, *De besnijdenis. Een ethnologische studie* (Amsterdam, 1947).

## 3. LOT AND ORACLE

a. On all kinds of occasions a decision or a choice was made by means of the lot (Hebrew *goral;* Greek *kleros*). Joshua occupied the land and concluded his life's work by allocating the land by lot, so that every tribe received an inheritance (Josh. 13:7). The piece of land itself was also called *goral* (Josh. 14:2; 15:1; 16:1). Clothes could be divided by lot (Ps. 22:19; cf. Mark 15:24 and parallels), as could an inheritance (Sir. 14:15; cf. Prov. 18:18) or the spoils of war (Prov. 1:14). The lot played a role, too, in sacral matters, such as the organization of the ministry (1 Chronicles 24–25; 26:13–16; Neh. 10:34; Luke 1:8). On the Day of Atonement the lot was cast for one of the goats (Lev. 16:8). Also, after the return from exile, lots were cast to determine who would live in Jerusalem (Neh. 11:1–2). In the book of Esther the word *pur* is explained as meaning "lot" (Esth. 3:7; 9:24). The lot is *cast* (Joel 3:3; Obad. 11; Nah. 3:10; Sir. 14:15; Ps. 22:19; cf. Mark 15:24 and parallels). It

can also *fall* on someone (Ezek. 24:6b; Jonah 1:7; Acts 1:26). Stones or pieces of wood that were inscribed or on which signs had been scratched were used for the lot (1 Chron. 26:13–16). The precise mode is not always clear.

## LITERATURE

W. Dommershausen, "Das 'Los' in der alttestamentlichen Theologie," *Trierer theologische Zeitschrift* 80 (1971) 195–206.

J. Lindblom, "Lot-Casting in the Old Testament," *Vetus Testamentum* 12 (1962) 164–78.

b. In the official cult the *urim* and *thummim* were used to obtain an oracle (cf. the blessing about Levi, Deut. 33:8–11). Later these objects became predominantly symbols of dignity (cf. Ezra 2:63; Neh. 7:65). They were carried by the high priest in his "breastpiece" (Exod. 25:7; 28:4–30; 29:5; 35:9–27; 39:8–21; Lev. 8:8). It is also called "breastpiece of judgment" (Exod. 28:15, 29–30; see also below under ephod). There is no clear explanation for the names of the sacred objects *urim* and *thummim* (probably having the shape of dice). Did they bear the first or the last letter of the alphabet? Was the one stone white and the other black? It has been suggested that *urim* (a word which despite its form is not a plural but expresses a superlative of intensity or quality) means "the perfect light" and *thummim* "perfection," or "cursed" and "innocent." The most plausible explanation is that there was a white stone meaning "yes" and a black stone meaning "no." There is, however, the possibility that beforehand an agreement was made about the significance of the stones. In any case, it always concerns the choice between two possibilities. The oracle could also "be silent," perhaps when both stones showed the same (cf. 1 Sam. 14:3, 37). An oracle such as that used by heathen priests and designated with another term (*qesem*) was forbidden in the Old Testament (e.g., Deut. 18:10). Divination by examining the liver (especially practiced in Mesopotamia) was forbidden in Israel (cf. Ezek. 21:21).

## LITERATURE

E. Lipiński, "Urim and Tummim," *Vetus Testamentum* 20 (1970) 495–96.

J. Maier, "Urim and Tummim," *Kairos* 11 (1969) 22–23.

E. Robertson, "The 'Urim and Tummim'; What Were They?" *Vetus Testamentum* 14 (1964) 67–74.

J. Schoneveld, "Urim en Tummim," *Orientalia Neerlandica* (1948) 216–22.

c. The *teraphim* (likely a mask) was also one of the objects used in ancient times to obtain an oracle. Later it is mentioned among the "abominable things" (cf. 2 Kings 23:24; Ezek. 21:21; Hos. 3:4—here in combination with the ephod). Only in 2 Kings 23:24 and Zechariah 10:2 does teraphim designate a plurality (see *urim* and *thummim* above); in other passages the word stands for one object (cf. Genesis 31; Jdgs. 17:5; 18:14–20; 1 Sam. 15:23; 19:11–17).

## LITERATURE

C. J. Labuschagne, "Teraphim—A New Proposal for its Etymology," *Vetus Testamentum* 16 (1966) 115ff.

E. Sellin, "Ephod und Terafim," *Journal of the Palestine Oriental Society* 14 (1934) 185–94.

_____, "Zu Ephod und Terafim," *Zeitschrift für die alttestamentliche Wissenschaft* 55 (1937) 296–98.

d. In 1 Samuel 23:1–13; 30:1–25 the *ephod* is mentioned as a means to "inquire" of God. The difficulty is that a piece of clothing of the high priest has the same name. Common to these diverse items may have been the root meaning of the word "clothing" or "dress." The oracular instrument may have been a skirt or bag used for shaking the stones. According to 1 Samuel 21:9, the sword of Goliath was behind the ephod, wrapped in a cloth. Judges 8:27 reports that Gideon made the gold that had been collected into an ephod. The weight mentioned there, more than

seventeen hundred shekels, is too large to make us think of a cloth covered with gold. In that passage the ephod may stand for an image of a god or a metal casing (in Isa. 30:22 a related word is used).

## LITERATURE

K. Elliger, "Ephod und Choshen," *Vetus Testamentum* 8 (1958) 19–35.

I. Friedrich, *Ephod und Choshen im Lichte des Alten Orients* (Vienna, 1968).

J. Morgenstern, *The Ark, the Ephod, and the Tent of Meeting* (Cincinnati, 1945).

H. Thiersch, *Ependytes und Ephod. Gottesbild und Priesterkleid im alten Vorderasien* (Stuttgart, 1936).

e. A special form of the oracle is the trial by *ordeal*. This too is found in the Old Testament. Here the concern is not to obtain guidance for the present or future (as is the case with the normal use of the lot), but to obtain a decision about something that has already happened; in other words, a legal judgment. God is here the One who determines the lot. Joshua 7:13–18 speaks of the curse of the devoted thing that lies on the people. The lot has to determine who is the guilty one. 1 Samuel 10:20–24 is about designating the person who is to be king. 1 Samuel 14 also speaks about the ordeal. Compare with this Jonah 1:7, where an ordeal is mentioned that was used by pagans to find the guilty one. A special form of an ordeal in old times was the "law of jealousy" (Num. 5:11–31).

## LITERATURE

O. Eissfeldt, "Wahrsagung im Alten Testament," *Kleine Schriften* IV (Tübingen, 1968) 271–75.

E. Grant, "Oracle in the Old Testament," *American Journal of Semitic Languages and Literatures* 39 (1922/23) 257–81.

F. Horst, "Der Eid im Alten Testament," *Evangelische Theologie* 17 (1957) 366–84.

A. Jirku, *Mantik in Alt-Israel* (Rostock, 1913).

R. Press, "Das Ordal im alten Israel," *Zeitschrift*

*für die alttestamentliche Wissenschaft* 51
(1933) 121–40, 227–55.

A. Schulz, "Die Ordalien in Alt-Israel," in *Fest-schrift G. von Hertling* (Munich, 1913),
pp. 29–35.

---

f. The casting of the lot, for an ordeal as well as
for an oracle, fell into disuse in later times. In
1 Samuel 14:44 it can already be seen that the
will of God in the ordeal and the voice of God in
the protests of the people could contradict each
other. According to the Talmud, the oracle by lot
ceased already at the time of Solomon.

# 4. SACRIFICIAL CULT AND PRAYERS

a. In the Old Testament, sacrifices belong to the
cultic means that are used, within the covenant of
YHWH with his people, to regulate the association of God with people, and, as the consequence
or condition of it, also the relationship of people to
each other. The origin of these sacrifices can be
traced only in part. There is considerable similarity, especially with the Canaanites. Israel,
however, always had to develop its peculiar religious beliefs, also in the area of sacrifices. The
meaning of blood is an illustration. Shortly after
their settlement in Canaan the Israelites still seem
to have used the blood of animals as food, as this
was done by the neighboring nations (1 Sam.
14:31–35). However, they had to realize that all
life belongs to God. That is why the absolute prohibition to use blood was given (Lev. 7:26). "The
life of all flesh is its blood" (cf. Gen. 9:4–6; Lev.
17:14; Deut. 12:23). This has played a large role
throughout Jewish history (cf. Acts 15:19–21).

The first Old Testament narrative to speak of
sacrifices is that of Cain and Abel (Gen. 4:3–5). A
term is used which later is the usual designation
for a food offering, but which originally meant a
"presentation," a "gift" (*minhah*). The story
shows at least that the bringing of sacrifices is an
act all people are familiar with. Israel's prophets
were sharply critical of sacrificial customs, but it
was never their intention to abolish the whole
cult. They denounced in scathing terms all out-
growths and trusting in the automatic efficacy of
the sacrificial service. If Israel did not live according to the rules of the covenant all sacrifices
would be meaningless (cf. Isa. 1:10–17; 29:13;
Jer. 7:21–23; Hos. 6:6; Amos 4:4–5; 5:4–6, 21–
26; 9:1; Micah 6:6–8).

To get some idea of the enormous variety of
sacrifices, we can distinguish three main categories: sacrifices intended as *gift,* those that establish
or support the *community,* and those that are *reconciling* in nature. It should be remembered,
however, that all three facets are more or less
present in all sacrificial ceremonies, though they
alternate as the most prominent.

(1) The Sacrifice as Gift. In everything that was
offered to God, Israel had always to be aware
that everthing comes from God. In David's hymn
of praise recorded in 1 Chronicles 29:10–19, this
confession is found: "for all things come from
thee, and of thy own have we given thee" (verse
14b). God does not "need" anything from man,
but with respect to God man should show that he
is willing to give himself. The sacrifice that most
clearly expresses this unconditional giving is the
"burnt offering" (*olah*), literally, "that which
goes up in smoke." The sacrificial laws of Leviticus (chapters 1–7) start with it (cf. Lev. 1:1–17;
6:8–13). The offerer himself receives nothing of
the sacrifice, in contrast to the communion and
meal offerings. The priest gets only the skin of the
animal. The offerer kills the animal himself: an ox,
sheep, or goat; for those less well-to-do, also birds
(cf. Lev. 1:14; 5:7; 12:8). However, the manipulation of the blood was to be done by the priest
(Lev. 1:11). The sacrificer was first to lay his hand
on the head of the sacrificial animal to indicate
that it was his sacrifice and that the atonement
that would be wrought was on his behalf (Lev.
1:4). In later times the official priests did much
more at all sacrificial ceremonies. In earlier times,
however, the offerer performed the acts himself.
The priests laid the cleaned parts of the animal on
the altar of burnt offering, on which there had
always to be a fire. The following morning the
ashes were to be put beside the altar. The burnt
offering was thus the unconditional "surrender to
YHWH." The going up in smoke undoubtedly
symbolized that what was sacrificed was
"given" to the invisible sphere, to God's domain.
The altar symbolized as it were the meeting place

of God with this world. Burnt offerings were also repeatedly mentioned in the old texts that reflect the situation before the existence of the temple (Jdgs. 6:26–28; 13:15–20; 1 Sam. 6:14; 7:9; 10:8).

Besides the term "burnt offering," other terms are used that emphasize the gift character of the sacrifice. The Hebrew *kalil* is one of them; it has in it the root of the word "whole." Buber renders it as *Ganzopfer* (1 Sam. 7:9; Deut. 33:10; Ps. 51:21). Another word that should be mentioned here is the earlier-mentioned *minhah*, which can stand for an ordinary gift (Gen. 32:14ff.) or a tribute to the king (1 Sam. 10:27; 2 Chron. 17:5). Occasionally the "gift" presented to YHWH and what is presented to the king are found in one sentence (2 Chron. 32:23). In the sacrificial laws a *minhah* always designated a nonbloody sacrifice. Usually, however, it was a sacrifice added to the burnt offering and consumed along with it. According to Lev. 2:1–16 it consisted of a cake of flour mixed with oil and sprinkled with incense. It was burnt in its entirety. Usually a drink offering (wine) was added to it. In a similar context such a gift offering is also called *qorban*, a term occurring only in the books of Leviticus, Numbers, and Ezekiel with that meaning. Its basic meaning is that of "making something approach" to God, that is, giving it to God. In later times it became a general word for sacrifice and still later a kind of formula that was pronounced over something that was withdrawn from ordinary use, but without actually bringing it as a sacrifice. In the New Testament the word occurs once in that sense (in a dispute of Jesus with the scribes, Mark 7:11). In Matthew 27:6 a similar word occurs, designating the temple treasury. The term *ishsheh* also belongs here. Usually, following the Septuagint, it is translated as "an offering by fire" (Lev. 1:9–10). Frequently it is added that it was "a pleasing odor" to the Lord, an old expression taken over by the biblical writers to indicate that the offering was accepted by God. The shewbread or bread of the Presence (see the description of the tabernacle and temple below) and the offerings of incense (incense mixed with other pleasant-smelling ingredients) also belong to gift offerings. The latter were burnt on the altar of incense (cf. Exod. 30:7–8 on morning and eve-

ning sacrifice). Only the sons of Aaron were permitted to bring the offering of incense (cf. 2 Chron. 26:16–18); it was regarded as a sacred privilege (Luke 1:9). It had a significant function on the Great Day of Atonement (see section B.10.f below).

(2) Communion Sacrifices. Though the term as such does not occur in the Bible, one can speak of communion sacrifices in cases where the victim was not only given to God but in part was also shared by the offerers and the priest. There are some who think that this was the original meaning of all sacrifices and that God was then as it were the One sharing in the meal. Leviticus 3:1–17 contains a description of these sacrifices under the name "peace offerings," a translation derived from the Greek rendering of the Hebrew *zebah shelamim*. There is no consensus about the original meaning of *shelamim*, though it is certain that *zebah* is a "sacrificial victim" (it is also used independently). The (plural) term *shelamim* may have a connection with *shalom* (hence "peace offerings"). It is, however, also explained as "final offering." More important than the original meaning is the purpose of these sacrifices, namely, to establish communion. Here we could point to the communion-establishing character of every meal and also think of the Old Testament Passover and the Lord's Supper in the Christian church. After the slaughtering, a part of the animal (only an ox or small livestock, no fowl) was burned as an offering by fire to YHWH, in particular the fat (like the blood it was regarded as the symbol of the vital power) and the kidneys (in the Old Testament viewed as the most important organ besides the heart, in man often as the seat of what we call the conscience; cf. Ps. 16:7). This part is the "food" for YHWH. This bold expression occurs a few times in the Old Testament (Lev. 3:11, 16; 21:6, 8, 17, 21–22; 22:25; 24:7; Num. 28:2; Ezek. 44:7), but it has an altogether different background than with the heathen peoples (cf. Ps. 50:13). There were various kinds of communion sacrifices, as is apparent from the prescriptions in Leviticus 7:11–18; 22:17–25; 28:30, namely as *todah* (thank or praise offering), as *nedabh* (voluntary sacrifice), and as *neder* (votive offering). For the communion sacrifices strict regulations were maintained as to what

might be eaten by those who brought the sacrifice. Compare with this Paul's admonitions for celebrating the Lord's Supper in a worthy manner (1 Cor. 11:17–34).

(3) Expiatory Sacrifices. If for one reason or another the covenant relationship with YHWH had been disrupted by a person, it could be restored (from God's side by his grace). That required the sacrifice that effects reconciliation. It is unnecessary to say it (but let it here be said again anyway!) that it does not concern an automatic ritual here. For that purpose read the detailed regulations in Leviticus 4:1–5:13 and 5:14–6:7, as well as the prophetic critique on all sacrifices (see above). Every sacrifice that required the shedding of blood possessed reconciling power (cf. Lev. 17:11), but for some cases, mentioned, for example, in the cited chapters of Leviticus, special sacrifices were required. Included here are the sacrifice for sin (*hattat*) and the guilt offering (*asham*). The offering for sin could be used in case someone had sinned "unintentionally." The regulations in Leviticus distinguish in that connection four types of people: the high priest (the anointed priest, Lev. 4:3), the whole nation (the whole congregation of Israel, Lev. 4:13), the ruler (Lev. 4:22), and one from the common people (presumably one of the free citizens is meant, Lev. 4:27). The sin offerings of the poor are mentioned separately (Lev. 5:7–13). In all cases the manipulations of the blood were very important. The fat was to be burned on the altar. The whole of the rites shows clearly that here we find ourselves at the heart of the cult: reconciliation as total removal of sins.

The sin offerings play a large role in the ritual of the Day of Atonement (Leviticus 16). In 2 Corinthians 5:21 Paul says: "For our sake God made him to be sin who knew no sin." With an allusion to the Old Testament sacrificial laws, the Greek word for "sin" is used here in a dual sense, namely, as "sin" and as "sin offering," even as is done in the Hebrew. The word for "guilt offering" has likewise a dual meaning; guilt or being guilty and the means to remove that guilt. In contrast to the sin offering, this sacrifice is not part of the ritual of the great feasts. In origin it designates rather the penalty imposed for a variety of offenses, and only secondarily the sacrifice. It should thus also be viewed as a penalty that is to be paid to YHWH, because every offense against the neighbor is also against God (e.g., in the case of false witness, Lev. 6:3, 5). Isaiah 53:10 speaks of the guilt offering of the servant of the Lord. The precise demarcation between a sin offering and a guilt offering is not clear. Leviticus 14:10–32, for example, prescribes that for the cleansing of a leper, the one as well as the other is to be brought (in addition to a burnt offering). The book of Deuteronomy does not mention these sacrifices. In the New Testament the entire sacrificial cult is regarded as fulfilled in the death of Jesus Christ. During his earthly life Jesus accepted the sacrificial cult and temple service as something sacred (Matt. 5:23–26; 23:16–22) and gave it his prophetic criticism (Matt. 9:13; 12:7). He institutes a new covenant, however (Matt. 12:6; 26:61; John 2:19; 4:21). Paul calls Christ the passover lamb that has been slain for us (1 Cor. 5:7). In the epistle to the Hebrews the bloody sacrifice, as this was brought by the high priest under the old dispensation, has become a foreshadowing of the sacrifice made by Christ once and for all (see especially Hebrews 8–10).

## LITERATURE

K. W. Clark, "Worship in the Jerusalem Temple after A.D. 70," *New Testament Studies* 6 (1959/1960) 269–80.

R. Dussaud, *Les origines cananéennes du sacrifice israélite* (Paris, 1941²).

G. B. Gray, *Sacrifice in the Old Testament* (Oxford, 1925).

B. A. Levine, *In the Presence of the Lord* (Leiden, 1974).

W. O. E. Oesterley, *Sacrifices in Ancient Israel* (London, 1937).

R. Rendtorff, *Studien zur Geschichte des Opfers im Alten Israel* (Neukirchen-Vluyn, 1967).

H. H. Rowley, "The Meaning of Sacrifice in the Old Testament," *Bulletin of the John Rylands Library* 33 (1950/51) 74–110.

R. de Vaux, *Studies in Old Testament Sacrifice* (London, 1964).

b. Sacrifice and prayer have from olden times been undoubtedly closely connected, though the Old Testament contains no prescriptions about that connection. Various psalms may have been used as prayers at certain cultic happenings. In Psalm 141:2 prayer itself is called an offering of incense (cf. Rev. 5:8; 8:3–4). Here we are not concerned with the content of prayer (petition, thanksgiving, praise, confession) but with the regulations with respect to the times, the posture, and the special dress to be used in prayer. The older parts of the Old Testament do not contain set times of prayer, though from 1 Samuel 1:3, 9–19 it can be gathered that a sacrifice was regarded as an opportunity to direct special prayers to God. Only in the late Old Testament era do we read of prayers three times a day (Dan. 6:11; Ps. 55:18). Also the New Testament mentions it in passing (Acts 3:1). Acts 16:13, 16 speaks of a special place of prayer. One could pray standing (1 Sam. 1:9, 26; 1 Kings 8:22; 2 Chron. 6:12; Luke 18:11), or prostrated on the ground (the so-called *proskynesis*, 1 Kings 8:54; 2 Chron. 6:13; Isa. 45:23; cf. Gen. 24:26; Exod. 34:8; Ps. 5:8). The hands were stretched out to heaven or toward the holy place (Exod. 9:29; 1 Kings 8:22; 2 Chron. 6:13; Ps. 28:2; cf. Exod. 17:8–9). Prayer was directed to (the place of) the name of YHWH (2 Chron. 6:21). That gave rise to the custom, by those living outside the Holy Land, of praying with the face toward Jerusalem (1 Kings 8:44; 2 Chron. 6:34; Dan. 6:11).

## LITERATURE

P. A. H. de Boer, *De voorbede in het Oude Testament* (= *Oudtestamentische Studiën* 3; Leiden, 1943).

I. Elbogen, *Der jüdische Gottesdienst in seiner geschichtlichen Entwicklung* (Frankfurt am Main, 1931[3]; repr. Hildesheim, 1962).

J. Heineman, *Prayer in the Talmud* (Berlin/New York, 1977).

H. J. Hermisson, *Sprache und Ritus im altisraelitischen Kult* (Neukirchen-Vluyn, 1965).

N. B. Johnson, *Prayer in the Apocrypha and Pseudepigrapha: A Study of the Jewish Concept of God* (Philadelphia, 1948).

G. Klinzing, *Die Umdeutung des Kultus in der Qumrangemeinde und im Neuen Testament* (Göttingen, 1971).

N. H. Ridderbos, *De plaats van het loven en het bidden in het Oude Testament* (Kampen, 1970).

Already before the time of the New Testament the prayer shawl (*tallit*) and the prayer belts (*tefillin*) were in use. The first, a square wrapping cloth with tassels, was originally an ordinary garment, which Jesus also wore (Matt. 9:20; 14:36; Luke 8:44). The tassels were a reminder of God's commands (Num. 15:38; Deut. 22:12; Matt. 23:5). The last passage shows that the Pharisees used it to demonstrate their piety. A kind of protective efficacy was also attributed to it, like an amulet. The prayer belts were to be attached to the left arm. The small box attached to it had to contain the texts Exodus 13:1–10, 11–16; Deuteronomy 6:4–9; 11:13–21, written on parchment. It is assumed that the prescriptions in those passages were originally meant symbolically. Later these boxes were also attached to the forehead during prayer. The *mezuzah* (the word means literally "doorpost"), which was used at a later time, contained the pericopes Deuteronomy 6:4–10; 11:13–20 on a small scroll of parchment.

## LITERATURE

H. L. Strack and P. Billerbeck, *Kommentar zum Neuen Testament aus Talmud und Midrasch* IV/1 (Munich, 1928) 250ff.

Y. Yadin, *Tefillin from Qumran* (Jerusalem, 1969).

## 5. PRIESTS AND LEVITES

The priesthood occupied an important place among the biblical institutions. Priests were to serve the people as their representatives with God and as God's representatives with the people. Different from the prophets, they were not charismatic (though they could certainly be called from those circles; cf. 2 Chron. 24:20). They were invested with an office (hence the detailed description of their official dress, Exodus 28 and 39) that was hereditary through the generations. The title given to them was *kohen*, a term which until today has remained a priestly name among the Jewish people. Attempts have been made to find a connection with other languages, for instance, with a similar word in Arabic meaning "soothsayer." Others associate it with a Hebrew verb meaning "stand" or "place before," so that originally a *kohen* would be someone who "stands before God" (cf. Deut. 10:8) or someone "who places (sacrifices) before God." Though none of the three is totally convincing, it is safest to say that a *kohen* is someone who on behalf of the people stands before God.

Only in the course of time did the priesthood receive its fixed form. In early times the father or the head of the family performed the priestly duties (Jdgs. 6:18; 13:19; Job 1:5; cf. Jdgs. 17:5, 12; Deut. 21:1–4). The backgrounds of the later developments are not always clear, but some lines can be pointed out. The two names continually surfacing in history in connection with the priestly office are the historical names Aaron and Levi. Beginning with them, two threads weave themselves through the history in the Old Testament. Those threads are interwoven with other traditions, however, for instance, the one concerning Zadok. That is why in later times there is a system in which (a) descent from Aaron and (b) descent from Levi played a role, and in which, moreover, (c) "Zadokite priests" are also mentioned.

a. Aaronic Priests. In the priestly parts of the Pentateuch, Aaron and his sons (Nadab, Abihu, Eleazar, Ithamar) occupied the priestly office. Moses was to clothe them with the priestly garments (Exod. 28:39–40), and to consecrate them for their office (Exodus 29; Leviticus 8). Commanded by Moses, the mediator of the Old Covenant, Aaron brought the first sacrifice to the tabernacle (Leviticus 9). After the death of Nadab and Abihu (Lev. 10:1–5; Num. 3:4; 26:61), "the tribe of Levi" was assigned to Aaron, Eleazar, and Ithamar as their servants. The Levites functioned as secondary priests and as representatives of the firstborn of the Israelites (Num. 3:9, 12–13, 44; cf. Exod. 13:2).

b. Levites and Levitical Priests. In Deuteronomy 18:1–8 no mention is made of Aaron and his sons. In fact, they are hardly mentioned in the whole book of Deuteronomy, only in 9:20 and 10:6 (many regard these as later additions that combine the various traditions). Mention is made of "the Levitical priests, the whole tribe of Levi." According to the Masoretic text of Judges 17:7, "Levite" designates a profession or office. The Levite mentioned there belongs to the tribe of Judah (cf. also Judges 17–20; Deut. 12:12; Exod. 33:25–29). In the "blessing of Moses" (Deuteronomy 33), the Levites were mentioned in the saying about (the tribe, the tribal ancestor) Levi. In Genesis 49:5–7 and Genesis 34, a dispersed tribe of Levi (and of Simeon) is mentioned. Some tribal lists mention Levi, others do not (see section A.5 above). It has been asked: did the tribe of Levi perish, are the similarities between the names Levi and Levite only coincidental? Did the Levites become priests and was Moses thereby the connecting link (according to Exod. 2:1 Moses was a man from the house of Levi)? Deuteronomy 27:9, 12, 14 speak successively about Levitical priests, about the tribe of Levi, and about Levites (who perform the service of "blessing"); the same is true to some extent of Deuteronomy 31:9, 24–26. The Levites received their income from the tithes (Num. 18:21–24), of which the priests also received a share (Num. 18:25–32). In Numbers 35:1–8; Joshua 21:1–42; 1 Chronicles 6:54–81, "Levitical cities" are mentioned (to which later also the cities of refuge belonged), which together with the pastures around it were given to the Kohathite, the Gershonite, and the Merarite families (in total, forty-eight cities). In its present form, the list of Joshua 21 is usually viewed as a literary product from the monarchical time, but its roots go back to a much older period. In the book of Deuteronomy the two titles of priest and Levite were identified in the sense that only Levites could be priests.

c. Zadokite Priests. During David's reign Zadok was one of the most important priests besides Abiathar (2 Sam. 8:17; 5:24, 35; 19:11; 20:25). During Solomon's reign he became high priest in Jerusalem (1 Kings 1:7–8; 2:26–27, 35). According to 2 Samuel 8:17 this Zadok was an Elide (that is, from the house of Eli), a grandson of Phinehas. Some, regarding this text as a later addition, are inclined to regard Zadok as a successor of the priest in the original Jebusite sanctuary in Jerusalem. It is certain that Ezekiel on behalf of God assigned the priestly office only to the sons of Zadok (Ezek. 44:15). For centuries the high priestly office was exclusively in Zadokite hands (cf. Ezra 3:2; Hag. 1:1). Yet also descendants of Abiathar were recognized as priests (1 Chronicles 24). Whether the later Sadducees derived their name and descent from Zadok (as is often assumed) is a moot question.

d. The later books of the Old Testament contain the system that requires that all priests had to be Levites (hence, "Levitical priests") but that not all Levites had priestly status. The ordinary Levites had become a lower type of cleric, who according to the books of Chronicles had important tasks, such as responsibility for the singing in the temple, the passing on of the old traditions through their preaching, the guarding of the temple, and the like. But unlike the Levitical priests, they did not perform the service at the altar. The consecration of the Levites is mentioned in Numbers 8:1–22. The same chapter speaks next about their age (Num. 8:23–26; cf., however, Numbers 4; 1 Chron. 23:3). The consecration of priests is sometimes called "the filling of the hand." Compare the Authorized Version with the RSV at passages such as Exodus 28:41; 29:9, 29; 32:29. It is an old expression which originally was probably connected with the income that the priest "received in the hand," but which later became a technical term for their consecration.

e. The priests were "anointed" (Exod. 28:41; 30:30; 40:12–15; Lev. 7:35–36; 10:7; Num. 3:3). It is not likely that this became a custom only after the Exile, as has been supposed. Separate mention is made of the anointing of the high priest (see also Exod. 29:4–9; Lev. 4:3, 16; 6:20–23; 8:12; 16:32; 1 Chron. 29:22). The precious oil mentioned in Ps. 133:2 (even if "the beard of Aaron" is not, as some say, regarded as a later addition) is only figurative language referring to the fragrant care of the hair. According to Exodus 28:36, the high priest wore a plate of pure gold on which was engraved "Holy to YHWH" (cf. Exod. 39:30; Lev. 8:9). This "diadem" was probably in the shape of a flower. Exodus 28:39–43 and 39:27–31 speak of the garments of the priest. The

high priest had special clothing (Exodus 28; 39:1–26). For the Urim and Thummim and the ephod see sections B.3.b and d above.

f. The work of the priests consisted in making the sacrifices, of which they usually received a part, and the performance of all kinds of cultic services in the sanctuary. There were also services that could only be done by the high priest (cf. the ritual of the Day of Atonement, section B.10.f below). From of old the priests also had a responsibility in the instruction in the sacred stories and laws. Numbers 6:22–27 mentions "the priestly benediction." Blessing was the privilege of the priests (cf. Lev. 9:22; Deut. 10:8; 27:14; 1 Chron. 23:13). Kings, however, also pronounced the blessing (2 Sam. 6:18; 1 Kings 8:55; cf. 2 Chron. 26:16–19).

g. In the postexilic period priests and Levites were divided into groups (1 Chron. 23:6–24; 24:1–19). The number of groups was not always constant (cf. Ezra 2:36–39; Neh. 10:3–9; 12:1–7; see also Luke 1:5).

## LITERATURE

W. W. von Baudissin, *Die Geschichte des alttestamentlichen Priesterthums* (Leipzig, 1889).

A. Cody, *A History of Old Testament Priesthood* (Rome, 1969).

A. H. J. Gunneweg, *Leviten und Priester* (Göttingen, 1965).

A. R. Johnson, *The Cultic Prophet in Ancient Israel* (Cardiff, 1962[2]).

R. de Vaux, " 'Lévites' minéens et lévites israélites," in *Lex tua veritas* (Festschrift H. Junker; Trier, 1961), pp. 265–73.

A. C. Welch, *Prophet and Priest in Old Israel* (Oxford, 1953).

## 6. THE ARK

a. In the Solomonic temple as well as in the earlier tabernacle (see section B.7 below) the ark occupied an important place. The word *aron* means chest or box. The box used for the transportation of the body of Joseph was an *aron* (Gen. 50:26). The treasury box of the priest Jehoiada and of King Joash was also designated by that term

XXXIV. A Mycenean gold death mask. (University Museum, University of Pennsylvania; picture Rosenthal Art Slides)

XXXV. A Persian gold daric from the time of Artaxerxes II (ca. 400 B.C.). The king is poised on one knee holding a bow and spear. (From the collection of G. L. Archer; picture W. S. LaSor)

XXXVI. Silver shekels struck in Jerusalem in "Year 3" (left) and "Year 5" of the Jewish revolt, ca. A.D. 68 and 70, respectively. (G. Nalbandian)

XXXVII. A coin of Vespasian wearing a victory wreath. He was emperor when his son Titus captured Jerusalem in A.D. 70. (G. Nalbandian)

XXXVIII. A replica of Aaron's breastplate in gold and precious stones representing the twelve tribes (cf. Exod. 28, 39). (American Baptist Assembly, Green Lake, Wisconsin)

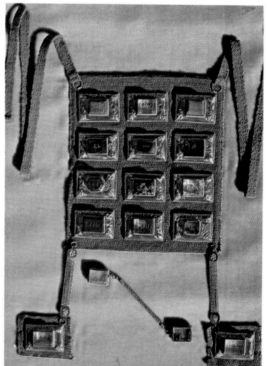

96. A reconstruction of an Israelite home from the period of the monarchy. Such reconstructions are always based on the interpretation of the foundations, since in most cases only the foundations are recovered. Yet the presence of a staircase of stones may be an indication that the building had more than one floor (cf. 2 Kings 4:10). The floor plan of this house shows that it consisted of four parts: three parallel rooms (the center one being the inner court) and another across the back adjoining them (this is the inner room, the actual sleeping area). Such homes were occupied by the more well-to-do commoners. See pp. 50ff., 350.

97. Part of the ivory headboard of an Ugaritic king's bed. (Direction Générale des Antiquités et des Musées, Damascus, Syria)

98. A panel from the Black Obelisk of Shalmaneser III showing Jehu (or his emissary) bowing before the Assyrian king (ca. 859–824 B.C.). This is the only contemporary representation of an Israelite king. Note the garments: hats, long robes, sandals. (Trustees of the British Museum)

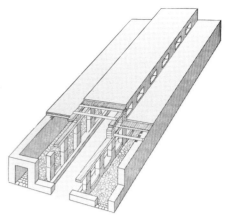

99. The sarcophagus of Ahiram, a tenth-century B.C. king of Byblos (Gebal). This side shows him seated on a throne and attendants approaching him. On the rim of the sarcophagus is a sepulchral inscription in Phoenician identifying the sarcophagus and invoking curses on anyone (particularly an official) who disturbs it. (Direction générale des antiquités, Republic of Lebanon)

100. A reconstruction of rectangular buildings of three large rooms with pillars. Such buildings were found in many cities in the monarchial period. Formerly scholars often thought these were stables for horses, but it is now believed that they were store houses, especially for goods that were used to pay taxes. There are also those who think that they were military barracks or bazaars (covered shopping streets).

101. Shekel weights of stone.

102. A bronze box with silver coins from.the 1st century A.D., including some shekels from the time of the Jewish revolt.

103. Part of Hezekiah's tunnel. Through it water flowed from the spring east of the city to a reservoir in southeast Jerusalem.

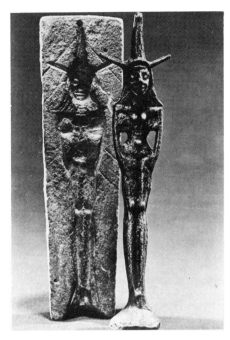

104. A relief from a tomb at Saqqara showing priests using flint knives to perform the rite of circumcision on a group of boys (6th Dynasty, 2350–2000 B.C.). (Egyptian Museum, Cairo)

105. A bronze figure, with its mold, of a god (Bronze Age). These images may have been given to believers after they had gone on a pilgrimage or perhaps bought as a memento. Such molds have been found at several temples.

106. The reconstructed foundations of the temple from the citadel of Arad in the Negeb (monarchial period). (1) Court (in it was also a wash basin). (2) Step on which the priest stood and the altar of burnt offering. It measured 3 by 5 by 5 meters and consisted of natural stone and loam with a slab of flint on it. (3) Elevated rear part of the court, open only to priests? (4) Sanctuary proper. Note the two symbolic columns flanking the entrance. (5) Niche for statue or symbol of the god. In this temple this niche is already in the shape of a cella. In it stood two small altars of incense and a so-called standing stone (masseba).

107. A group of limestone horned altars from Megiddo. (Oriental Institute, University of Chicago)

109. A page from the Birds' Head Haggadah (Germany, ca. A.D. 1300). The birds' heads were used to avoid depicting human features. (Israel Museum, Jerusalem)

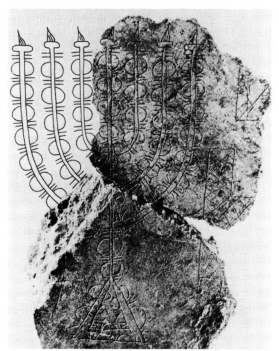

108. Fragments of wall plaster from a house in Jerusalem in New Testament times. Pictures of objects had been carved into the plaster, including one of the seven-branched candlestick in the temple. Aside from the picture on the Arch of Titus, this is the only one from that particular time. And because this comes from Jerusalem, it is believed to be more reliable.

110. A bitumen stone "cup of Elijah." (Israel Museum, Jerusalem)

111. Title page of Ecclesiastes from a prayerbook (Italy, A.D. 1492). Ecclesiastes is traditionally read in the synagogue during the Feast of Tabernacles (Sukkot). See pp. 390–92. (Jewish Theological Seminary Library)

112. Lower left: Title page of the Ethics of the Fathers (a mishnaic tractate also called Pirke Aboth) from a prayerbook (Italy, A.D. 1452). Since the Ethics of the Fathers begins with the events at Mt. Sinai, it is customarily read during the seven weeks between Passover and Pentecost (Feast of Weeks). The latter feast celebrates the giving of the Torah. See pp. 389–390. (Jewish Theological Seminary Library)

113. Title page of the book of Esther (Cologne, A.D. 1843). Esther is traditionally read at the Feast of Purim. See p. 392. (Jewish Theological Seminary Library)

*114. Reproduction of Solomon's temple by C. F. Stevens from specifications by W. F. Albright and G. E. Wright. See pp. 377–79. (Biblical Archaeologist)*

*115. Aerial view of Jerusalem from the south. In the center is the Haram esh-Sherif (the temple mount). To its left, running through the center of the city, is the Tyropeon (Central) Valley. To the right of the Haram is the Kidron Valley, which joins the Hinnom Valley just southwest of the Haram. (Matson Photo Service)*

XXXIX. A view from the southwest of part of the Jerusalem Temple Model. Visible above the wall surrounding the temple mount are the temple (upper left) and the royal stoa (upper right). The Central (Tyropeon) Valley runs below the Western (Wailing) Wall (upper left) and next to the hippodrome (right center). (W. S. LaSor)

XL. Bronze Age pottery from Bab edh-Dhra (ca. 3000–2000 B.C.). Decorations include red slip, ledge handles, lug handles, punctate design, and beaded bands. (R. H. Johnston)

(2 Kings 12:9–10; 2 Chron. 24:8ff.). In the description of the ark as a cultic object this root meaning should be remembered (cf. Exod. 25:16; 40:20; Deut. 10:1–5; see sections d and e below). However, the parts that go with the ark, the mercy seat and the cherubim, seem to point to a throne function (see section c below).

b. For information about the shape and the making of the ark we are virtually limited to the book of Exodus, namely, Exodus 25:10–22 and 37:1–9. The latter pericope speaks about the construction of the ark per se. It was to be made of hard acacia wood, on the inside and outside covered with gold. Its length was two and half cubits, breadth and height each a cubit and a half (a cubit is slightly less than half a meter or 18 in.). Four gold rings were to be attached to it, two on each side. Through these the poles for carrying it were to be passed. These poles, also to be covered with gold, were to remain in the rings.

c. The ark was to have a *kapporet* of pure gold. The word is translated as "mercy seat" or "atonement cover" (NIV). That translation includes two meanings of the verb from which *kapporet* is derived, namely, "to cover" and "to reconcile." Yet the above-mentioned Exodus 25 does not speak about "reconciliation," though it is done in many other passages, especially in connection with the ritual of the Day of Atonement (Leviticus 16; see B.10.f below). Compare also Romans 3:25, where Paul alludes to the meaning of *kapporet*, though in his day the ark and thus also the mercy seat had long since disappeared. The Septuagint often translates *kapporet* with the Greek word for "means of reconciliation" (cf. also Heb. 9:5). The importance of the object, especially in later Old Testament times, is evidenced by 1 Chronicles 28:11, where the most holy place in the temple is called "the room for the mercy seat" (Luther: *Haus des Gnadenstuhls*). The Old Testament does not say, however, as some contend, that originally it was not the lid of the ark but a separate cultic object. In Numbers 7:89 (which speaks of the voice of God that came to Moses from above the atonement cover) it is also indicated as lying on the ark. On the mercy seat, and forming part of it, were two cherubim made of gold. These were to be viewed as guardians and also as bearers of God's invisible throne. In later days the ark was also called "footstool" (1 Chron. 28:2; cf. Ps. 132:7). In the Old Testament it is said of God that he dwells on or above the cherubim (1 Sam. 4:4; 2 Sam. 6:2; 1 Chron. 13:6; etc.). It is uncertain, however, whether this expression originally referred to the cherubim figures on the ark or to cherubim as personification of the clouds ("the rider on the clouds" was an Ugaritic divine title; cf. Ps. 68:5).

d. According to Exodus 37:1–9 the ark was constructed by Bezalel. According to Deuteronomy 10:1–3 Moses was the maker; he was to deposit the (new) tablets of stone in it. It is pure conjecture that originally there may have been something else in the ark, for example, covenant documents or even a statue of a god or oracular stones. There is a later rabbinic tradition that says that the ark contained a jar with manna. According to Hebrews 9:4 Aaron's staff was in it. Those traditions are based on a (wrong) interpretation of Exodus 16:33 and Numbers 17:10. Often the term "ark of the covenant" is used (Josh. 3:1–17; 4:9; 6:6); also "of the covenant of the Lord" or "of the covenant of God" (e.g. Num. 10:33; 14:44; Deut. 10:8; 1 Sam. 4:3–5; 1 Chron. 16:6; cf. Rev. 11:19). Also used is "ark of the testimony" (Exod. 25:22–23) or in brief "the testimony" (e.g., Num. 17:4), whereby the "testimony" (*edut*) refers to the tables of the law that were kept in the ark.

e. Some have attempted to explain the ark as an originally empty divine seat, on the analogy of other nations. But that theory runs aground on the designation "ark" or "chest." We did note, however, that the cherubim may imply a reference to the throne of God. The theory of the ark as throne is based especially on Jeremiah 3:16–17, because there the ark and the city of Jerusalem are mentioned after each other, and because it is said that at that time the city will be called "the throne of the Lord." The most that can be argued is that in that passage this is also said of the ark, but symbolically. More cannot be inferred from it. The prophets use the image more often, for instance, in reference to heaven, whereby earth is the footstool (Isa. 66:1; Ps. 99:5; 132:7; Lam. 2:1; compare also Jer. 14:21). The throne character of the ark is rather to be connected with the cherubim (see above). Another theory holds that the ark is to be regarded as a war palladium, a sacred object carried along into battle. This idea is based on the story in 1 Samuel 4. Desperate about the threatened defeat by the Philistines, Israel asks for the ark to be brought into the army camp (verses 3–4). The story speaks of God as "the Lord of hosts who is enthroned on the cherubim." The theory assumes that the "hosts" are the armies of the Israelite tribes, and thus the ark is the throne of the war-god. However, the word "hosts" (*sebaot*), in combination with the name of God, is to be understood as a plural of intensity: the God who has all power! The ark can, however, be viewed as a symbol of YHWH's accompaniment, especially during the desert time. But how easily such a symbol changed into a presumed guarantee may be seen in the account of 1 Samuel 4.

The symbolic accompaniment character is also expressed in the saying concerning the ark (Num. 10:35–36; also called "the signal words"; cf. Josh. 3:1–4:1; 6:1–27; 2 Sam. 11:11).

f. In contrast to the view that the ark would be a cultic object taken over from the Canaanites (a theory found in many older studies), today there is greater confidence in the biblical reports. The ark was already in existence in the desert and must have been made at Sinai (see the pericopes mentioned under b above). After the journey through the wilderness the ark functioned in the crossing of the Jordan (see Joshua 3–6). We also met the ark in the scene at Mount Ebal and Mount Gerizim (Josh. 8:30–35). In the days of the judges we find it mentioned in Judges 20:27, and after that especially in 1 Samuel 1–3. At that time there was a sanctuary in Shiloh where the ark was stored, guarded by the priest Eli. After Israel's defeat the Philistines captured the ark (1 Samuel 4), but they experienced nothing but trouble from it (1 Samuel 5) and therefore sent it back to Israel's border. The men of Kiriath-jearim hauled it from there and placed it in the house of Abinadab (1 Sam. 7:1). Then for a long time there is silence about the sacred object. An exception to that is 1 Samuel 14:18 where, however, the Septuagint does not read "ark" but "ephod." The Chronicler presumably based himself on this tradition when he said that in the days of Saul the ark was neglected (1 Chron. 13:3). David had the ark carried to Jerusalem (with some delay when it was put in the house of Obed-edom), where a

tent becomes its temporary home (2 Samuel 6). It has been suggested that on that occasion Psalm 24 was written (see also section B.7 below). Because David was not allowed to build the temple in Jerusalem, the ark did not receive its final place in the most holy place until the temple had been built by his son Solomon. 1 Kings 8:1–11 and 2 Chronicles 5:2–14 give an account of these happenings. The fortunes of the ark after that are unknown. Whether Shishak of Egypt took it away (1 Kings 14:26) or whether one of Israel's own kings, for fear of paganism (Hezekiah, 2 Kings 18:4) or to make room for pagan objects (Manasseh, 2 Kings 21:7), removed the ark, we do not know. It is certain that the ark did not survive the capture of Jerusalem by the Babylonians and that no new one was made (cf. Jer. 3:16). It is not mentioned in Ezekiel's description of the temple, nor was there an ark in the second temple built after the captivity. According to 2 Maccabees 2:5 Jeremiah hid the ark on the mountain of Moses, without wanting others to know precisely where it was buried. In the New Testament the ark is only mentioned in passing (Heb. 9:4; Rev. 11:19).

## LITERATURE

W. R. Arnold, *Ephod and Ark* (Cambridge, 1917).

H. A. Brongers, "Einige Aspekte der gegenwärtigen Lage der Lade-Forschung," *Nederlands Theologisch Tijdschrift* 25 (1971) 6–27.

O. Eissfeldt, "Lade und Gesetzestafeln," *Kleine Schriften* III (Tübingen, 1967) 526–29.

_____, "Lade und Stierbild," *Kleine Schriften* II (Tübingen, 1964) 282–305.

M. Haran, "The Ark and the Cherubim: Their Symbolic Significance in Biblical Ritual," *Israel Exploration Journal* 9 (1959) 30–38, 89–94.

J. Jeremias, "Lade und Zion," in H. W. Wolff, ed., *Probleme biblischer Theologie* (Festschrift G. von Rad; Munich, 1971), pp. 183–98.

J. Maier, *Das israelitische Ladeheiligtum* (Berlin, 1965).

## 7. THE TENT AND THE TABERNACLE

The "tent," usually called "tabernacle," was the most important sanctuary before there was a temple in Jerusalem, and especially during Israel's journey through the desert. "Tabernacle" comes from the Latin and means "tent" or "barrack." Luther used *Hutte des Stifts* or the *Stiftshutte*. In some parts of the Pentateuch this desert sanctuary, which had to be movable, is simply called an *ohel* ("tent"), to which later the designation *mishkan* ("dwelling") is added.

a. In Exodus 33:7–11 we are told that Moses made a tent and pitched it outside the camp. He called it "tent of meeting." The name does not mean, as has been supposed, that the people used it for their festive gatherings, but that God used it to meet with Moses. Outwardly it resembled a tent such as was also used by ordinary people (see section A.1 above), though the Bible says nothing more specific about it. It is not said either that it contained some kind of object (but see under d below) or that sacrifices were brought to it. The old stories about the tent or the tent of meeting are found in the above-mentioned Exodus 33:7–11 and in Numbers 11:16–29; 12:1–16; Deuteronomy 31:14–15. The accounts are always about Moses, who is allowed to speak with God. In the last-mentioned passage his successor Joshua is also involved. The people have to stand outside the tent, where Moses as mediator communicates the word of God to them. The pillar of cloud stood at the entrance of the tent.

b. Later accounts (all priestly) contain a very elaborate and detailed description of the tent, which, however, is then no longer called by that name but by various other names. The data about it are found especially in Exodus 25–31 (prescriptions) and Exodus 35–40 (execution of the prescriptions). The other names are "dwelling" (e.g., Exod. 25:9), "dwelling of YHWH" (RSV "tabernacle of the Lord"; e.g., Lev. 17:4; alongside of it, "tent of meeting" in one sentence), "tabernacle of the testimony" (Exod. 38:21; etc.), or "tent of the testimony" (Num. 9:15; 17:7; 18:2). In some passages (Exod. 39:32; 40:2, 6, 29) the double designation "the tabernacle of the tent of meeting" is used. The meaning of this combination is "the dwelling or tabernacle *is* the tent of meeting." The same equation of "tent" and "dwelling" is found in 2 Samuel 7:6. In the New Testament an allusion to the tent of the testimony is found in Acts 7:44 (Stephen's speech), which reflects the description in Exodus 25. Revelation 15:5 men-

tions "the temple of the tent of witness." The tent is especially mentioned in the epistle to the Hebrews (chapters 8 and 9) where the true, heavenly tabernacle is contrasted with the temporary, earthly tent.

c. The tabernacle described in the priestly traditions is a complicated structure, a kind of rectangular tent with wooden supports. According to Exodus 25:9 it was to be made after the pattern that had been shown to Moses on the mountain. It is not clear whether Exodus 26 originally spoke of one structure (which in many ways makes us think of the later temple) or of two interwoven traditions. Exodus 26:1–14 speaks first about the *tentlike part*. That tent is to be made of four kinds of superimposed curtains or skins. The bottom layer (the layer one looks at from within the tent) consists of two large curtains of twenty-eight by twenty cubits, each consisting of five strips four cubits in width that were to be sewn together along their length. The material must be "fine twined linen and blue, purple, and scarlet yarn" with figures of cherubim worked into them on the visible inside. The curtains were to be connected with loops and gold clasps. For transport they could be taken apart. Over this bottom layer a second layer of curtains was laid, made of goat hair, together constituting a larger surface than the first layer so as to afford greater protection, and measuring thirty by forty-four cubits. (Bear in mind that the biblical passages always speak of "length" when they refer to the largest sizes; cf. Exod. 26:2, 8.) The curtains were to be placed over the wooden frame in such a way that they covered the north side, the upper side, and the south side. Over these curtains still another double layer was placed, first of ram skins dyed red and then of hides of sea cows (probably a dolphinlike animal; Exod. 26:14). We can visualize only in part what the *wooden frame* looked like. "Every reconstruction remains hypothetical" (Fensham, *Exodus,* p. 191). Especially Exodus 26:28 causes problems. Exodus 26:15–30 describes how the upright frames of acacia wood (overlaid with gold) are to be put in silver bases. They are all to be attached to each other by means of taps, rings, and crossbars and so form the supporting pavilion.

d. The tabernacle was divided into two compartments, the holy place and the most holy place.

The two were to be separated by a "veil" (*paroket*) made of the same precious material as the bottom tent curtain and likewise decorated with cherubim. It was to be hung on four acacia wood pillars overlaid with gold. Also the front (east side) of the tabernacle was to be closed, with a curtain (*masak*) of the same precious material, decorated with many-colored, finely twisted linen. It was to be hung on five pillars. In the back compartment of the tabernacle, the most holy place, the ark of the covenant (see section B.6 above) was to be placed, invisible and inaccessible to the people *and* to the priests. One day per year (Day of Atonement) the high priest could enter there as mediator (see also section 8 below). The front compartment (the holy place) contained the table of the bread of the presence on the north side, to the right viewed from the entrance. These loaves were also called "bread of the (divine) face." They were to be replaced every day (Exod. 25:30; cf. 1 Sam. 21:6). The table was to be two cubits in length, one cubit wide, and one and a half cubits high, made of acacia wood, overlaid with gold (Exod. 25:23–30), and to be carried by poles through rings. Right before the entrance, by the veil, was the incense altar, a cubit square and two cubits high, with "horns" projecting at the four corners (see Exod. 30:1–10). On the left side in the holy place stood the golden, seven-branched lampstand (*menorah;* see Exod. 25:31–39). It was artistically decorated with buds shaped like almond blossoms. On the seven branches were to be seven lamps casting their light in front of it. In the holy place, accessible only to the priests, there were also plates, dishes, pitchers, and bowls to be used in worship (Exod. 25:29).

e. The tabernacle itself was positioned in a separate courtyard, measuring fifty by a hundred cubits. It was bounded by colored curtains of finely twisted linen, suspended on pillars (Exod. 27:9–19). The height was only five cubits, so that the top half of the tabernacle remained visible. In the courtyard stood the altar of burnt offering, five by five by three cubits, with horns on the corners, the whole overlaid with copper (Exod. 27:1–8). This too was made portable by poles and rings. Pots for the ashes, shovels, sprinkling bowls (bowls used for sprinkling in the sacrificial

cult), forks, and firepans went with it. The firepans were used for keeping the smoldering fire (cf. Lev. 10:1). Separate mention should be made of the bronze basin filled with water for the cultic purification of the hands and feet of the priests (Exod. 30:17–21; cf. the "bronze sea" in the later temple).

---

## LITERATURE

F. M. Cross, "The Priestly Tabernacle," *Biblical Archaeologist* 10 (1947) 45–68.

R. E. Friedman, "The Tabernacle in the Temple," *Biblical Archaeologist* 43 (1980) 241–48.

V. Fritz, *Tempel und Zelt. Studien zum Tempelbau in Israel und zu dem Zeltheiligtum der Priesterschrift* (Neukirchen-Vluyn, 1977).

D. W. Gooding, *The Account of the Tabernacle* (Cambridge, 1959).

M. Görg, *Das Zelt der Begegnung. Untersuchung der sakralen Zelttraditionen Altisraels* (Bonn, 1967).

G. von Rad, "The Tent and the Ark," in *The Problem of the Hexateuch and Other Essays* (New York, 1966), pp. 103–24.

---

## 8. THE TEMPLE

### a. Introductory Observations

Besides the tabernacle, the Old Testament knows of a number of fixed sanctuaries (see section B.11, introduction). But best known is the temple in Jerusalem, built by Solomon. David already had in mind building it, but was not permitted to because he was a "man of wars" (1 Chron. 28:3). The wood for the building was furnished by the Tyrian king Hiram (1 Kings 5:1–18) or Huram (2 Chron. 2:3–16), with whom Solomon had an alliance. At Solomon's request he also sent a skilled artisan, called Hiram according to 1 Kings 7:13, while in 2 Chron. 2:13 he is also called Huram-Abi, that is, Huram the master (literally, "the father"). The Solomonic temple was destroyed by the Babylonians in 587 (see further section c below). After the Babylonian captivity it was rebuilt (520–515) and enlarged and beautified. The temple was located on the present site of the Dome of the Rock (also incorrectly called Mosque of Omar) in modern Jerusalem. Inside, the "sacred rock" can be seen. It is agreed that the temple was built over this rock, but there is no agreement about the precise location of the temple. Some point to the rock as the place where the altar of burnt offering stood in the courtyard. Others are inclined to think that the most holy place must have been over the rock. Today the second theory is favored. In 2 Chronicles 3:1 the place where the temple would be built was indicated as Mount Moriah (cf. Gen. 22:2).

## b. Solomon's Temple

(1) Form and Arrangement. A description of the shape and arrangement of the temple is found in 1 Kings 6 and 7, chapters that seem to have incorporated an official document for the builders. Another description (with some remarkable differences) is found in 2 Chronicles 3 and 4. The author of 2 Chronicles regularly gives evidence that he was personally acquainted only with the temple of Zerubbabel. Much in the construction is unclear, especially as concerns the foundations and the side storage chambers. But it is possible to visualize what the whole looked like. It was an elongated building, but one not conspicuous on account of its measurements. The total length of the temple proper (holy place and most holy place) was sixty cubits (about 30 m. or 100 ft.). In front of it was a porch or portal (*ulam*) with a length of ten cubits. It should be remembered, for example, with the report in 1 Kings 6:3, that the longest side was always called "length." The "house" can alternately refer to the main room of the temple or also to the whole temple. All measurements pertain to the inside of the building. The thickness of the walls, probably two and a half meters (8 ft.), at least at the base, is to be added to that. The height was about 15 meters (50 ft.; 1 Kings 6:2), that of the most holy place 10 meters (35 ft.). The temple was facing in a west-east direction. This can be inferred from 1 Kings 7:39 and from the orientation of the temple in the book of Ezekiel (Ezek. 40:6; 43:4) and of the later Herodian structure. In all likelihood the temple was not precisely facing the rising sun but was slightly turned in an east-northeast direc-

tion, thus more in the direction of the first visible rays of the sun. The portal mentioned above was its entrance. See ill. 106.

(2) Detailed Description. East of the temple building, in front of the *ulam*, stood two pillars, named Jachin and Boaz. Their names evoke recollections of old pagan symbols of life. The name of the first, on the north side, right in front of the entrance, may refer to a verb meaning "confirm" or "establish," the name of the second to "strength." The translation of "Boaz" by "in him is strength" seems to be only a popular etymology, however. It has been suggested that the pillars were signs of Solomon's royal power or indications of God's sovereignty. The latter seems the most plausible. Such pillars (made of stone or, like those of Solomon, hollow and of metal) have also been found at heathen temples. The Old Testament, however, does not tell whatever symbolic meaning they may have had. According to 1 Kings 7:15 their height was eighteen cubits, their circumference twelve cubits. Each pillar was crowned by a capital, five cubits high. Probably due to copyists' errors, the text of 2 Chronicler 3 has different measurements. Woven garlands were around the capitals. That is also how 2 Chronicles 3:16 is to be understood.

Right behind the pillars was first of all the porch, which was the entrance to the actual temple. The latter was closed by two large doors, ornamented with "cherubim, palms, and open flowerbuds" (1 Kings 6:33–35). The main room (*hekal*), later usually called "the holy place," had a length of forty cubits, a width of twenty, and a height of thirty. The side walls contained "windows with recessed frames" (1 Kings 6:4), that is, latticed windows, likely with stone bars. Nothing more is said about them, but we should think of them as having been high up in the walls, allowing the light to come in from the top. The floor was of cypress wood. The walls were lined with cedar wood (1 Kings 6:15). 2 Chronicles 3:5 also mentions cypress wood. The report in 1 Kings 6:30 that the floor of the house was overlaid with gold (as translated in the RSV) is not clear. What seems to be meant is that the borders of the front and the back of the room were ornamented with gold. It is not likely that the whole floor was covered with gold. Inside the main room there was first of all an altar of cedar wood (1 Kings 6:20), covered with gold. It is called the "golden altar" (1 Kings 7:48; cf. Isa. 6:6). Incense was offered on it (cf. Luke 1:9). There was furthermore the table of the bread of the presence (see section 7 above). Mention is made of ten golden lampstands, five on each of the long sides (1 Kings 7:49; 2 Chron. 4:7). Many, however, believe that those texts originally mentioned only one golden lampstand, as in the tabernacle and the second temple (ill. 108; cf. 2 Chron. 13:11). Furthermore, there were all kinds of golden untensils in the holy place, required for the worship service.

The most holy place, having the shape of a cube, was twenty cubits on all three sides. It was behind the main room and could only be entered by the high priest once per year. A comparison of the measurements shows that the height of the main room varied from that of the most holy place at least ten cubits (about 5 m. or 16 ft.). We are not told what was done with that extra space in the structure. Some have thought of a podium or elevation on which the most holy place was built. But that would have required a flight of stairs, which is not mentioned anywhere. Others, with a reference to 2 Chronicles 3:9, have thought of a room above the most holy place, but that is not likely either. An intermediate solution has also been suggested, namely, that half of the height would be below and half of it above the most holy place. Today it is usually assumed that the most holy place was on ground level and that the space above the ceiling was empty, unused space.

In the Old Testament this room is called not only holy of holies or most holy place (Ezek. 41:4), but also *debir*. The AV rendered this "oracle"; it used to be thought that there was a connection with the verb "speak" (*dabar*). Today the word is correctly derived from a verb meaning "be behind," hence the translation "inner sanctuary" in the RSV (1 Kings 6:5, 16, 19–23, 31; 7:49; 8:6, 8; 2 Chron. 4:20; 5:7, 9; Ps. 28:2; Sir. 45:9). The space was without light. It is debated whether the Solomonic temple had a curtain between the holy pace and the most holy place. It is mentioned by the Chronicler (2 Chron. 3:14), but 1 Kings 6:31 speaks of doors of olive wood. The curtain of 2 Chronicles 3:14 was made of fine linen in beautiful colors, with cherubim worked into it.

The ark of the covenant was in the most holy place (see section B.6 above). Two cherubim functioned as guards; few details are given of these cherubim (see, however, the description of the four creatures in Ezekiel 1 and 10:20). In the Syro-Phoenician world of 1200 to 800 B.C., cherubim were known as hybrid beings, winged sphinxes (lions with a human head). An Israelite postage stamp from 1966 contains a picture of a Phoenician ivory sphinx. Unlike those in the tabernacle, the faces of the cherubim were oriented toward the entrance of the holy of holies (2 Chron. 3:13). Extending over the whole space, the wings of the cherubim covered the ark.

After the completion of the temple, the ark was put in place with elaborate ceremonies (1 Kings 8:1–11). Reporting on it, Chronicles stressed the special position of the Levites: only they were allowed to carry the ark, while the Levitical priests carried in the other objects and from then on performed the actual service in the temple (2 Chron. 5:2–14). The temple building constructed by Solomon also had side rooms (1 Kings 8:5–8), built as three stories; because of the indentation of the temple wall the second was a cubit wider than the first, the third a cubit wider than the second.

(3) The Courtyard. Around the temple was an "inner courtyard" (1 Kings 6:36; 7:12) and a "great courtyard" (1 Kings 7:9, 12). The first was a walled-in square on which the temple itself stood; later it was called the "courtyard of the priests" (cf. 2 Chron. 4:9). The great courtyard was likewise a walled-in square, in which, however, was also built the palace of the king. In the inner courtyard stood the altar of burnt offering with the four horns (to which one could go for refuge; see section A.7 above). It is mentioned in 2 Chronicles 4:1 but not in the building report of 1 Kings 7. One would have expected it there between verses 22 and 23. Many assume that it has dropped out there for unknown reasons (see 1 Kings 9:25). According to the text of Chronicles, the measurements were twenty by twenty cubits, with a height of ten cubits. Solomon probably did not build a new (another) altar, but renewed the one built by David (cf. 1 Chron. 21:26; 2 Sam. 24:25) by adding a copper grating to the stone foundation.

The courtyard also contained, on the southeast

side of the temple, the so-called brass (molten) sea, a huge basin with a circumference of about thirty cubits and a radius of five cubits. In 1 Kings 7:26 the capacity is said to be two thousand baths. According to 2 Chronicles 4:5, however, the capacity is three thousand baths. Some believe that this remarkable difference is not due to a copyist's error but comes from the fact that the Chronicler imagined it as a cylinder (on the basis of 2 Kings 16:17) and not as a half-sphere. Whether one thinks of the "royal bath" of forty-five liters (12 gals.) or of the ordinary bath of twenty-two or twenty-three liters (about 6 gals.; the latter must have been the case for the sea), it was an immense basin! Though in the pagan world such a sea might be an indication of the threatening primeval sea, in Israel the brass sea (though the name remained) became a utensil. 2 Chronicles 4:6b must not be read as if it says that the priests washed themselves *in* the sea (so the AV and the RSV), but "that they washed themselves with it," that is, with the water. On the upper rim, and also around the basin itself, were ornamental gourds, cast in two rows in one piece with the sea. In nature they are cucumberlike fruits with a highly purgative effect (1 Kings 7:24). The Chronicler, maybe because he did not understand the word, replaced it by "bulls," small representations of the large bulls that supported the basin. The twelve statues of bulls that supported the sea were looking in all four directions, three in each direction. In the courtyard were also found all kinds of utensils, for the most part of gold, such as wash basins for rinsing the sacrificial victims, pots for boiling, bowls for sprinkling, tongs, snuffers, knives and scissors, and basins on wheeled supports (wagons).

## c. Zerubbabel's Temple

Being allowed to return home to their land in 538 B.C., the exiles were given permission to rebuild the temple, especially under the leadership of Zerubbabel, a descendant of David. The work was completed in 515. Not much is known of this postexilic temple. The measurements were the same as those of Solomon's temple, because the foundations were repaired (Ezra 4:12; 5:16). The altar had been restored earlier (Ezra 3:2-4). Its measurements were those of 2 Chronicles 4:1 (cf.

Ezek. 43:13-17). The money for the rebuilding was given by the Persian government (Ezra 6:4, 8). The ark of the covenant had perished and was not replaced (cf. Jer. 3:16). The temple of Solomon had doors of olive wood between the holy place and the most holy place and perhaps also a curtain, but with respect to the temple of Zerubbabel only a curtain is mentioned (1 Macc. 1:23; 4:51). The copper pillars were absent (cf. Jer. 52:17-23 and 2 Kings 25:13-17). Also, the sea of bronze is not mentioned. It had one seven-branched lampstand (1 Macc. 1:23; 4:49). Storage rooms or side chambers are also mentioned (Ezra 8:29).

From the books of Maccabees it is known that the temple was plundered and desecrated in 169 B.C. In 167 a statue of an idol was erected in it (cf. also Dan. 9:27; 11:31). The cleansing and rededication happened in 164 B.C. under Judas Maccabeus (cf. 1 Macc. 4:36-51, 52-59; see section B.12.b below). The second temple was certainly not as lavish as the first, though the difference was probably not too great. Indeed, Haggai 2:4 says of the second temple, "Is it not in your sight as nothing?" But it should be remembered that this was said at the beginning of the rebuilding (in the year 520). The weeping with a loud voice, mentioned in Ezra 3:12, is rather an old rite at the laying of the first stone. Shouting of praise is also mentioned, probably by the younger generation that was unacquainted with such an old rite.

A separate discussion could be devoted to the temple in the prophecies of Ezekel, but this was not a real temple. It was a theological-prophetic design, a vision, in which Ezekiel (with recollections of the temple of Solomon) saw a kind of ideal temple, a building, protected by walls in a "sacred square." It has been thought that the temple of Zerubbabel was constructed according to this design, but this idea has, especially lately, been abandoned (W. Zimmerli, *Ezekiel* II [Hermeneia; Philadelphia, 1983] 360). In the centuries following Solomon there were changes, however: the profane was more and more distinguished from the cultic-sacred, the priests became more important (cf. 2 Chron. 4:9), and considering the palace of the king as being part of the temple area was regarded as sacrilege (cf. Ezek. 43:8). Especially remarkable in the vision (Ezek. 40:1-

42:20) is the emphasis on the most important part of the temple, the "inner chamber," called "the most holy place." The name *debir* (see section B.8.b above) is not used (Ezek. 41:4). This vision of the prophet certainly influenced the building plans carried out by Herod in the renovation of the temple.

### d. Herod's Temple

During the reign of Herod the Great, the expansion and beautification of the temple was begun in 20/19 B.C. Ten years later the building was dedicated, but the renovation of the whole building was not complete until A.D. 64. That temple was the place Jesus frequented, where God wished to reveal himself in a unique way, and where man might approach God (Luke 2:49; Matt. 21:13; 23:21; John 4:22). At the same time Jesus was denounced because of what he said about the temple (Matt. 26:61 and parallels). The temple was totally destroyed in the year 70 and never rebuilt.

The main temple structure had the same length and width as the one of Zerubbabel, but it was higher. An upper story was added to the holy place and the most holy place. Spears of gold ("scarecrows") were placed on the flat roof. It was also surrounded by attached side chambers of three floors. The information about this can be gathered from the Mishnaic tractate Middoth and from a work of Flavius Josephus (1st century A.D.). There is some discrepancy in the evidence, however. According to Josephus (*Jewish Wars* 5.5.4), the temple had a portal of a height of 100 cubits, which according to him had sunk twenty cubits. Josephus was also aware of the present text of 2 Chronicles 3:4, where the height of the portal (of the temple of Solomon!) is listed as 120 cubits (*Antiquities* 15.11). About the beginning of our era a "correction" must have been made by a believer who felt that the temple of Solomon should surpass everything; the original reading must have been "twenty cubits."

The entire temple complex, annexes, portals, and porticoes had a surface area of one hundred and forty-four thousand square meters (about 35 acres). The area was bounded by porticoes, one of which was called "the portico of Solomon" (on

the east side; cf. John 10:23; Acts 3:11; 5:12). The southeast corner of the square had still another building, "the corner of the sanctuary," probably referred to in Matthew 4:5 and Luke 4:9. In the center of the outer courtyard there was a higher terrace. On the east side the inner courtyard could be reached by way of a flight of stairs; Gentiles were forbidden to enter there on penalty of death.

First one entered the court of women. This must be the place where the incident recorded in John 8:1–11 took place. There are some who believe that Paul in Acts 21:31–39 was on those stairs; others prefer to think of the stairs of the Fortress Antonia. The gate called "Beautiful" (Acts 3:2) was the east entrance to the court of women. That courtyard must have been the place where the trumpetlike treasuries stood (cf. Mark 12:41ff.; Luke 21:1ff.). A semicircular stairway led from the court of women to the inner courtyard through another, higher gate. In the "court of Israel" stood the altar of burnt offering. There the men could participate in the sacrificial cult, for instance, the laying of their hands on the passover lamb. The women could only *observe* what happened. Walking around the altar, the believers also came between the altar and the temple proper. On such an occasion (Feast of Booths) Jesus spoke the words in John 7:38. From the porch the curtain, covering the door, could be seen. The furniture in the holy place included the altar of incense (Luke 1:9). In the most holy place, at the place where the (lost) ark used to stand, was the "stone." There was also a curtain between the holy place and the most holy place. Matthew 27:51 likely refers to this inner curtain. In the northwest corner of the temple area was the Fortress Antonia.

---

### LITERATURE

Y. Aharoni, "The Solomonic Temple, the Tabernacle and the Arad Sanctuary," in *Orient and Occident* (Festschrift Cyrus H. Gordon; Kevelaer/Neukirchen-Vluyn, 1973), pp. 1–8.

A. Th. Busink, *Der Tempel von Jerusalem von Salomo bis Herodes, I: Der Tempel Salomos* (Leiden, 1970).

W. Eltester, "Der siebenarmige Leuchter und der

Titusbogen," in *Judentum, Christentum und Kirche* (Berlin, 1960), pp. 62–76.

V. Fritz, *Tempel und Zelt* (Neukirchen-Vluyn, 1977).

B. Gärtner, *The Temple and the Community in Qumran and the New Testament* (Oxford, 1965).

A. M. Goldberg, "Der siebenarmige Leuchter," *Zeitschrift der Deutschen Morgenlandischen Gesellschaft* 117 (1967) 232–46.

J. Gutmann, ed., *The Temple of Solomon* (Missoula, 1976).

M. Haran, *Temples and Temple Service in Ancient Israel* (Oxford, 1978).

J. Jeremias, *Jerusalem in the Time of Jesus* (Philadelphia, 1969; repr. 1975), pp. 77–84, 140–44, 147–267.

H. J. Kraus, *Gottesdienst in Israel* (Munich, 1962²).

A. Kuschke, "Der Tempel Salomos und der 'syrische Tempeltypus'," in F. Maass, ed., *Das ferne und nahe Wort* (Festschrift L. Rost; Berlin, 1967), pp. 124–32.

C. L. Meyers, "The Elusive Temple," *Biblical Archaeologist* 45 (1982) 33–41.

N. Poulssen, *König und Tempel im Glaubenszeugnis des Alten Testaments* (Stuttgart, 1967).

K. Rupprecht, *Der Tempel von Jerusalem* (Berlin/New York, 1977).

J. Schmid, "Der Tempelbau Salomos in religionsgeschichtlicher Sicht," in A. Kuschke and E. Kutsch, eds., *Archäologie und Altes Testament* (Festschrift K. Galling; Tübingen, 1970), pp. 241–50.

H. Schult, "Der Debir im salomonischen Tempel," *Zeitschrift des Deutschen Palästinavereins* 80 (1964) 46–54.

F. Stolz, *Strukturen und Figuren im Kult von Jerusalem* (Berlin, 1970).

R. de Vaux, "Le caractère du temple salomonien," *Mélanges bibliques A. Robert* (Paris, 1957), pp. 137–48.

---

# 9. THE CALENDAR

## a. General

Very early in human history, according to some during the last ice age, about thirty thousand years ago, the need must have been felt to capture and record the rhythm of time. From the tenth century B.C. we possess an "agricultural calendar," uncovered in 1908 in excavations at Gezer, that speaks of eight periods, some of two months, others of a month. It mentions the operations in the field, beginning with September-October. The ancient Egyptians calculated that a solar year was three hundred and sixty-five days plus a quarter of a day. In reality it is three hundred sixty-five days, five hours, forty-eight minutes, and forty-six seconds. The ancient Babylonians used the lunar year, in which they combined twelve periods from new moon to new moon. Twelve lunar months together constituted three hundred fifty-four days, eight hours, forty-eight minutes, and thirty-six seconds. The solar as well as the lunar system caused great difficulties, because the solar and lunar years are not equal in length. A calendar was not only needed to distinguish the seasons, but also to be able to observe the various festivals and commemorative days. For centuries the determination of the calendar was the work of the priests. Agricultural and liturgical calendars cannot be separated from each other.

## b. Divisions of Time in Israel

In Old Testament times Israel had a calendar that took into account the solar year but was determined by the phases of the moon. According to the later Jewish conception, the nations go by the sun but Israel by the moon. For this idea Psalm 104:19 was invoked. Each month had to begin with the first visible appearance of the lunar crescent of the "first quarter." We do not know how in ancient times Israel always managed to reconcile solar year and lunar year. Today the Jews add a leap month, called "second Adar," seven times in nine years. Originally Israel used Canaanite names for the months. Four are mentioned in the Bible: Abib or Aviv, the first month (Exod. 13:4; 23:15; 34:18; Deut. 16:1); Ziv, the second month (1 Kings 6:1, 37); Etanim, the seventh month (1 Kings 8:2); Bul, the eighth month (1 Kings 6:38). During Josiah's reform a change in calendar must have taken place. After that frequently only the number of the months was indicated. In the Exile the Babylonian names were more and more adopted, alongside the use of the numbers. Those later names for the months are: (1) Nisan, middle of March to middle of April; (2) Iyyar; (3) Siwan; (4) Tammuz; (5) Ab; (6) Elul; (7) Tishri; (8) Marcheshwan; (9) Kislev; (10) Tebet; (11) Shebat; (12) Adar, middle of February to middle of March. If a "second Adar" is to be inserted, it is regarded as the real Adar month. Not all names occur in the Old Testament.

Another division of time is that into weeks. The septad constituting the week is not a natural division of the solar year. The ancient Egyptians originally divided the month into three decades (tenths). The division into seven approximates more the lunar calculation (with four moon phases). The Babylonians, who applied the lunar system, were not familiar with the regular weekly sequence. As far as we know, Israel was the only nation that consistently used a seven-day week through all seasons and years.

## c. Background of the Liturgical Calendar

Ancient peoples were greatly dependent on nature. At the changing of the seasons there was a celebration and the favor of the gods was implored. Though taking over many customs, Israel was not permitted to celebrate its festivals like the *goyim*. The "nature festivals" were or became also "historical festivals." The focal point was the celebration of the sabbath. The other days of the week were indicated only with a sequential number. The number seven plays an important role. The most important festive month is the seventh.

---

### LITERATURE

P. Carrington, *The Primitive Christian Calendar* (Cambridge, 1952).

J. van Goudoever, *Biblical Calendars* (Leiden, 1961²).

L. Rost, "Weidewechsel und Festkalender," *Zeitschrift des Deutschen Palästinavereins* 67 (1943) 205–16.

S. Talmon, "Divergencies in Calendar-Reckoning in Ephraim and Judah," *Vetus Testamentum* 8 (1958) 48–74.

See also under sections B.6, 7.

---

## 10. SPECIAL DAYS AND YEARS

### a. Days of Commemoration and Fasting

Of the special days we should mention first of all the day of Midian, the day of Jerusalem, and the feast of Nicanor (Isa. 9:4; Ps. 137:7; 2 Macc. 15:37). These are to be regarded as commemorative days. In addition, days of fasting were observed on special occasions (Jer. 36:9). Only the Day of Atonement was a prescribed day of fasting (see under e below). During the Babylonian captivity all kinds of days of mourning and fasting were introduced (Zech. 7:3; 8:19). These had to do with the remembrance of the destruction of Jerusalem and of the temple. According to the prophetic word, after the return those days could be dropped. They were reintroduced after the destruction of the Herodian temple. Even before that, however, fasting was practiced in Israel, as preparation or as an act of penance (1 Macc. 3:47; 2 Macc. 13:12). In New Testament times the Pharisees strictly kept two days of fasting per week (Monday and Thursday; Luke 18:12; cf. Matt. 9:14; Mark 2:18; Luke 5:33; Acts 9:9, 19). Jesus rejected fasting as an occasion for religious boasting, but for his disciples he approved of it as a voluntary discipline (Matt. 6:16–18; cf. Acts 13:3; 14:23). He fasted himself in preparation for his messianic task (Matt. 4:2; Luke 4:2).

---

### LITERATURE

H. A. Brongers, "Fasting in Israel in Biblical and Post-Biblical Times," *Oudtestamentische Studiën* 20 (1977) 1–21.

M. Freiberger, *Das Fasten im alten Israel* (Zagreb, 1927).

A. W. Groenman, *Het wasten bij Israël* (Leiden, 1906).

---

### b. The Day of the New Moon

In some passages in the Old Testament the new moon and sabbath are mentioned together (2 Kings 4:23; Isa. 1:13; 66:23; Ezek. 45:17; Hos. 2:10; Amos 8:5; cf. Col. 2:16; also in reverse order, 1 Chron. 23:31; 2:4; 8:13; 31:3; cf. Judith

8:6). The passages intimate that in some ways the two days belonged together. From the combination it has been inferred that both were lunar festivals, but with respect to the sabbath this is nowhere supported in the Bible. They are mentioned together because they were regularly recurring festive days. Also, the observance of the new moon, at least in the official religion, had nothing to do with moon worship. It can safely be said, however, that especially the celebration of the new moon or month provided occasion for mixing with the Baal cult (is not this a threat present with every observance?). That may be the reason why in the postexilic passages (see above) the sabbath is preferably mentioned first. The prophets frequently denounced the celebration (see also section B.4.a above). There was, however, also a legitimate celebration of the day of the new moon, not as an oracle day as among many ancient peoples, but more as a festive day on which work ceased. In 2 Kings 4:8–37 we have the account of a woman who wants to visit the prophet Elisha to ask for help. "Why will you go to him today?" says her husband. "It is neither new moon nor sabbath" (verse 23). In these words is still heard the recollection of "oracle day." From the time of King Saul we have the story in 1 Samuel 20 which mentions a festival celebration of the day of the new moon (verse 6, "yearly sacrifice"). David seizes the celebration of this day as an occasion to test the king's disposition toward him. The joyful character of this day is attested by the law prescribing the sounding of trumpets. According to Numbers 10:10 this was to be done on days of rejoicing, at appointed feasts and new moon festivals. In Psalm 81:4 not the trumpet but the horn (*shophar*) is mentioned for announcing the new moon and full moon (here it probably concerns the celebration of the autumn feast). Various sacrifices were to be brought that day (cf. Num. 10:10; 28:11–15; Neh. 10:33; 2 Chron. 4:4; Ezek. 46:1–3, 6–7). Later Judaism called the day before the new moon the "small day of atonement."

## c. The New Year Feast

It is certain that ancient Israel had a New Year feast even as other nations did. From Ugaritic texts it is evident that the Canaanites made a big celebration of the day of the new moon of the autumn month. Old narratives in the Bible still preserve recollections of similar celebrations in Israel (cf. Jdgs. 21:1; 1 Samuel 1). Later the New Year feast became part of the feast of the autumn month. The anointing of King Saul seems to have been done on a New Year feast day. Perhaps the renewal of his kingship also happened on such a day (1 Sam. 13:11). For the expression "the days appointed" in this text can also be translated as "the feast of days," which might refer to the New Year feast.

For centuries the Jews celebrated the day of the New Year on the first of the month Tishri. Observing the official beginning of the year as happening in the spring was begun under Babylonian influence. Later Jewish expositors even mention four different dates for the New Year: for the kings and for the festivals, in the month Nisan; for the tithe of the flock, in the month Elul; for the number of the year, the sabbatical year, and the Year of Jubilee, in the month Tishri; and for the tithe of the trees, in the month Shebat.

### LITERATURE

J. C. de Moor, *New Year with Canaanites and Israelites* (Kampen, 1972).

S. Mowinckel, *Zum israelitischen Neujahr und zur Deutung der Thronbesteigungspsalmen* (Oslo, 1952).

L. I. Pap, *Das israelitische Neujahrsfest* (Kampen, 1933).

N. H. Snaith, *The Jewish New Year Festival* (London, 1947).

## d. The Sabbath

(1) Name. There are Babylonian texts that speak of a *shabattu* or *shapattu* day. The supposition, defended by some, of a linguistic connection between *shabattu/shapattu* and the Old Testament word sabbath must be rejected. "Every attempt to derive the word sabbath from a non-Hebrew verbal stem must be deemed unsuccessful" (Meesters, p. 15). Moreover, such a determination

would not help at all, because the sabbath is a unique institution in Israel. During and after the Exile, when particularly Israel's religious independence was severely threatened, Israel more and more emphasized that uniqueness. In the later Roman empire the Jewish keeping of the sabbath created a lot of offense, even though the division into weeks was taken over from the Jews. The day was not holy in itself or due to events in nature (phase of the moon and the like), but it must be sanctified to YHWH. So it should become clear that all of time and all of life belong to YHWH. The sabbath is a "delight" (Isa. 58:13).

(2) Background. As concerns the reasons for the sabbath commandment, both Decalogs offer different backgrounds and traditions (Exod. 20:8–11; Deut. 5:12–15). The first, the priestly tradition, sees the sabbath against the background of *creation*: "YHWH rested [*wayyanah*] on the seventh day." Compare this with Genesis 2:1–3, where it is said that God rested from all the work he had created. Here the sabbath is not mentioned by name, but "seventh day" is used (cf. 23:12; 34:12). In contrast to Exodus 20:11, in Genesis 2:2 "rest" rendered *shabat*, which we could translate with the verb "keep sabbath." The verb occurs repeatedly in the Old Testament with the meaning "celebrate the sabbath." Therefore one should not be too ready to derive the noun from the verb and trace the positive form of the commandment back to a prohibition: "you may not work (on the seventh day)." The opposite is just as possible, if not more likely. In the Decalog another verb is used that indeed means "rest," but with the secondary meaning "wait" (cf. 1 Sam. 25:9; Dan. 12:13). In Exodus 31:17 the verb "catch one's breath" (be refreshed) is used (cf. Exod. 23:12). Man may observe sabbath to catch his breath. God's sabbath is the ur-pattern. Hebrews 4:9 speaks of the sabbath rest for God's people based on the accomplished work of Christ.

The second, the (probably older) Deuteronomic redaction of the Decalog, points to the *deliverance* from slavery as the foundation of the commandment. It is proper to speak of a salvation-history background. Each sabbath celebration may be an occasion of joy for the Israelite because God has given him deliverance and freedom. Implied in this is its social aspect: other people and all creatures must also profit from the gift (cf. Exod. 23:12). Even today in the consecration of the sabbath there is a reminder both of creation and of deliverance. In the early Christian church, the resurrection day became the special day for celebrating the deliverance.

(3) The Practice of the Observance. The Old Testament nowhere records when Israel began the celebration of the sabbath. In the story about the manna it seems as if the sabbath was "discovered" (Exod. 16:23, 26). On that day everyone was to remain where he was (16:29). Exodus 35:1–3 prescribes death for working on the sabbath; no fire may be lit (cf. also Num. 15:32–36). Many, mainly later texts contain all kinds of prohibitions (Isa. 58:13; Jer. 17:19–27; Neh. 10:31). The Mishnaic tractate on the sabbath enumerates forty-less-one prohibitions. In the books of Maccabees we are told that the Jews at first refused to fight on the sabbath (1 Macc. 2:35–48). In later times one spoke of a "sabbath day journey," a distance of two thousand cubits (cf. Acts 1:12). That calculation is based on Exodus 16:29; Numbers 35:5; Joshua 3:4. In the old days, however, the sabbath was certainly not yet regarded as a day surrounded by prohibitions (cf. 2 Kings 11:5–12; 2 Chron. 23:4–8). For the writing prophets it was a festal day; the removal of this day was a hard judgment (Hos. 2:10; Amos 8:5; Isa. 1:13; cf. Lam. 2:6). In the modern Jewish celebration it is also primarily a festive day. If a day of penance or a day of fasting should fall on the same day as the sabbath, the sabbath takes priority! In its early years the Christian church retained the sabbath, but in the freedom with which Jesus observed it (cf. Mark 3:1–6; John 5:10; 9:14, etc.). The gentile churches did not consider themselves bound by the commandment. The New Testament speaks of the "breaking of bread" on the evening of the first day of the week (Acts 20:7; cf. Luke 24:30–35; John 20:19–29; Acts 1:4). On that first day or "day of the Lord" everyone set something aside as a gift (1 Cor. 16:2; cf. Rev. 1:10). The Talmud speaks of the "day of the Lord" as "the day of the Nazarene." During the reign of Constantine the Great, Sunday became an official day of rest.

## LITERATURE

N. E. Andreasen, *The Old Testament Sabbath* (Missoula, Montana, 1972).

_____, "Recent Studies of the OT Sabbath," *Zeitschrift für die alttestamentliche Wissenschaft* 86 (1974) 453–69.

N. A. Barack, *A History of the Sabbath* (New York, 1965).

E. Jenni, *Die theologische Begründung des Sabbatgebotes im Alten Testament* (Zurich, 1956).

J. H. Meesters, *Op zoek naar de oorsprong van de sabbat* (Assen, 1966).

N. Negretti, *Il settimo giorno* (Rome, 1973).

## e. The Sabbatical Year and the Year of Jubilee

(1) Every seventh year was a total sabbath in ancient Israel. Its purpose was to reorient the community to God, also with respect to the neighbor and to the land. Perhaps in the olden days every seventh year the land was again redistributed by lottery. The seventh year belonged to YHWH and to the community (Exod. 20:10–12), the land must have "a sabbath of solemn rest" (Lev. 25:3–4). In Deuteronomy 15:1–18 the expression "the year of release" is used (cf. Exod. 21:2). The observance encountered obstacles (read Jer. 34:13–14; cf. Lev. 26:35). After the Exile the people again assumed the obligation of the law (Neh. 10:31). Deuteronomy 31:10 stipulates that this law was to be read at the Feast of Tabernacles (this may imply a reminder of the New Year Festival; de Moor, I, 22). 1 Maccabees 6:49 shows how seriously the people in the so-called intertestamental period tried to keep the sabbatical year.

(2) Jubilee, the year that concludes a period of seven times seven years, is mentioned a few times. It was to be announced on the Day of Atonement with the joyful sound of the trumpet (*shophar*). The Hebrew expression is "year of the *yobel*"; the Latin translation is *annus jubilaris*. Freedom was to be announced to the inhabitants of the land. There were not to be "slave families"

in Israel (Lev. 25:8–17). The land was to be returned to the original owner (Lev. 27:16–24). In passing it is mentioned in Numbers 36:4. In Ezekiel 46:17 "the year of liberty" refers to the Jubilee and not to the sabbatical year (Roubos, p. 74; cf. the rendering in the Targum). In the book of Jubilees all of world history is divided into periods of jubilee. In Luke 4:19 Jesus refers to the messianic period as "the acceptable year of the Lord," a kind of Jubilee (cf. Isa. 61:2).

## LITERATURE

S. B. Hoenig, "Sabbatical Years and the Year of Jubilee," *Jewish Quarterly Review* 59 (1968/69) 222–36.

J. Lewy, "The Biblical Institution of Deror in the Light of Akkadian Documents," *Eretz Israel* 5 (1958) 21–31.

E. Neufeld, "Socio-Economic Background of Yobel and Semitta," *Revista degli Studi Orientali* 33 (1958) 53–124.

R. North, *Sociology of the Biblical Jubilee* (Rome, 1954).

K. Roubos, *Feesten in Israël ten tijde van het Oude Testament* (Baarn, 1960).

G. Wallis, "Das Jobeljahr-Gesetz, eine Novelle zum Sabbathjahr-Gesetz," *Mitteilungen des Instituts für Orientforschung* 15 (1969) 337–45.

(3) The Day of Atonement. The tenth day of the month Tishri is very significant. Sometimes that day has no special name in the Old Testament (Leviticus 16), but sometimes it is called *yom hakkipurim*, "(great) day of atonement" (Lev. 23:26–32; 25:9). It is a day of fasting and penance, a "great sabbath" on which a holy convocation is to be held (Lev. 23:26–32; Num. 29:7–11). "On that day two streams of love spring forth, one from the heart of the sinners as a longing for atonement and one from above as grace from God," as a later Jewish commentator writes about it. Leviticus 16 is not only concerned with the atonement for the uncleanness of the priests and the people, but also with that of the tabernacle. It was inherent in the Old Testament cult that the place where God met with his people must be

"freed from sin." The prophet Ezekiel (45:18, 20) also speaks of such a freeing from sin. After bathing, Aaron was to put on simple linen clothing, then wash himself again and put on his ordinary clothing (Lev. 16:4, 23–28). As sacrifices for himself he had to bring along a young bullock and a ram, for the people two he-goats and a ram. Putting incense on a bowl with burning coals, upon entering he was not to look at the mercy seat. Then the blood was to be sprinkled, that of the bullock and of one of the goats. The second goat had been chosen by lot "for Azazel" (verse 10). In the Authorized Version (following the Septuagint), this has been translated as "for a scapegoat," because it was thought to be derived from a verb "go away." In origin Azazel is a desert demon. According to Leviticus 16:21 the goat was to be sent away into the desert after the high priest had put the sins of the people on the animal by laying his hands on it. God would no longer remember the sins (cf. Micah 7:19b). Later Jewish writings mention that the goat was led to a high rock and then pushed off. In the centuries after the Exile an elaborate ritual evolved. Later, after the disappearance of the temple, the bloody sacrifices ceased. Hebrews 9:7, 12; 10:3, 20 refer to the Day of Atonement to indicate Christ's function as sacrifice and as priest. In Acts 27:9 the day is called "the fast."

## LITERATURE

E. Auerbach, "Neujahrs- und Versöhnungsfest in den biblischen Quellen," *Vetus Testamentum* 8 (1958) 337–43.

K. Elliger, *Leviticus* (Handbuch zum Alten Testament I/4; Tübingen, 1966), pp. 200ff.

J. G. Frazer, *The Scapegoat* (London, 1913).

S. Landersdorfer, *Studien zum biblischen Versöhnungstag* (Münster, 1924).

M. Lohr, *Das Ritual von Lev. 16* (Berlin, 1925).

Th. C. Vriezen, "The Term hizza: Lustration and Consecration," *Oudtestamentische Studiën* 7 (1950) 201–35.

# 11. THE MAJOR FEASTS

## a. Introduction

The three major festivals, which were "pilgrim festivals" when there was a temple in Jerusalem, constitute the framework of Israel's calendar of feasts. Nevertheless, this was already their character in the previous centuries when the people journeyed to the smaller sanctuaries. Such smaller shrines mentioned in the Old Testament are: Shechem (Jdgs. 9:27), Shiloh (Jdgs. 21:19; 1 Samuel 1), Bethel (1 Samuel 9–10), Gilgal (1 Samuel 10; 11:14–15; 13:7ff.), Mizpah (1 Samuel 10), Hebron (2 Sam. 15:7ff.), and Bethlehem (1 Sam. 20:6, 28–29). Each of the three feasts has gone through a development that can be traced only in part. A variety of actors contributed to that. Of particular importance is that Israel began to reflect its history in these festivals as a history that was guided by YHWH and interpreted by prophetic voices.

## b. Passover

This feast grew out of two elements. The first is *pesah*, from which, by way of Aramaic and Greek, the Dutch word *pasen* (English Easter) is derived. This is how it is briefly called in the Old Testament. Only once (Exod. 34:25) do we read of "the feast of *pesah*" (cf. Exod. 12:14). This is different in the New Testament. The second element is the Feast of Unleavened Bread (*massot*). The fusion of both elements into one Passover happened after the destruction of the first temple. In later times it was designated "the days of unleavened bread" (Acts 20:6) or "the Feast of Unleavened Bread, which is called the Passover" (e.g., Luke 22:1) or, in brief, "Passover" (Matt. 26:2).

(1) Pesah (Passover). The etymology does not help us with the significance of the feast. In Exodus 12:13, 23, 27 a connection is made with a Hebrew verb, which, however, occurs only here with the meaning "to pass over" (and so "to spare"). In 1 Kings 18:21, 26 the same verb refers to the limping dance of pagan priests. In 2 Samuel 4:4 a word likely coming from the same root

means "crippled, lame." In Isaiah 31:5 it is usually translated "protect," but the meaning "celebrate Passover" has also been advocated. The suggestion that the word originally referred to the passing of the full moon is no more than conjecture. *Pesah* had to be celebrated with the killing of an animal from the flock, a male lamb, either a sheep or a goat (Exod. 12:5, 21), later also a sheep or an ox (Deut. 16:2). In Exodus 12:12 the killing is connected with the death of the firstborn. This is followed by a communal meal (see under [3] below). The sacrifice and the meal must have been known already before the exodus out of Egypt. The account preceding the Exodus already mentioned that the people had to celebrate a feast in honor of YHWH (Exod. 3:11, 18; 5:1ff.; 7:16; 10:24–26). Later it was totally historicized and combined with the bringing of the firstfruits of the barley harvest.

(2) Matsot. The *massot* are loaves or cakes, baked without leaven or yeast. The eating of it goes back to an age-old custom. In Exodus 12:34, 39 the explanation is given that it reflects the haste with which the Israelites had to leave Egypt, but before that we read already about the preparation of the lamb. Deuteronomy 16:3 speaks of "the bread of affliction." The Canaanites ate unleavened bread at the beginning of the harvest. This contains the idea of the "sanctification" of the harvest that might not "be spoiled." Something of that sanctification is still reflected in Leviticus 23:9–11. See ill. 109.

(3) The Passover Regulations. According to Exodus 12, on the tenth day of the month Nisan an animal was to be selected that was to be used as a meal for one household, and if the household was too small it had to be shared with a neighbor. Nothing of the edible parts was to be left over. The time of slaughter (on the fourteenth day) is indicated with an expression that literally means "between the two evenings." The Pharisees later explained this as the time before sunset; the Samaritans explained it as the brief twilight between sunset and night (this is today the most generally accepted explanation; cf. also Exod. 16:12; 26:39, 41; 30:8; Num. 9:3, 5, 11; 28:4, 8). In origin the Passover was a family feast. Though according to the stipulations the animal was to be

killed in the temple (Deut. 16:2, 6), the celebration of the feast was done in the family circle. According to the Synoptic Gospels, Jesus celebrated the Passover in Jerusalem, though not in the temple. The killing of the lamb had to be done in a ritual manner. No bone could be broken (Exod. 12:46; cf. John 19:36). The head had to remain connected to the bones and the inner part of the animal. The blood had to be smeared both on doorposts and on the lintel. After the centralization of the cult, the blood was sprinkled near the altar of burnt offering (2 Chron. 35:11). According to Exodus 12:22, a bunch of hyssop was to be used for the application of the blood. The hyssop was generally regarded as a plant that could ward off evil (cf. Lev. 14:4; Num. 19:6; Ps. 51:9). According to some, a plant was meant that retarded the coagulation of blood. Owing to its red color, the smearing of the blood also had an apotropaic effect (cf. Num. 19:2–4). Through the centuries the dark background of death and destruction remained part of the celebration of Passover. While the Israelites were in their homes (Exod. 12:22), destruction went around, but YHWH was their protector.

The preparation of the animal for the meal was also carefully described. The meat had to be roasted in fire; it could not be eaten raw or boiled. This regulation was not always valid as is shown by a comparison of Exodus 12:8–9 with Deuteronomy 16:7. The change was no doubt due to the changed circumstances of the people. Bitter herbs had to be eaten with it (Exod. 12:8; Num. 9:11). The significance of that is not further described. Sometimes a reference is made to Exodus 1:14. What was customary among many peoples (the eating of spring herbs to increase one's vitality) was in Israel totally embedded in the historical framework.

The dress and actions at Passover are also described. The loins were to be girded, the feet shod with sandals, and the staff in the hand (Exod. 12:11). One must be ready for travel!

A week of celebration followed upon the Passover evening and night. For bread only *massot* could be eaten. Only food that was actually to be eaten could be prepared (Exod. 12:16). It was very important that following generations would understand the significance of the feast. Therefore instruction about it had to be given in the family circle. Exodus 13:8–10 describes how it is to be taught to the son: it is because of what YHWH did for me when I came out of Egypt. This must be as "a sign on your hand" (compare the later use of prayer straps). For the regulations pertaining to the celebration, see also Exodus 13:3–10; 23:14–15; 34:18–26; Leviticus 23:5–8; Numbers 28:16–25; Deuteronomy 16:1–8; Ezekiel 45:21–24.

(4) Illustrations of Passover Celebrations. In addition to the pericopes mentioned above, we refer first to Joshua 5:10–12. This passage concerns the time immediately after the crossing of the Jordan at Gilgal. On the evening after the fourteenth of Nisan, the people ate unleavened bread and roasted grain from the produce of the land. The latter was prohibited according to Leviticus 23:6, 14, while Exodus 12 makes no mention of it. 2 Chronicles 30 speaks of a Passover under King Hezekiah. Because the cleansing of the temple was not complete until the sixteenth of Nisan, the king consulted with his chiefs and the people to celebrate the feast in the following month. For that Numbers 9:6–11 was invoked (2 Chron. 30:4). The feast was celebrated for seven days, after which it was extended by seven days. The remarkable thing is that those who had not purified themselves could also eat of the *pesah*. The king himself prayed for pardon (30:19). Since the days of Solomon there had not been such a great feast (30:26). 2 Kings 23:21–23 and (in greater detail) 2 Chronicles 35:1–19 describe a feast under King Josiah. Chronicles devotes special attention to the familiar character of the feast. None of the kings celebrated it like Josiah (this refers to the following of the prescriptions in Deuteronomy). Ezra 6:19–22 speaks of the first celebration after the dedication of the postexilic temple. It is striking that neither here nor at the celebration in Chronicles is deliberate mention made of the exodus out of Egypt.

(5) Further Developments. In the Gospels, Passover celebrations are sometimes the background of accounts and events, for instance, Luke 2:41–51. This is particularly so in the case of Jesus' last meal with his disciples. The singing of hymns of praise (Psalms 113–118) occupies an important place at that meal. Mention is also made of the drinking of the cup of wine (Matt. 26:26–29; Mark 14:22–25; Luke 22:14–20). Paul exhorts his readers to celebrate the feast with the unleavened bread of sincerity and truth (1 Cor. 5:6–8). In Hebrews 11:28 it is said of Moses that he proved his faith in God's promises by keeping the Passover. It is not possible to reconstruct in every detail the entire course of events on the eve of Jesus' death and the eating of the Passover. Yet we can find in it the major elements of the later Jewish celebrations. The Jewish Passover haggadah, containing the liturgy for the celebration of the *seder* evening (*seder* really means "ordering"), mentions the cup of wine that was to be passed five times. The fifth cup is called "the cup of Elijah." According to Old Testament expectation Elijah would return to announce the messianic age (cf. Mal. 4:5). The expectation of the future was indeed more and more linked with the celebration of the Passover. Perhaps this was aided by the Septuagint text of Jeremiah 31:8, which (different from the Hebrew text) reads: "I . . . gather them together from the ends of the earth for the Passover." See ill. 110.

---

## LITERATURE

E. Auerbach, "Die Feste im alten Israel," *Vetus Testamentum* 8 (1958) 1–18.

T. H. Gaster, *Passover. Its History and Traditions* (London/New York, 1958).

P. Grelot and J. Pierron, *Osternacht und Osterfeier im Alten und Neuen Bund* (Düsseldorf, 1959).

H. Haag, *Vom alten zum neuen Pascha. Geschichte und Theologie des Osterfestes* (Stuttgart, 1971).

M. Haran, "The Passover Sacrifice," in *Studies in the Religion of Ancient Israel* (Supplements to Vetus Testamentum 23; Leiden, 1972), pp. 86–116.

J. Jeremias, *Die Passahfeier der Samaritaner und ihrer Bedeutung für das Verständnis der alttestamentlichen Passahüberlieferung* (Giessen, 1932).

H. J. Kraus, *Gottesdienst in Israel* (Munich, 1962), pp. 61–72.

P. Laaf, *Die Pascha-Feier Israels. Eine literarkritische und überlieferungsgeschichtliche Studie* (Bonn, 1970).

J. B. Segal, *The Hebrew Passover from the Earliest Time to* A.D. *70* (London, 1963).

R. de Vaux, *Studies in Old Testament Sacrifice* (London, 1964).

---

## c. The Feast of Weeks

(1) Name. The second pilgrim festival is variously designated. In the Old Testament it is usually called Feast of Weeks (*hag shabuot*), also feast of harvest (wheat) or of the firstfruits (Exod. 23:16a; 34:22a; Lev. 23:15–22; Num. 28:26–31; Deut. 16:9–12; 2 Chron. 8:13). The Greek name *pentecoste* (fiftieth) or pentecost does not occur in the canonical books of the Old Testament (this would have to be in the Septuagint), but it is found in some noncanonical books (cf. 2 Macc. 12:32), and further also in the New Testament (cf. Acts 2:1; 20:16; 1 Cor. 16:8). According to 2 Chronicles 15:10, the time at which Asa renewed the covenant may have been the Day of Pentecost. For very early already the Feast of Weeks (following the reading *hag shebuot*) has been interpreted as "feast of oaths" (cf. 2 Chron. 15:14; Kraus, *Gottesdienst*, p. 77). It was connected with the law-giving at Sinai with an appeal to Exodus 19:1. From the details in the passages two things can be inferred: it was a harvest feast and it was a feast that was dependent on the Passover. It is often called *aseret*, which generally designates a free or festive day in the Old Testament, later, however, a concluding (feast) day (cf. Lev. 23:36; Num. 29:35; Deut. 16:8; 2 Chron. 7:9; Neh. 8:19). The Feast of Weeks lasted only one day, though in the diaspora a second day was added to it because officials feared that not all Israelites would be acquainted with the calendar days.

(2) Date. Before the celebration of the Feast of Weeks, present-day Jews have their *omer* time. In the Old Testament this word means the cut-off corn, the sheaf. Besides that it also means (but then usually designated as *gomer*) a measure (cf. Exod. 16:36). In later references to the omer time, both meanings are implied. According to rabbinic exegesis it can also designate a special offering or gift. In the land of the Bible the grain harvest begins with the barley and ends with the wheat.

The period of seven weeks (among later Jews a period of abstinence, with the exception of the thirty-third day) is not further indicated in the Pentateuch; all that is mentioned is the beginning day from which one is to count and the last day (the feast day). After the time of the Old Testament there are different ideas among the Jews as to the day constituting the *terminus a quo* of the seven weeks (Van Goudoever, pp. 18, 29). It concerns here the exegesis of Leviticus 23:11, 15, which speaks of "the day after the sabbath." The Sadducees (and also the Samaritans) took the text as literally as possible. They understood the sabbath mentioned there as being the seventh day of the week, the day on which Passover was celebrated. In that case the Feast of Weeks was always on the first day (Sunday). The Council of Nicea more or less went along with this and put Pentecost (even as Easter) on a Sunday. The Pharisees counted differently. Their calculation became officially accepted in Jewish orthodoxy from the second century A.D. According to them the "sabbath" in these texts refers to the first feast day of the Passover. On the following day the sheaf was to be brought and the fiftieth day was to be calculated from that.

(3) Harvest Feast. The Feast of Weeks was originally a harvest feast. Even as on the first day after the Passover sabbath the sheaf of barley was to be brought, so on the fiftieth day part of the wheat was to be brought, namely, two "wave loaves," baked from two-tenths of an ephah of fine flour with leaven (unlike the matsot). At a later time, on the basis of Exodus 23:16a and Numbers 28:26, the presentation was viewed as the first in the series of all the items that are enumerated in Deuteronomy 8:8: barley, wheat, vines, fig trees, pomegranates, olive trees, honey. Those other fruits could be brought at a later time. The festival retained its harvest character, even in countries with different harvest times. The book of Ruth became the scroll for the Feast of Weeks (cf. Ruth 1:22; 2:23). By bringing the firstfruits blessing rested on the house (Ezek. 44:30). The word "firstfruit" means both "first" and "best." The enumeration of the added sacrifices for the Feast of Weeks in Leviticus 23 differs from the one in Numbers 28. The later tradition explains this difference in this way: Leviticus 23 mentions the

sacrifices for the first year, whereas Numbers 28 mentions the regular sacrifices for the feast that pertained later.

(4) Background. The prescriptions regarding the Feast of Weeks included a social law. When a field was harvested, that which grew on the very edges had to be left standing. Also whatever was not gathered the first time had to be left for the poor and the stranger. The remainder was for the community (Lev. 23:15–22). The book of Deuteronomy (which centers the celebration in Jerusalem; cf. Acts 2) adds the admonition: "You shall remember that you were a slave in Egypt" (Deut. 16:12). The Israelite must consider himself responsible also for the slaves and the socially weak. It would be too much to say that there we have a historical-redemptive foundation, for the reminder is not to the Exodus but to the bondage in Egypt. Yet it does come into focus. In any case, the Feast of Weeks is also historically anchored. After the Old Testament era this historicization is greatly extended. In the book of Jubilees the feast is grounded in the covenant with Noah and Abraham; also the children of Jacob celebrated the feast, after which it passed into oblivion until God gave the law at Sinai. The Qumran community celebrated it as "covenant feast." Until A.D. 70 its harvest and thanksgiving character remained predominant. About that time it must have become the feast of the giving of the law (cf. Exod. 19:1). Tradition develops the meaningful interpretation: liberation apart from law is empty. Passover is the feast of the liberation, Pentecost that of the giving of the law.

According to data from the second century, the ancient church understood by "Pentecost" the fifty days after Easter, but later the name was reserved for the fiftieth day after Easter.

## LITERATURE

E. Auerbach, "Die Feste im alten Israel," *Vetus Testamentum* 8 (1958) 1–18.

H. J. Kraus, *Gottesdienst in Israel* (Munich, 1962), pp. 72ff.

E. Lohse, *"pentekoste,"* in G. Kittel and G. Friedrich, eds., *Theological Dictionary of the New Testament* VI (Grand Rapids, 1968) 44–53.

## d. The Feast of Tabernacles

(1) Name. The third in the series is the Feast of Tabernacles or the Feast of Ingathering. In the later passages of the Old Testament it is designated as "the feast" (1 Kings 8:2, 65; 12:32; 2 Chron. 5:3; 7:8–9; Neh. 8:15; Ezek. 45:25). In Leviticus 23:39 it is called "the feast of YHWH." Compare also the linguistic usage in the time of the New Testament (John 7:2, 37), even though in the time shortly before the destruction of the temple the Feast of Passover enjoyed the greatest popularity.

The biblical Feast of Tabernacles contains three elements: it is a harvest and thanksgiving festival (during which in old times one used to live in "booths" or "tabernacles" in the vineyard), it became a feast in memory of the Exodus, and finally it also became an altar and temple feast. In Exodus 23:14–17 and 34:22–24 the name "feast of ingathering" (*asiph*) is used. These passages employ two datings. Reference is made to the time of the harvesting of the fruits and to "the end or the change of the year," that is, to the autumn equinox. Actually the entire autumn season is a combination of feast days (the first day of the month, the Feast of Tabernacles, and the Day of Atonement). In Deuteronomy 16:13–15 the name *sukkot* feast is used. No explanation of the term is given there, since apparently it is presumed to be familiar. The noun *sukkot* (from *sukkah, sok*) is connected with a verb meaning "weave" or "plait" and also (derived from it) "cover" or "protect." A *sukkah* is a hut or lean-to with a roof of branches and foliage as a protection against the sun (Isa. 4:6; Jonah 4:5). Jacob built booths for his flock (Gen. 33:17). King Benhadad of Aram constructed huts or summer houses as shelters outside the besieged city of Samaria (1 Kings 20:12, 16). During the monarchical era Israel was probably also familiar with the custom that on a campaign the soldiers lived in tents and the kings and the generals in huts (2 Sam. 11:11). However, the term also designates the hut that was placed in the vineyard during the time of the ripening of the fruits, a hut plaited from branches and foliage (cf. Isa. 1:8). It became a symbol of the inconstancy and fleetingness of life (Job 27:18), in general also the designation of a simple shelter or house (Amos 9:11; Ps. 18:12; 27:5). In Deuteronomy 16 the *sukkot* reminds one of guard huts in the vineyard, for there the feast is only referred to as a harvest and thanksgiving feast; no historical perspectives are associated with it. Joy is to be dominant. The feast is to be celebrated for seven days with the family and the stranger.

The Mishnaic tractate on the Feast of Tabernacles carefully describes the hut. It must stand in the open air and must have a roof constructed of vegetative components. For eight days one lives as much as possible in the open field. The feast is characterized by exuberance. "Whoever has not experienced the joy at the water procession has never seen joy in his life." That water procession was also known in the time of the New Testament. The court of women was magnificently illuminated. In John 7:1–8:19 the carnival-like character of the feast is clearly evident from the inserted story about the adulterous woman. In the book of Jubilees customs are mentioned that do not occur in the Old Testament canon. The symbolism of light played a large role. The Mishnaic tractate emphatically opposes a kind of light cult (at sunset two priests from where they stand must turn their face to the west, to the temple, and not to the east). Leviticus 23:34–38 contains something not found in the biblical passages already referred to; there the feast is not dated according to the agricultural calendar but by referring to the seventh month. There may thus be no doubt about the date. The first and the last days have the character of a semi-sabbath. The feast lasted seven days. Yet the last day was called the eighth day. Tradition apparently added it. Also 1 Kings 8:65 speaks of seven (and still another seven) days, after which the king dismissed the people on the eighth day (cf. 2 Chron. 7:8–10). In John 7:37 the last day is called "the great day" of the feast.

(2) Historicization. In Leviticus 23:39–44 (regarded by some as a later, by others as an older passage) the living in *sukkot* is historically explained. The people were ordered to pick fruits and all kinds of branches. It is not stated that those branches were to be used for constructing the booth (cf., however, Nehemiah 8). One may be joyful before the face of the Lord. From the branches and fruits a bouquet was made (later called *lulab*). A custom coming into vogue later was to keep apart a fruit (the citronlike etrog) and

to bind together a folded palm branch with twigs and branches. There the etrog is also called (following rabbinic exegesis) "apple of paradise." The historicization in Leviticus 23:39–44 does present some problems. During the Exodus and the journey through the desert (Lev. 23:43), the people did not live in huts but in tents (cf. Hos. 12:10). Especially the connection between the desert and the leafy trees seems strange. There are clearly two traditions interwoven here. On the one hand the Feast of Thanksgiving for the harvest (the Canaanites celebrated the New Year Festival with huts of branches in which images of deities were given a temporary home; de Moor I, 22, 29). On the other hand it must have been a feast in commemoration of Israel's wandering existence as well as a feast in which the covenant was renewed (therefore according to Lev. 23:42 the feast was not for strangers). Numbers 29:12–38 informs us about the many sacrifices that were to be brought.

(3) Some Celebrations. In Nehemiah 8:14–19 we are told how Ezra, while reading the Torah, came upon regulations regarding the feast. The people had not kept the regulations, yet they knew (though nowhere mentioned in the biblical passages discussed above) how to construct a *sukkot* (Neh. 8:18). The people went and got leaves from the trees. They made themselves booths, everyone on his roof or in the courts by the homes, also in the courts of the house of God and on two squares. The twenty-fourth day of Tishri was a day of penance and prayer. Ezra 3:2–4 speaks about the celebration of the feast in connection with the dedication of the altar (cf. 2 Chron. 7:8–10). A separate problem is why, according to 1 Kings 12:32, King Jeroboam had a Feast of Tabernacles celebrated in the northern kingdom, not in the seventh month but in the eighth. The biblical writer openly states that Jeroboam wanted to detach himself from the southern kingdom and the temple of Solomon. But why a month later? We wonder whether the effect would not have been heightened if he had taken the same date so as to bind the people to Bethel and Dan. Some believe that Jeroboam here accommodated a heathen custom of celebrating a harvest and fertility feast in the eighth month. Others are of the opinion that he interspersed a month in the calendar.

(4) Later Elements. The later elements of the feast of *sukkot* are (Ehrlich, p. 56): (a) Covering the altar with green twigs. (b) Walking about the altar with the *lulab;* this was likely the only occasion when the ordinary Israelite came between altar and temple proper. (c) Striking the altar with branches. (d) Lighting of the candlesticks. (e) The torch dance. (f) Singing to the accompaniment of various musical instruments, sounding of the shophar. (g) Procession to the spring of Siloam at the dawn of day. (h) Dipping of water, whereby the high priest sprinkled water on the altar (at that moment Jesus may have uttered the words in John 7:38). (i) Offerings of wine. The loss of the temple brought about a change in various customs as well. The feast has not been taken over by the Christian church, in name or in substance.

## LITERATURE

A. Alt, "Zelt und Hütten," *Kleine Schriften* III (Munich, 1959) 233–42.

E. L. Ehrlich, *Kultsymbolik im Alten Testament und im nachbiblischen Judentum* (Stuttgart, 1959).

G. W. McRae, "The Meaning and Evolution of the Feast of Tabernacles," *Catholic Biblical Quarterly* 22 (1960) 251–76.

L. I. Pap, *Das israelitische Neujahrfest* (Kampen, 1933), pp. 33–47.

## 12. SOME FEASTS FROM LATER TIMES

### a. Purim

Among the Jews this feast is of a lower order, and it was celebrated with the giving of gifts and the eating of the typical pastry, the "Haman's ears." Nevertheless, some rabbis, basing themselves on the Jerusalem Talmud at Esther 9:28, said that when the messiah has come there will be no more sabbaths or feast days, but there will be Purim. In the synagogue the book of Esther is read, the only biblical book besides the Pentateuch to be used in the form of a scroll. It belongs to the five *megilloth*, of which Canticles is to be read at Passover, Ruth at the Feast of Weeks, Ecclesiastes at the Feast of Tabernacles, and Lamentations at the commemoration of the destruction of the temple. The account in the book of Esther concludes with the institution of the Feast of Purim on the fourteenth and fifteenth of the month of Adar. Days of fasting and mourning are to precede the actual feast, as a reminder of the casting of the lot (*pur;* see section B.3.b above). In 2 Maccabees 15:37 Purim is called "Mordecai's day," after the name of the "prince of the exile."

## LITERATURE

V. Christian, "Zur Herkunft des Purim-Festes," in H. Junker and J. Botterweck, eds., *Alttestamentliche Studien* (Festschrift F. Nötscher; Bonn, 1950), pp. 33–37.

T. H. Gaster, *Purim and Hanukkah in Custom and Tradition* (New York, 1950).

W. W. Hallo, "The First Purim," *Biblical Archaeologist* 46 (1983) 19–29.

### b. Hanukkah

This goes back to an event described in the books of Maccabees, namely, the rededication of the temple in 164 B.C. The Jews had been compelled by the Seleucids to offer sacrifices to Zeus in the temple. Judas defeated the enemies and cleansed the temple from all heathen pollution (1 Macc. 4:36–51). Then he instituted the Feast of the Dedication of the Temple on the twenty-fifth of Kislev (1 Macc. 4:59; 2 Macc. 1:9; 2:18; 10:5–9). A symbolism of light is associated with the Feast of Hanukkah. Today the so-called hanukkah candelabra (also called "Maccabees lamp") has eight lights that are lighted on successive nights with the help of a ninth light, the "servant." It is sometimes said that this is done to avoid "strange fire." In the heading of Psalm 30 (in content a hymn of thanks by one delivered from dire need) it is said that this song in later times was sung at the celebration of the Feast of Hanukkah. In the New Testament the feast is mentioned in John 10:22 as *ta enkainia* ("renewal, dedication").

## LITERATURE

J. Morgenstern, "The Chanukkah Festival and the Calendar of Ancient Israel," *Hebrew Union College Annual* 20 (1947) 1–136; 21 (1948) 365–496.

O. S. Rankin, *The Origins of the Festival of Hanukkah* (Edinburgh, 1930).

# Index